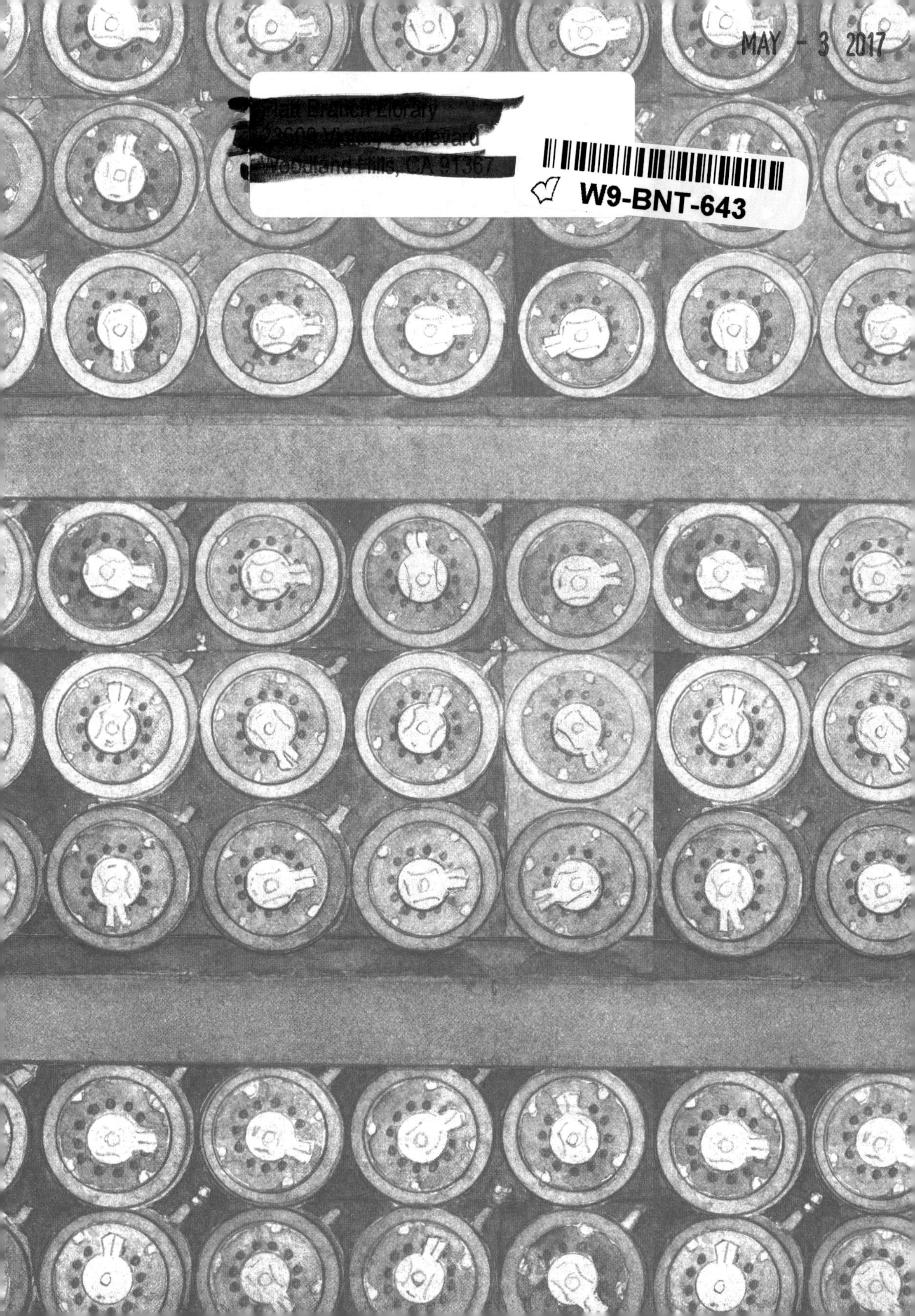

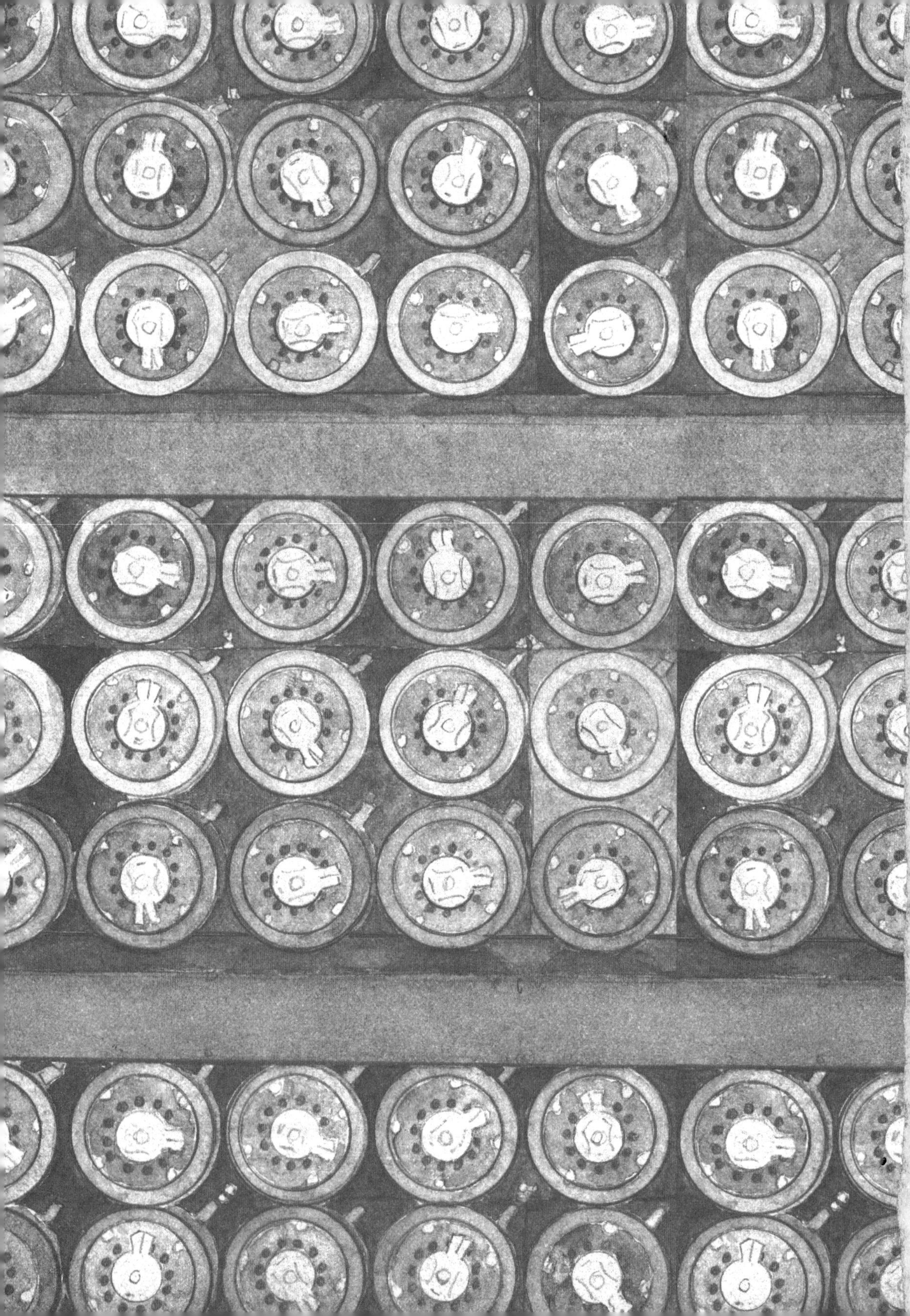

THE IMITATION GAME

Alan Turing Decoded

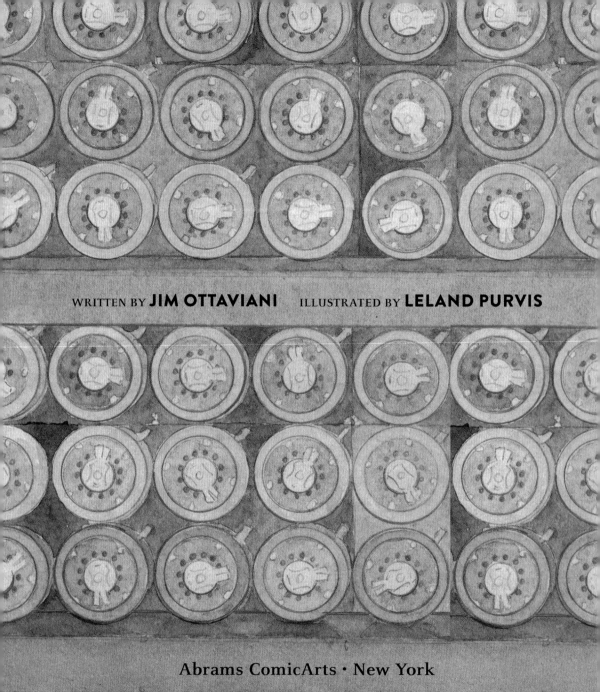

WRITTEN BY **JIM OTTAVIANI**   ILLUSTRATED BY **LELAND PURVIS**

Abrams ComicArts · New York

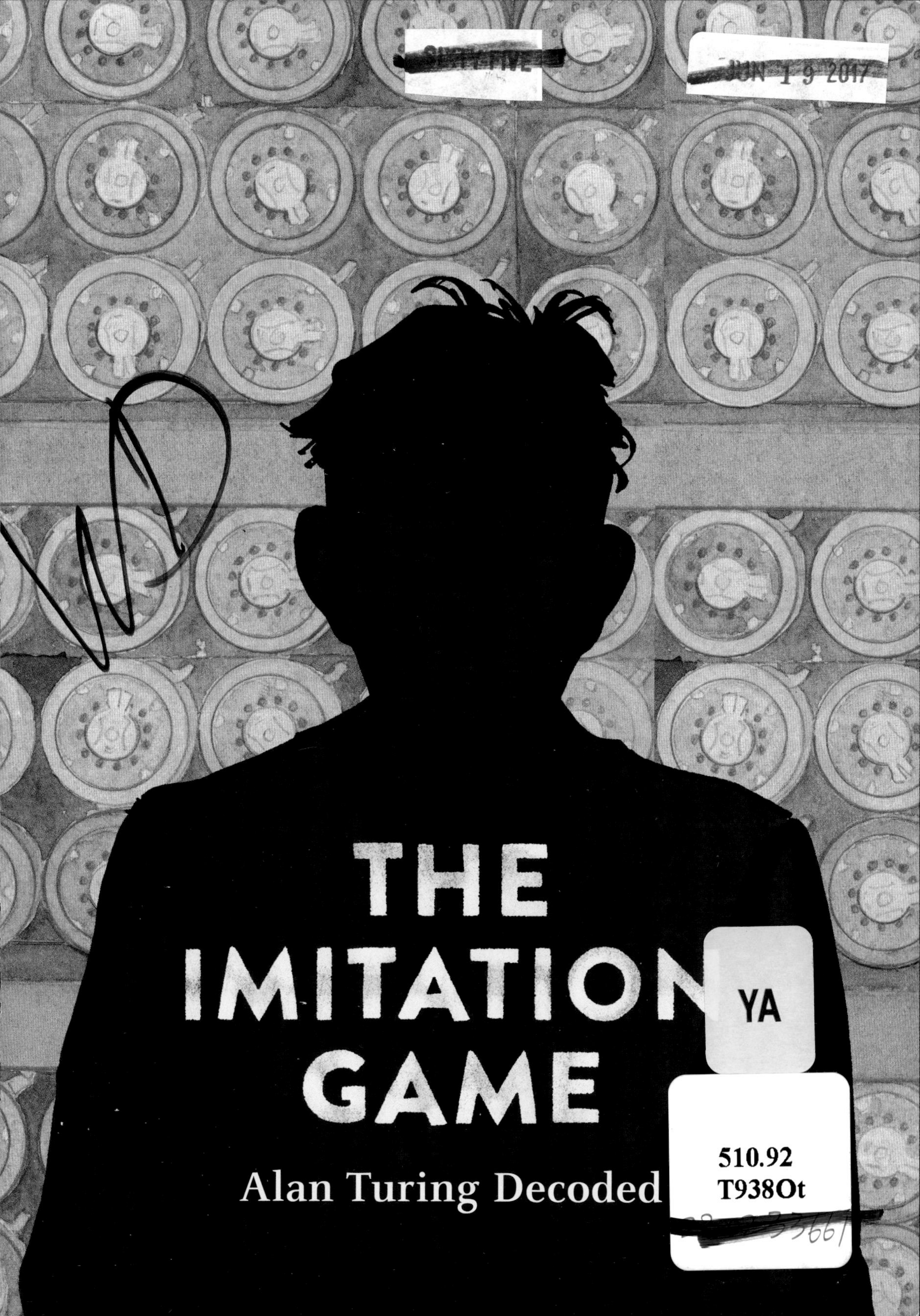

THE IMITATION GAME

Alan Turing Decoded

Editors: Orlando Dos Reis, Nicole Sclama, and Carol Burrell
Project Manager: Charles Kochman
Designer: Pam Notarantonio
Managing Editor: Jen Graham
Production Manager: Elizabeth Peskin

Library of Congress Control Number: 2015946819

ISBN: 978-1-4197-1893-9

Printed and bound in China
11 10 9 8 7 6 5 4 3 2

Abrams ComicArts books are available at special discounts when purchased in
quantity for premiums and promotions as well as fundraising or educational
use. Special editions can also be created to specification. For details, contact
specialsales@abramsbooks.com or the address below.

ABRAMS The Art of Books
115 West 18th Street, New York, NY 10011
abramsbooks.com

ACKNOWLEDGMENTS

Nicole Sclama and, before her, Joan Hilty edited the story. Things you might have found unclear are no doubt the result of us ignoring one of their many excellent suggestions. Nick Abadzis worked through the dialogue, correcting our idioms and suggesting better and more British ways to say things. Kat Hagedorn and Carol Burrell worked behind the scenes to make this edition possible, and the folks at Tor.com gave the story its first run around the house. At Abrams, thanks also to Orlando Dos Reis (Editorial), Pamela Notarantonio and Chad W. Beckerman (Design), Charles Kochman (Editorial), Jen Graham and Leily Kleinbard (Managing Editorial), and Elizabeth Peskin and Alison Gervais (Production).

```
01001001001000000111000001110 01001
101111011000001101111011101101 10010
100100000111010001101110010000 00011
00011011011110110111001110011011010
01011001000110010101110010001 00000
0111010001101000011001010010 0000
01110001011101010110010101110 01101
110100011010001011011110110111000101
```

UNIVERSAL COMPUTING

```
000         UNIVERSAL 0001001000101000011011
00001011011100010000001101101011000
01011000110110100001101001011011
10011001010111001100100000001101001
010000110100101101110011010110 0111
11100100100010000001      COMPUTING 0
10000110100101110011001000000011100 11
0110100001101111011101010110110 00110
010001000000110001001100101 0110
011101101001011011100010000001110 11
1011010101110100011010000010000
0011001001100101011001100110100101 1
011100110100101110100011010010110 1111
011011100111001100100000001101111 0110
011000100000011101000110100001100 10
1001000000110110101100101011000 01011
0111001101001011011100110011100 100000
01101111011001100010000001110100 0110
100001100101001000000111010001100 10
```

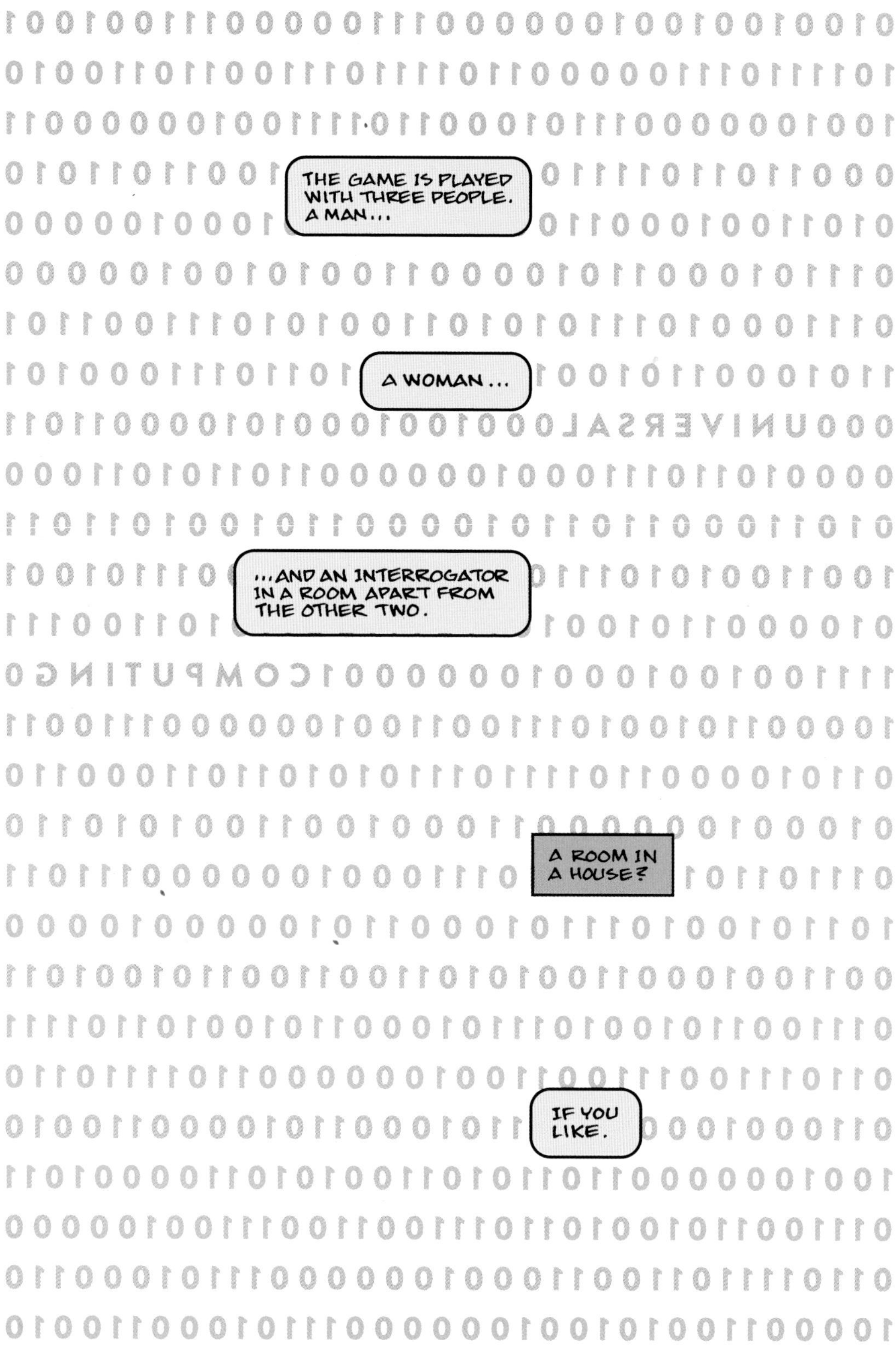
THE GAME IS PLAYED WITH THREE PEOPLE. A MAN...
A WOMAN...
...AND AN INTERROGATOR IN A ROOM APART FROM THE OTHER TWO.
A ROOM IN A HOUSE?
IF YOU LIKE.

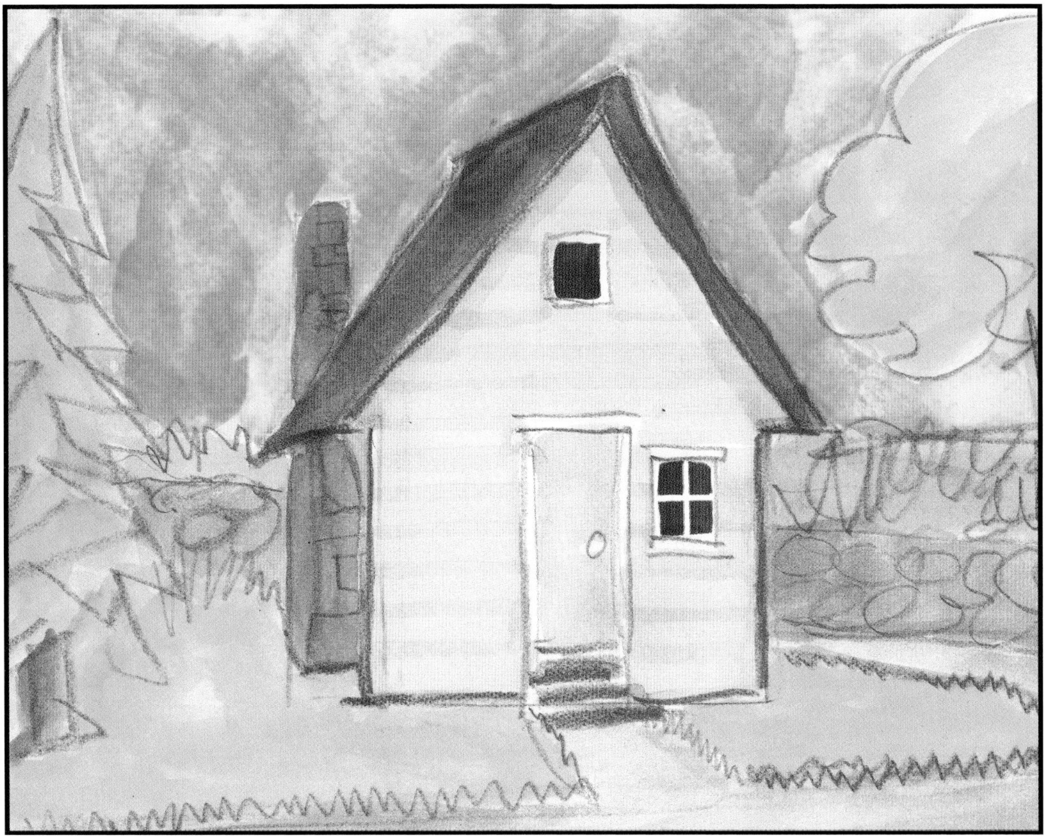

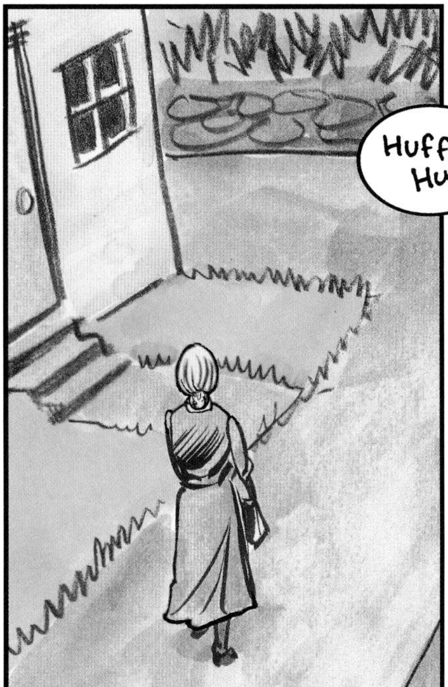
Huff
Huff

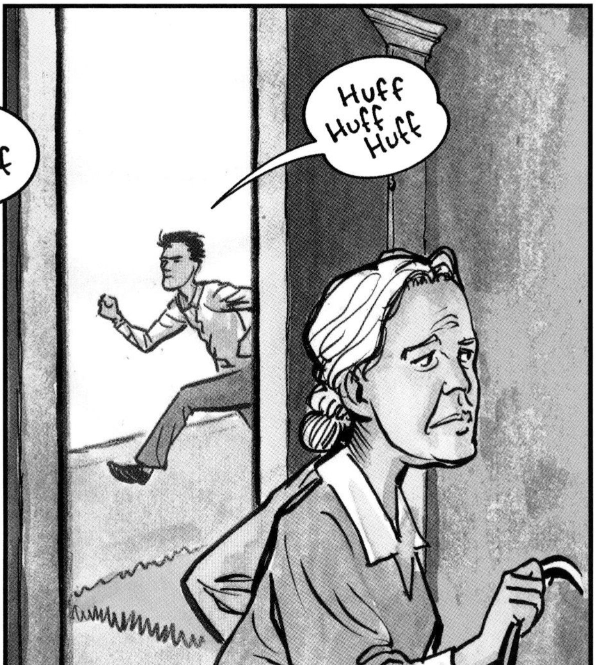
Huff
Huff
Huff

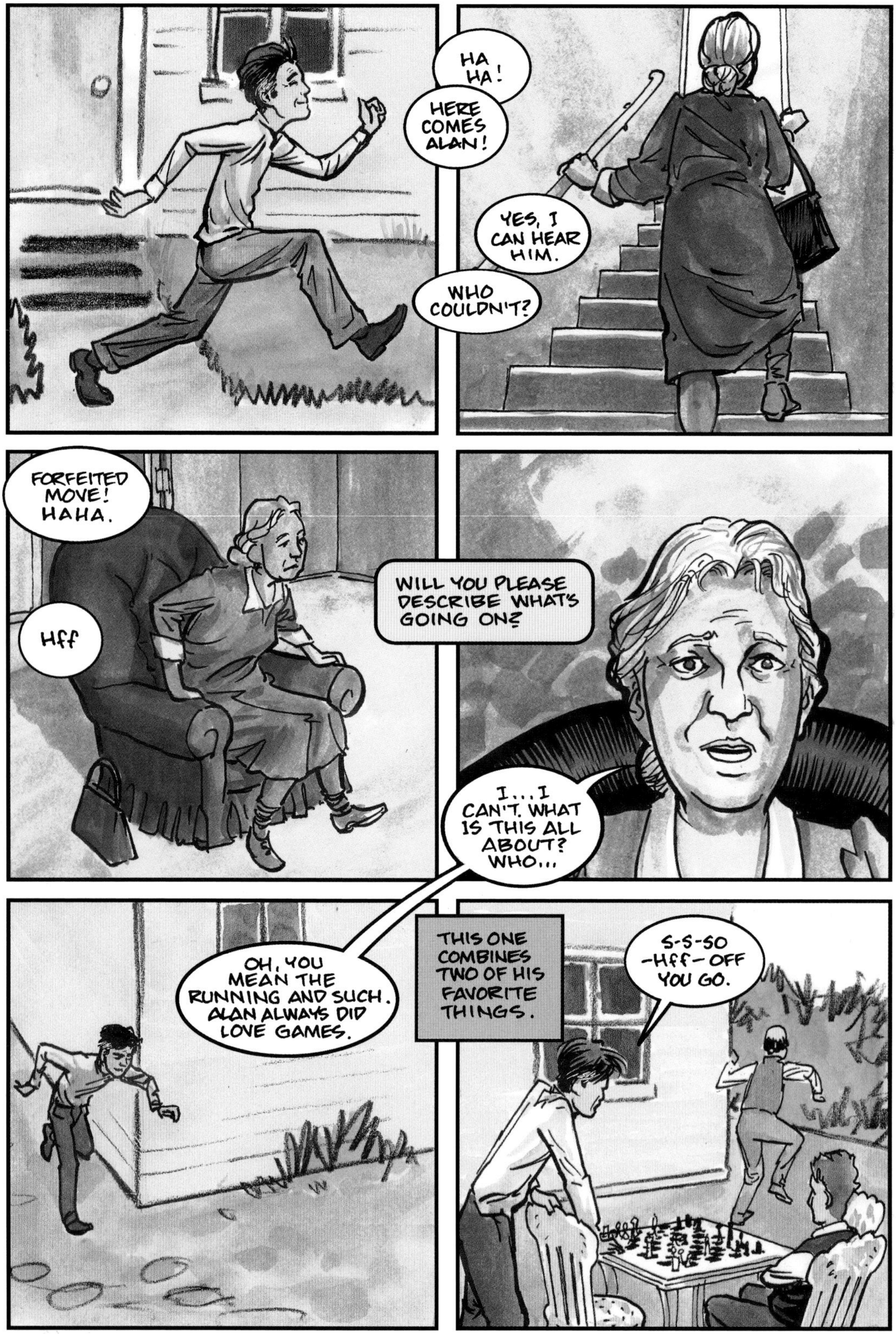
HA HA!
HERE COMES ALAN!
YES, I CAN HEAR HIM.
WHO COULDN'T?
FORFEITED MOVE! HAHA.
Hff
WILL YOU PLEASE DESCRIBE WHAT'S GOING ON?
I... I CAN'T. WHAT IS THIS ALL ABOUT? WHO...
OH, YOU MEAN THE RUNNING AND SUCH. ALAN ALWAYS DID LOVE GAMES.
THIS ONE COMBINES TWO OF HIS FAVORITE THINGS.
S-S-SO -Hff- OFF YOU GO.

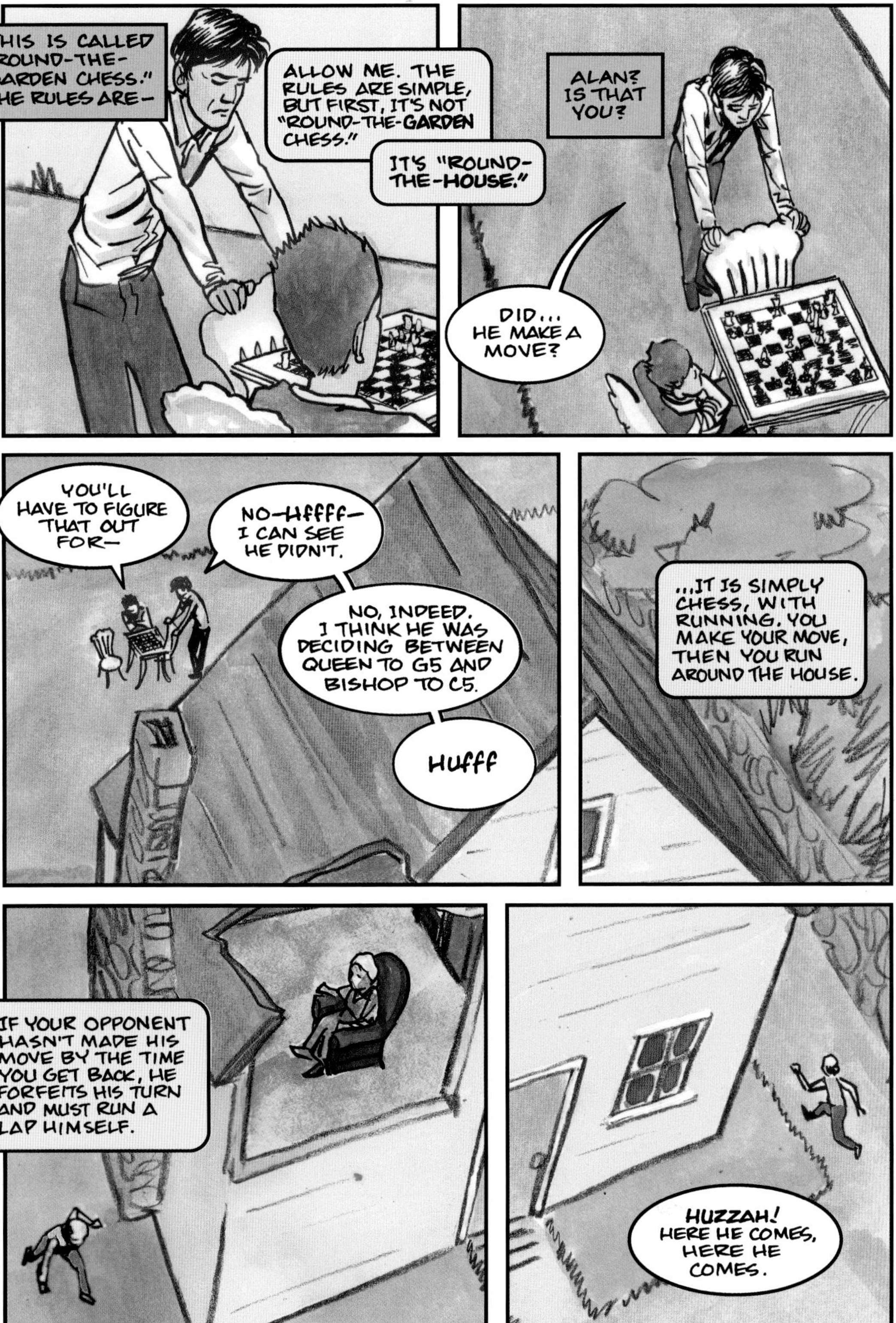
THIS IS CALLED "ROUND-THE-GARDEN CHESS." THE RULES ARE—
ALLOW ME. THE RULES ARE SIMPLE, BUT FIRST, IT'S NOT "ROUND-THE-GARDEN CHESS."
IT'S "ROUND-THE-HOUSE."
ALAN? IS THAT YOU?
DID... HE MAKE A MOVE?
YOU'LL HAVE TO FIGURE THAT OUT FOR—
NO—Hffff— I CAN SEE HE DIDN'T.
NO, INDEED. I THINK HE WAS DECIDING BETWEEN QUEEN TO G5 AND BISHOP TO C5.
Hufff
...IT IS SIMPLY CHESS, WITH RUNNING. YOU MAKE YOUR MOVE, THEN YOU RUN AROUND THE HOUSE.
IF YOUR OPPONENT HASN'T MADE HIS MOVE BY THE TIME YOU GET BACK, HE FORFEITS HIS TURN AND MUST RUN A LAP HIMSELF.
HUZZAH! HERE HE COMES, HERE HE COMES.

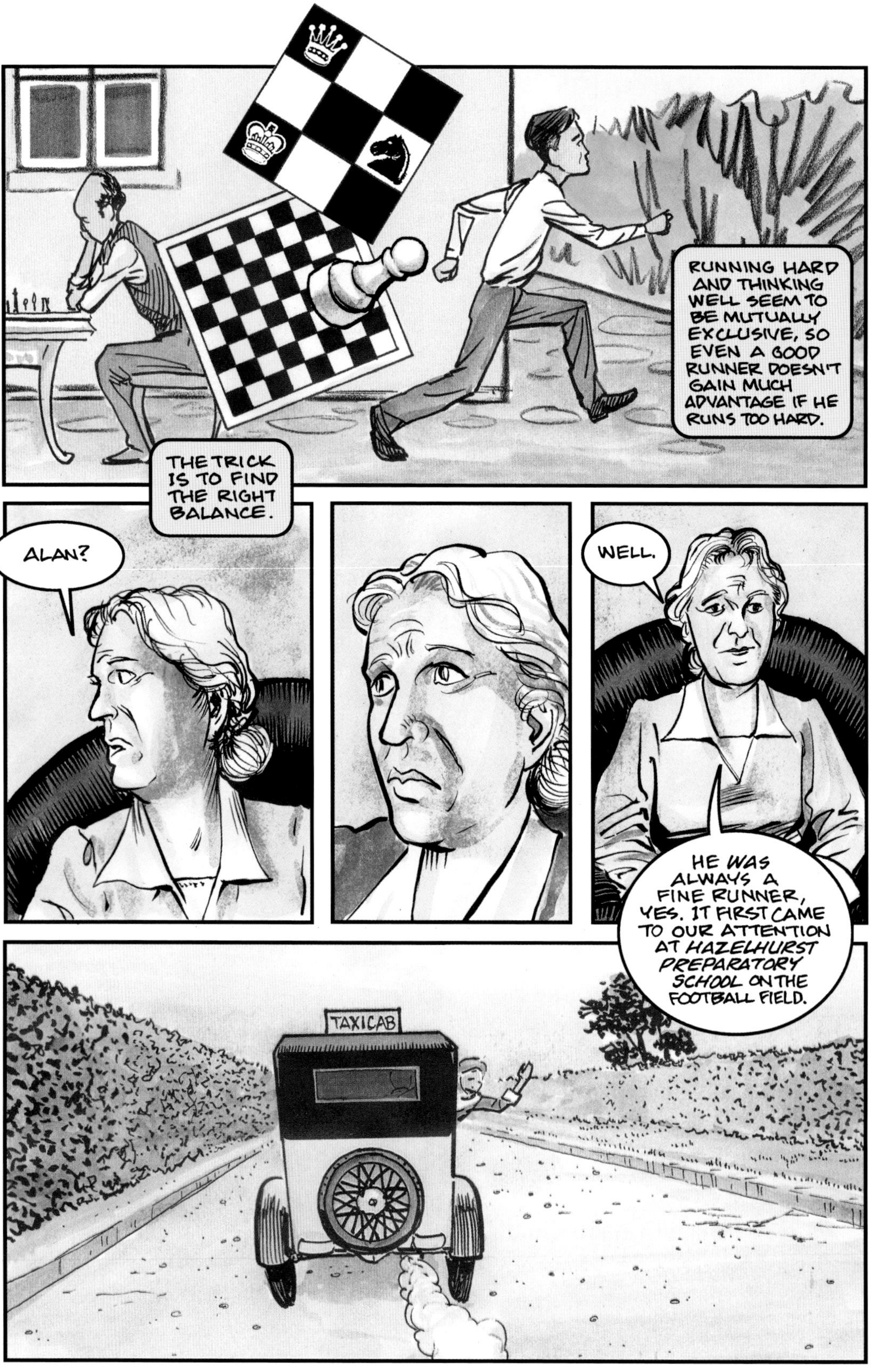
RUNNING HARD AND THINKING WELL SEEM TO BE MUTUALLY EXCLUSIVE, SO EVEN A GOOD RUNNER DOESN'T GAIN MUCH ADVANTAGE IF HE RUNS TOO HARD.
THE TRICK IS TO FIND THE RIGHT BALANCE.
ALAN?
WELL.
HE *WAS* ALWAYS A FINE RUNNER, YES. IT FIRST CAME TO OUR ATTENTION AT *HAZELHURST PREPARATORY SCHOOL* ON THE FOOTBALL FIELD.
TAXICAB

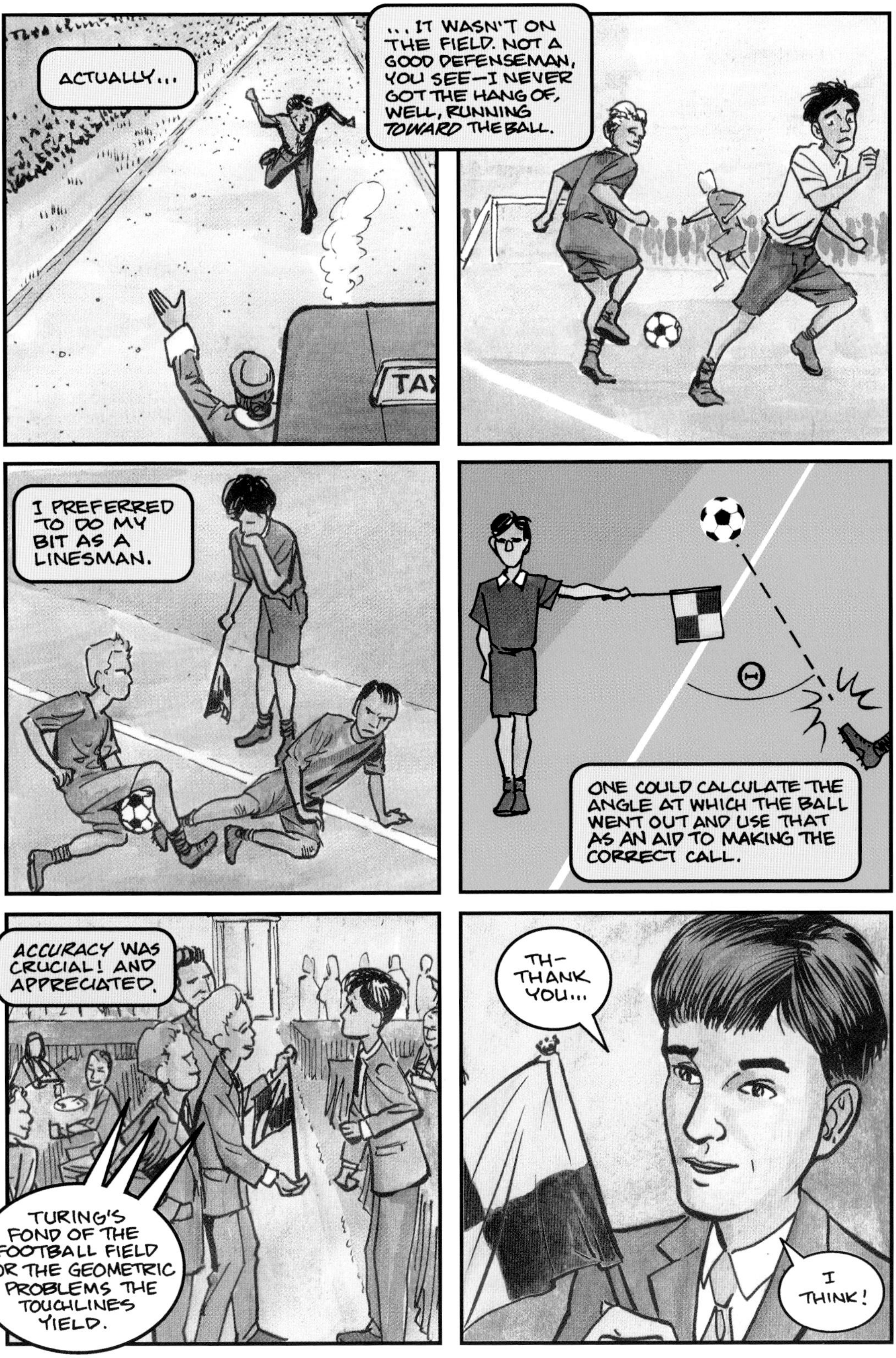
ACTUALLY...
...IT WASN'T ON THE FIELD. NOT A GOOD DEFENSEMAN, YOU SEE—I NEVER GOT THE HANG OF, WELL, RUNNING *TOWARD* THE BALL.
I PREFERRED TO DO MY BIT AS A LINESMAN.
Θ
ONE COULD CALCULATE THE ANGLE AT WHICH THE BALL WENT OUT AND USE THAT AS AN AID TO MAKING THE CORRECT CALL.
ACCURACY WAS CRUCIAL! AND APPRECIATED.
TURING'S FOND OF THE FOOTBALL FIELD FOR THE GEOMETRIC PROBLEMS THE TOUCHLINES YIELD.
TH-THANK YOU...
I THINK!

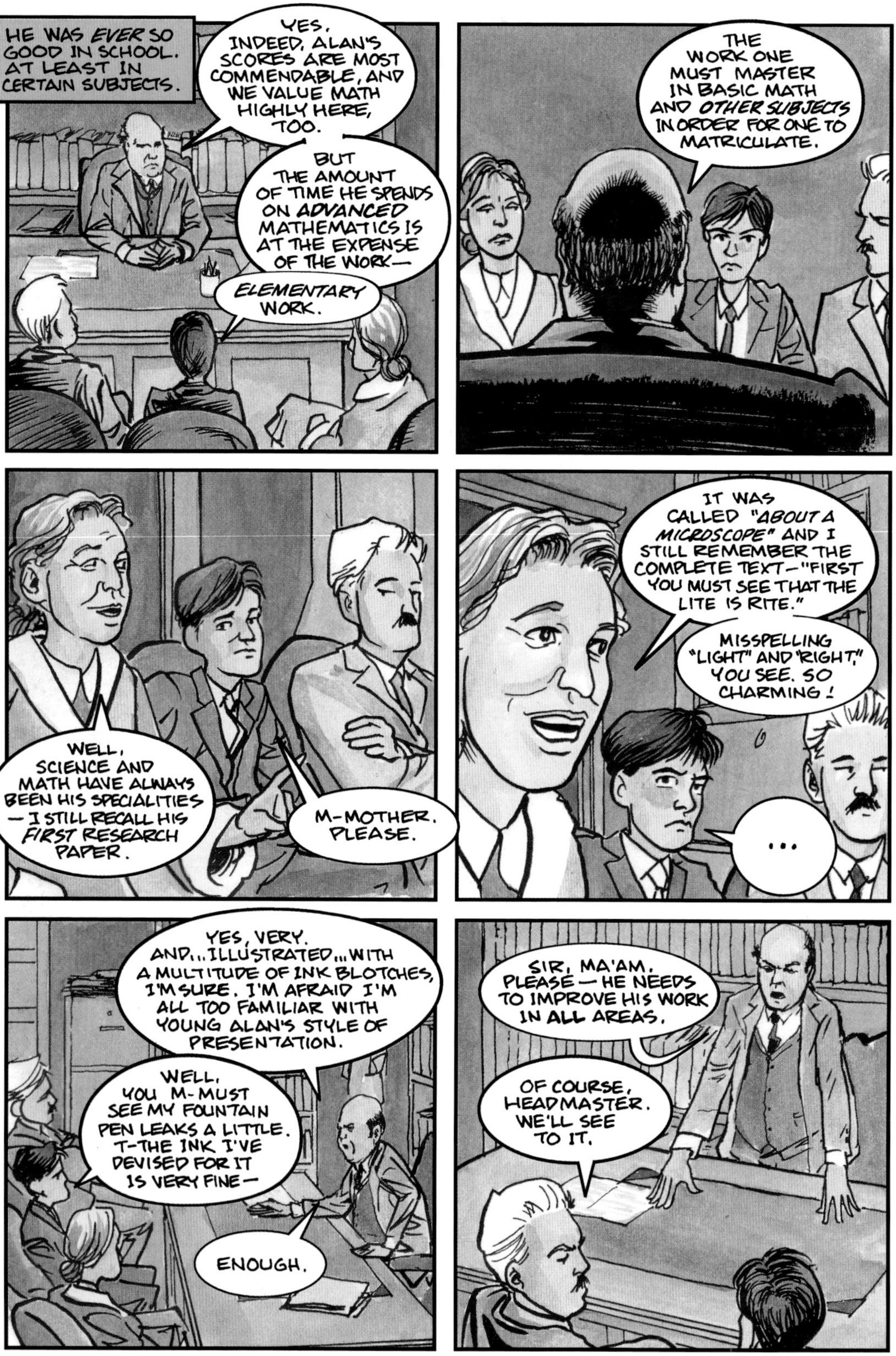
HE WAS *EVER* SO GOOD IN SCHOOL. AT LEAST IN CERTAIN SUBJECTS.
YES. INDEED, ALAN'S SCORES ARE MOST COMMENDABLE, AND WE VALUE MATH HIGHLY HERE, TOO.
BUT THE AMOUNT OF TIME HE SPENDS ON *ADVANCED* MATHEMATICS IS AT THE EXPENSE OF THE WORK—
ELEMENTARY WORK.
THE WORK ONE MUST MASTER IN BASIC MATH AND *OTHER SUBJECTS* IN ORDER FOR ONE TO MATRICULATE.
WELL, SCIENCE AND MATH HAVE ALWAYS BEEN HIS SPECIALITIES — I STILL RECALL HIS *FIRST* RESEARCH PAPER.
M-MOTHER. PLEASE.
IT WAS CALLED *"ABOUT A MICROSCOPE"* AND I STILL REMEMBER THE COMPLETE TEXT—"FIRST YOU MUST SEE THAT THE LITE IS RITE."
MISSPELLING "LIGHT" AND "RIGHT," YOU SEE. SO CHARMING!
...
YES, VERY. AND... ILLUSTRATED... WITH A MULTITUDE OF INK BLOTCHES, I'M SURE. I'M AFRAID I'M ALL TOO FAMILIAR WITH YOUNG ALAN'S STYLE OF PRESENTATION.
WELL, YOU M-MUST SEE MY FOUNTAIN PEN LEAKS A LITTLE. T-THE INK I'VE DEVISED FOR IT IS VERY FINE—
ENOUGH.
SIR, MA'AM. PLEASE — HE NEEDS TO IMPROVE HIS WORK IN **ALL AREAS**.
OF COURSE, HEADMASTER. WE'LL SEE TO IT.

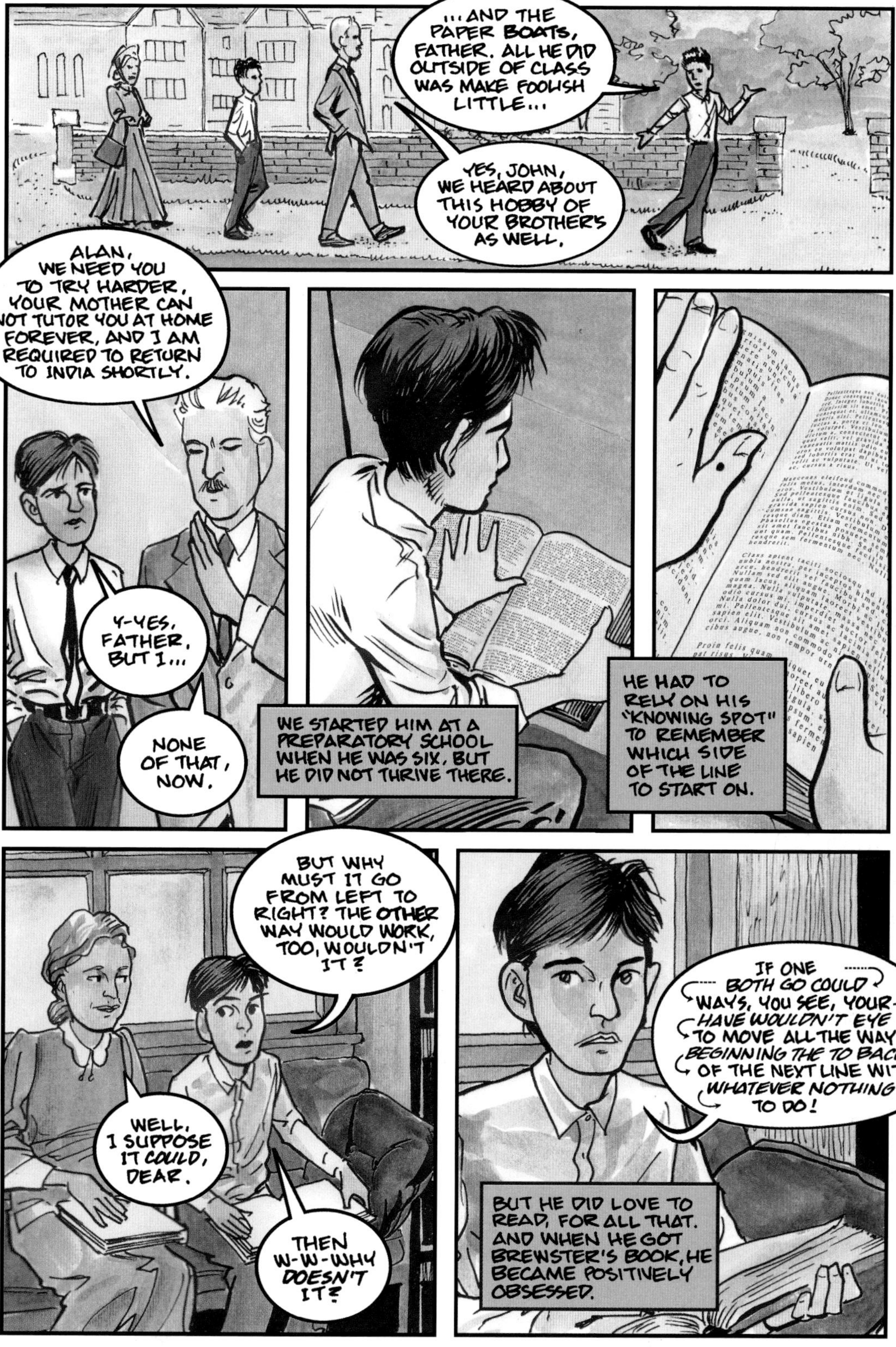
...AND THE PAPER BOATS, FATHER. ALL HE DID OUTSIDE OF CLASS WAS MAKE FOOLISH LITTLE...
YES, JOHN, WE HEARD ABOUT THIS HOBBY OF YOUR BROTHER'S AS WELL.
ALAN, WE NEED YOU TO TRY HARDER. YOUR MOTHER CAN NOT TUTOR YOU AT HOME FOREVER, AND I AM REQUIRED TO RETURN TO INDIA SHORTLY.
Y-YES, FATHER, BUT I...
NONE OF THAT, NOW.
WE STARTED HIM AT A PREPARATORY SCHOOL WHEN HE WAS SIX, BUT HE DID NOT THRIVE THERE.
HE HAD TO RELY ON HIS "KNOWING SPOT" TO REMEMBER WHICH SIDE OF THE LINE TO START ON.
BUT WHY MUST IT GO FROM LEFT TO RIGHT? THE OTHER WAY WOULD WORK, TOO, WOULDN'T IT?
WELL, I SUPPOSE IT COULD, DEAR.
THEN W-W-WHY DOESN'T IT?
IF ONE
BOTH GO COULD
WAYS, YOU SEE, YOUR
HAVE WOULDN'T EYE
TO MOVE ALL THE WAY
BEGINNING THE TO BACK
OF THE NEXT LINE WITH
WHATEVER NOTHING
TO DO!
BUT HE DID LOVE TO READ, FOR ALL THAT. AND WHEN HE GOT BREWSTER'S BOOK, HE BECAME POSITIVELY OBSESSED.

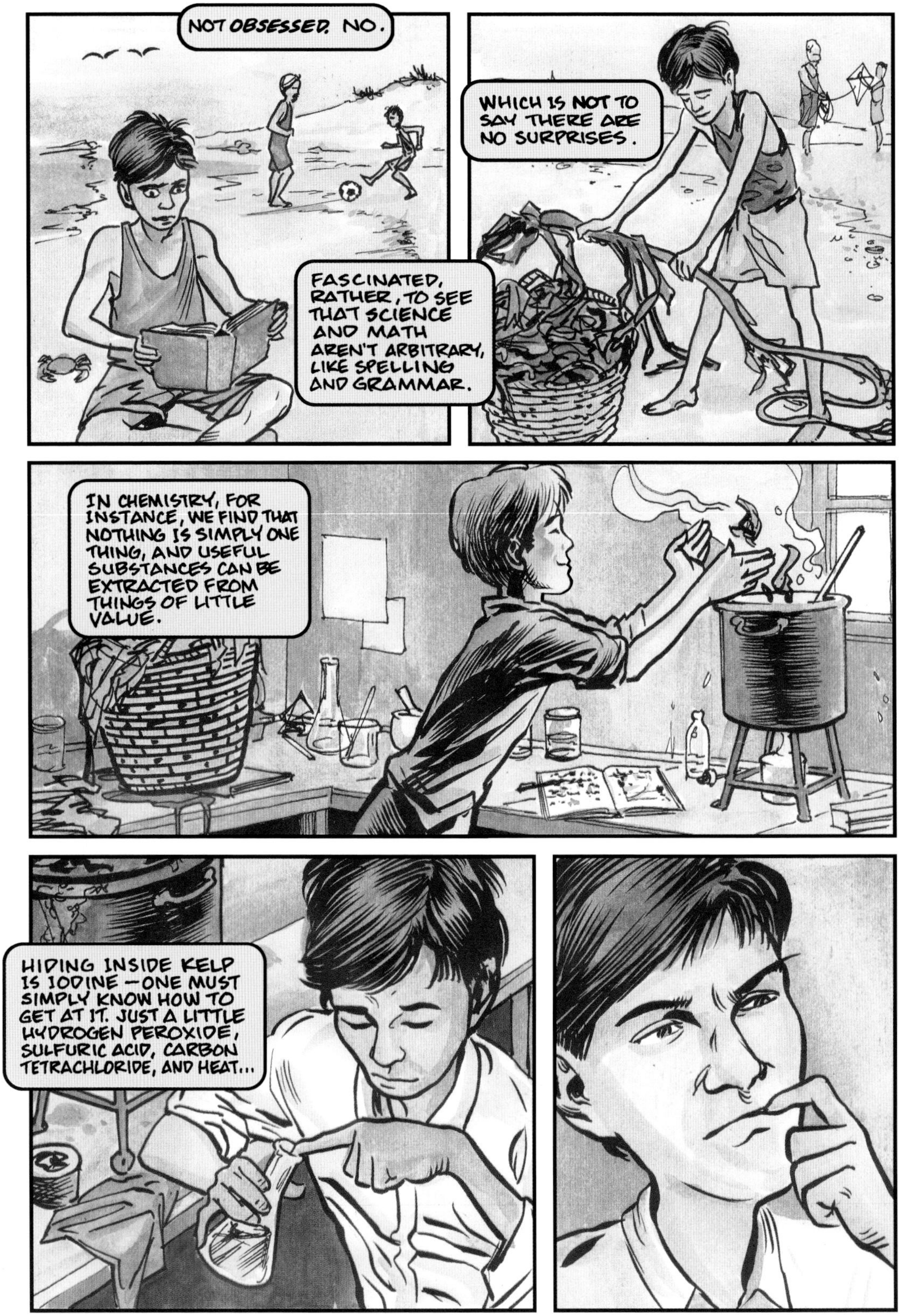
NOT OBSESSED. NO.
FASCINATED, RATHER, TO SEE THAT SCIENCE AND MATH AREN'T ARBITRARY, LIKE SPELLING AND GRAMMAR.
WHICH IS NOT TO SAY THERE ARE NO SURPRISES.
IN CHEMISTRY, FOR INSTANCE, WE FIND THAT NOTHING IS SIMPLY ONE THING, AND USEFUL SUBSTANCES CAN BE EXTRACTED FROM THINGS OF LITTLE VALUE.
HIDING INSIDE KELP IS IODINE—ONE MUST SIMPLY KNOW HOW TO GET AT IT. JUST A LITTLE HYDROGEN PEROXIDE, SULFURIC ACID, CARBON TETRACHLORIDE, AND HEAT...

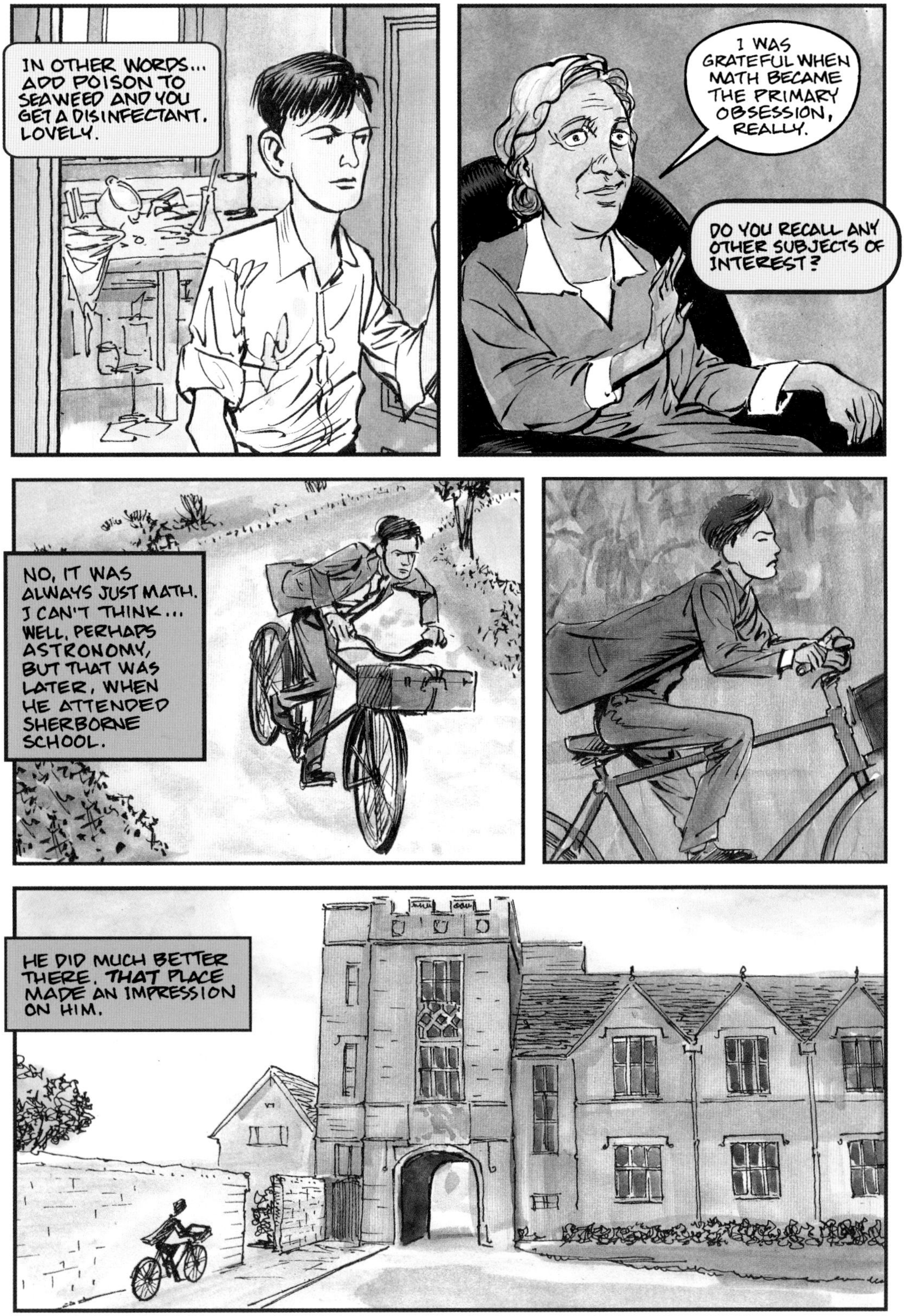

IN OTHER WORDS... ADD POISON TO SEAWEED AND YOU GET A DISINFECTANT. LOVELY.
I WAS GRATEFUL WHEN MATH BECAME THE PRIMARY OBSESSION, REALLY.
DO YOU RECALL ANY OTHER SUBJECTS OF INTEREST?
NO, IT WAS ALWAYS JUST MATH. I CAN'T THINK... WELL, PERHAPS ASTRONOMY, BUT THAT WAS LATER, WHEN HE ATTENDED SHERBORNE SCHOOL.
HE DID MUCH BETTER THERE. THAT PLACE MADE AN IMPRESSION ON HIM.

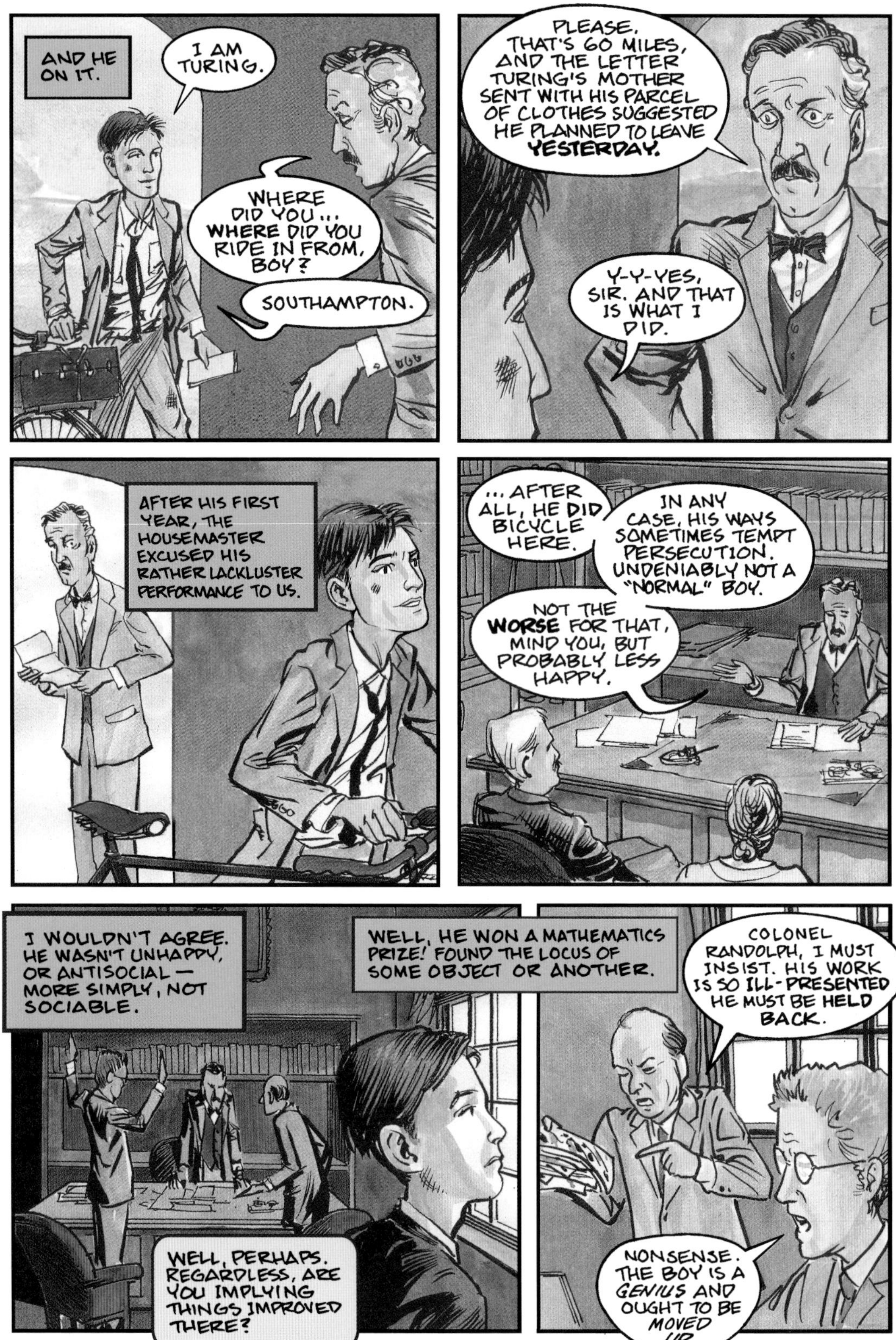

AND HE ON IT.
I AM TURING.
WHERE DID YOU... WHERE DID YOU RIDE IN FROM, BOY?
SOUTHAMPTON.
PLEASE. THAT'S 60 MILES, AND THE LETTER TURING'S MOTHER SENT WITH HIS PARCEL OF CLOTHES SUGGESTED HE PLANNED TO LEAVE YESTERDAY.
Y-Y-YES, SIR. AND THAT IS WHAT I DID.
AFTER HIS FIRST YEAR, THE HOUSEMASTER EXCUSED HIS RATHER LACKLUSTER PERFORMANCE TO US.
...AFTER ALL, HE DID BICYCLE HERE.
IN ANY CASE, HIS WAYS SOMETIMES TEMPT PERSECUTION. UNDENIABLY NOT A "NORMAL" BOY.
NOT THE WORSE FOR THAT, MIND YOU, BUT PROBABLY LESS HAPPY.
I WOULDN'T AGREE. HE WASN'T UNHAPPY, OR ANTISOCIAL — MORE SIMPLY, NOT SOCIABLE.
WELL, PERHAPS. REGARDLESS, ARE YOU IMPLYING THINGS IMPROVED THERE?
WELL, HE WON A MATHEMATICS PRIZE! FOUND THE LOCUS OF SOME OBJECT OR ANOTHER.
COLONEL RANDOLPH, I MUST INSIST. HIS WORK IS SO ILL-PRESENTED HE MUST BE HELD BACK.
NONSENSE. THE BOY IS A GENIUS AND OUGHT TO BE MOVED UP.

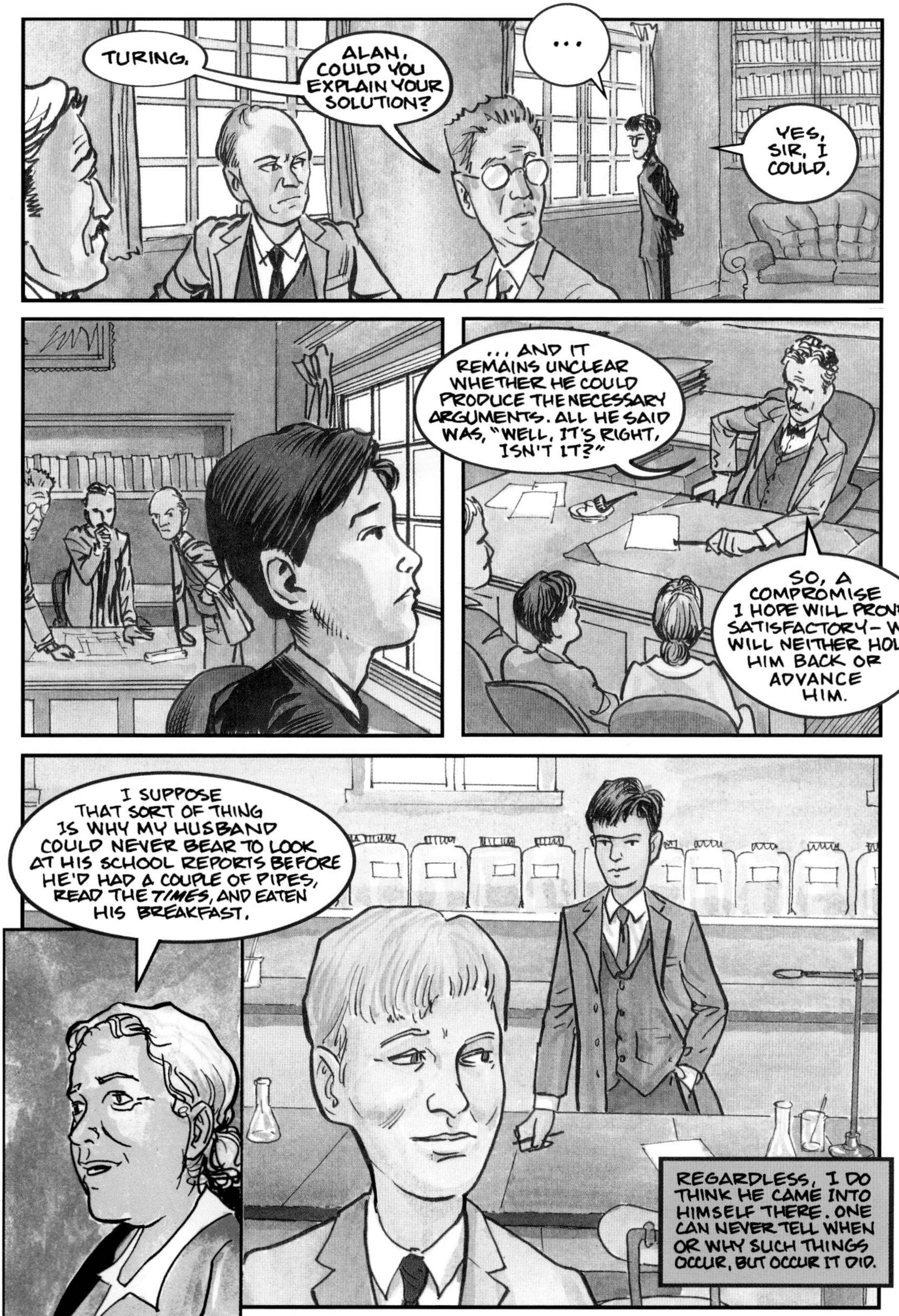
TURING.
ALAN, COULD YOU EXPLAIN YOUR SOLUTION?
...
YES, SIR, I COULD.
..., AND IT REMAINS UNCLEAR WHETHER HE COULD PRODUCE THE NECESSARY ARGUMENTS. ALL HE SAID WAS, "WELL, IT'S RIGHT, ISN'T IT?"
SO, A COMPROMISE I HOPE WILL PROVE SATISFACTORY– WE WILL NEITHER HOLD HIM BACK OR ADVANCE HIM.
I SUPPOSE THAT SORT OF THING IS WHY MY HUSBAND COULD NEVER BEAR TO LOOK AT HIS SCHOOL REPORTS BEFORE HE'D HAD A COUPLE OF PIPES, READ THE *TIMES*, AND EATEN HIS BREAKFAST.
REGARDLESS, I DO THINK HE CAME INTO HIMSELF THERE. ONE CAN NEVER TELL WHEN OR WHY SUCH THINGS OCCUR, BUT OCCUR IT DID.

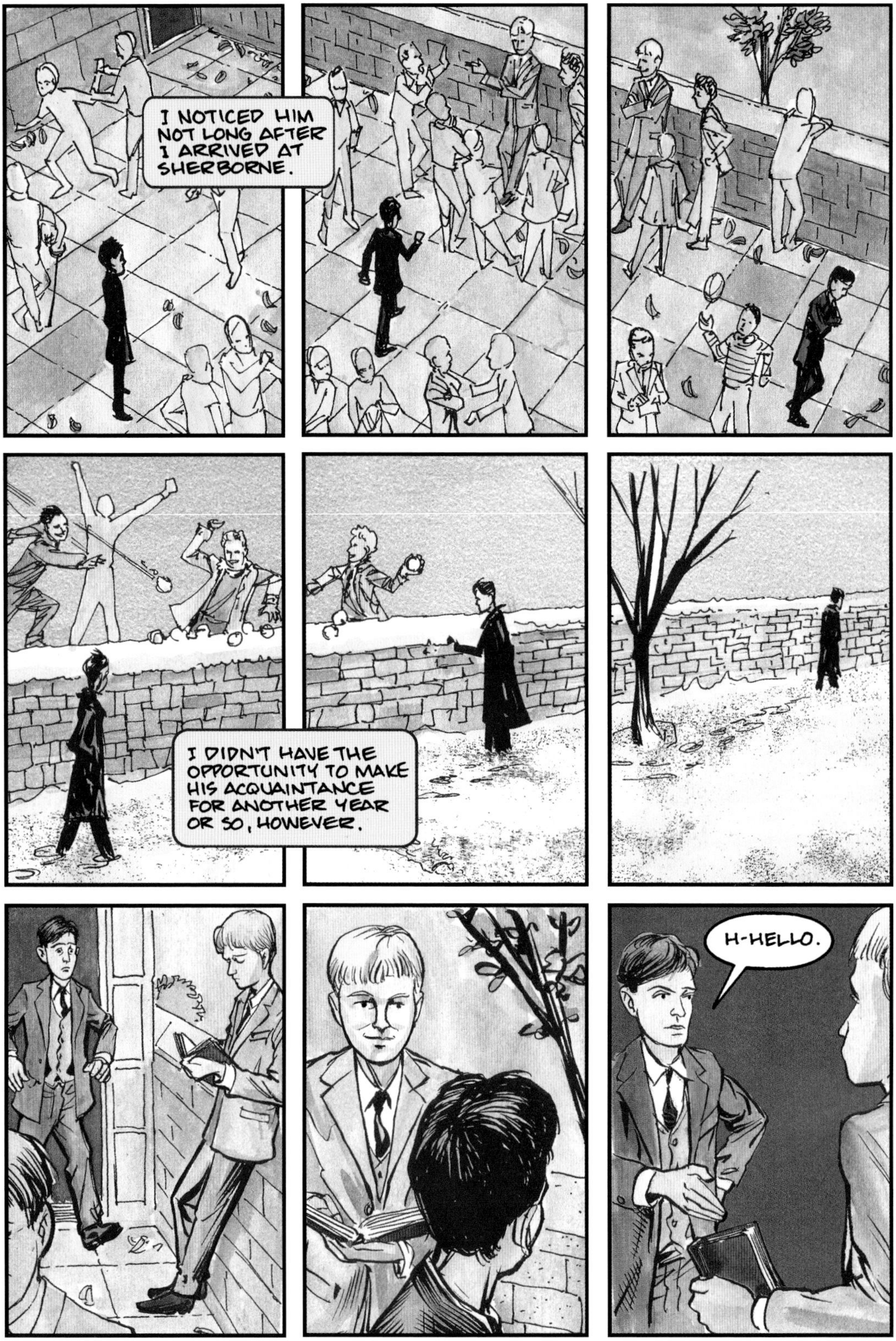
I NOTICED HIM NOT LONG AFTER I ARRIVED AT SHERBORNE.
I DIDN'T HAVE THE OPPORTUNITY TO MAKE HIS ACQUAINTANCE FOR ANOTHER YEAR OR SO, HOWEVER.
H-HELLO.

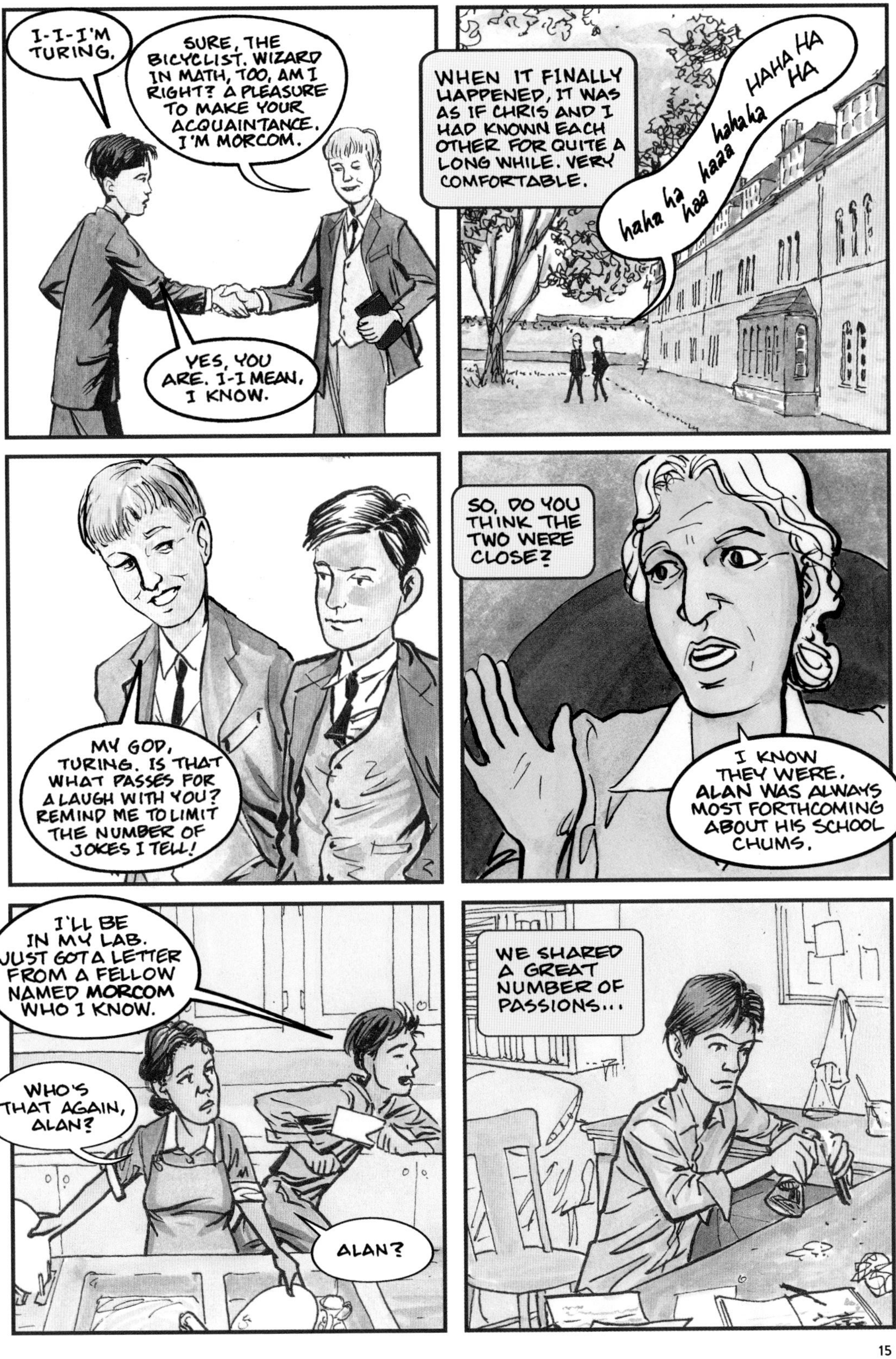
I-I-I'M TURING.
SURE, THE BICYCLIST. WIZARD IN MATH, TOO, AM I RIGHT? A PLEASURE TO MAKE YOUR ACQUAINTANCE. I'M MORCOM.
YES, YOU ARE. I-I MEAN, I KNOW.
WHEN IT FINALLY HAPPENED, IT WAS AS IF CHRIS AND I HAD KNOWN EACH OTHER FOR QUITE A LONG WHILE. VERY COMFORTABLE.
haha ha haa haaa hahaha HAHA HA HA
MY GOD, TURING. IS THAT WHAT PASSES FOR A LAUGH WITH YOU? REMIND ME TO LIMIT THE NUMBER OF JOKES I TELL!
SO, DO YOU THINK THE TWO WERE CLOSE?
I KNOW THEY WERE. ALAN WAS ALWAYS MOST FORTHCOMING ABOUT HIS SCHOOL CHUMS.
I'LL BE IN MY LAB. JUST GOT A LETTER FROM A FELLOW NAMED MORCOM WHO I KNOW.
WHO'S THAT AGAIN, ALAN?
ALAN?
WE SHARED A GREAT NUMBER OF PASSIONS...

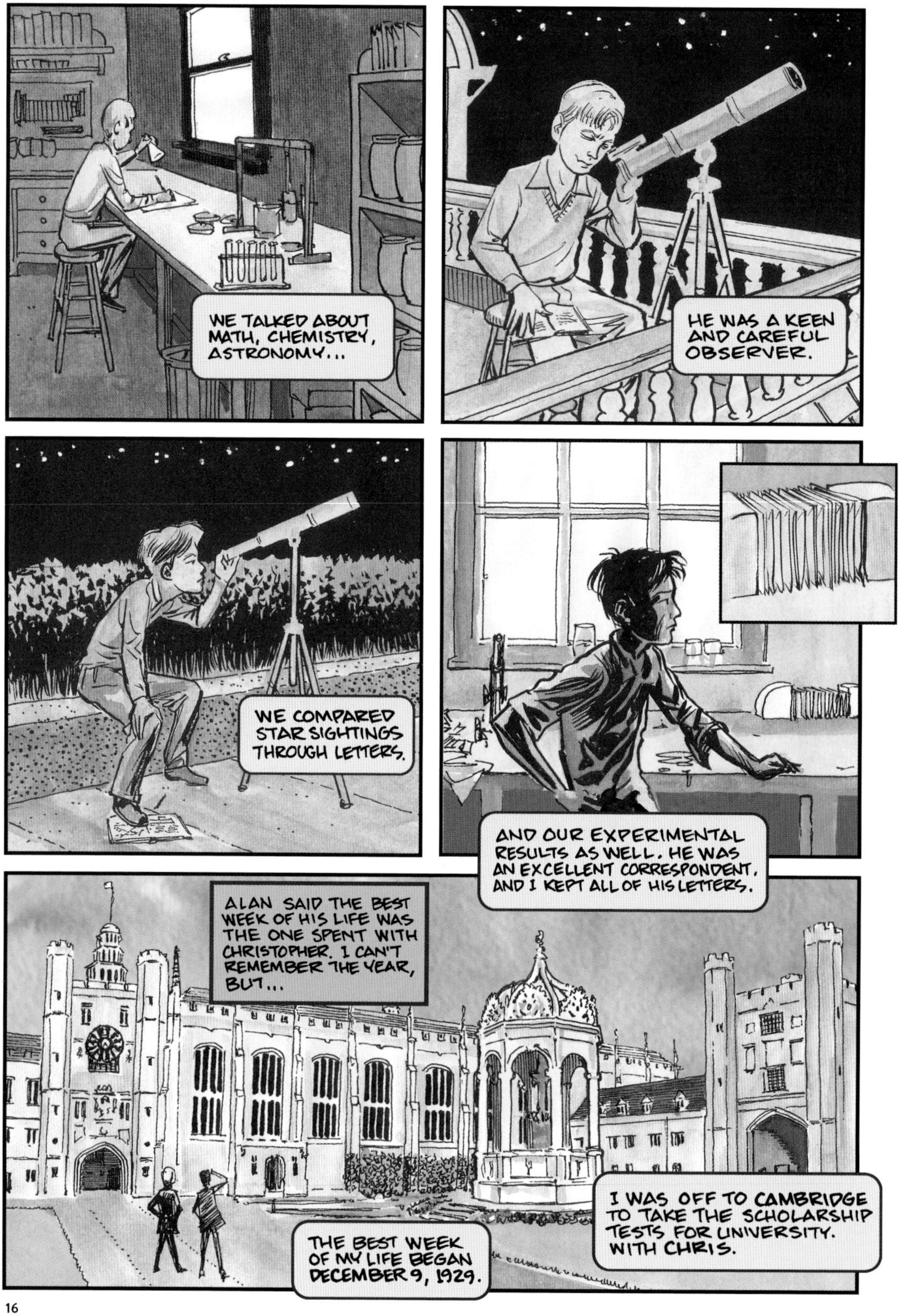
WE TALKED ABOUT MATH, CHEMISTRY, ASTRONOMY...
HE WAS A KEEN AND CAREFUL OBSERVER.
WE COMPARED STAR SIGHTINGS THROUGH LETTERS.
AND OUR EXPERIMENTAL RESULTS AS WELL. HE WAS AN EXCELLENT CORRESPONDENT, AND I KEPT ALL OF HIS LETTERS.
ALAN SAID THE BEST WEEK OF HIS LIFE WAS THE ONE SPENT WITH CHRISTOPHER. I CAN'T REMEMBER THE YEAR, BUT...
THE BEST WEEK OF MY LIFE BEGAN DECEMBER 9, 1929.
I WAS OFF TO CAMBRIDGE TO TAKE THE SCHOLARSHIP TESTS FOR UNIVERSITY. WITH CHRIS.

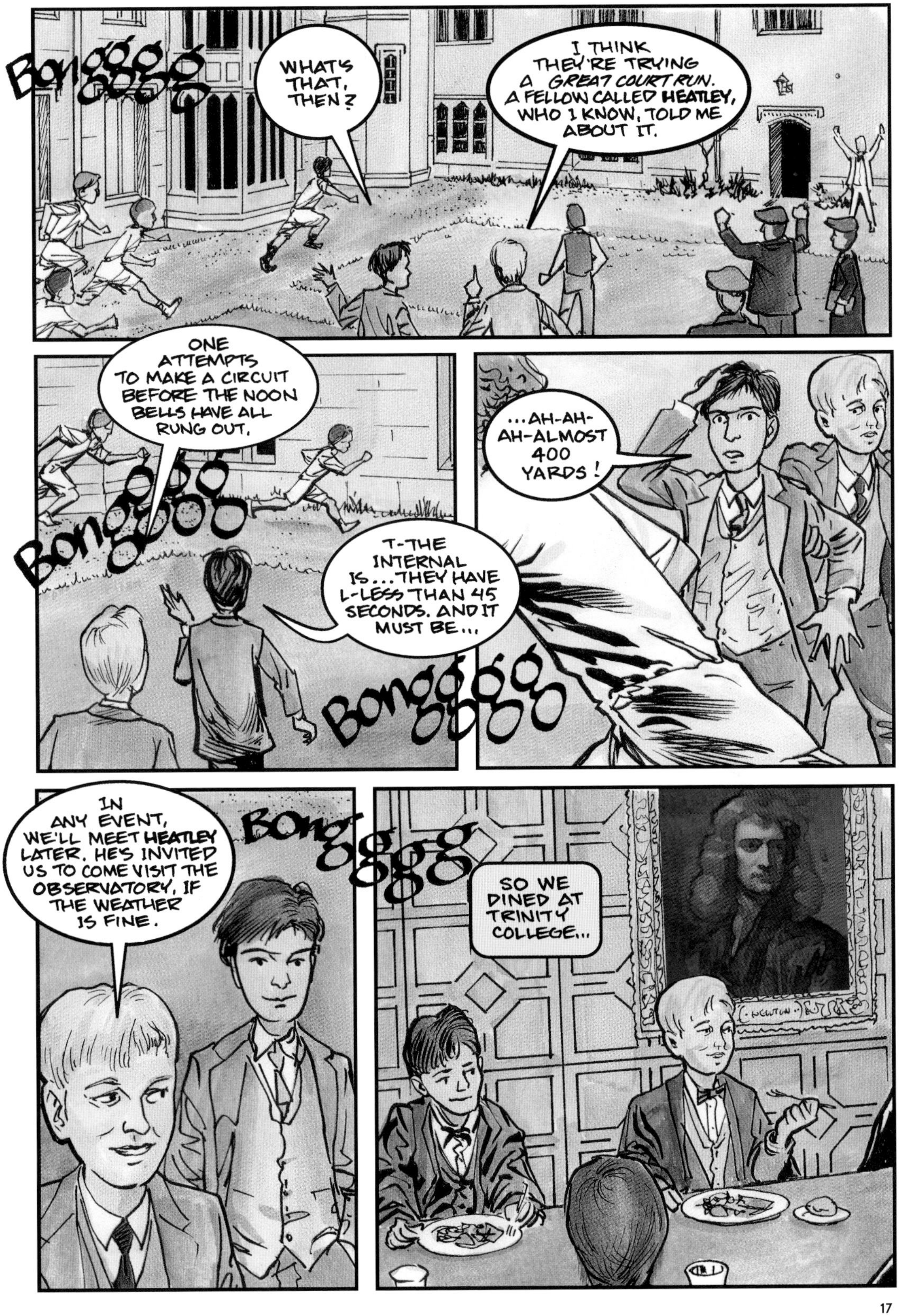
Bonggggg
WHAT'S THAT, THEN?
I THINK THEY'RE TRYING A GREAT COURT RUN. A FELLOW CALLED HEATLEY, WHO I KNOW, TOLD ME ABOUT IT.
ONE ATTEMPTS TO MAKE A CIRCUIT BEFORE THE NOON BELLS HAVE ALL RUNG OUT.
Bonggggggg
T-THE INTERNAL IS... THEY HAVE L-LESS THAN 45 SECONDS. AND IT MUST BE...
...AH-AH-AH-ALMOST 400 YARDS!
Bonggggggg
IN ANY EVENT, WE'LL MEET HEATLEY LATER. HE'S INVITED US TO COME VISIT THE OBSERVATORY, IF THE WEATHER IS FINE.
Bonggggg
SO WE DINED AT TRINITY COLLEGE...
NEWTON

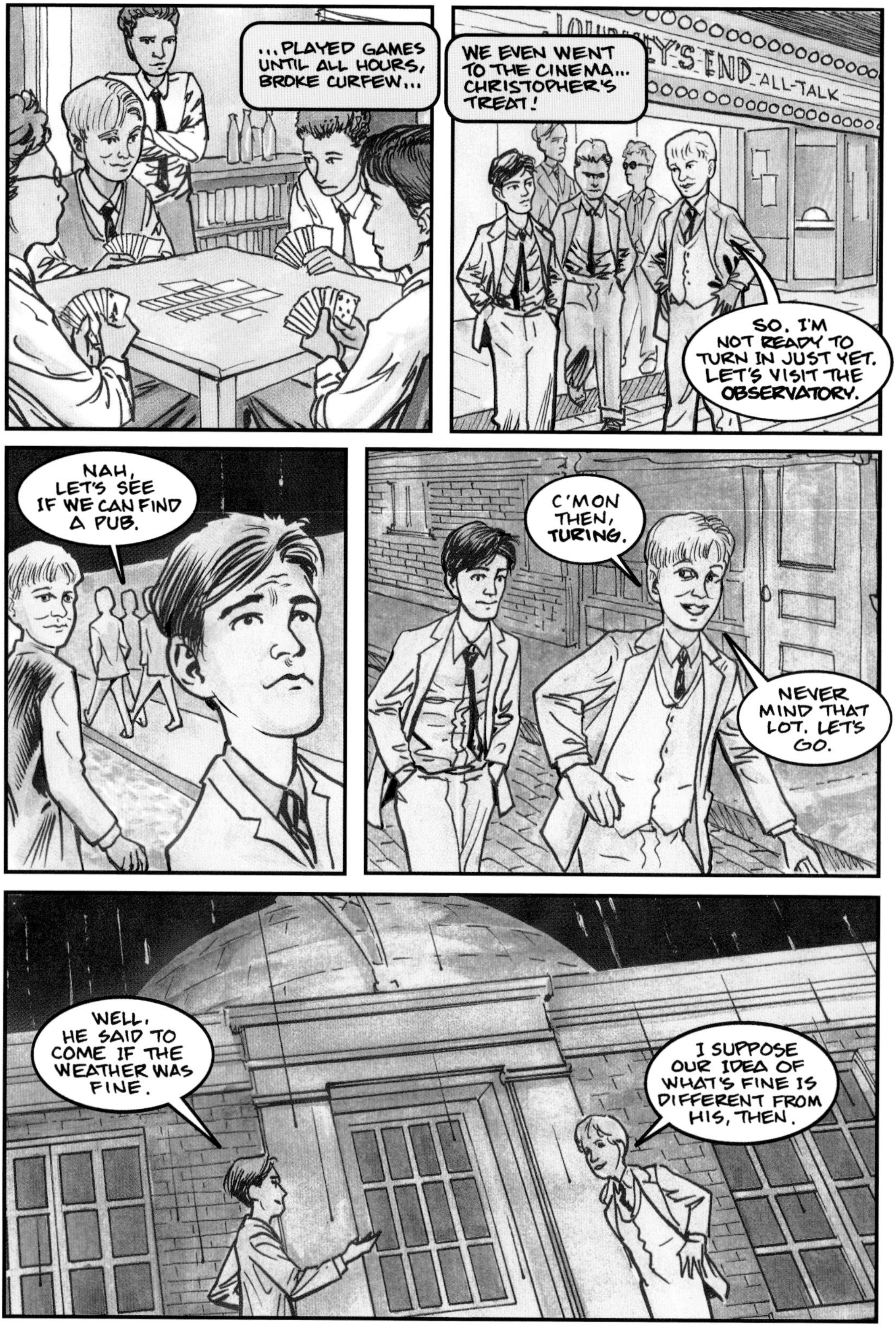
...PLAYED GAMES UNTIL ALL HOURS, BROKE CURFEW...
WE EVEN WENT TO THE CINEMA... CHRISTOPHER'S TREAT!
ALL-TALK
SO. I'M NOT READY TO TURN IN JUST YET. LET'S VISIT THE OBSERVATORY.
NAH, LET'S SEE IF WE CAN FIND A PUB.
C'MON THEN, TURING.
NEVER MIND THAT LOT. LET'S GO.
WELL, HE SAID TO COME IF THE WEATHER WAS FINE.
I SUPPOSE OUR IDEA OF WHAT'S FINE IS DIFFERENT FROM HIS, THEN.

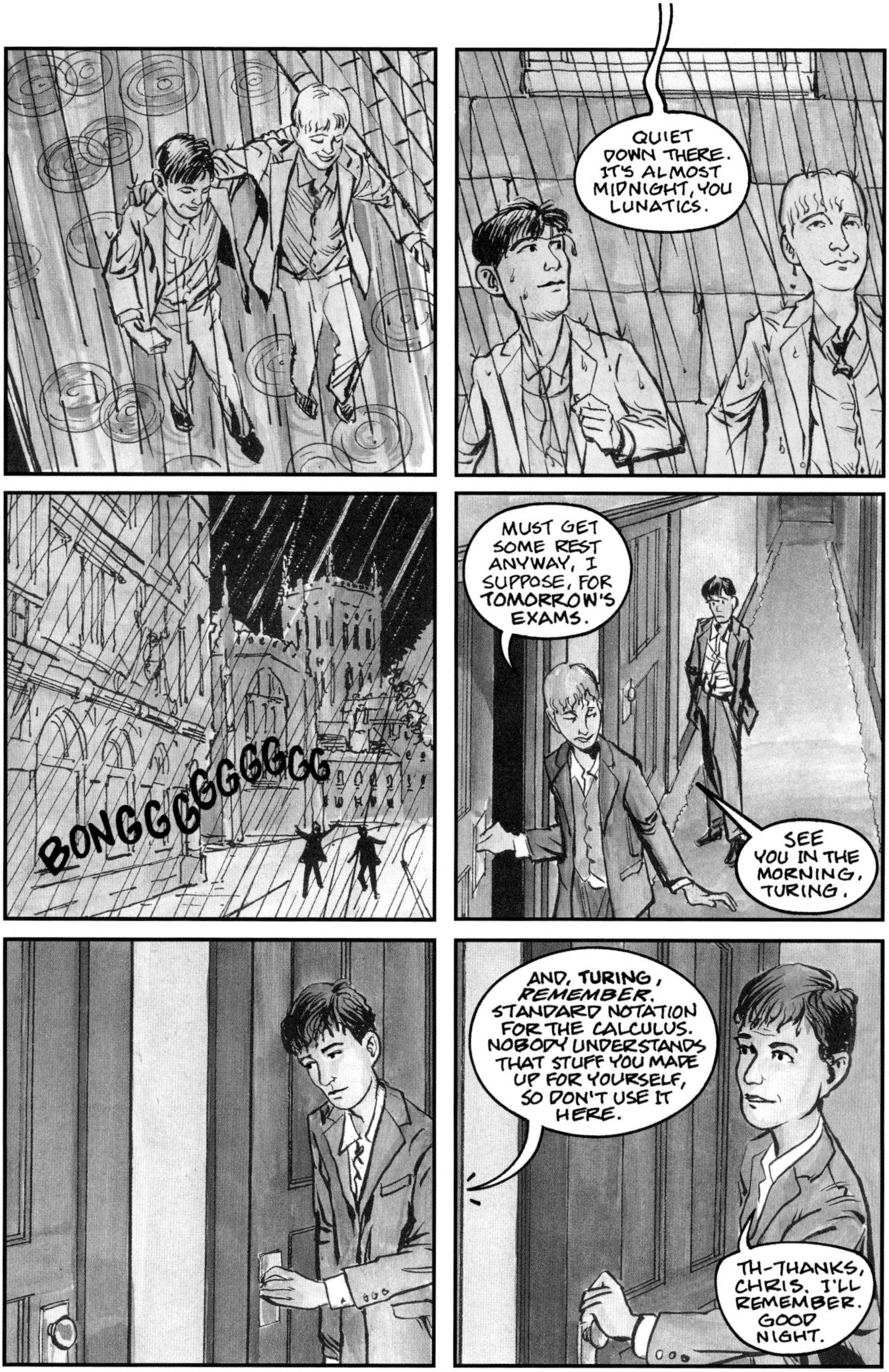
QUIET DOWN THERE. IT'S ALMOST MIDNIGHT, YOU LUNATICS.
BONGGGGGGGGG
MUST GET SOME REST ANYWAY, I SUPPOSE, FOR TOMORROW'S EXAMS.
SEE YOU IN THE MORNING, TURING.
AND, TURING, *REMEMBER*. STANDARD NOTATION FOR THE CALCULUS. NOBODY UNDERSTANDS THAT STUFF YOU MADE UP FOR YOURSELF, SO DON'T USE IT HERE.
TH-THANKS, CHRIS. I'LL REMEMBER. GOOD NIGHT.

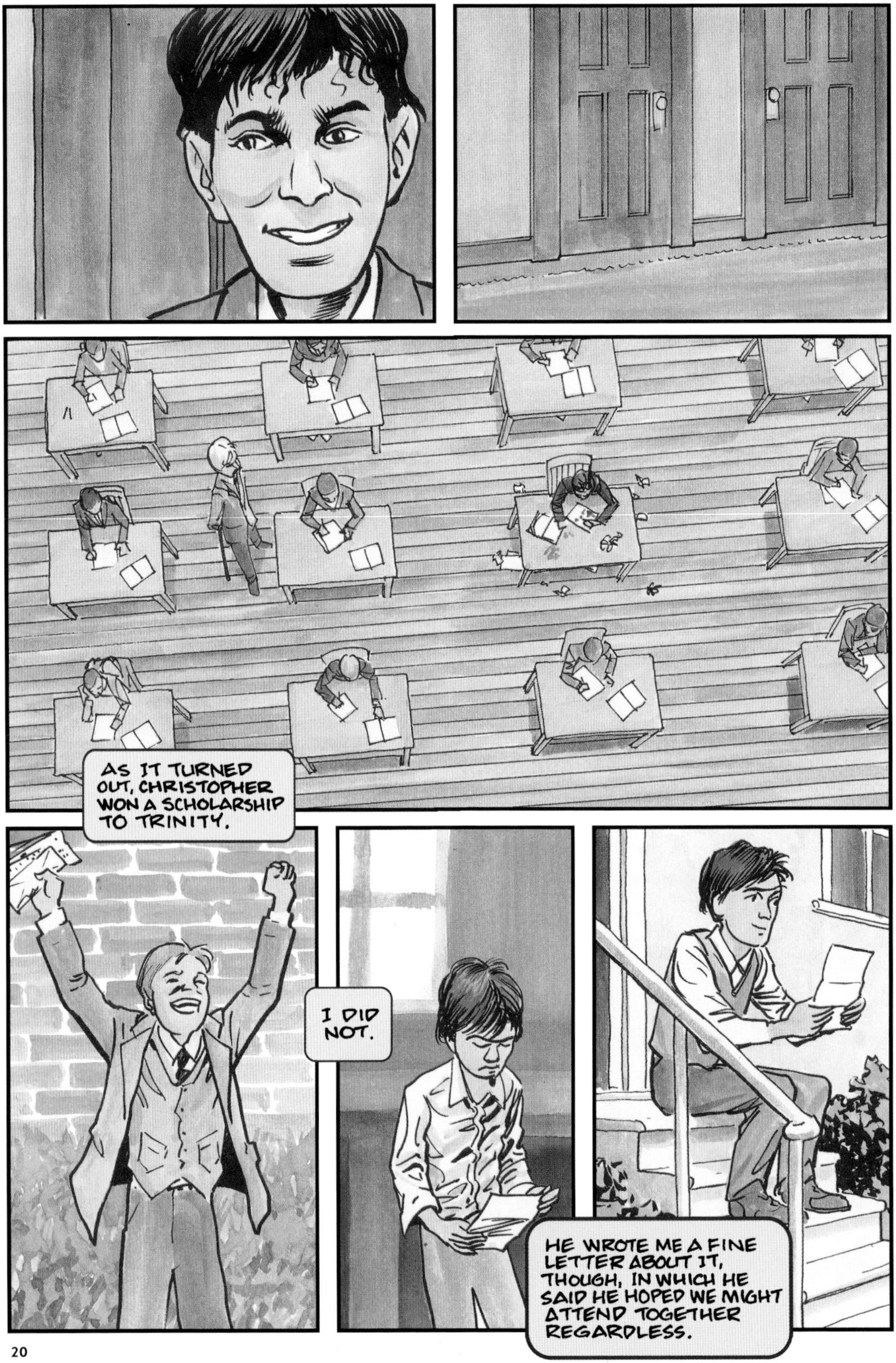
AS IT TURNED OUT, CHRISTOPHER WON A SCHOLARSHIP TO TRINITY.
I DID NOT.
HE WROTE ME A FINE LETTER ABOUT IT, THOUGH, IN WHICH HE SAID HE HOPED WE MIGHT ATTEND TOGETHER REGARDLESS.

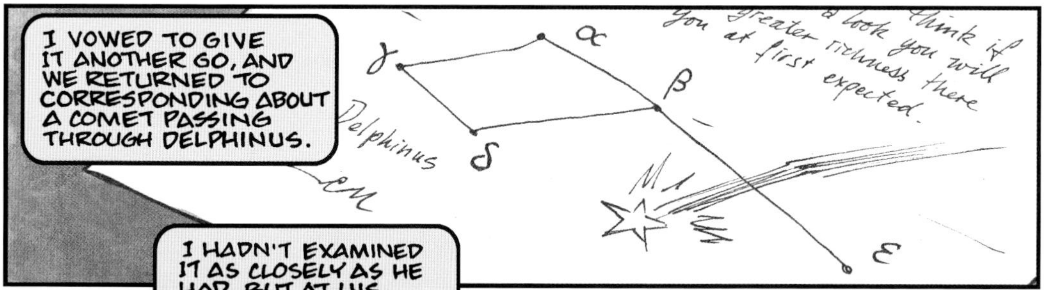
I VOWED TO GIVE IT ANOTHER GO, AND WE RETURNED TO CORRESPONDING ABOUT A COMET PASSING THROUGH DELPHINUS.
Delphinus
γ
α
β
δ
ε

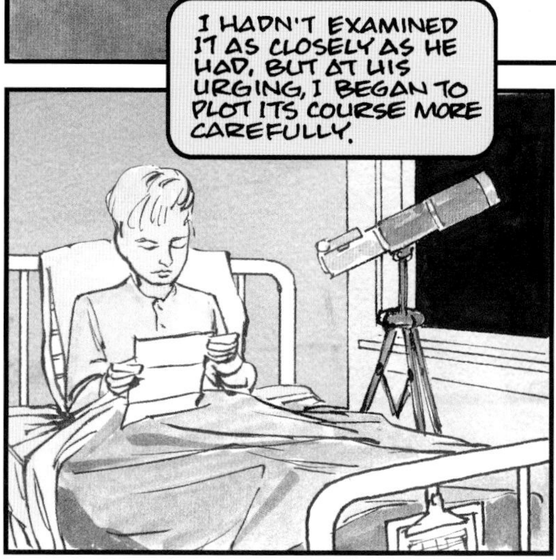
I HADN'T EXAMINED IT AS CLOSELY AS HE HAD, BUT AT HIS URGING, I BEGAN TO PLOT ITS COURSE MORE CAREFULLY.

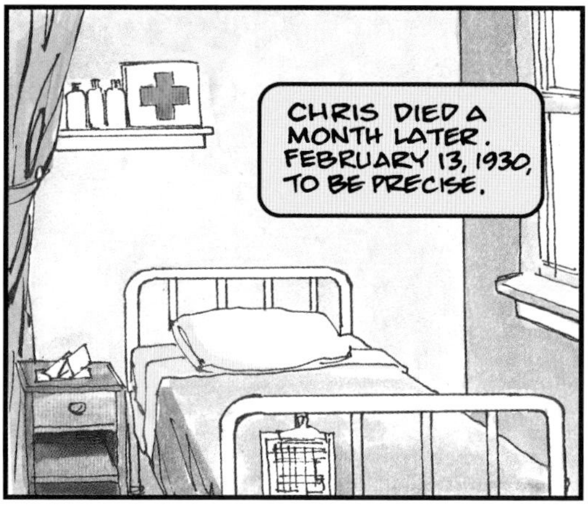
CHRIS DIED A MONTH LATER. FEBRUARY 13, 1930, TO BE PRECISE.

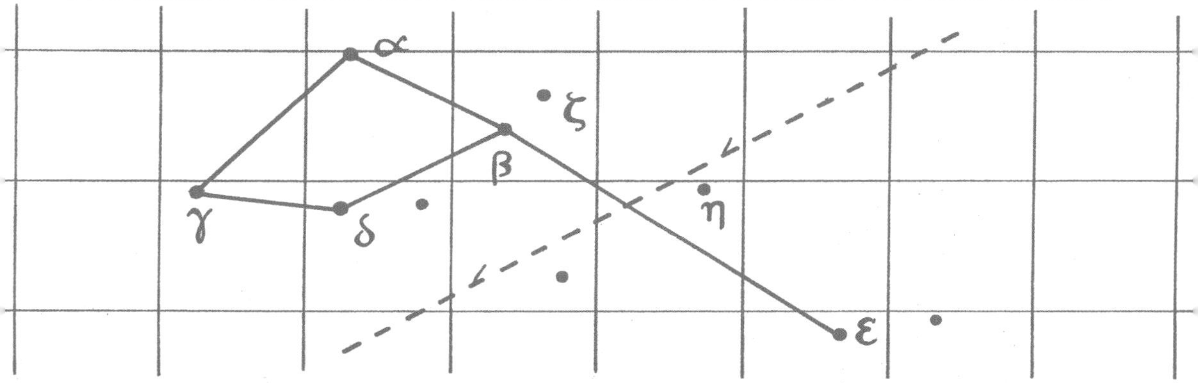
α
ζ
β
γ
δ
η
ε

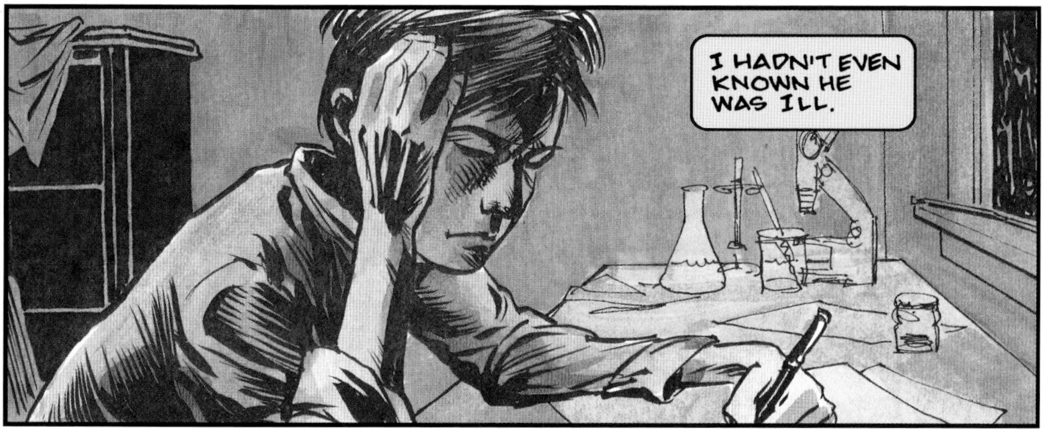
I HADN'T EVEN KNOWN HE WAS ILL.

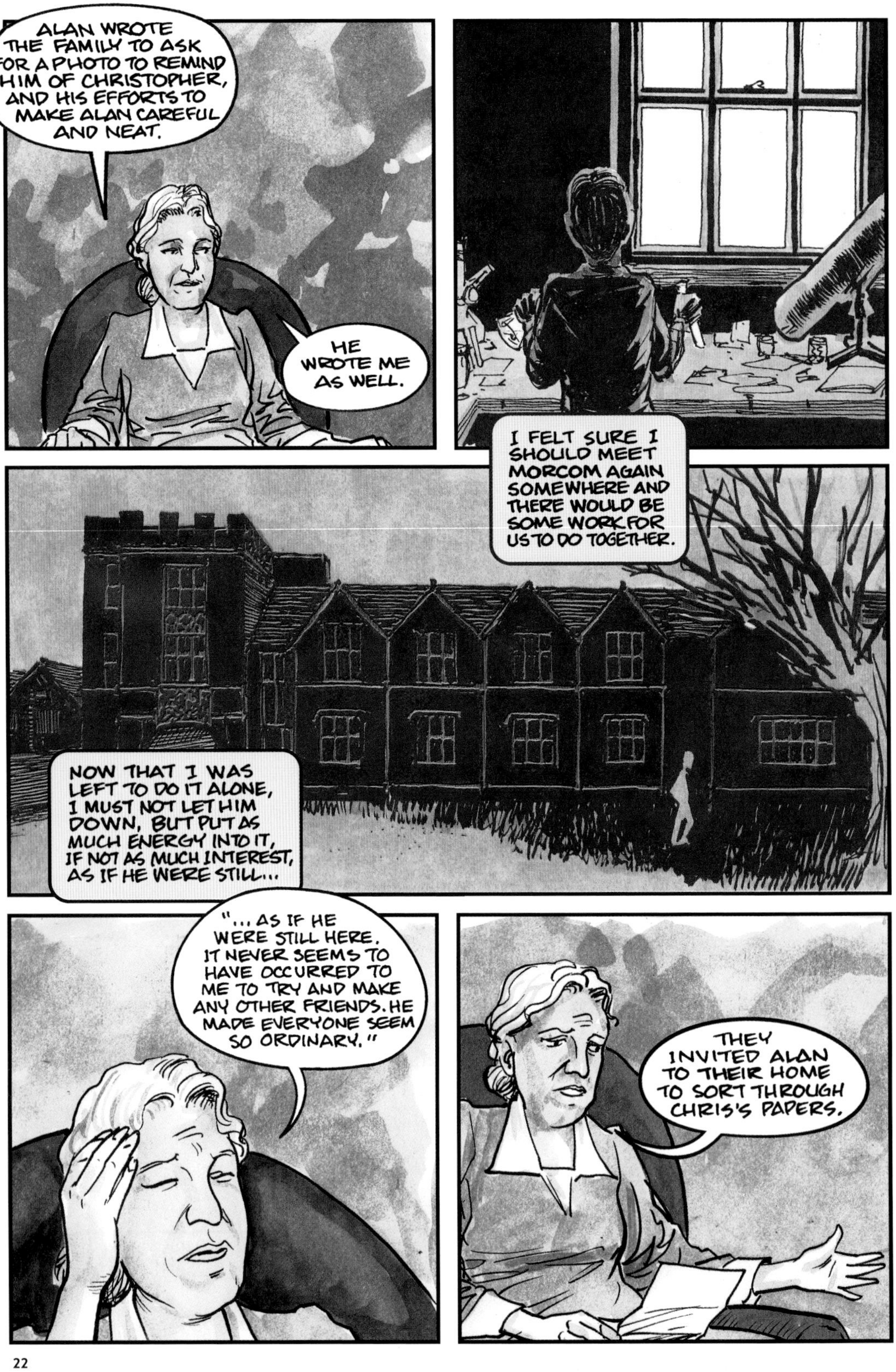
ALAN WROTE THE FAMILY TO ASK FOR A PHOTO TO REMIND HIM OF CHRISTOPHER, AND HIS EFFORTS TO MAKE ALAN CAREFUL AND NEAT.
HE WROTE ME AS WELL.
I FELT SURE I SHOULD MEET MORCOM AGAIN SOMEWHERE AND THERE WOULD BE SOME WORK FOR US TO DO TOGETHER.
NOW THAT I WAS LEFT TO DO IT ALONE, I MUST NOT LET HIM DOWN, BUT PUT AS MUCH ENERGY INTO IT, IF NOT AS MUCH INTEREST, AS IF HE WERE STILL...
"... AS IF HE WERE STILL HERE. IT NEVER SEEMS TO HAVE OCCURRED TO ME TO TRY AND MAKE ANY OTHER FRIENDS. HE MADE EVERYONE SEEM SO ORDINARY."
THEY INVITED ALAN TO THEIR HOME TO SORT THROUGH CHRIS'S PAPERS.

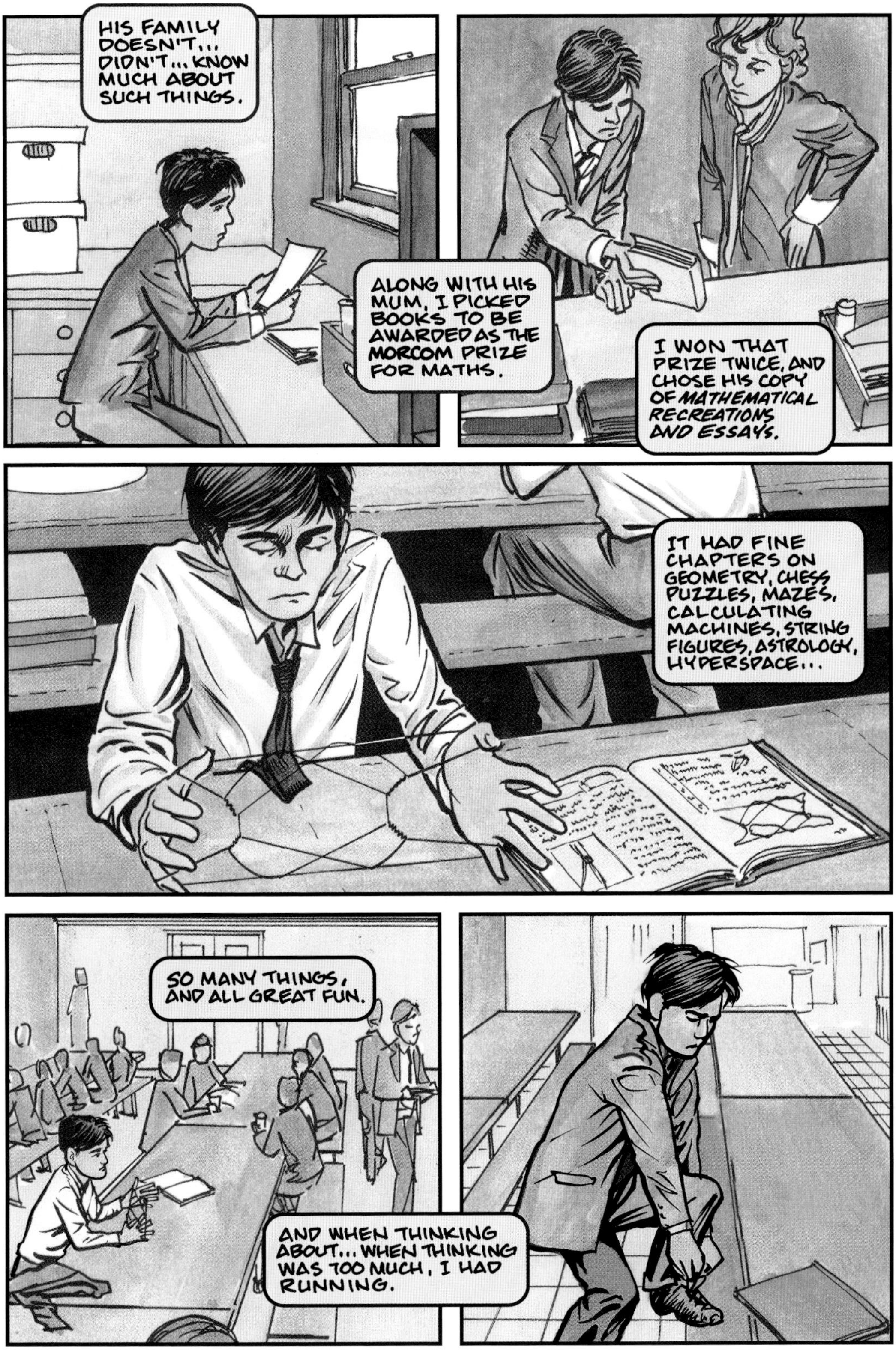
HIS FAMILY DOESN'T... DIDN'T... KNOW MUCH ABOUT SUCH THINGS.
ALONG WITH HIS MUM, I PICKED BOOKS TO BE AWARDED AS THE MORCOM PRIZE FOR MATHS.
I WON THAT PRIZE TWICE, AND CHOSE HIS COPY OF *MATHEMATICAL RECREATIONS AND ESSAYS*.
IT HAD FINE CHAPTERS ON GEOMETRY, CHESS PUZZLES, MAZES, CALCULATING MACHINES, STRING FIGURES, ASTROLOGY, HYPERSPACE...
SO MANY THINGS, AND ALL GREAT FUN.
AND WHEN THINKING ABOUT... WHEN THINKING WAS TOO MUCH, I HAD RUNNING.

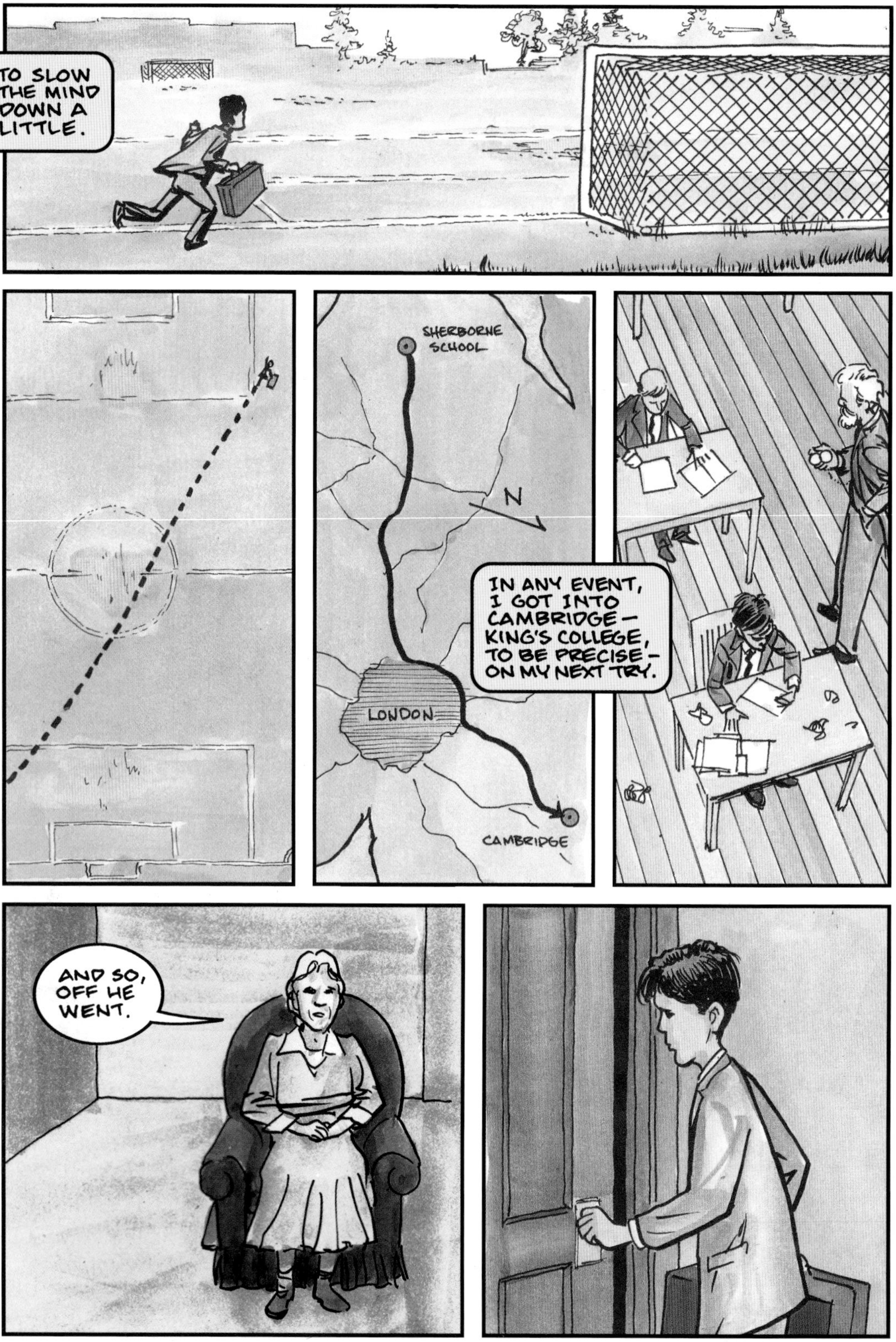
TO SLOW THE MIND DOWN A LITTLE.
SHERBORNE SCHOOL
N
LONDON
CAMBRIDGE
IN ANY EVENT, I GOT INTO CAMBRIDGE – KING'S COLLEGE, TO BE PRECISE – ON MY NEXT TRY.
AND SO, OFF HE WENT.

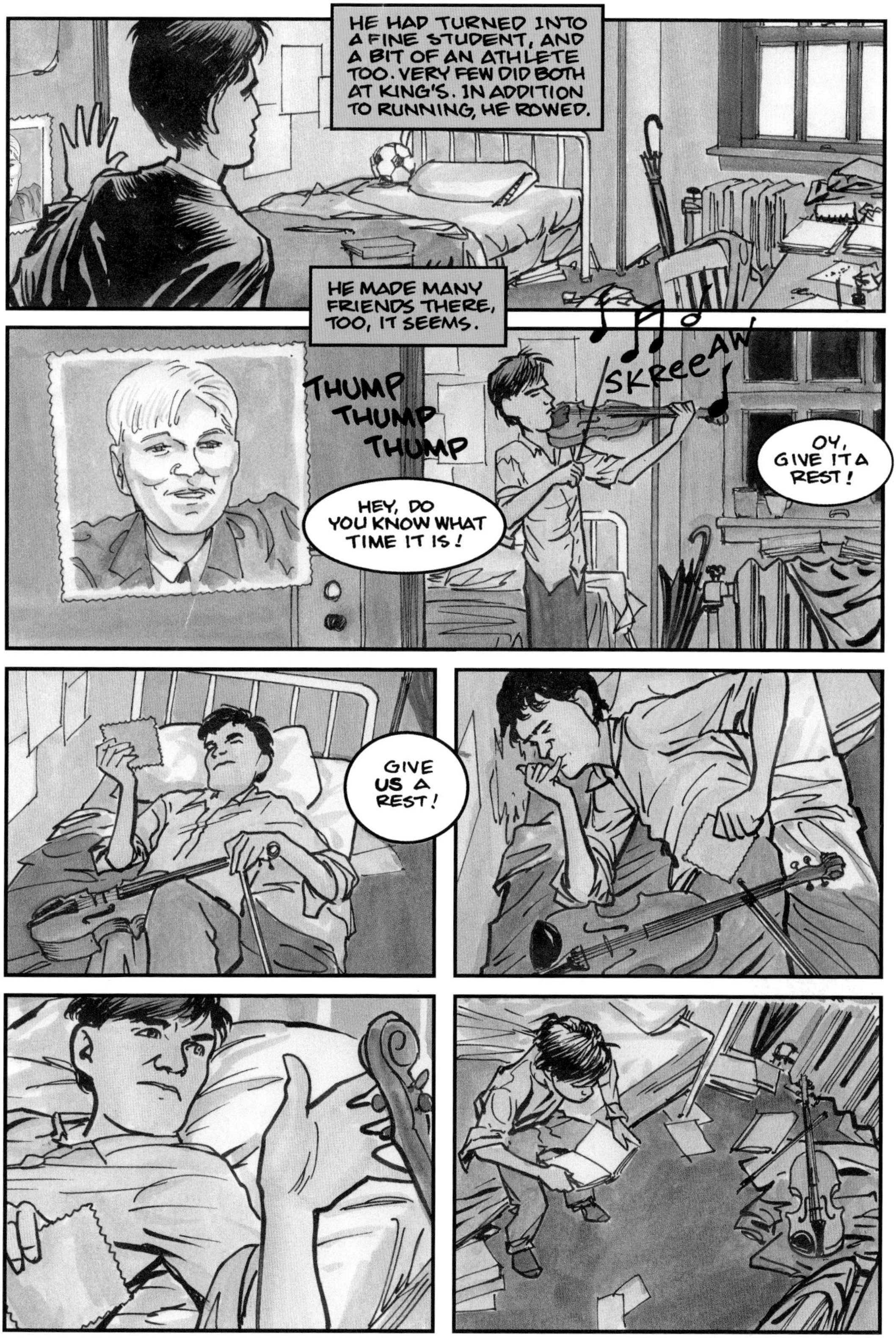
HE HAD TURNED INTO A FINE STUDENT, AND A BIT OF AN ATHLETE TOO. VERY FEW DID BOTH AT KING'S. IN ADDITION TO RUNNING, HE ROWED.
HE MADE MANY FRIENDS THERE, TOO, IT SEEMS.
SKREEAW
THUMP THUMP THUMP
HEY, DO YOU KNOW WHAT TIME IT IS!
OY, GIVE IT A REST!
GIVE US A REST!

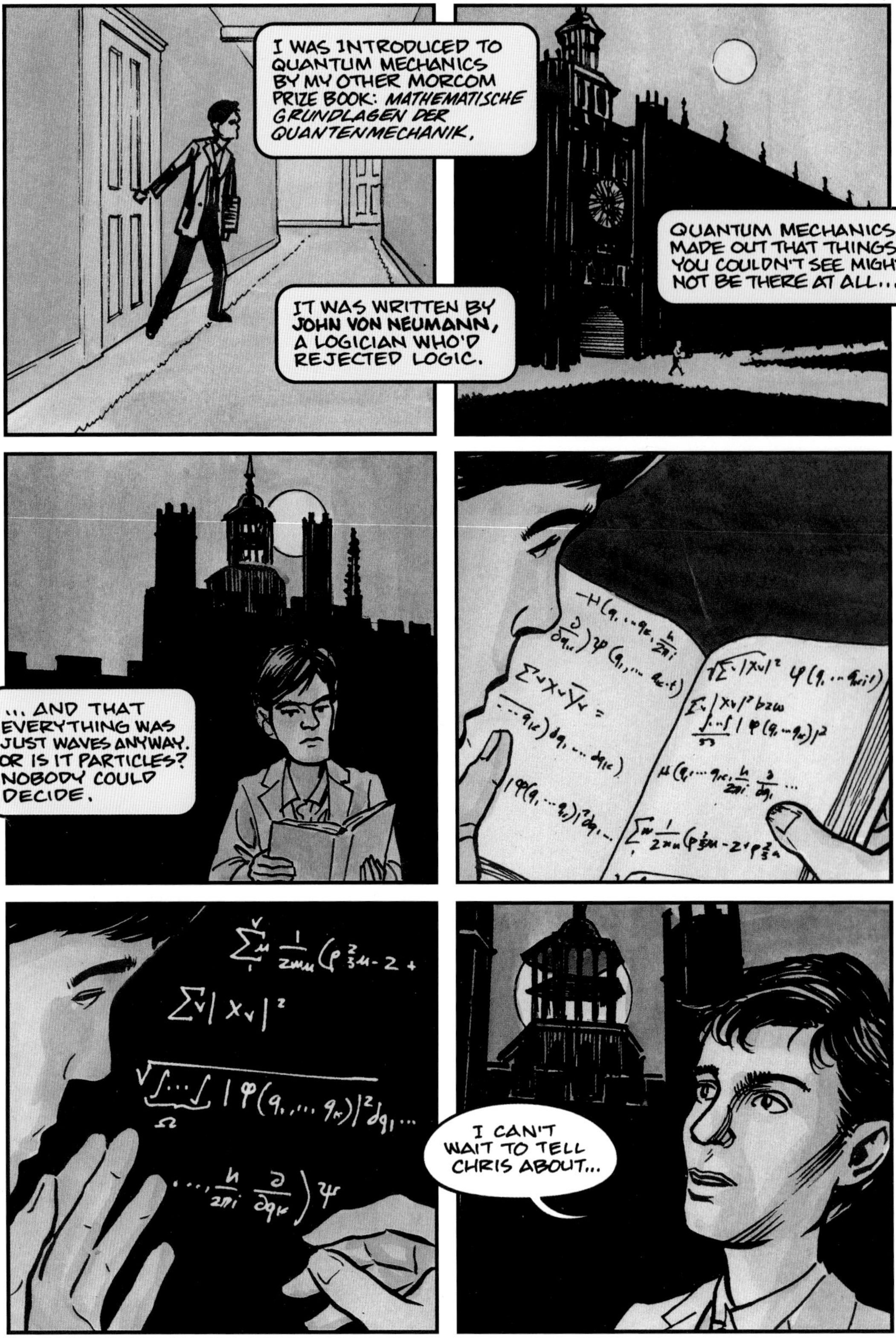
I WAS INTRODUCED TO QUANTUM MECHANICS BY MY OTHER MORCOM PRIZE BOOK: *MATHEMATISCHE GRUNDLAGEN DER QUANTENMECHANIK*.
IT WAS WRITTEN BY **JOHN VON NEUMANN**, A LOGICIAN WHO'D REJECTED LOGIC.
QUANTUM MECHANICS MADE OUT THAT THINGS YOU COULDN'T SEE MIGHT NOT BE THERE AT ALL...
... AND THAT EVERYTHING WAS JUST WAVES ANYWAY. OR IS IT PARTICLES? NOBODY COULD DECIDE.
I CAN'T WAIT TO TELL CHRIS ABOUT...

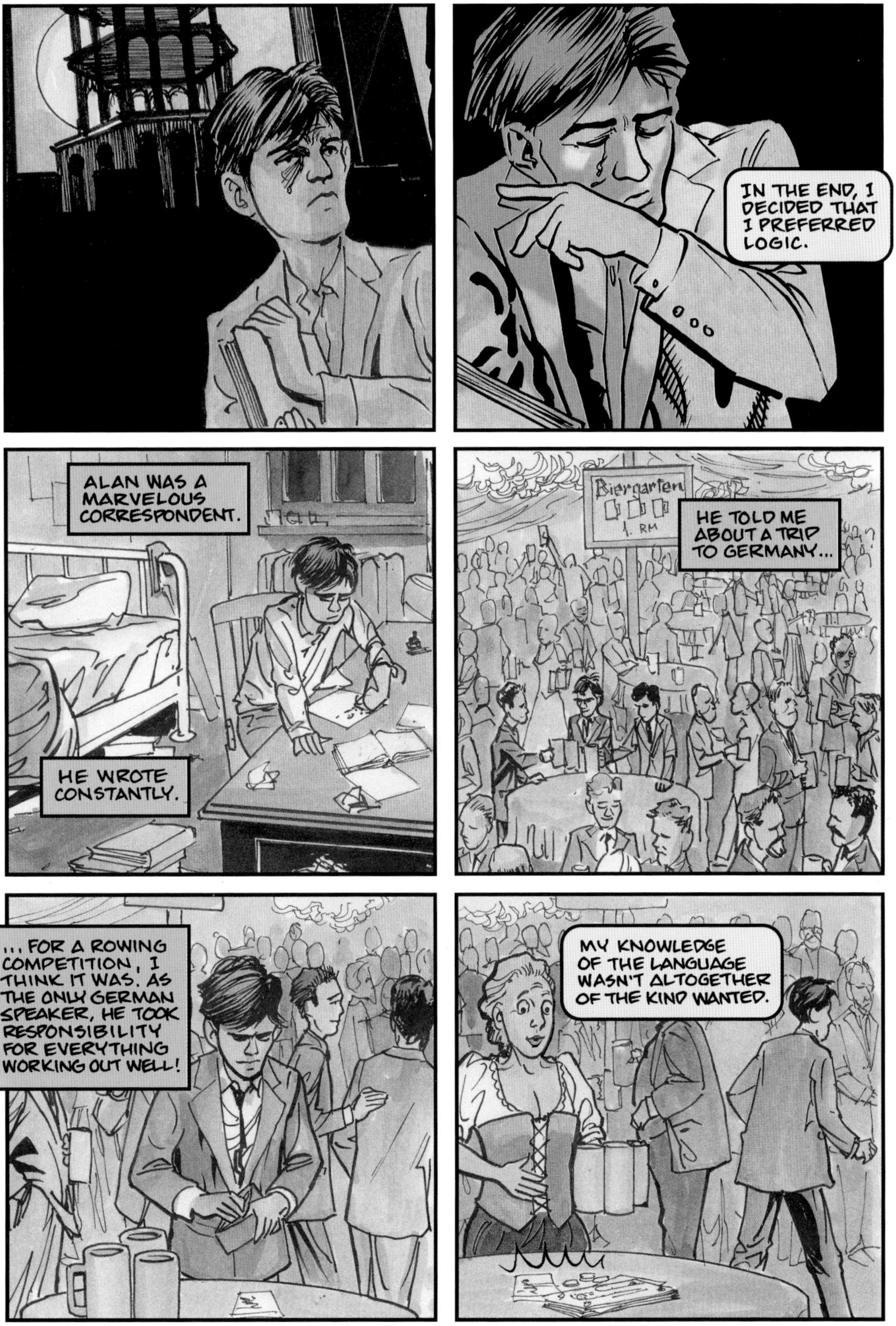

IN THE END, I DECIDED THAT I PREFERRED LOGIC.
ALAN WAS A MARVELOUS CORRESPONDENT.
HE WROTE CONSTANTLY.
Biergarten
1. RM
HE TOLD ME ABOUT A TRIP TO GERMANY...
...FOR A ROWING COMPETITION, I THINK IT WAS. AS THE ONLY GERMAN SPEAKER, HE TOOK RESPONSIBILITY FOR EVERYTHING WORKING OUT WELL!
MY KNOWLEDGE OF THE LANGUAGE WASN'T ALTOGETHER OF THE KIND WANTED.

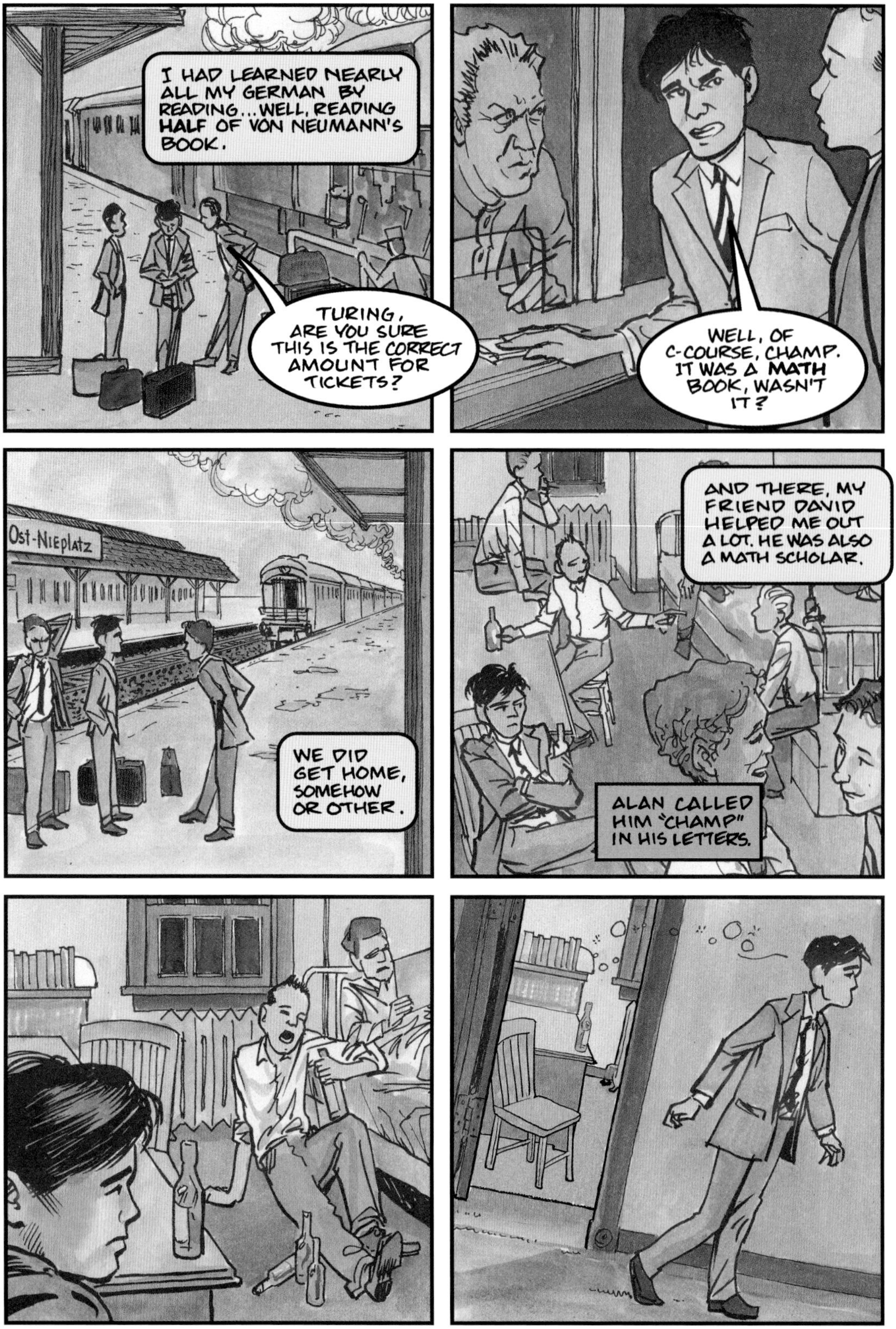
I HAD LEARNED NEARLY ALL MY GERMAN BY READING... WELL, READING HALF OF VON NEUMANN'S BOOK.
TURING, ARE YOU SURE THIS IS THE CORRECT AMOUNT FOR TICKETS?
WELL, OF C-COURSE, CHAMP. IT WAS A MATH BOOK, WASN'T IT?
Ost-Nieplatz
WE DID GET HOME, SOMEHOW OR OTHER.
AND THERE, MY FRIEND DAVID HELPED ME OUT A LOT. HE WAS ALSO A MATH SCHOLAR.
ALAN CALLED HIM "CHAMP" IN HIS LETTERS.

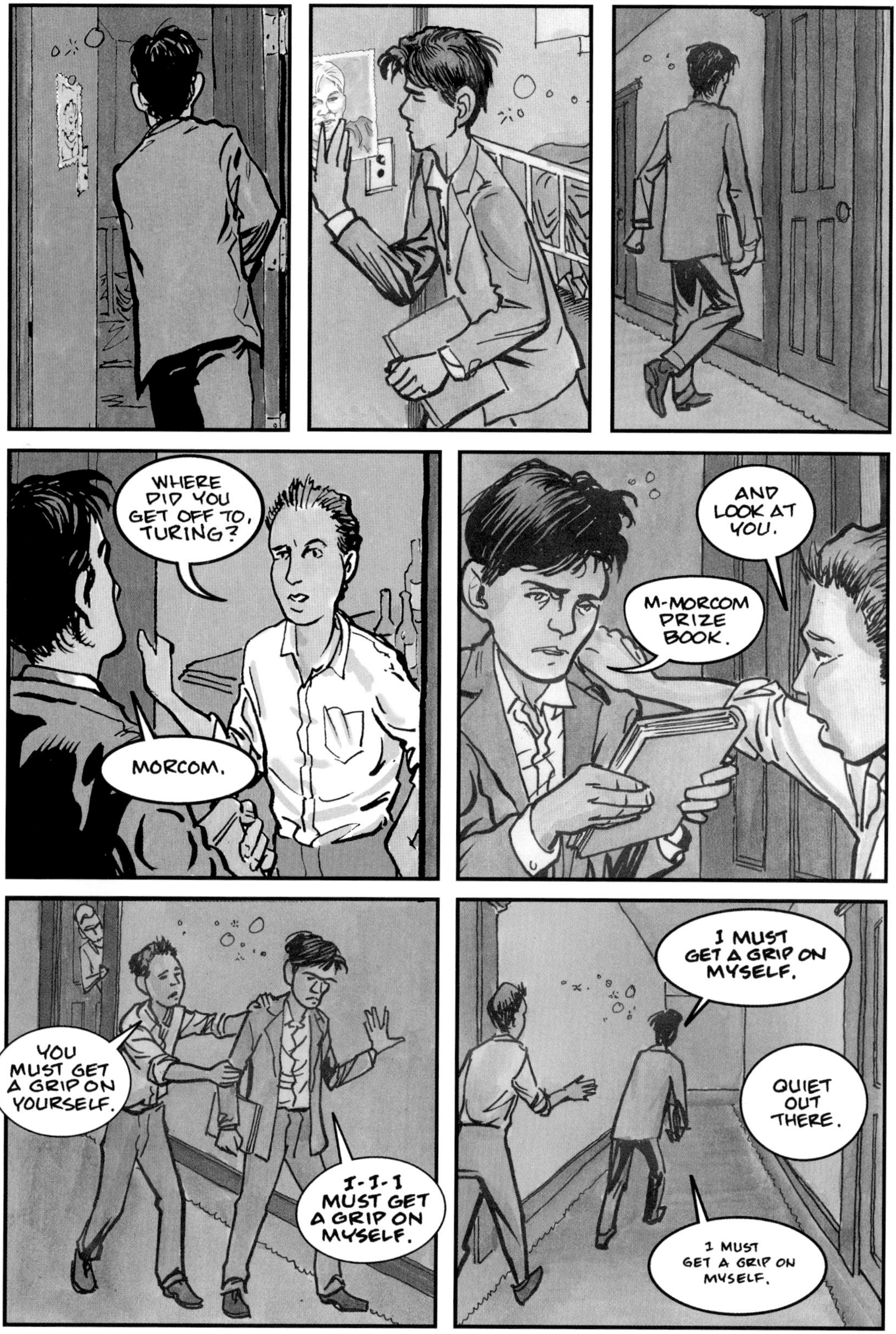
WHERE DID YOU GET OFF TO, TURING?
MORCOM.
AND LOOK AT YOU.
M-MORCOM PRIZE BOOK.
YOU MUST GET A GRIP ON YOURSELF.
I-I-I MUST GET A GRIP ON MYSELF.
I MUST GET A GRIP ON MYSELF.
QUIET OUT THERE.
I MUST GET A GRIP ON MYSELF.

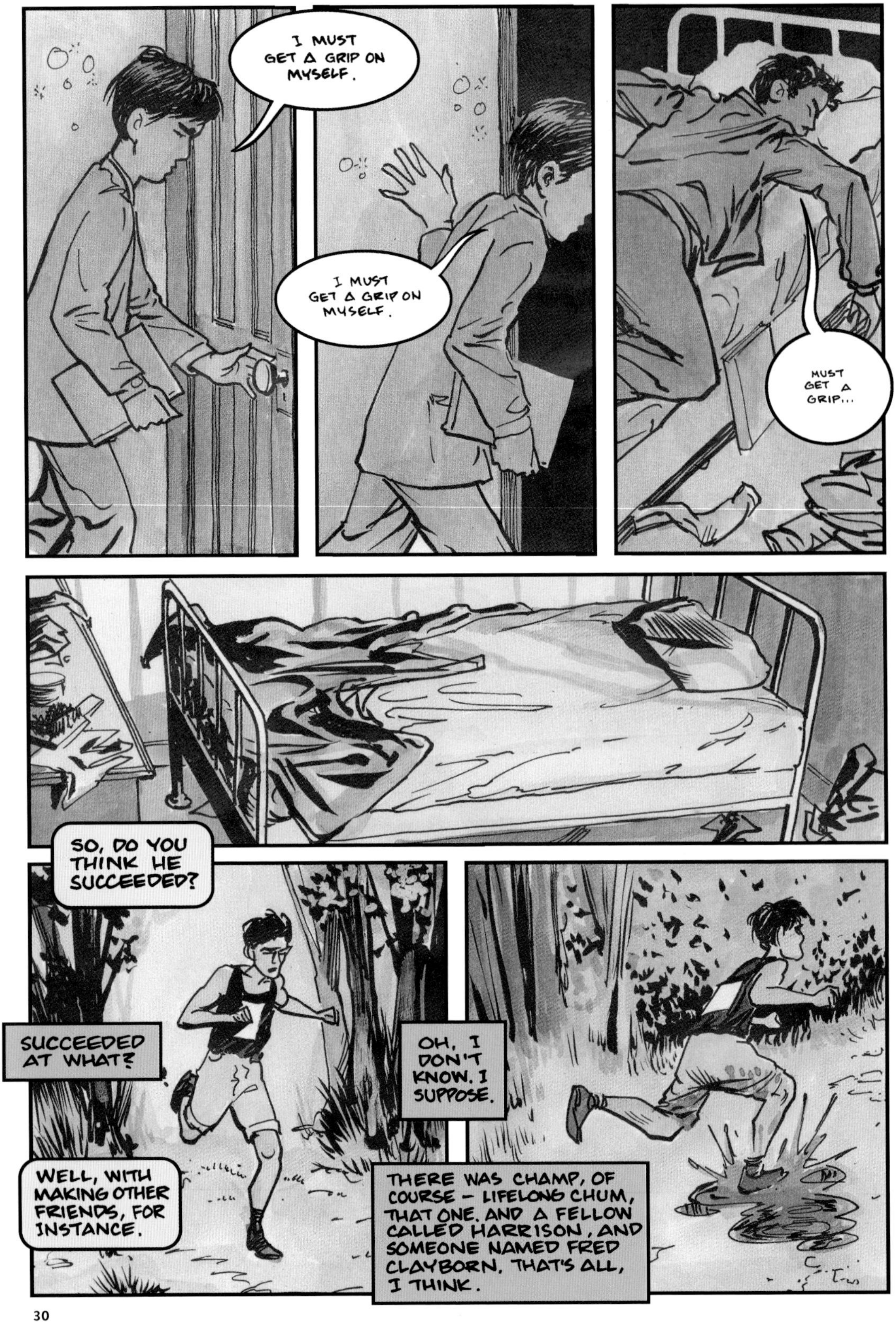
I MUST GET A GRIP ON MYSELF.
I MUST GET A GRIP ON MYSELF.
MUST GET A GRIP...
SO, DO YOU THINK HE SUCCEEDED?
SUCCEEDED AT WHAT?
OH, I DON'T KNOW. I SUPPOSE.
WELL, WITH MAKING OTHER FRIENDS, FOR INSTANCE.
THERE WAS CHAMP, OF COURSE – LIFELONG CHUM, THAT ONE. AND A FELLOW CALLED HARRISON, AND SOMEONE NAMED FRED CLAYBORN. THAT'S ALL, I THINK.

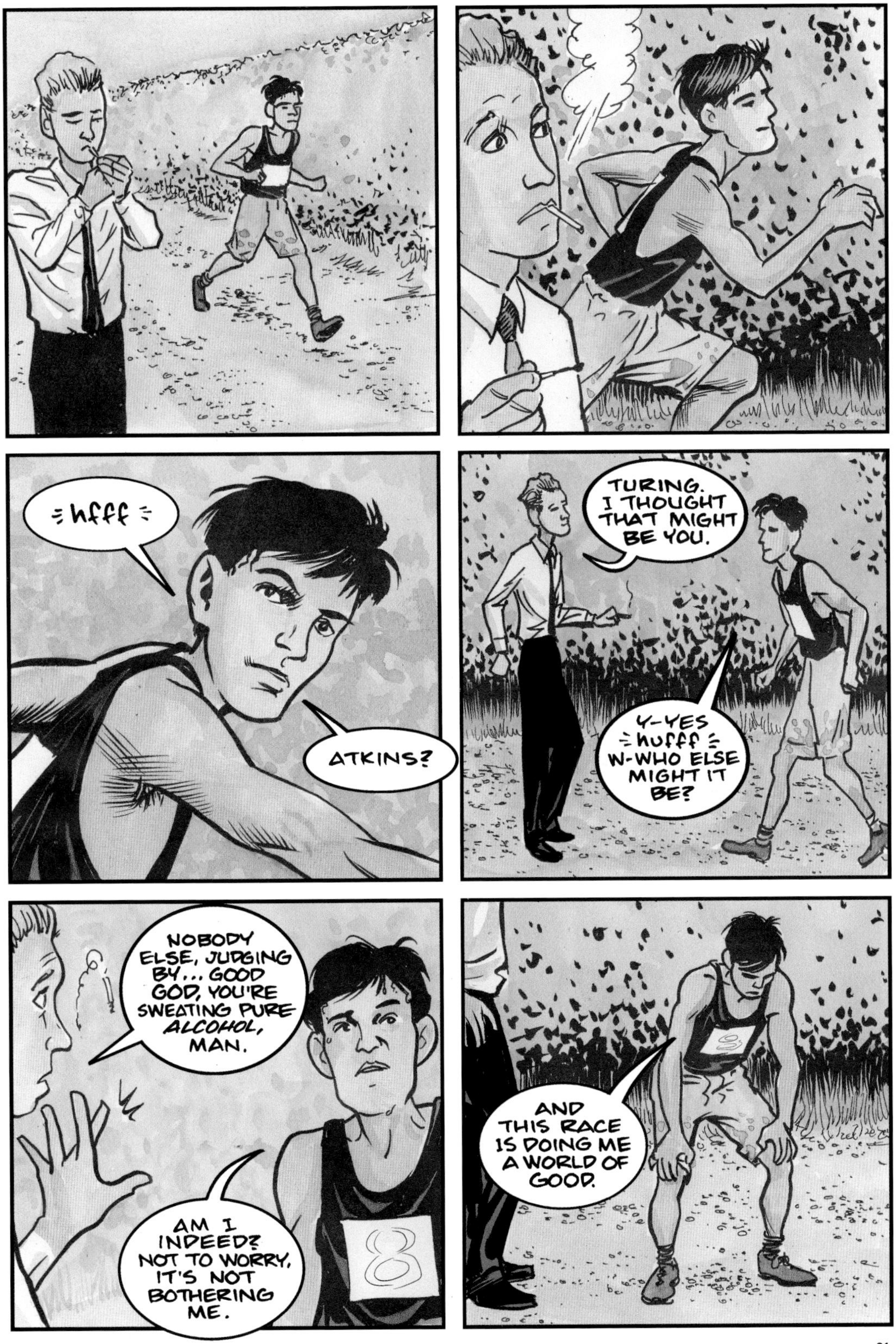

≈ hfff ≈
ATKINS?
TURING. I THOUGHT THAT MIGHT BE YOU.
Y-YES ≈ huffff ≈ W-WHO ELSE MIGHT IT BE?
NOBODY ELSE, JUDGING BY... GOOD GOD, YOU'RE SWEATING PURE ALCOHOL, MAN.
AM I INDEED? NOT TO WORRY, IT'S NOT BOTHERING ME.
AND THIS RACE IS DOING ME A WORLD OF GOOD.

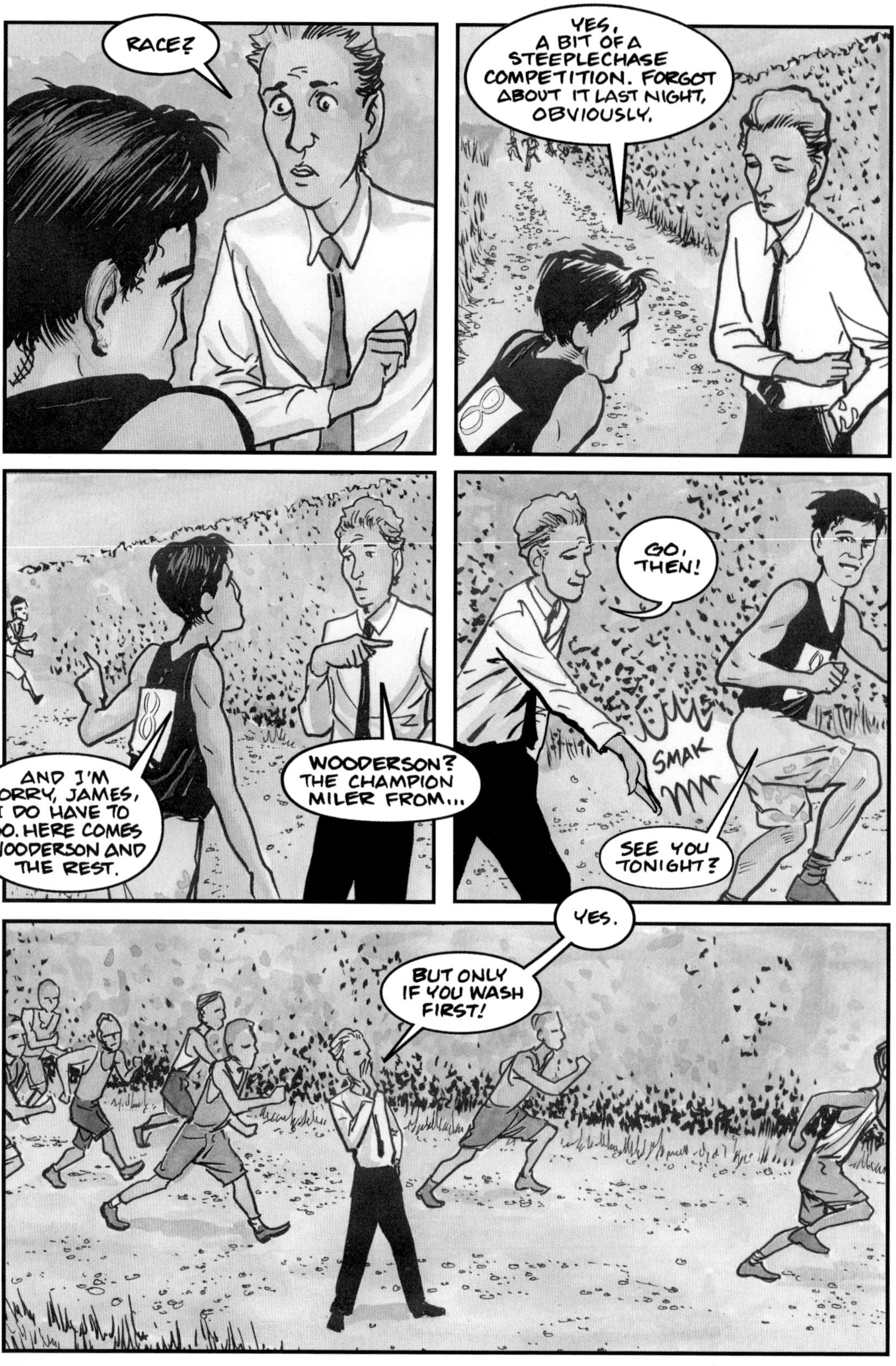
RACE?
YES, A BIT OF A STEEPLECHASE COMPETITION. FORGOT ABOUT IT LAST NIGHT, OBVIOUSLY.
AND I'M SORRY, JAMES, I DO HAVE TO GO. HERE COMES WOODERSON AND THE REST.
WOODERSON? THE CHAMPION MILER FROM...
GO, THEN!
SMAK
SEE YOU TONIGHT?
YES.
BUT ONLY IF YOU WASH FIRST!

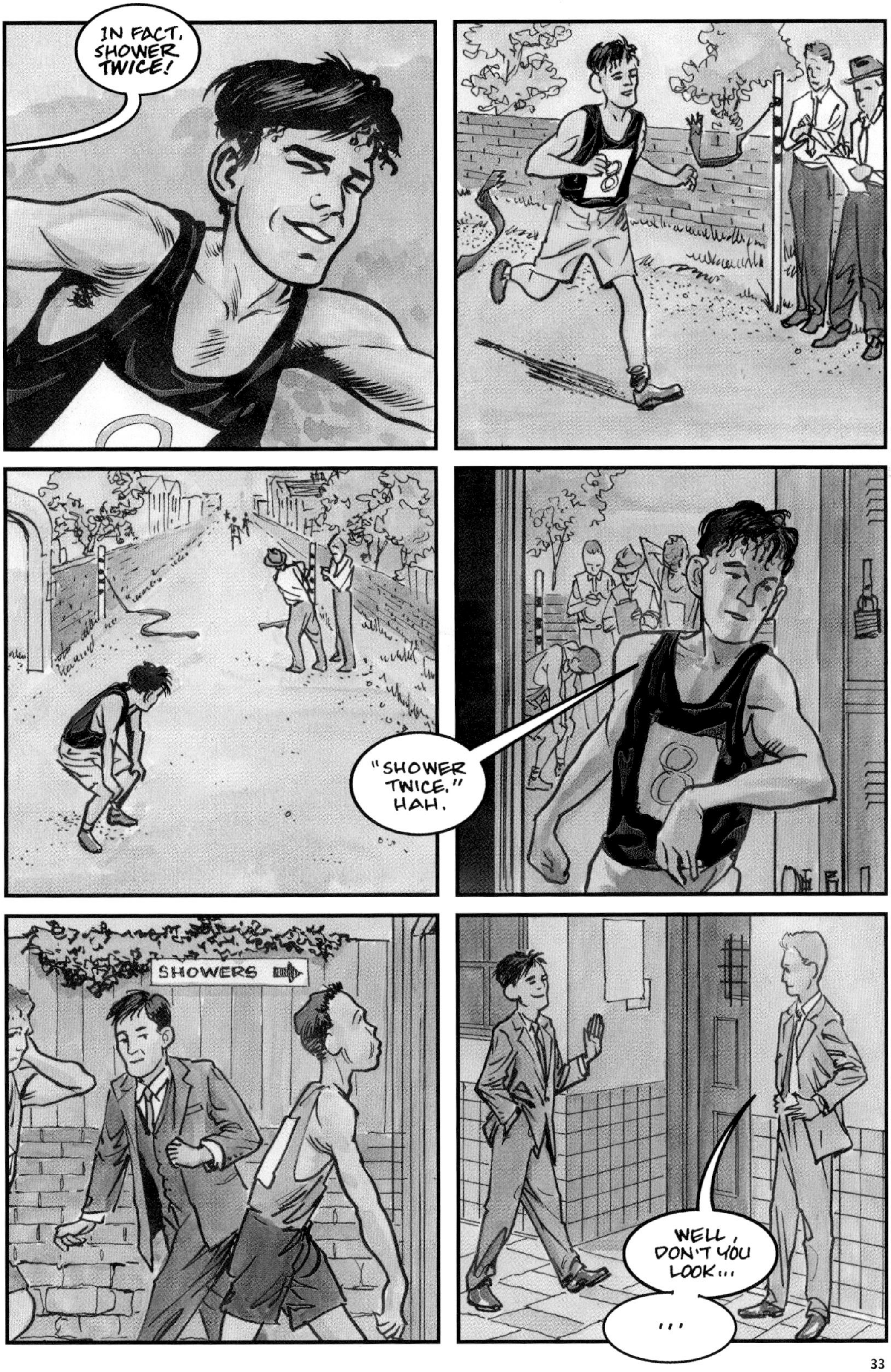
IN FACT, SHOWER TWICE!
SHOWERS
"SHOWER TWICE." HAH.
WELL, DON'T YOU LOOK...
...

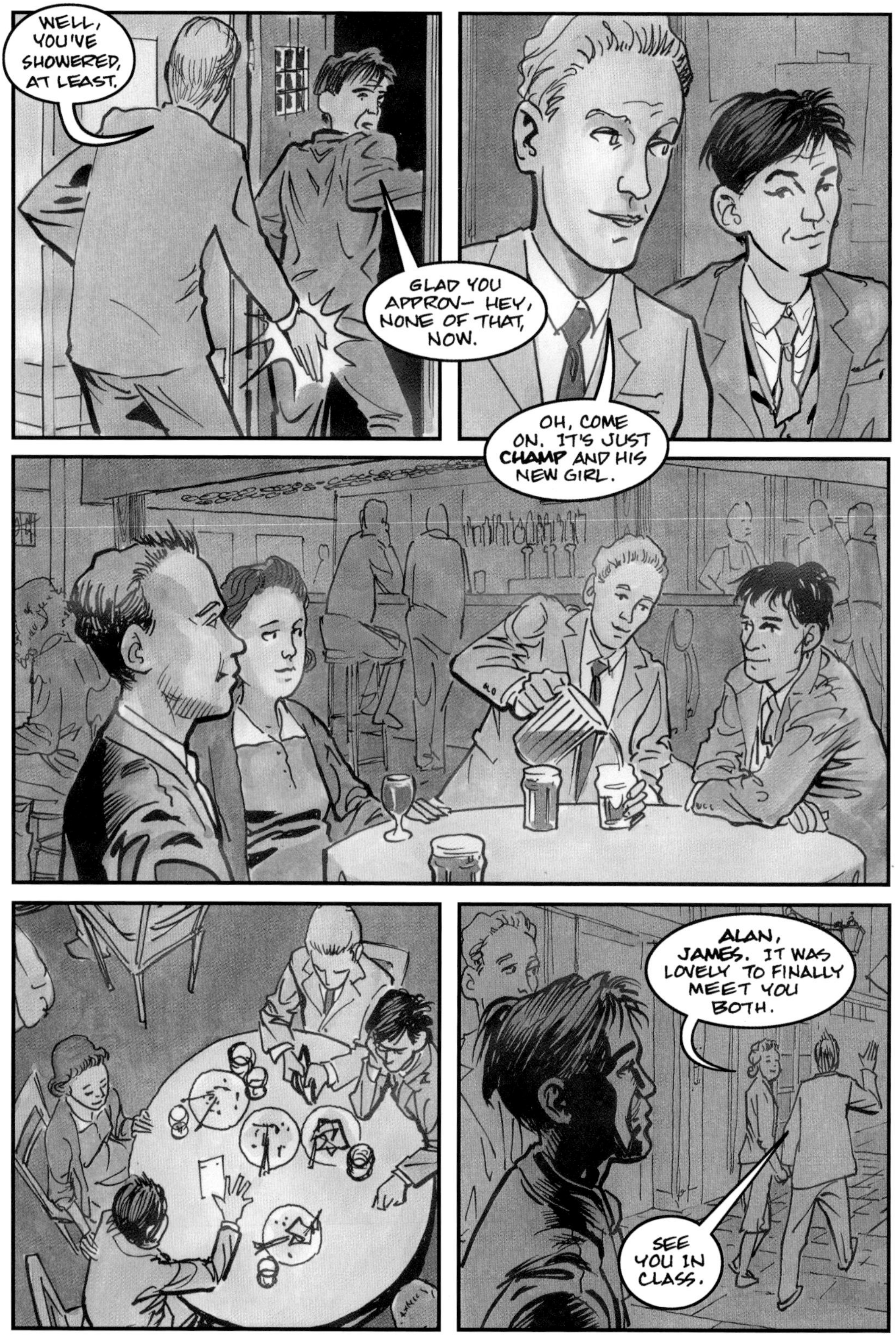
WELL, YOU'VE SHOWERED, AT LEAST.
GLAD YOU APPROV- HEY, NONE OF THAT, NOW.
OH, COME ON. IT'S JUST CHAMP AND HIS NEW GIRL.
ALAN, JAMES. IT WAS LOVELY TO FINALLY MEET YOU BOTH.
SEE YOU IN CLASS.

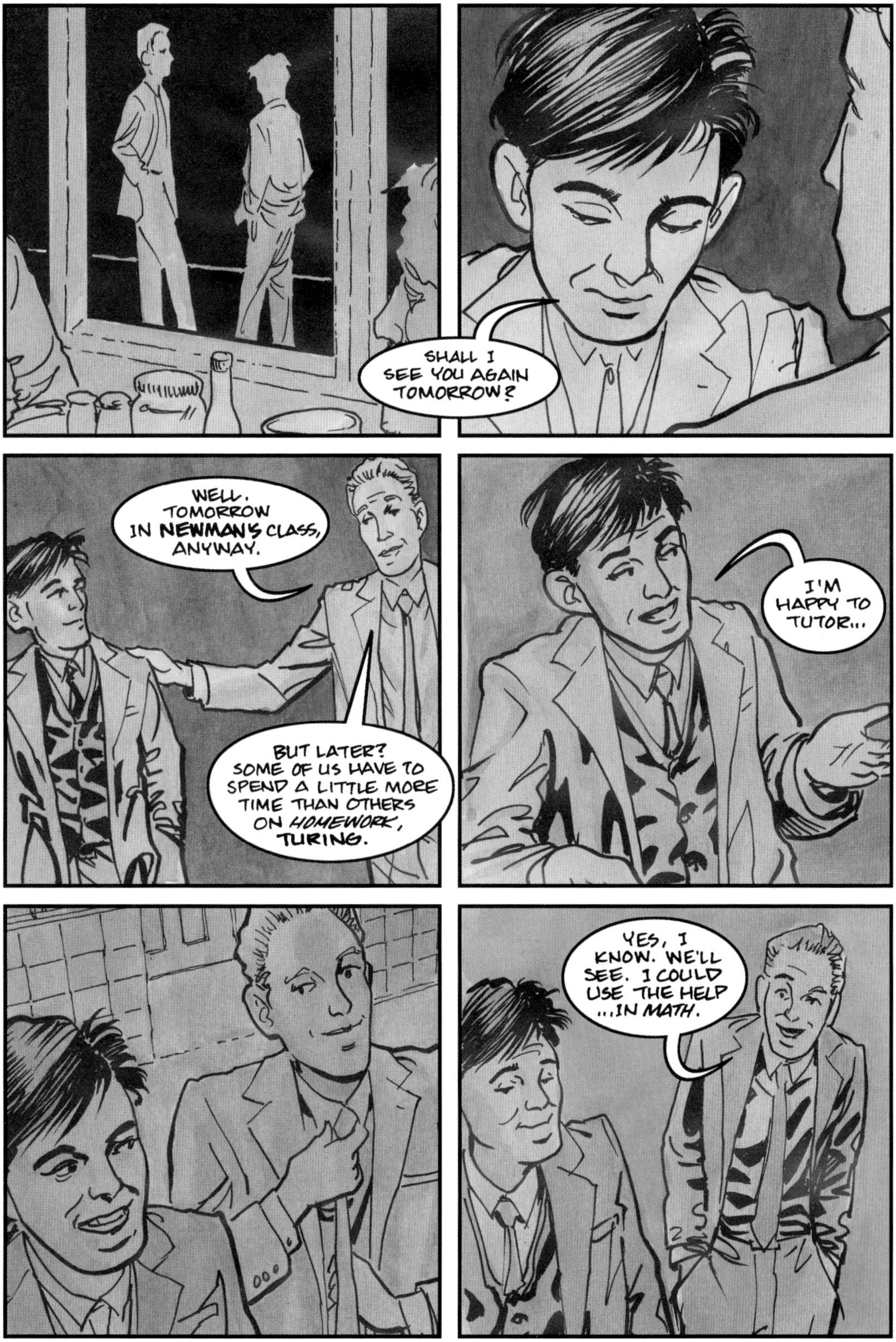

SHALL I SEE YOU AGAIN TOMORROW?
WELL. TOMORROW IN NEWMAN'S CLASS, ANYWAY.
BUT LATER? SOME OF US HAVE TO SPEND A LITTLE MORE TIME THAN OTHERS ON *HOMEWORK*, **TURING**.
I'M HAPPY TO TUTOR...
YES, I KNOW. WE'LL SEE. I COULD USE THE HELP ...IN *MATH*.

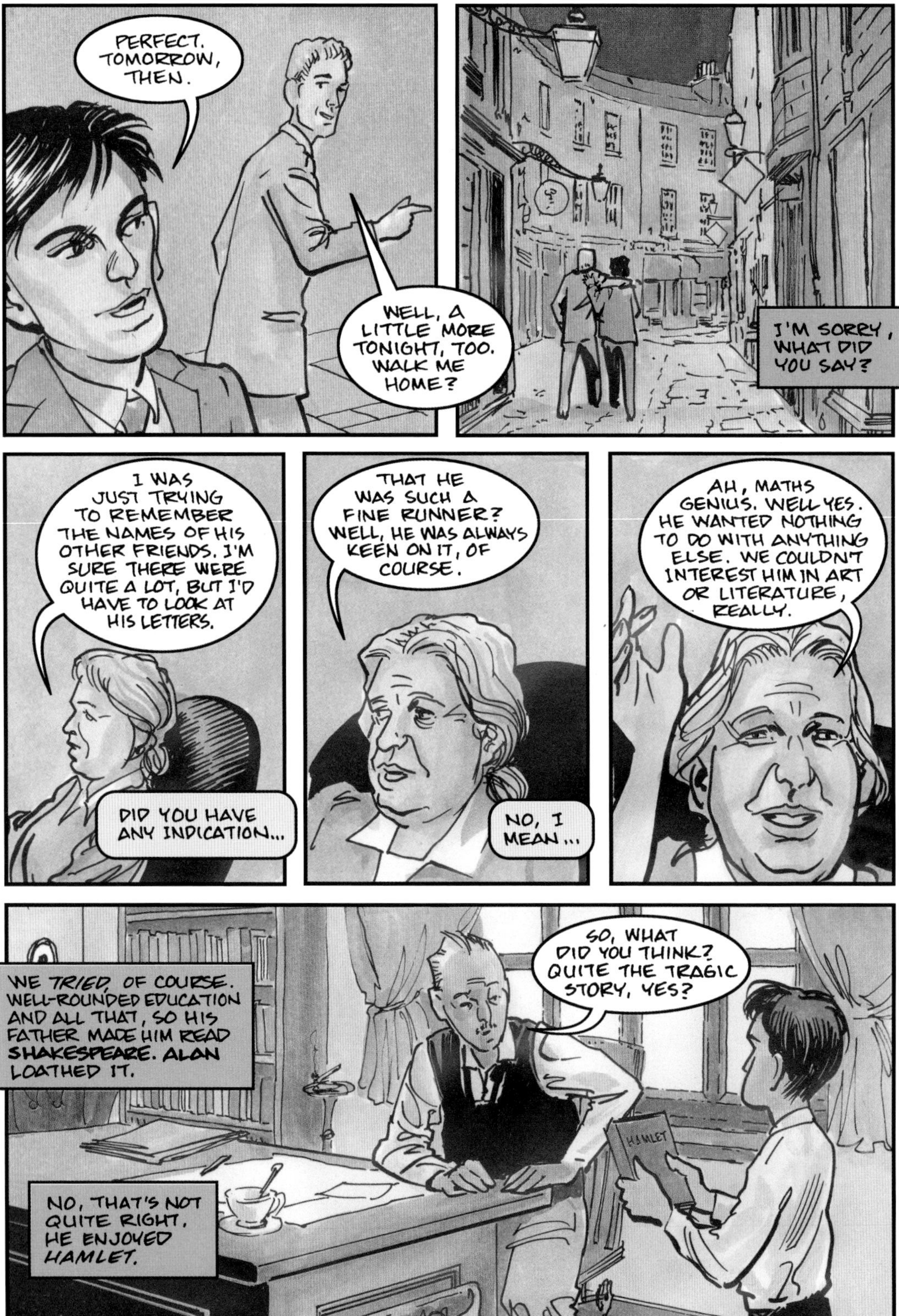
PERFECT. TOMORROW, THEN.
WELL, A LITTLE MORE TONIGHT, TOO. WALK ME HOME?
I'M SORRY, WHAT DID YOU SAY?
I WAS JUST TRYING TO REMEMBER THE NAMES OF HIS OTHER FRIENDS. I'M SURE THERE WERE QUITE A LOT, BUT I'D HAVE TO LOOK AT HIS LETTERS.
DID YOU HAVE ANY INDICATION...
THAT HE WAS SUCH A FINE RUNNER? WELL, HE WAS ALWAYS KEEN ON IT, OF COURSE.
NO, I MEAN...
AH, MATHS GENIUS. WELL YES. HE WANTED NOTHING TO DO WITH ANYTHING ELSE. WE COULDN'T INTEREST HIM IN ART OR LITERATURE, REALLY.
WE *TRIED*, OF COURSE. WELL-ROUNDED EDUCATION AND ALL THAT, SO HIS FATHER MADE HIM READ **SHAKESPEARE. ALAN** LOATHED IT.
SO, WHAT DID YOU THINK? QUITE THE TRAGIC STORY, YES?
HAMLET
NO, THAT'S NOT QUITE RIGHT. HE ENJOYED *HAMLET*.

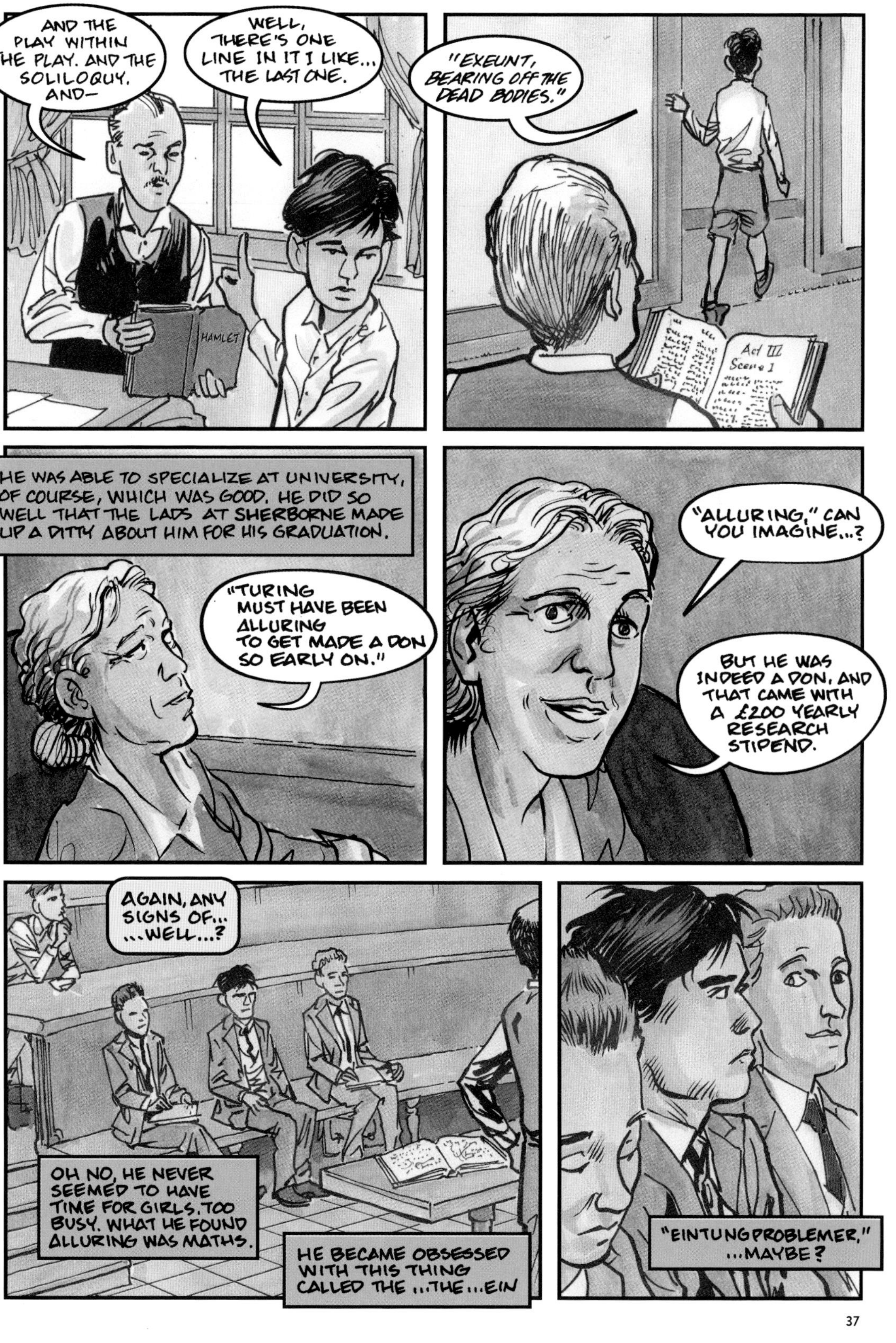
AND THE PLAY WITHIN THE PLAY. AND THE SOLILOQUY. AND—
WELL, THERE'S ONE LINE IN IT I LIKE... THE LAST ONE.
HAMLET
"EXEUNT, BEARING OFF THE DEAD BODIES."
Act III Scene 1
HE WAS ABLE TO SPECIALIZE AT UNIVERSITY, OF COURSE, WHICH WAS GOOD. HE DID SO WELL THAT THE LADS AT SHERBORNE MADE UP A DITTY ABOUT HIM FOR HIS GRADUATION.
"TURING MUST HAVE BEEN ALLURING TO GET MADE A DON SO EARLY ON."
"ALLURING," CAN YOU IMAGINE...?
BUT HE WAS INDEED A DON, AND THAT CAME WITH A £200 YEARLY RESEARCH STIPEND.
AGAIN, ANY SIGNS OF... ...WELL...?
OH NO, HE NEVER SEEMED TO HAVE TIME FOR GIRLS. TOO BUSY. WHAT HE FOUND ALLURING WAS MATHS.
HE BECAME OBSESSED WITH THIS THING CALLED THE ...THE... EIN
"EINTUNGPROBLEMER," ...MAYBE?

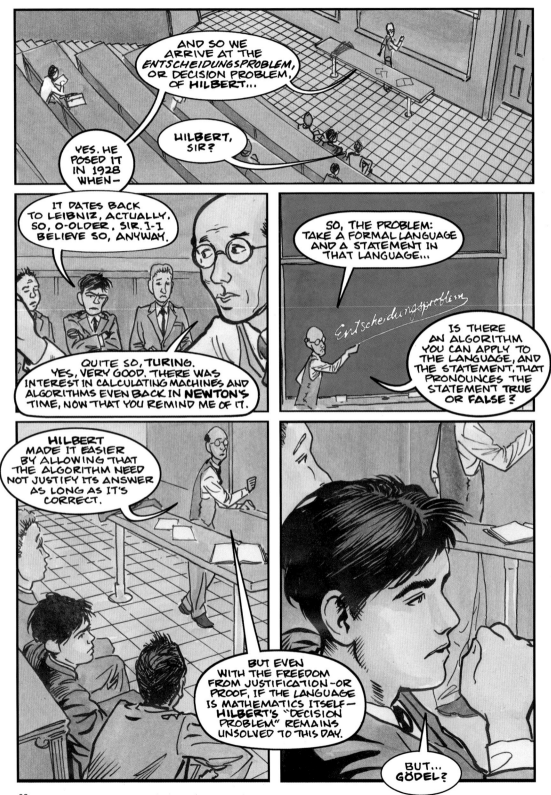

AND SO WE ARRIVE AT THE *ENTSCHEIDUNGSPROBLEM,* OR DECISION PROBLEM, OF HILBERT...

HILBERT, SIR?

YES. HE POSED IT IN 1928 WHEN—

IT DATES BACK TO LEIBNIZ, ACTUALLY, SO, O-OLDER, SIR. I—I BELIEVE SO, ANYWAY.

QUITE SO, TURING. YES, VERY GOOD. THERE WAS INTEREST IN CALCULATING MACHINES AND ALGORITHMS EVEN BACK IN **NEWTON'S** TIME, NOW THAT YOU REMIND ME OF IT.

SO, THE PROBLEM: TAKE A FORMAL LANGUAGE AND A STATEMENT IN THAT LANGUAGE...

Entscheidungsproblem

IS THERE AN ALGORITHM YOU CAN APPLY TO THE LANGUAGE, AND THE STATEMENT, THAT PRONOUNCES THE STATEMENT TRUE OR FALSE?

HILBERT MADE IT EASIER BY ALLOWING THAT THE ALGORITHM NEED NOT JUSTIFY ITS ANSWER AS LONG AS IT'S CORRECT.

BUT EVEN WITH THE FREEDOM FROM JUSTIFICATION—OR PROOF, IF THE LANGUAGE IS MATHEMATICS ITSELF— **HILBERT'S** "DECISION PROBLEM" REMAINS UNSOLVED TO THIS DAY.

BUT... GÖDEL?

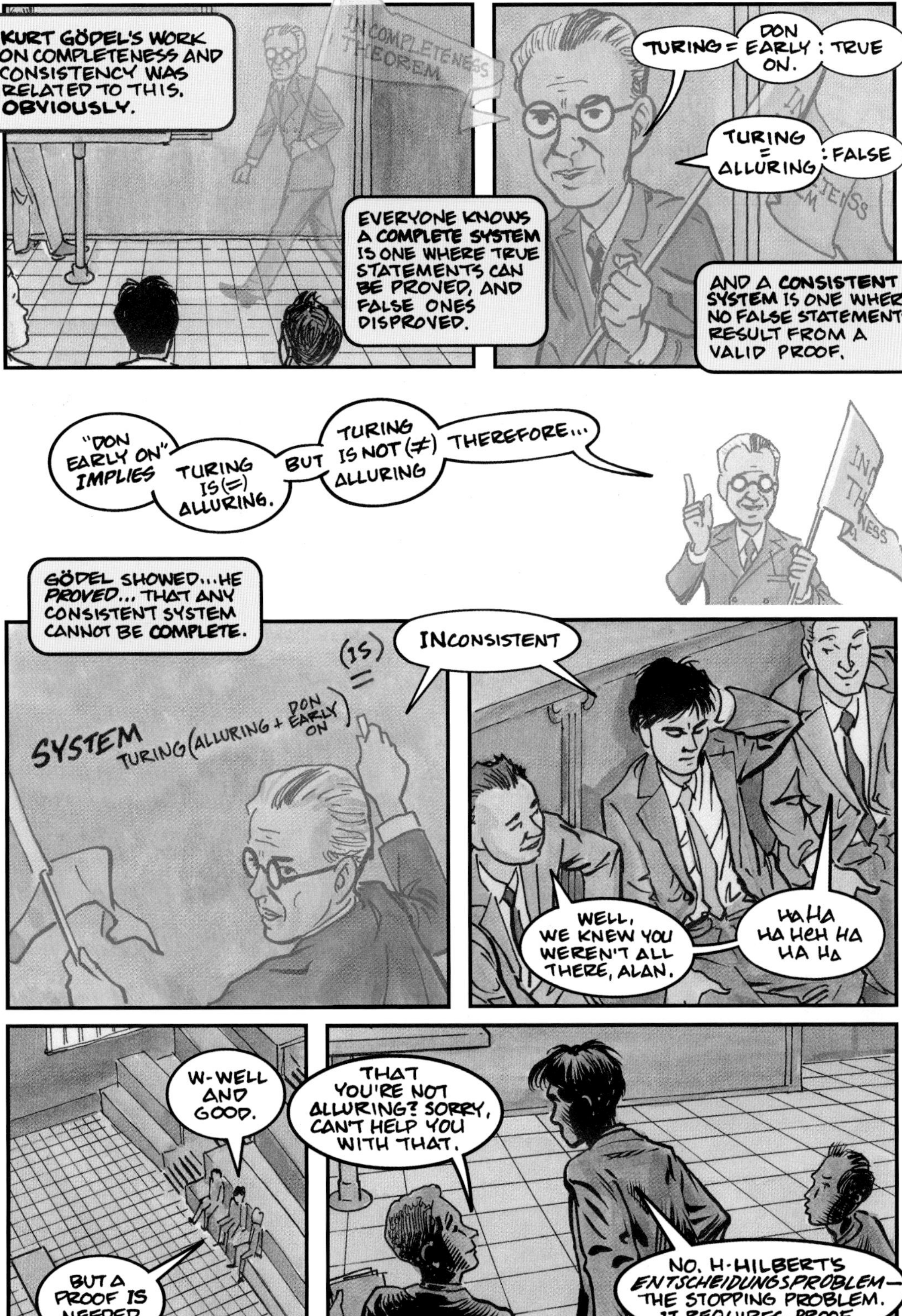
KURT GÖDEL'S WORK ON COMPLETENESS AND CONSISTENCY WAS RELATED TO THIS. OBVIOUSLY.
INCOMPLETENESS THEOREM
EVERYONE KNOWS A COMPLETE SYSTEM IS ONE WHERE TRUE STATEMENTS CAN BE PROVED, AND FALSE ONES DISPROVED.
TURING = DON EARLY ON. : TRUE
TURING = ALLURING : FALSE
AND A CONSISTENT SYSTEM IS ONE WHERE NO FALSE STATEMENTS RESULT FROM A VALID PROOF.
"DON EARLY ON" IMPLIES
TURING IS(=) ALLURING.
BUT
TURING IS NOT(≠) ALLURING
THEREFORE...
GÖDEL SHOWED...HE PROVED... THAT ANY CONSISTENT SYSTEM CANNOT BE COMPLETE.
SYSTEM TURING(ALLURING + DON EARLY ON) = (IS)
INCONSISTENT
WELL, WE KNEW YOU WEREN'T ALL THERE, ALAN.
HA HA HA HEH HA HA HA
W-WELL AND GOOD.
BUT A PROOF IS NEEDED.
THAT YOU'RE NOT ALLURING? SORRY, CAN'T HELP YOU WITH THAT.
NO. H-HILBERT'S ENTSCHEIDUNGSPROBLEM— THE STOPPING PROBLEM. IT REQUIRES PROOF.

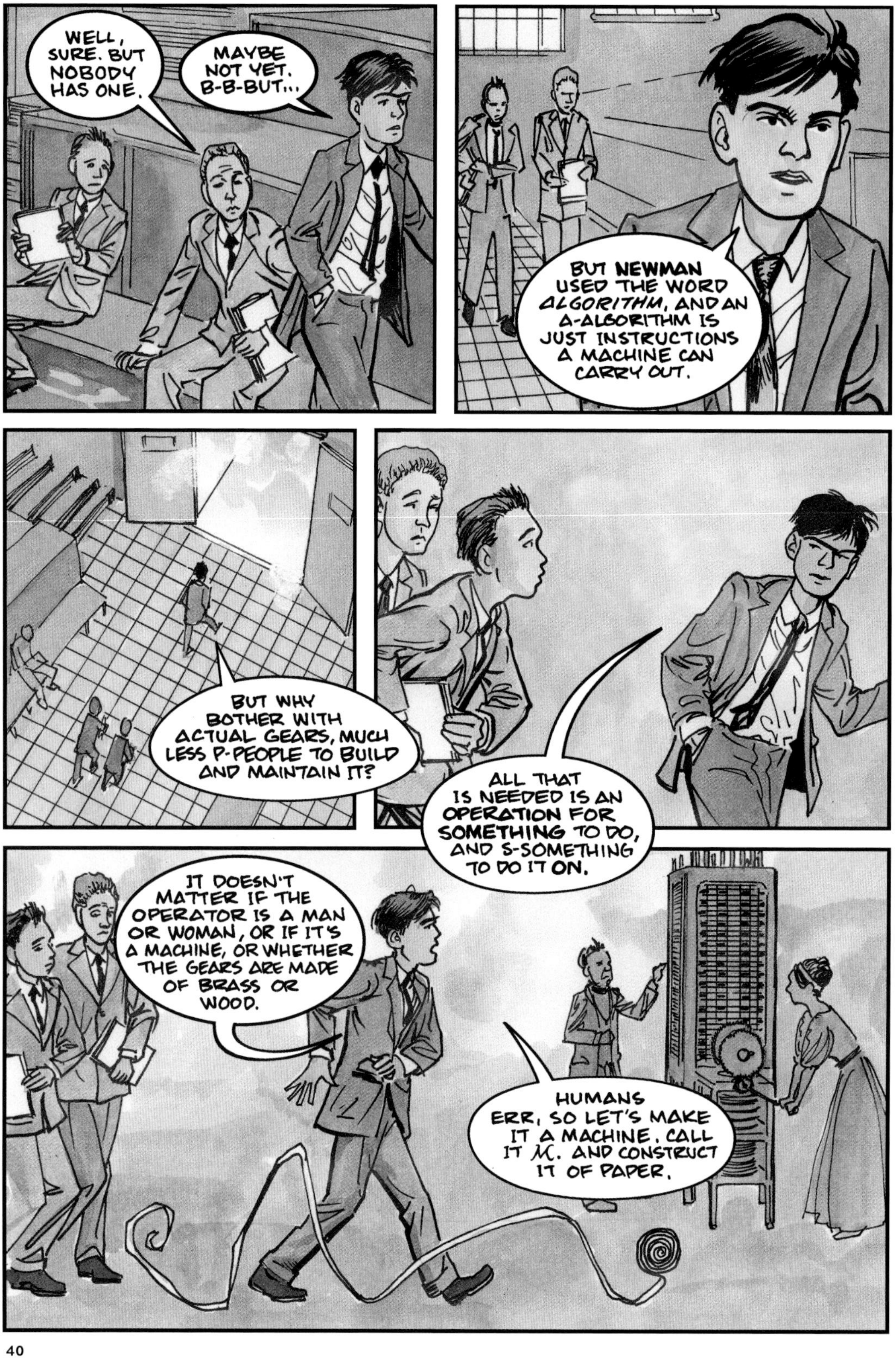
WELL, SURE. BUT NOBODY HAS ONE.
MAYBE NOT YET. B-B-BUT...
BUT NEWMAN USED THE WORD ALGORITHM, AND AN A-ALGORITHM IS JUST INSTRUCTIONS A MACHINE CAN CARRY OUT.
BUT WHY BOTHER WITH ACTUAL GEARS, MUCH LESS P-PEOPLE TO BUILD AND MAINTAIN IT?
ALL THAT IS NEEDED IS AN OPERATION FOR SOMETHING TO DO, AND S-SOMETHING TO DO IT ON.
IT DOESN'T MATTER IF THE OPERATOR IS A MAN OR WOMAN, OR IF IT'S A MACHINE, OR WHETHER THE GEARS ARE MADE OF BRASS OR WOOD.
HUMANS ERR, SO LET'S MAKE IT A MACHINE. CALL IT M. AND CONSTRUCT IT OF PAPER.

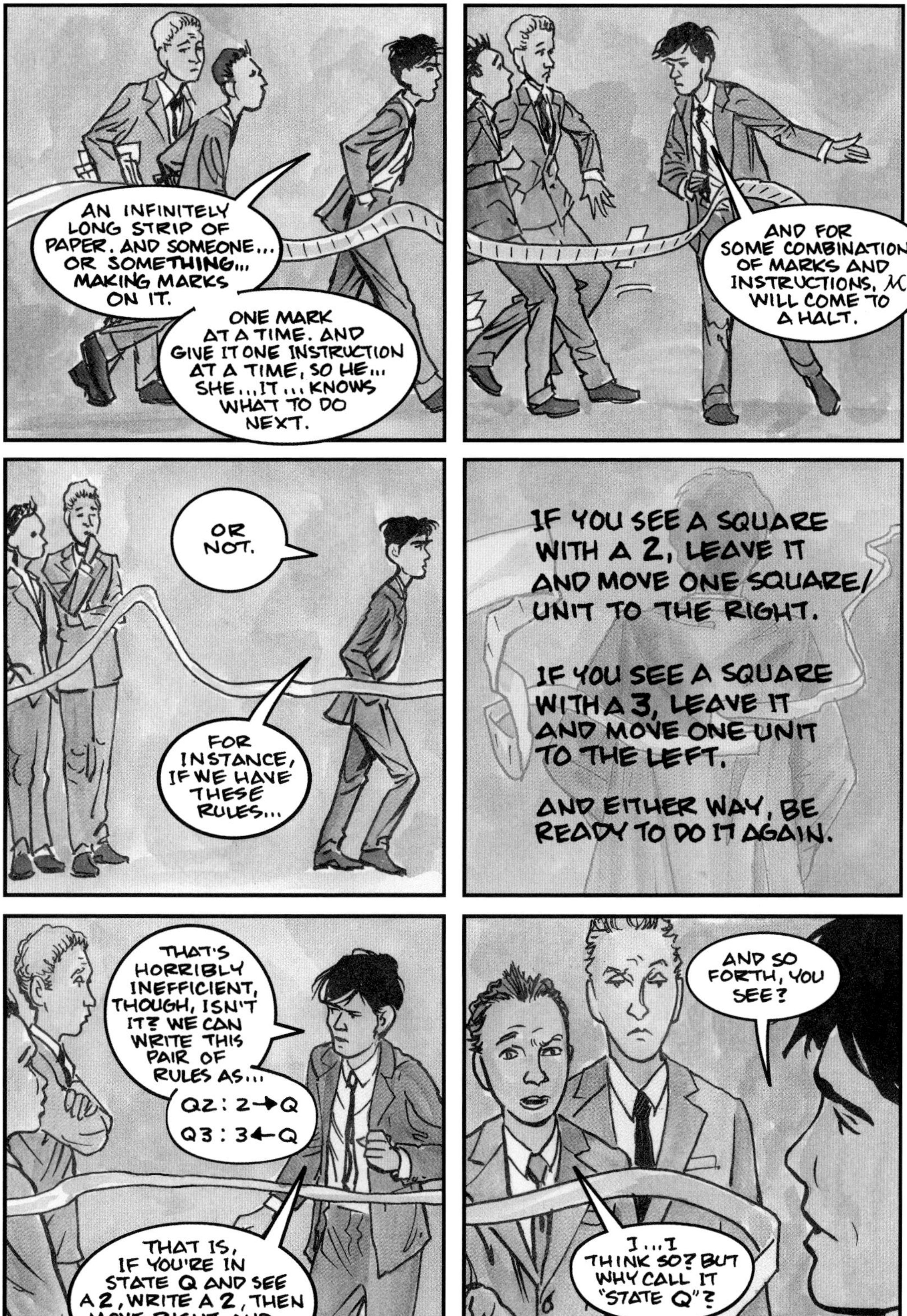
AN INFINITELY LONG STRIP OF PAPER. AND SOMEONE... OR SOMETHING... MAKING MARKS ON IT.
ONE MARK AT A TIME. AND GIVE IT ONE INSTRUCTION AT A TIME, SO HE... SHE... IT... KNOWS WHAT TO DO NEXT.
AND FOR SOME COMBINATION OF MARKS AND INSTRUCTIONS, $\mathcal{M}$ WILL COME TO A HALT.
OR NOT.
FOR INSTANCE, IF WE HAVE THESE RULES...
IF YOU SEE A SQUARE WITH A 2, LEAVE IT AND MOVE ONE SQUARE/UNIT TO THE RIGHT.
IF YOU SEE A SQUARE WITH A 3, LEAVE IT AND MOVE ONE UNIT TO THE LEFT.
AND EITHER WAY, BE READY TO DO IT AGAIN.
THAT'S HORRIBLY INEFFICIENT, THOUGH, ISN'T IT? WE CAN WRITE THIS PAIR OF RULES AS...
Q2 : 2→Q
Q3 : 3←Q
THAT IS, IF YOU'RE IN STATE Q AND SEE A 2, WRITE A 2, THEN MOVE RIGHT AND STAY IN STATE Q.
AND SO FORTH, YOU SEE?
I... I THINK SO? BUT WHY CALL IT "STATE Q"?

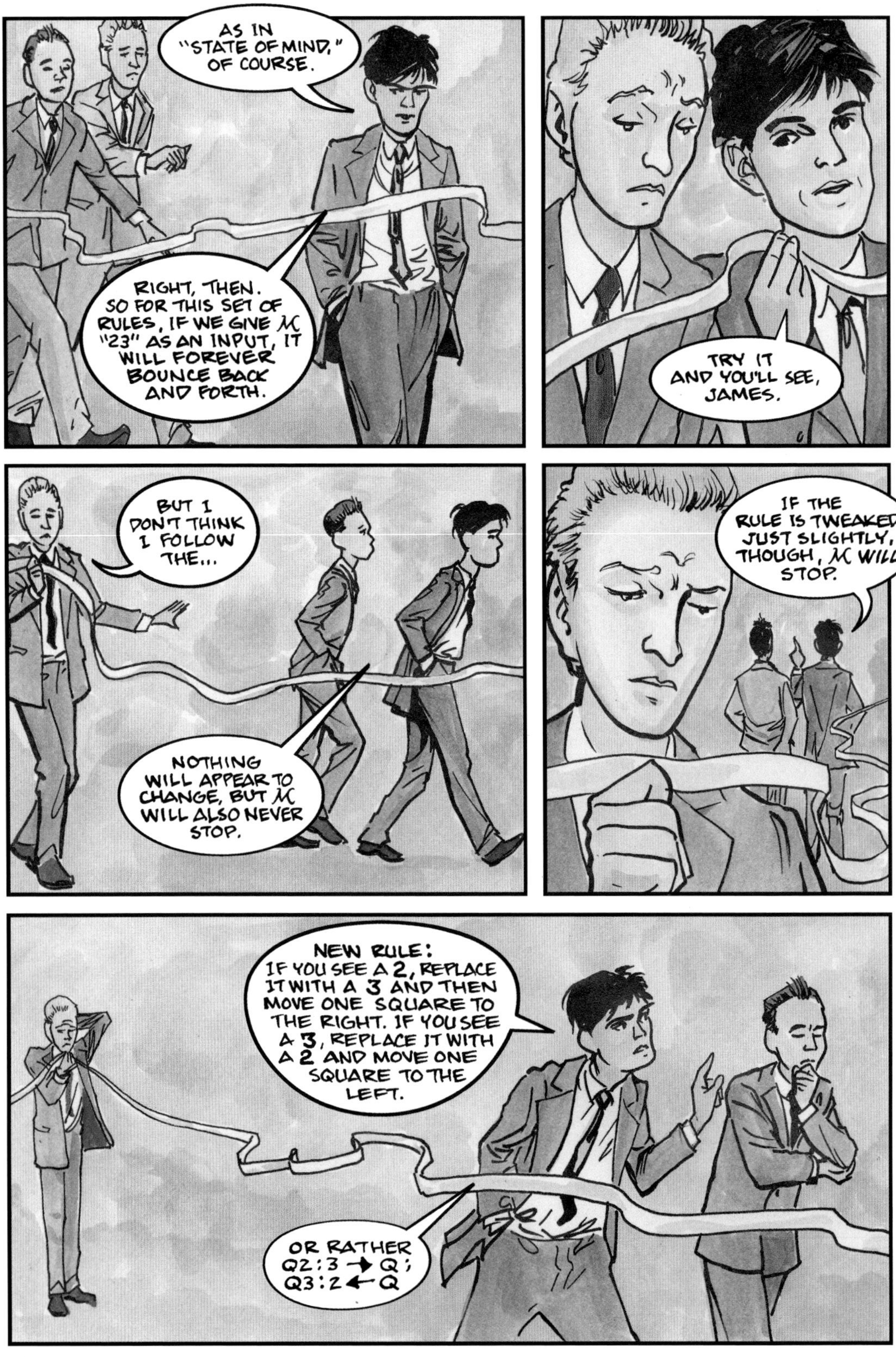
AS IN "STATE OF MIND," OF COURSE.
RIGHT, THEN. SO FOR THIS SET OF RULES, IF WE GIVE M "23" AS AN INPUT, IT WILL FOREVER BOUNCE BACK AND FORTH.
TRY IT AND YOU'LL SEE, JAMES.
BUT I DON'T THINK I FOLLOW THE...
NOTHING WILL APPEAR TO CHANGE, BUT M WILL ALSO NEVER STOP.
IF THE RULE IS TWEAKED JUST SLIGHTLY, THOUGH, M WILL STOP.
NEW RULE: IF YOU SEE A 2, REPLACE IT WITH A 3 AND THEN MOVE ONE SQUARE TO THE RIGHT. IF YOU SEE A 3, REPLACE IT WITH A 2 AND MOVE ONE SQUARE TO THE LEFT.
OR RATHER Q2 : 3 → Q ; Q3 : 2 ← Q

THIS MACHINE ℳ, WHEN GIVEN "23" AS AN INPUT, DOES THIS.
AND THEN... ℳ HALTS FOR WANT OF FURTHER INSTRUCTIONS?
INDEED. NOW, ABOUT ALL THESE Qs AND →s AND :s AND ;s...?
WOULDN'T IT BE BETTER TO REPLACE THEM WITH NUMBERS?

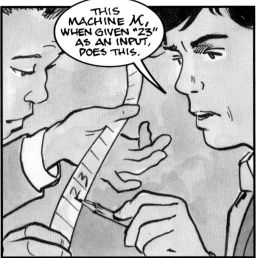

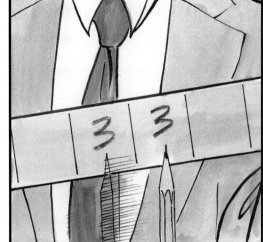

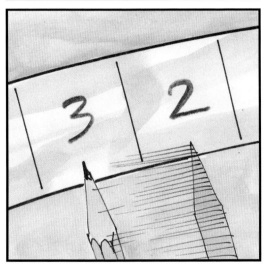

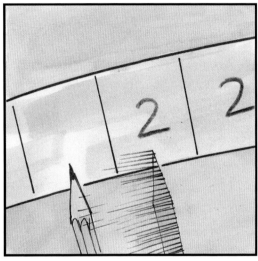

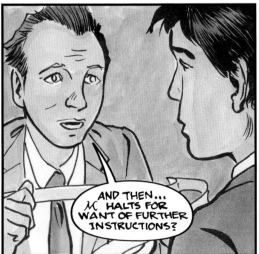

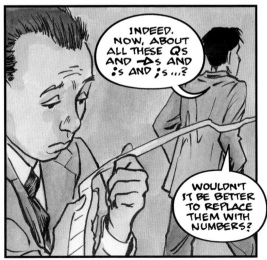

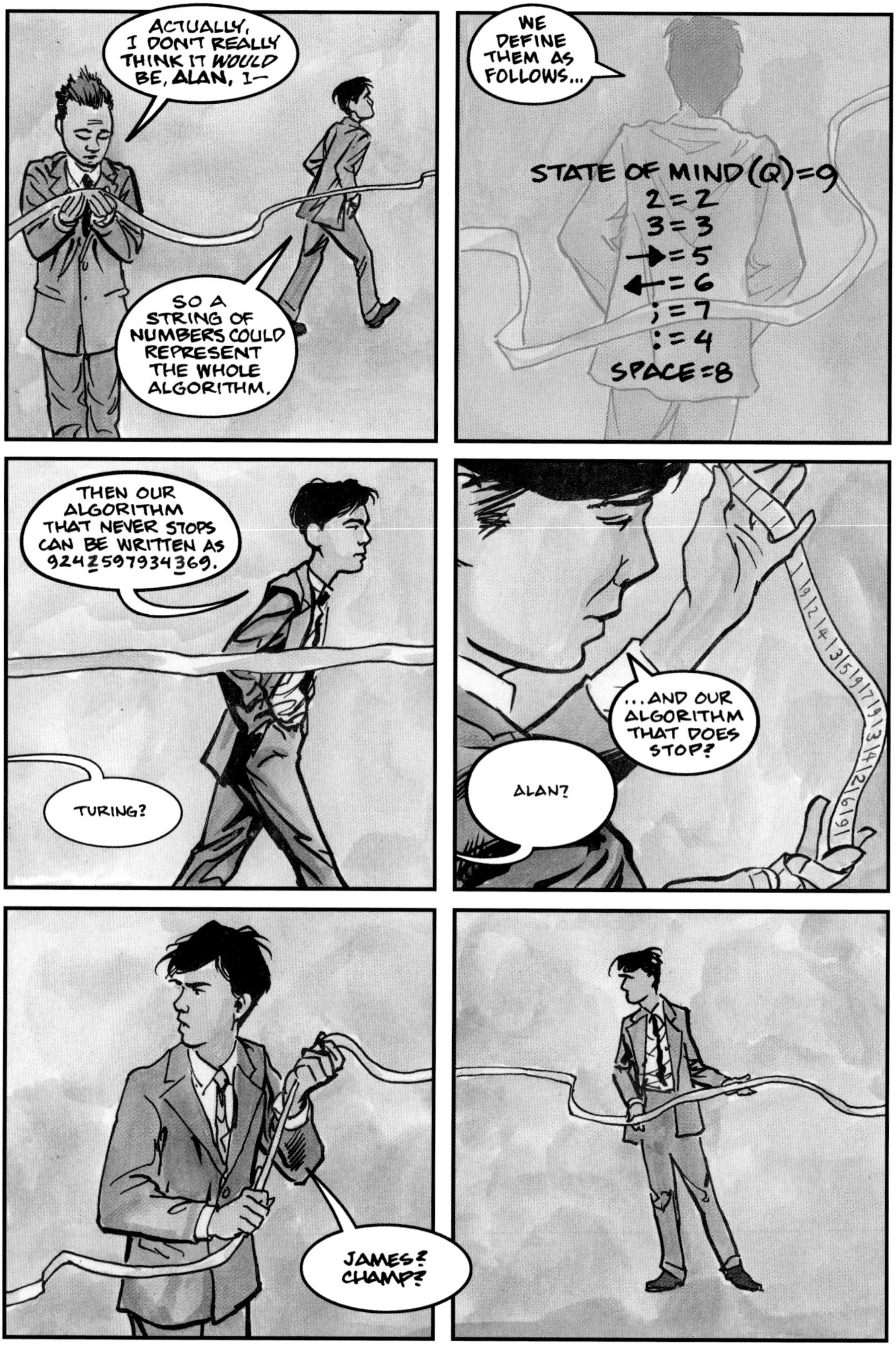
ACTUALLY, I DON'T REALLY THINK IT WOULD BE, ALAN, I—
SO A STRING OF NUMBERS COULD REPRESENT THE WHOLE ALGORITHM.
WE DEFINE THEM AS FOLLOWS...
STATE OF MIND (Q)=9
2=2
3=3
→=5
←=6
;=7
:=4
SPACE=8
THEN OUR ALGORITHM THAT NEVER STOPS CAN BE WRITTEN AS 9242597934369.
TURING?
...AND OUR ALGORITHM THAT DOES STOP?
ALAN?
JAMES? CHAMP?

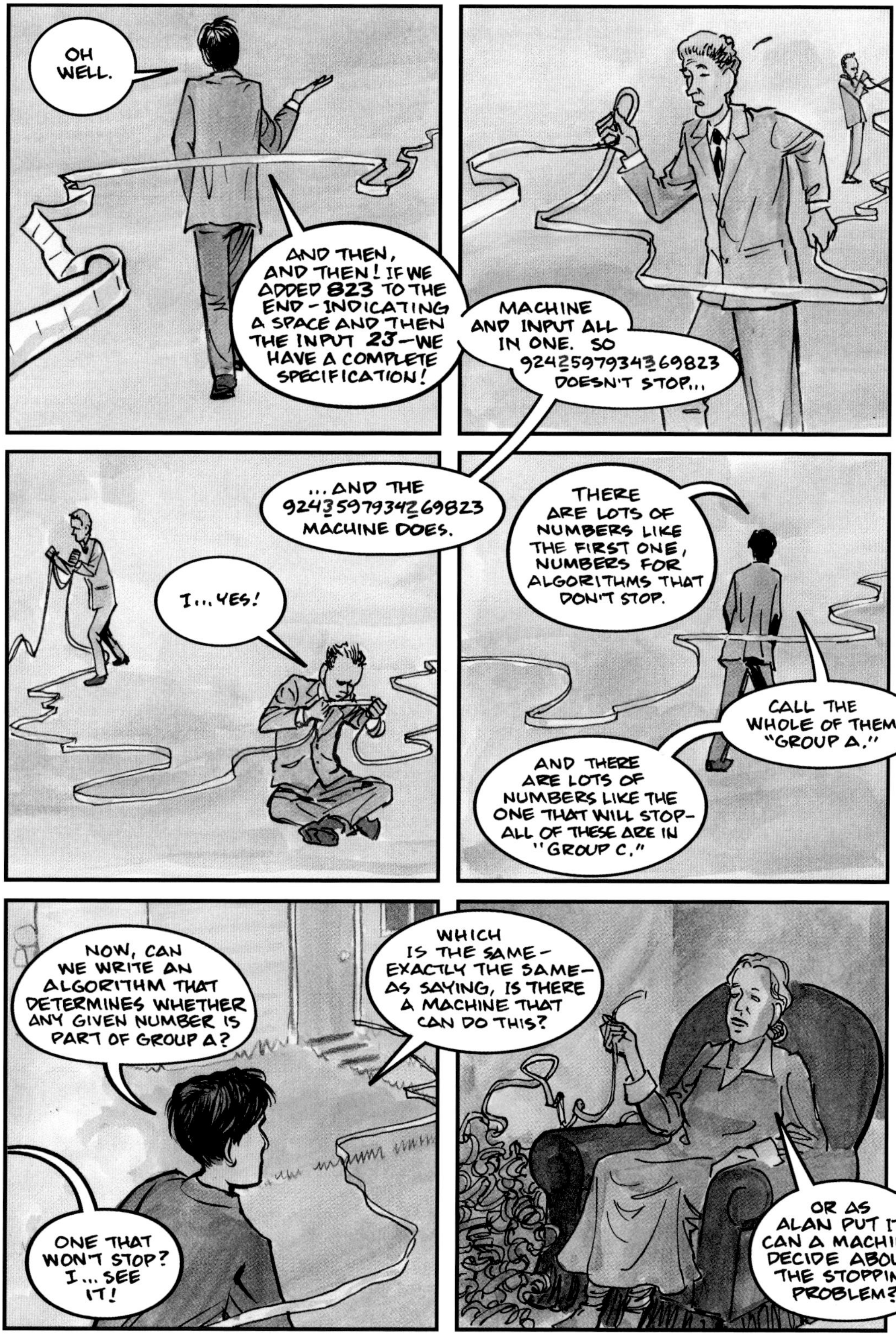
OH WELL.
AND THEN, AND THEN! IF WE ADDED 823 TO THE END - INDICATING A SPACE AND THEN THE INPUT 23—WE HAVE A COMPLETE SPECIFICATION!
MACHINE AND INPUT ALL IN ONE. SO 9242597934369823 DOESN'T STOP...
...AND THE 9243597934269823 MACHINE DOES.
I... YES!
THERE ARE LOTS OF NUMBERS LIKE THE FIRST ONE, NUMBERS FOR ALGORITHMS THAT DON'T STOP.
CALL THE WHOLE OF THEM "GROUP A."
AND THERE ARE LOTS OF NUMBERS LIKE THE ONE THAT WILL STOP- ALL OF THESE ARE IN "GROUP C."
NOW, CAN WE WRITE AN ALGORITHM THAT DETERMINES WHETHER ANY GIVEN NUMBER IS PART OF GROUP A?
WHICH IS THE SAME- EXACTLY THE SAME- AS SAYING, IS THERE A MACHINE THAT CAN DO THIS?
ONE THAT WON'T STOP? I... SEE IT!
OR AS ALAN PUT IT, CAN A MACHINE DECIDE ABOUT THE STOPPING PROBLEM?

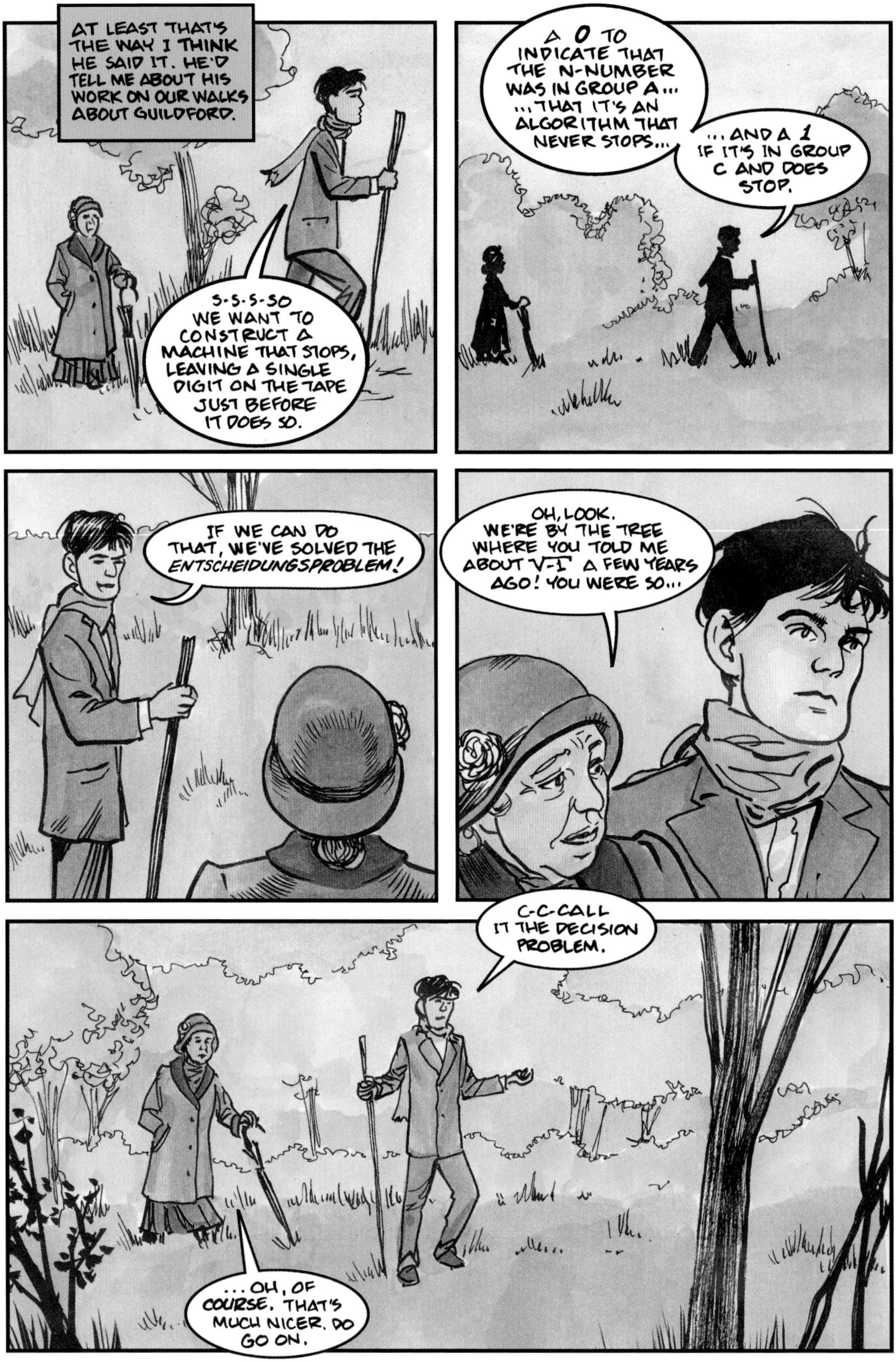
AT LEAST THAT'S THE WAY I THINK HE SAID IT. HE'D TELL ME ABOUT HIS WORK ON OUR WALKS ABOUT GUILDFORD.
S-S-S-SO WE WANT TO CONSTRUCT A MACHINE THAT STOPS, LEAVING A SINGLE DIGIT ON THE TAPE JUST BEFORE IT DOES SO.
A 0 TO INDICATE THAT THE N-NUMBER WAS IN GROUP A... ...THAT IT'S AN ALGORITHM THAT NEVER STOPS...
...AND A 1 IF IT'S IN GROUP C AND DOES STOP.
IF WE CAN DO THAT, WE'VE SOLVED THE *ENTSCHEIDUNGSPROBLEM!*
OH, LOOK. WE'RE BY THE TREE WHERE YOU TOLD ME ABOUT '√-1' A FEW YEARS AGO! YOU WERE SO...
C-C-CALL IT THE DECISION PROBLEM.
...OH, OF COURSE. THAT'S MUCH NICER. DO GO ON.

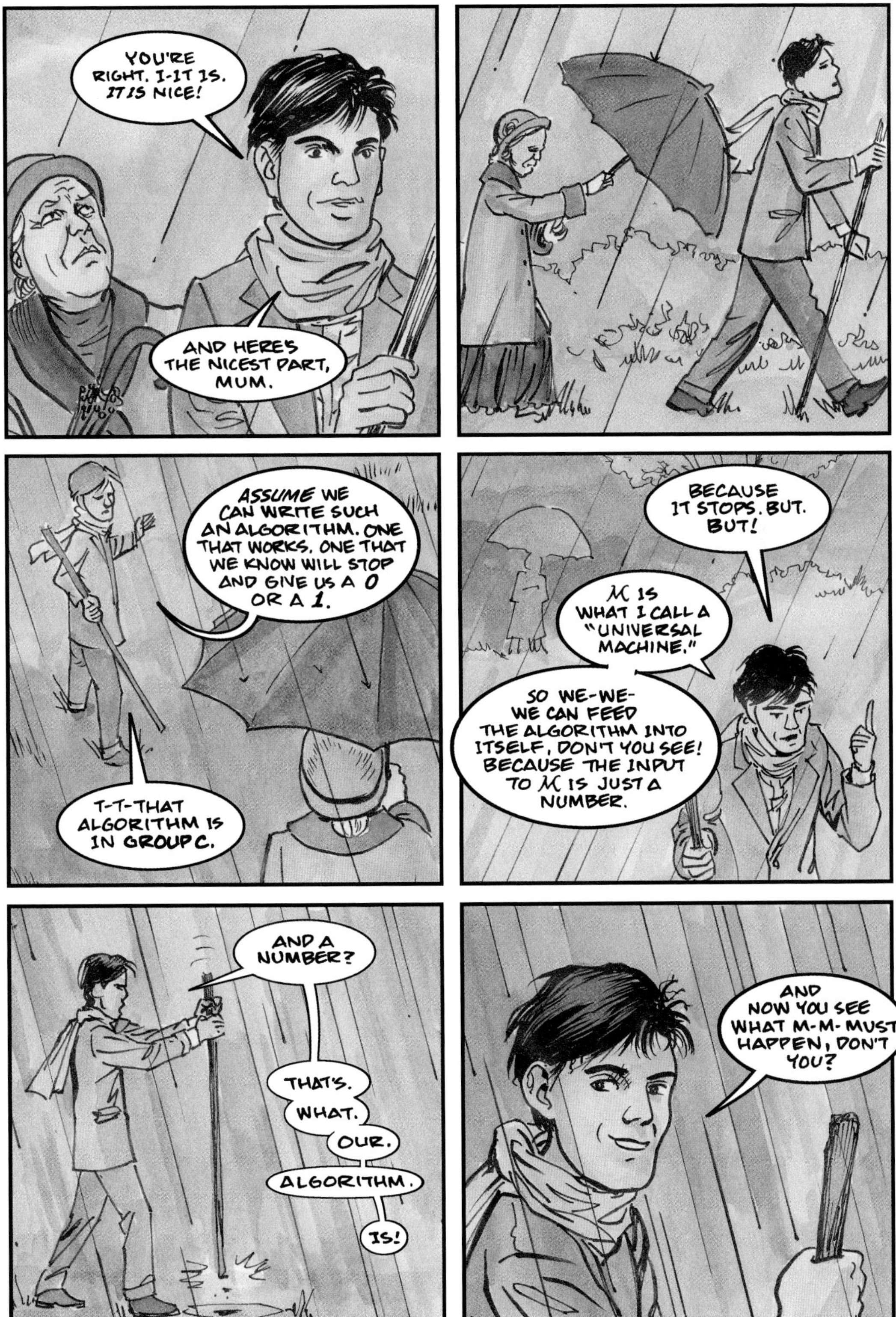
YOU'RE RIGHT. I-IT IS. IT IS NICE!
AND HERE'S THE NICEST PART, MUM.
ASSUME WE CAN WRITE SUCH AN ALGORITHM. ONE THAT WORKS. ONE THAT WE KNOW WILL STOP AND GIVE US A 0 OR A 1.
T-T-THAT ALGORITHM IS IN GROUP C.
BECAUSE IT STOPS. BUT. BUT!
M IS WHAT I CALL A "UNIVERSAL MACHINE."
SO WE-WE- WE CAN FEED THE ALGORITHM INTO ITSELF, DON'T YOU SEE! BECAUSE THE INPUT TO M IS JUST A NUMBER.
AND A NUMBER?
THAT'S.
WHAT.
OUR.
ALGORITHM.
IS!
AND NOW YOU SEE WHAT M-M-MUST HAPPEN, DON'T YOU?

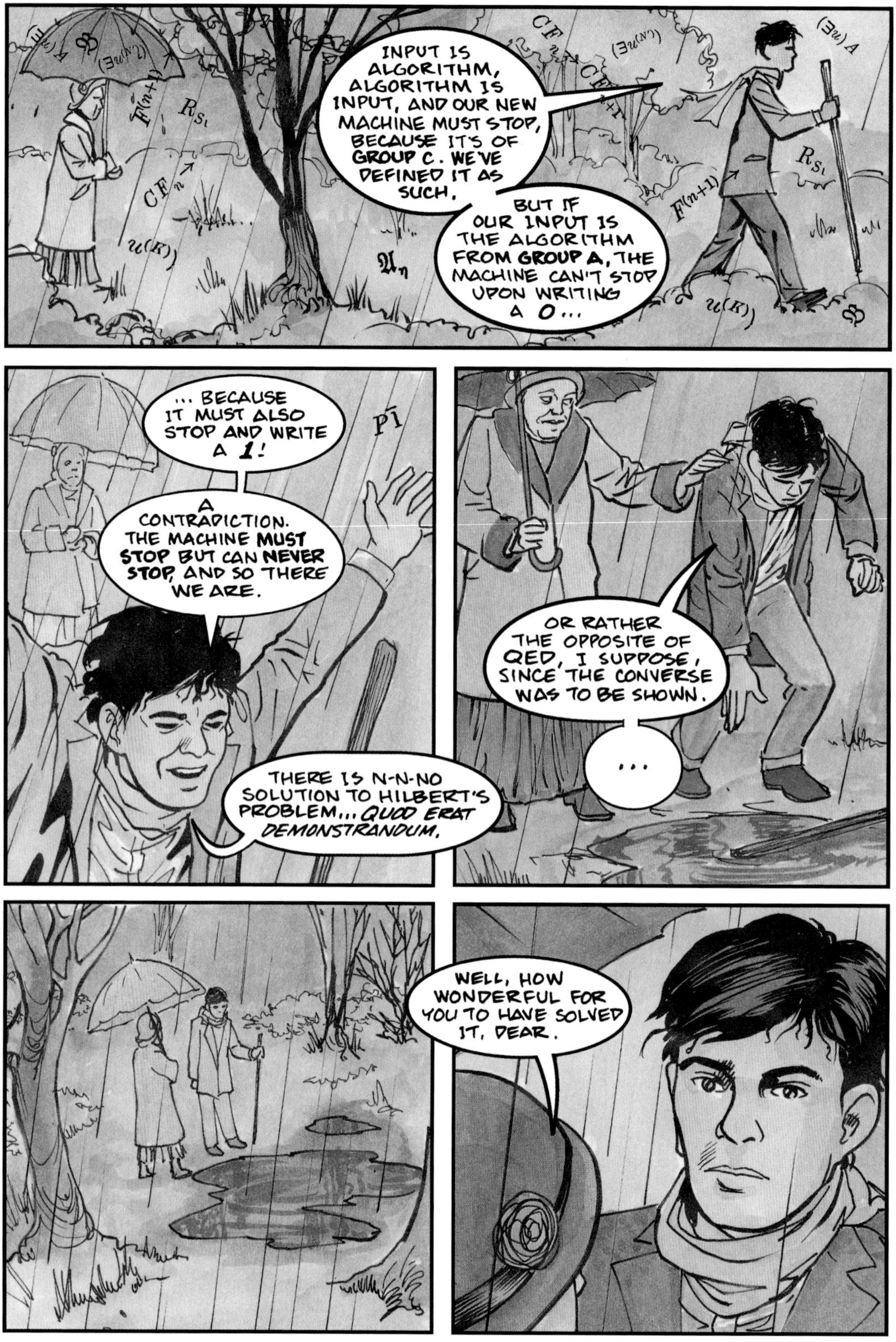
INPUT IS ALGORITHM, ALGORITHM IS INPUT, AND OUR NEW MACHINE MUST STOP, BECAUSE IT'S OF GROUP C. WE'VE DEFINED IT AS SUCH.
BUT IF OUR INPUT IS THE ALGORITHM FROM GROUP A, THE MACHINE CAN'T STOP UPON WRITING A 0...
... BECAUSE IT MUST ALSO STOP AND WRITE A 1!
A CONTRADICTION. THE MACHINE MUST STOP BUT CAN NEVER STOP, AND SO THERE WE ARE.
THERE IS N-N-NO SOLUTION TO HILBERT'S PROBLEM... QUOD ERAT DEMONSTRANDUM.
OR RATHER THE OPPOSITE OF QED, I SUPPOSE, SINCE THE CONVERSE WAS TO BE SHOWN.
...
WELL, HOW WONDERFUL FOR YOU TO HAVE SOLVED IT, DEAR.

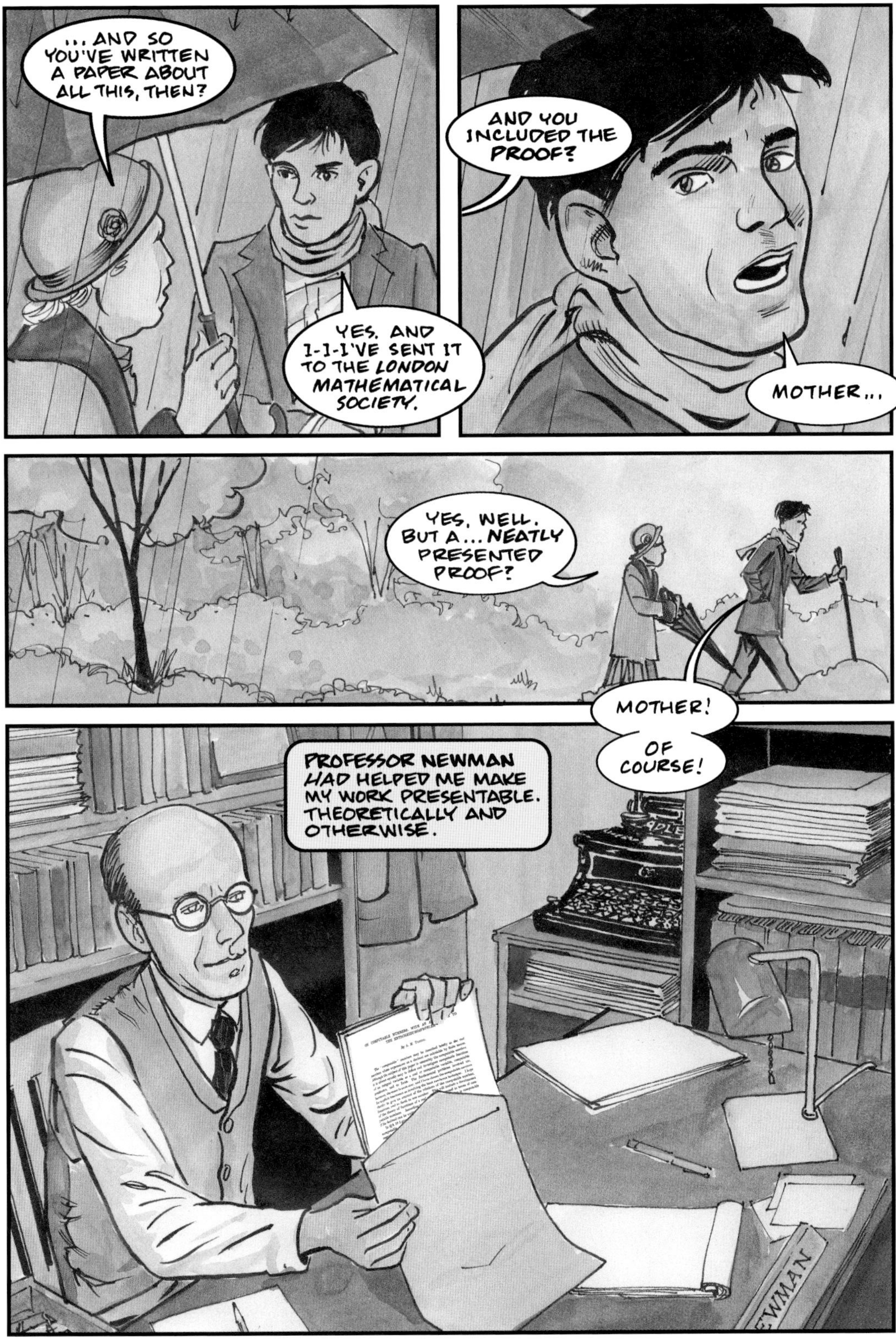
...AND SO YOU'VE WRITTEN A PAPER ABOUT ALL THIS, THEN?
YES. AND I-I-I'VE SENT IT TO THE *LONDON MATHEMATICAL SOCIETY.*
AND YOU INCLUDED THE **PROOF?**
MOTHER...
YES, WELL. BUT A... **NEATLY** PRESENTED PROOF?
MOTHER!
OF COURSE!
PROFESSOR NEWMAN *HAD* HELPED ME MAKE MY WORK PRESENTABLE. THEORETICALLY AND OTHERWISE.

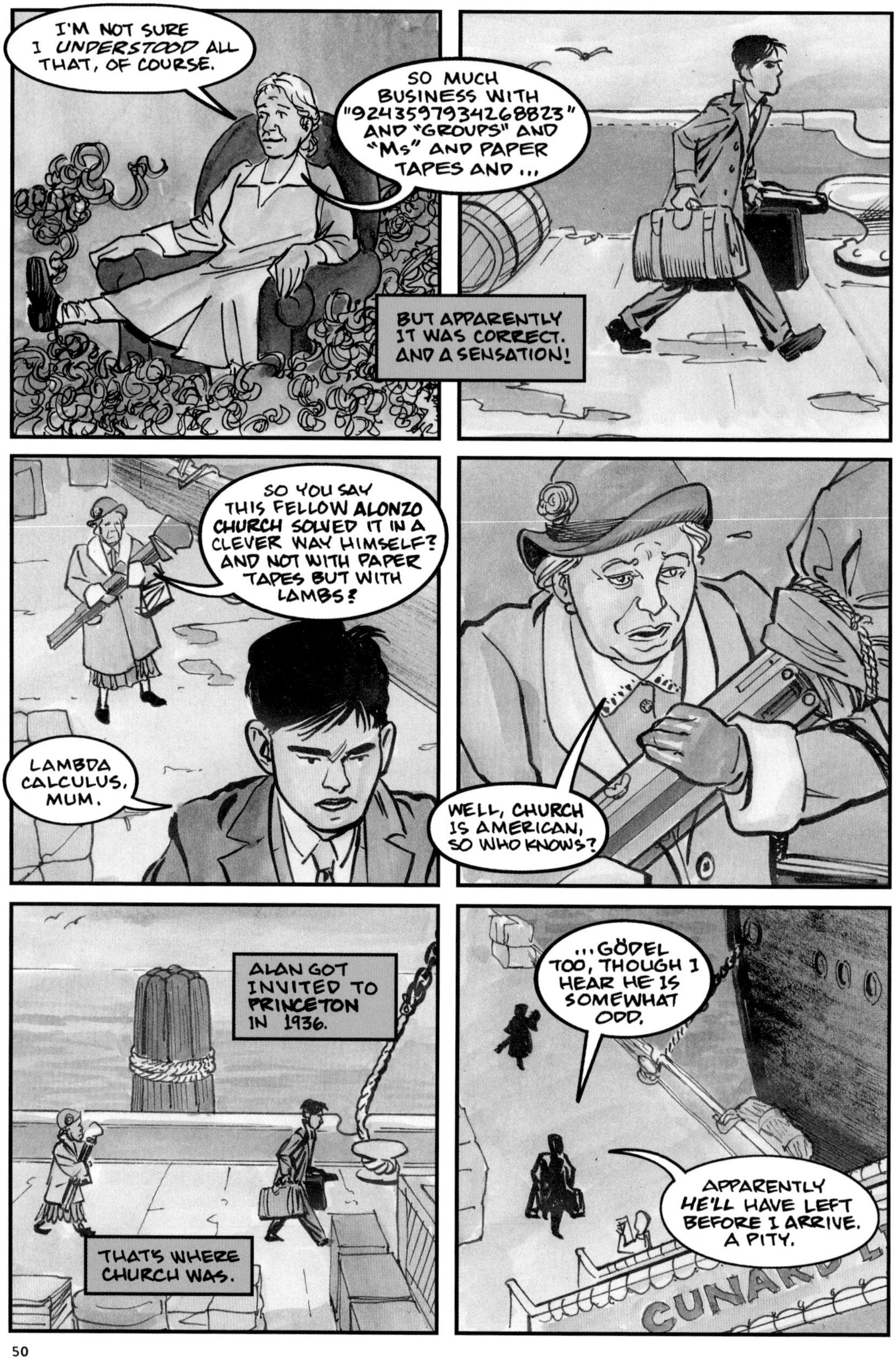

I'M NOT SURE I UNDERSTOOD ALL THAT, OF COURSE.
SO MUCH BUSINESS WITH "924359793426 8823" AND "GROUPS" AND "Ms" AND PAPER TAPES AND ...
BUT APPARENTLY IT WAS CORRECT. AND A SENSATION!
SO YOU SAY THIS FELLOW ALONZO CHURCH SOLVED IT IN A CLEVER WAY HIMSELF? AND NOT WITH PAPER TAPES BUT WITH LAMBS?
LAMBDA CALCULUS, MUM.
WELL, CHURCH IS AMERICAN, SO WHO KNOWS?
ALAN GOT INVITED TO PRINCETON IN 1936.
THAT'S WHERE CHURCH WAS.
...GÖDEL TOO, THOUGH I HEAR HE IS SOMEWHAT ODD.
APPARENTLY HE'LL HAVE LEFT BEFORE I ARRIVE. A PITY.
CUNARD

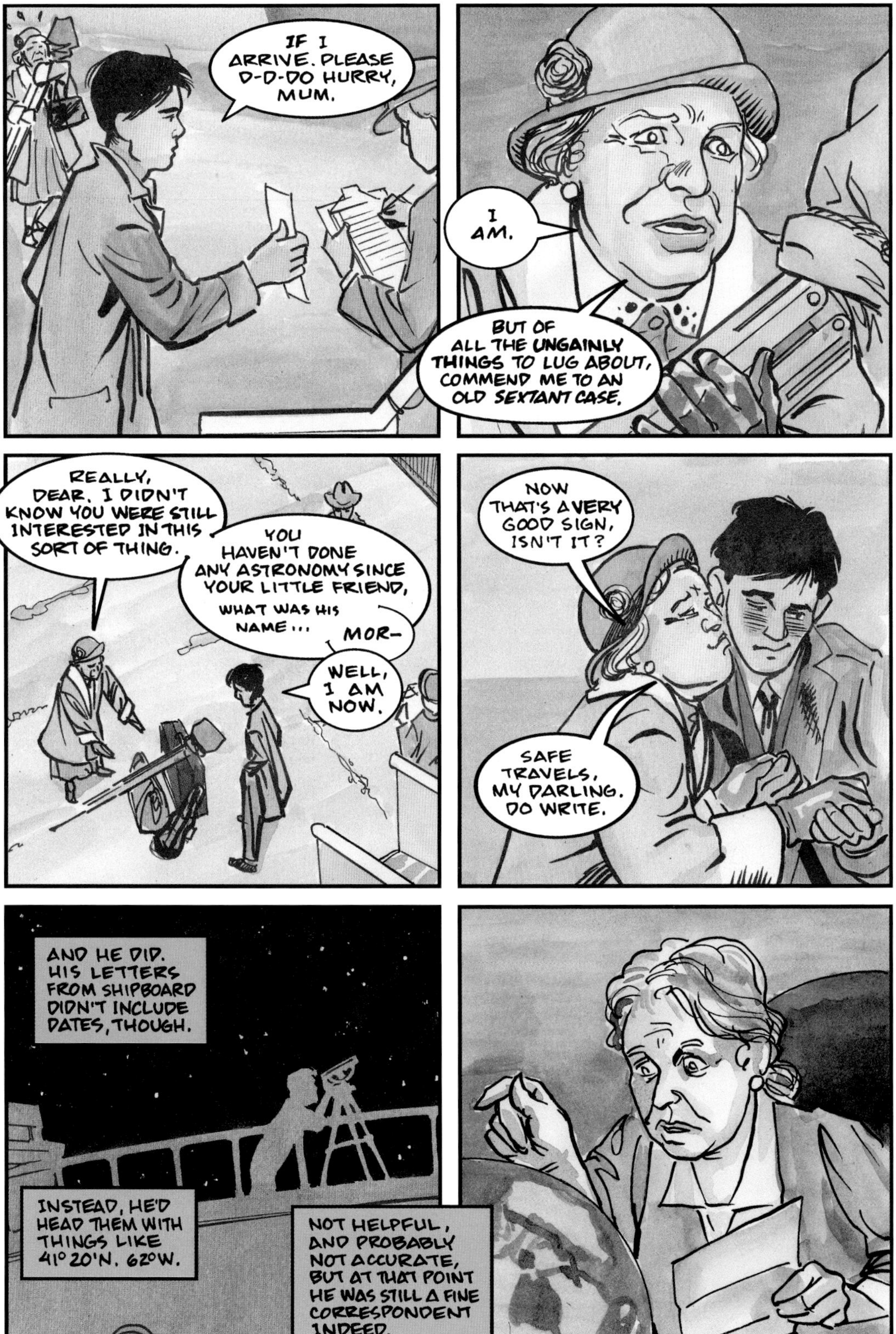
IF I ARRIVE. PLEASE D-D-DO HURRY, MUM.
I AM.
BUT OF ALL THE UNGAINLY THINGS TO LUG ABOUT, COMMEND ME TO AN OLD SEXTANT CASE.
REALLY, DEAR. I DIDN'T KNOW YOU WERE STILL INTERESTED IN THIS SORT OF THING.
YOU HAVEN'T DONE ANY ASTRONOMY SINCE YOUR LITTLE FRIEND, WHAT WAS HIS NAME... MOR-
WELL, I AM NOW.
NOW THAT'S A VERY GOOD SIGN, ISN'T IT?
SAFE TRAVELS, MY DARLING. DO WRITE.
AND HE DID. HIS LETTERS FROM SHIPBOARD DIDN'T INCLUDE DATES, THOUGH.
INSTEAD, HE'D HEAD THEM WITH THINGS LIKE 41° 20'N. 62°W.
NOT HELPFUL, AND PROBABLY NOT ACCURATE, BUT AT THAT POINT HE WAS STILL A FINE CORRESPONDENT INDEED.

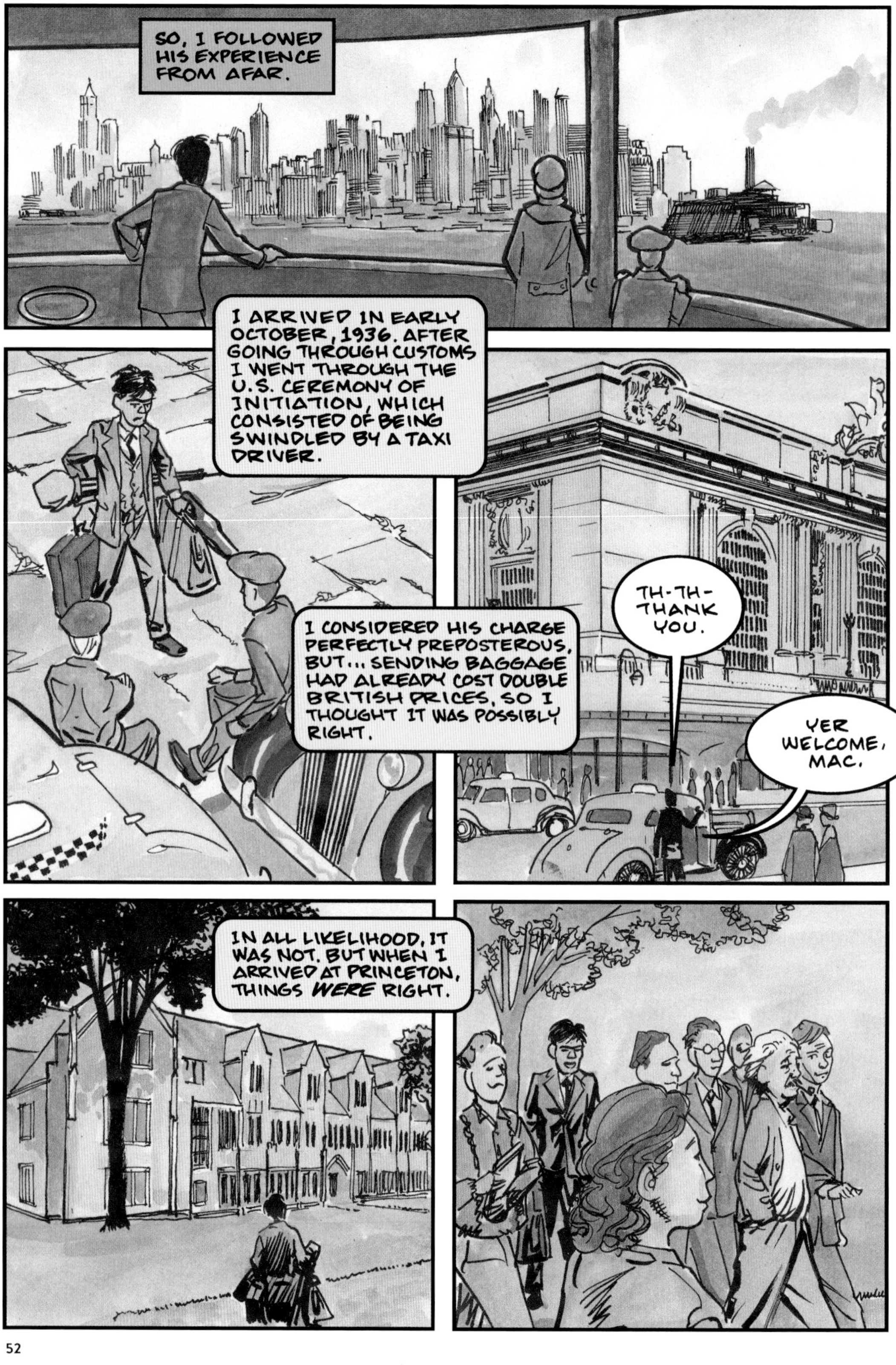
SO, I FOLLOWED HIS EXPERIENCE FROM AFAR.
I ARRIVED IN EARLY OCTOBER, 1936. AFTER GOING THROUGH CUSTOMS I WENT THROUGH THE U.S. CEREMONY OF INITIATION, WHICH CONSISTED OF BEING SWINDLED BY A TAXI DRIVER.
I CONSIDERED HIS CHARGE PERFECTLY PREPOSTEROUS, BUT... SENDING BAGGAGE HAD ALREADY COST DOUBLE BRITISH PRICES, SO I THOUGHT IT WAS POSSIBLY RIGHT.
TH-TH-THANK YOU.
YER WELCOME, MAC.
IN ALL LIKELIHOOD, IT WAS NOT. BUT WHEN I ARRIVED AT PRINCETON, THINGS *WERE* RIGHT.

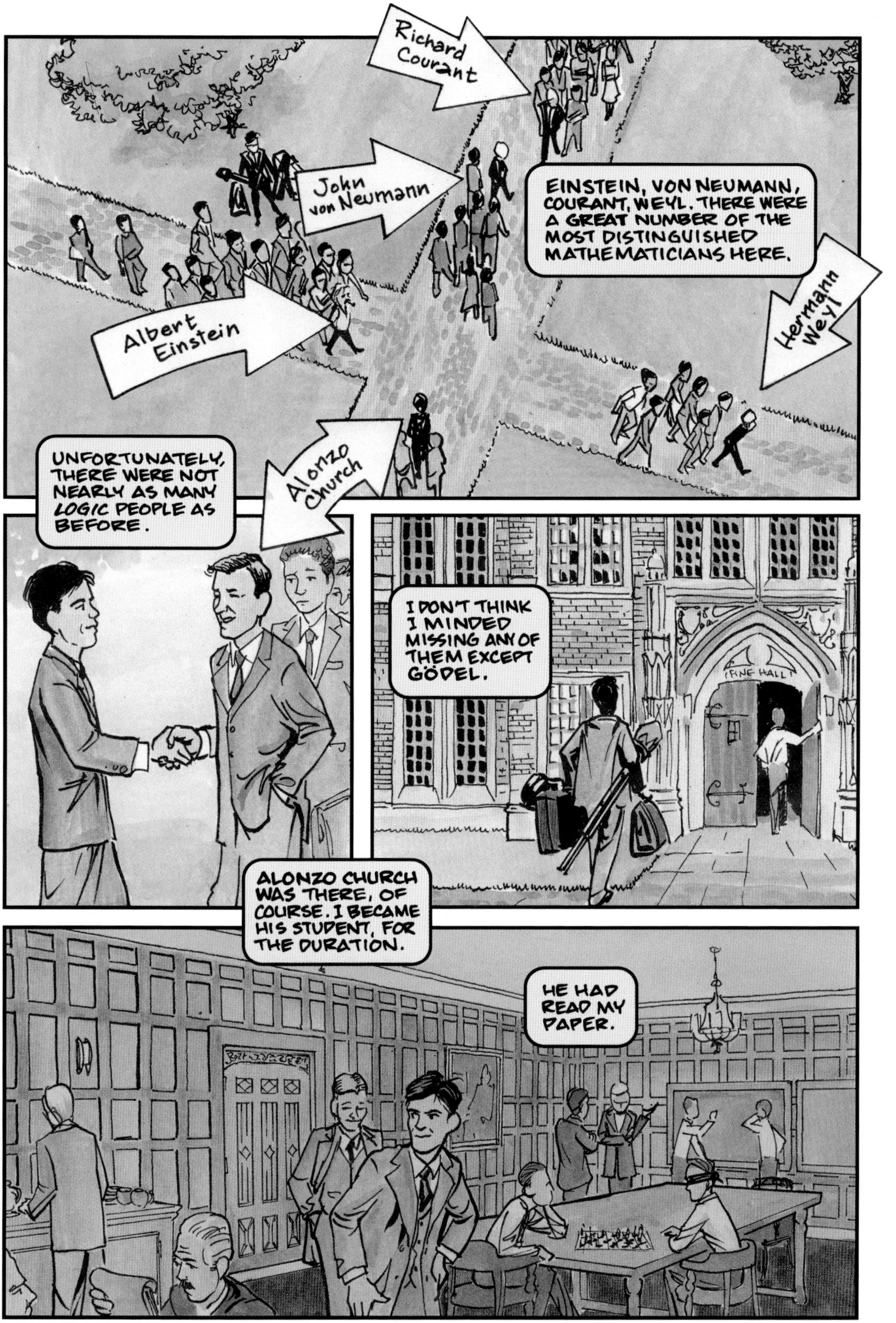
Richard Courant
John von Neumann
EINSTEIN, VON NEUMANN, COURANT, WEYL. THERE WERE A GREAT NUMBER OF THE MOST DISTINGUISHED MATHEMATICIANS HERE.
Hermann Weyl
Albert Einstein
Alonzo Church
UNFORTUNATELY, THERE WERE NOT NEARLY AS MANY LOGIC PEOPLE AS BEFORE.
I DON'T THINK I MINDED MISSING ANY OF THEM EXCEPT GÖDEL.
FINE HALL
ALONZO CHURCH WAS THERE, OF COURSE. I BECAME HIS STUDENT, FOR THE DURATION.
HE HAD READ MY PAPER.

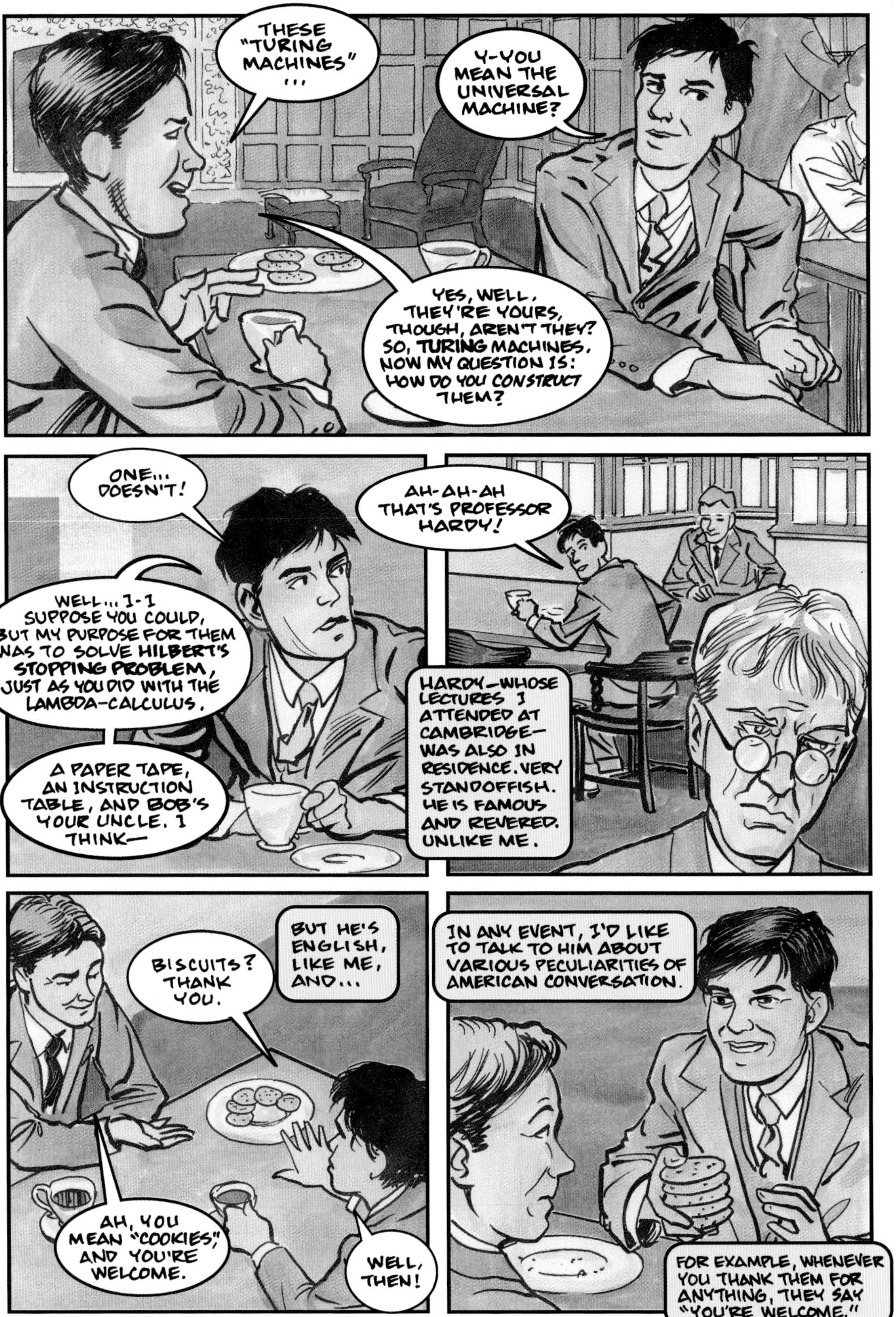
THESE "TURING MACHINES" ...
Y-YOU MEAN THE UNIVERSAL MACHINE?
YES, WELL, THEY'RE YOURS, THOUGH, AREN'T THEY? SO, TURING MACHINES. NOW MY QUESTION IS: HOW DO YOU CONSTRUCT THEM?
ONE... DOESN'T!
WELL... I-I SUPPOSE YOU COULD, BUT MY PURPOSE FOR THEM WAS TO SOLVE HILBERT'S STOPPING PROBLEM, JUST AS YOU DID WITH THE LAMBDA-CALCULUS.
A PAPER TAPE, AN INSTRUCTION TABLE, AND BOB'S YOUR UNCLE. I THINK—
AH-AH-AH THAT'S PROFESSOR HARDY!
HARDY—WHOSE LECTURES I ATTENDED AT CAMBRIDGE—WAS ALSO IN RESIDENCE. VERY STANDOFFISH. HE IS FAMOUS AND REVERED. UNLIKE ME.
BISCUITS? THANK YOU.
BUT HE'S ENGLISH, LIKE ME, AND...
AH, YOU MEAN "COOKIES," AND YOU'RE WELCOME.
WELL, THEN!
IN ANY EVENT, I'D LIKE TO TALK TO HIM ABOUT VARIOUS PECULIARITIES OF AMERICAN CONVERSATION.
FOR EXAMPLE, WHENEVER YOU THANK THEM FOR ANYTHING, THEY SAY "YOU'RE WELCOME."

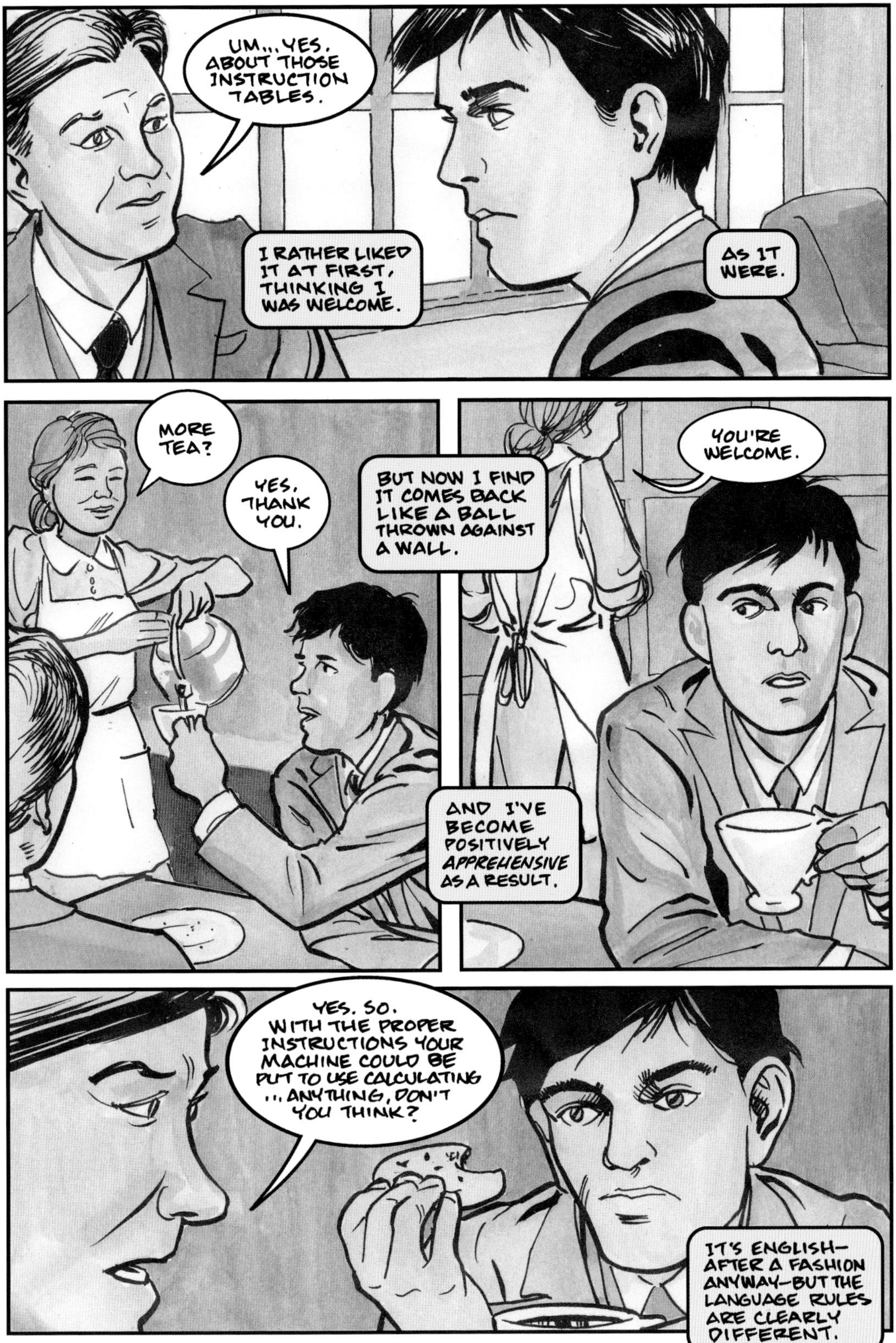
UM... YES. ABOUT THOSE INSTRUCTION TABLES.
I RATHER LIKED IT AT FIRST, THINKING I WAS WELCOME.
AS IT WERE.
MORE TEA?
YES, THANK YOU.
BUT NOW I FIND IT COMES BACK LIKE A BALL THROWN AGAINST A WALL.
YOU'RE WELCOME.
AND I'VE BECOME POSITIVELY *APPREHENSIVE* AS A RESULT.
YES. SO. WITH THE PROPER INSTRUCTIONS YOUR MACHINE COULD BE PUT TO USE CALCULATING ...ANYTHING, DON'T YOU THINK?
IT'S ENGLISH—AFTER A FASHION ANYWAY—BUT THE LANGUAGE RULES ARE CLEARLY DIFFERENT.

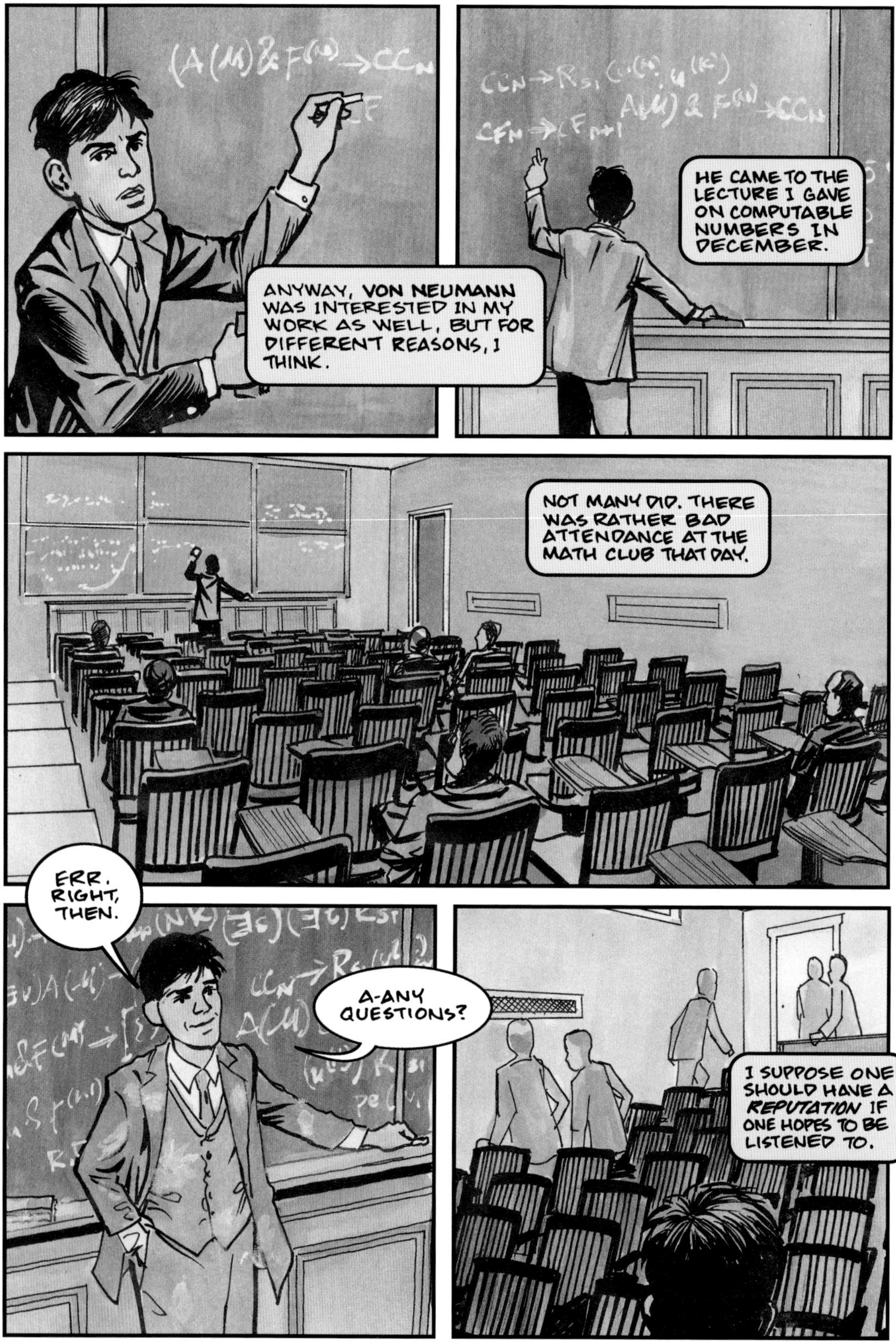
ANYWAY, VON NEUMANN WAS INTERESTED IN MY WORK AS WELL, BUT FOR DIFFERENT REASONS, I THINK.
HE CAME TO THE LECTURE I GAVE ON COMPUTABLE NUMBERS IN DECEMBER.
NOT MANY DID. THERE WAS RATHER BAD ATTENDANCE AT THE MATH CLUB THAT DAY.
ERR. RIGHT, THEN.
A-ANY QUESTIONS?
I SUPPOSE ONE SHOULD HAVE A *REPUTATION* IF ONE HOPES TO BE LISTENED TO.

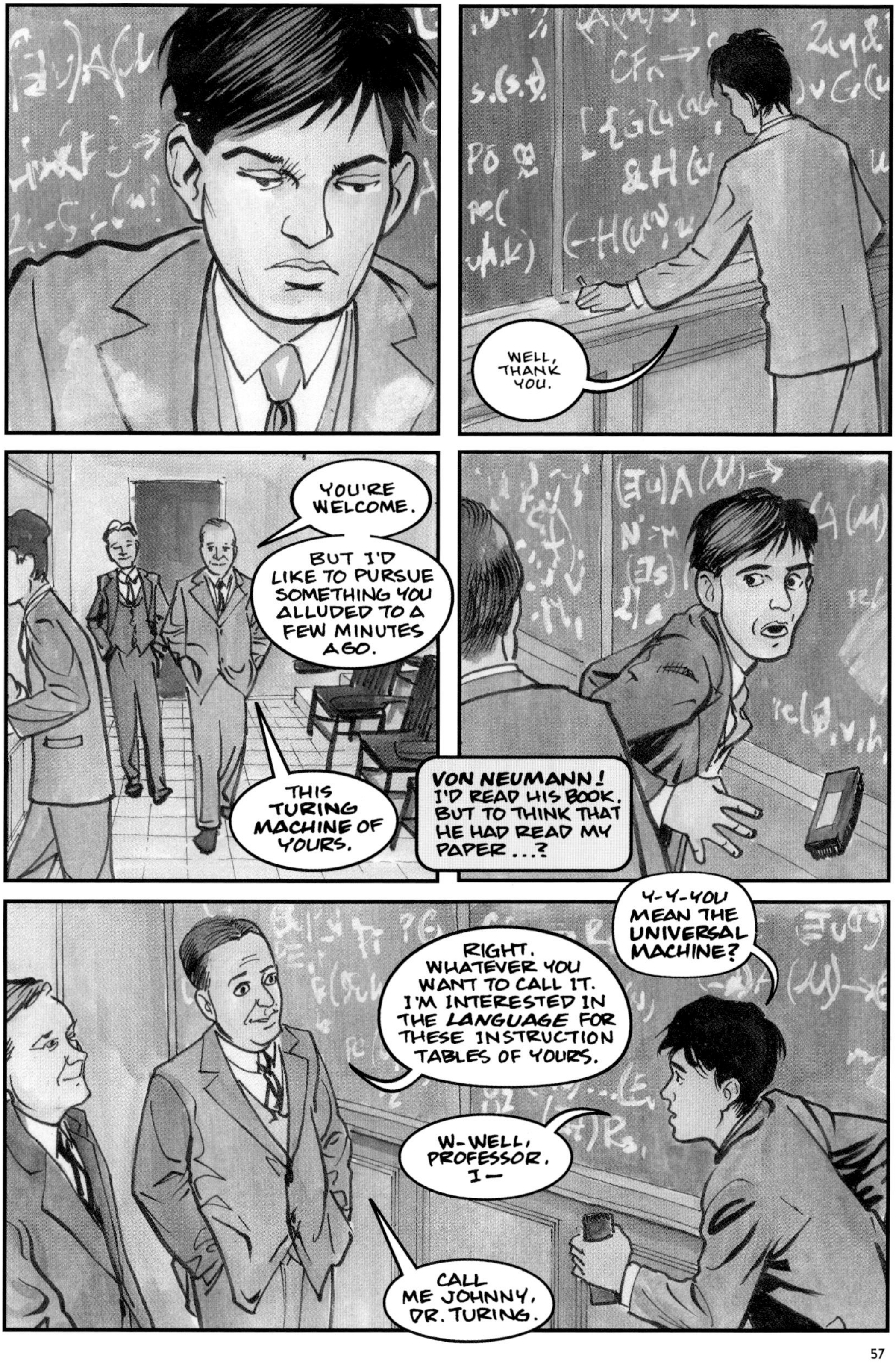

WELL, THANK YOU.
YOU'RE WELCOME.
BUT I'D LIKE TO PURSUE SOMETHING YOU ALLUDED TO A FEW MINUTES AGO.
THIS TURING MACHINE OF YOURS.
VON NEUMANN! I'D READ HIS BOOK. BUT TO THINK THAT HE HAD READ MY PAPER ...?
Y-Y-YOU MEAN THE UNIVERSAL MACHINE?
RIGHT. WHATEVER YOU WANT TO CALL IT. I'M INTERESTED IN THE *LANGUAGE* FOR THESE INSTRUCTION TABLES OF YOURS.
W-WELL, PROFESSOR. I—
CALL ME JOHNNY, DR. TURING.

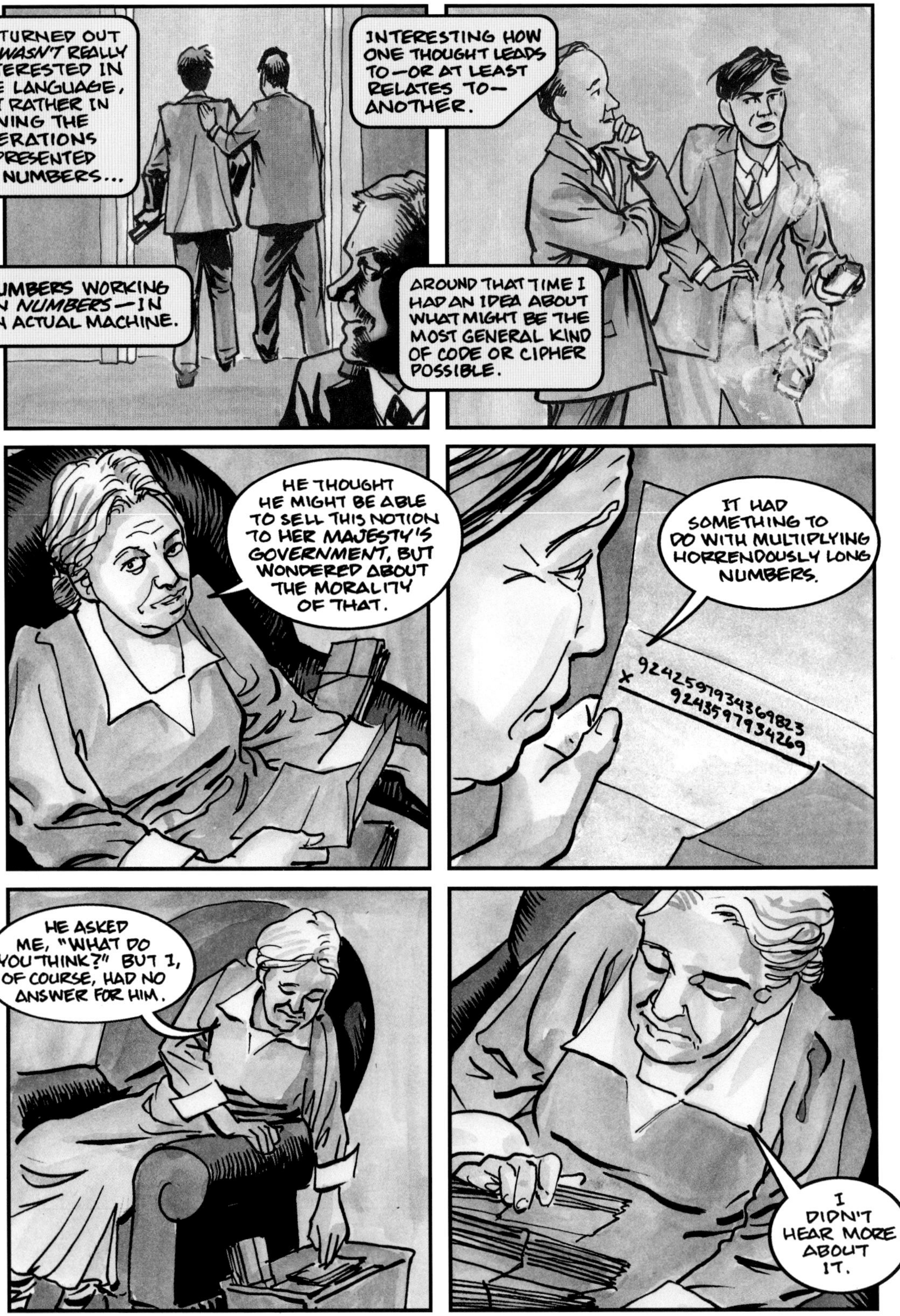
IT TURNED OUT HE *WASN'T* REALLY INTERESTED IN THE LANGUAGE, BUT RATHER IN HAVING THE OPERATIONS REPRESENTED AS NUMBERS...
NUMBERS WORKING ON *NUMBERS*—IN AN ACTUAL MACHINE.
INTERESTING HOW ONE THOUGHT LEADS TO—OR AT LEAST RELATES TO—ANOTHER.
AROUND THAT TIME I HAD AN IDEA ABOUT WHAT MIGHT BE THE MOST GENERAL KIND OF CODE OR CIPHER POSSIBLE.
HE THOUGHT HE MIGHT BE ABLE TO SELL THIS NOTION TO HER MAJESTY'S GOVERNMENT, BUT WONDERED ABOUT THE MORALITY OF THAT.
IT HAD SOMETHING TO DO WITH MULTIPLYING HORRENDOUSLY LONG NUMBERS.
9242597934369823
x 9243597934269
HE ASKED ME, "WHAT DO YOU THINK?" BUT I, OF COURSE, HAD NO ANSWER FOR HIM.
I DIDN'T HEAR MORE ABOUT IT.

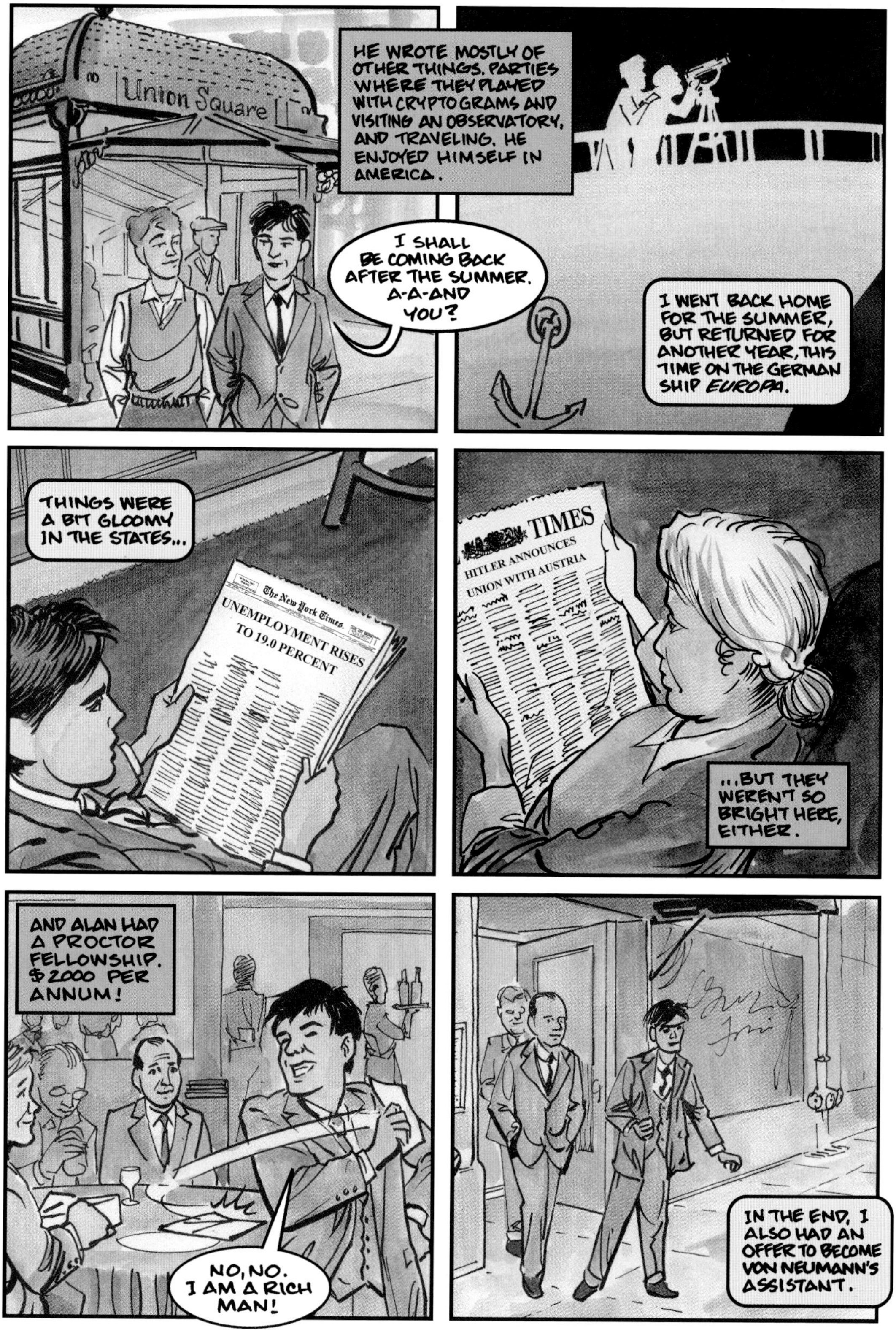
Union Square
HE WROTE MOSTLY OF OTHER THINGS. PARTIES WHERE THEY PLAYED WITH CRYPTOGRAMS AND VISITING AN OBSERVATORY, AND TRAVELING. HE ENJOYED HIMSELF IN AMERICA.
I SHALL BE COMING BACK AFTER THE SUMMER. A-A-AND YOU?
I WENT BACK HOME FOR THE SUMMER, BUT RETURNED FOR ANOTHER YEAR, THIS TIME ON THE GERMAN SHIP *EUROPA*.
THINGS WERE A BIT GLOOMY IN THE STATES...
The New York Times.
UNEMPLOYMENT RISES TO 19.0 PERCENT
TIMES
HITLER ANNOUNCES UNION WITH AUSTRIA
...BUT THEY WEREN'T SO BRIGHT HERE, EITHER.
AND ALAN HAD A PROCTOR FELLOWSHIP. $2000 PER ANNUM!
NO, NO. I AM A RICH MAN!
IN THE END, I ALSO HAD AN OFFER TO BECOME VON NEUMANN'S ASSISTANT.

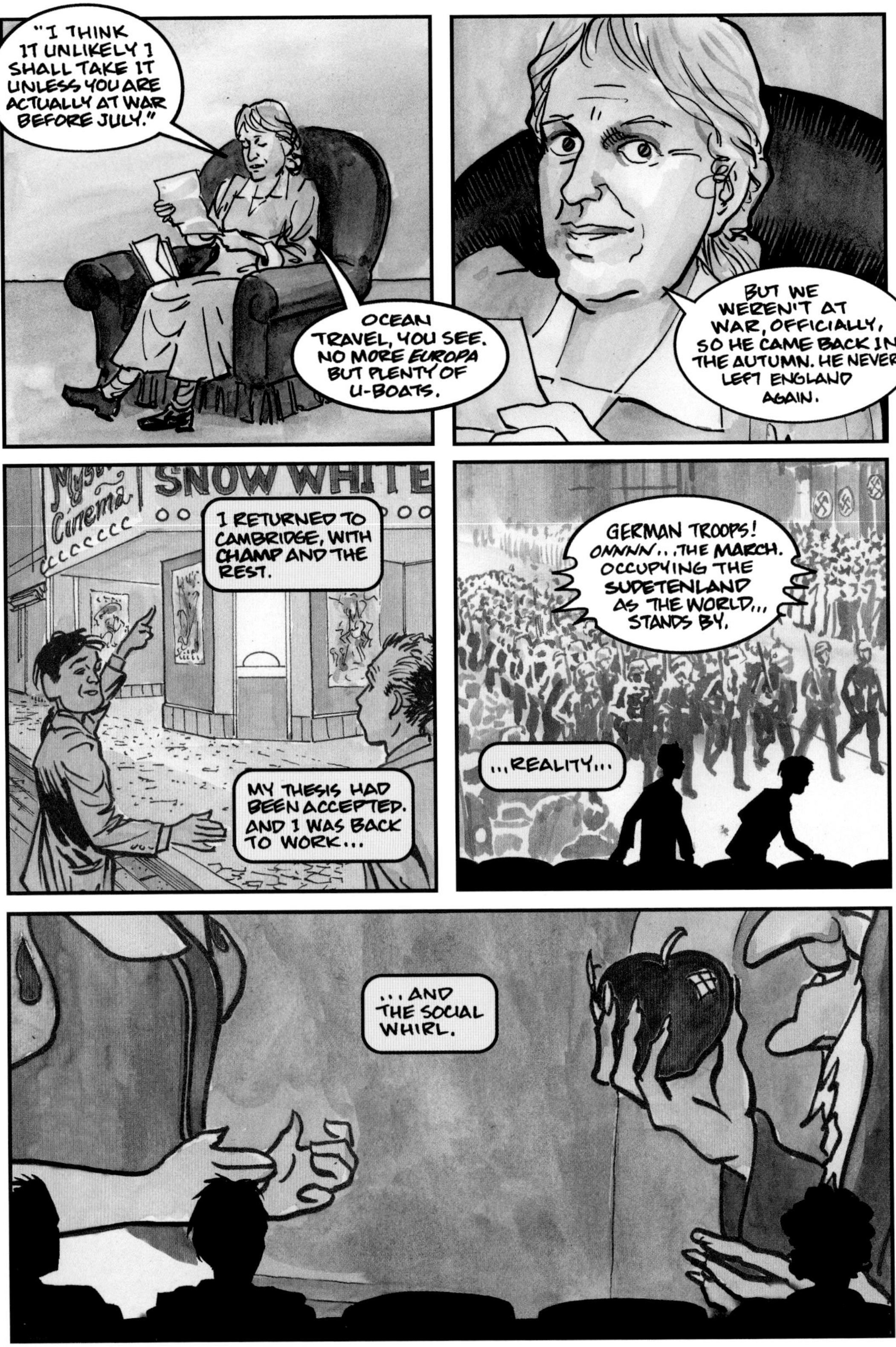
"I THINK IT UNLIKELY I SHALL TAKE IT UNLESS YOU ARE ACTUALLY AT WAR BEFORE JULY."
OCEAN TRAVEL, YOU SEE. NO MORE *EUROPA* BUT PLENTY OF U-BOATS.
BUT WE WEREN'T AT WAR, OFFICIALLY, SO HE CAME BACK IN THE AUTUMN. HE NEVER LEFT ENGLAND AGAIN.
Mystic Cinema
SNOW WHITE
I RETURNED TO CAMBRIDGE, WITH CHAMP AND THE REST.
MY THESIS HAD BEEN ACCEPTED. AND I WAS BACK TO WORK...
GERMAN TROOPS! ONNNN...THE MARCH. OCCUPYING THE SUDETENLAND AS THE WORLD... STANDS BY.
...REALITY...
...AND THE SOCIAL WHIRL.

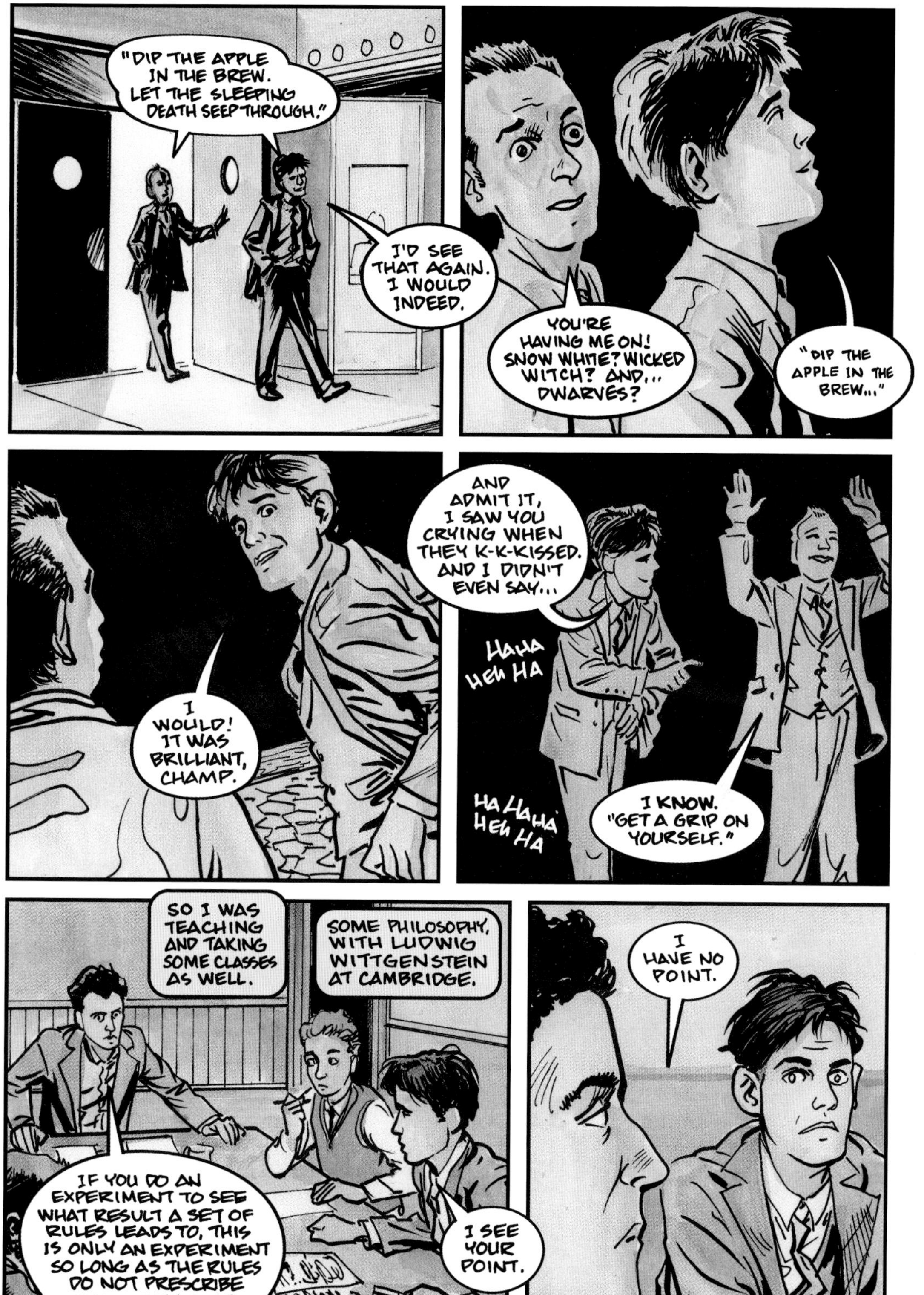

"DIP THE APPLE IN THE BREW. LET THE SLEEPING DEATH SEEP THROUGH."
I'D SEE THAT AGAIN. I WOULD INDEED.
YOU'RE HAVING ME ON! SNOW WHITE? WICKED WITCH? AND... DWARVES?
"DIP THE APPLE IN THE BREW..."
I WOULD! IT WAS BRILLIANT, CHAMP.
AND ADMIT IT, I SAW YOU CRYING WHEN THEY K-K-KISSED. AND I DIDN'T EVEN SAY...
HAHA HEH HA
HA HAHA HEH HA
I KNOW. "GET A GRIP ON YOURSELF."
SO I WAS TEACHING AND TAKING SOME CLASSES AS WELL.
SOME PHILOSOPHY, WITH LUDWIG WITTGENSTEIN AT CAMBRIDGE.
IF YOU DO AN EXPERIMENT TO SEE WHAT RESULT A SET OF RULES LEADS TO, THIS IS ONLY AN EXPERIMENT SO LONG AS THE RULES DO NOT PRESCRIBE WHAT THEY HAVE TO LEAD TO.
I SEE YOUR POINT.
I HAVE NO POINT.

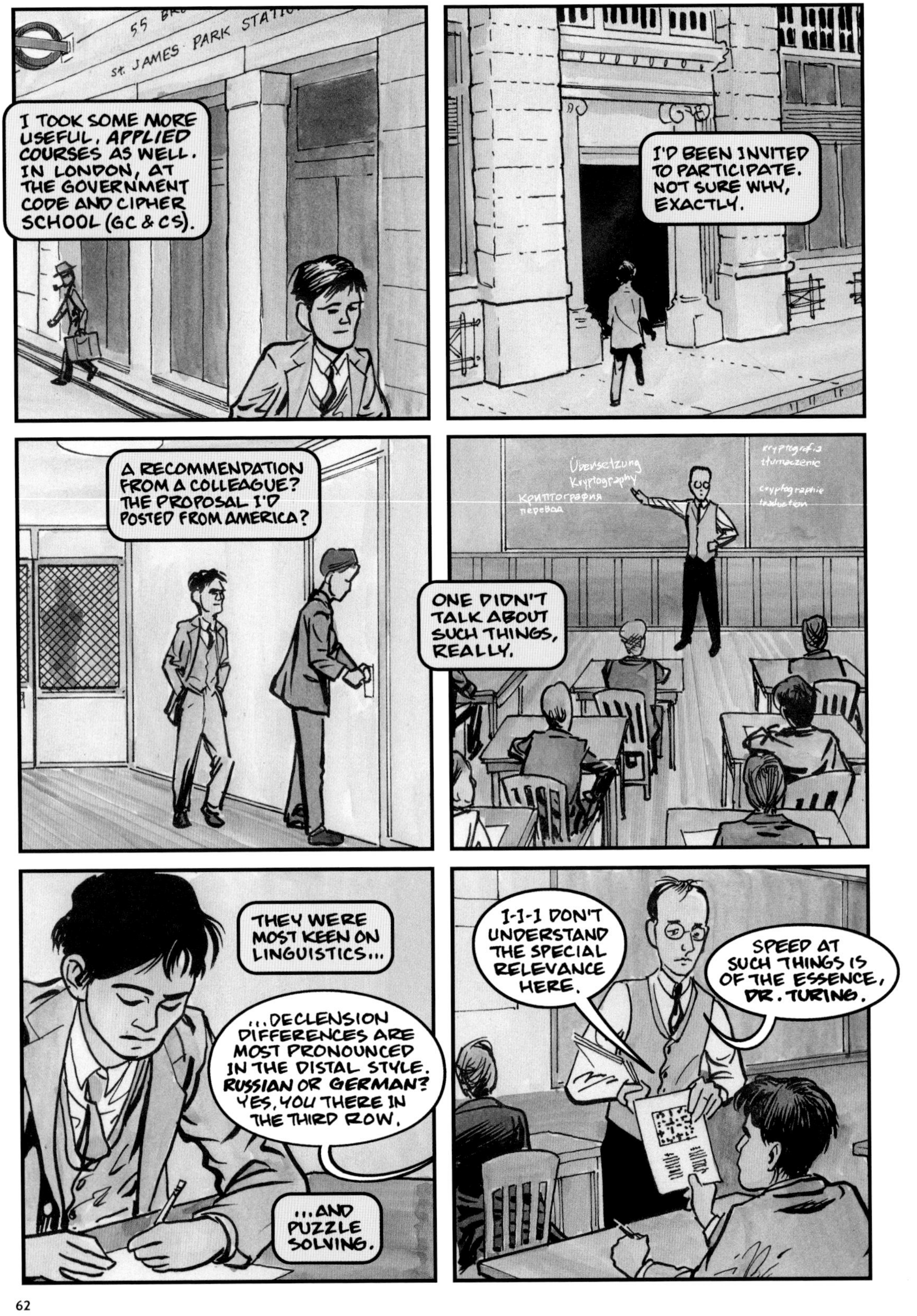
55 BR
ST. JAMES PARK STATION
I TOOK SOME MORE USEFUL, APPLIED COURSES AS WELL. IN LONDON, AT THE GOVERNMENT CODE AND CIPHER SCHOOL (GC & CS).
I'D BEEN INVITED TO PARTICIPATE. NOT SURE WHY, EXACTLY.
A RECOMMENDATION FROM A COLLEAGUE? THE PROPOSAL I'D POSTED FROM AMERICA?
Übersetzung
Kryptography
Криптография
перевод
cryptographie
ONE DIDN'T TALK ABOUT SUCH THINGS, REALLY.
THEY WERE MOST KEEN ON LINGUISTICS...
...DECLENSION DIFFERENCES ARE MOST PRONOUNCED IN THE DISTAL STYLE. RUSSIAN OR GERMAN? YES, YOU THERE IN THE THIRD ROW.
...AND PUZZLE SOLVING.
I-I-I DON'T UNDERSTAND THE SPECIAL RELEVANCE HERE.
SPEED AT SUCH THINGS IS OF THE ESSENCE, DR. TURING.

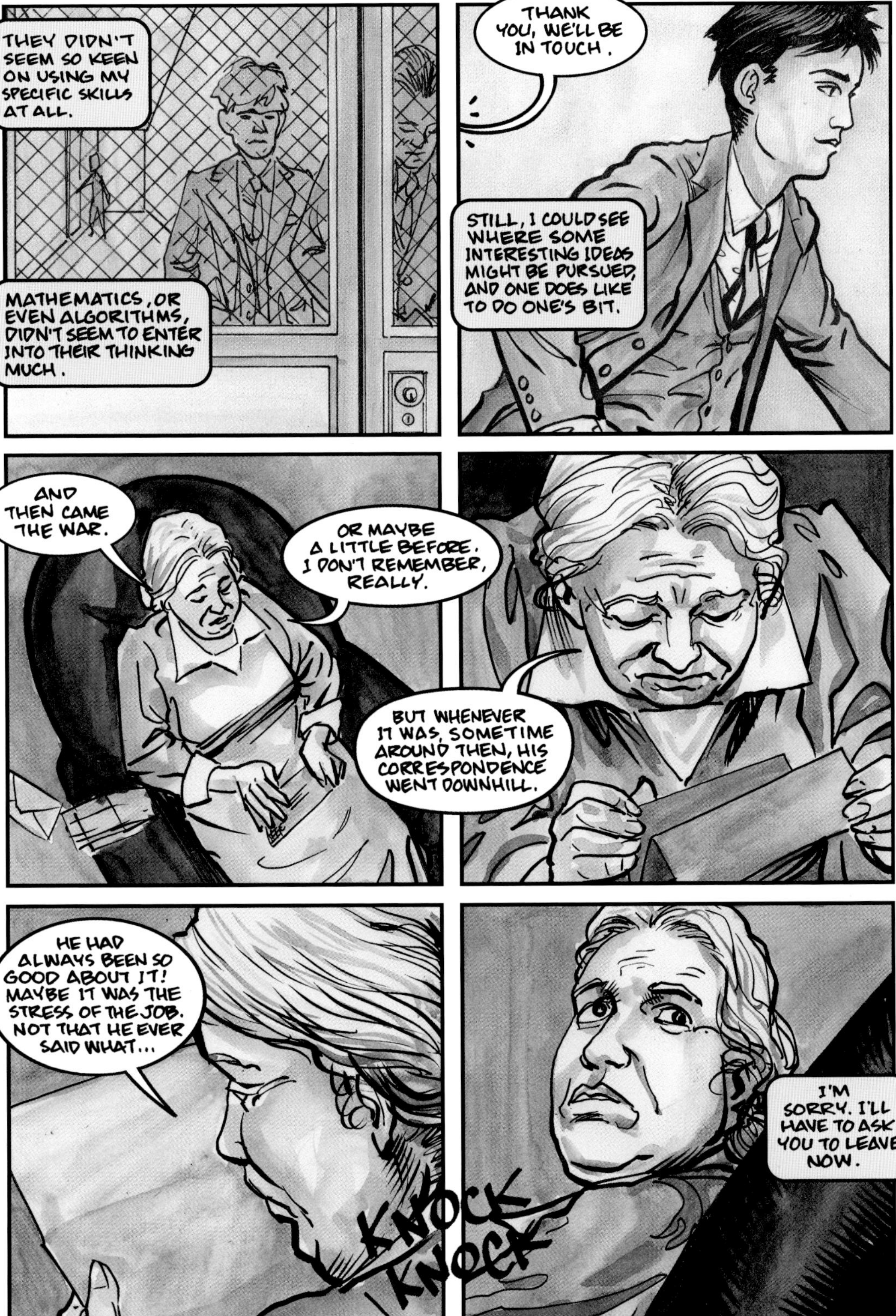
THEY DIDN'T SEEM SO KEEN ON USING MY SPECIFIC SKILLS AT ALL.
MATHEMATICS, OR EVEN ALGORITHMS, DIDN'T SEEM TO ENTER INTO THEIR THINKING MUCH.
THANK YOU, WE'LL BE IN TOUCH.
STILL, I COULD SEE WHERE SOME INTERESTING IDEAS MIGHT BE PURSUED, AND ONE DOES LIKE TO DO ONE'S BIT.
AND THEN CAME THE WAR.
OR MAYBE A LITTLE BEFORE. I DON'T REMEMBER, REALLY.
BUT WHENEVER IT WAS, SOMETIME AROUND THEN, HIS CORRESPONDENCE WENT DOWNHILL.
HE HAD ALWAYS BEEN SO GOOD ABOUT IT! MAYBE IT WAS THE STRESS OF THE JOB. NOT THAT HE EVER SAID WHAT...
KNOCK KNOCK
I'M SORRY. I'LL HAVE TO ASK YOU TO LEAVE NOW.

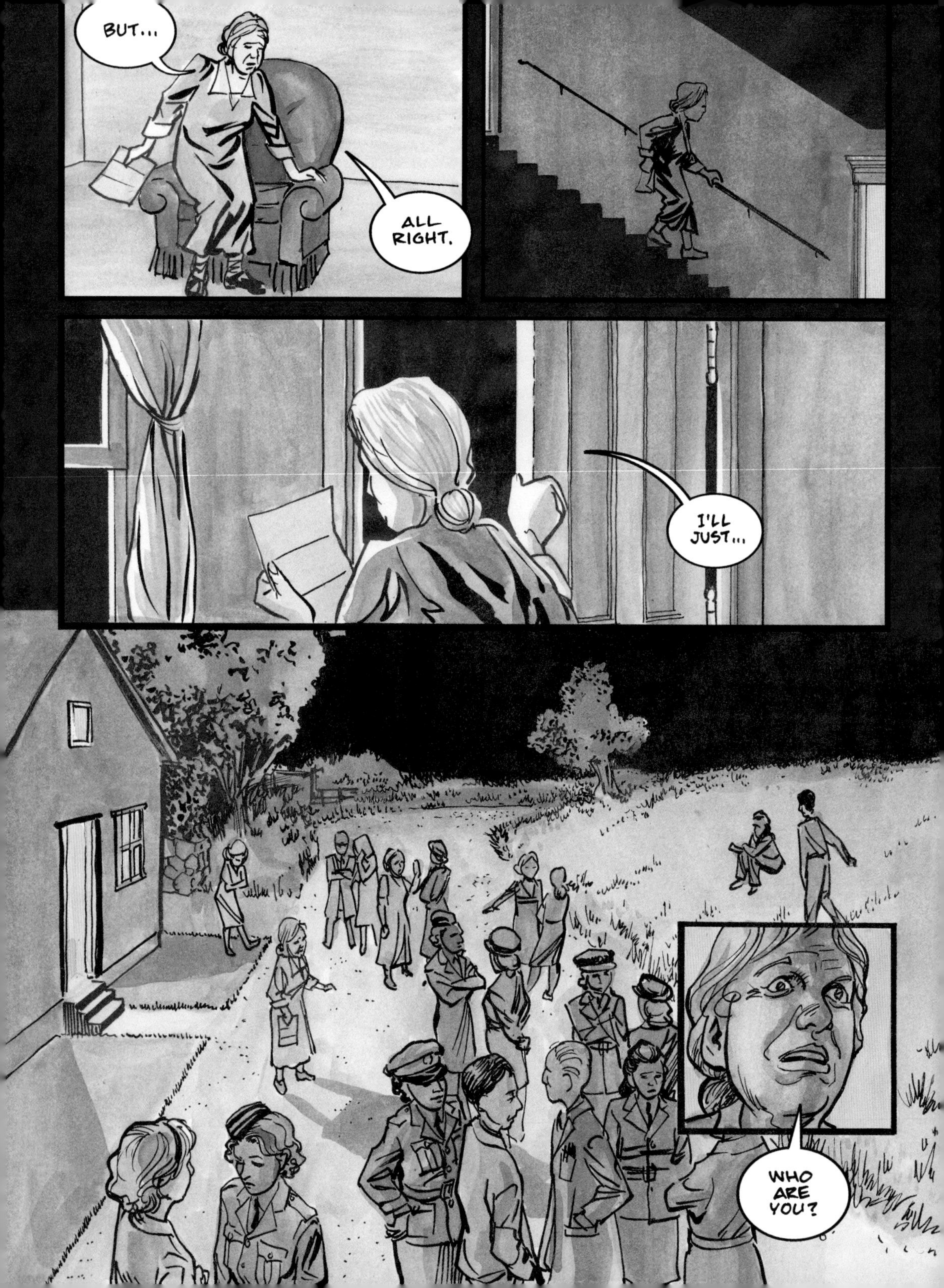
BUT...
ALL RIGHT.
I'LL JUST...
WHO ARE YOU?

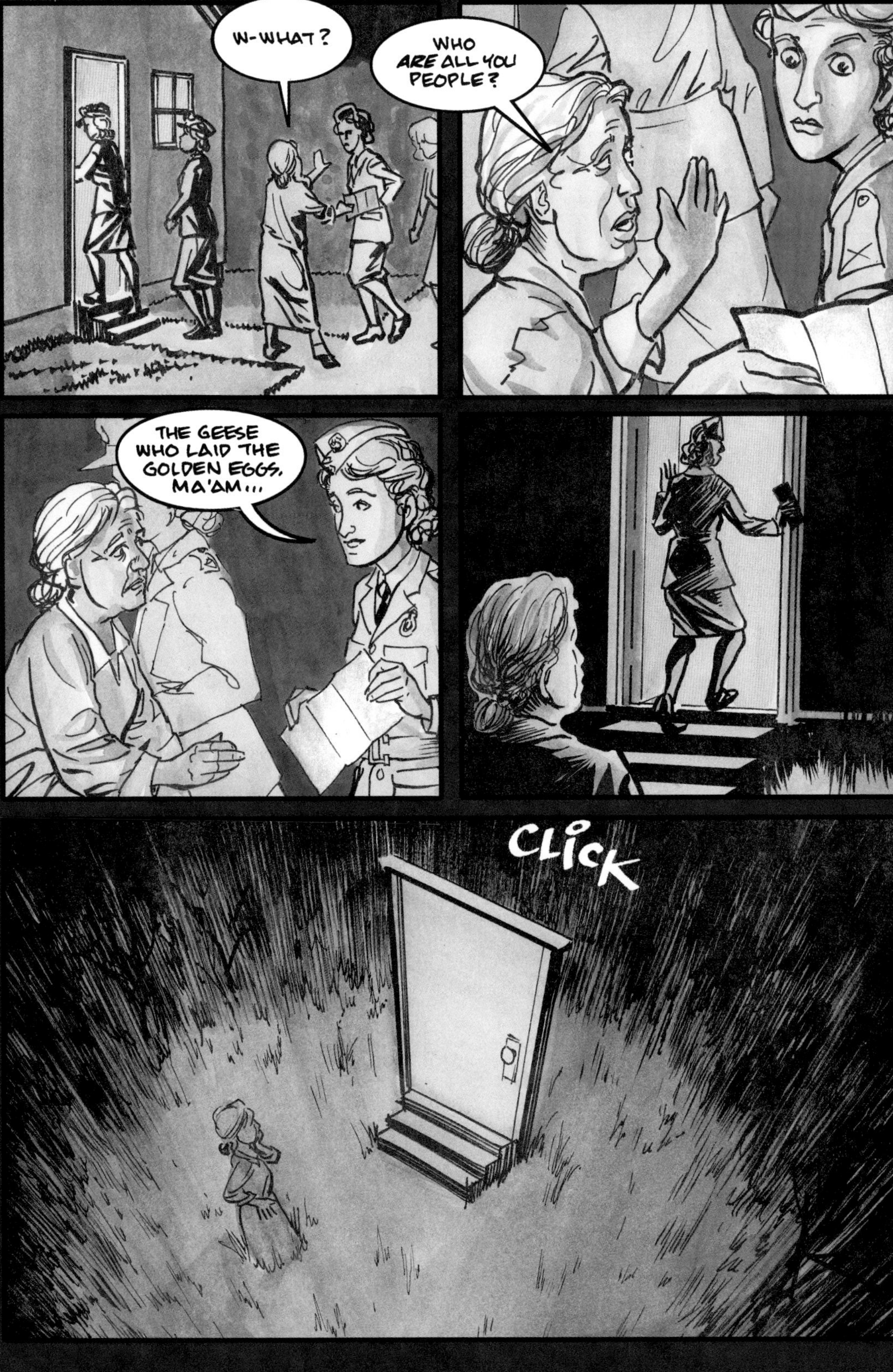
W-WHAT?
WHO ARE ALL YOU PEOPLE?
THE GEESE WHO LAID THE GOLDEN EGGS, MA'AM...
CLICK

```
HHXMJ   KVYHS   WHTNZ   STOGQ
YRJZN   KFLDU   ZTISL   GAANW
RLRHN   EZPPX   CFLRV   OCLUX
PTGFW   TWQGL   GDXJX   TGMJY
JUTOP   XBZQK   RNPIJ   TWVZH
NHXED   FRVOF   MAFNO   USDBR
ANASZ   BPHDZ   SZBTE   KAKSK
QMCVI   KWZIK   MIRPO   JCYWW
HKHNR   MKVRS   YSUUB   GXEMH
OMTYE   ABXNO   RCQFA   AGUWY
OTAAH   IRNHC   FHXMK   TPJUQ
GUCYM   RSECR   ETRCB   HQAUS
LIRJO   FVBOM   KBVTS   VILNX
PLONR   ZHUOF   FLXRA   BUESY
YFUVM   OESHQ   HFWAL   YGWOK
UTCZN   JUZCO   OAIAP   OYNHB
FPYWQ   RAJRC   ENSIZ   HKMGJ
IMVYJ   VJFDC   IQCBV   LMCVX
VBNWK   QLHMS   ROFFR   ZPGCD
HGRKF   POJJZ   ULTRA   TSUOA
QBVBY   HPIPF   WTJKK   UQKVO
JLDCO   LGKBP   ZHOCA   NHYZE
```

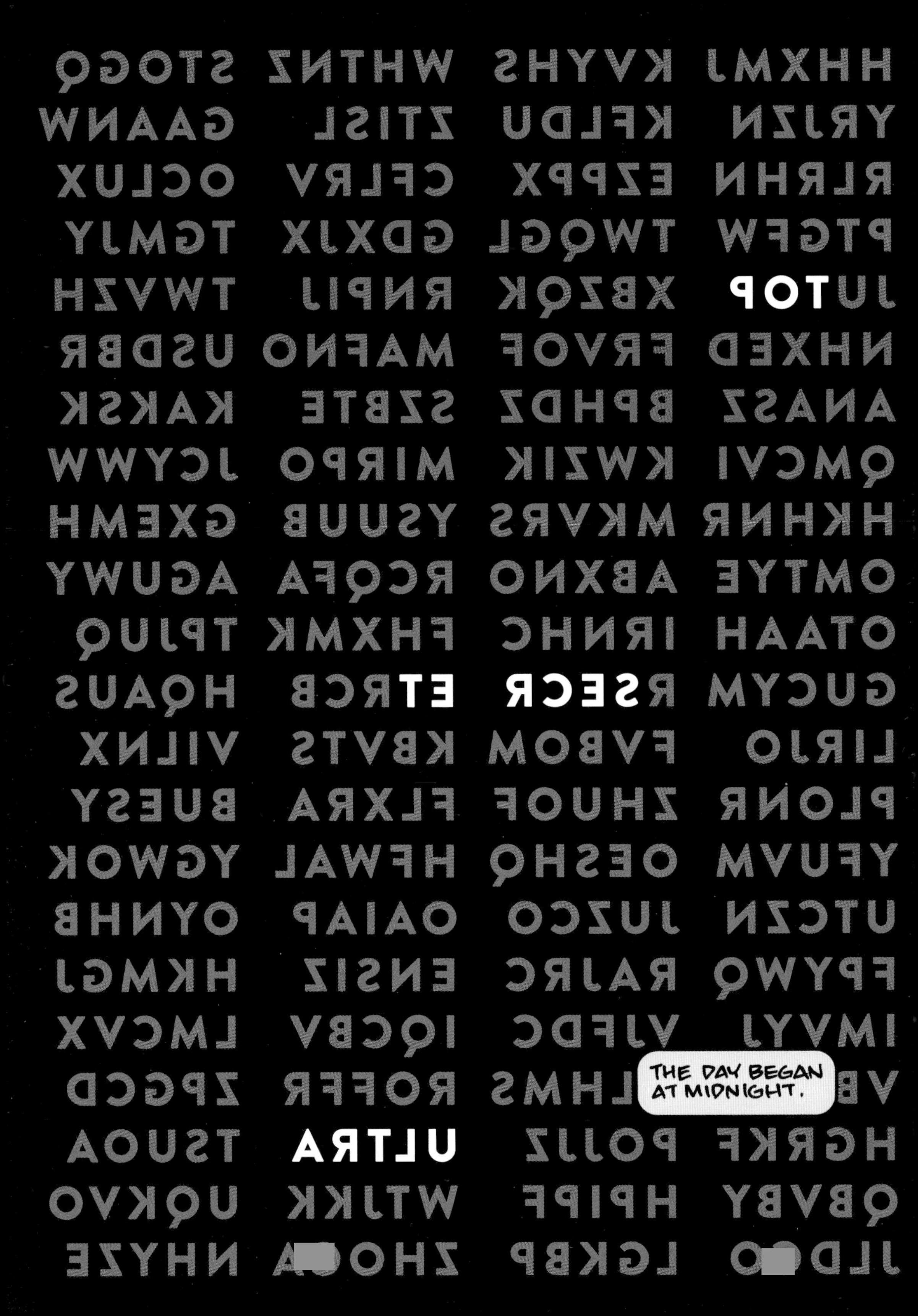
THE DAY BEGAN AT MIDNIGHT.

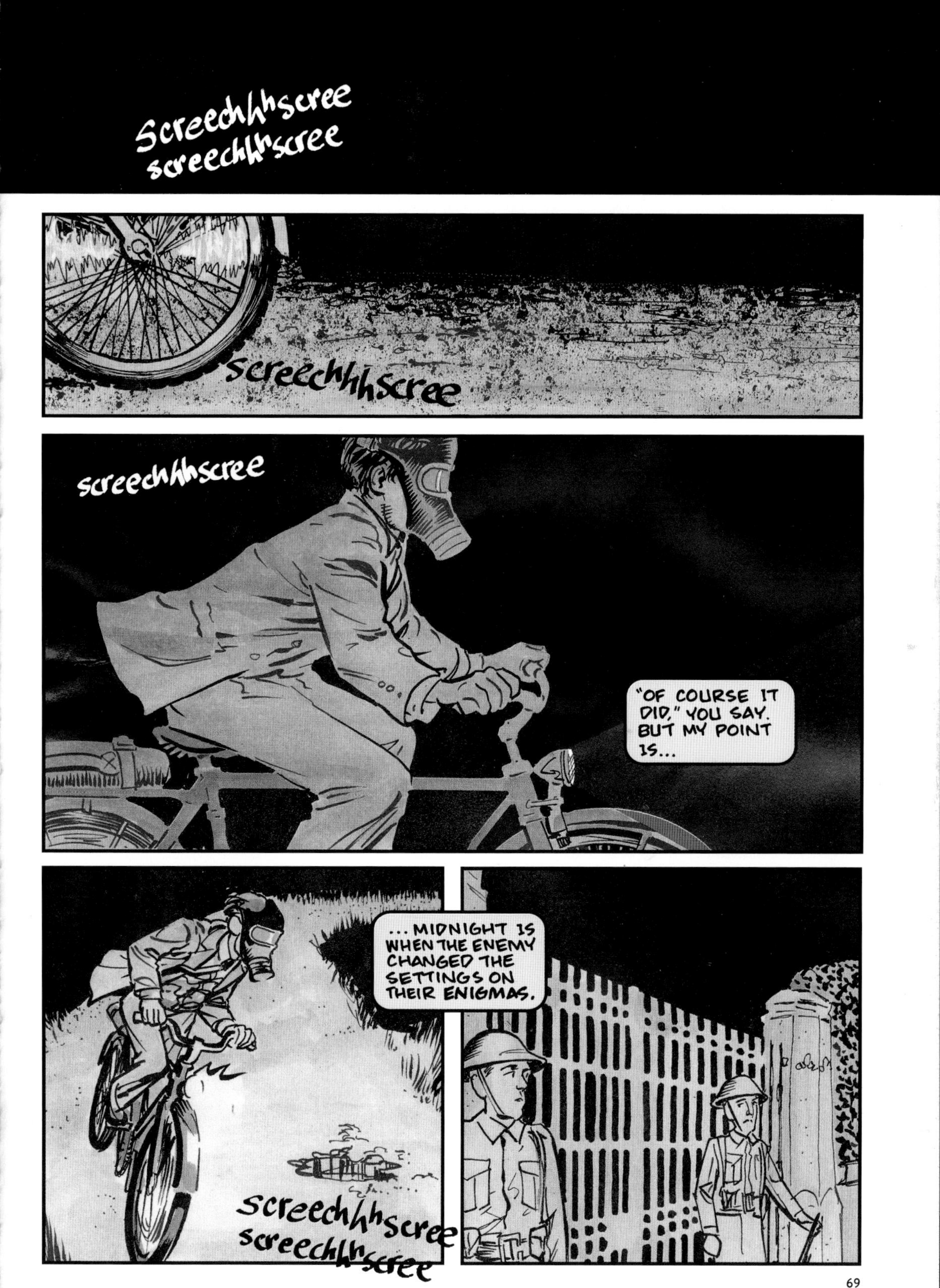
Screechhhscree
screechhhscree
screechhhscree
screechhhscree
"OF COURSE IT DID," YOU SAY. BUT MY POINT IS...
...MIDNIGHT IS WHEN THE ENEMY CHANGED THE SETTINGS ON THEIR ENIGMAS.
screechhhscree
screechhhscree

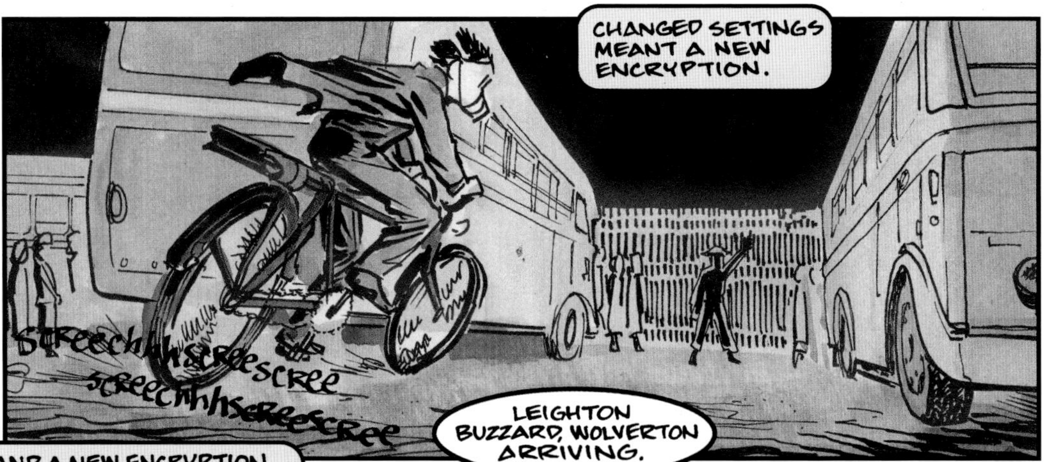
CHANGED SETTINGS MEANT A NEW ENCRYPTION.
SCREECHHHSCREESCREE
SCREECHHHSCREESCREE
SCREECHHHSCREESCREE
LEIGHTON BUZZARD, WOLVERTON ARRIVING.

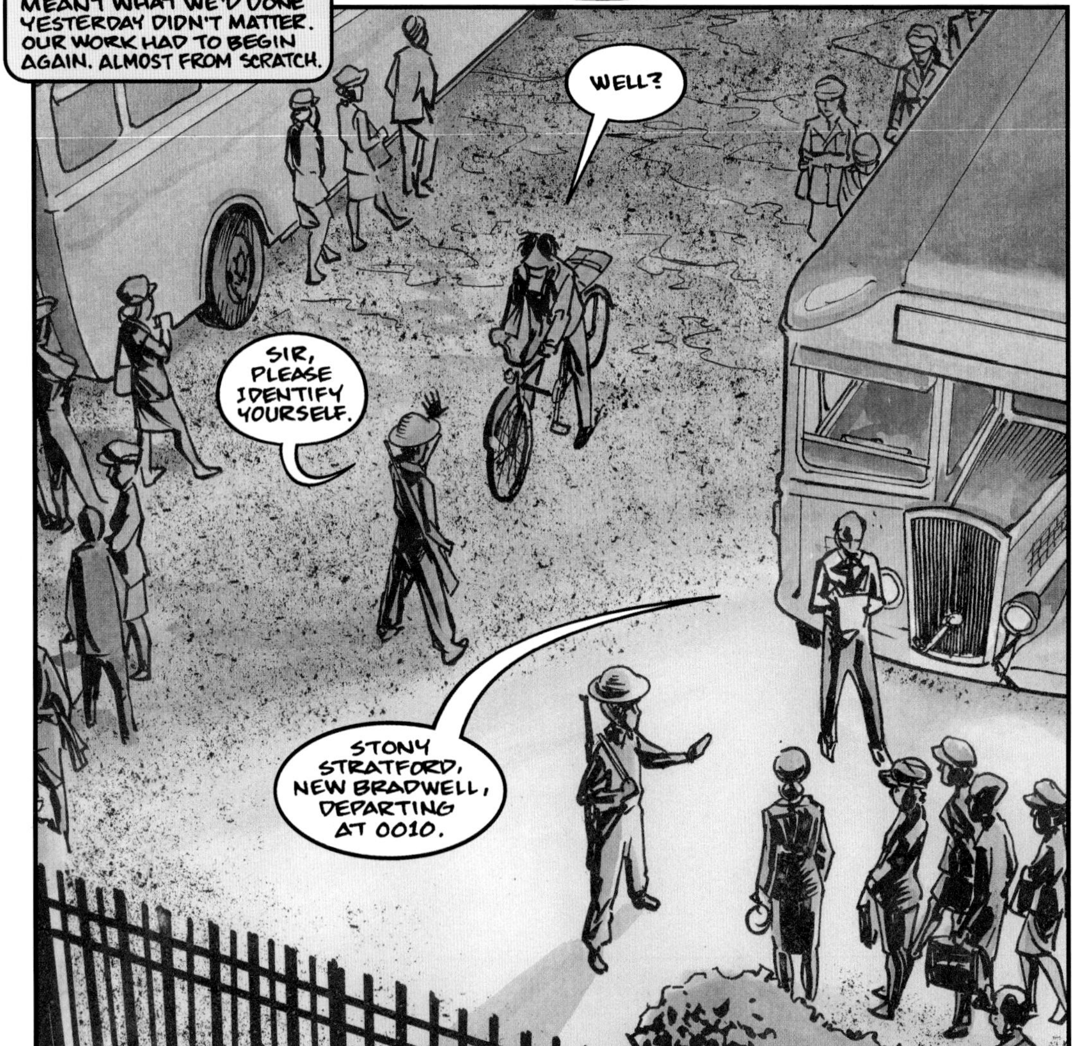
AND A NEW ENCRYPTION MEANT WHAT WE'D DONE YESTERDAY DIDN'T MATTER. OUR WORK HAD TO BEGIN AGAIN. ALMOST FROM SCRATCH.
WELL?
SIR, PLEASE IDENTIFY YOURSELF.
STONY STRATFORD, NEW BRADWELL, DEPARTING AT 0010.

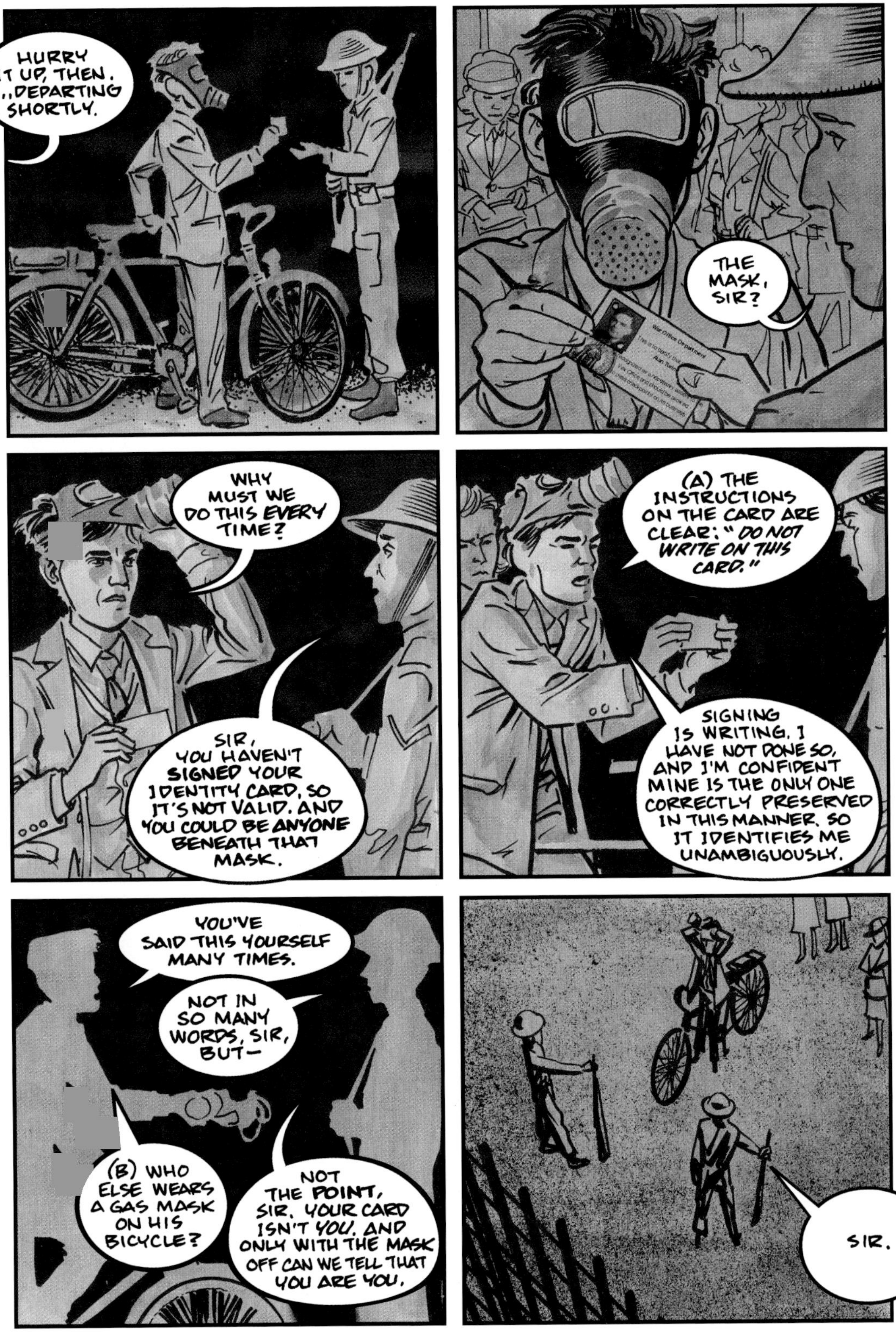
HURRY IT UP, THEN. ...DEPARTING SHORTLY.
THE MASK, SIR?
WHY MUST WE DO THIS EVERY TIME?
SIR, YOU HAVEN'T SIGNED YOUR IDENTITY CARD, SO IT'S NOT VALID. AND YOU COULD BE ANYONE BENEATH THAT MASK.
(A) THE INSTRUCTIONS ON THE CARD ARE CLEAR: "DO NOT WRITE ON THIS CARD."
SIGNING IS WRITING. I HAVE NOT DONE SO, AND I'M CONFIDENT MINE IS THE ONLY ONE CORRECTLY PRESERVED IN THIS MANNER. SO IT IDENTIFIES ME UNAMBIGUOUSLY.
YOU'VE SAID THIS YOURSELF MANY TIMES.
NOT IN SO MANY WORDS, SIR, BUT—
(B) WHO ELSE WEARS A GAS MASK ON HIS BICYCLE?
NOT THE POINT, SIR. YOUR CARD ISN'T YOU. AND ONLY WITH THE MASK OFF CAN WE TELL THAT YOU ARE YOU.
SIR.

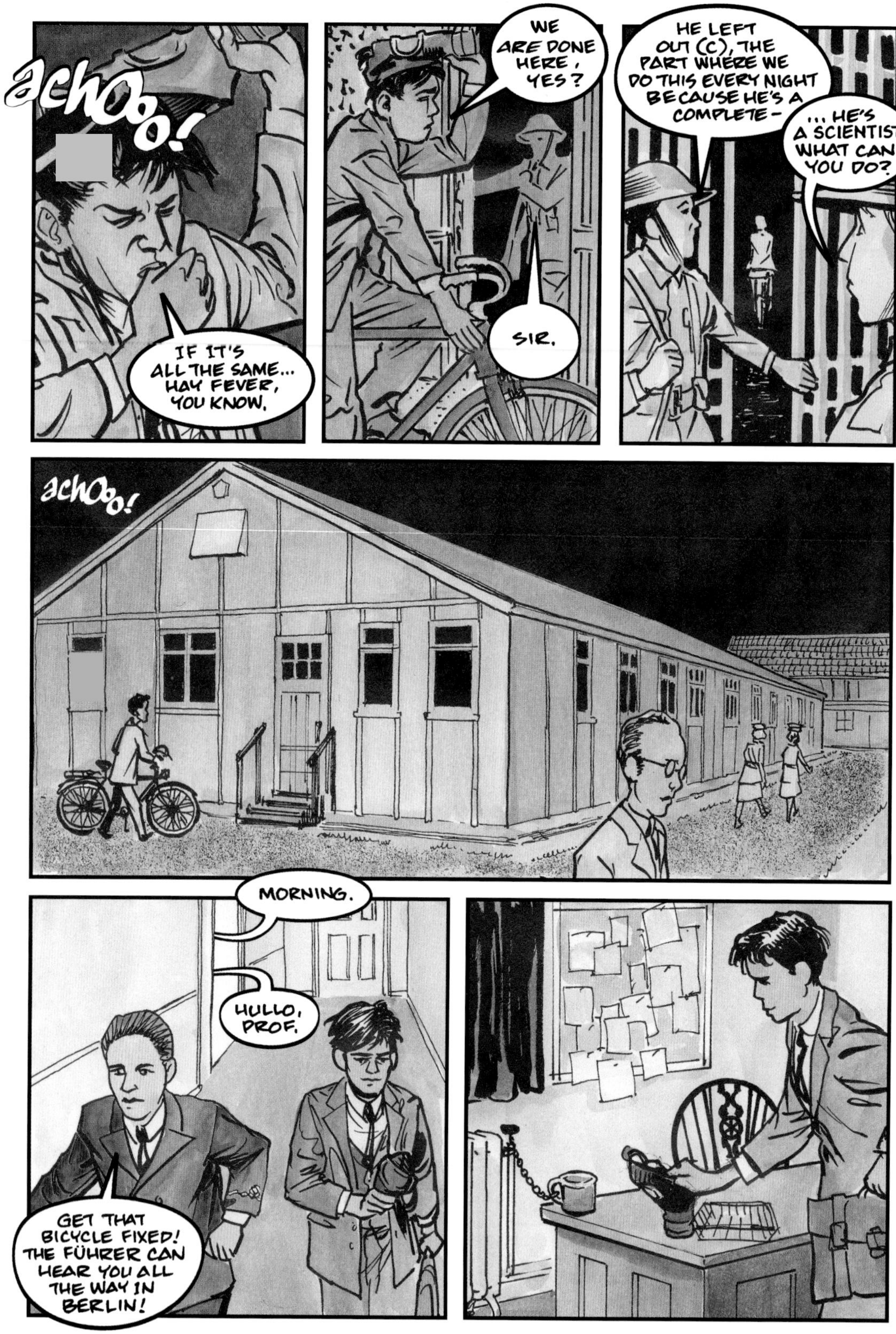
achoooo!
IF IT'S ALL THE SAME... HAY FEVER, YOU KNOW.
WE ARE DONE HERE, YES?
SIR.
HE LEFT OUT (C), THE PART WHERE WE DO THIS EVERY NIGHT BECAUSE HE'S A COMPLETE –
... HE'S A SCIENTIST. WHAT CAN YOU DO?
achooo!
MORNING.
HULLO, PROF.
GET THAT BICYCLE FIXED! THE FÜHRER CAN HEAR YOU ALL THE WAY IN BERLIN!

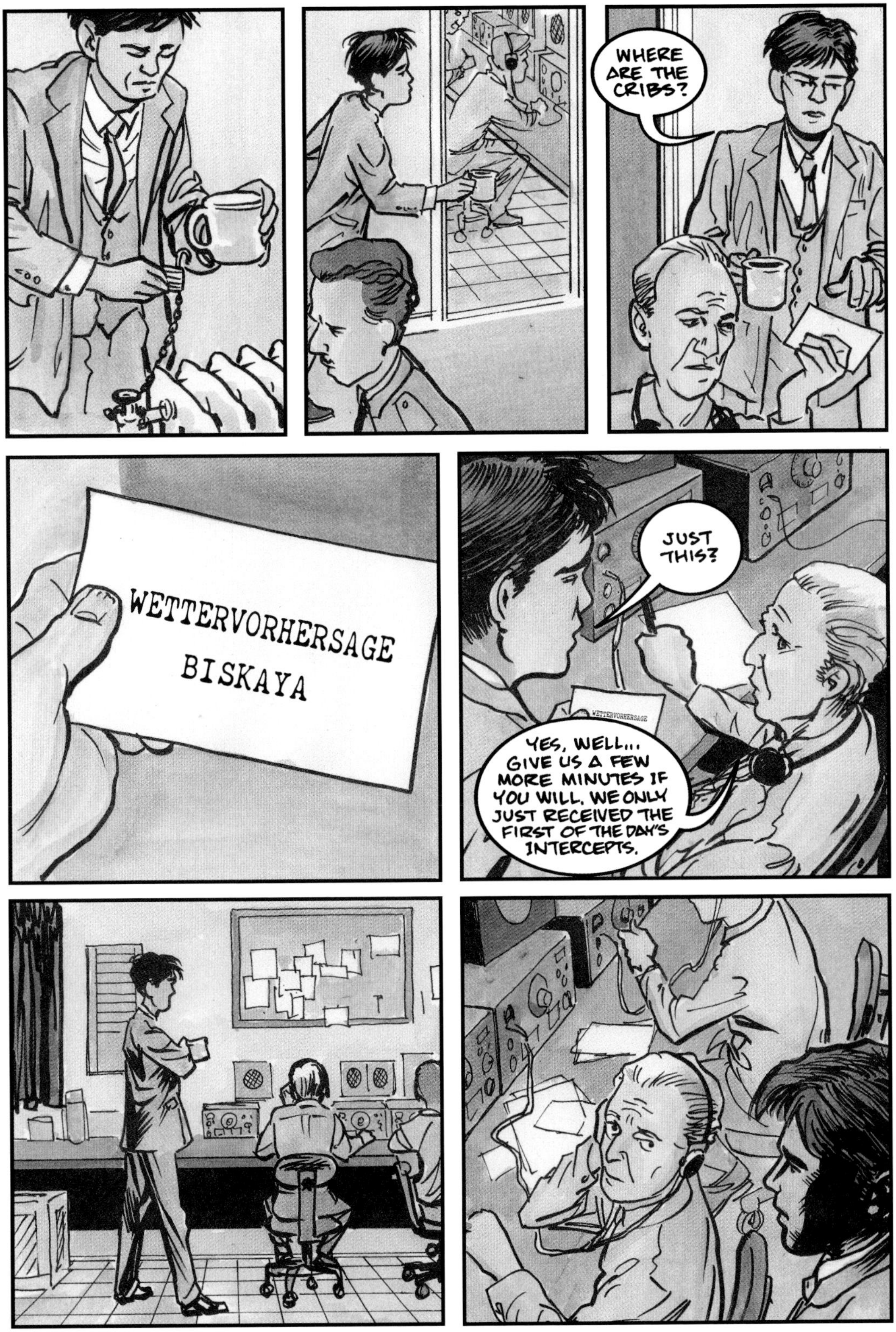
WHERE ARE THE CRIBS?
WETTERVORHERSAGE BISKAYA
JUST THIS?
WETTERVORHERSAGE
YES, WELL... GIVE US A FEW MORE MINUTES IF YOU WILL. WE ONLY JUST RECEIVED THE FIRST OF THE DAY'S INTERCEPTS.

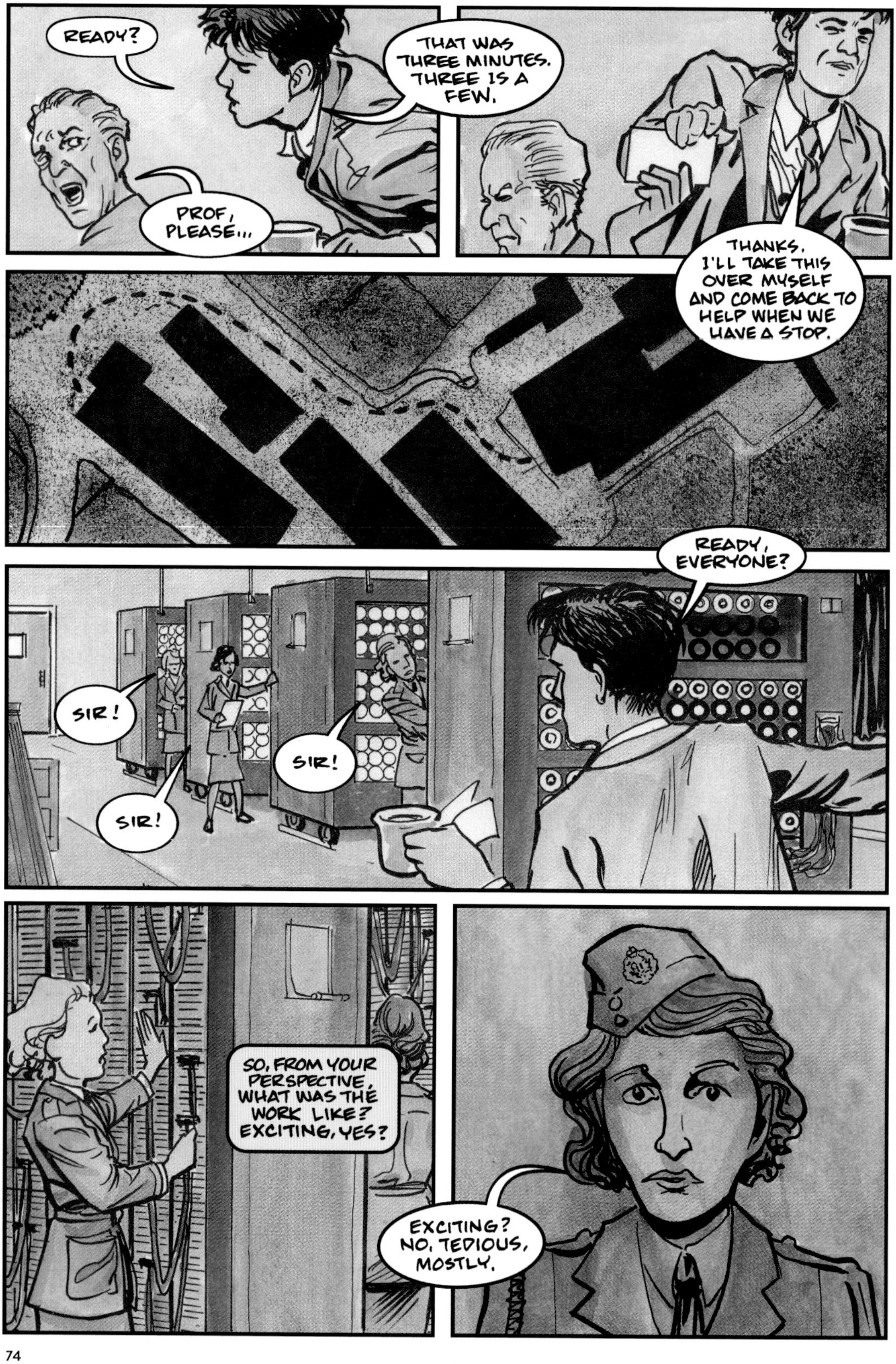
READY?
THAT WAS THREE MINUTES. THREE IS A FEW.
PROF, PLEASE...
THANKS. I'LL TAKE THIS OVER MYSELF AND COME BACK TO HELP WHEN WE HAVE A STOP.
READY, EVERYONE?
SIR!
SIR!
SIR!
SO, FROM YOUR PERSPECTIVE, WHAT WAS THE WORK LIKE? EXCITING, YES?
EXCITING? NO. TEDIOUS, MOSTLY.

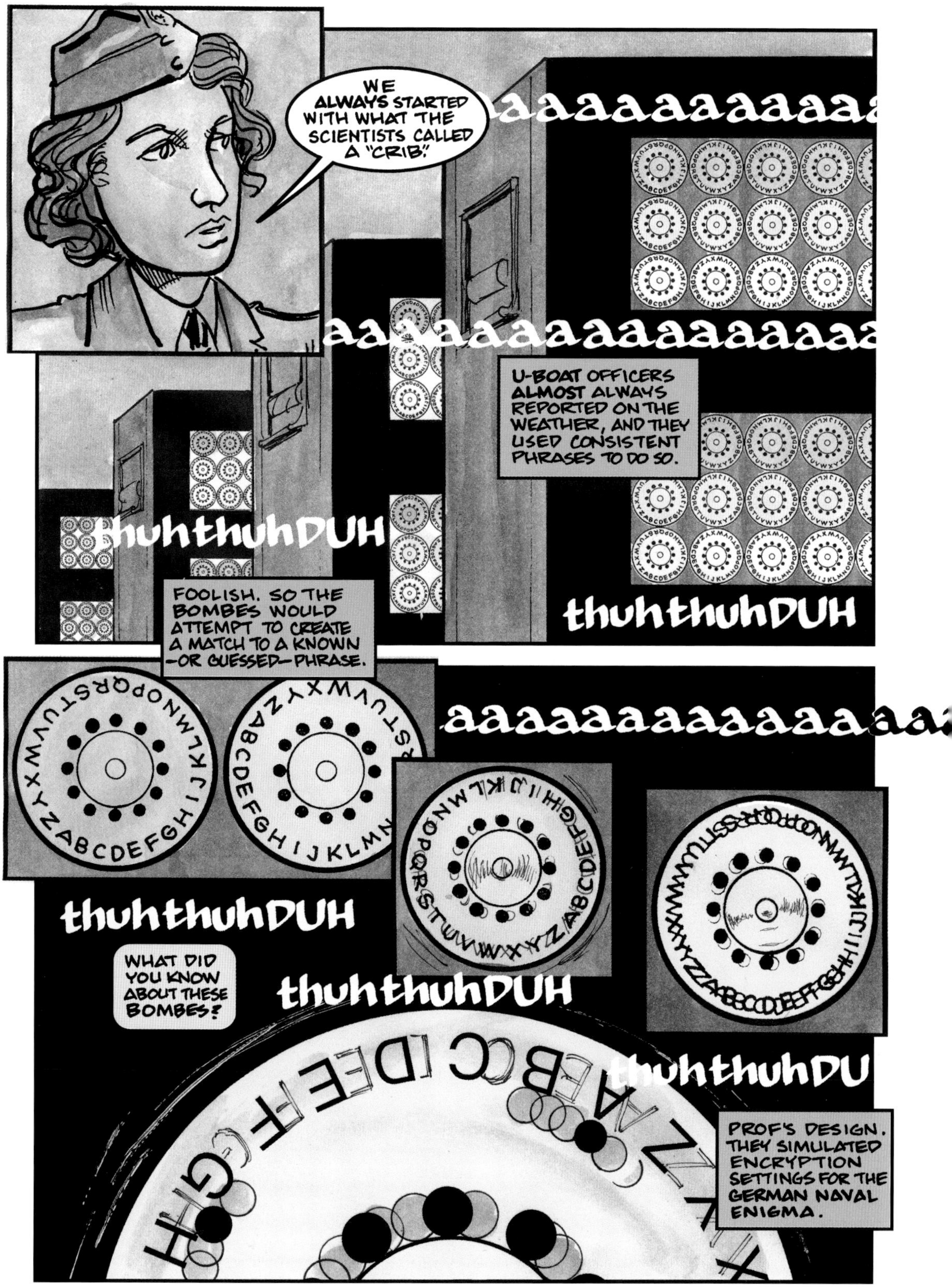
WE ALWAYS STARTED WITH WHAT THE SCIENTISTS CALLED A "CRIB."
aaaaaaaaaaa
aaaaaaaaaaaaa
U-BOAT OFFICERS ALMOST ALWAYS REPORTED ON THE WEATHER, AND THEY USED CONSISTENT PHRASES TO DO SO.
thuhthuhDUH
thuhthuhDUH
FOOLISH. SO THE BOMBES WOULD ATTEMPT TO CREATE A MATCH TO A KNOWN —OR GUESSED— PHRASE.
aaaaaaaaaaaaa
thuhthuhDUH
WHAT DID YOU KNOW ABOUT THESE BOMBES?
thuhthuhDUH
thuhthuhDU
PROF'S DESIGN. THEY SIMULATED ENCRYPTION SETTINGS FOR THE GERMAN NAVAL ENIGMA.

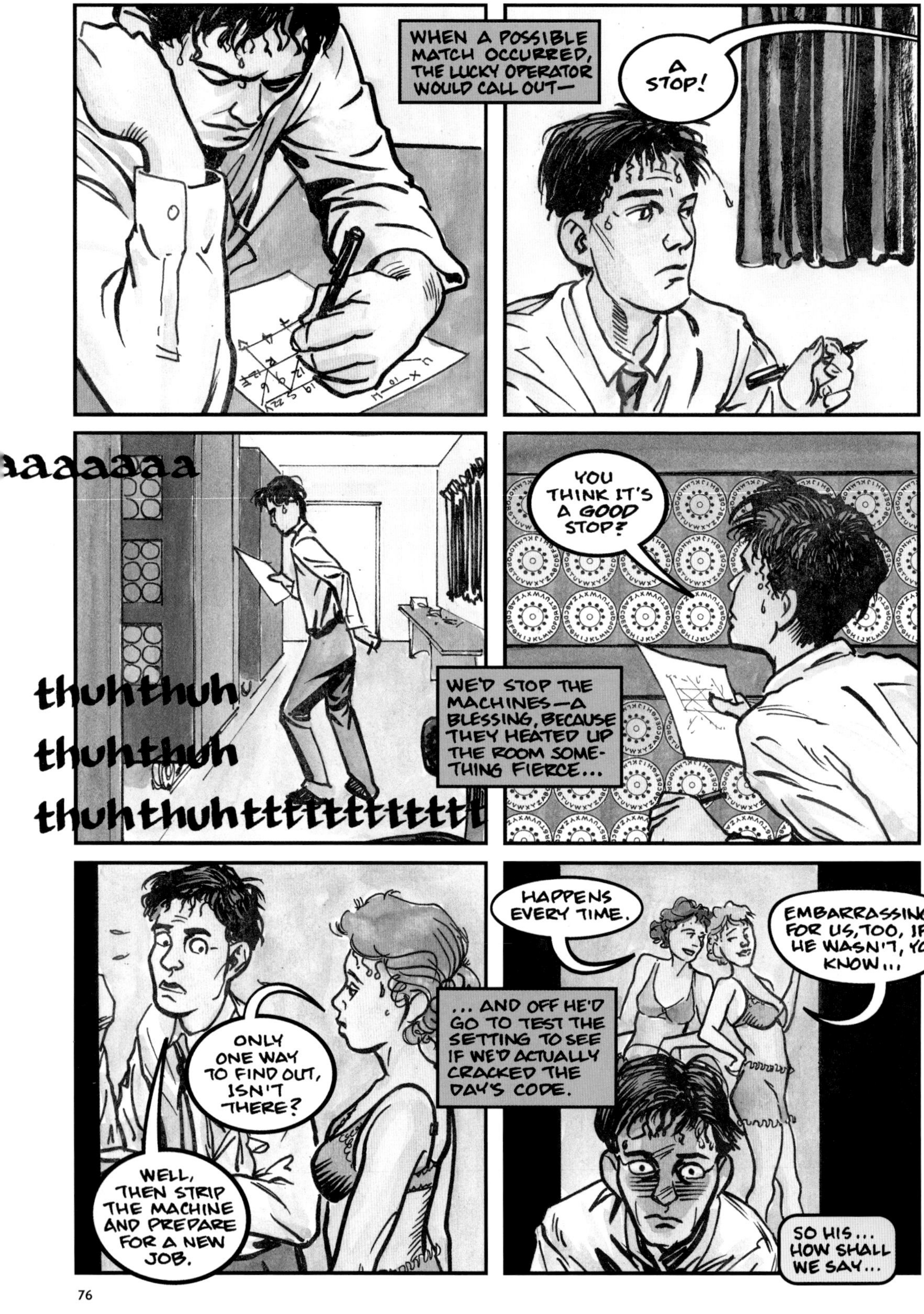
WHEN A POSSIBLE MATCH OCCURRED, THE LUCKY OPERATOR WOULD CALL OUT—
A STOP!
aaaaaaa
thuhthuh
thuhthuh
thuhthuhttttttttttt
YOU THINK IT'S A GOOD STOP?
WE'D STOP THE MACHINES—A BLESSING, BECAUSE THEY HEATED UP THE ROOM SOME-THING FIERCE...
ONLY ONE WAY TO FIND OUT, ISN'T THERE?
WELL, THEN STRIP THE MACHINE AND PREPARE FOR A NEW JOB.
... AND OFF HE'D GO TO TEST THE SETTING TO SEE IF WE'D ACTUALLY CRACKED THE DAY'S CODE.
HAPPENS EVERY TIME.
EMBARRASSING FOR US, TOO, IF HE WASN'T, YOU KNOW...
SO HIS... HOW SHALL WE SAY...

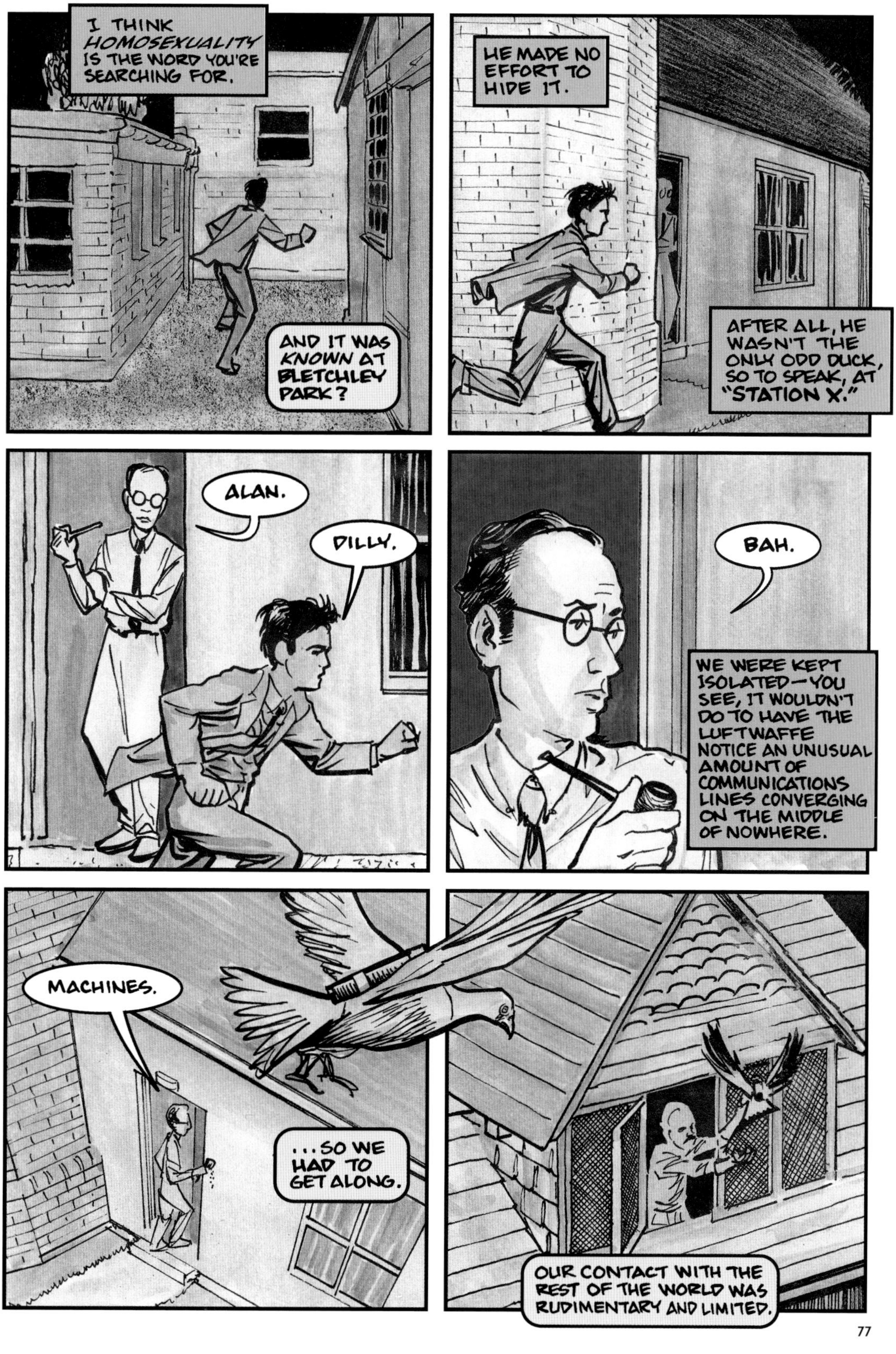
I THINK *HOMOSEXUALITY* IS THE WORD YOU'RE SEARCHING FOR.
AND IT WAS *KNOWN* AT BLETCHLEY PARK?
HE MADE NO EFFORT TO HIDE IT.
AFTER ALL, HE WASN'T THE ONLY ODD DUCK, SO TO SPEAK, AT "STATION X."
ALAN.
DILLY.
BAH.
WE WERE KEPT ISOLATED—YOU SEE, IT WOULDN'T DO TO HAVE THE LUFTWAFFE NOTICE AN UNUSUAL AMOUNT OF COMMUNICATIONS LINES CONVERGING ON THE MIDDLE OF NOWHERE.
MACHINES.
...SO WE HAD TO GET ALONG.
OUR CONTACT WITH THE REST OF THE WORLD WAS RUDIMENTARY AND LIMITED.

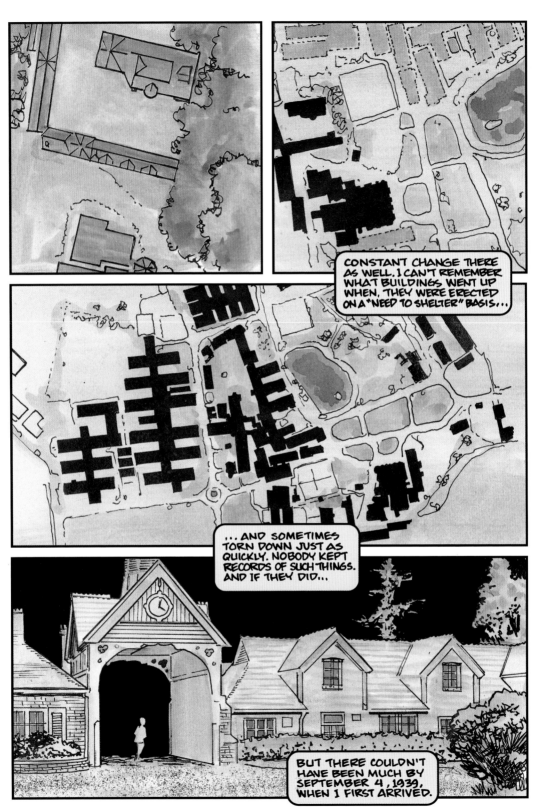

CONSTANT CHANGE THERE AS WELL. I CAN'T REMEMBER WHAT BUILDINGS WENT UP WHEN, THEY WERE ERECTED ON A "NEED TO SHELTER" BASIS...

...AND SOMETIMES TORN DOWN JUST AS QUICKLY. NOBODY KEPT RECORDS OF SUCH THINGS. AND IF THEY DID...

BUT THERE COULDN'T HAVE BEEN MUCH BY SEPTEMBER 4, 1939, WHEN I FIRST ARRIVED.

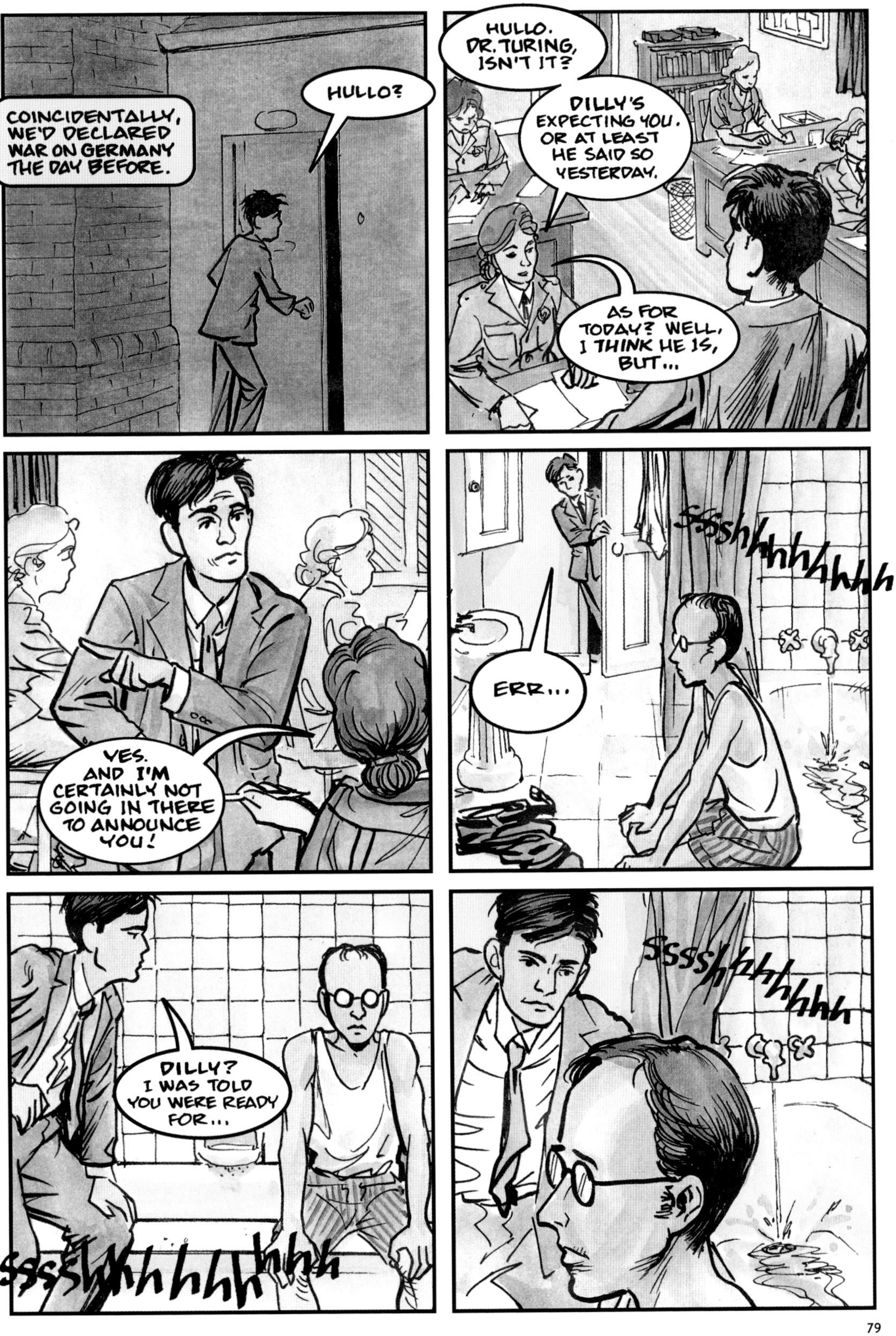
COINCIDENTALLY, WE'D DECLARED WAR ON GERMANY THE DAY BEFORE.
HULLO?
HULLO. DR. TURING, ISN'T IT?
DILLY'S EXPECTING YOU. OR AT LEAST HE SAID SO YESTERDAY.
AS FOR TODAY? WELL, I THINK HE IS, BUT...
YES. AND I'M CERTAINLY NOT GOING IN THERE TO ANNOUNCE YOU!
SSSHHHHHHHH
ERR...
DILLY? I WAS TOLD YOU WERE READY FOR...
SSSHHHHHHHHH
SSSHHHHHHHH

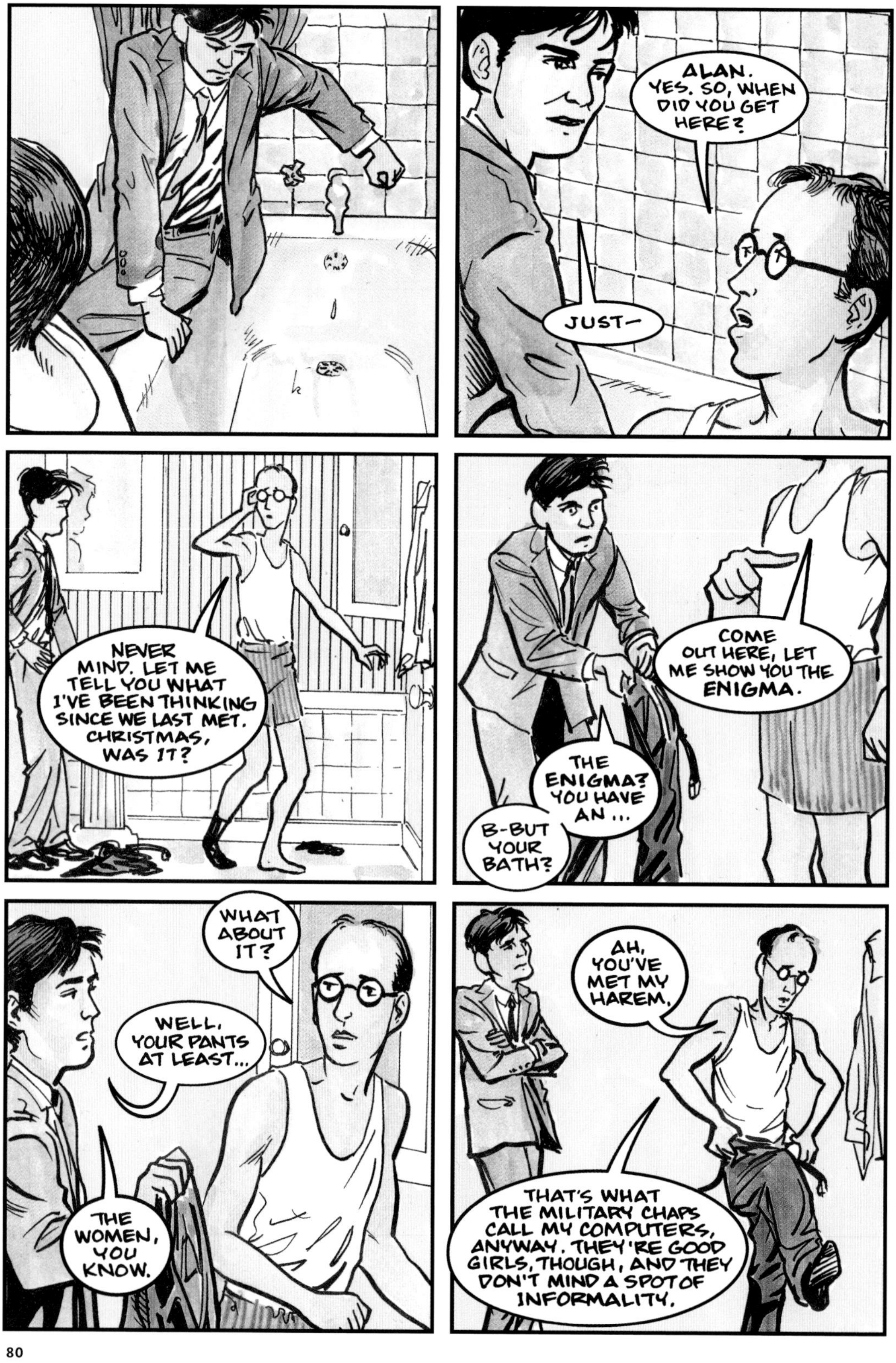
ALAN. YES. SO, WHEN DID YOU GET HERE?
JUST—
NEVER MIND. LET ME TELL YOU WHAT I'VE BEEN THINKING SINCE WE LAST MET. CHRISTMAS, WAS IT?
COME OUT HERE, LET ME SHOW YOU THE ENIGMA.
THE ENIGMA? YOU HAVE AN...
B-BUT YOUR BATH?
WHAT ABOUT IT?
WELL, YOUR PANTS AT LEAST...
THE WOMEN, YOU KNOW.
AH, YOU'VE MET MY HAREM.
THAT'S WHAT THE MILITARY CHAPS CALL MY COMPUTERS, ANYWAY. THEY'RE GOOD GIRLS, THOUGH, AND THEY DON'T MIND A SPOT OF INFORMALITY.

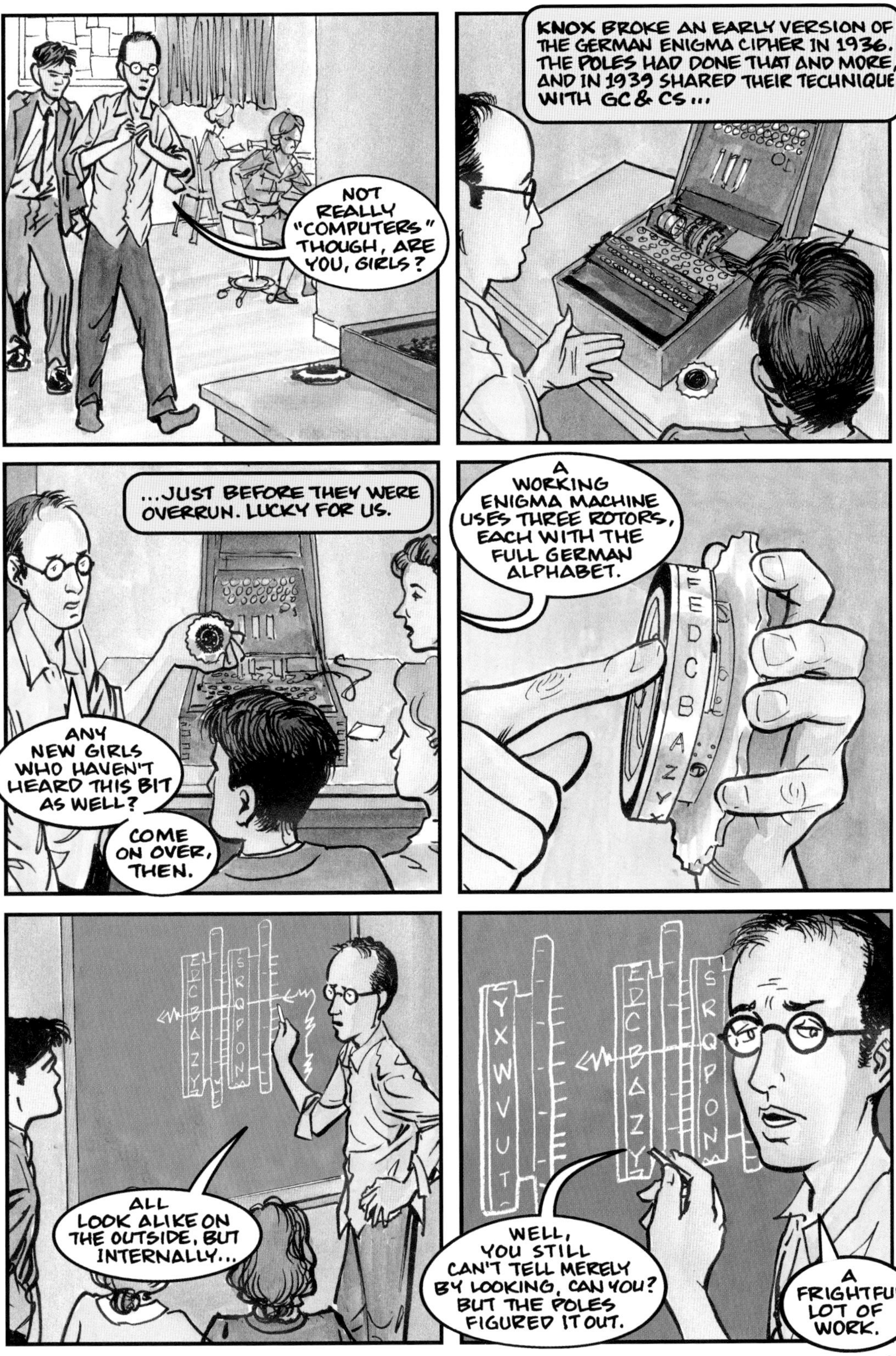
NOT REALLY "COMPUTERS" THOUGH, ARE YOU, GIRLS?
KNOX BROKE AN EARLY VERSION OF THE GERMAN ENIGMA CIPHER IN 1936. THE POLES HAD DONE THAT AND MORE, AND IN 1939 SHARED THEIR TECHNIQUE WITH GC & CS...
...JUST BEFORE THEY WERE OVERRUN. LUCKY FOR US.
ANY NEW GIRLS WHO HAVEN'T HEARD THIS BIT AS WELL?
COME ON OVER, THEN.
A WORKING ENIGMA MACHINE USES THREE ROTORS, EACH WITH THE FULL GERMAN ALPHABET.
ALL LOOK ALIKE ON THE OUTSIDE, BUT INTERNALLY...
WELL, YOU STILL CAN'T TELL MERELY BY LOOKING, CAN YOU? BUT THE POLES FIGURED IT OUT.
A FRIGHTFUL LOT OF WORK.

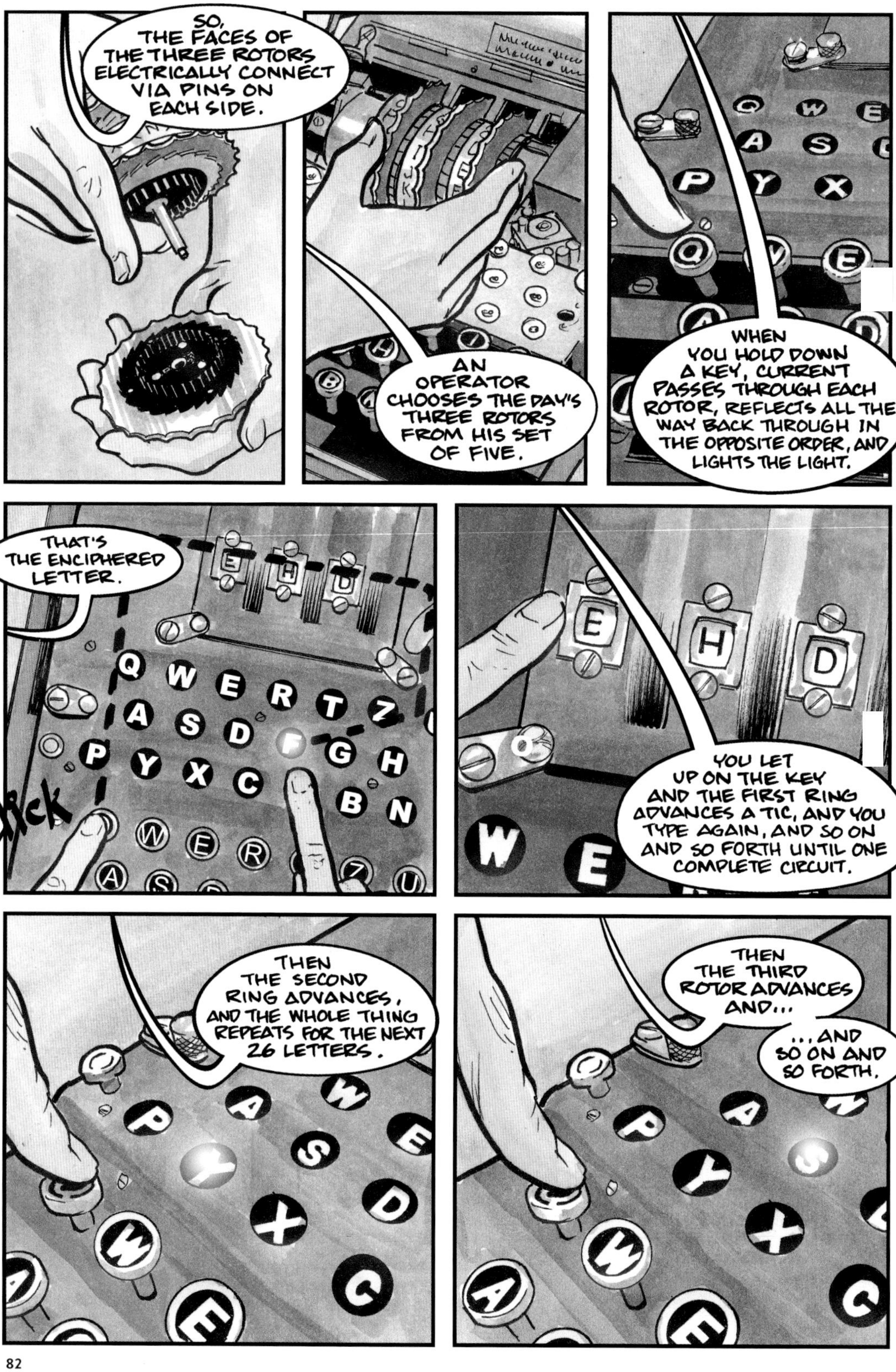
SO, THE FACES OF THE THREE ROTORS ELECTRICALLY CONNECT VIA PINS ON EACH SIDE.
AN OPERATOR CHOOSES THE DAY'S THREE ROTORS FROM HIS SET OF FIVE.
WHEN YOU HOLD DOWN A KEY, CURRENT PASSES THROUGH EACH ROTOR, REFLECTS ALL THE WAY BACK THROUGH IN THE OPPOSITE ORDER, AND LIGHTS THE LIGHT.
THAT'S THE ENCIPHERED LETTER.
CLICK
YOU LET UP ON THE KEY AND THE FIRST RING ADVANCES A TIC, AND YOU TYPE AGAIN, AND SO ON AND SO FORTH UNTIL ONE COMPLETE CIRCUIT.
THEN THE SECOND RING ADVANCES, AND THE WHOLE THING REPEATS FOR THE NEXT 26 LETTERS.
THEN THE THIRD ROTOR ADVANCES AND...
...AND SO ON AND SO FORTH.

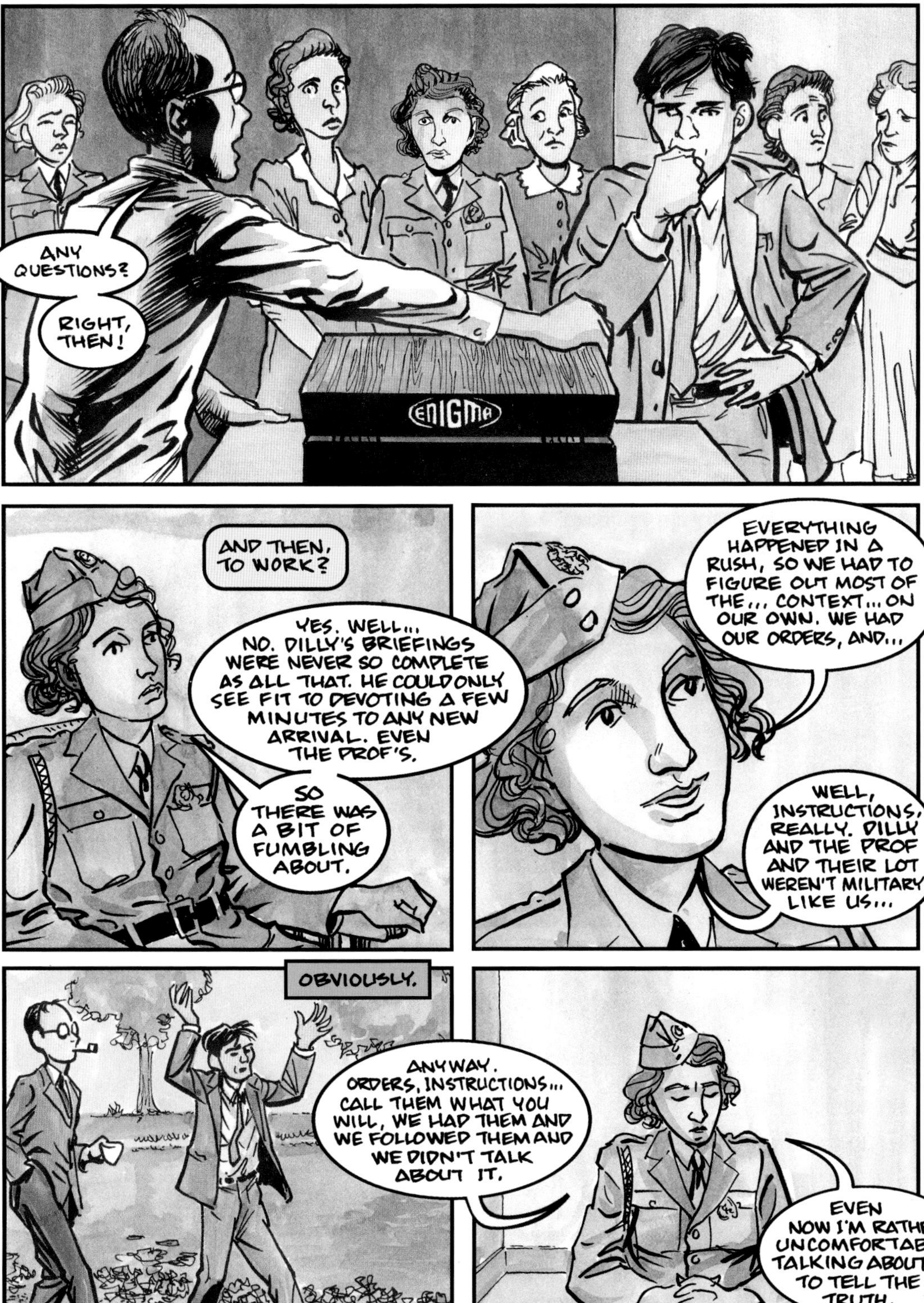
ANY QUESTIONS?
RIGHT, THEN!
ENIGMA
AND THEN, TO WORK?
YES. WELL... NO. DILLY'S BRIEFINGS WERE NEVER SO COMPLETE AS ALL THAT. HE COULD ONLY SEE FIT TO DEVOTING A FEW MINUTES TO ANY NEW ARRIVAL. EVEN THE PROF'S.
SO THERE WAS A BIT OF FUMBLING ABOUT.
EVERYTHING HAPPENED IN A RUSH, SO WE HAD TO FIGURE OUT MOST OF THE... CONTEXT... ON OUR OWN. WE HAD OUR ORDERS, AND...
WELL, INSTRUCTIONS, REALLY. DILLY AND THE PROF AND THEIR LOT WEREN'T MILITARY LIKE US...
OBVIOUSLY.
ANYWAY. ORDERS, INSTRUCTIONS... CALL THEM WHAT YOU WILL, WE HAD THEM AND WE FOLLOWED THEM AND WE DIDN'T TALK ABOUT IT.
EVEN NOW I'M RATHER UNCOMFORTABLE TALKING ABOUT IT, TO TELL THE TRUTH.

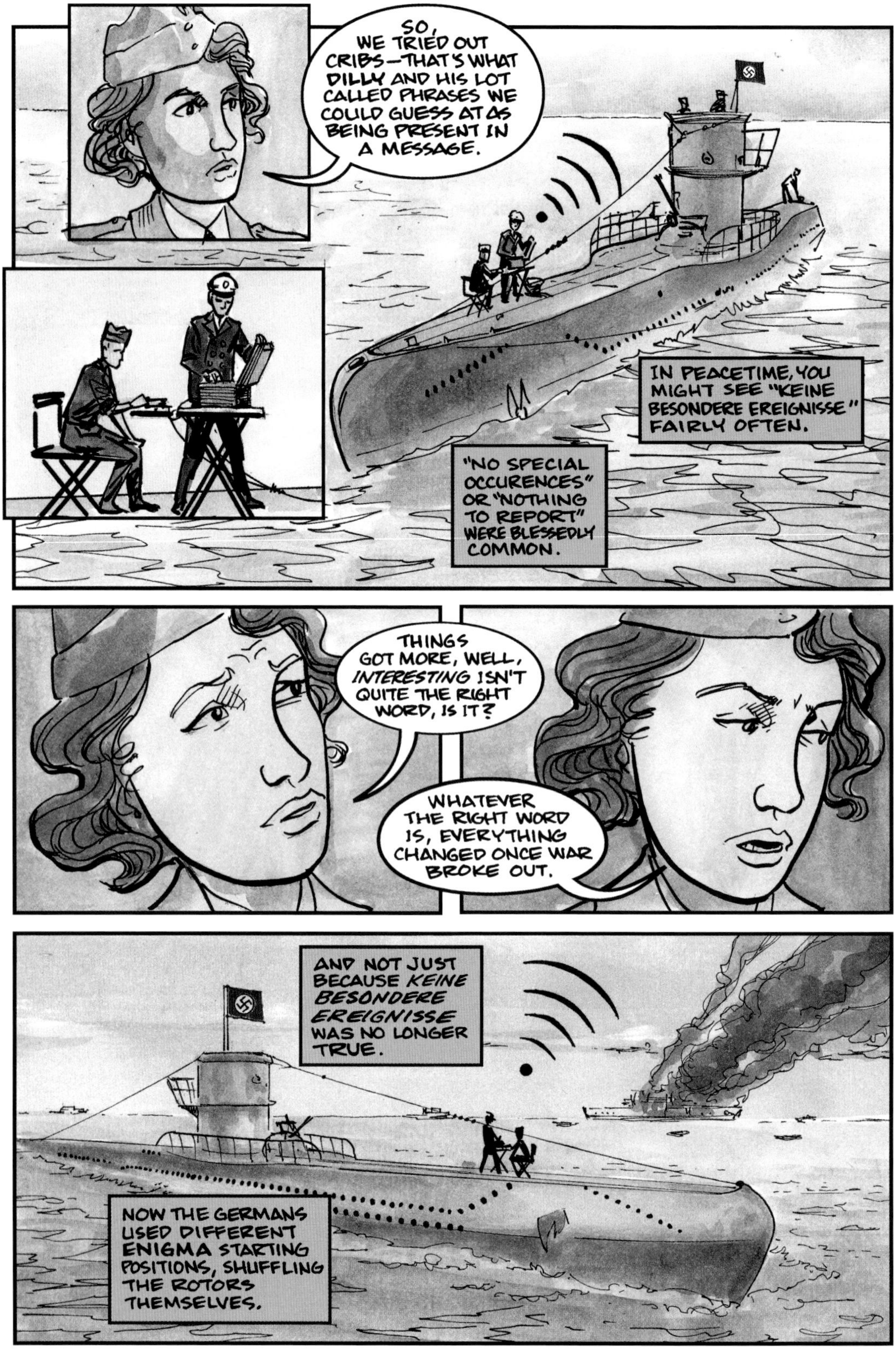
SO, WE TRIED OUT CRIBS—THAT'S WHAT DILLY AND HIS LOT CALLED PHRASES WE COULD GUESS AT AS BEING PRESENT IN A MESSAGE.
IN PEACETIME, YOU MIGHT SEE "KEINE BESONDERE EREIGNISSE" FAIRLY OFTEN.
"NO SPECIAL OCCURENCES" OR "NOTHING TO REPORT" WERE BLESSEDLY COMMON.
THINGS GOT MORE, WELL, INTERESTING ISN'T QUITE THE RIGHT WORD, IS IT?
WHATEVER THE RIGHT WORD IS, EVERYTHING CHANGED ONCE WAR BROKE OUT.
AND NOT JUST BECAUSE KEINE BESONDERE EREIGNISSE WAS NO LONGER TRUE.
NOW THE GERMANS USED DIFFERENT ENIGMA STARTING POSITIONS, SHUFFLING THE ROTORS THEMSELVES.

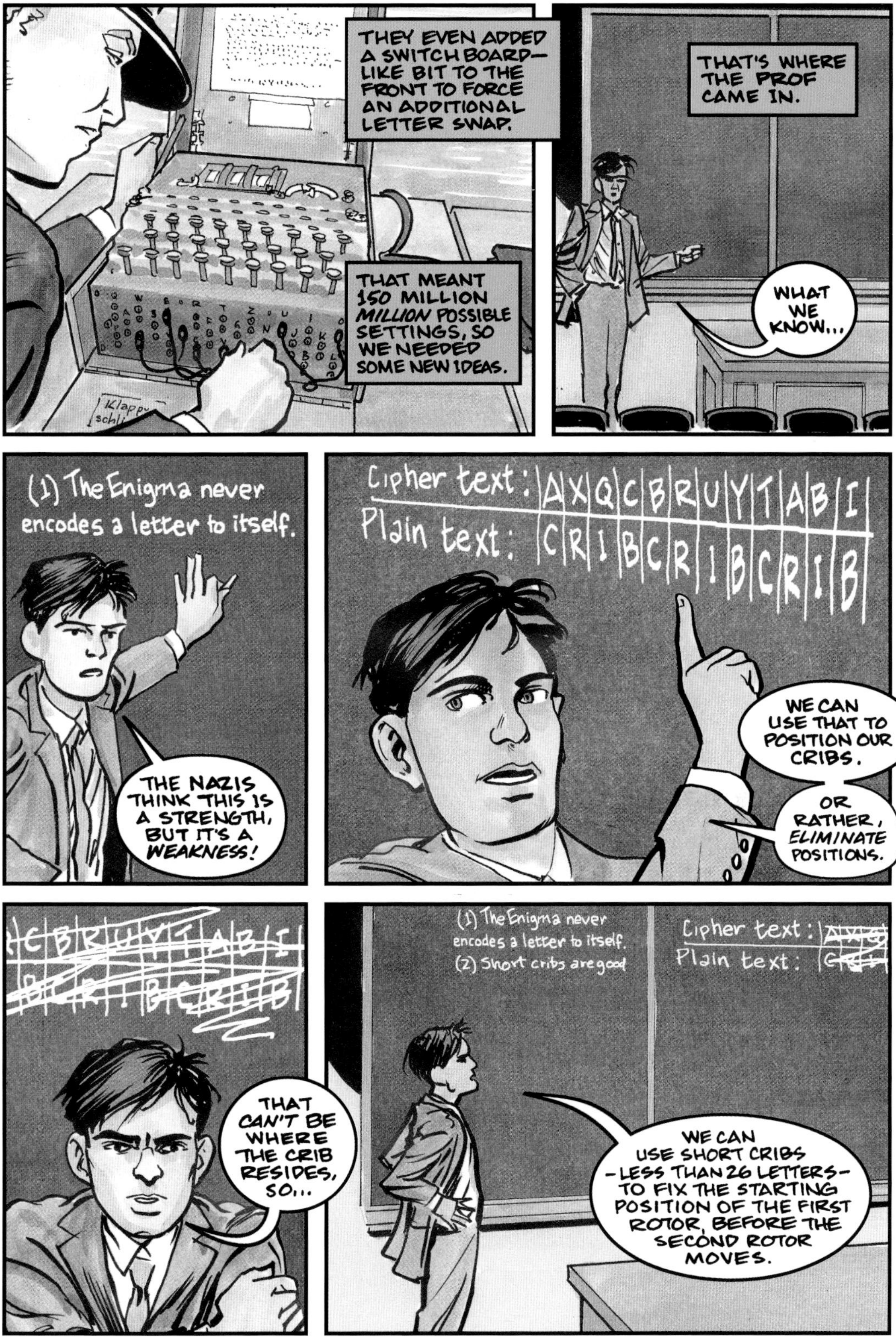
THEY EVEN ADDED A SWITCH BOARD-LIKE BIT TO THE FRONT TO FORCE AN ADDITIONAL LETTER SWAP.
THAT MEANT 150 MILLION *MILLION* POSSIBLE SETTINGS, SO WE NEEDED SOME NEW IDEAS.
THAT'S WHERE THE PROF CAME IN.
WHAT WE KNOW...
(1) The Enigma never encodes a letter to itself.
THE NAZIS THINK THIS IS A STRENGTH, BUT IT'S A *WEAKNESS*!
Cipher text: A X Q C B R U Y T A B I
Plain text: C R I B C R I B C R I B
WE CAN USE THAT TO POSITION OUR CRIBS.
OR RATHER, *ELIMINATE* POSITIONS.
THAT *CAN'T* BE WHERE THE CRIB RESIDES, SO...
(1) The Enigma never encodes a letter to itself.
(2) Short cribs are good
Cipher text:
Plain text:
WE CAN USE SHORT CRIBS -LESS THAN 26 LETTERS- TO FIX THE STARTING POSITION OF THE FIRST ROTOR, BEFORE THE SECOND ROTOR MOVES.

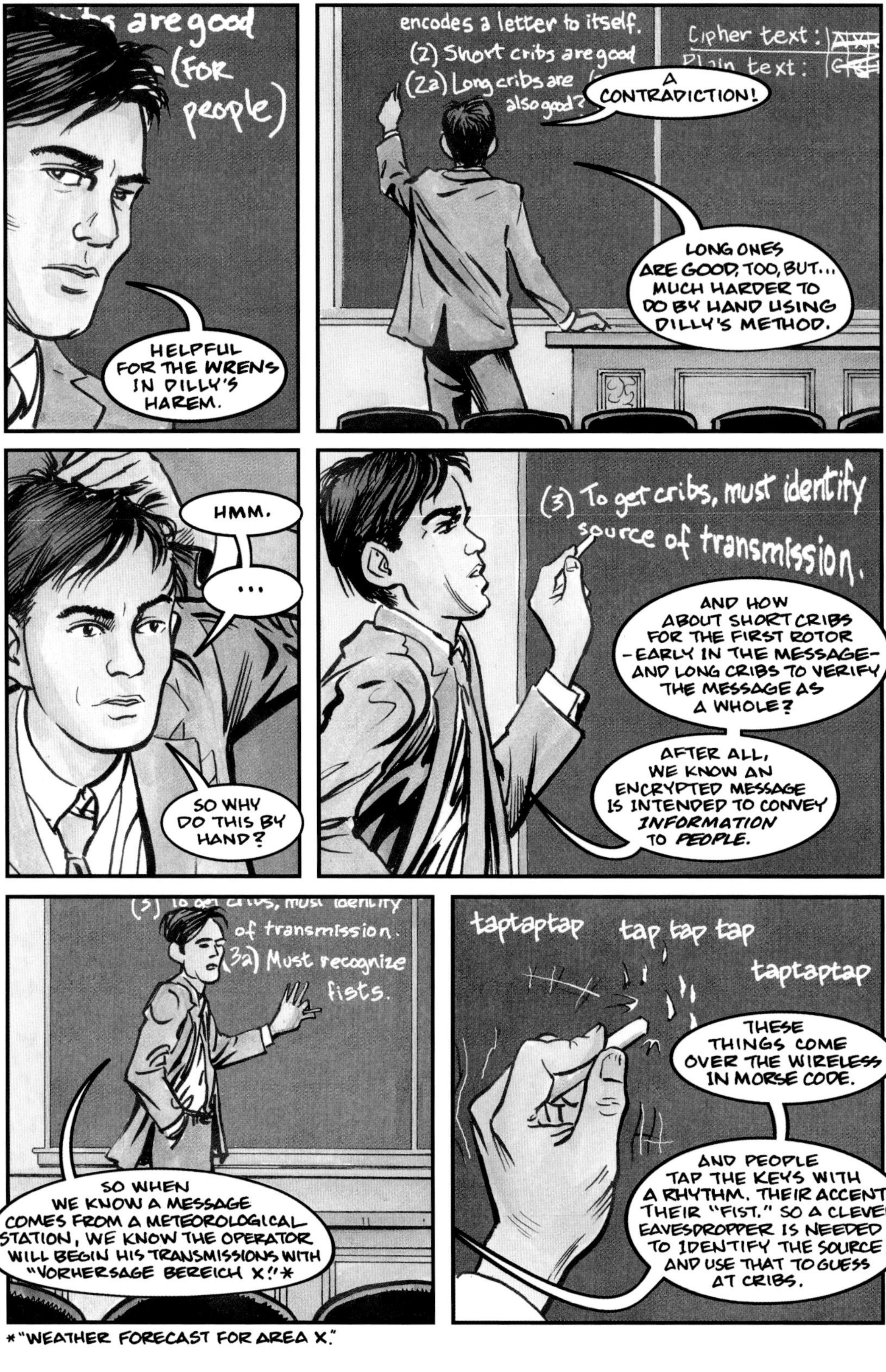
are good
(FOR people)
HELPFUL FOR THE WRENS IN DILLY'S HAREM.
encodes a letter to itself.
(2) Short cribs are good
(2a) Long cribs are
also good?
Cipher text :
Plain text :
A CONTRADICTION!
LONG ONES ARE GOOD, TOO, BUT... MUCH HARDER TO DO BY HAND USING DILLY'S METHOD.
HMM.
...
SO WHY DO THIS BY HAND?
(3) To get cribs, must identify source of transmission.
AND HOW ABOUT SHORT CRIBS FOR THE FIRST ROTOR -EARLY IN THE MESSAGE- AND LONG CRIBS TO VERIFY THE MESSAGE AS A WHOLE?
AFTER ALL, WE KNOW AN ENCRYPTED MESSAGE IS INTENDED TO CONVEY INFORMATION TO PEOPLE.
of transmission.
(3a) Must recognize fists.
SO WHEN WE KNOW A MESSAGE COMES FROM A METEOROLOGICAL STATION, WE KNOW THE OPERATOR WILL BEGIN HIS TRANSMISSIONS WITH "VORHERSAGE BEREICH X!"*
taptaptap
tap tap tap
taptaptap
THESE THINGS COME OVER THE WIRELESS IN MORSE CODE.
AND PEOPLE TAP THE KEYS WITH A RHYTHM. THEIR ACCENT. THEIR "FIST." SO A CLEVER EAVESDROPPER IS NEEDED TO IDENTIFY THE SOURCE, AND USE THAT TO GUESS AT CRIBS.

* "WEATHER FORECAST FOR AREA X."

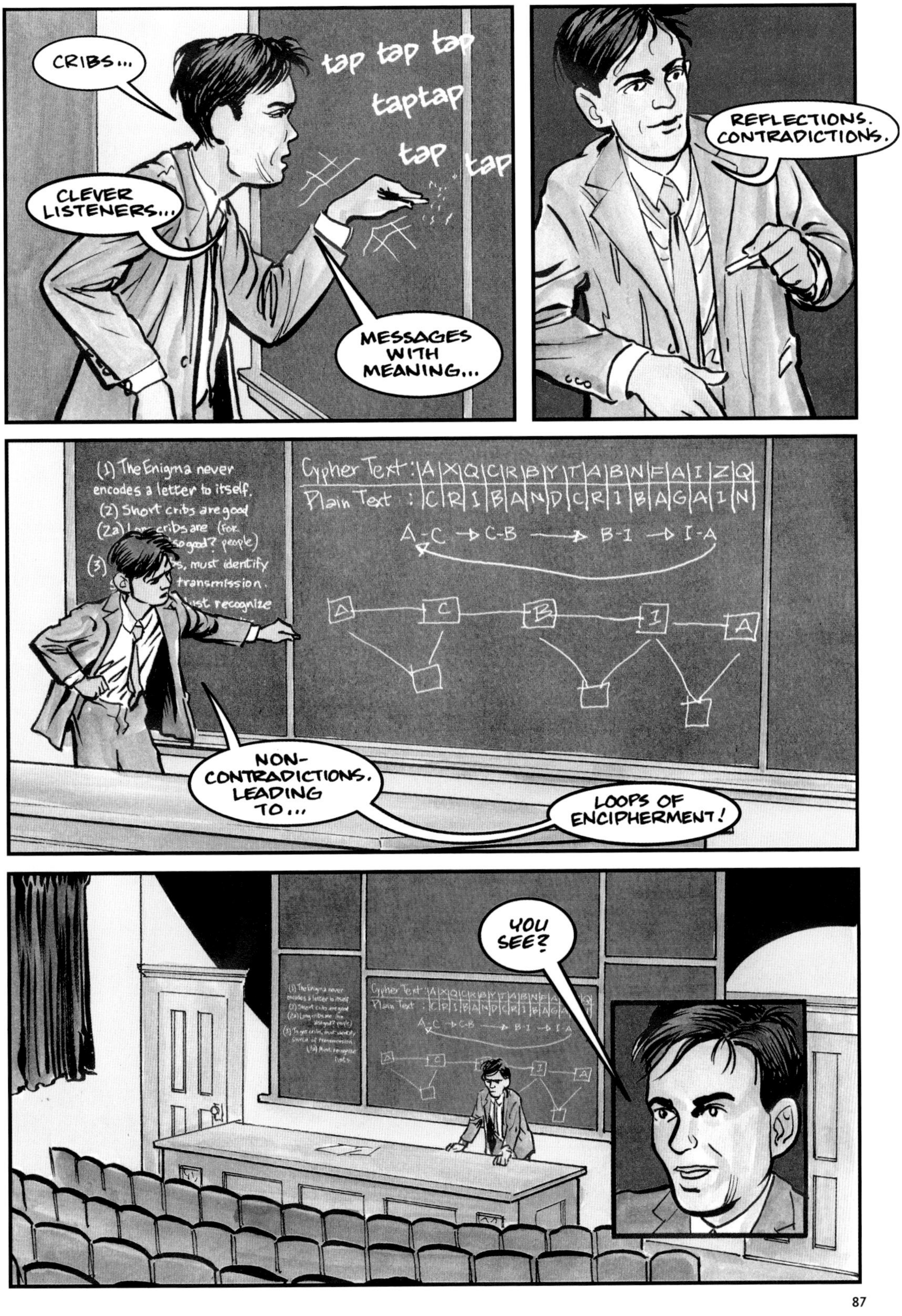
CRIBS...
tap tap tap
taptap
tap
tap
CLEVER LISTENERS...
MESSAGES WITH MEANING...
REFLECTIONS. CONTRADICTIONS.
(1) The Enigma never encodes a letter to itself.
(2) Short cribs are good
Cypher Text : A X Q C R B Y T A B N F A I Z Q
Plain Text : C R I B A N D C R I B A G A I N
A-C → C-B → B-I → I-A
A
C
B
I
A
NON-CONTRADICTIONS. LEADING TO...
LOOPS OF ENCIPHERMENT!
YOU SEE?

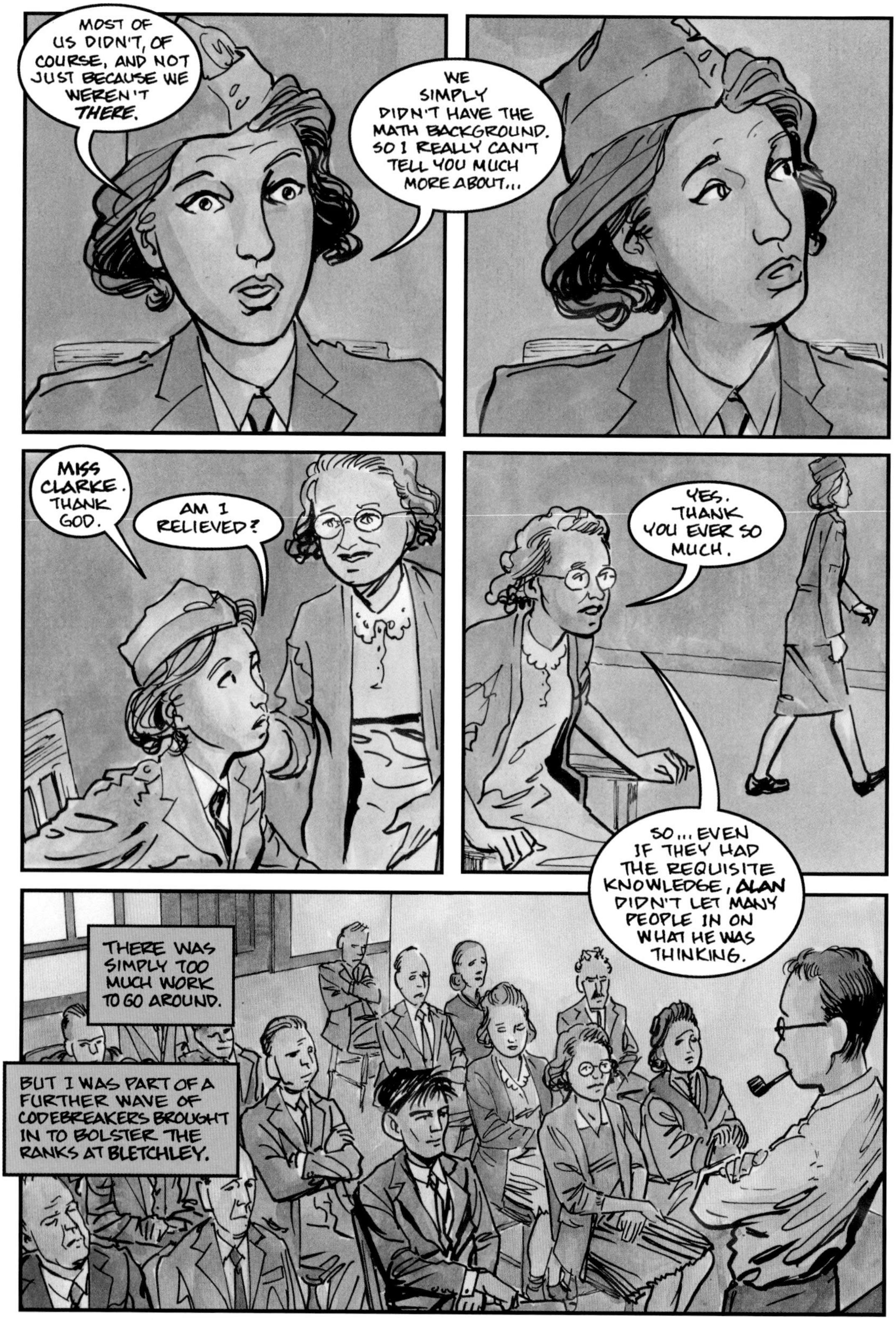
MOST OF US DIDN'T, OF COURSE, AND NOT JUST BECAUSE WE WEREN'T THERE.
WE SIMPLY DIDN'T HAVE THE MATH BACKGROUND. SO I REALLY CAN'T TELL YOU MUCH MORE ABOUT...
MISS CLARKE. THANK GOD.
AM I RELIEVED?
YES. THANK YOU EVER SO MUCH.
SO... EVEN IF THEY HAD THE REQUISITE KNOWLEDGE, ALAN DIDN'T LET MANY PEOPLE IN ON WHAT HE WAS THINKING.
THERE WAS SIMPLY TOO MUCH WORK TO GO AROUND.
BUT I WAS PART OF A FURTHER WAVE OF CODEBREAKERS BROUGHT IN TO BOLSTER THE RANKS AT BLETCHLEY.

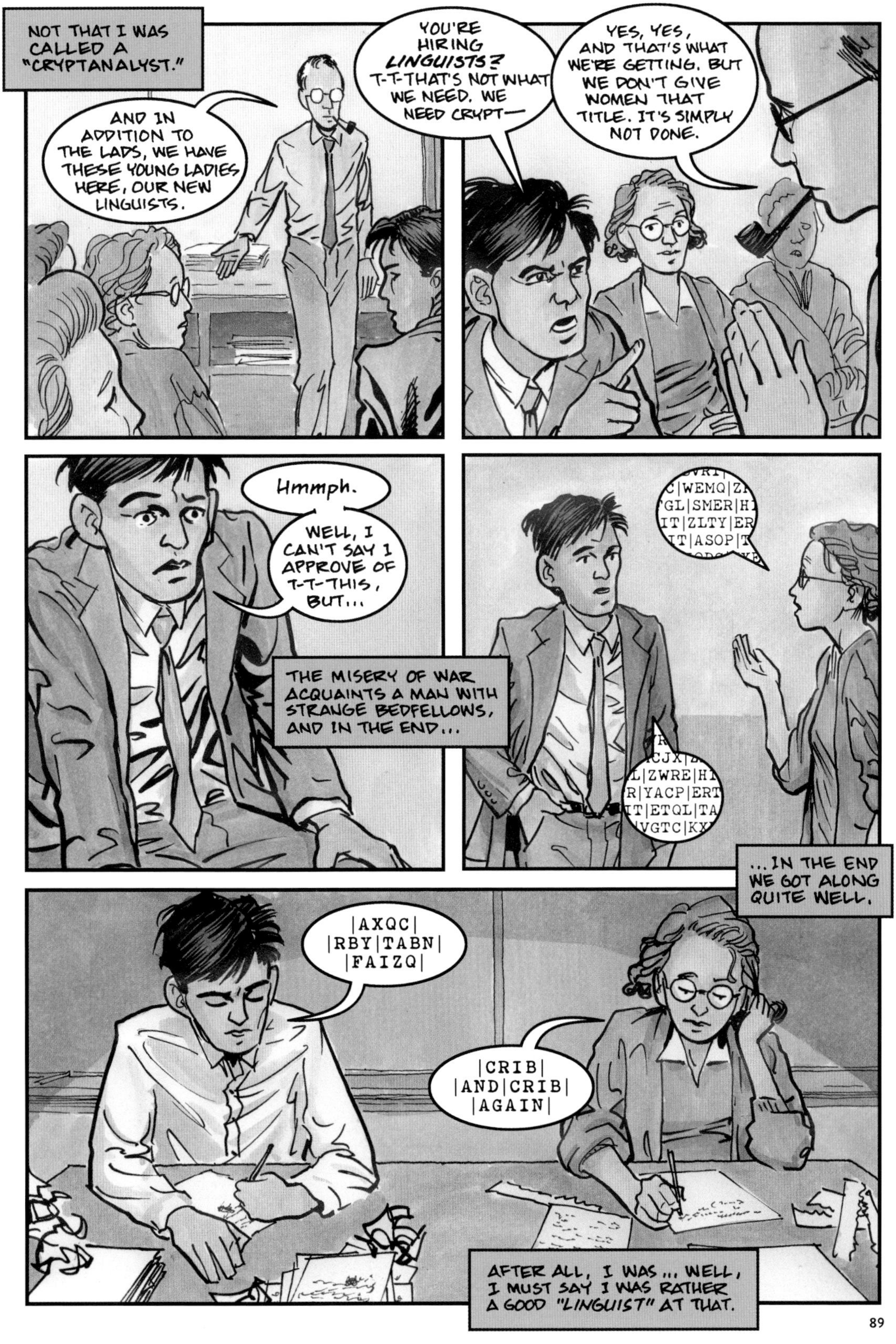
NOT THAT I WAS CALLED A "CRYPTANALYST."
AND IN ADDITION TO THE LADS, WE HAVE THESE YOUNG LADIES HERE, OUR NEW LINGUISTS.
YOU'RE HIRING *LINGUISTS?* T-T-THAT'S NOT WHAT WE NEED. WE NEED CRYPT—
YES, YES, AND THAT'S WHAT WE'RE GETTING. BUT WE DON'T GIVE WOMEN THAT TITLE. IT'S SIMPLY NOT DONE.
Hmmph.
WELL, I CAN'T SAY I APPROVE OF T-T-THIS, BUT...
THE MISERY OF WAR ACQUAINTS A MAN WITH STRANGE BEDFELLOWS, AND IN THE END...
...IN THE END WE GOT ALONG QUITE WELL.
|AXQC| |RBY|TABN| |FAIZQ|
|CRIB| |AND|CRIB| |AGAIN|
AFTER ALL, I WAS... WELL, I MUST SAY I WAS RATHER A GOOD *"LINGUIST"* AT THAT.

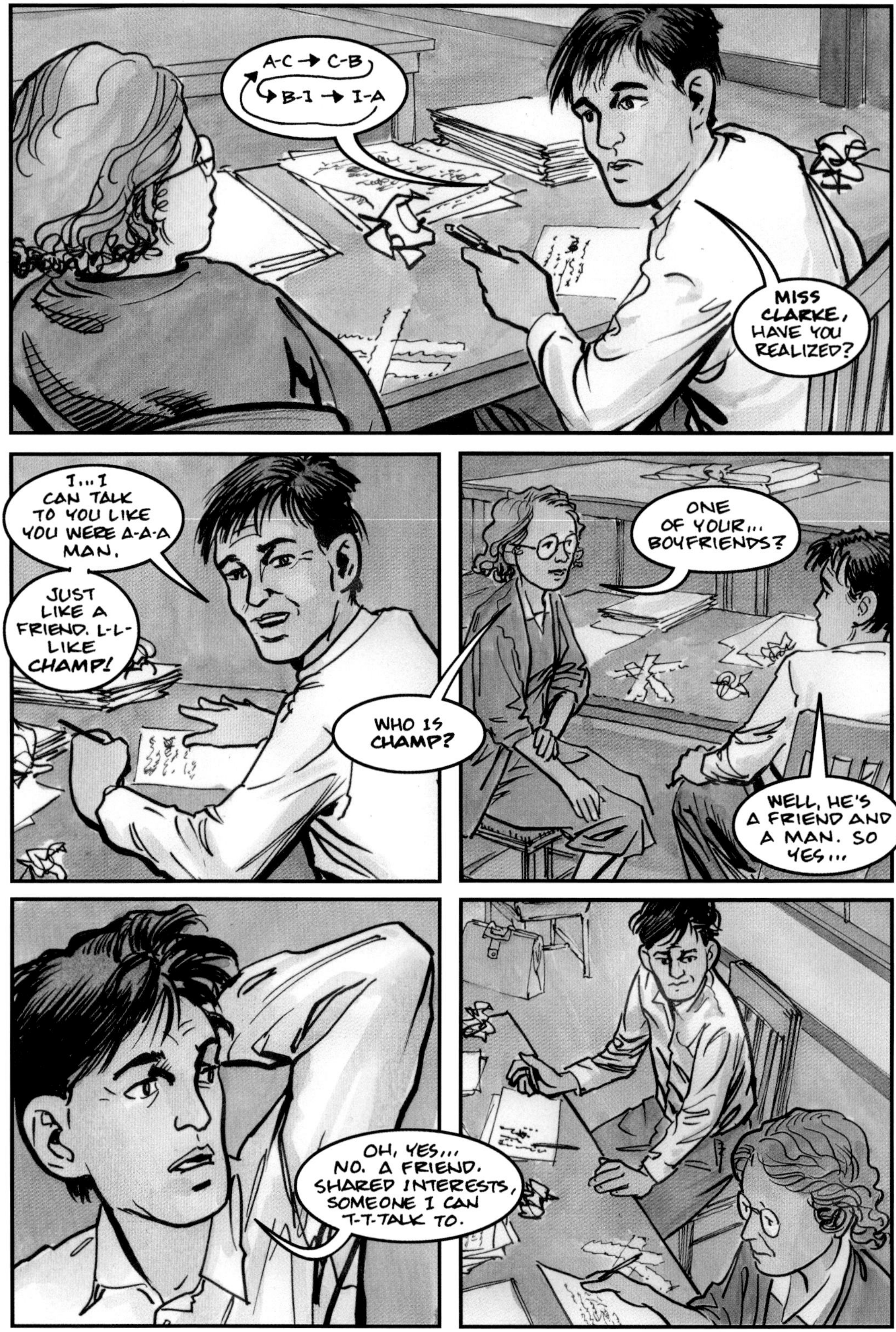
A-C → C-B
B-I → I-A
MISS CLARKE, HAVE YOU REALIZED?
I... I CAN TALK TO YOU LIKE YOU WERE A-A-A MAN.
JUST LIKE A FRIEND. L-L-LIKE CHAMP!
WHO IS CHAMP?
ONE OF YOUR... BOYFRIENDS?
WELL, HE'S A FRIEND AND A MAN. SO YES...
OH, YES... NO. A FRIEND. SHARED INTERESTS, SOMEONE I CAN T-T-TALK TO.

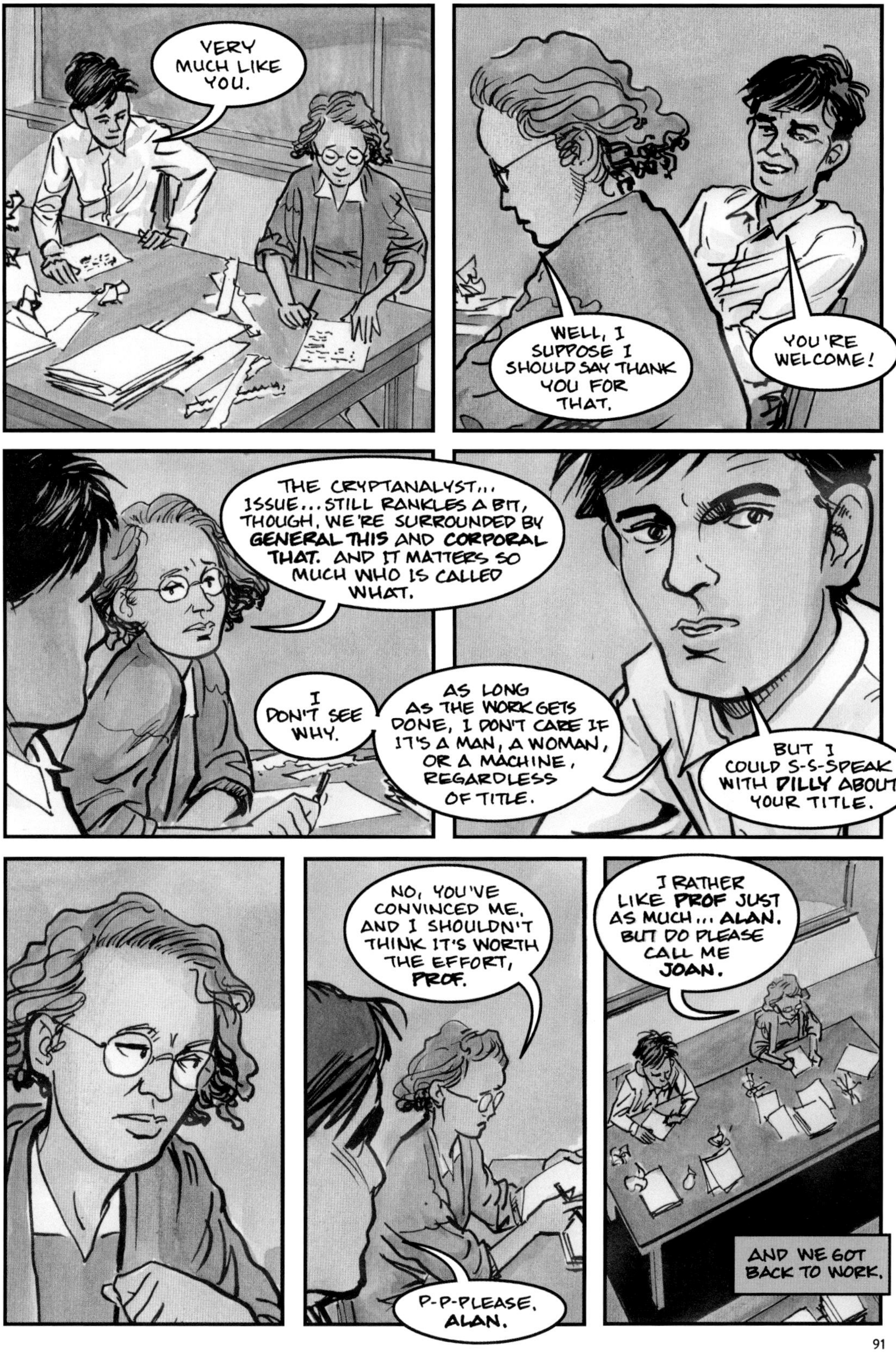

VERY MUCH LIKE YOU.
WELL, I SUPPOSE I SHOULD SAY THANK YOU FOR THAT.
YOU'RE WELCOME!
THE CRYPTANALYST... ISSUE... STILL RANKLES A BIT, THOUGH. WE'RE SURROUNDED BY GENERAL THIS AND CORPORAL THAT. AND IT MATTERS SO MUCH WHO IS CALLED WHAT.
I DON'T SEE WHY.
AS LONG AS THE WORK GETS DONE, I DON'T CARE IF IT'S A MAN, A WOMAN, OR A MACHINE, REGARDLESS OF TITLE.
BUT I COULD S-S-SPEAK WITH DILLY ABOUT YOUR TITLE.
NO, YOU'VE CONVINCED ME. AND I SHOULDN'T THINK IT'S WORTH THE EFFORT, PROF.
P-P-PLEASE, ALAN.
I RATHER LIKE PROF JUST AS MUCH... ALAN. BUT DO PLEASE CALL ME JOAN.
AND WE GOT BACK TO WORK.

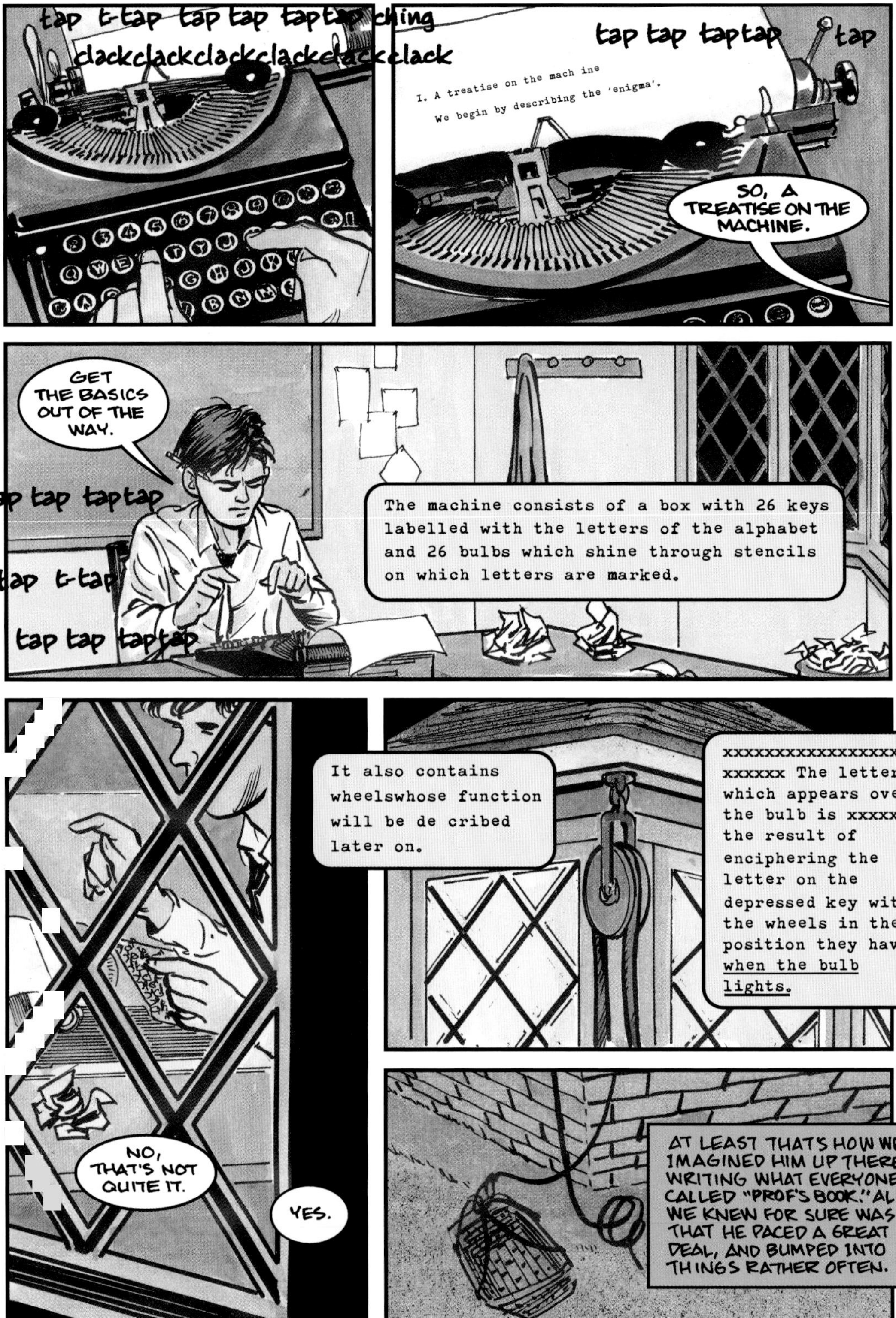

tap t-tap tap tap taptap ching
clackclackclackclackclackclack
tap tap taptap tap
I. A treatise on the mach ine
We begin by describing the 'enigma'.
SO, A TREATISE ON THE MACHINE.
GET THE BASICS OUT OF THE WAY.
tap tap taptap
tap t-tap
tap tap taptap
The machine consists of a box with 26 keys labelled with the letters of the alphabet and 26 bulbs which shine through stencils on which letters are marked.
NO, THAT'S NOT QUITE IT.
YES.
It also contains wheelswhose function will be de cribed later on.
xxxxxxxxxxxxxxxxxx xxxxxx The letter which appears over the bulb is xxxxxx the result of enciphering the letter on the depressed key with the wheels in the position they have when the bulb lights.
AT LEAST THAT'S HOW WE IMAGINED HIM UP THERE, WRITING WHAT EVERYONE CALLED "PROF'S BOOK." ALL WE KNEW FOR SURE WAS THAT HE PACED A GREAT DEAL, AND BUMPED INTO THINGS RATHER OFTEN.

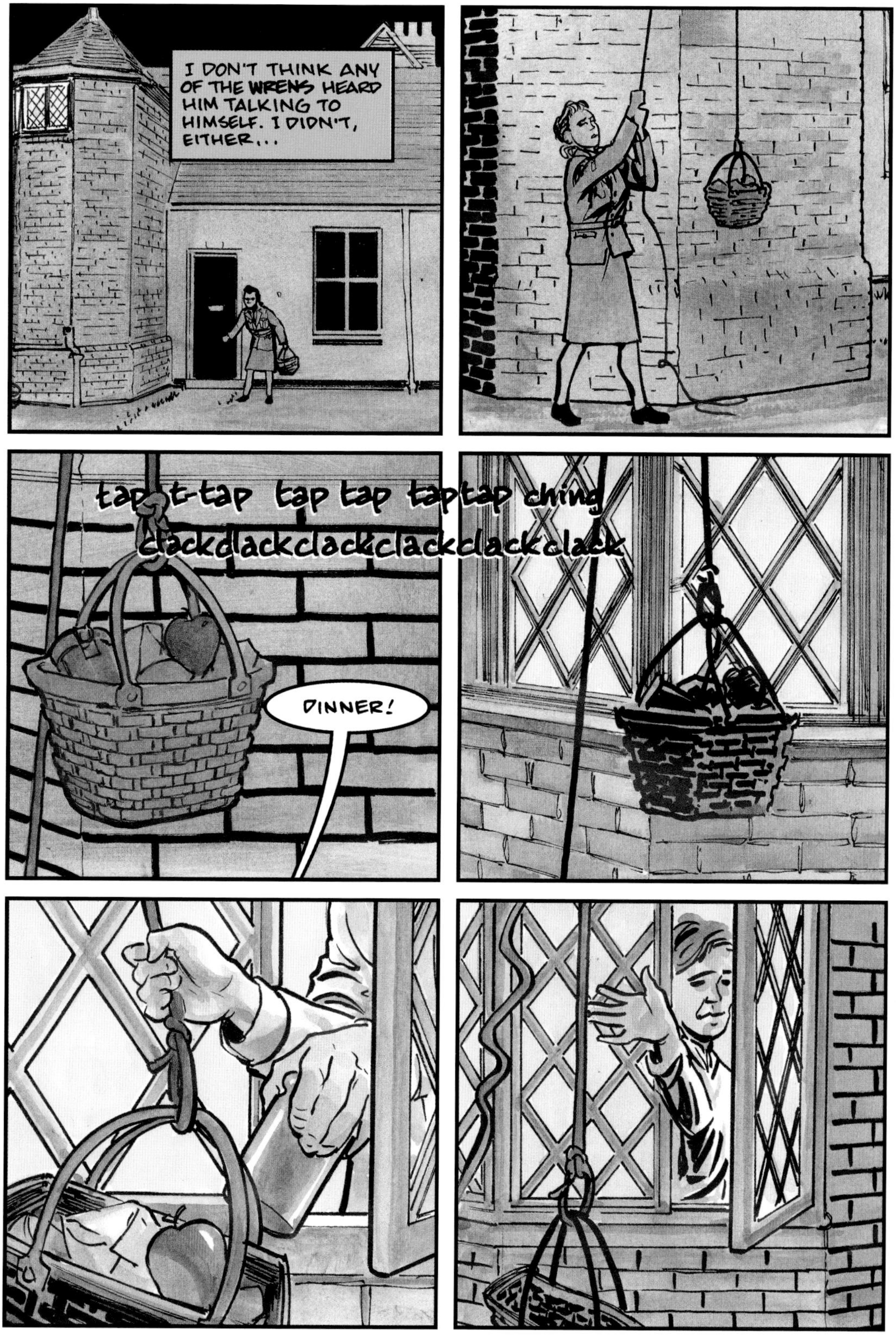
I DON'T THINK ANY OF THE WRENS HEARD HIM TALKING TO HIMSELF. I DIDN'T, EITHER...
tap t-tap tap tap taptap ching
clackclackclackclackclackclack
DINNER!

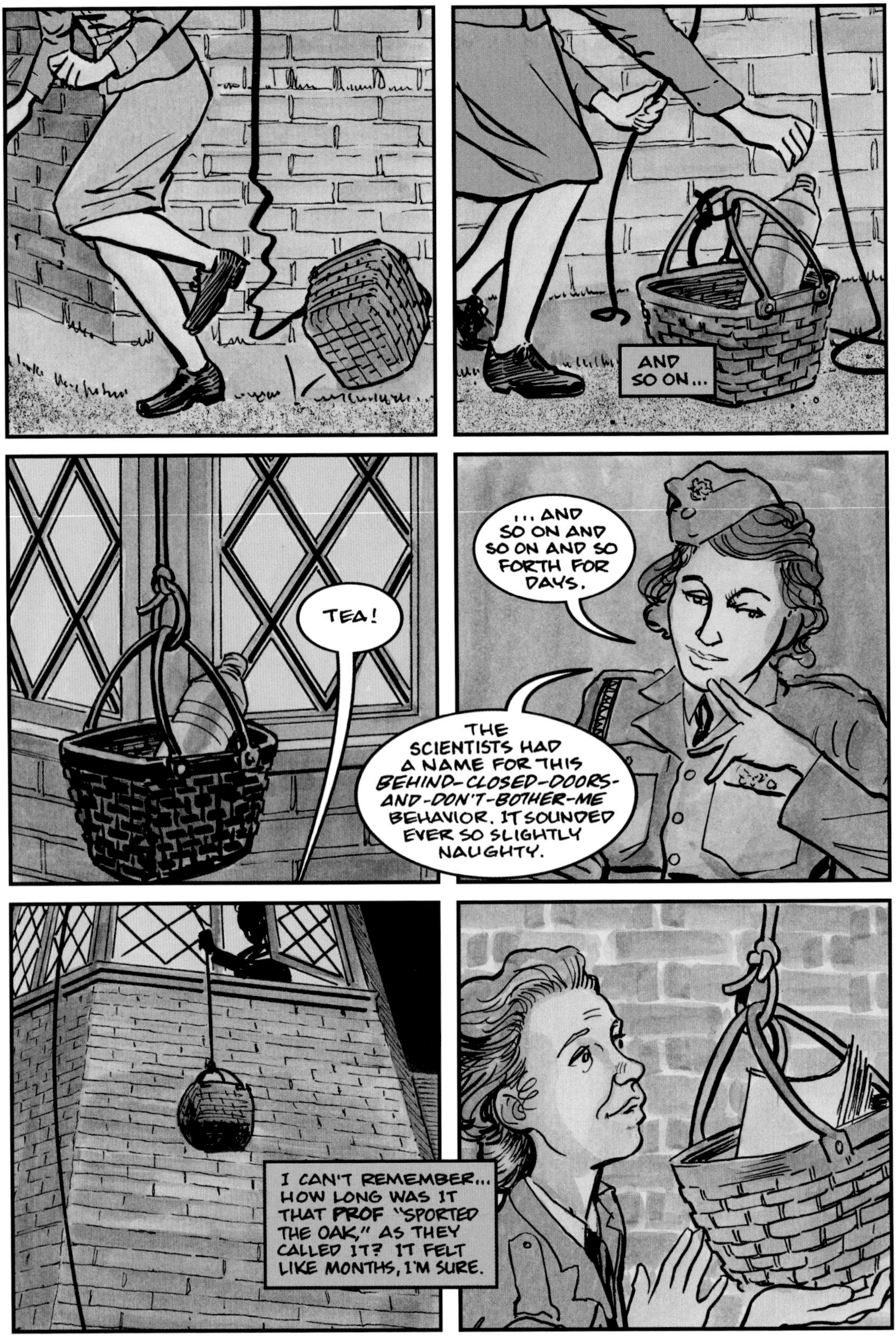
AND SO ON...
TEA!
...AND SO ON AND SO ON AND SO FORTH FOR DAYS.
THE SCIENTISTS HAD A NAME FOR THIS *BEHIND-CLOSED-DOORS-AND-DON'T-BOTHER-ME* BEHAVIOR. IT SOUNDED EVER SO SLIGHTLY NAUGHTY.
I CAN'T REMEMBER... HOW LONG WAS IT THAT **PROF** "SPORTED THE OAK," AS THEY CALLED IT? IT FELT LIKE MONTHS, I'M SURE.

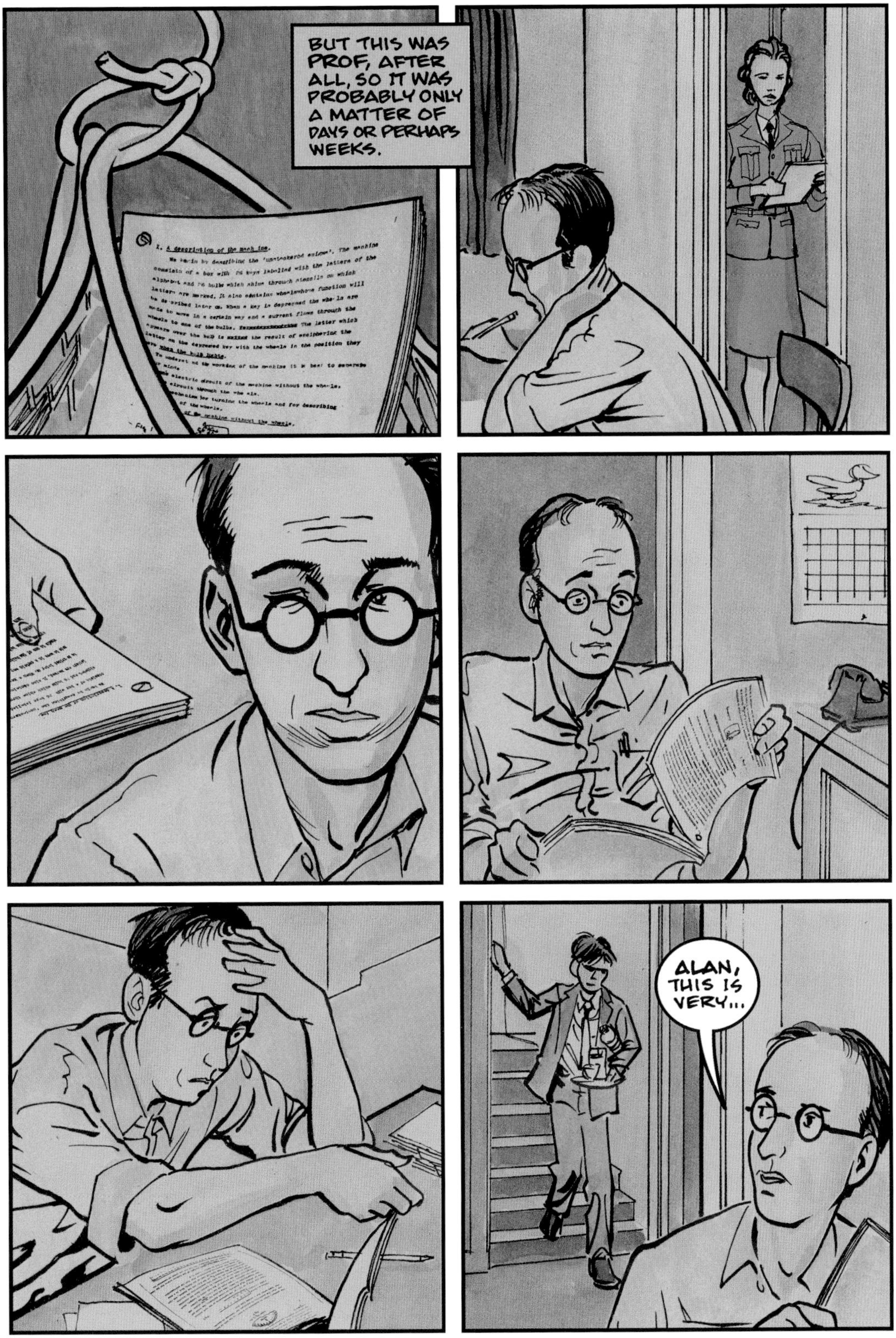
BUT THIS WAS PROF, AFTER ALL, SO IT WAS PROBABLY ONLY A MATTER OF DAYS OR PERHAPS WEEKS.
ALAN, THIS IS VERY...

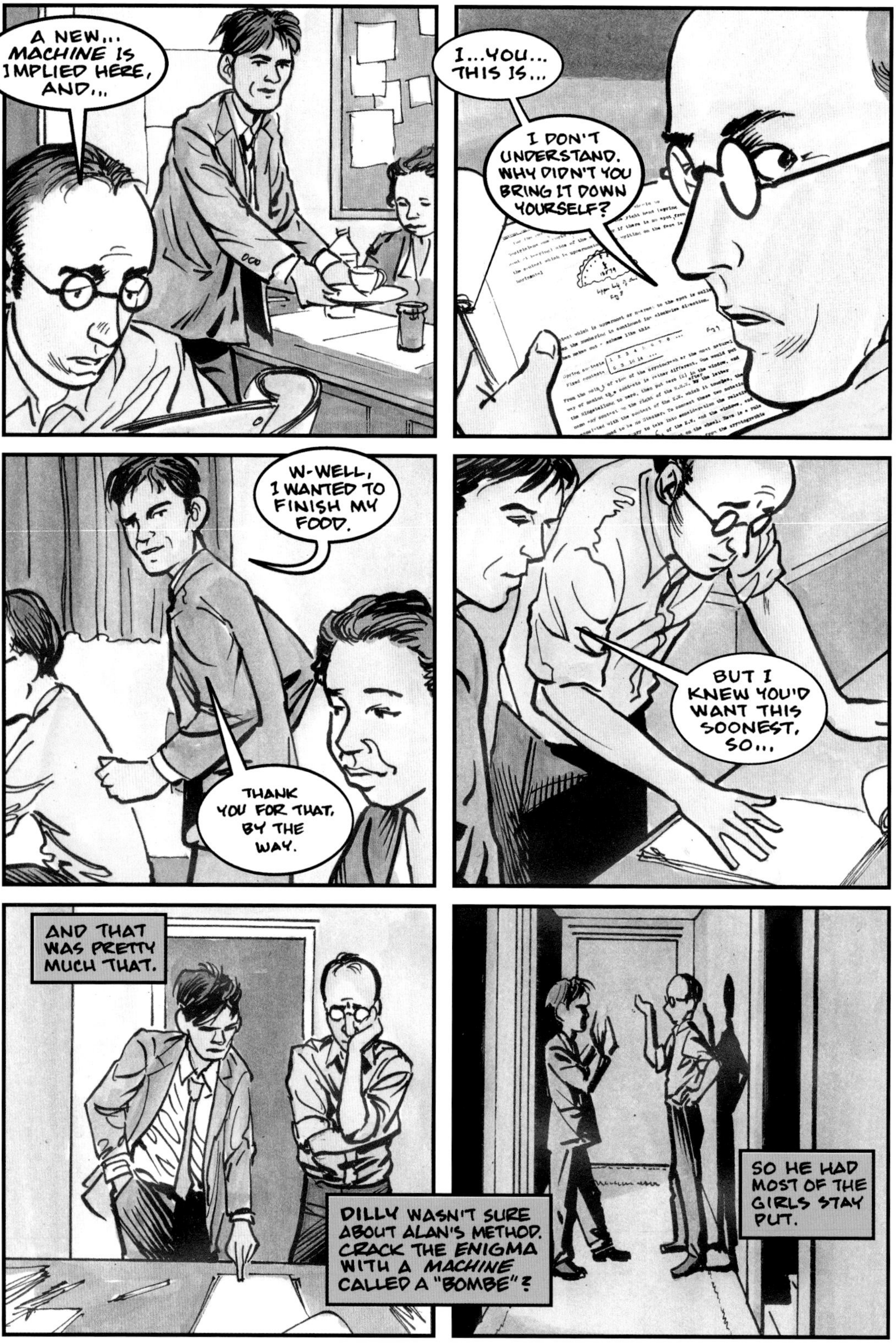
A NEW... MACHINE IS IMPLIED HERE, AND...
I...YOU... THIS IS...
I DON'T UNDERSTAND. WHY DIDN'T YOU BRING IT DOWN YOURSELF?
W-WELL, I WANTED TO FINISH MY FOOD.
THANK YOU FOR THAT, BY THE WAY.
BUT I KNEW YOU'D WANT THIS SOONEST, SO...
AND THAT WAS PRETTY MUCH THAT.
DILLY WASN'T SURE ABOUT ALAN'S METHOD. CRACK THE ENIGMA WITH A MACHINE CALLED A "BOMBE"?
SO HE HAD MOST OF THE GIRLS STAY PUT.

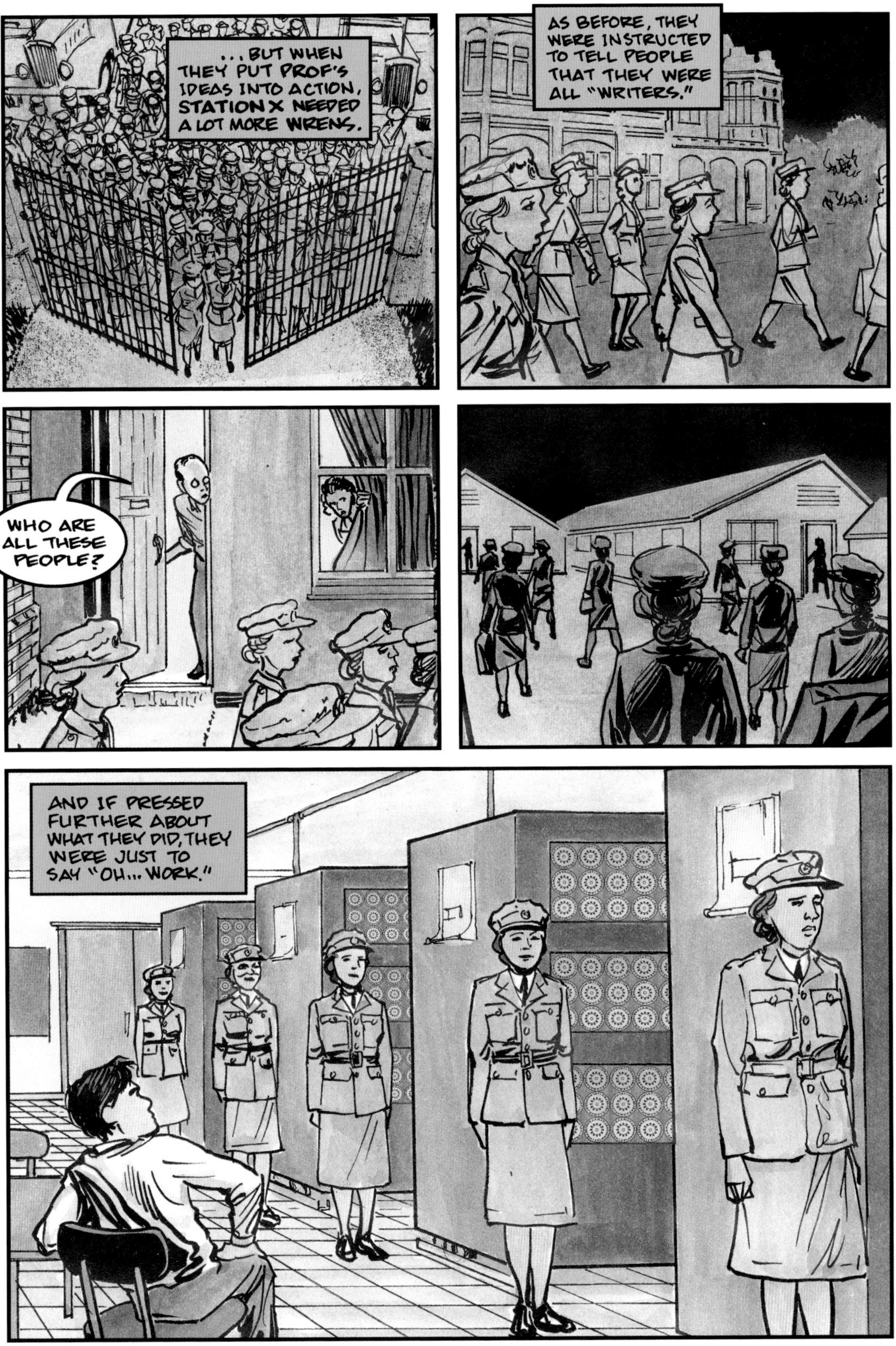

...BUT WHEN THEY PUT PROF'S IDEAS INTO ACTION, STATION X NEEDED A LOT MORE WRENS.
AS BEFORE, THEY WERE INSTRUCTED TO TELL PEOPLE THAT THEY WERE ALL "WRITERS."
WHO ARE ALL THESE PEOPLE?
AND IF PRESSED FURTHER ABOUT WHAT THEY DID, THEY WERE JUST TO SAY "OH... WORK."

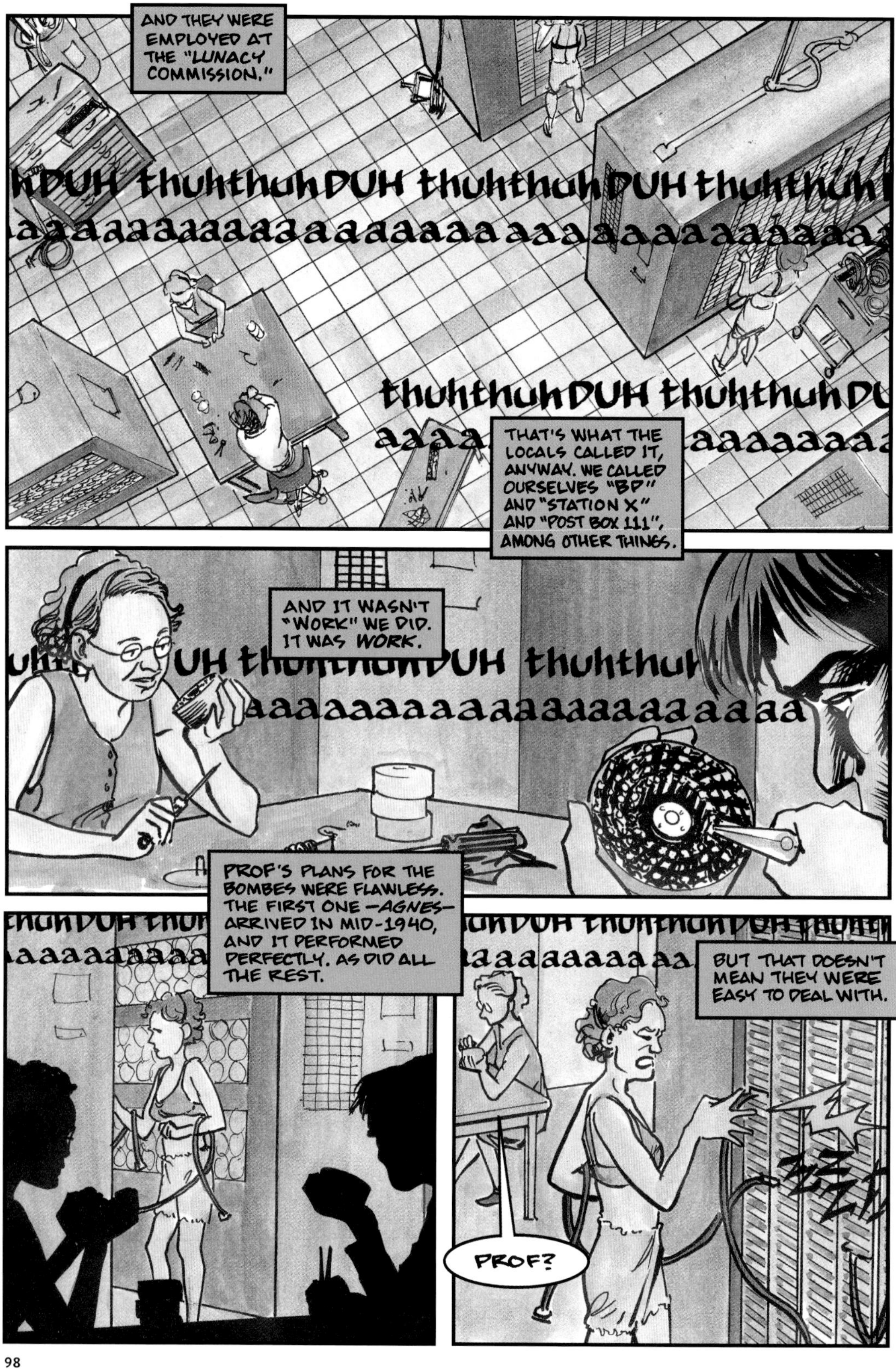

AND THEY WERE EMPLOYED AT THE "LUNACY COMMISSION."
thuhthuhDUH thuhthuhDUH thuhthuh
aaaaaaaaaaaaaaaaaaaaaaaaaaaa
THAT'S WHAT THE LOCALS CALLED IT, ANYWAY. WE CALLED OURSELVES "BP" AND "STATION X" AND "POST BOX 111", AMONG OTHER THINGS.
AND IT WASN'T "WORK" WE DID. IT WAS WORK.
PROF'S PLANS FOR THE BOMBES WERE FLAWLESS. THE FIRST ONE —AGNES— ARRIVED IN MID-1940, AND IT PERFORMED PERFECTLY. AS DID ALL THE REST.
BUT THAT DOESN'T MEAN THEY WERE EASY TO DEAL WITH.
PROF?

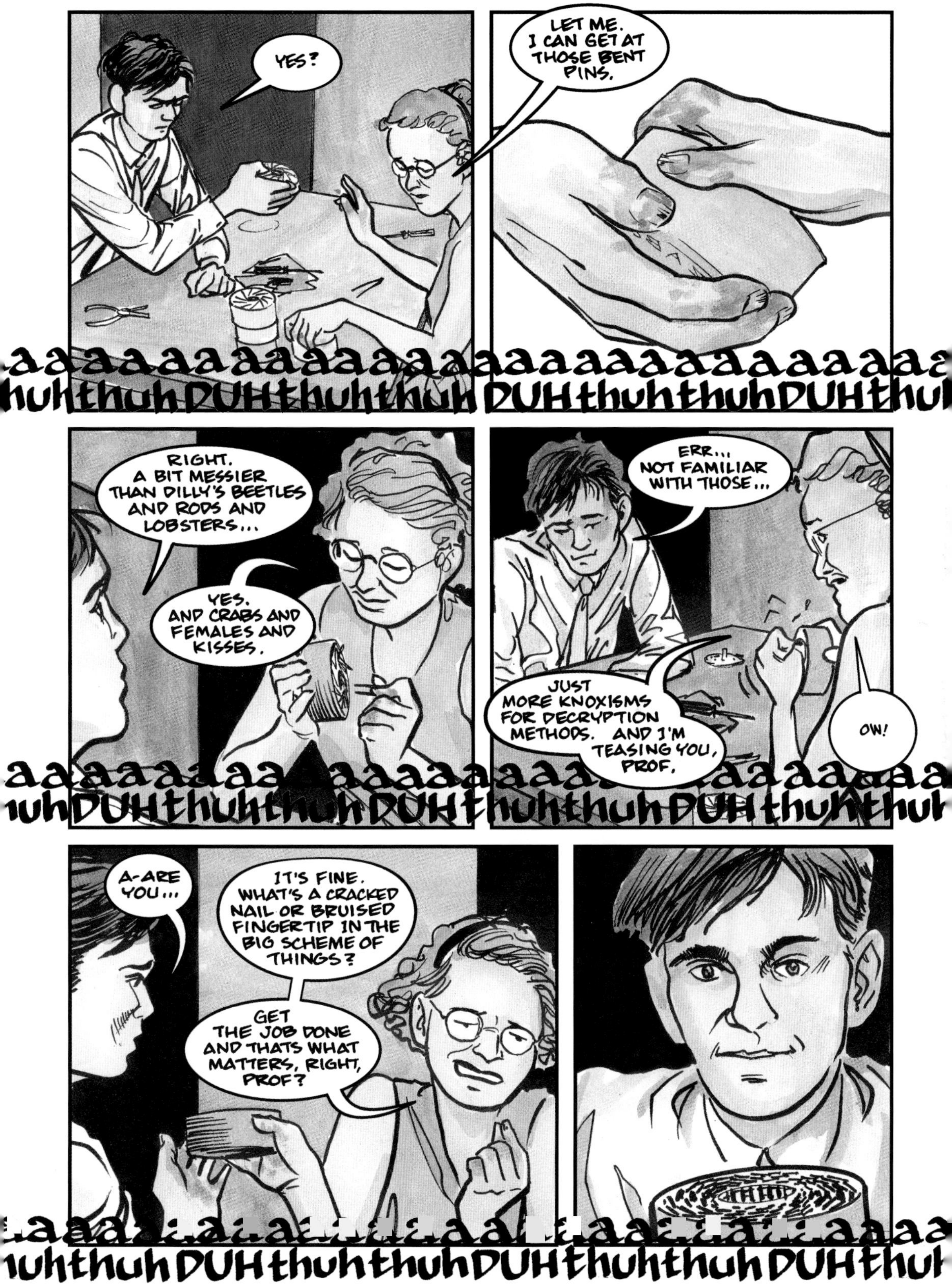
YES?
LET ME. I CAN GET AT THOSE BENT PINS.
aaaaaaaaaaaaaaaaaaaaaaaaa
thuhthuhDUHthuhthuhDUHthuhthuhDUHthuh
RIGHT. A BIT MESSIER THAN DILLY'S BEETLES AND RODS AND LOBSTERS...
YES. AND CRABS AND FEMALES AND KISSES.
ERR... NOT FAMILIAR WITH THOSE...
JUST MORE KNOXISMS FOR DECRYPTION METHODS. AND I'M TEASING YOU, PROF.
OW!
aaaaaaaaaaaaaaaaaaaaaaaaa
thuhDUHthuhthuhDUHthuhthuhDUHthuhthuh
A-ARE YOU...
IT'S FINE. WHAT'S A CRACKED NAIL OR BRUISED FINGERTIP IN THE BIG SCHEME OF THINGS?
GET THE JOB DONE AND THATS WHAT MATTERS, RIGHT, PROF?
aaaaaaaaaaaaaaaaaaaaaaaaa
thuhthuhDUHthuhthuhDUHthuhthuhDUHthuh

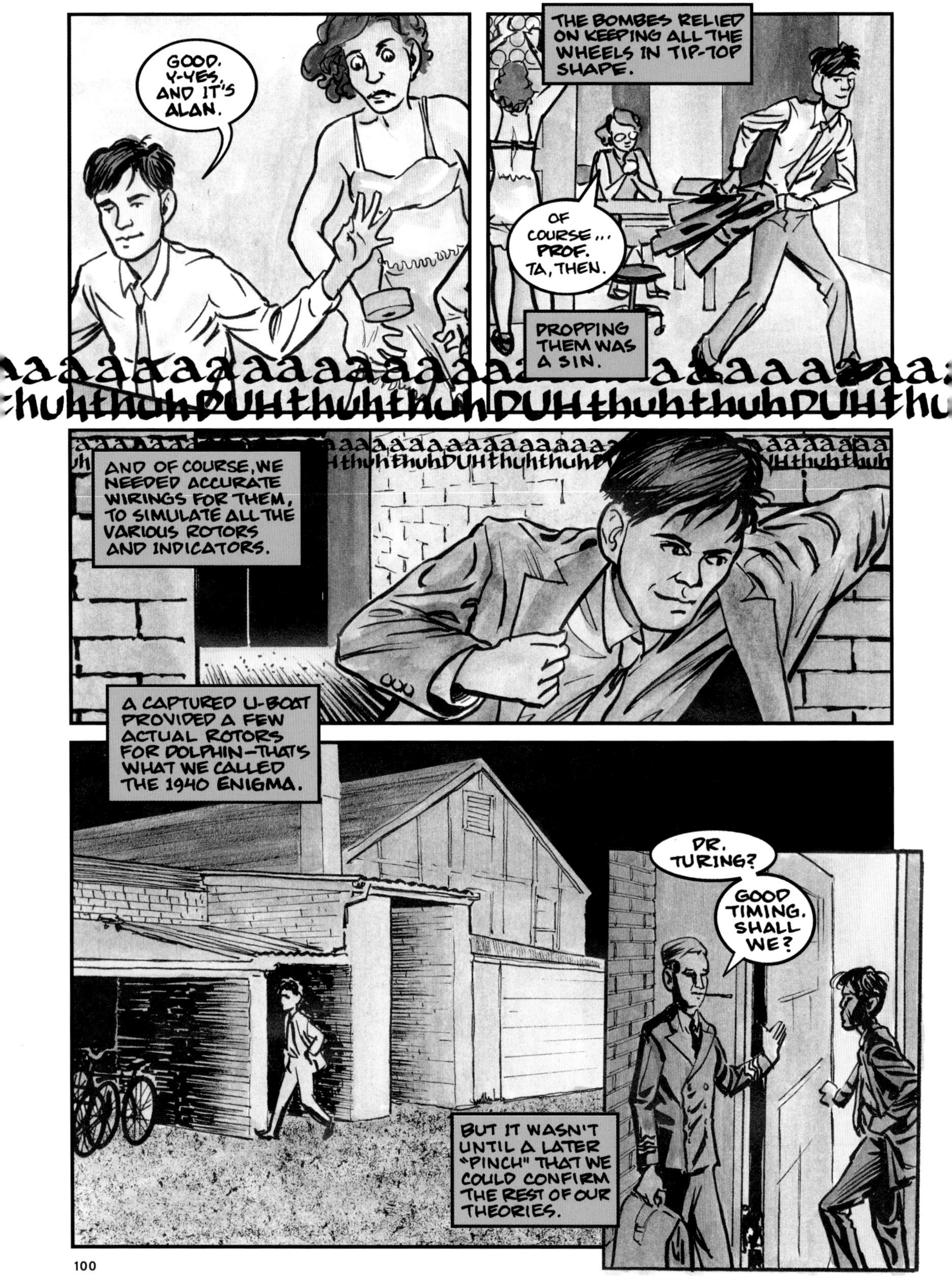
GOOD. Y-YES, AND IT'S ALAN.
THE BOMBES RELIED ON KEEPING ALL THE WHEELS IN TIP-TOP SHAPE.
OF COURSE... PROF. TA, THEN.
DROPPING THEM WAS A SIN.
aaaaaaaaaaaaaaaaaaaaa
thuhthuhDUHthuhthuhDUHthuhthuhDUHthu
AND OF COURSE, WE NEEDED ACCURATE WIRINGS FOR THEM, TO SIMULATE ALL THE VARIOUS ROTORS AND INDICATORS.
A CAPTURED U-BOAT PROVIDED A FEW ACTUAL ROTORS FOR DOLPHIN—THAT'S WHAT WE CALLED THE 1940 ENIGMA.
DR. TURING?
GOOD TIMING. SHALL WE?
BUT IT WASN'T UNTIL A LATER "PINCH" THAT WE COULD CONFIRM THE REST OF OUR THEORIES.

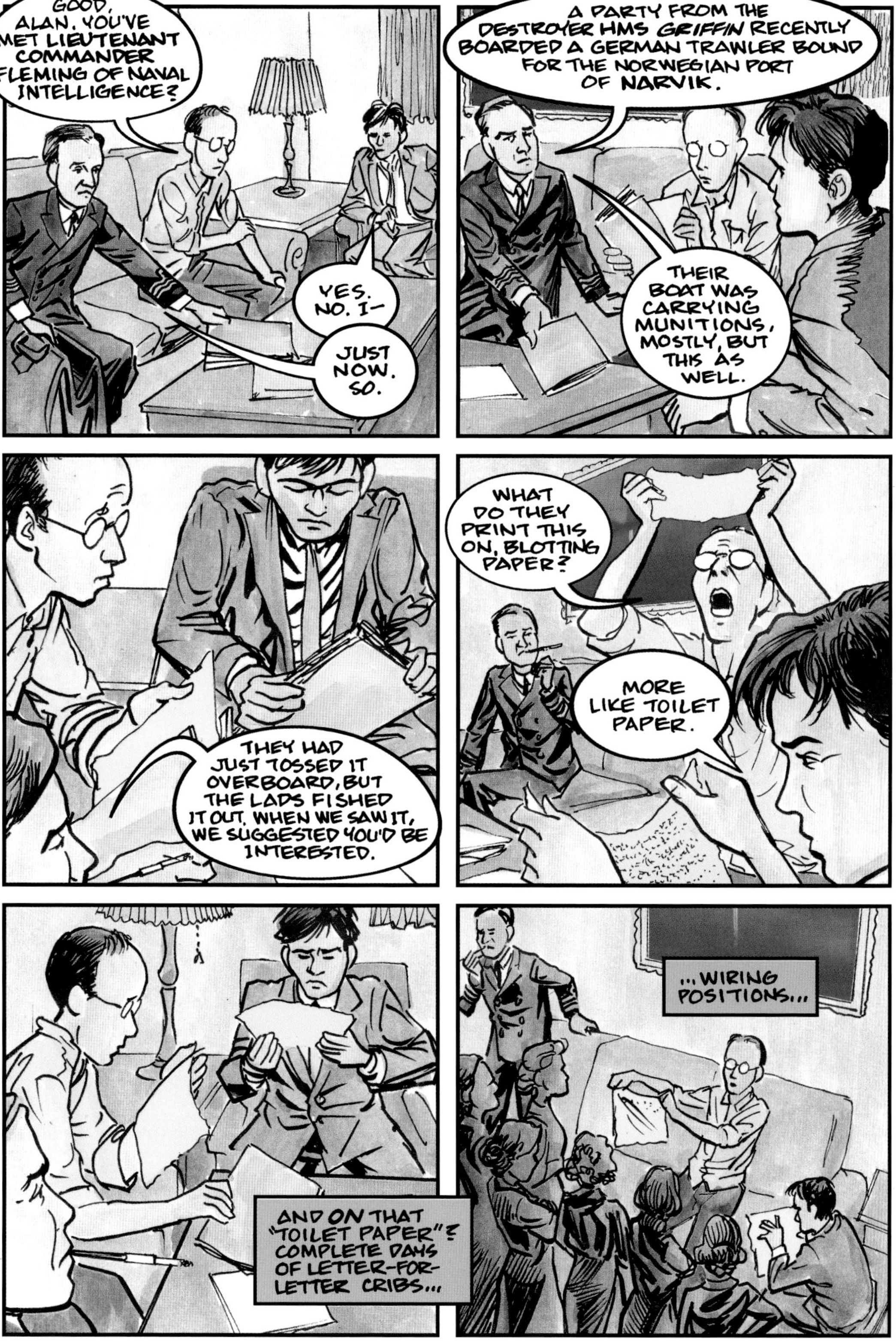
GOOD, ALAN. YOU'VE MET LIEUTENANT COMMANDER FLEMING OF NAVAL INTELLIGENCE?
YES. NO. I-
JUST NOW. SO.
A PARTY FROM THE DESTROYER HMS *GRIFFIN* RECENTLY BOARDED A GERMAN TRAWLER BOUND FOR THE NORWEGIAN PORT OF NARVIK.
THEIR BOAT WAS CARRYING MUNITIONS, MOSTLY, BUT THIS AS WELL.
THEY HAD JUST TOSSED IT OVERBOARD, BUT THE LADS FISHED IT OUT. WHEN WE SAW IT, WE SUGGESTED YOU'D BE INTERESTED.
WHAT DO THEY PRINT THIS ON, BLOTTING PAPER?
MORE LIKE TOILET PAPER.
AND ON THAT "TOILET PAPER"? COMPLETE DAYS OF LETTER-FOR-LETTER CRIBS...
...WIRING POSITIONS...

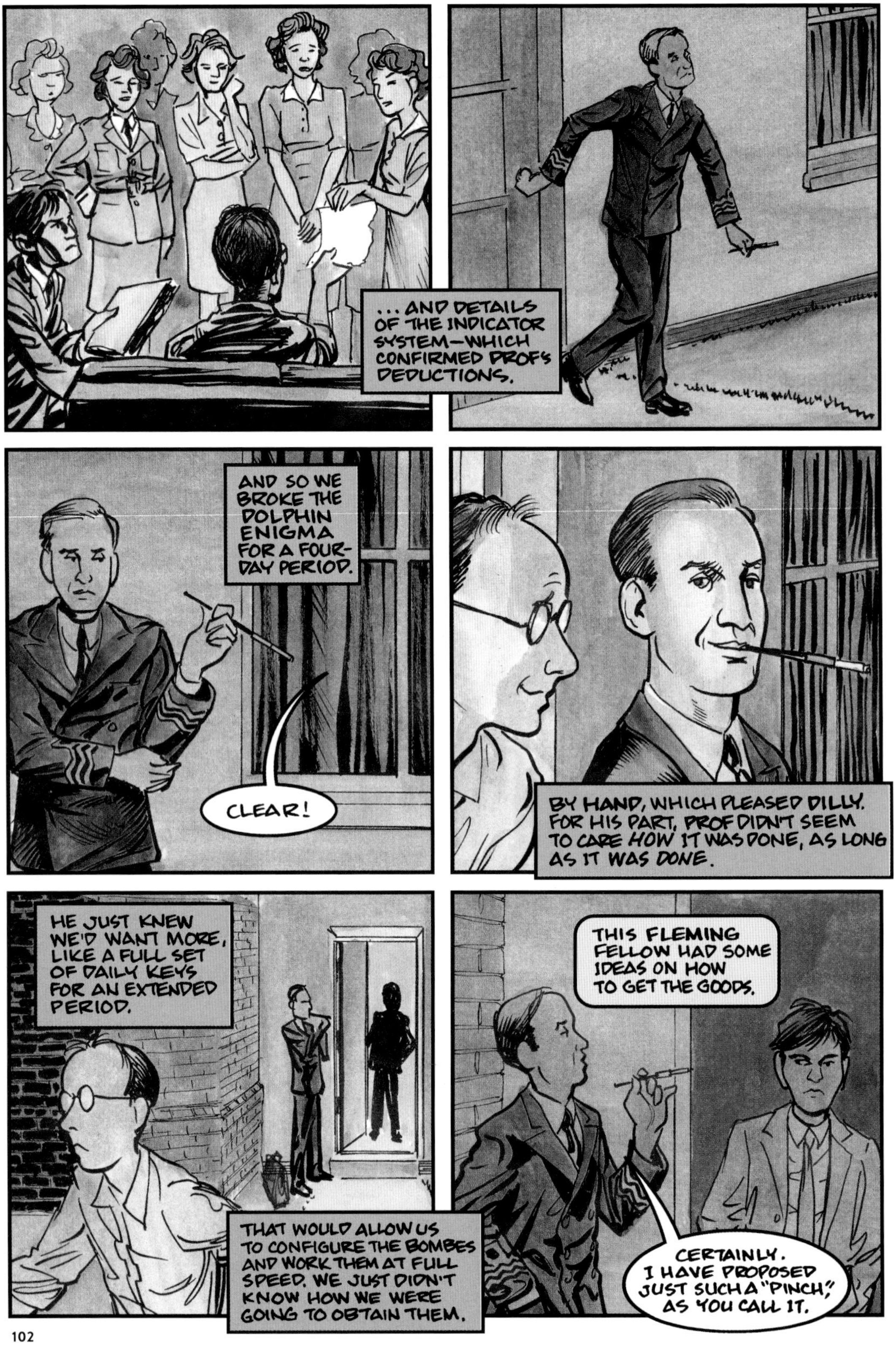
...AND DETAILS OF THE INDICATOR SYSTEM—WHICH CONFIRMED PROF'S DEDUCTIONS.
AND SO WE BROKE THE DOLPHIN ENIGMA FOR A FOUR-DAY PERIOD.
CLEAR!
BY HAND, WHICH PLEASED DILLY. FOR HIS PART, PROF DIDN'T SEEM TO CARE HOW IT WAS DONE, AS LONG AS IT WAS DONE.
HE JUST KNEW WE'D WANT MORE, LIKE A FULL SET OF DAILY KEYS FOR AN EXTENDED PERIOD.
THAT WOULD ALLOW US TO CONFIGURE THE BOMBES AND WORK THEM AT FULL SPEED. WE JUST DIDN'T KNOW HOW WE WERE GOING TO OBTAIN THEM.
THIS FLEMING FELLOW HAD SOME IDEAS ON HOW TO GET THE GOODS.
CERTAINLY. I HAVE PROPOSED JUST SUCH A "PINCH," AS YOU CALL IT.

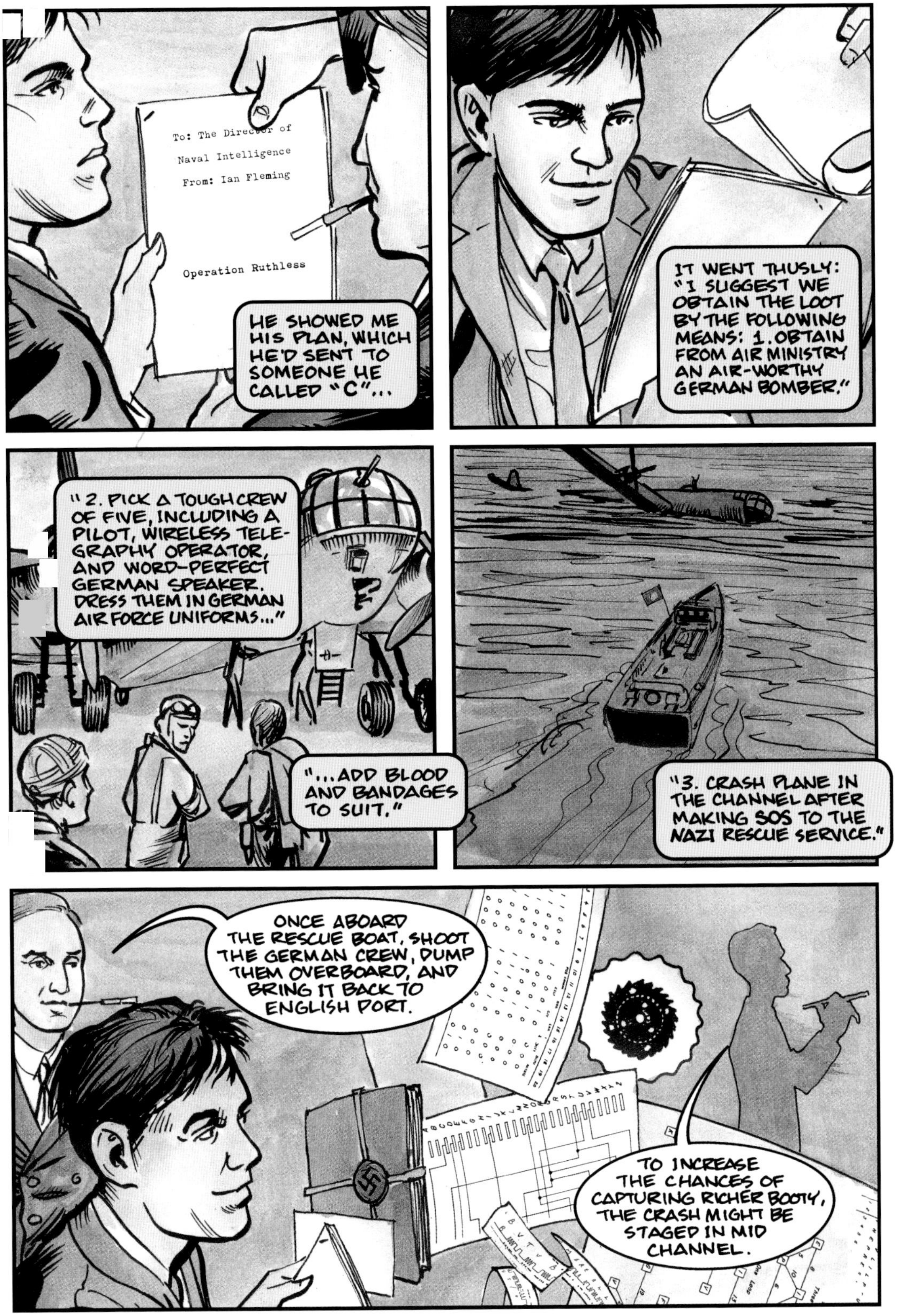
To: The Director of
Naval Intelligence
From: Ian Fleming
Operation Ruthless
HE SHOWED ME HIS PLAN, WHICH HE'D SENT TO SOMEONE HE CALLED "C"...
IT WENT THUSLY: "I SUGGEST WE OBTAIN THE LOOT BY THE FOLLOWING MEANS: 1. OBTAIN FROM AIR MINISTRY AN AIR-WORTHY GERMAN BOMBER."
"2. PICK A TOUGH CREW OF FIVE, INCLUDING A PILOT, WIRELESS TELEGRAPHY OPERATOR, AND WORD-PERFECT GERMAN SPEAKER. DRESS THEM IN GERMAN AIR FORCE UNIFORMS..."
"...ADD BLOOD AND BANDAGES TO SUIT."
"3. CRASH PLANE IN THE CHANNEL AFTER MAKING SOS TO THE NAZI RESCUE SERVICE."
ONCE ABOARD THE RESCUE BOAT, SHOOT THE GERMAN CREW, DUMP THEM OVERBOARD, AND BRING IT BACK TO ENGLISH PORT.
TO INCREASE THE CHANCES OF CAPTURING RICHER BOOTY, THE CRASH MIGHT BE STAGED IN MID CHANNEL.

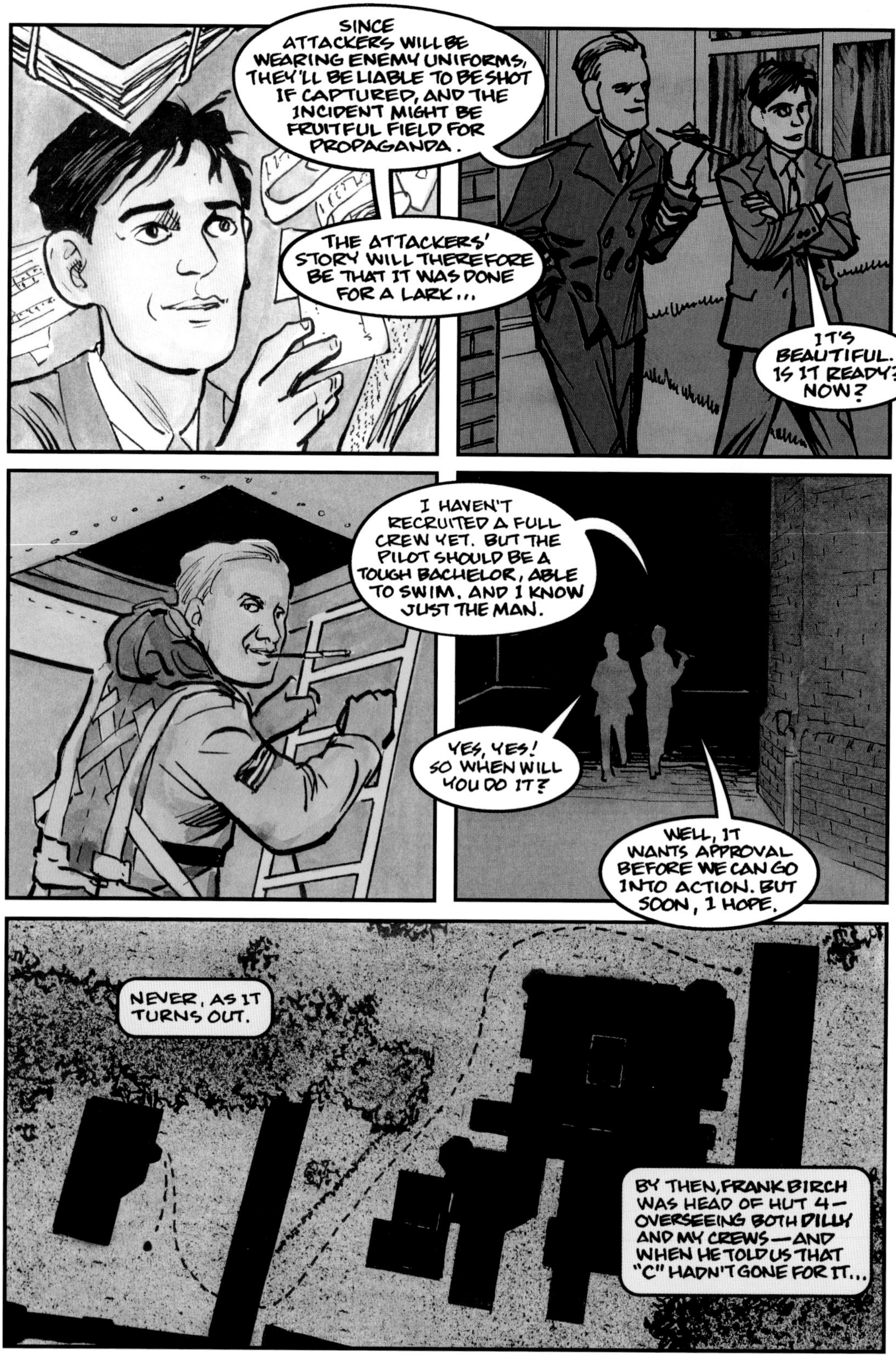
SINCE ATTACKERS WILL BE WEARING ENEMY UNIFORMS, THEY'LL BE LIABLE TO BE SHOT IF CAPTURED, AND THE INCIDENT MIGHT BE FRUITFUL FIELD FOR PROPAGANDA.
THE ATTACKERS' STORY WILL THEREFORE BE THAT IT WAS DONE FOR A LARK...
IT'S BEAUTIFUL. IS IT READY? NOW?
I HAVEN'T RECRUITED A FULL CREW YET. BUT THE PILOT SHOULD BE A TOUGH BACHELOR, ABLE TO SWIM. AND I KNOW JUST THE MAN.
YES, YES! SO WHEN WILL YOU DO IT?
WELL, IT WANTS APPROVAL BEFORE WE CAN GO INTO ACTION. BUT SOON, I HOPE.
NEVER, AS IT TURNS OUT.
BY THEN, FRANK BIRCH WAS HEAD OF HUT 4— OVERSEEING BOTH DILLY AND MY CREWS—AND WHEN HE TOLD US THAT "C" HADN'T GONE FOR IT...

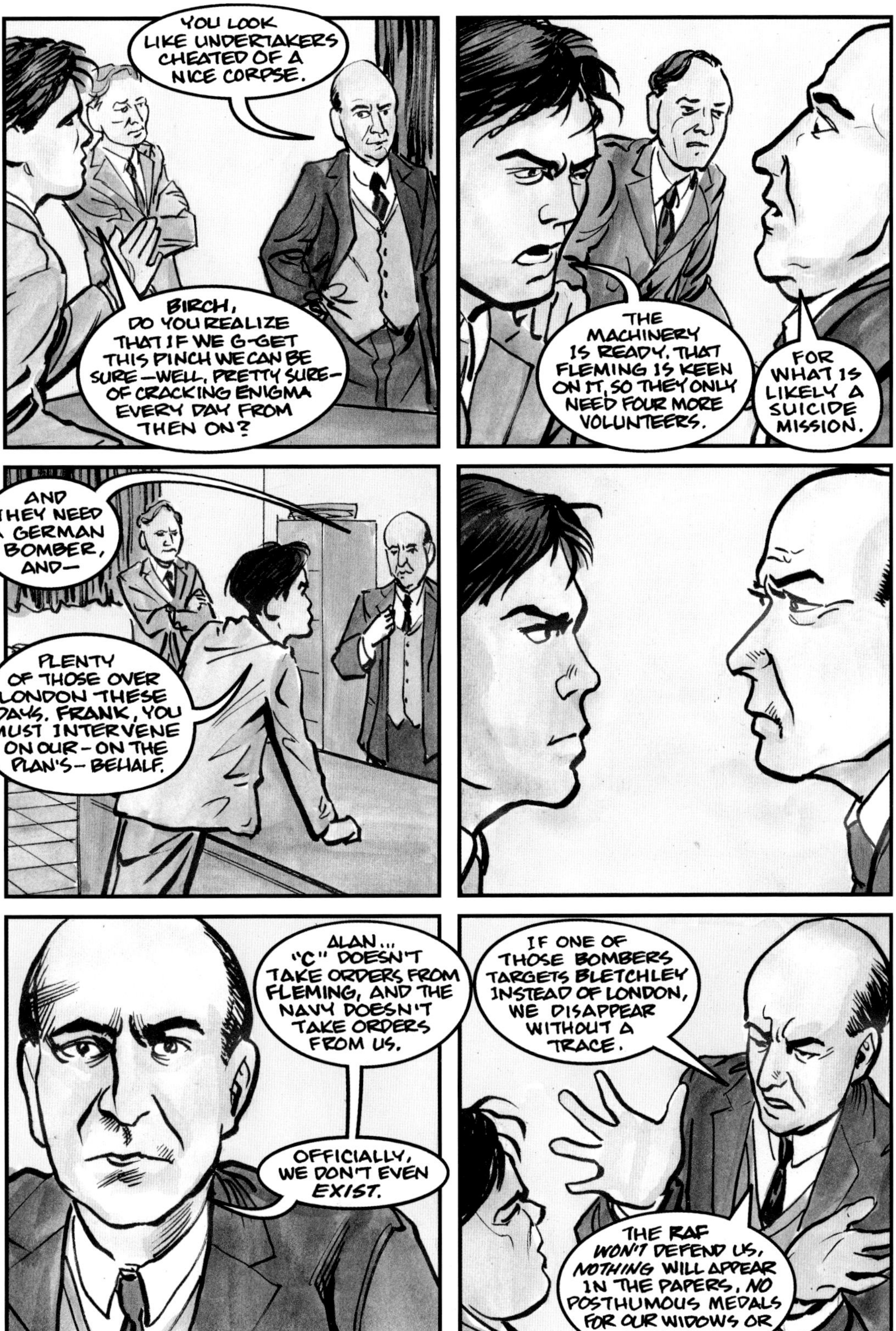
YOU LOOK LIKE UNDERTAKERS CHEATED OF A NICE CORPSE.
BIRCH, DO YOU REALIZE THAT IF WE G-GET THIS PINCH WE CAN BE SURE—WELL, PRETTY SURE—OF CRACKING ENIGMA EVERY DAY FROM THEN ON?
THE MACHINERY IS READY. THAT FLEMING IS KEEN ON IT, SO THEY ONLY NEED FOUR MORE VOLUNTEERS.
FOR WHAT IS LIKELY A SUICIDE MISSION.
AND THEY NEED A GERMAN BOMBER, AND—
PLENTY OF THOSE OVER LONDON THESE DAYS. FRANK, YOU MUST INTERVENE ON OUR—ON THE PLAN'S—BEHALF.
ALAN... "C" DOESN'T TAKE ORDERS FROM FLEMING, AND THE NAVY DOESN'T TAKE ORDERS FROM US.
OFFICIALLY, WE DON'T EVEN *EXIST*.
IF ONE OF THOSE BOMBERS TARGETS BLETCHLEY INSTEAD OF LONDON, WE DISAPPEAR WITHOUT A TRACE.
THE RAF *WON'T* DEFEND US, *NOTHING* WILL APPEAR IN THE PAPERS, *NO* POSTHUMOUS MEDALS FOR OUR WIDOWS OR MOTHERS.

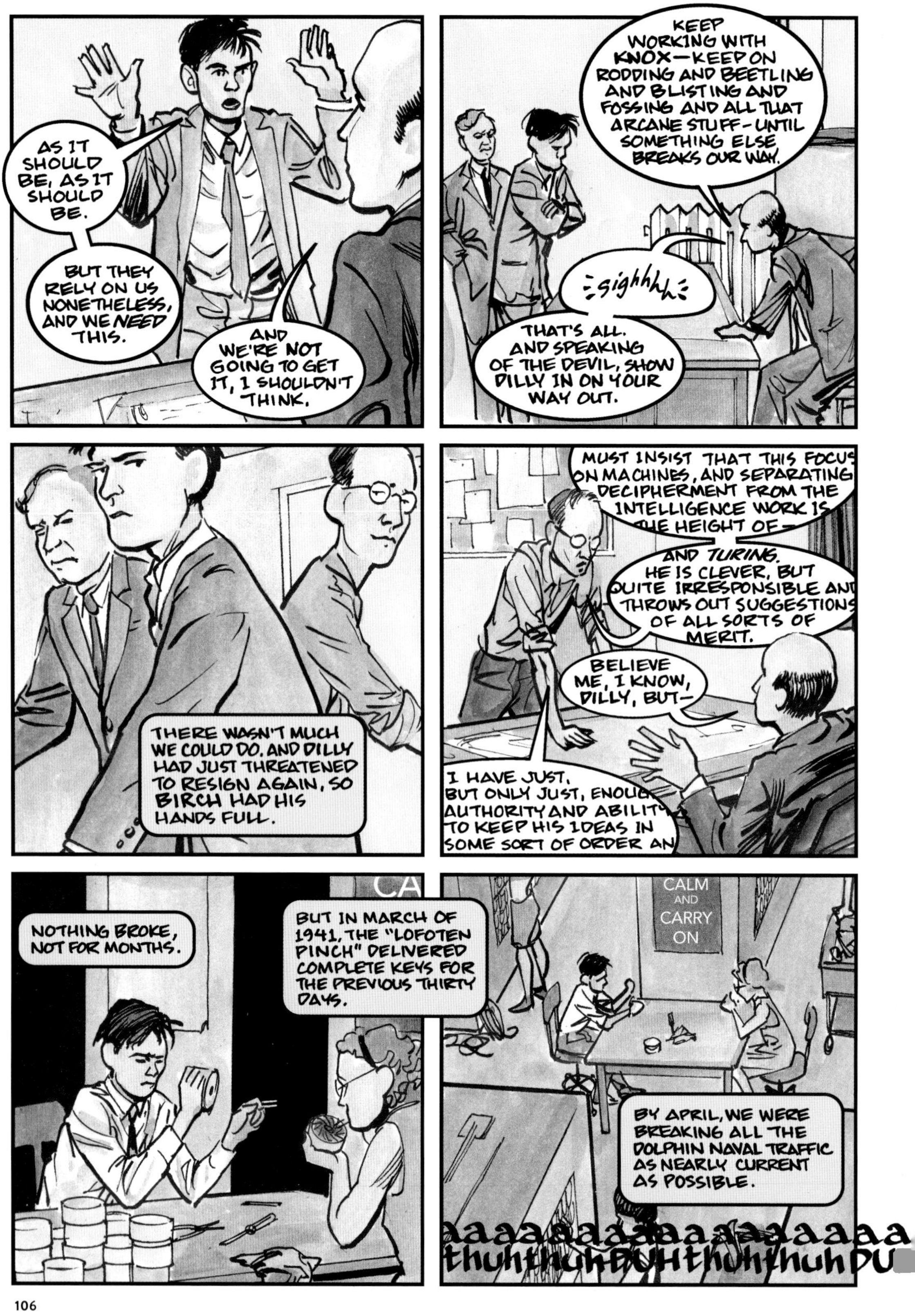
AS IT SHOULD BE, AS IT SHOULD BE.
BUT THEY RELY ON US NONETHELESS, AND WE *NEED* THIS.
AND WE'RE **NOT** GOING TO GET IT, I SHOULDN'T THINK.
KEEP WORKING WITH KNOX—KEEP ON RODDING AND BEETLING AND BLISTING AND FOSSING AND ALL THAT ARCANE STUFF—UNTIL SOMETHING ELSE BREAKS OUR WAY.
sighhhhh
THAT'S ALL. AND SPEAKING OF THE DEVIL, SHOW DILLY IN ON YOUR WAY OUT.
THERE WASN'T MUCH WE COULD DO, AND DILLY HAD JUST THREATENED TO RESIGN AGAIN, SO BIRCH HAD HIS HANDS FULL.
MUST INSIST THAT THIS FOCUS ON MACHINES, AND SEPARATING DECIPHERMENT FROM THE INTELLIGENCE WORK IS THE HEIGHT OF—
AND *TURING*. HE IS CLEVER, BUT QUITE IRRESPONSIBLE AND THROWS OUT SUGGESTIONS OF ALL SORTS OF MERIT.
BELIEVE ME, I KNOW, DILLY, BUT—
I HAVE JUST, BUT ONLY JUST, ENOUGH AUTHORITY AND ABILITY TO KEEP HIS IDEAS IN SOME SORT OF ORDER AN
CA
NOTHING BROKE, NOT FOR MONTHS.
BUT IN MARCH OF 1941, THE "LOFOTEN PINCH" DELIVERED COMPLETE KEYS FOR THE PREVIOUS THIRTY DAYS.
CALM AND CARRY ON
BY APRIL, WE WERE BREAKING ALL THE DOLPHIN NAVAL TRAFFIC AS NEARLY CURRENT AS POSSIBLE.
aaaaaaaaaaaaaaaa
thuhthuhDUHthuhthuhDU

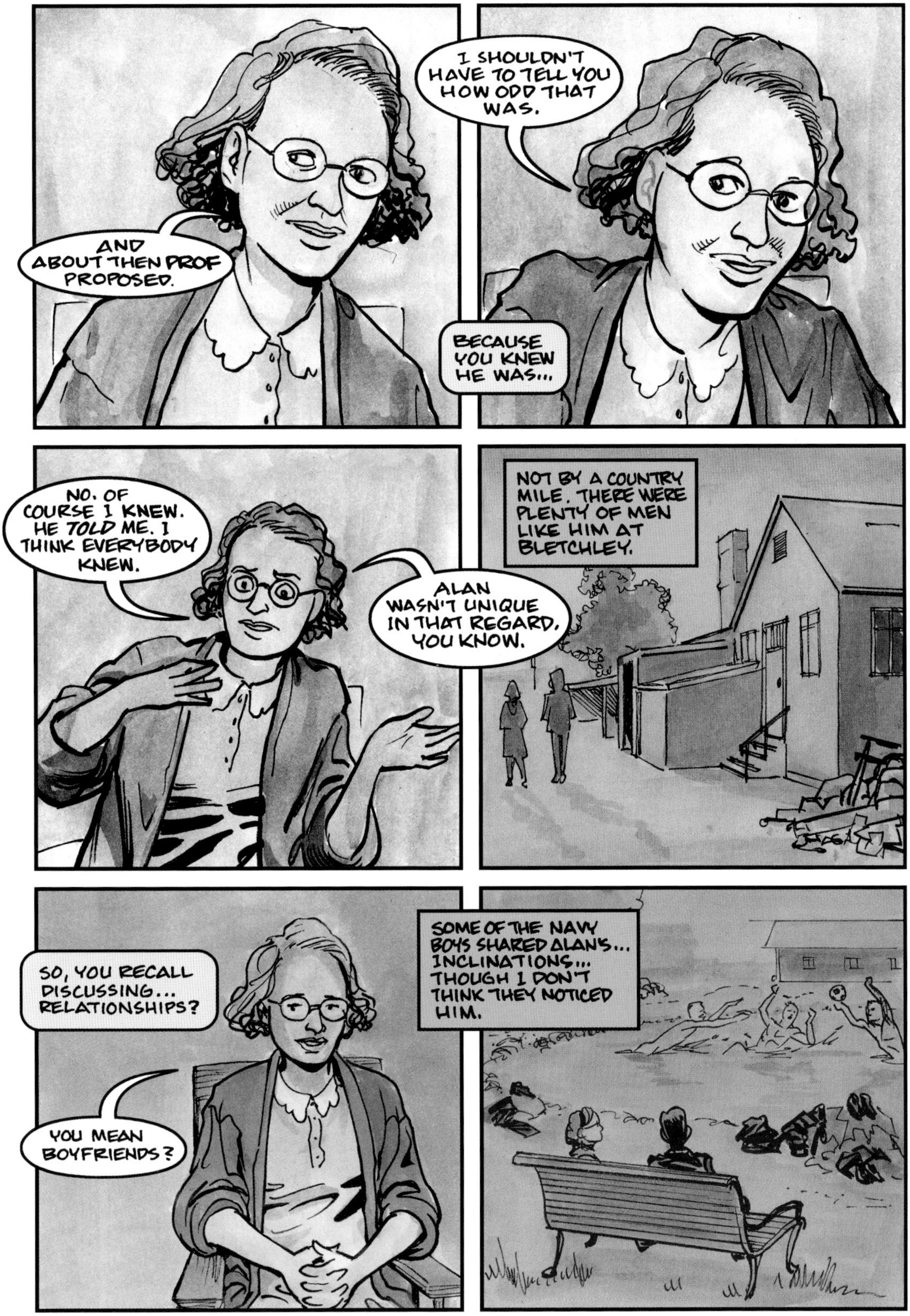
AND ABOUT THEN PROF PROPOSED.
I SHOULDN'T HAVE TO TELL YOU HOW ODD THAT WAS.
BECAUSE YOU KNEW HE WAS...
NO. OF COURSE I KNEW. HE *TOLD* ME. I THINK EVERYBODY KNEW.
ALAN WASN'T UNIQUE IN THAT REGARD, YOU KNOW.
NOT BY A COUNTRY MILE. THERE WERE PLENTY OF MEN LIKE HIM AT BLETCHLEY.
SO, YOU RECALL DISCUSSING... RELATIONSHIPS?
YOU MEAN BOYFRIENDS?
SOME OF THE NAVY BOYS SHARED ALAN'S... INCLINATIONS... THOUGH I DON'T THINK THEY NOTICED HIM.

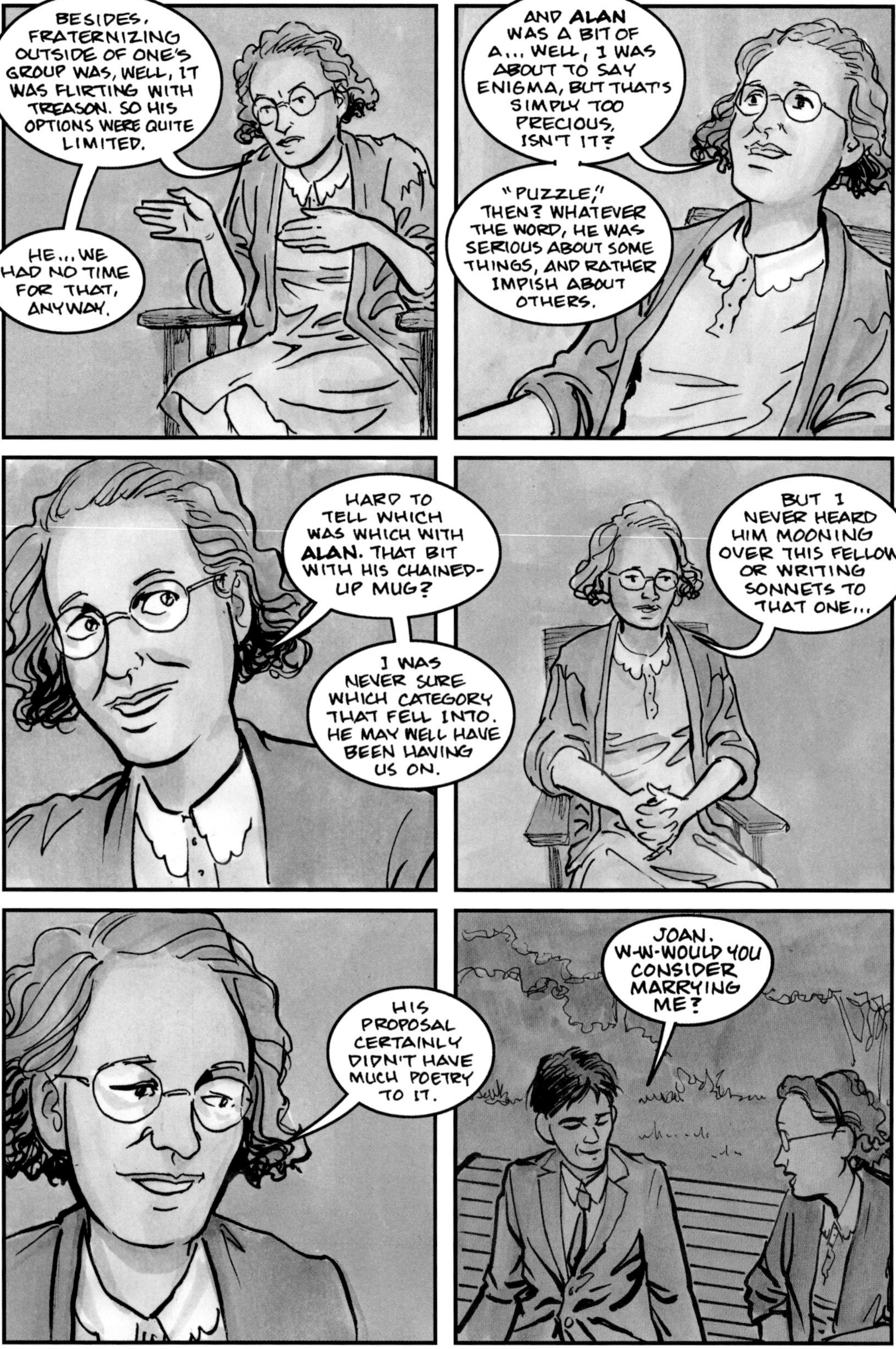
BESIDES, FRATERNIZING OUTSIDE OF ONE'S GROUP WAS, WELL, IT WAS FLIRTING WITH TREASON. SO HIS OPTIONS WERE QUITE LIMITED.
HE... WE HAD NO TIME FOR THAT, ANYWAY.
AND ALAN WAS A BIT OF A... WELL, I WAS ABOUT TO SAY ENIGMA, BUT THAT'S SIMPLY TOO PRECIOUS, ISN'T IT?
"PUZZLE," THEN? WHATEVER THE WORD, HE WAS SERIOUS ABOUT SOME THINGS, AND RATHER IMPISH ABOUT OTHERS.
HARD TO TELL WHICH WAS WHICH WITH ALAN. THAT BIT WITH HIS CHAINED-UP MUG?
I WAS NEVER SURE WHICH CATEGORY THAT FELL INTO. HE MAY WELL HAVE BEEN HAVING US ON.
BUT I NEVER HEARD HIM MOONING OVER THIS FELLOW OR WRITING SONNETS TO THAT ONE...
HIS PROPOSAL CERTAINLY DIDN'T HAVE MUCH POETRY TO IT.
JOAN. W-W-WOULD YOU CONSIDER MARRYING ME?

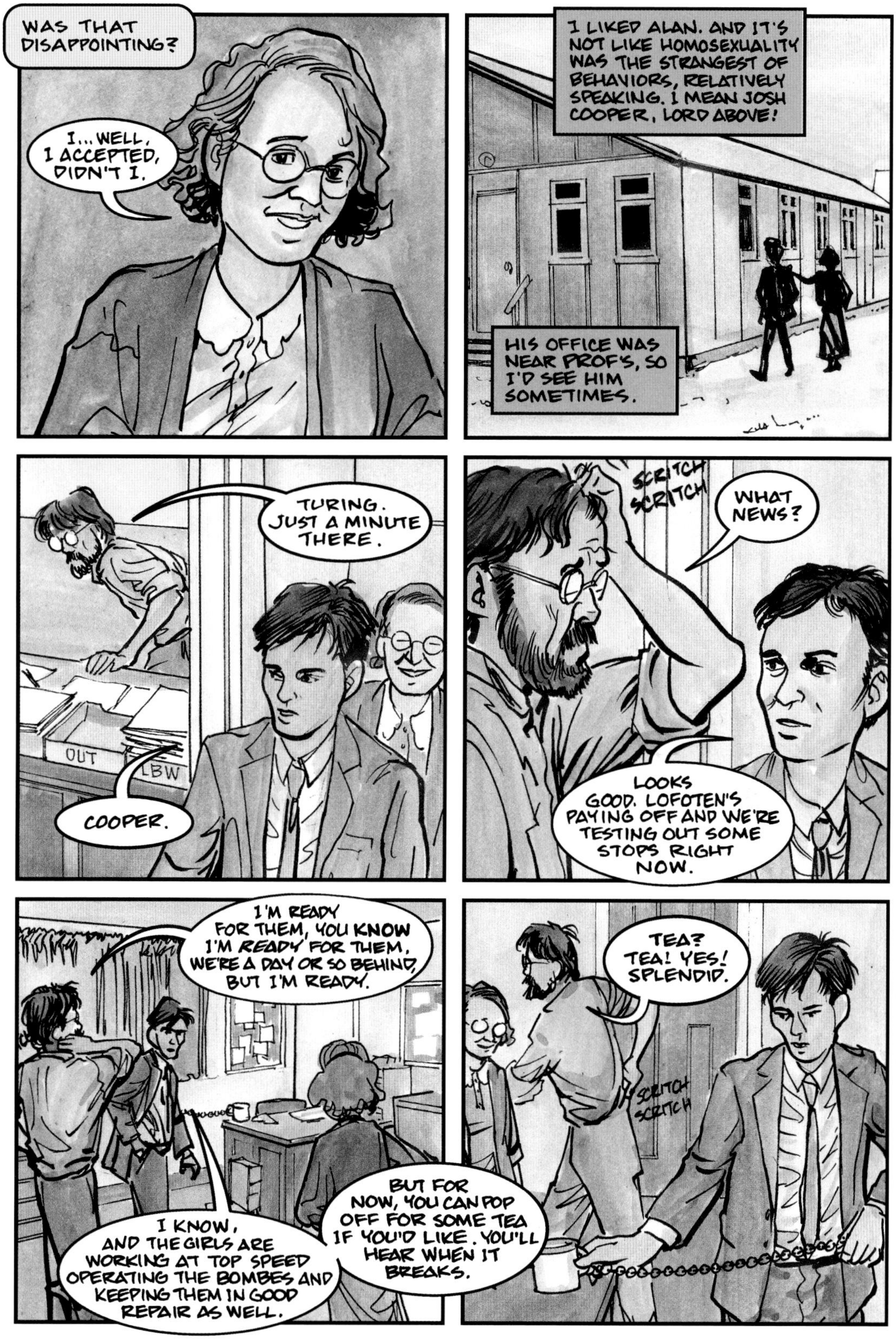

WAS THAT DISAPPOINTING?
I... WELL, I ACCEPTED, DIDN'T I.
I LIKED ALAN. AND IT'S NOT LIKE HOMOSEXUALITY WAS THE STRANGEST OF BEHAVIORS, RELATIVELY SPEAKING. I MEAN JOSH COOPER, LORD ABOVE!
HIS OFFICE WAS NEAR PROF'S, SO I'D SEE HIM SOMETIMES.
TURING. JUST A MINUTE THERE.
OUT
LBW
COOPER.
SCRITCH SCRITCH
WHAT NEWS?
LOOKS GOOD. LOFOTEN'S PAYING OFF AND WE'RE TESTING OUT SOME STOPS RIGHT NOW.
I'M READY FOR THEM, YOU KNOW I'M *READY* FOR THEM. WE'RE A DAY OR SO BEHIND, BUT I'M READY.
I KNOW, AND THE GIRLS ARE WORKING AT TOP SPEED OPERATING THE BOMBES AND KEEPING THEM IN GOOD REPAIR AS WELL.
BUT FOR NOW, YOU CAN POP OFF FOR SOME TEA IF YOU'D LIKE. YOU'LL HEAR WHEN IT BREAKS.
TEA? TEA! YES! SPLENDID.
SCRITCH SCRITCH

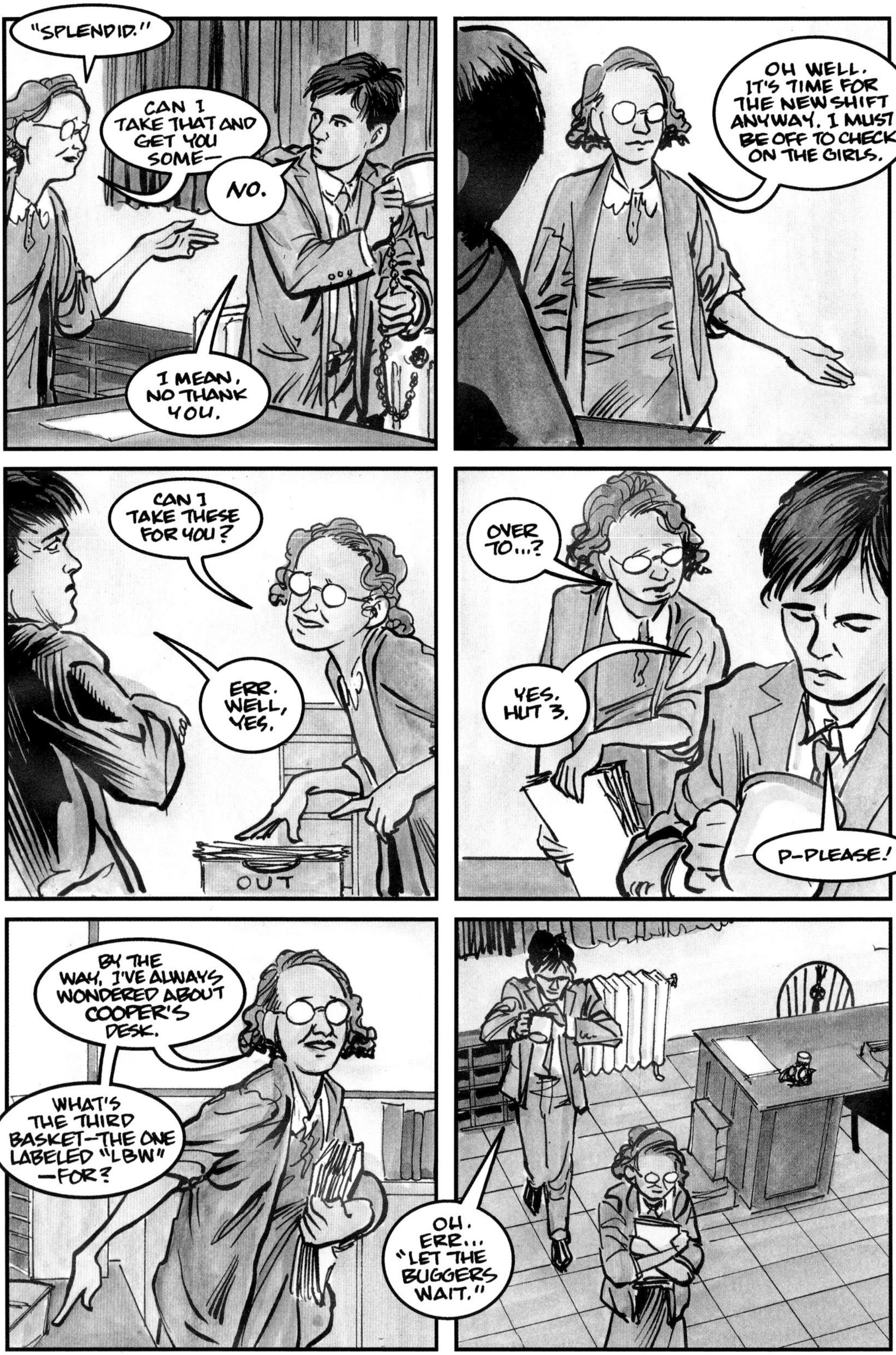
"SPLENDID."
CAN I TAKE THAT AND GET YOU SOME—
NO.
I MEAN, NO THANK YOU.
OH WELL. IT'S TIME FOR THE NEW SHIFT ANYWAY. I MUST BE OFF TO CHECK ON THE GIRLS.
CAN I TAKE THESE FOR YOU?
ERR. WELL, YES.
OUT
OVER TO...?
YES. HUT 3.
P-PLEASE!
BY THE WAY, I'VE ALWAYS WONDERED ABOUT COOPER'S DESK.
WHAT'S THE THIRD BASKET—THE ONE LABELED "LBW"—FOR?
OH. ERR... "LET THE BUGGERS WAIT."

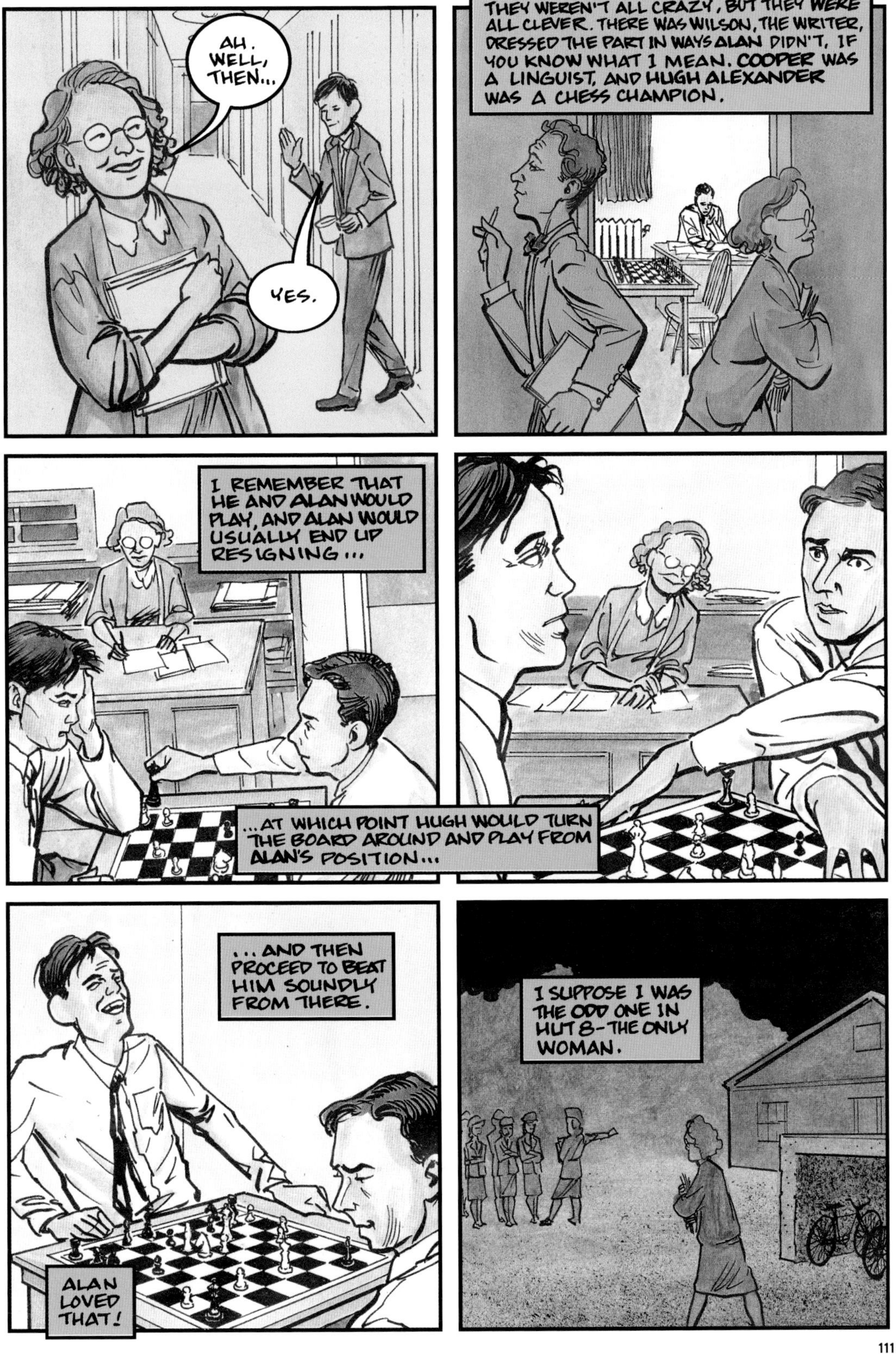
AH. WELL, THEN...
YES.
THEY WEREN'T ALL CRAZY, BUT THEY WERE ALL CLEVER. THERE WAS WILSON, THE WRITER, DRESSED THE PART IN WAYS ALAN DIDN'T, IF YOU KNOW WHAT I MEAN. COOPER WAS A LINGUIST, AND HUGH ALEXANDER WAS A CHESS CHAMPION.
I REMEMBER THAT HE AND ALAN WOULD PLAY, AND ALAN WOULD USUALLY END UP RESIGNING...
...AT WHICH POINT HUGH WOULD TURN THE BOARD AROUND AND PLAY FROM ALAN'S POSITION...
...AND THEN PROCEED TO BEAT HIM SOUNDLY FROM THERE.
ALAN LOVED THAT!
I SUPPOSE I WAS THE ODD ONE IN HUT 8- THE ONLY WOMAN.

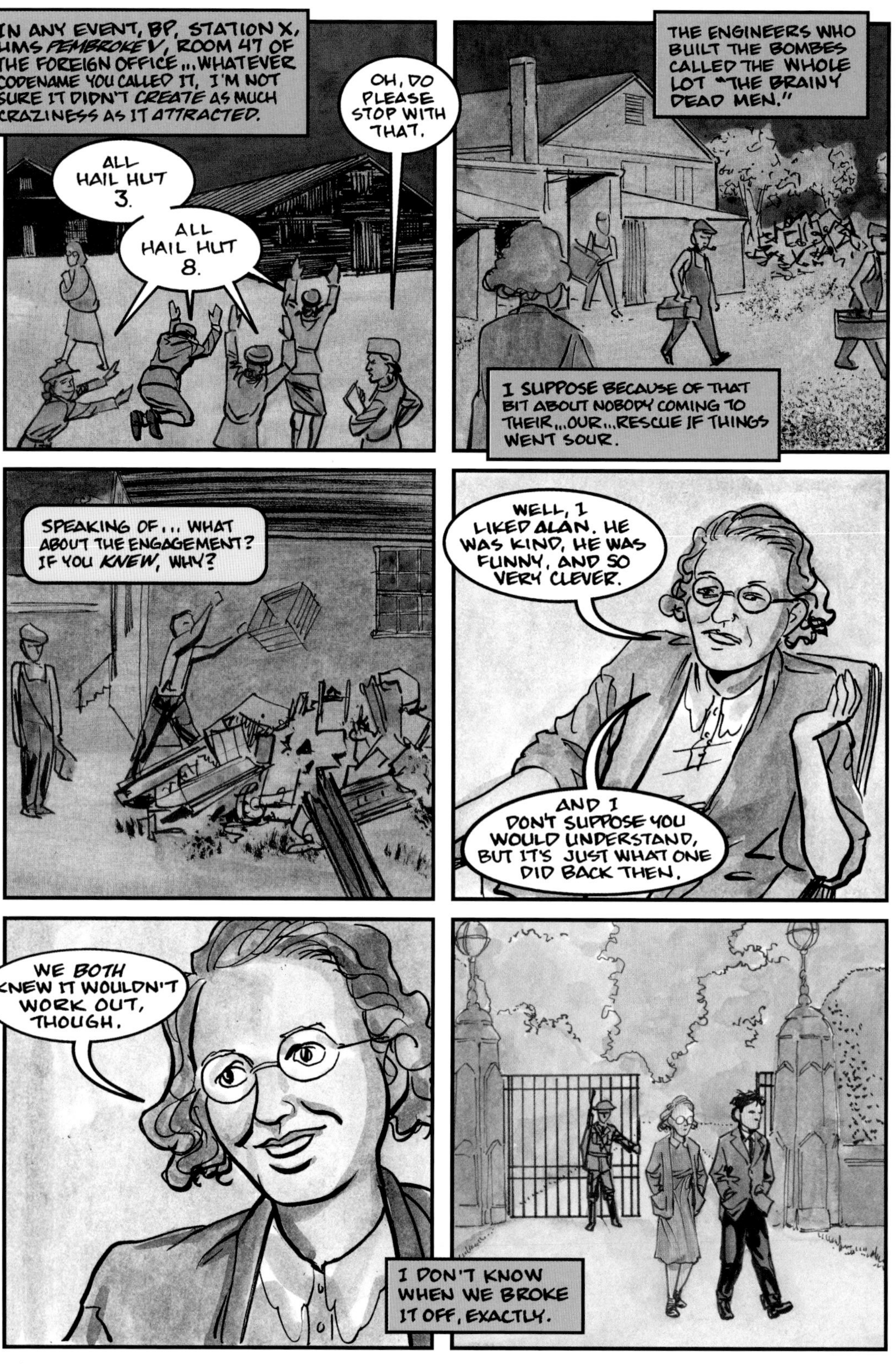
IN ANY EVENT, BP, STATION X, HMS PEMBROKE V, ROOM 47 OF THE FOREIGN OFFICE ... WHATEVER CODENAME YOU CALLED IT, I'M NOT SURE IT DIDN'T CREATE AS MUCH CRAZINESS AS IT ATTRACTED.
OH, DO PLEASE STOP WITH THAT.
ALL HAIL HUT 3.
ALL HAIL HUT 8.
THE ENGINEERS WHO BUILT THE BOMBES CALLED THE WHOLE LOT "THE BRAINY DEAD MEN."
I SUPPOSE BECAUSE OF THAT BIT ABOUT NOBODY COMING TO THEIR... OUR... RESCUE IF THINGS WENT SOUR.
SPEAKING OF ... WHAT ABOUT THE ENGAGEMENT? IF YOU KNEW, WHY?
WELL, I LIKED ALAN. HE WAS KIND, HE WAS FUNNY, AND SO VERY CLEVER.
AND I DON'T SUPPOSE YOU WOULD UNDERSTAND, BUT IT'S JUST WHAT ONE DID BACK THEN.
WE BOTH KNEW IT WOULDN'T WORK OUT, THOUGH.
I DON'T KNOW WHEN WE BROKE IT OFF, EXACTLY.

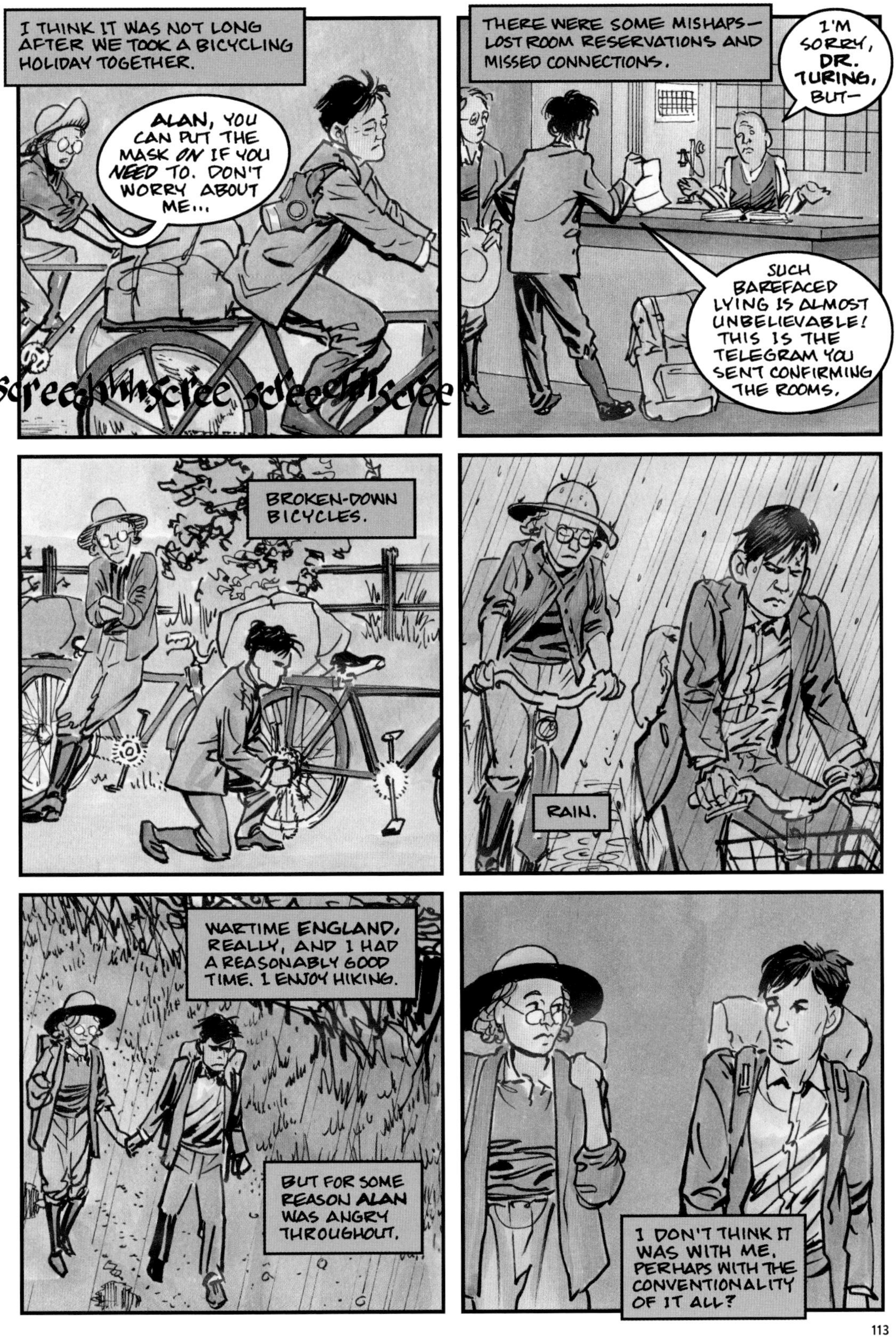
I THINK IT WAS NOT LONG AFTER WE TOOK A BICYCLING HOLIDAY TOGETHER.
ALAN, YOU CAN PUT THE MASK ON IF YOU NEED TO. DON'T WORRY ABOUT ME...
screech screee screech screee
THERE WERE SOME MISHAPS— LOST ROOM RESERVATIONS AND MISSED CONNECTIONS.
I'M SORRY, DR. TURING, BUT—
SUCH BAREFACED LYING IS ALMOST UNBELIEVABLE! THIS IS THE TELEGRAM YOU SENT CONFIRMING THE ROOMS.
BROKEN-DOWN BICYCLES.
RAIN.
WARTIME ENGLAND, REALLY, AND I HAD A REASONABLY GOOD TIME. I ENJOY HIKING.
BUT FOR SOME REASON ALAN WAS ANGRY THROUGHOUT.
I DON'T THINK IT WAS WITH ME, PERHAPS WITH THE CONVENTIONALITY OF IT ALL?

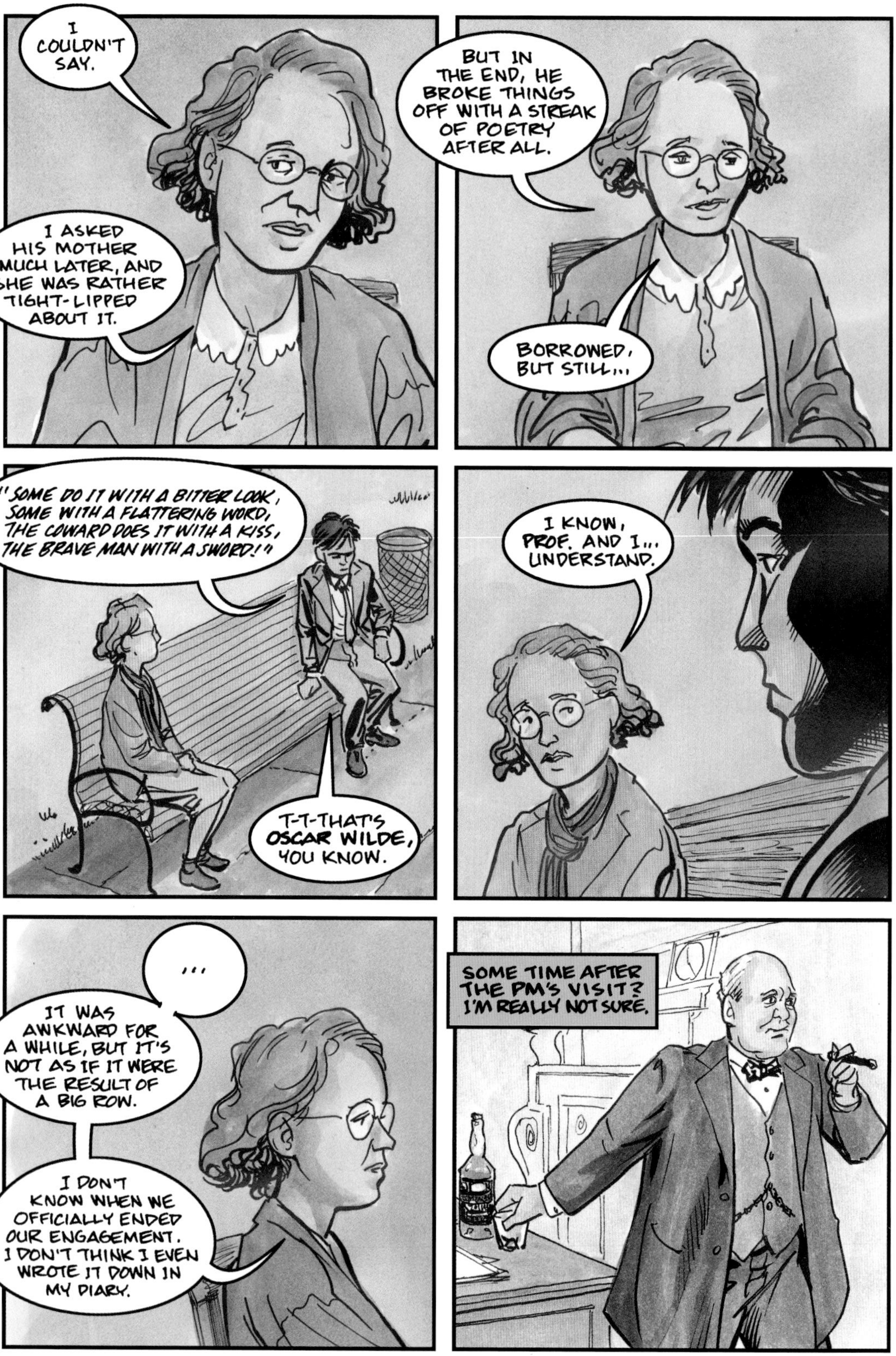

I COULDN'T SAY.
I ASKED HIS MOTHER MUCH LATER, AND SHE WAS RATHER TIGHT-LIPPED ABOUT IT.
BUT IN THE END, HE BROKE THINGS OFF WITH A STREAK OF POETRY AFTER ALL.
BORROWED, BUT STILL...
"SOME DO IT WITH A BITTER LOOK, SOME WITH A FLATTERING WORD, THE COWARD DOES IT WITH A KISS, THE BRAVE MAN WITH A SWORD!"
T-T-THAT'S OSCAR WILDE, YOU KNOW.
I KNOW, PROF. AND I... UNDERSTAND.
...
IT WAS AWKWARD FOR A WHILE, BUT IT'S NOT AS IF IT WERE THE RESULT OF A BIG ROW.
I DON'T KNOW WHEN WE OFFICIALLY ENDED OUR ENGAGEMENT. I DON'T THINK I EVEN WROTE IT DOWN IN MY DIARY.
SOME TIME AFTER THE PM'S VISIT? I'M REALLY NOT SURE.

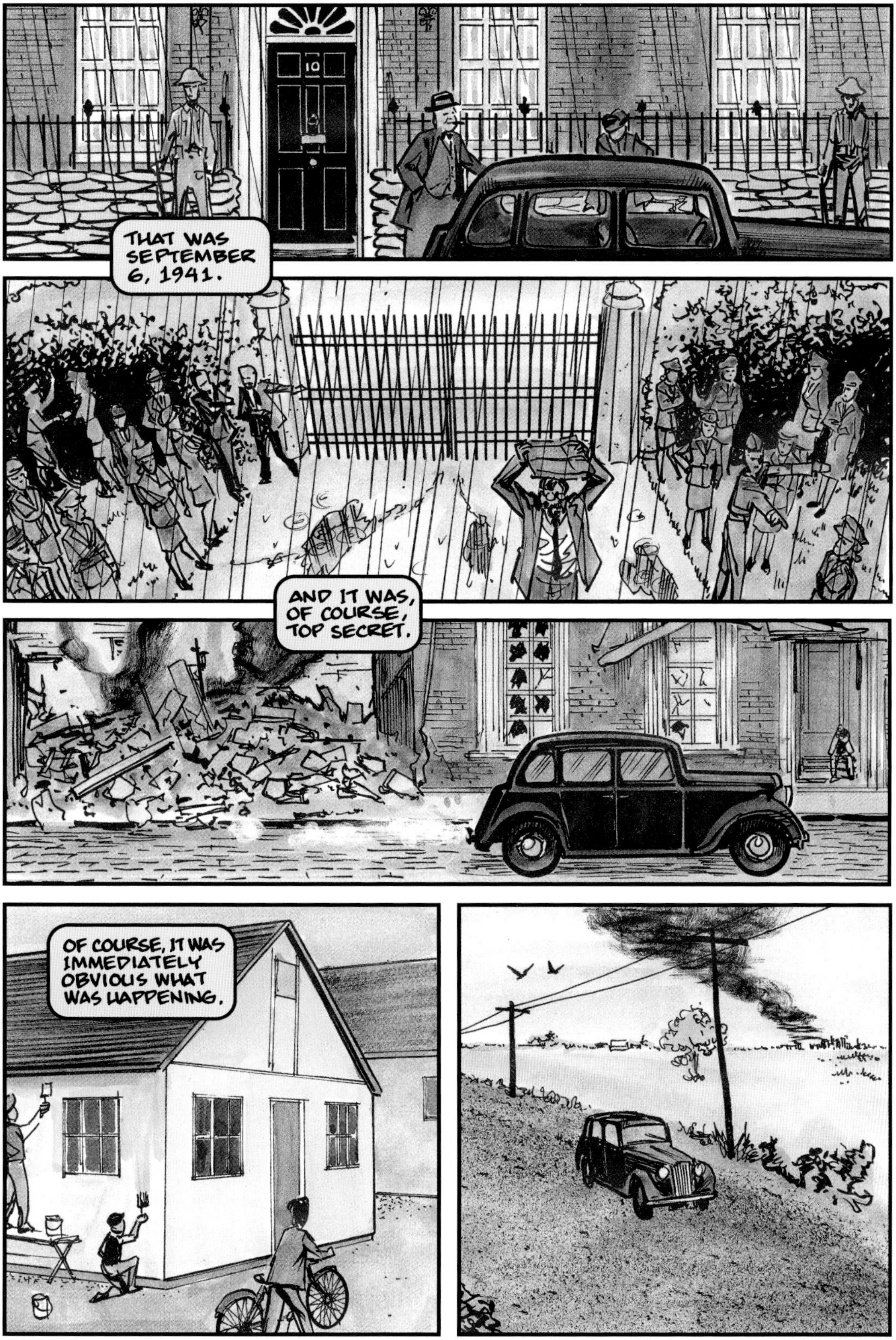
THAT WAS SEPTEMBER 6, 1941.
AND IT WAS, OF COURSE, TOP SECRET.
OF COURSE, IT WAS IMMEDIATELY OBVIOUS WHAT WAS HAPPENING.

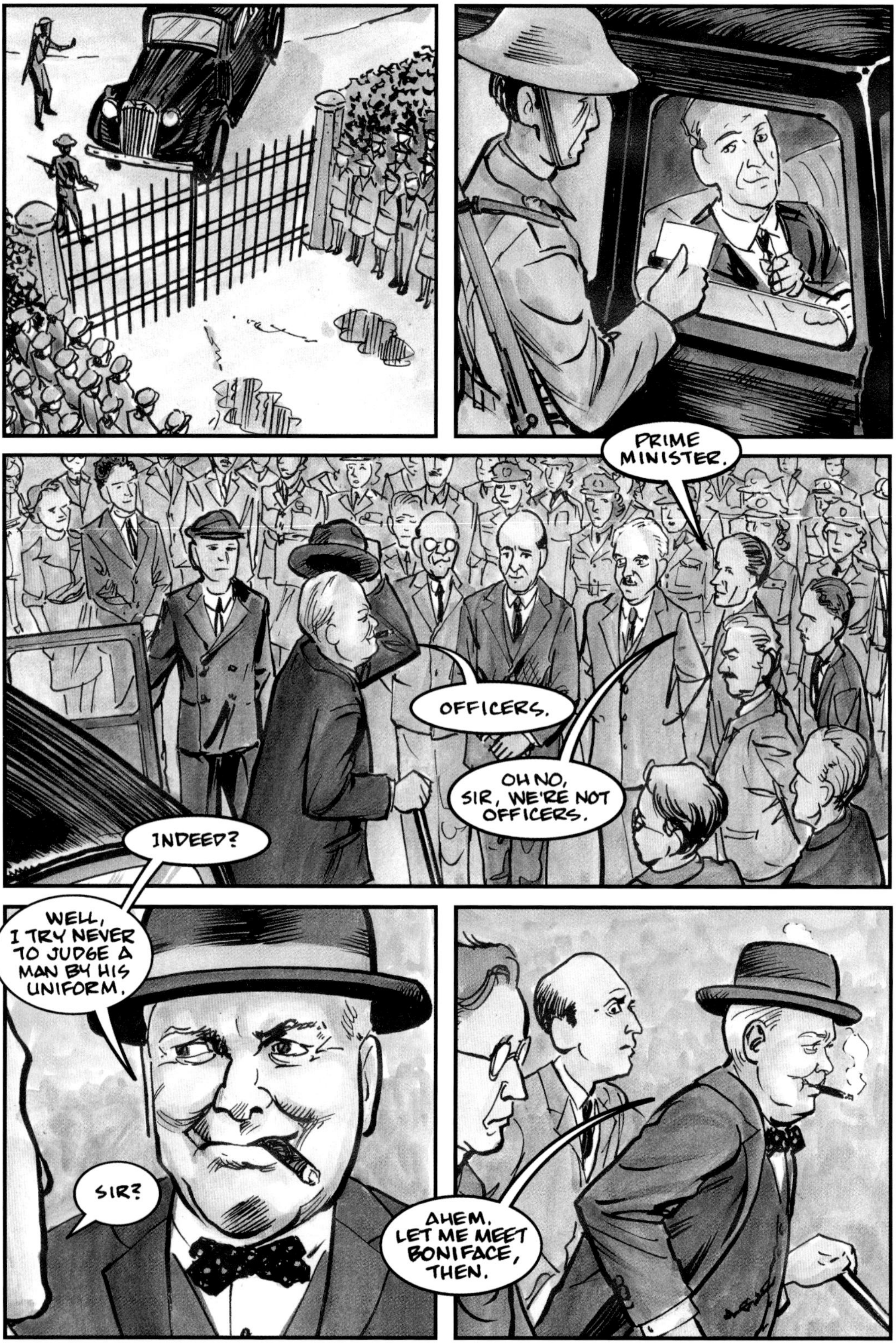
PRIME MINISTER.
OFFICERS.
OH NO, SIR, WE'RE NOT OFFICERS.
INDEED?
WELL, I TRY NEVER TO JUDGE A MAN BY HIS UNIFORM.
SIR?
AHEM. LET ME MEET BONIFACE, THEN.

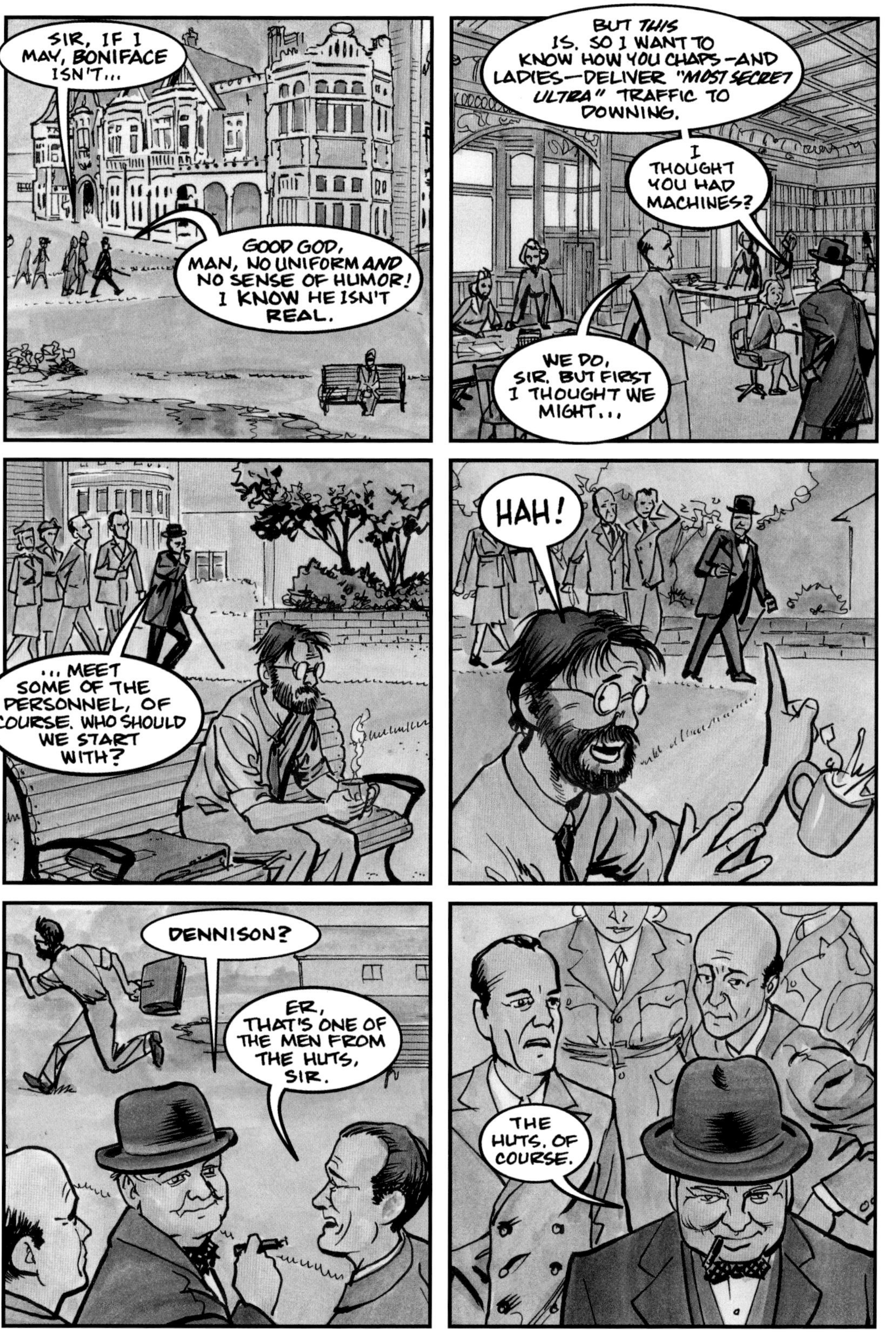
SIR, IF I MAY, BONIFACE ISN'T...
GOOD GOD, MAN, NO UNIFORM AND NO SENSE OF HUMOR! I KNOW HE ISN'T REAL.
BUT THIS IS. SO I WANT TO KNOW HOW YOU CHAPS—AND LADIES—DELIVER "MOST SECRET ULTRA" TRAFFIC TO DOWNING.
I THOUGHT YOU HAD MACHINES?
WE DO, SIR. BUT FIRST I THOUGHT WE MIGHT...
...MEET SOME OF THE PERSONNEL, OF COURSE. WHO SHOULD WE START WITH?
HAH!
DENNISON?
ER, THAT'S ONE OF THE MEN FROM THE HUTS, SIR.
THE HUTS, OF COURSE.

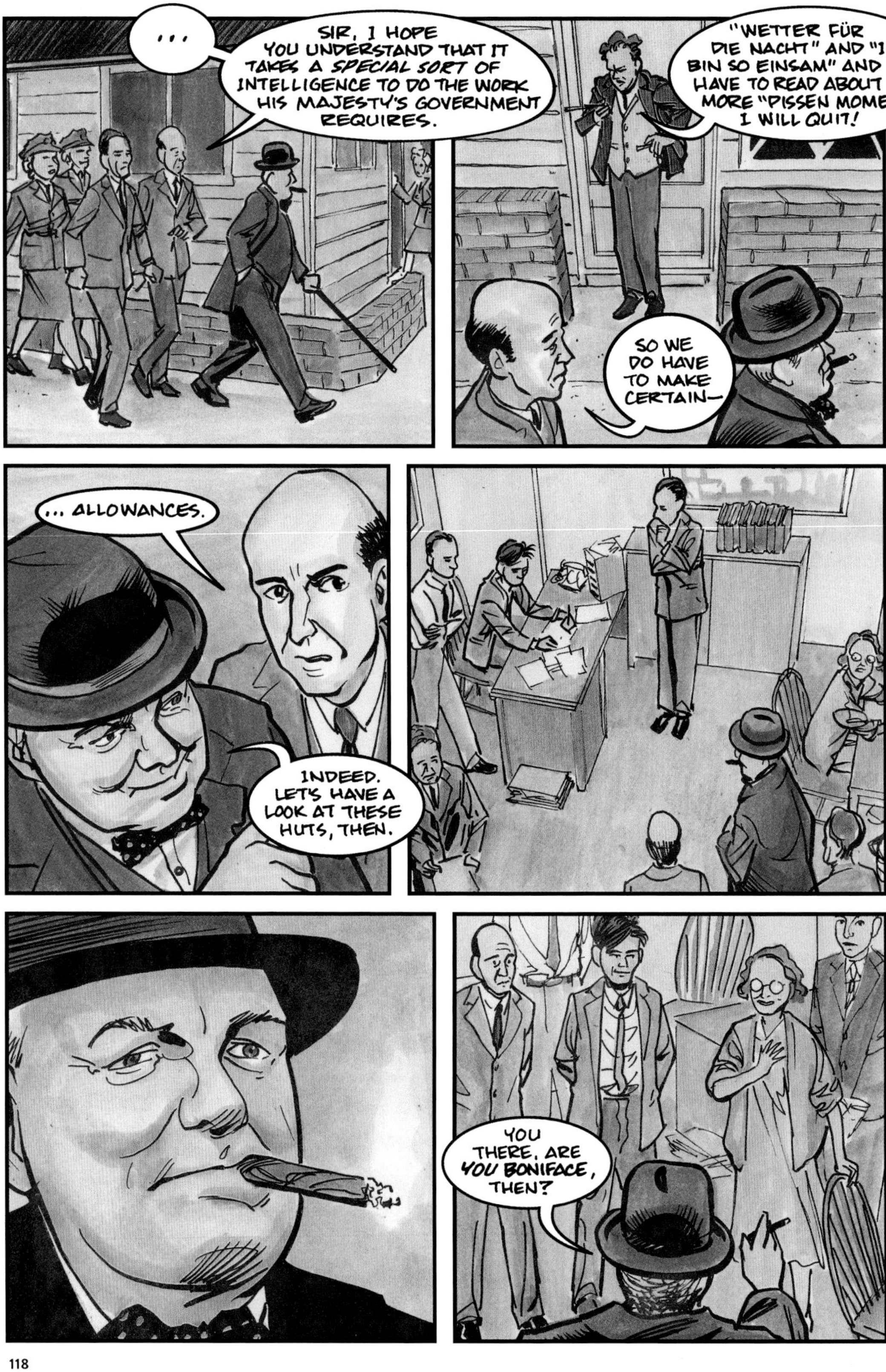
...
SIR, I HOPE YOU UNDERSTAND THAT IT TAKES A *SPECIAL SORT* OF INTELLIGENCE TO DO THE WORK HIS MAJESTY'S GOVERNMENT REQUIRES.
"WETTER FÜR DIE NACHT" AND "ICH BIN SO EINSAM" AND IF I HAVE TO READ ABOUT ONE MORE "PISSEN MOMENT" I WILL QUIT!
SO WE DO HAVE TO MAKE CERTAIN—
... ALLOWANCES.
INDEED. LET'S HAVE A LOOK AT THESE HUTS, THEN.
YOU THERE. ARE ***YOU*** BONIFACE, THEN?

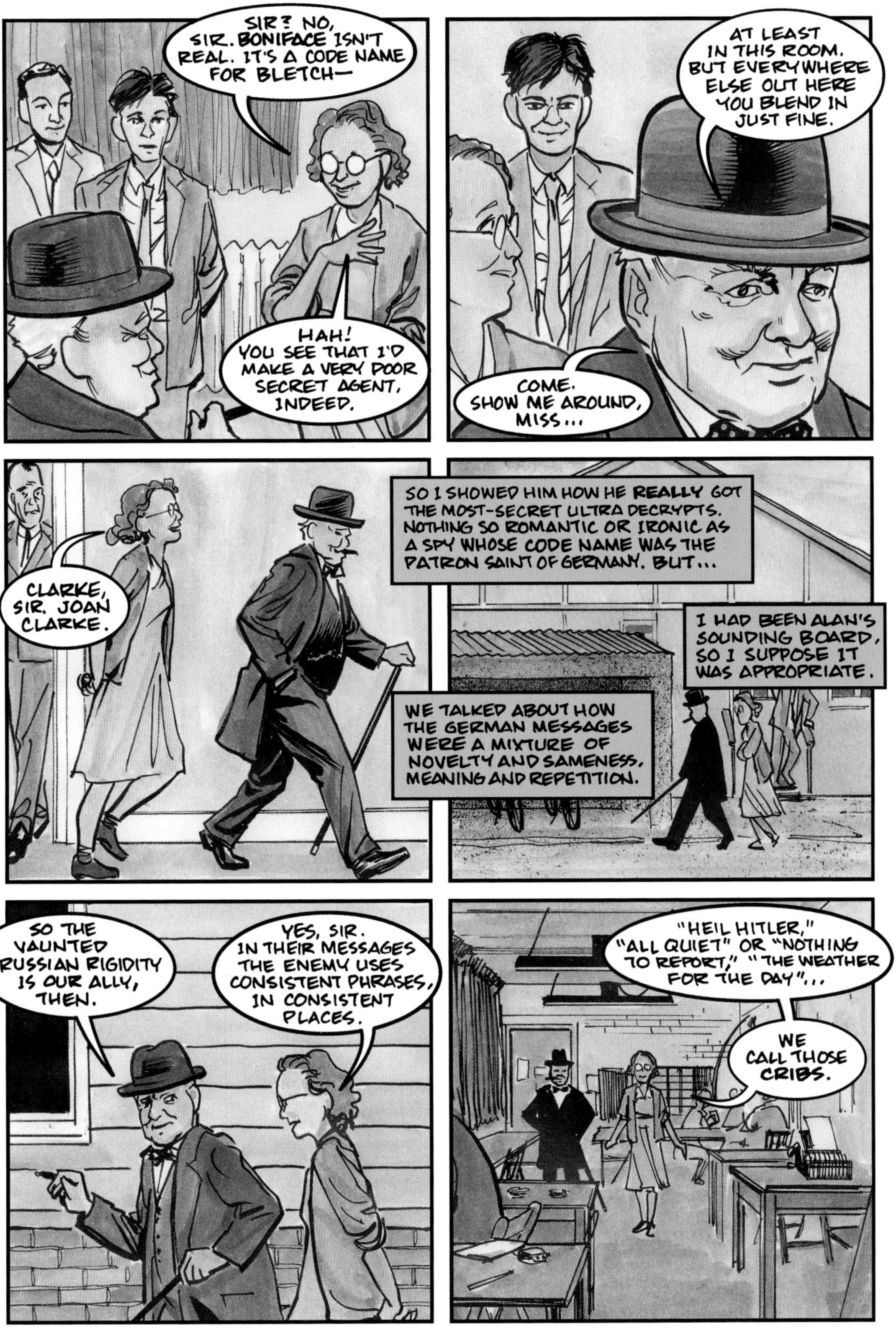
SIR? NO, SIR. BONIFACE ISN'T REAL. IT'S A CODE NAME FOR BLETCH—
HAH! YOU SEE THAT I'D MAKE A VERY POOR SECRET AGENT, INDEED.
AT LEAST IN THIS ROOM. BUT EVERYWHERE ELSE OUT HERE YOU BLEND IN JUST FINE.
COME. SHOW ME AROUND, MISS...
CLARKE, SIR. JOAN CLARKE.
SO I SHOWED HIM HOW HE REALLY GOT THE MOST-SECRET ULTRA DECRYPTS. NOTHING SO ROMANTIC OR IRONIC AS A SPY WHOSE CODE NAME WAS THE PATRON SAINT OF GERMANY. BUT...
I HAD BEEN ALAN'S SOUNDING BOARD, SO I SUPPOSE IT WAS APPROPRIATE.
WE TALKED ABOUT HOW THE GERMAN MESSAGES WERE A MIXTURE OF NOVELTY AND SAMENESS, MEANING AND REPETITION.
SO THE VAUNTED PRUSSIAN RIGIDITY IS OUR ALLY, THEN.
YES, SIR. IN THEIR MESSAGES THE ENEMY USES CONSISTENT PHRASES, IN CONSISTENT PLACES.
"HEIL HITLER," "ALL QUIET" OR "NOTHING TO REPORT," "THE WEATHER FOR THE DAY"...
WE CALL THOSE CRIBS.

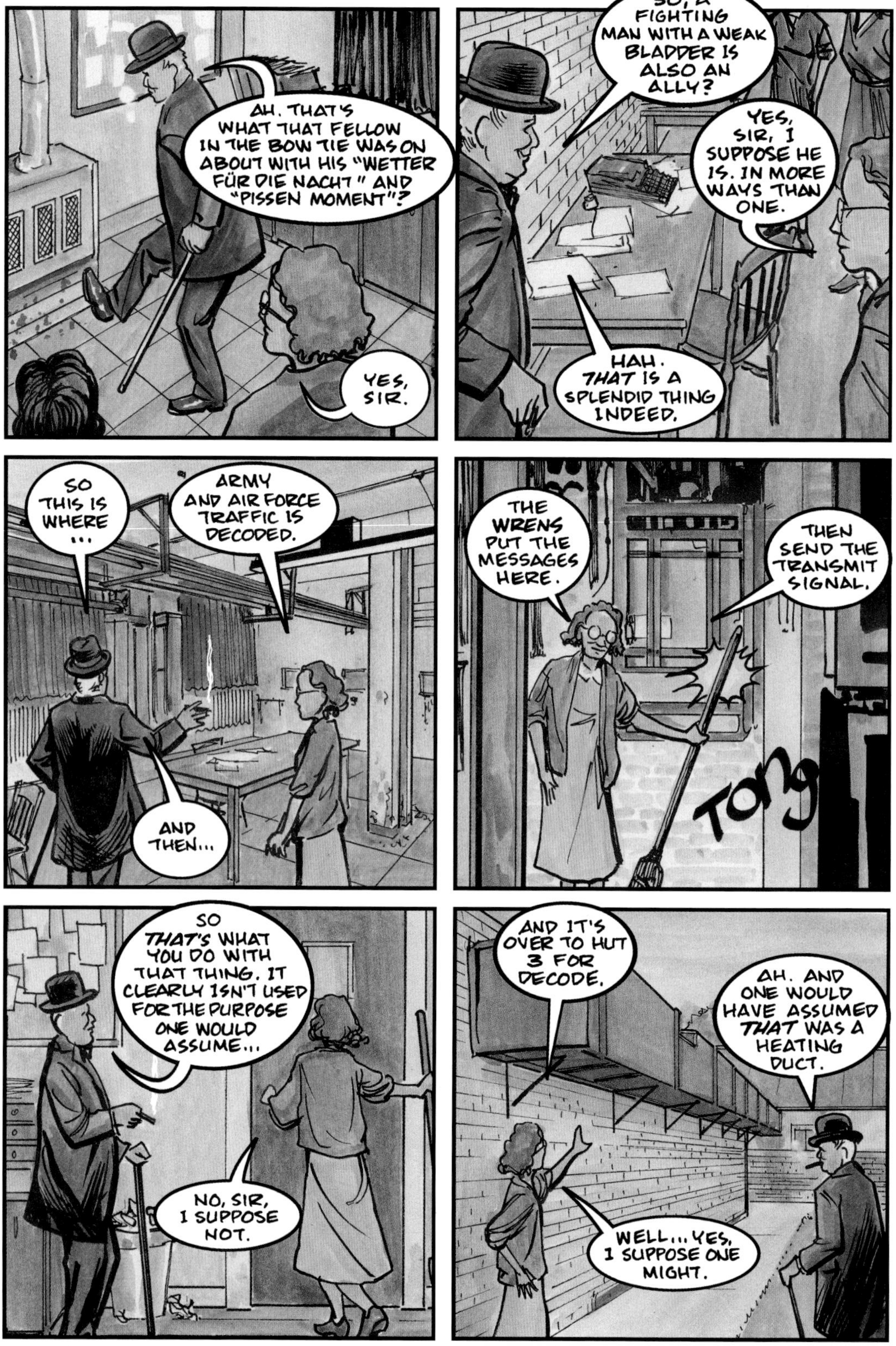

AH. THAT'S WHAT THAT FELLOW IN THE BOW TIE WAS ON ABOUT WITH HIS "WETTER FÜR DIE NACHT" AND "PISSEN MOMENT"?
YES, SIR.
SO, A FIGHTING MAN WITH A WEAK BLADDER IS ALSO AN ALLY?
YES, SIR, I SUPPOSE HE IS. IN MORE WAYS THAN ONE.
HAH. THAT IS A SPLENDID THING INDEED.
SO THIS IS WHERE ...
ARMY AND AIR FORCE TRAFFIC IS DECODED.
AND THEN...
THE WRENS PUT THE MESSAGES HERE.
THEN SEND THE TRANSMIT SIGNAL.
TONG
SO THAT'S WHAT YOU DO WITH THAT THING. IT CLEARLY ISN'T USED FOR THE PURPOSE ONE WOULD ASSUME...
NO, SIR, I SUPPOSE NOT.
AND IT'S OVER TO HUT 3 FOR DECODE.
AH. AND ONE WOULD HAVE ASSUMED THAT WAS A HEATING DUCT.
WELL... YES, I SUPPOSE ONE MIGHT.

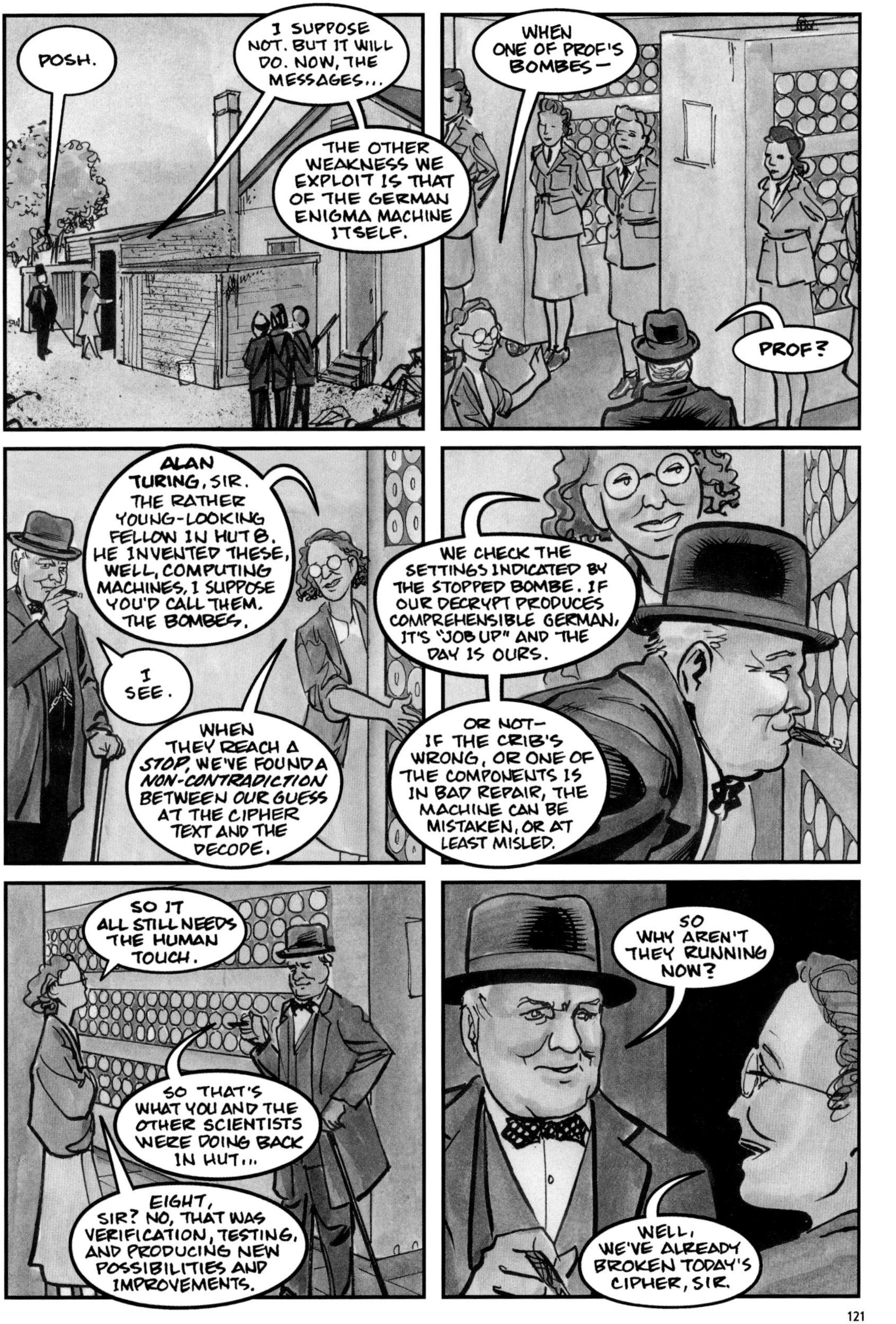
POSH.
I SUPPOSE NOT. BUT IT WILL DO. NOW, THE MESSAGES...
THE OTHER WEAKNESS WE EXPLOIT IS THAT OF THE GERMAN ENIGMA MACHINE ITSELF.
WHEN ONE OF PROF'S BOMBES—
PROF?
ALAN TURING, SIR. THE RATHER YOUNG-LOOKING FELLOW IN HUT 8. HE INVENTED THESE, WELL, COMPUTING MACHINES, I SUPPOSE YOU'D CALL THEM. THE BOMBES.
I SEE.
WHEN THEY REACH A STOP, WE'VE FOUND A NON-CONTRADICTION BETWEEN OUR GUESS AT THE CIPHER TEXT AND THE DECODE.
WE CHECK THE SETTINGS INDICATED BY THE STOPPED BOMBE. IF OUR DECRYPT PRODUCES COMPREHENSIBLE GERMAN, IT'S "JOB UP" AND THE DAY IS OURS.
OR NOT— IF THE CRIB'S WRONG, OR ONE OF THE COMPONENTS IS IN BAD REPAIR, THE MACHINE CAN BE MISTAKEN, OR AT LEAST MISLED.
SO IT ALL STILL NEEDS THE HUMAN TOUCH.
SO THAT'S WHAT YOU AND THE OTHER SCIENTISTS WERE DOING BACK IN HUT...
EIGHT, SIR? NO, THAT WAS VERIFICATION, TESTING, AND PRODUCING NEW POSSIBILITIES AND IMPROVEMENTS.
SO WHY AREN'T THEY RUNNING NOW?
WELL, WE'VE ALREADY BROKEN TODAY'S CIPHER, SIR.

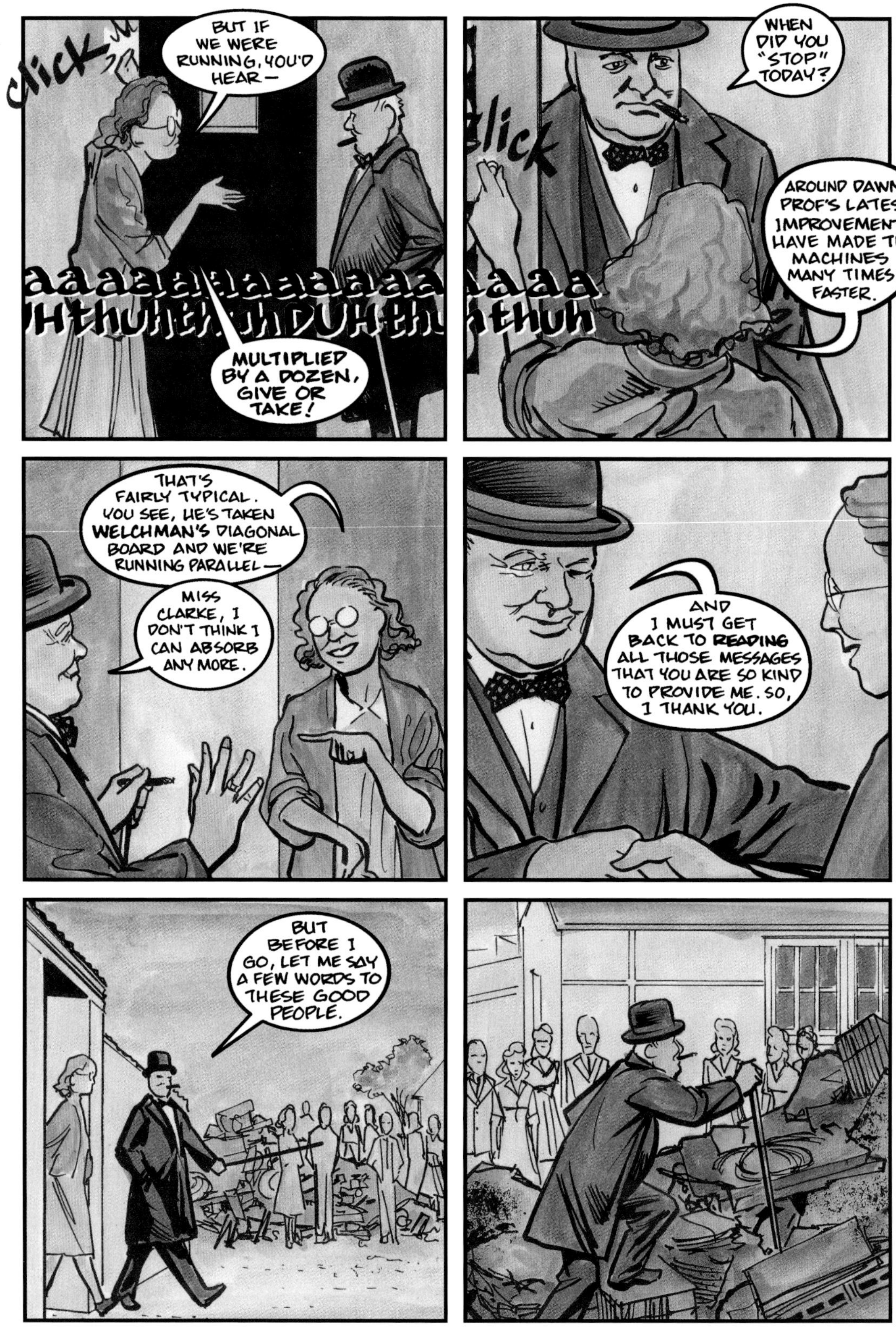
click
BUT IF WE WERE RUNNING, YOU'D HEAR—
MULTIPLIED BY A DOZEN, GIVE OR TAKE!
WHEN DID YOU "STOP" TODAY?
AROUND DAWN. PROF'S LATEST IMPROVEMENTS HAVE MADE THE MACHINES MANY TIMES FASTER.
THAT'S FAIRLY TYPICAL. YOU SEE, HE'S TAKEN WELCHMAN'S DIAGONAL BOARD AND WE'RE RUNNING PARALLEL—
MISS CLARKE, I DON'T THINK I CAN ABSORB ANY MORE.
AND I MUST GET BACK TO READING ALL THOSE MESSAGES THAT YOU ARE SO KIND TO PROVIDE ME. SO, I THANK YOU.
BUT BEFORE I GO, LET ME SAY A FEW WORDS TO THESE GOOD PEOPLE.

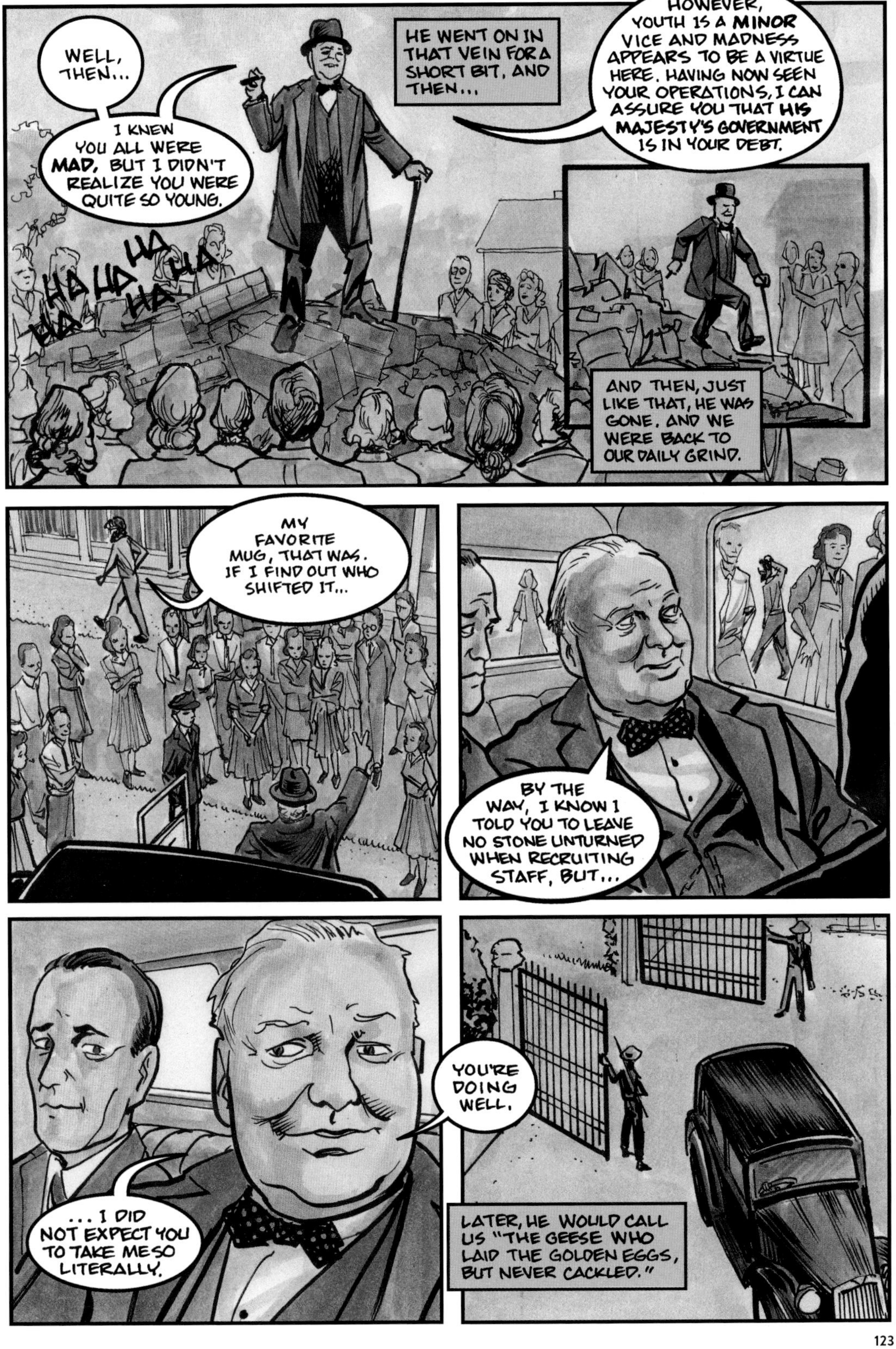
WELL, THEN...
I KNEW YOU ALL WERE MAD, BUT I DIDN'T REALIZE YOU WERE QUITE SO YOUNG.
HA HA HA HA HA HA
HE WENT ON IN THAT VEIN FOR A SHORT BIT, AND THEN...
HOWEVER, YOUTH IS A MINOR VICE AND MADNESS APPEARS TO BE A VIRTUE HERE. HAVING NOW SEEN YOUR OPERATIONS, I CAN ASSURE YOU THAT HIS MAJESTY'S GOVERNMENT IS IN YOUR DEBT.
AND THEN, JUST LIKE THAT, HE WAS GONE. AND WE WERE BACK TO OUR DAILY GRIND.
MY FAVORITE MUG, THAT WAS. IF I FIND OUT WHO SHIFTED IT...
BY THE WAY, I KNOW I TOLD YOU TO LEAVE NO STONE UNTURNED WHEN RECRUITING STAFF, BUT...
YOU'RE DOING WELL.
...I DID NOT EXPECT YOU TO TAKE ME SO LITERALLY.
LATER, HE WOULD CALL US "THE GEESE WHO LAID THE GOLDEN EGGS, BUT NEVER CACKLED."

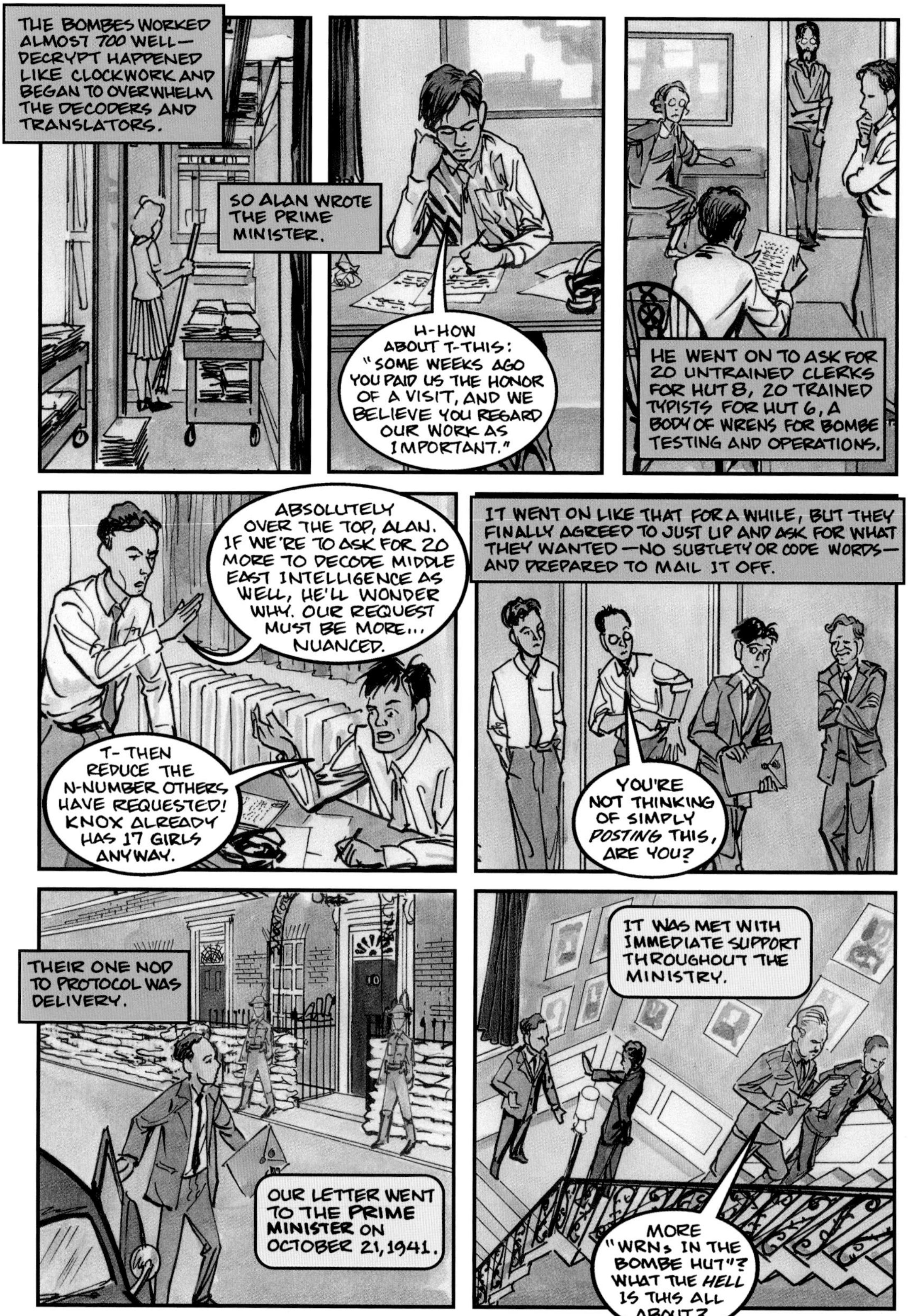
THE BOMBES WORKED ALMOST TOO WELL—DECRYPT HAPPENED LIKE CLOCKWORK AND BEGAN TO OVERWHELM THE DECODERS AND TRANSLATORS.
SO ALAN WROTE THE PRIME MINISTER.
H-HOW ABOUT T-THIS: "SOME WEEKS AGO YOU PAID US THE HONOR OF A VISIT, AND WE BELIEVE YOU REGARD OUR WORK AS IMPORTANT."
HE WENT ON TO ASK FOR 20 UNTRAINED CLERKS FOR HUT 8, 20 TRAINED TYPISTS FOR HUT 6, A BODY OF WRENS FOR BOMBE TESTING AND OPERATIONS.
ABSOLUTELY OVER THE TOP, ALAN. IF WE'RE TO ASK FOR 20 MORE TO DECODE MIDDLE EAST INTELLIGENCE AS WELL, HE'LL WONDER WHY. OUR REQUEST MUST BE MORE... NUANCED.
T-THEN REDUCE THE N-NUMBER OTHERS HAVE REQUESTED! KNOX ALREADY HAS 17 GIRLS ANYWAY.
IT WENT ON LIKE THAT FOR A WHILE, BUT THEY FINALLY AGREED TO JUST UP AND ASK FOR WHAT THEY WANTED—NO SUBTLETY OR CODE WORDS—AND PREPARED TO MAIL IT OFF.
YOU'RE NOT THINKING OF SIMPLY *POSTING* THIS, ARE YOU?
THEIR ONE NOD TO PROTOCOL WAS DELIVERY.
10
OUR LETTER WENT TO THE **PRIME MINISTER** ON OCTOBER 21, 1941.
IT WAS MET WITH IMMEDIATE SUPPORT THROUGHOUT THE MINISTRY.
MORE "WRNs IN THE BOMBE HUT"? WHAT THE *HELL* IS THIS ALL ABOUT?

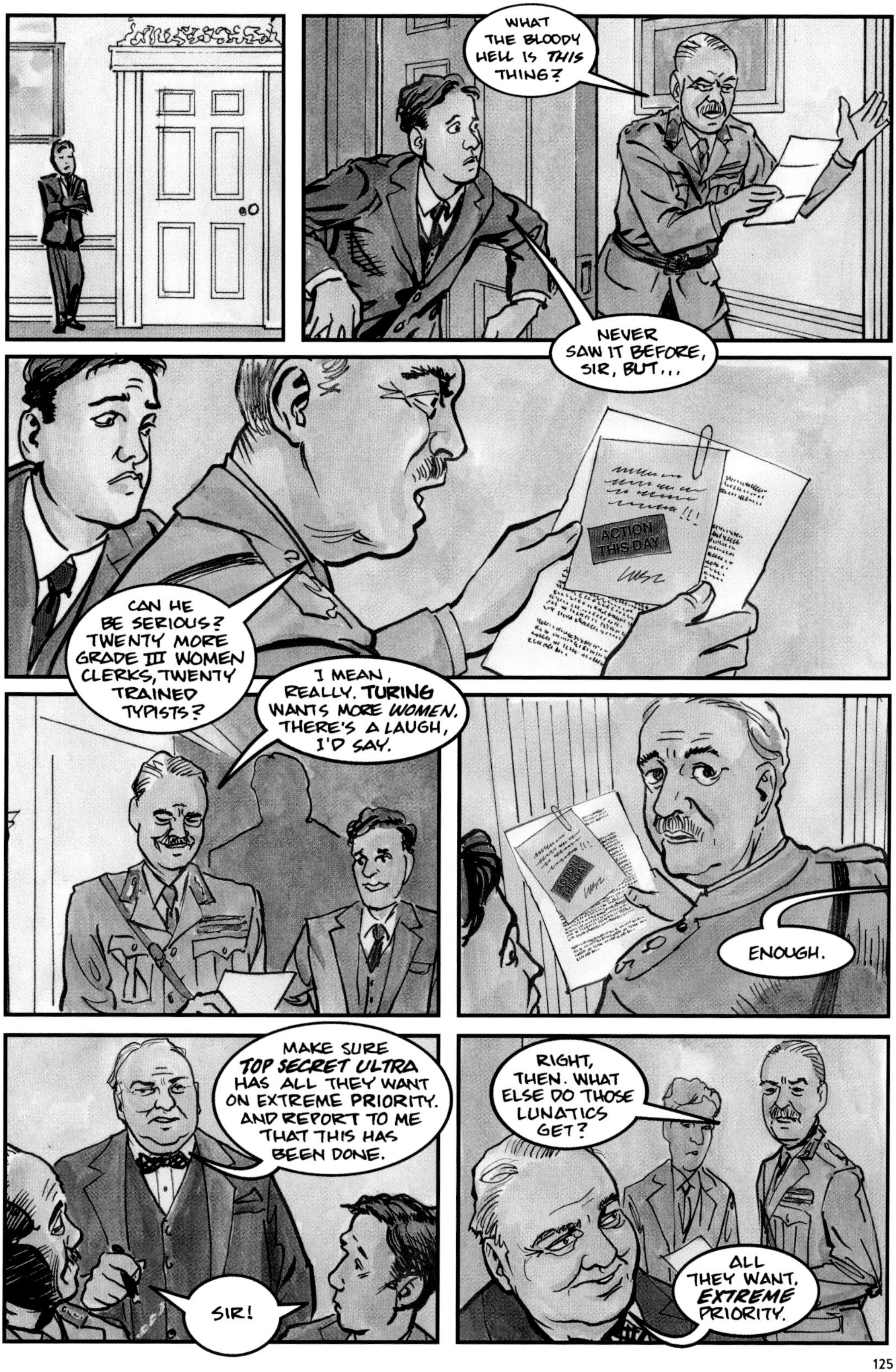
WHAT THE BLOODY HELL IS THIS THING?
NEVER SAW IT BEFORE, SIR, BUT...
ACTION THIS DAY
CAN HE BE SERIOUS? TWENTY MORE GRADE III WOMEN CLERKS, TWENTY TRAINED TYPISTS?
I MEAN, REALLY. TURING WANTS MORE WOMEN. THERE'S A LAUGH, I'D SAY.
ACTION THIS DAY
ENOUGH.
MAKE SURE TOP SECRET ULTRA HAS ALL THEY WANT ON EXTREME PRIORITY. AND REPORT TO ME THAT THIS HAS BEEN DONE.
SIR!
RIGHT, THEN. WHAT ELSE DO THOSE LUNATICS GET?
ALL THEY WANT. EXTREME PRIORITY.

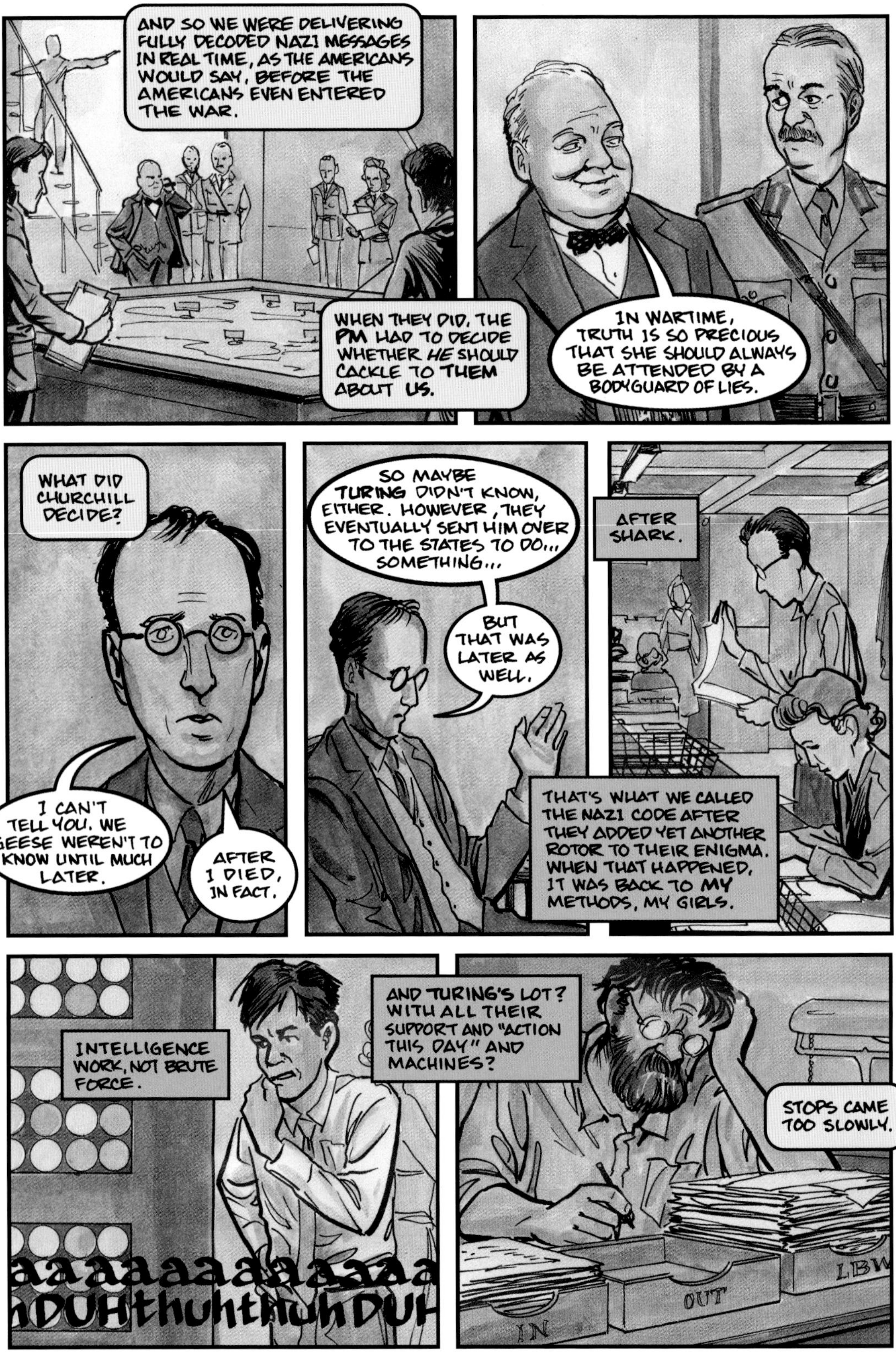
AND SO WE WERE DELIVERING FULLY DECODED NAZI MESSAGES IN REAL TIME, AS THE AMERICANS WOULD SAY, BEFORE THE AMERICANS EVEN ENTERED THE WAR.
WHEN THEY DID, THE PM HAD TO DECIDE WHETHER HE SHOULD CACKLE TO THEM ABOUT US.
IN WARTIME, TRUTH IS SO PRECIOUS THAT SHE SHOULD ALWAYS BE ATTENDED BY A BODYGUARD OF LIES.
WHAT DID CHURCHILL DECIDE?
I CAN'T TELL YOU. WE GEESE WEREN'T TO KNOW UNTIL MUCH LATER.
AFTER I DIED, IN FACT.
SO MAYBE TURING DIDN'T KNOW, EITHER. HOWEVER, THEY EVENTUALLY SENT HIM OVER TO THE STATES TO DO... SOMETHING...
BUT THAT WAS LATER AS WELL.
AFTER SHARK.
THAT'S WHAT WE CALLED THE NAZI CODE AFTER THEY ADDED YET ANOTHER ROTOR TO THEIR ENIGMA. WHEN THAT HAPPENED, IT WAS BACK TO MY METHODS, MY GIRLS.
INTELLIGENCE WORK, NOT BRUTE FORCE.
aaaaaaaaaaaaaa
hDUHthuhthuhDUH
AND TURING'S LOT? WITH ALL THEIR SUPPORT AND "ACTION THIS DAY" AND MACHINES?
STOPS CAME TOO SLOWLY.
IN
OUT
LBW

SO, BACK TO CRYPTOGRAPHY AND INTELLIGENCE —INSEPARABLE AS THEY SHOULD BE. I WAS GLAD TO HAVE HAD MY LETTERS OF RESIGNATION GO UNHEEDED.

aaaaaaaaaaaa nuhthuh DUH thuht!

SOMETIMES THE BOMBES WORKED-INITIALLY NOT ALL GERMAN RECEIVING STATIONS HAD THE NEW MACHINE.

BUT EVENTUALLY ALL STATIONS DID, AND EVERYONE WAS BACK TO DOING "DILLYISMUS" AND OTHER KNOX METHODS.

BY HAND.

UNTIL OCTOBER 30 ...

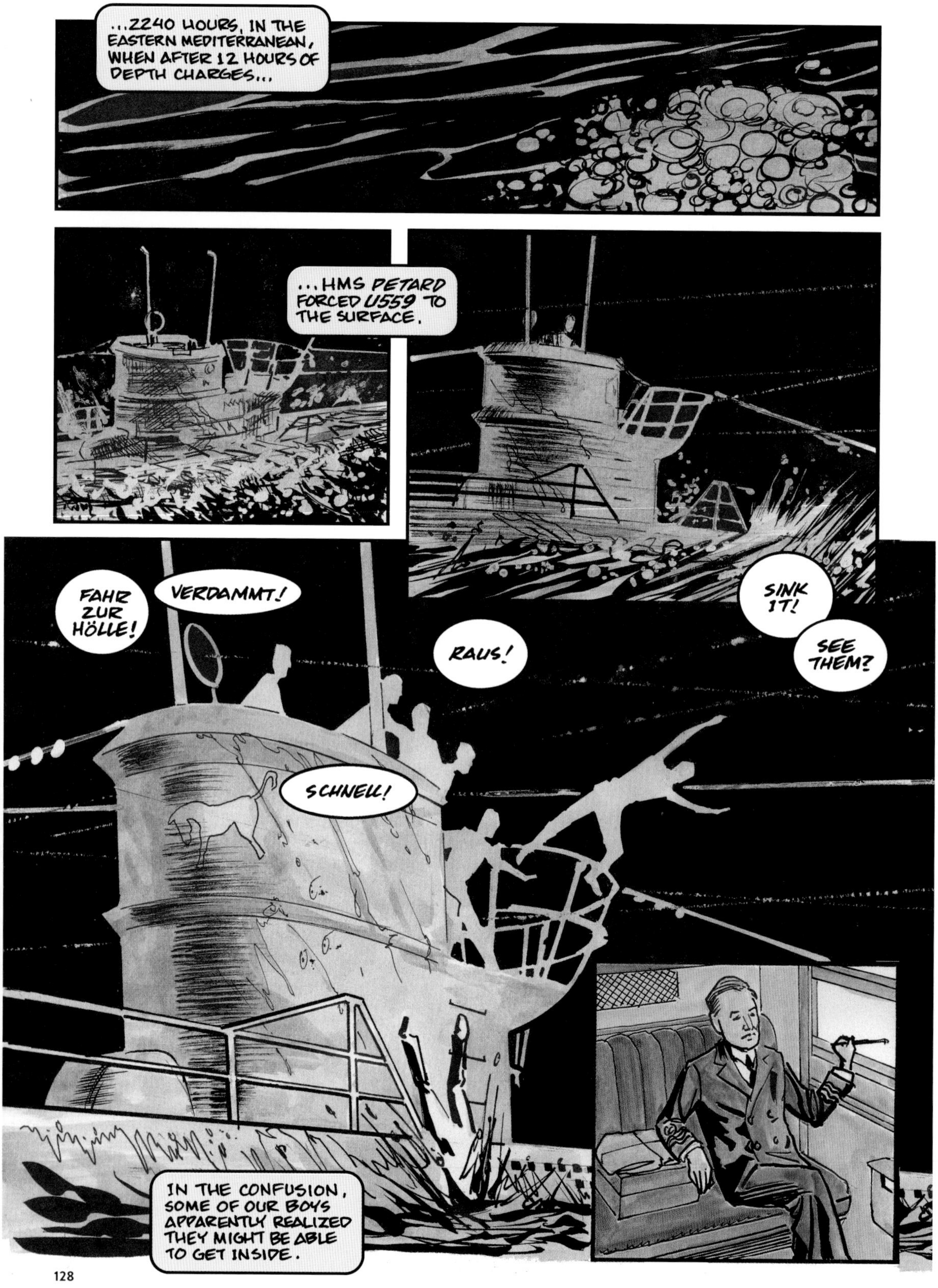
...2240 HOURS, IN THE EASTERN MEDITERRANEAN, WHEN AFTER 12 HOURS OF DEPTH CHARGES...
...HMS *PETARD* FORCED *U559* TO THE SURFACE.
FAHR ZUR HÖLLE!
VERDAMMT!
RAUS!
SINK IT!
SEE THEM?
SCHNELL!
IN THE CONFUSION, SOME OF OUR BOYS APPARENTLY REALIZED THEY MIGHT BE ABLE TO GET INSIDE.

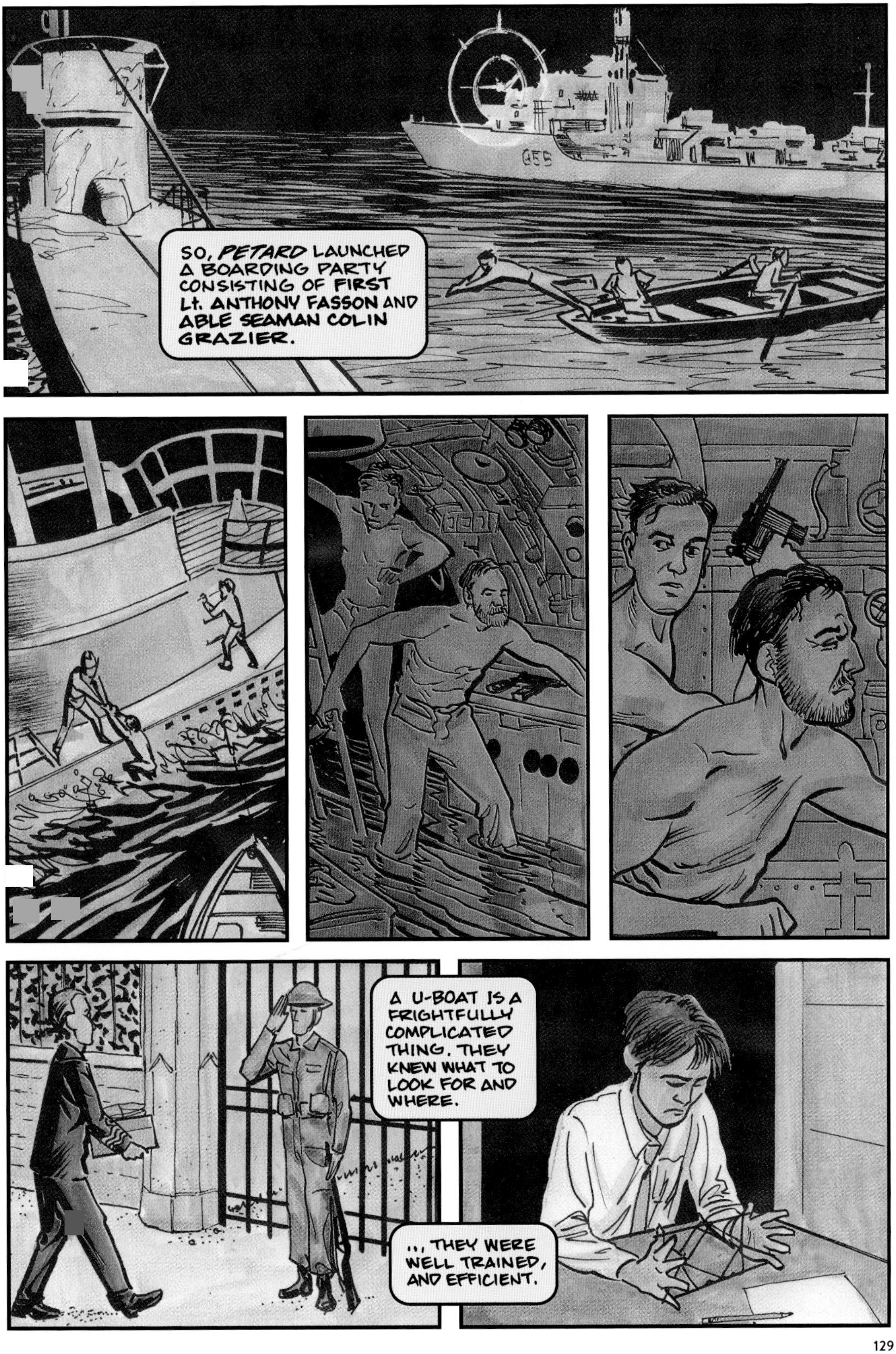
SO, PETARD LAUNCHED A BOARDING PARTY CONSISTING OF FIRST Lt. ANTHONY FASSON AND ABLE SEAMAN COLIN GRAZIER.
A U-BOAT IS A FRIGHTFULLY COMPLICATED THING. THEY KNEW WHAT TO LOOK FOR AND WHERE.
..., THEY WERE WELL TRAINED, AND EFFICIENT.

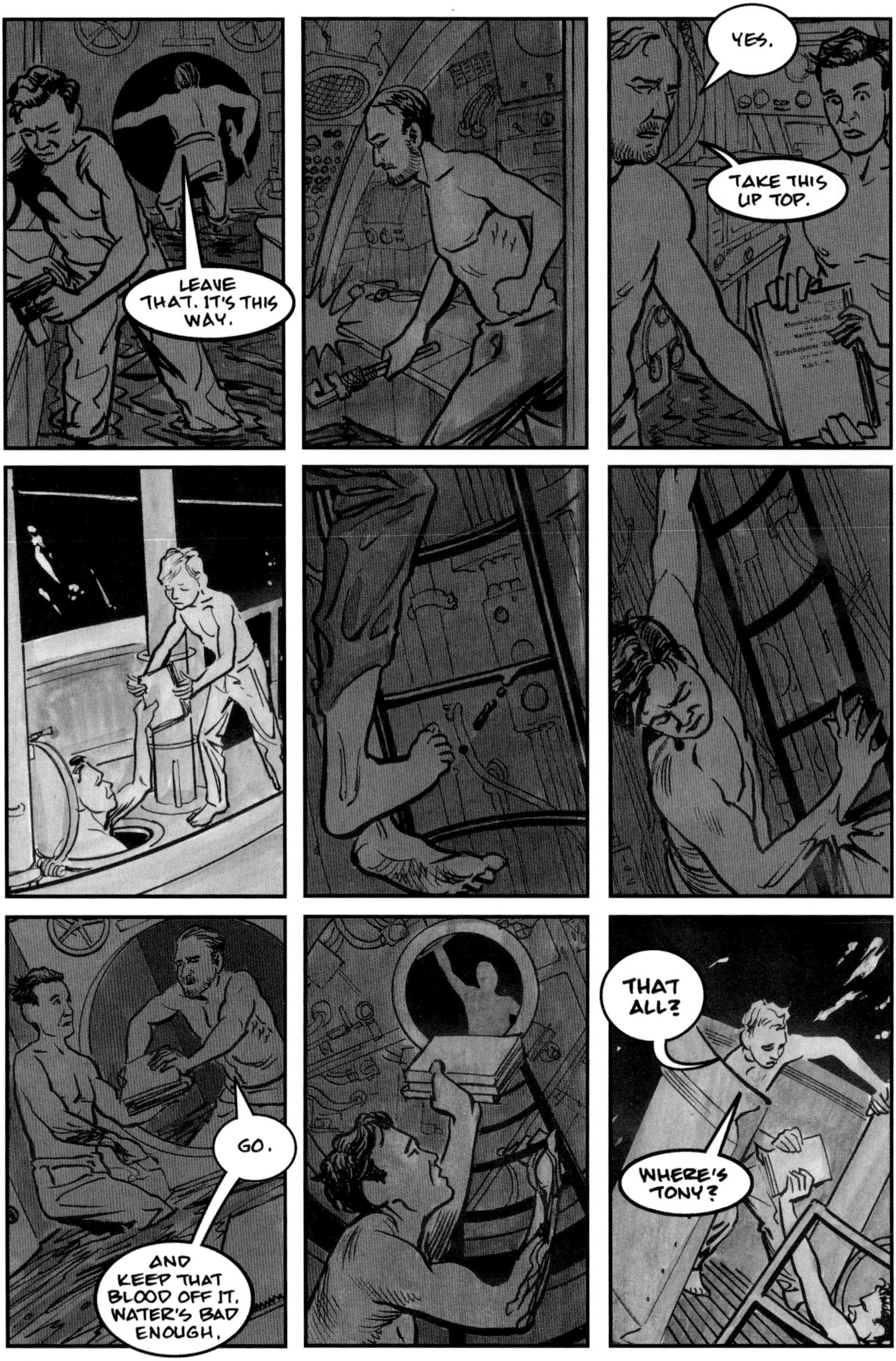
LEAVE THAT. IT'S THIS WAY.
YES.
TAKE THIS UP TOP.
GO.
AND KEEP THAT BLOOD OFF IT. WATER'S BAD ENOUGH.
THAT ALL?
WHERE'S TONY?

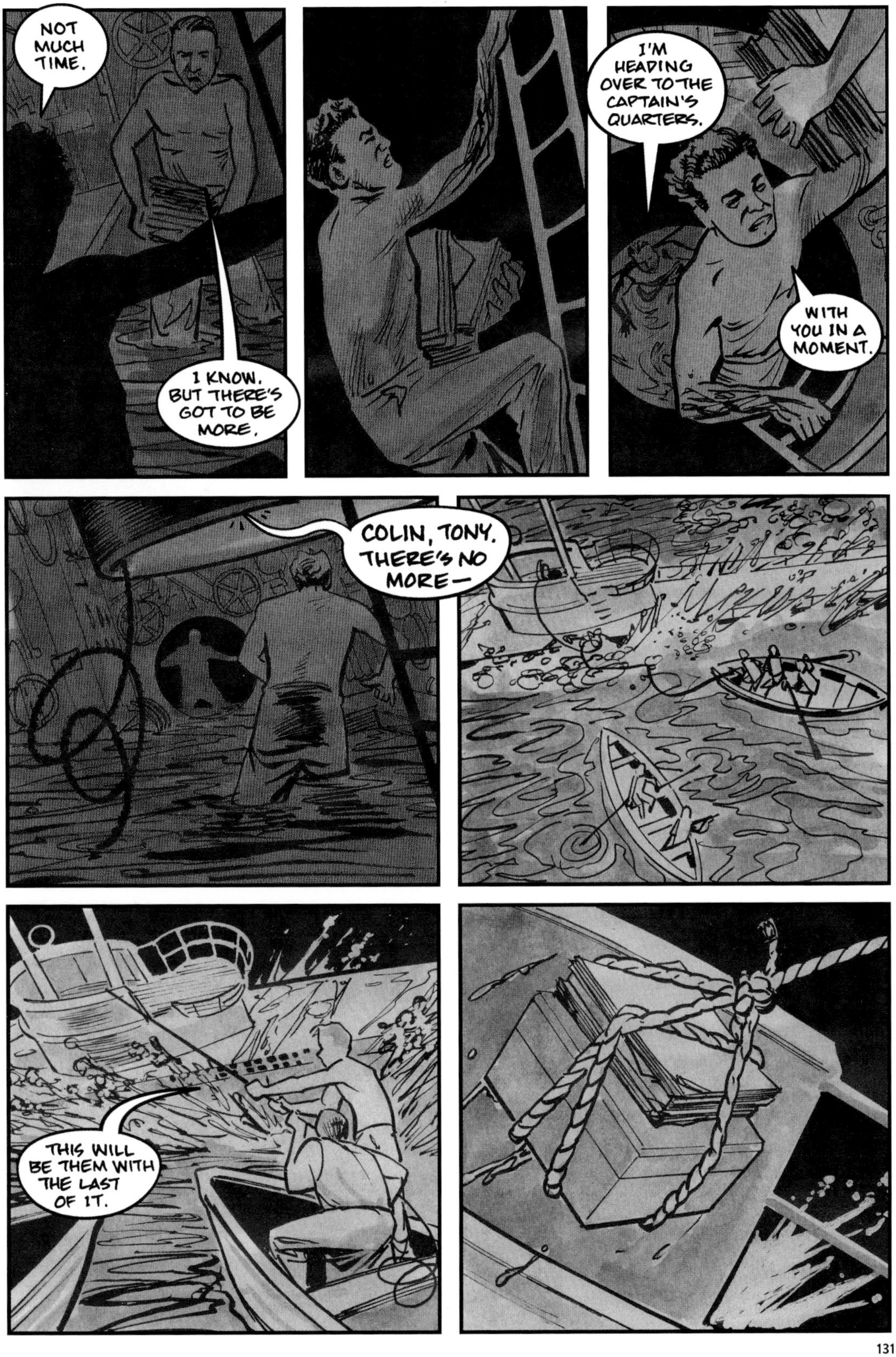
NOT MUCH TIME.
I KNOW. BUT THERE'S GOT TO BE MORE.
I'M HEADING OVER TO THE CAPTAIN'S QUARTERS.
WITH YOU IN A MOMENT.
COLIN, TONY. THERE'S NO MORE—
THIS WILL BE THEM WITH THE LAST OF IT.

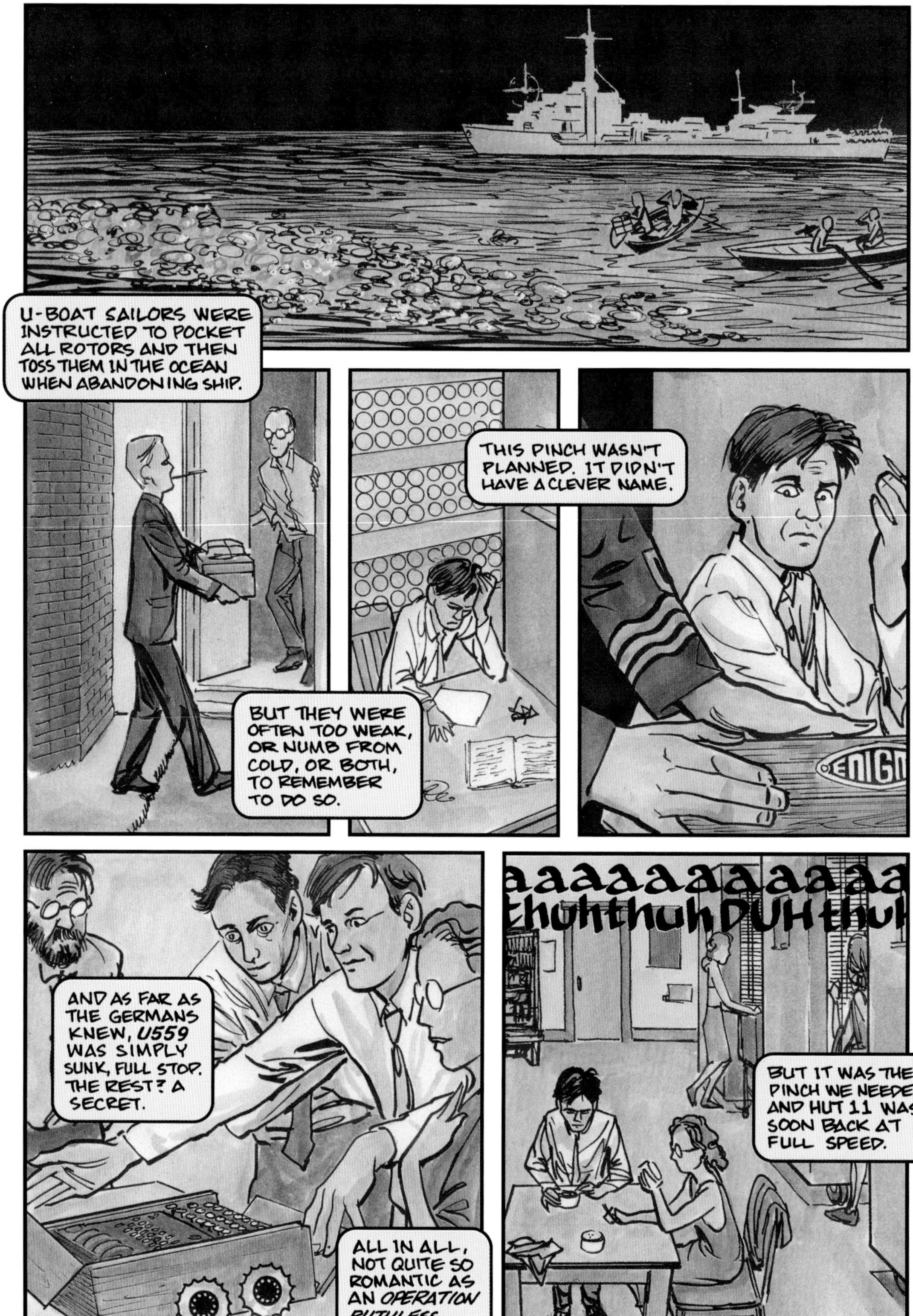
U-BOAT SAILORS WERE INSTRUCTED TO POCKET ALL ROTORS AND THEN TOSS THEM IN THE OCEAN WHEN ABANDONING SHIP.
BUT THEY WERE OFTEN TOO WEAK, OR NUMB FROM COLD, OR BOTH, TO REMEMBER TO DO SO.
THIS PINCH WASN'T PLANNED. IT DIDN'T HAVE A CLEVER NAME.
ENIGM
AND AS FAR AS THE GERMANS KNEW, *U559* WAS SIMPLY SUNK, FULL STOP. THE REST? A SECRET.
ALL IN ALL, NOT QUITE SO ROMANTIC AS AN *OPERATION RUTHLESS*.
aaaaaaaaaaaa
thuhthuhDUHthuh
BUT IT WAS THE PINCH WE NEEDED, AND HUT 11 WAS SOON BACK AT FULL SPEED.

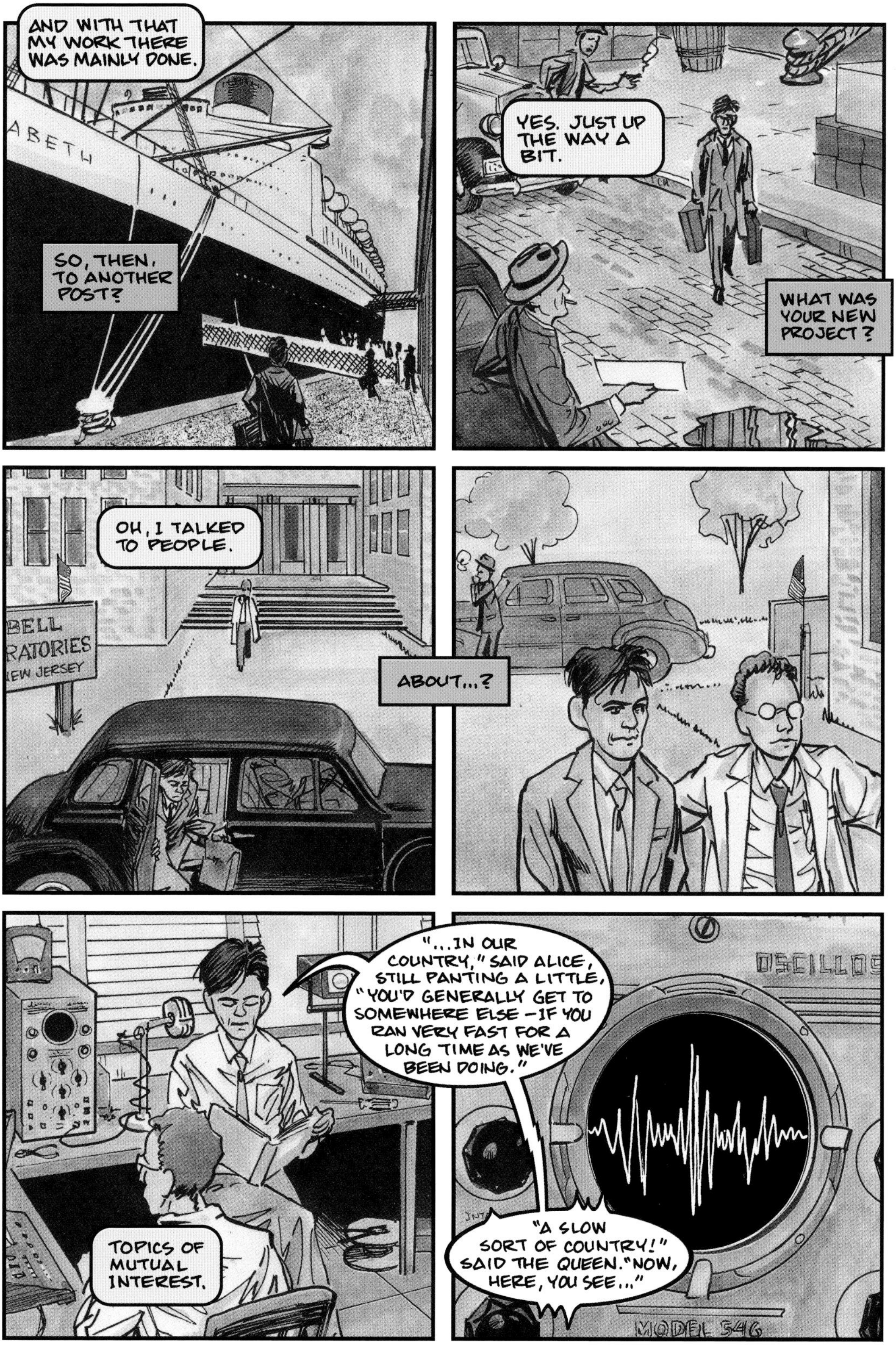
AND WITH THAT MY WORK THERE WAS MAINLY DONE.
ABETH
SO, THEN, TO ANOTHER POST?
YES. JUST UP THE WAY A BIT.
WHAT WAS YOUR NEW PROJECT?
OH, I TALKED TO PEOPLE.
BELL
RATORIES
NEW JERSEY
ABOUT...?
TOPICS OF MUTUAL INTEREST.
"...IN OUR COUNTRY," SAID ALICE, STILL PANTING A LITTLE, "YOU'D GENERALLY GET TO SOMEWHERE ELSE—IF YOU RAN VERY FAST FOR A LONG TIME AS WE'VE BEEN DOING."
OSCILLOS
"A SLOW SORT OF COUNTRY!" SAID THE QUEEN. "NOW, HERE, YOU SEE..."
MODEL 546

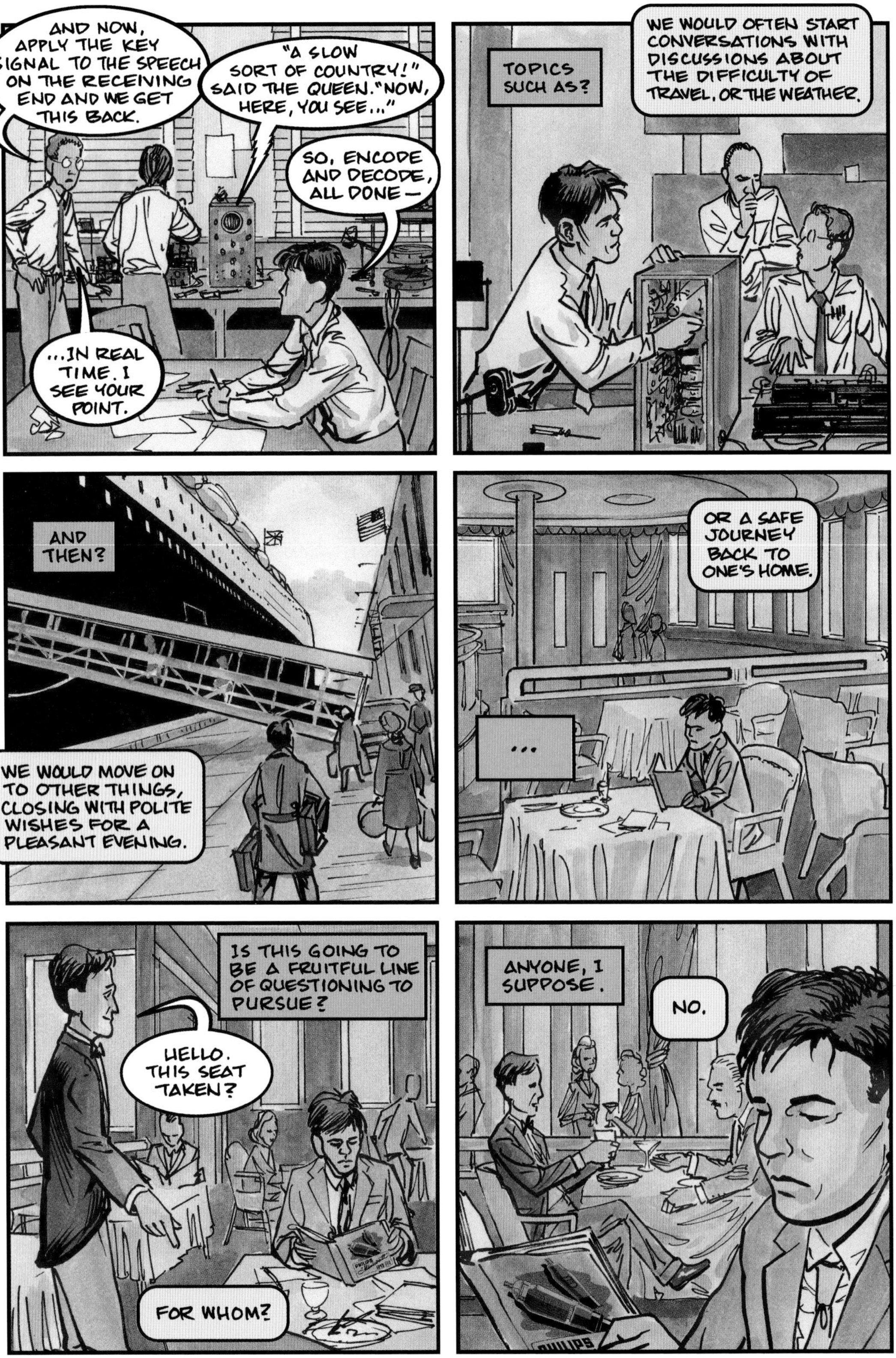
AND NOW, APPLY THE KEY SIGNAL TO THE SPEECH ON THE RECEIVING END AND WE GET THIS BACK.
"A SLOW SORT OF COUNTRY!" SAID THE QUEEN. "NOW, HERE, YOU SEE..."
SO, ENCODE AND DECODE, ALL DONE—
...IN REAL TIME. I SEE YOUR POINT.
TOPICS SUCH AS?
WE WOULD OFTEN START CONVERSATIONS WITH DISCUSSIONS ABOUT THE DIFFICULTY OF TRAVEL, OR THE WEATHER.
AND THEN?
WE WOULD MOVE ON TO OTHER THINGS, CLOSING WITH POLITE WISHES FOR A PLEASANT EVENING.
OR A SAFE JOURNEY BACK TO ONE'S HOME.
...
IS THIS GOING TO BE A FRUITFUL LINE OF QUESTIONING TO PURSUE?
HELLO. THIS SEAT TAKEN?
FOR WHOM?
ANYONE, I SUPPOSE.
NO.
PHILIPS

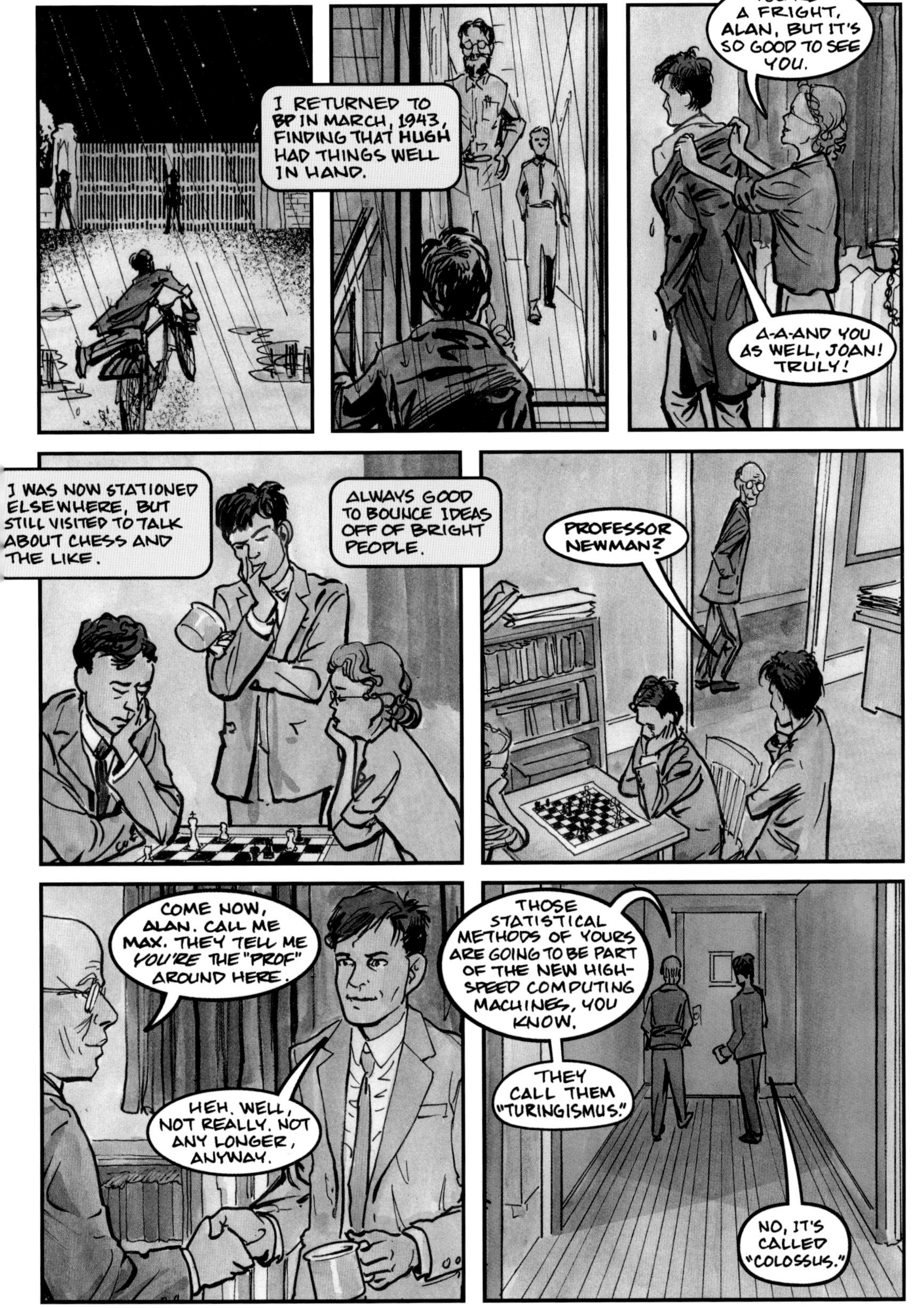
I RETURNED TO BP IN MARCH, 1943, FINDING THAT HUGH HAD THINGS WELL IN HAND.
YOU'RE A FRIGHT, ALAN, BUT IT'S SO GOOD TO SEE YOU.
A-A-AND YOU AS WELL, JOAN! TRULY!
I WAS NOW STATIONED ELSEWHERE, BUT STILL VISITED TO TALK ABOUT CHESS AND THE LIKE.
ALWAYS GOOD TO BOUNCE IDEAS OFF OF BRIGHT PEOPLE.
PROFESSOR NEWMAN?
COME NOW, ALAN. CALL ME MAX. THEY TELL ME *YOU'RE* THE "PROF" AROUND HERE.
HEH. WELL, NOT REALLY. NOT ANY LONGER, ANYWAY.
THOSE STATISTICAL METHODS OF YOURS ARE GOING TO BE PART OF THE NEW HIGH-SPEED COMPUTING MACHINES, YOU KNOW.
THEY CALL THEM "TURINGISMUS."
NO, IT'S CALLED "COLOSSUS."

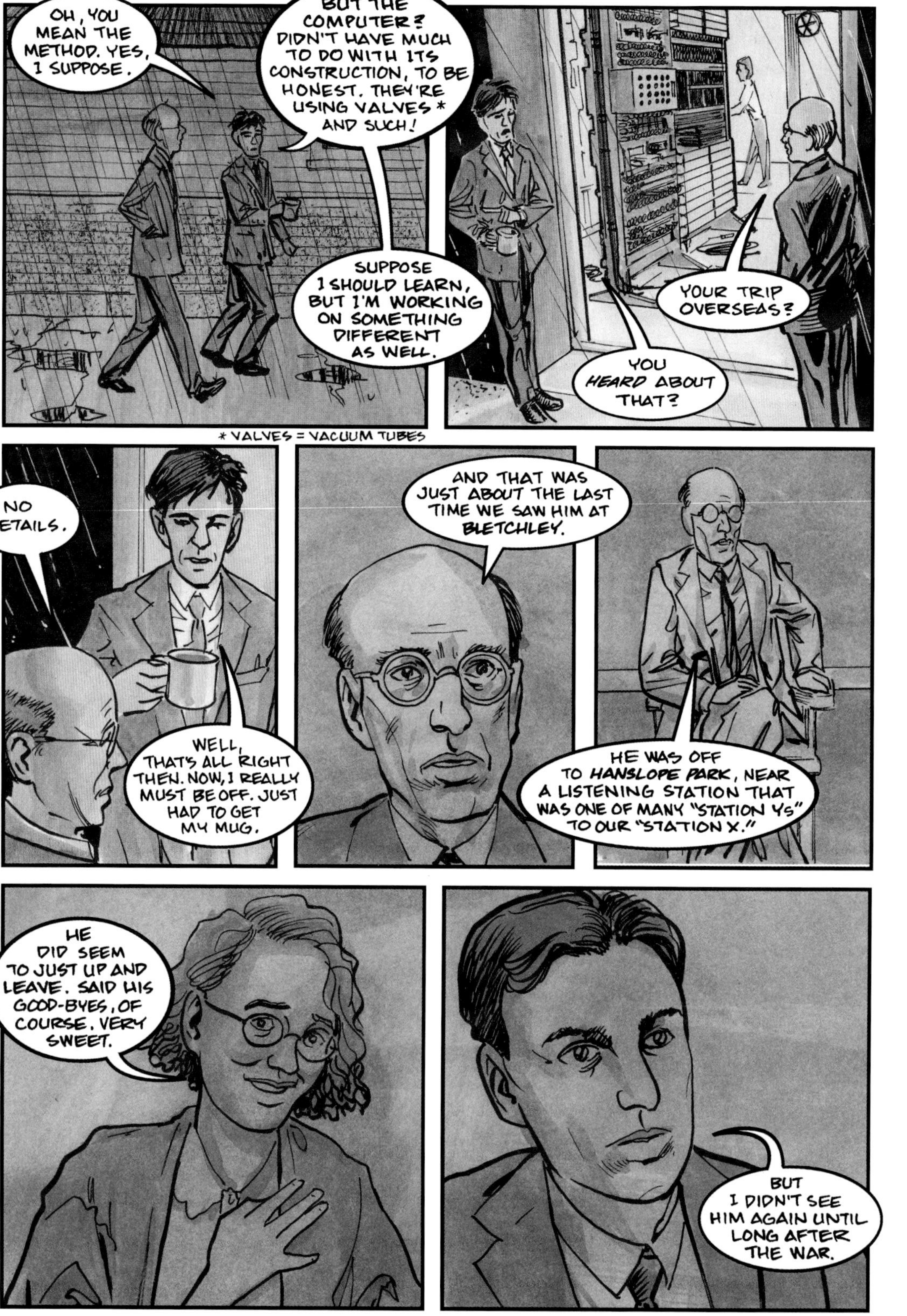
OH, YOU MEAN THE METHOD. YES, I SUPPOSE.
BUT THE COMPUTER? DIDN'T HAVE MUCH TO DO WITH ITS CONSTRUCTION, TO BE HONEST. THEY'RE USING VALVES * AND SUCH!
SUPPOSE I SHOULD LEARN, BUT I'M WORKING ON SOMETHING DIFFERENT AS WELL.
YOUR TRIP OVERSEAS?
YOU HEARD ABOUT THAT?
* VALVES = VACUUM TUBES
NO DETAILS.
WELL, THAT'S ALL RIGHT THEN. NOW, I REALLY MUST BE OFF. JUST HAD TO GET MY MUG.
AND THAT WAS JUST ABOUT THE LAST TIME WE SAW HIM AT BLETCHLEY.
HE WAS OFF TO HANSLOPE PARK, NEAR A LISTENING STATION THAT WAS ONE OF MANY "STATION YS" TO OUR "STATION X."
HE DID SEEM TO JUST UP AND LEAVE. SAID HIS GOOD-BYES, OF COURSE. VERY SWEET.
BUT I DIDN'T SEE HIM AGAIN UNTIL LONG AFTER THE WAR.

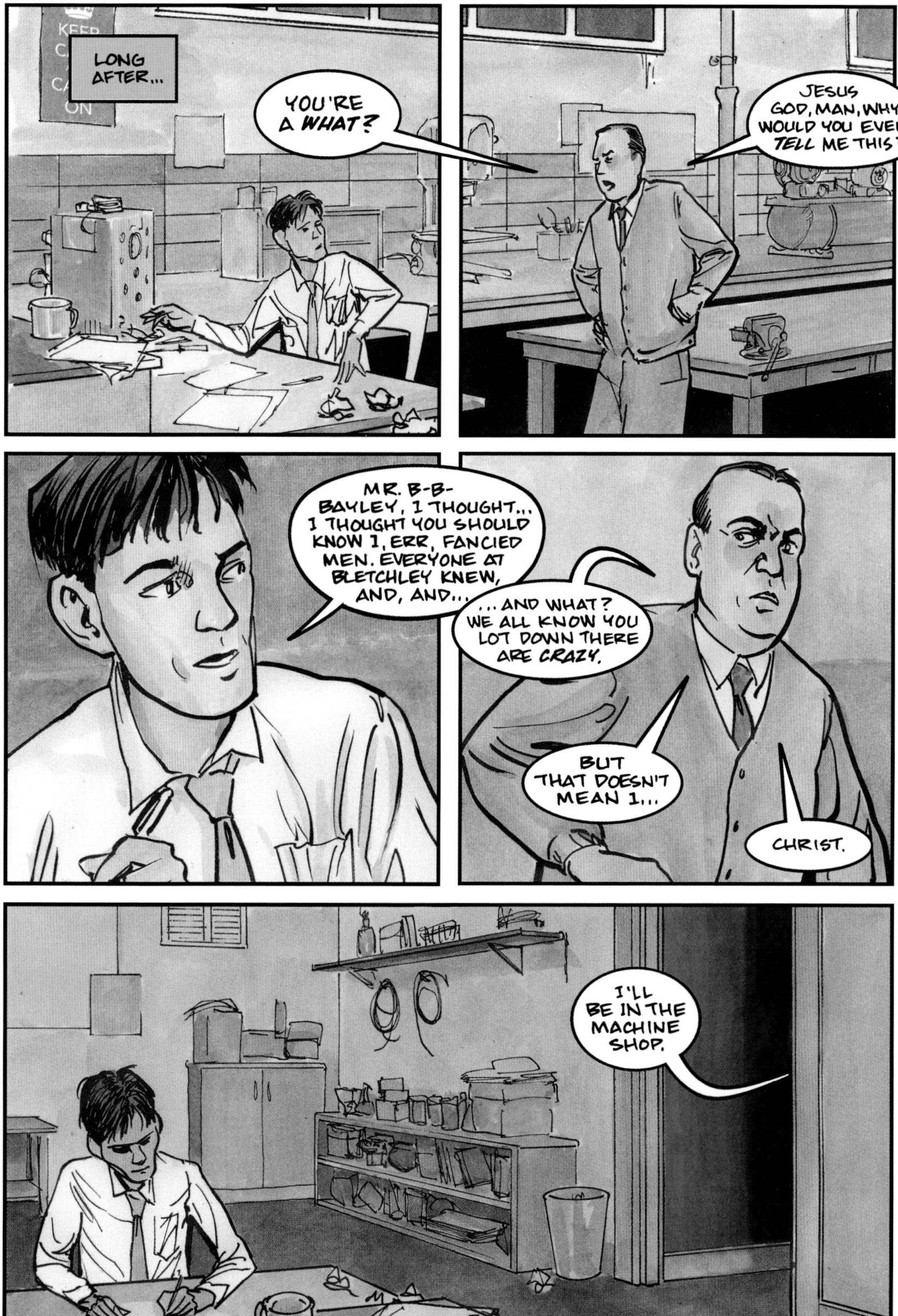
LONG AFTER...
YOU'RE A WHAT?
JESUS GOD, MAN, WHY WOULD YOU EVEN TELL ME THIS?
MR. B-B-BAYLEY, I THOUGHT... I THOUGHT YOU SHOULD KNOW I, ERR, FANCIED MEN. EVERYONE AT BLETCHLEY KNEW, AND, AND...
...AND WHAT? WE ALL KNOW YOU LOT DOWN THERE ARE CRAZY.
BUT THAT DOESN'T MEAN I...
CHRIST.
I'LL BE IN THE MACHINE SHOP.

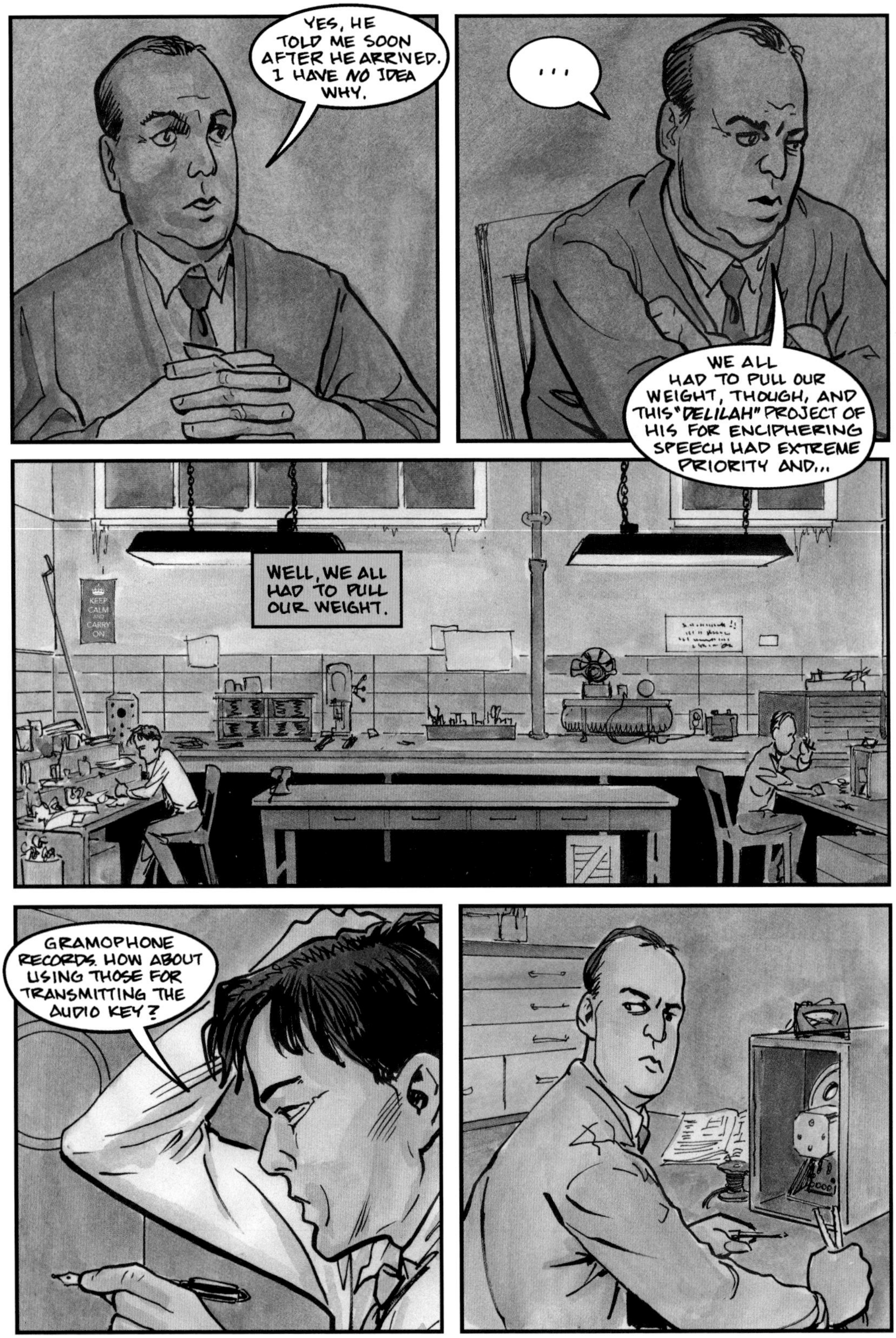
YES, HE TOLD ME SOON AFTER HE ARRIVED. I HAVE *NO* IDEA WHY.
...
WE ALL HAD TO PULL OUR WEIGHT, THOUGH, AND THIS "*DELILAH*" PROJECT OF HIS FOR ENCIPHERING SPEECH HAD EXTREME PRIORITY AND...
WELL, WE ALL HAD TO PULL OUR WEIGHT.
KEEP CALM AND CARRY ON
GRAMOPHONE RECORDS. HOW ABOUT USING THOSE FOR TRANSMITTING THE AUDIO KEY?

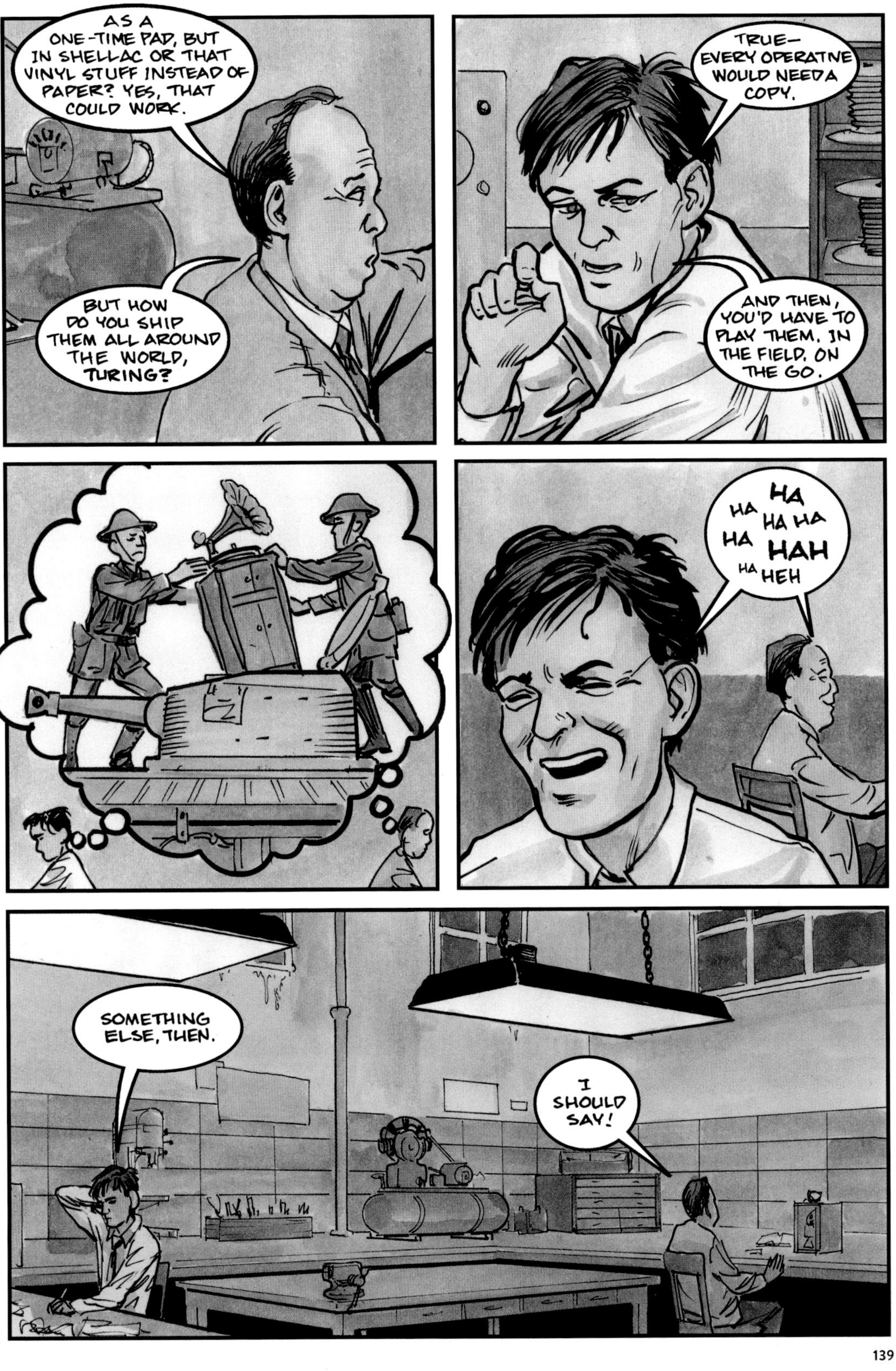

AS A ONE-TIME PAD, BUT IN SHELLAC OR THAT VINYL STUFF INSTEAD OF PAPER? YES, THAT COULD WORK.
BUT HOW DO YOU SHIP THEM ALL AROUND THE WORLD, TURING?
TRUE— EVERY OPERATNE WOULD NEEDA COPY.
AND THEN, YOU'D HAVE TO PLAY THEM. IN THE FIELD. ON THE GO.
HA HA HA HA HA HA HAH HA HEH
SOMETHING ELSE, THEN.
I SHOULD SAY!

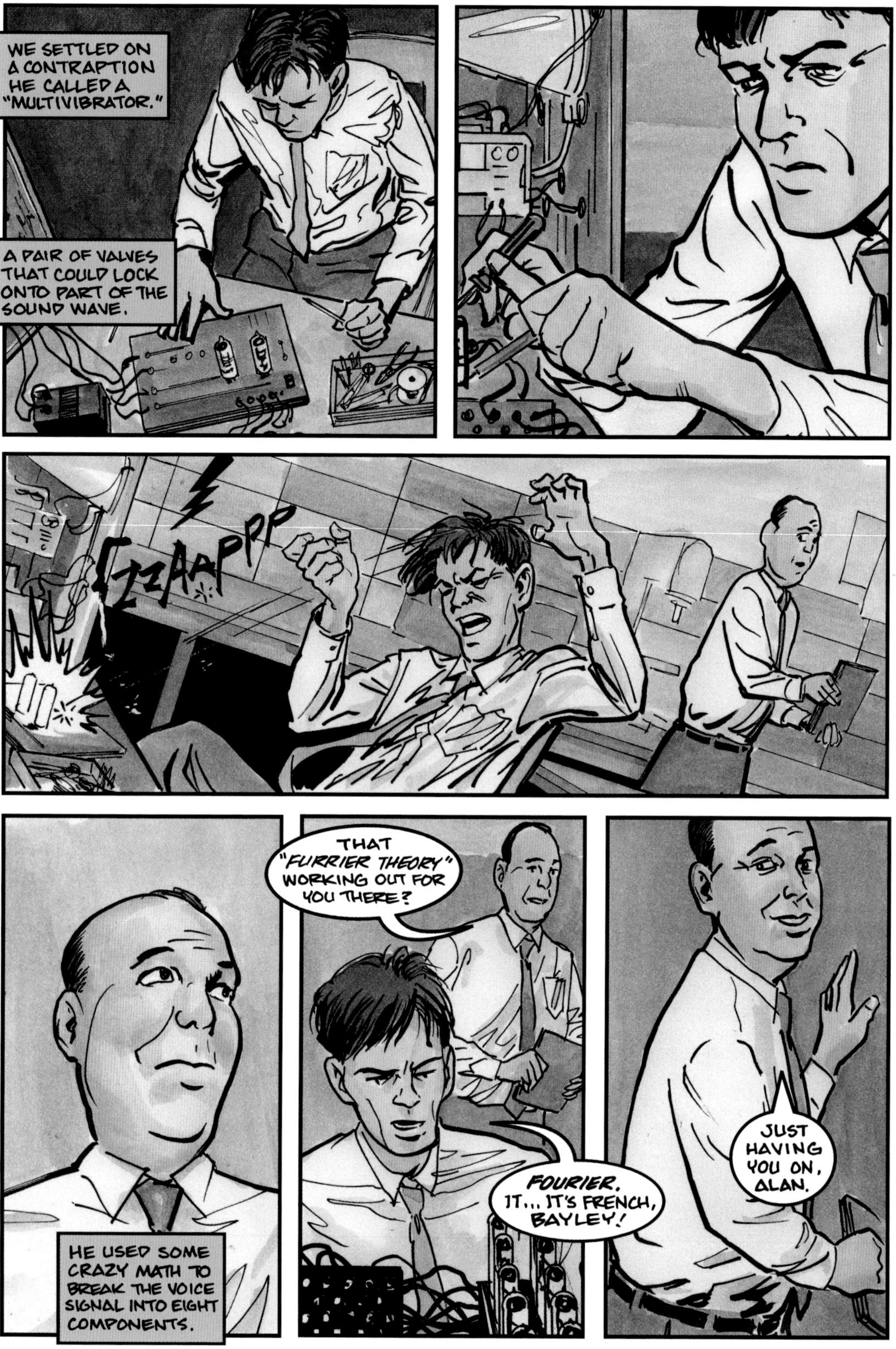
WE SETTLED ON A CONTRAPTION HE CALLED A "MULTIVIBRATOR."
A PAIR OF VALVES THAT COULD LOCK ONTO PART OF THE SOUND WAVE.
ZZAAPPP
HE USED SOME CRAZY MATH TO BREAK THE VOICE SIGNAL INTO EIGHT COMPONENTS.
THAT "FURRIER THEORY" WORKING OUT FOR YOU THERE?
FOURIER. IT... IT'S FRENCH, BAYLEY!
JUST HAVING YOU ON, ALAN.

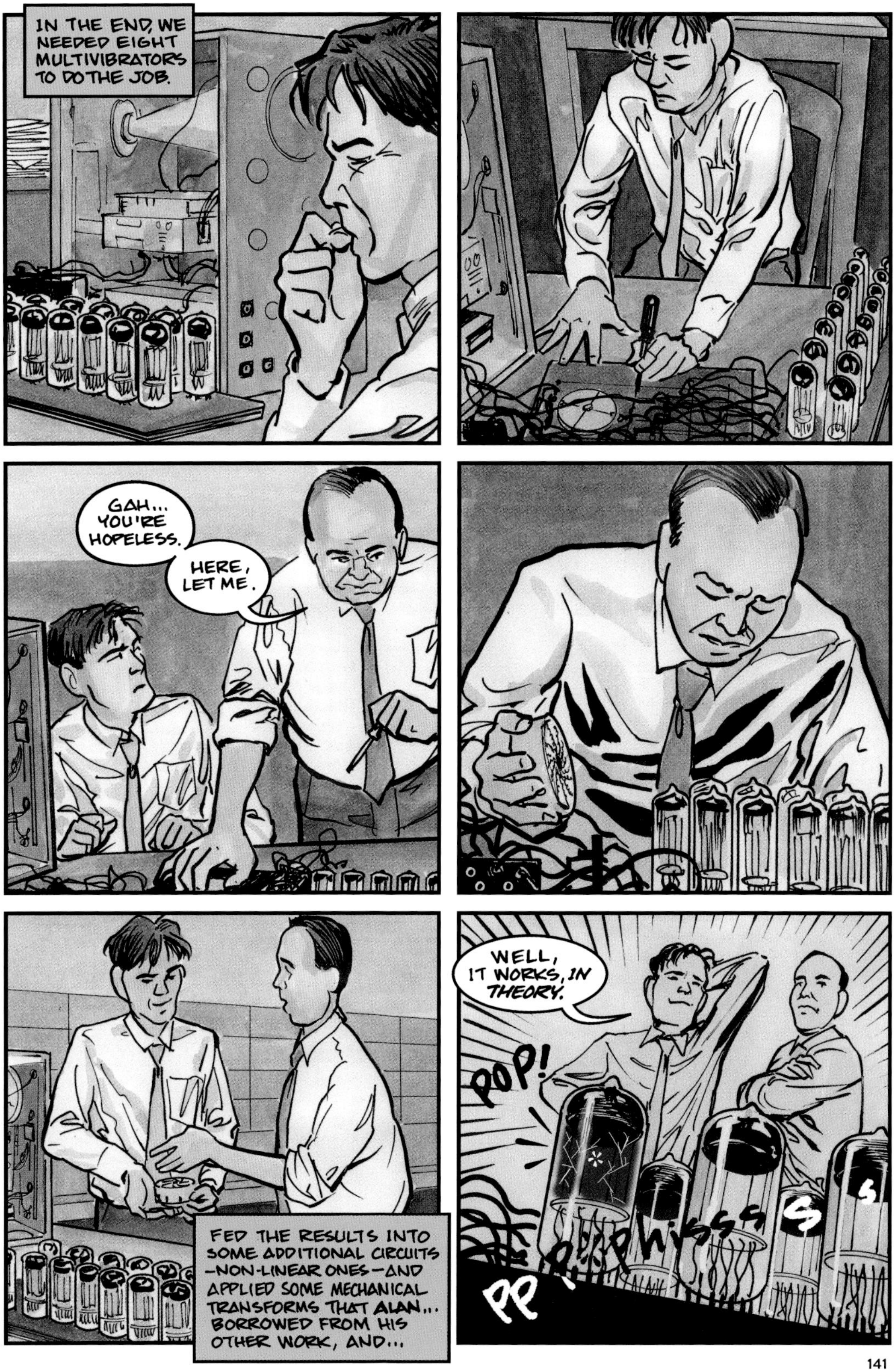
IN THE END, WE NEEDED EIGHT MULTIVIBRATORS TO DO THE JOB.
GAH... YOU'RE HOPELESS.
HERE, LET ME.
FED THE RESULTS INTO SOME ADDITIONAL CIRCUITS —NON-LINEAR ONES—AND APPLIED SOME MECHANICAL TRANSFORMS THAT ALAN... BORROWED FROM HIS OTHER WORK, AND...
WELL, IT WORKS, IN THEORY.
POP!

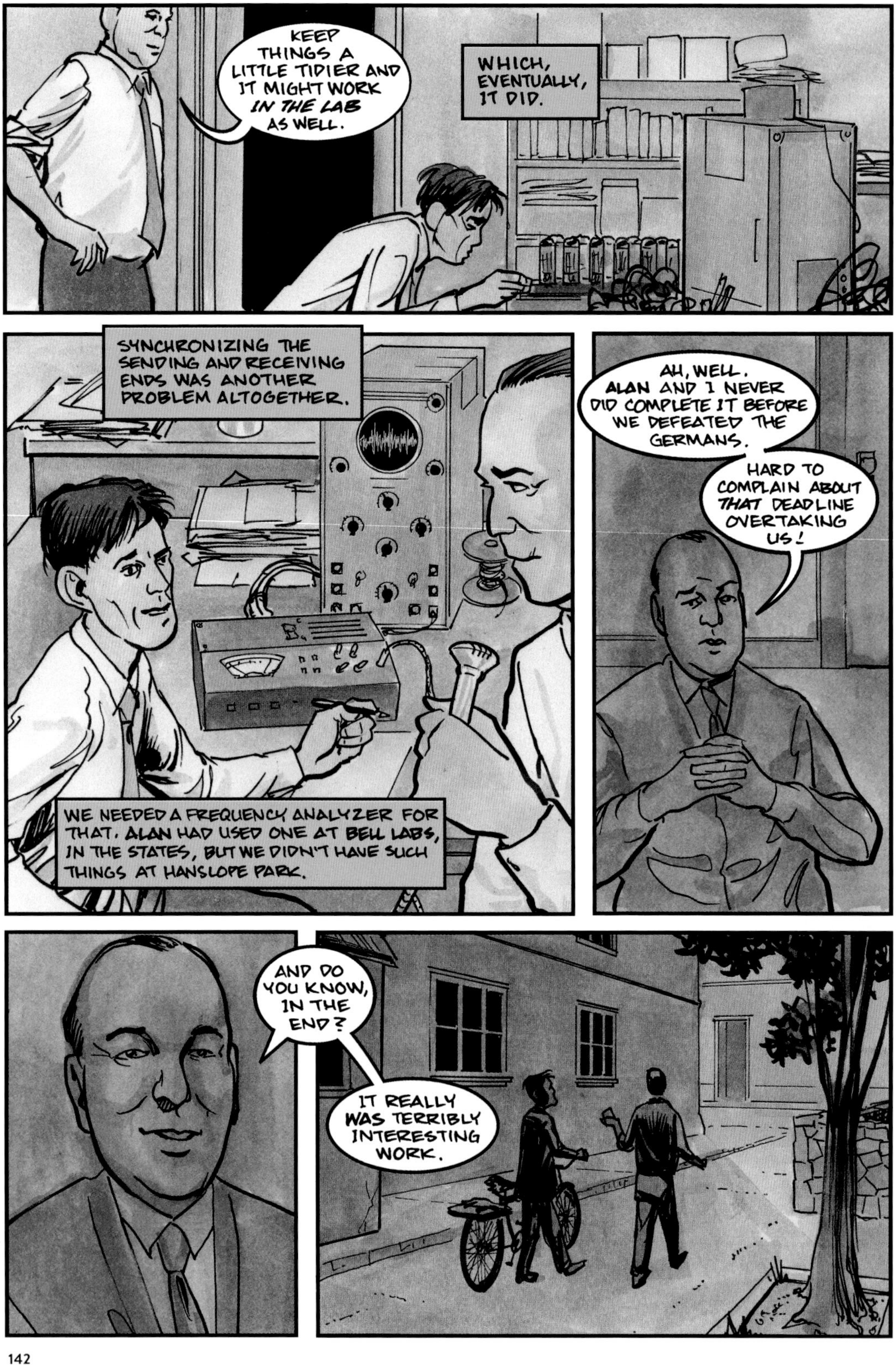
KEEP THINGS A LITTLE TIDIER AND IT MIGHT WORK *IN THE LAB* AS WELL.
WHICH, EVENTUALLY, IT DID.
SYNCHRONIZING THE SENDING AND RECEIVING ENDS WAS ANOTHER PROBLEM ALTOGETHER.
WE NEEDED A FREQUENCY ANALYZER FOR THAT. ALAN HAD USED ONE AT BELL LABS, IN THE STATES, BUT WE DIDN'T HAVE SUCH THINGS AT HANSLOPE PARK.
AH, WELL. ALAN AND I NEVER DID COMPLETE IT BEFORE WE DEFEATED THE GERMANS.
HARD TO COMPLAIN ABOUT *THAT* DEADLINE OVERTAKING US!
AND DO YOU KNOW, IN THE END?
IT REALLY WAS TERRIBLY INTERESTING WORK.

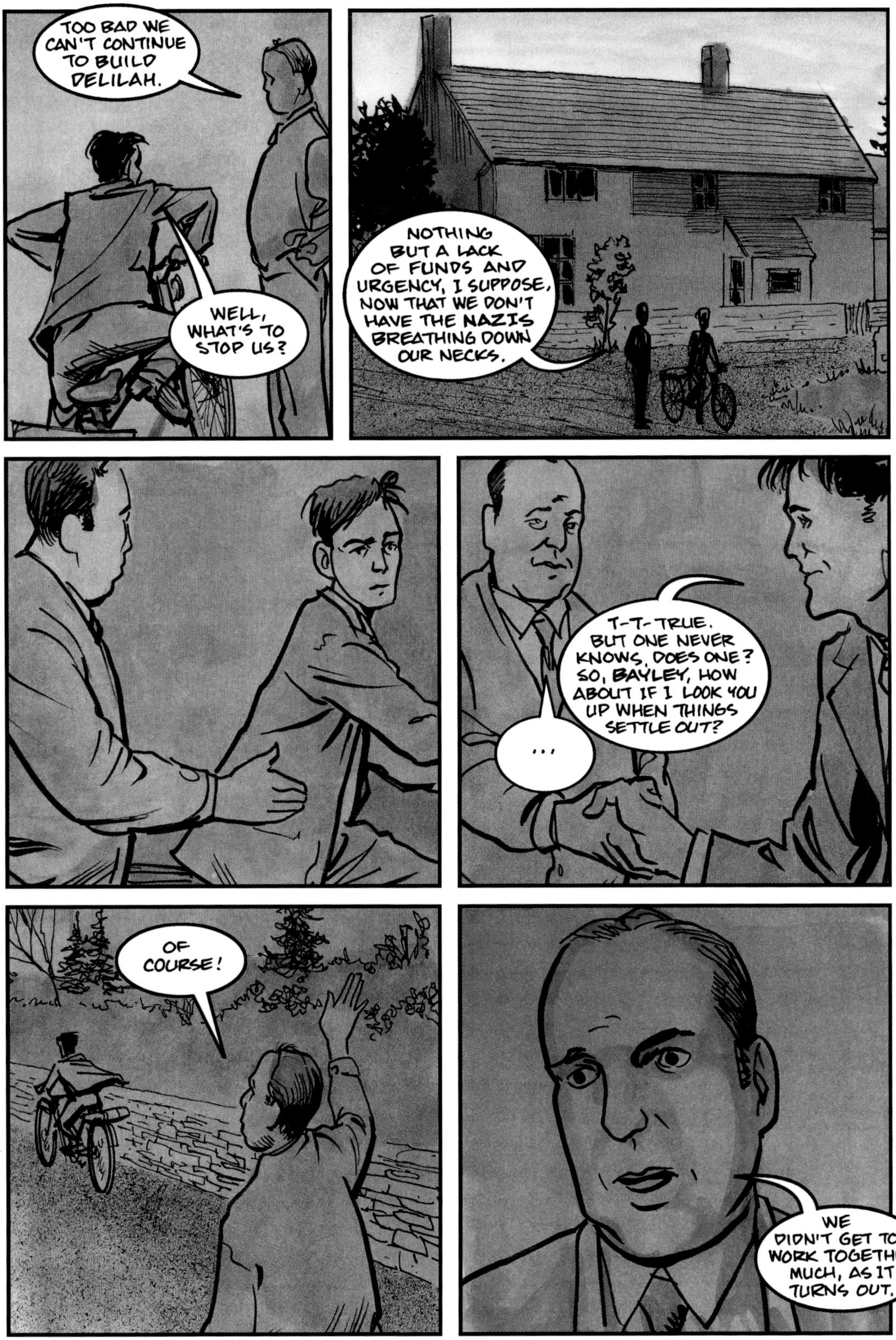
TOO BAD WE CAN'T CONTINUE TO BUILD DELILAH.
WELL, WHAT'S TO STOP US?
NOTHING BUT A LACK OF FUNDS AND URGENCY, I SUPPOSE, NOW THAT WE DON'T HAVE THE NAZIS BREATHING DOWN OUR NECKS.
T-T-TRUE. BUT ONE NEVER KNOWS, DOES ONE? SO, BAYLEY, HOW ABOUT IF I LOOK YOU UP WHEN THINGS SETTLE OUT?
...
OF COURSE!
WE DIDN'T GET TO WORK TOGETHER MUCH, AS IT TURNS OUT.

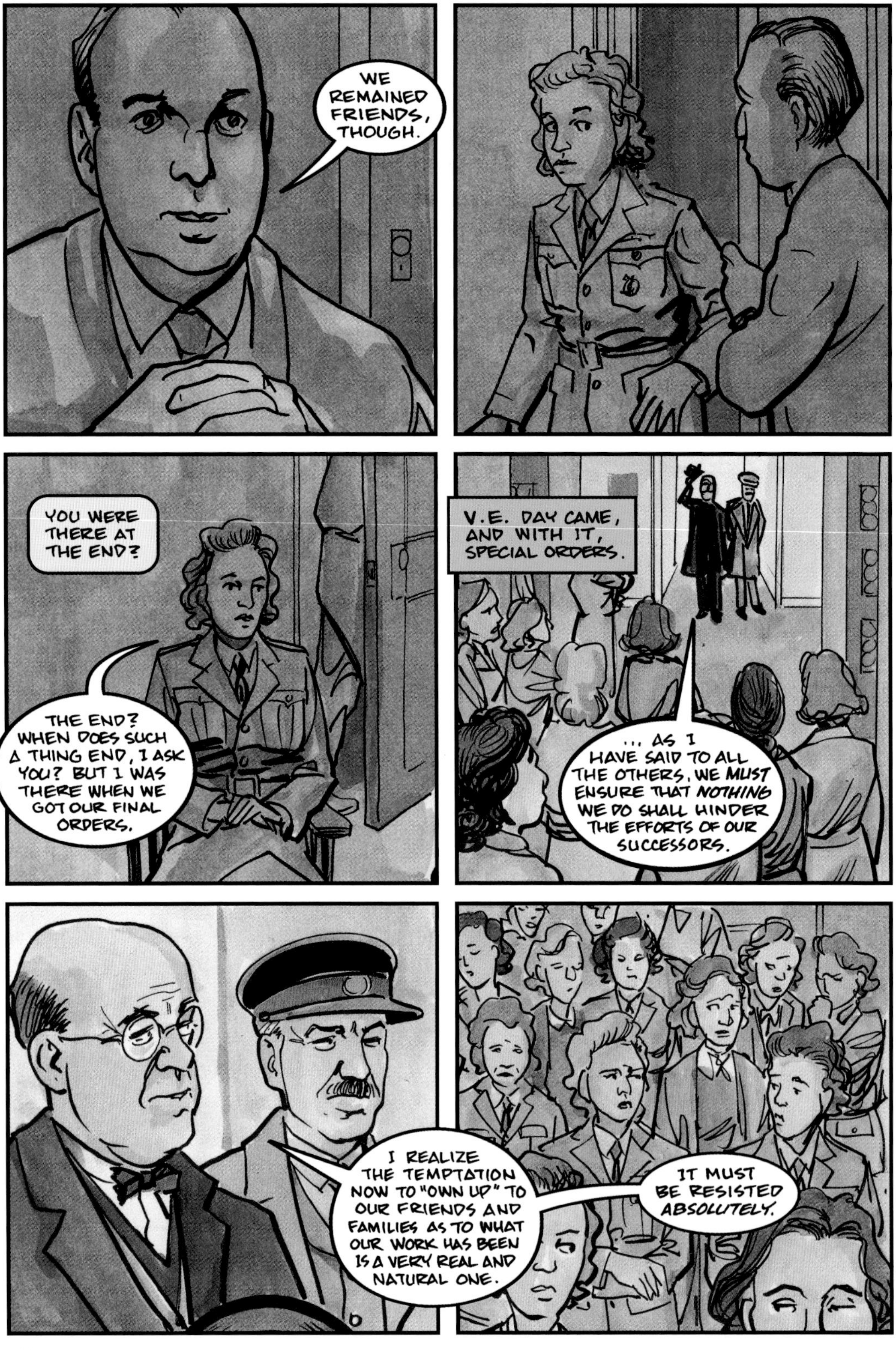
WE REMAINED FRIENDS, THOUGH.
YOU WERE THERE AT THE END?
THE END? WHEN DOES SUCH A THING END, I ASK YOU? BUT I WAS THERE WHEN WE GOT OUR FINAL ORDERS.
V.E. DAY CAME, AND WITH IT, SPECIAL ORDERS.
... AS I HAVE SAID TO ALL THE OTHERS, WE MUST ENSURE THAT NOTHING WE DO SHALL HINDER THE EFFORTS OF OUR SUCCESSORS.
I REALIZE THE TEMPTATION NOW TO "OWN UP" TO OUR FRIENDS AND FAMILIES AS TO WHAT OUR WORK HAS BEEN IS A VERY REAL AND NATURAL ONE.
IT MUST BE RESISTED ABSOLUTELY.

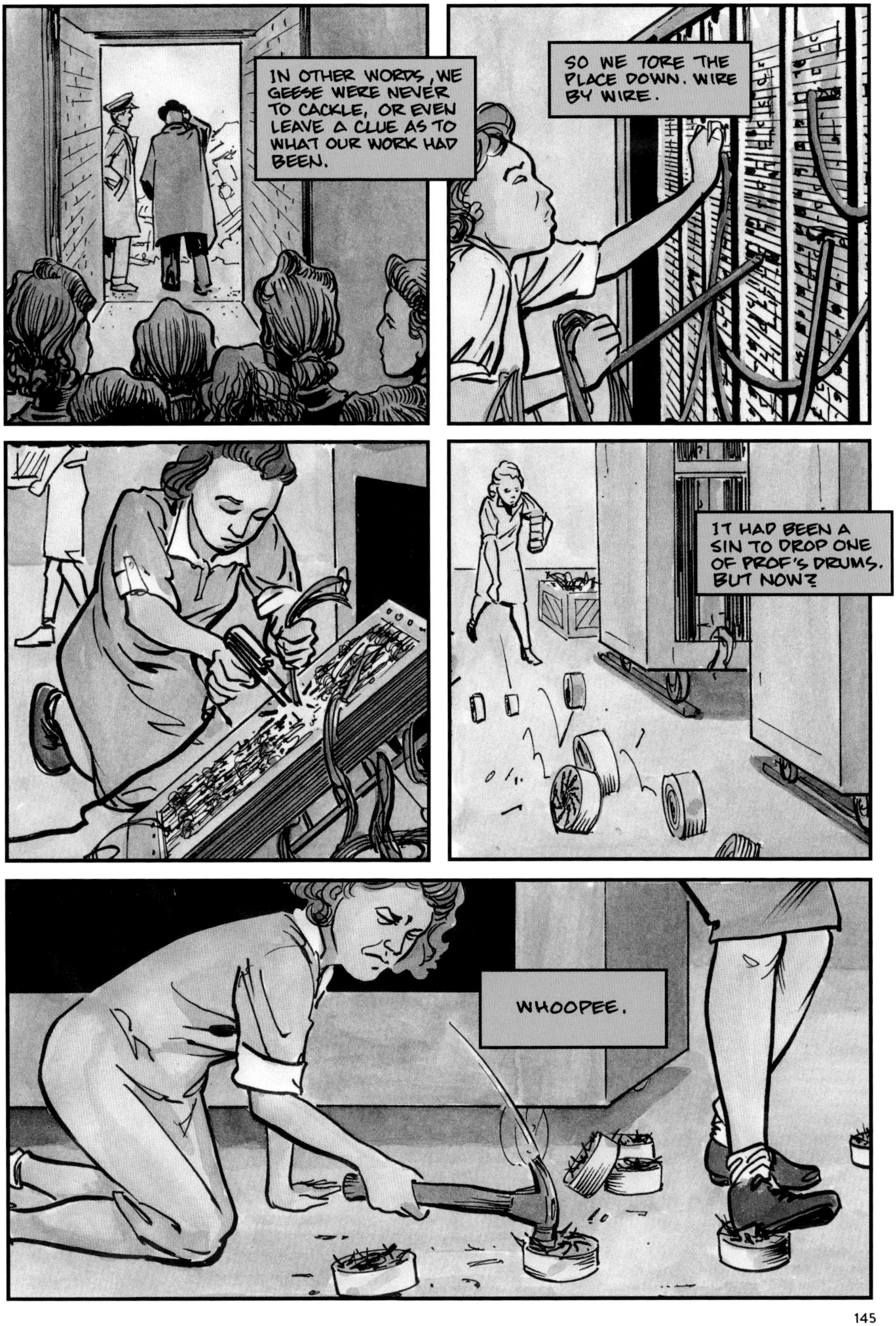
IN OTHER WORDS, WE GEESE WERE NEVER TO CACKLE, OR EVEN LEAVE A CLUE AS TO WHAT OUR WORK HAD BEEN.
SO WE TORE THE PLACE DOWN. WIRE BY WIRE.
IT HAD BEEN A SIN TO DROP ONE OF PROF'S DRUMS. BUT NOW?
WHOOPEE.

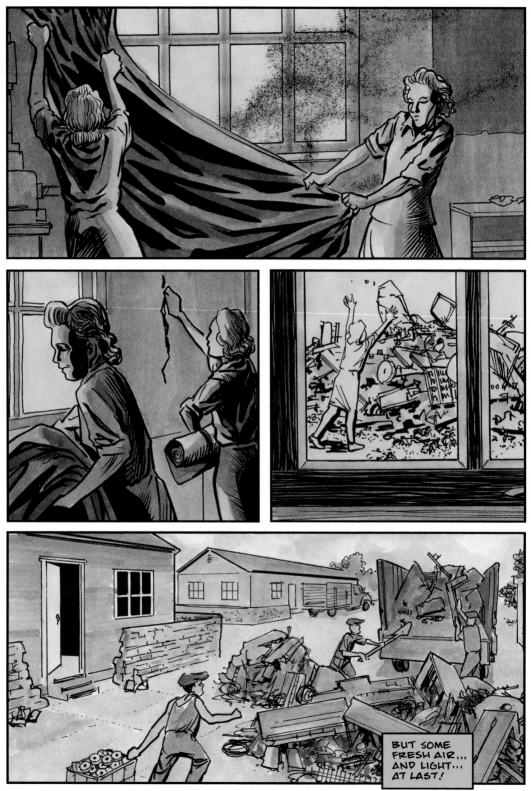

BUT SOME
FRESH AIR...
AND LIGHT...
AT LAST!

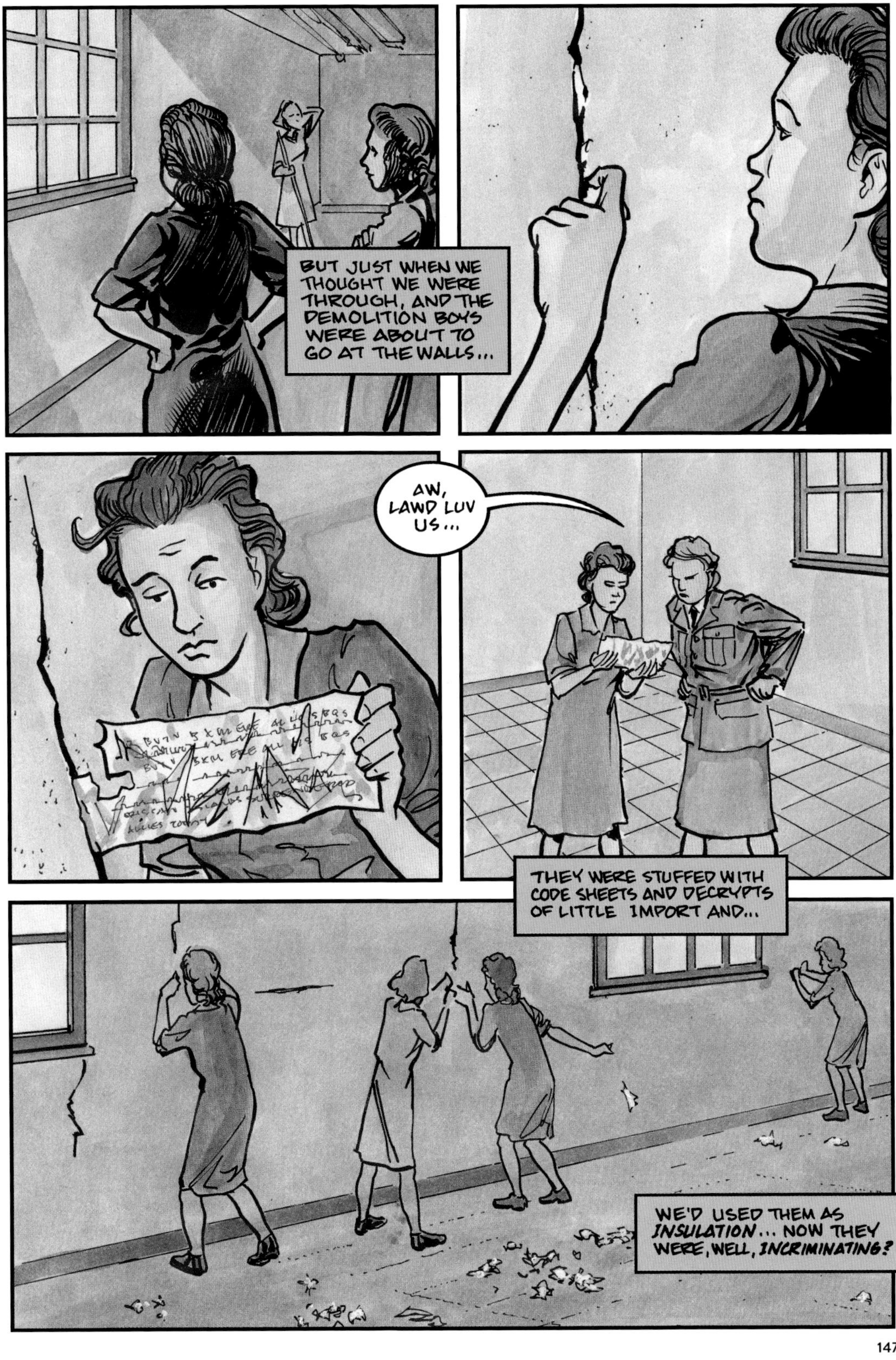
BUT JUST WHEN WE THOUGHT WE WERE THROUGH, AND THE DEMOLITION BOYS WERE ABOUT TO GO AT THE WALLS...
AW, LAWD LUV US...
THEY WERE STUFFED WITH CODE SHEETS AND DECRYPTS OF LITTLE IMPORT AND...
WE'D USED THEM AS *INSULATION*... NOW THEY WERE, WELL, *INCRIMINATING?*

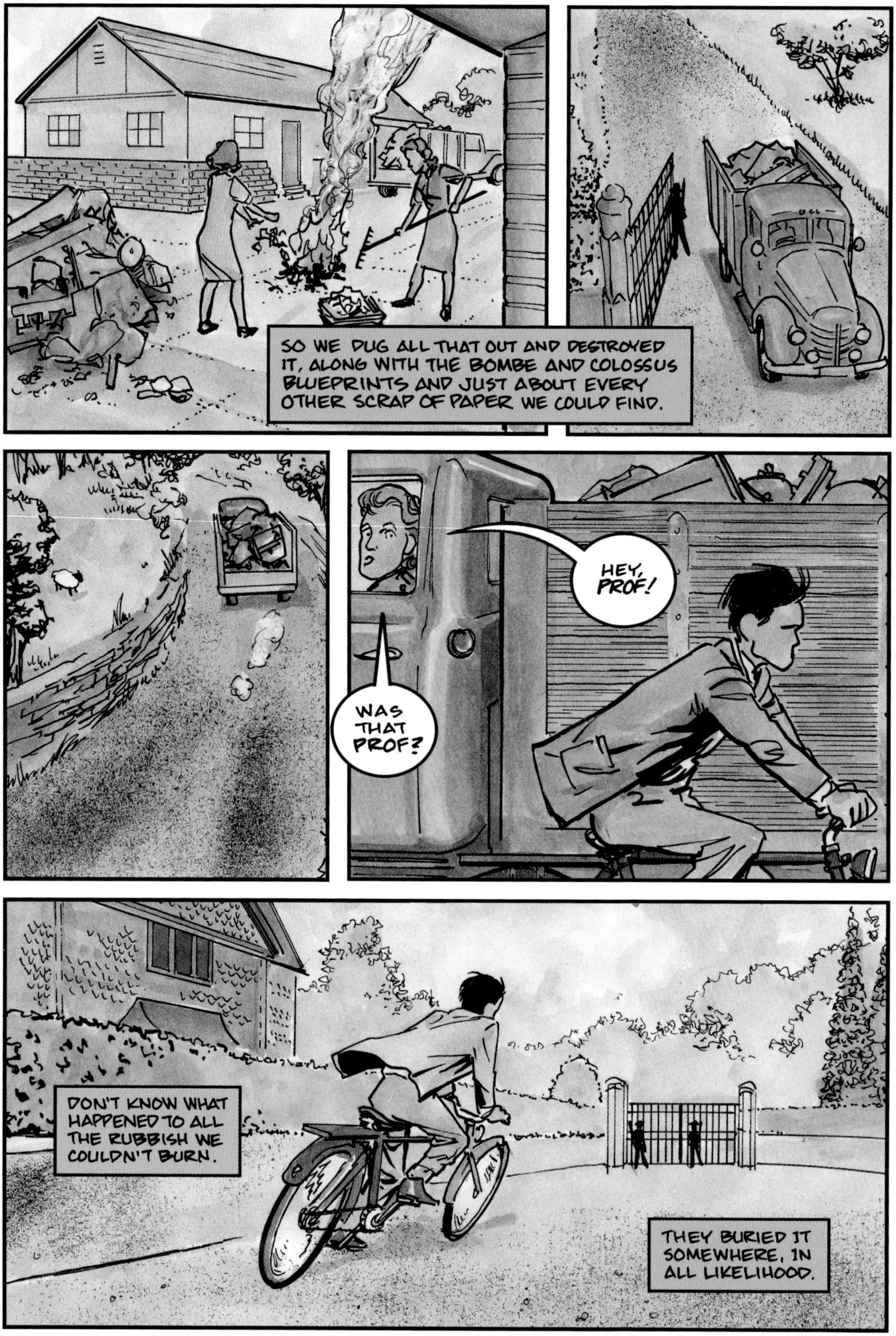
SO WE DUG ALL THAT OUT AND DESTROYED IT, ALONG WITH THE BOMBE AND COLOSSUS BLUEPRINTS AND JUST ABOUT EVERY OTHER SCRAP OF PAPER WE COULD FIND.
HEY, PROF!
WAS THAT PROF?
DON'T KNOW WHAT HAPPENED TO ALL THE RUBBISH WE COULDN'T BURN.
THEY BURIED IT SOMEWHERE, IN ALL LIKELIHOOD.

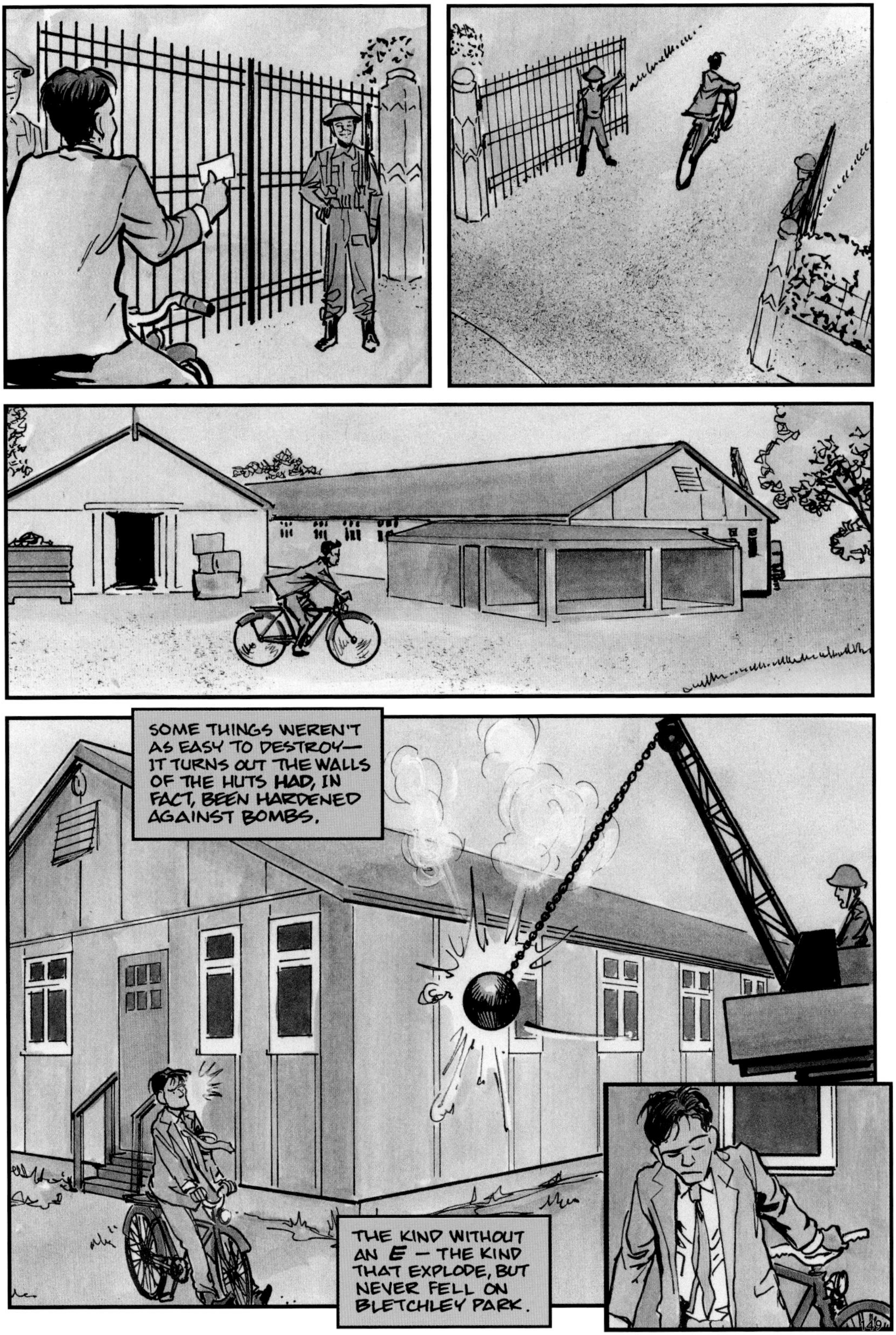
SOME THINGS WEREN'T AS EASY TO DESTROY— IT TURNS OUT THE WALLS OF THE HUTS HAD, IN FACT, BEEN HARDENED AGAINST BOMBS.
THE KIND WITHOUT AN E — THE KIND THAT EXPLODE, BUT NEVER FELL ON BLETCHLEY PARK.

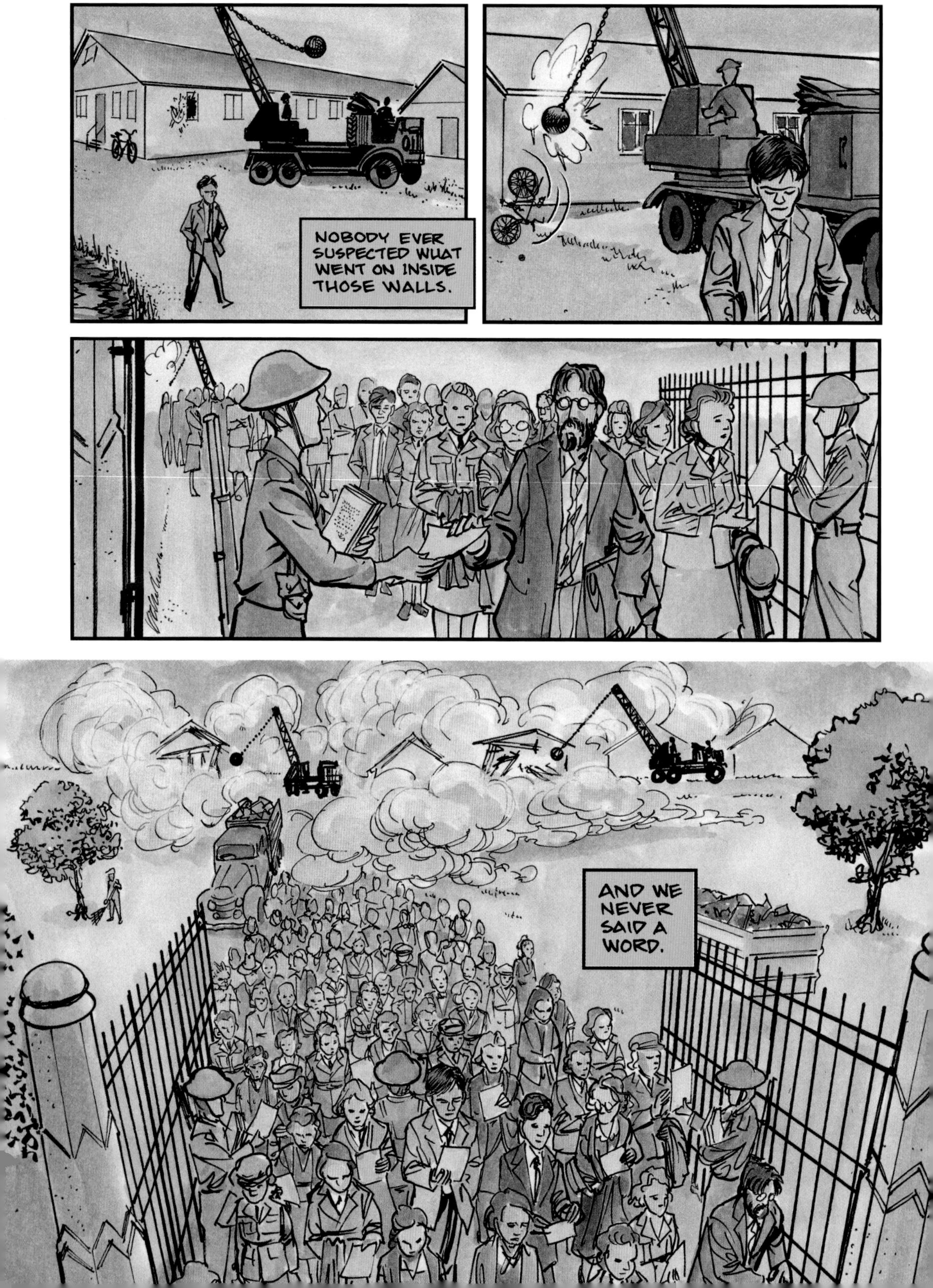
NOBODY EVER SUSPECTED WHAT WENT ON INSIDE THOSE WALLS.
AND WE NEVER SAID A WORD.

WE NEVER
SAID A WORD.

IF THE MEANING OF THE WORDS
MACHINE AND *THINK* ARE TO BE
FOUND BY EXAMINING HOW THEY
ARE COMMONLY USED, IT IS DIFFICULT
TO ESCAPE THE CONCLUSION THAT
THE MEANING AND THE ANSWER TO
THE QUESTION, "CAN MACHINES
THINK?" IS TO BE SOUGHT IN A
STATISTICAL SURVEY SUCH AS A
GALLUP POLL. BUT THIS IS ABSURD.
INSTEAD OF ATTEMPTING SUCH
A DEFINITION, I SHALL REPLACE
THE QUESTION BY ANOTHER,
WHICH IS CLOSELY RELATED TO IT
AND IS EXPRESSED IN RELATIVELY
UNAMBIGUOUS WORDS. THE NEW
FORM OF THE PROBLEM CAN BE
DESCRIBED IN TERMS OF A GAME
WHICH WE CALL . . .

THE IMITATION GAME

IT MIGHT BE URGED THAT WHEN PLAYING **THE IMITATION GAME** THE BEST STRATEGY FOR THE MACHINE MAY POSSIBLY BE SOMETHING OTHER THAN IMITATION OF THE BEHAVIOR OF A MAN. THIS MAY BE, BUT I THINK IT IS UNLIKELY THAT THERE IS ANY GREAT EFFECT OF THIS KIND. IN ANY CASE, THERE IS NO INTENTION TO INVESTIGATE HERE THE THEORY OF THE GAME, AND IT WILL BE ASSUMED THAT THE BEST STRATEGY IS TO TRY TO PROVIDE ANSWERS THAT WOULD NATURALLY BE GIVEN BY A MAN.

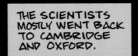

THE SCIENTISTS MOSTLY WENT BACK TO CAMBRIDGE AND OXFORD.

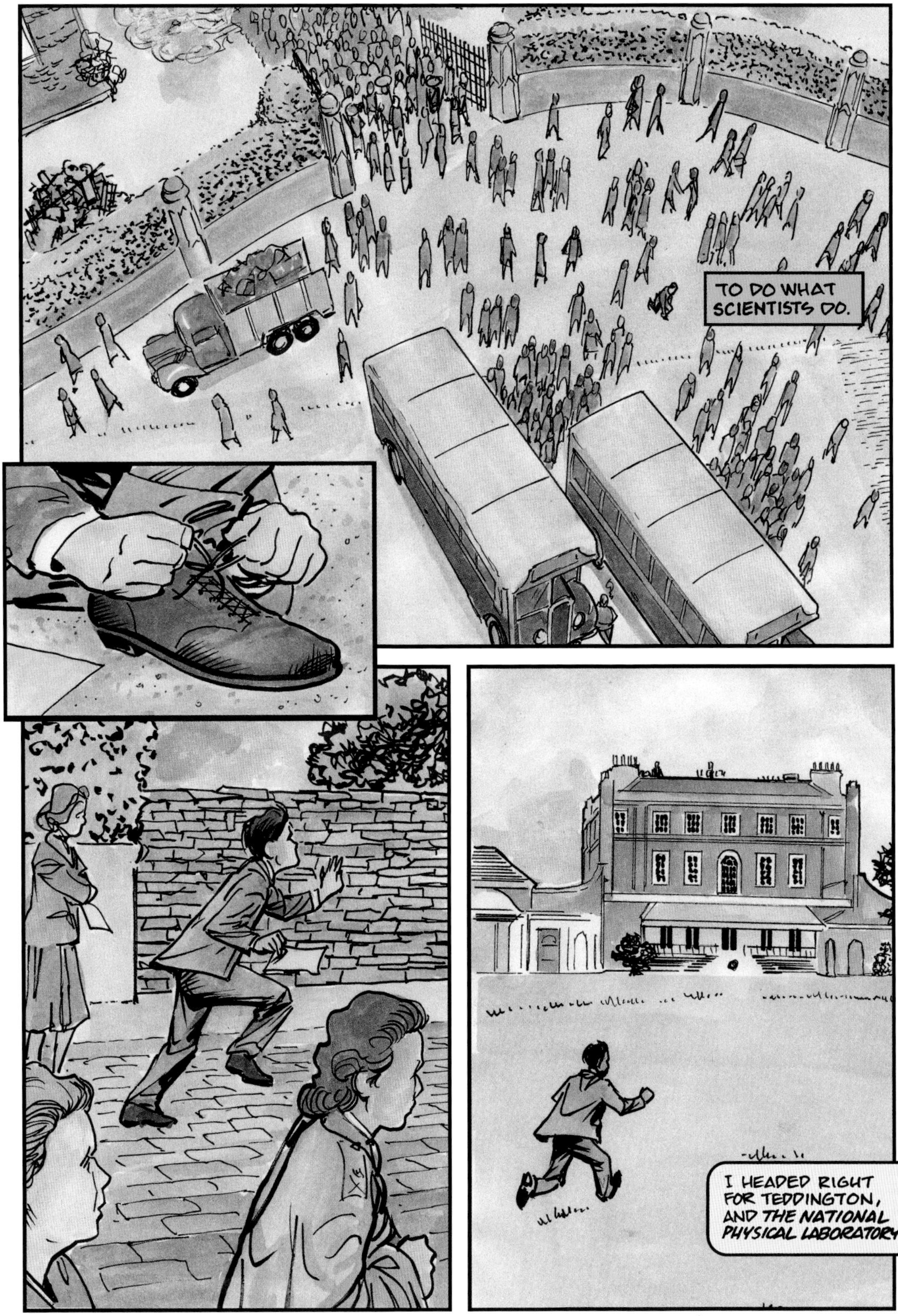
TO DO WHAT SCIENTISTS DO.
I HEADED RIGHT FOR TEDDINGTON, AND *THE NATIONAL PHYSICAL LABORATORY.*

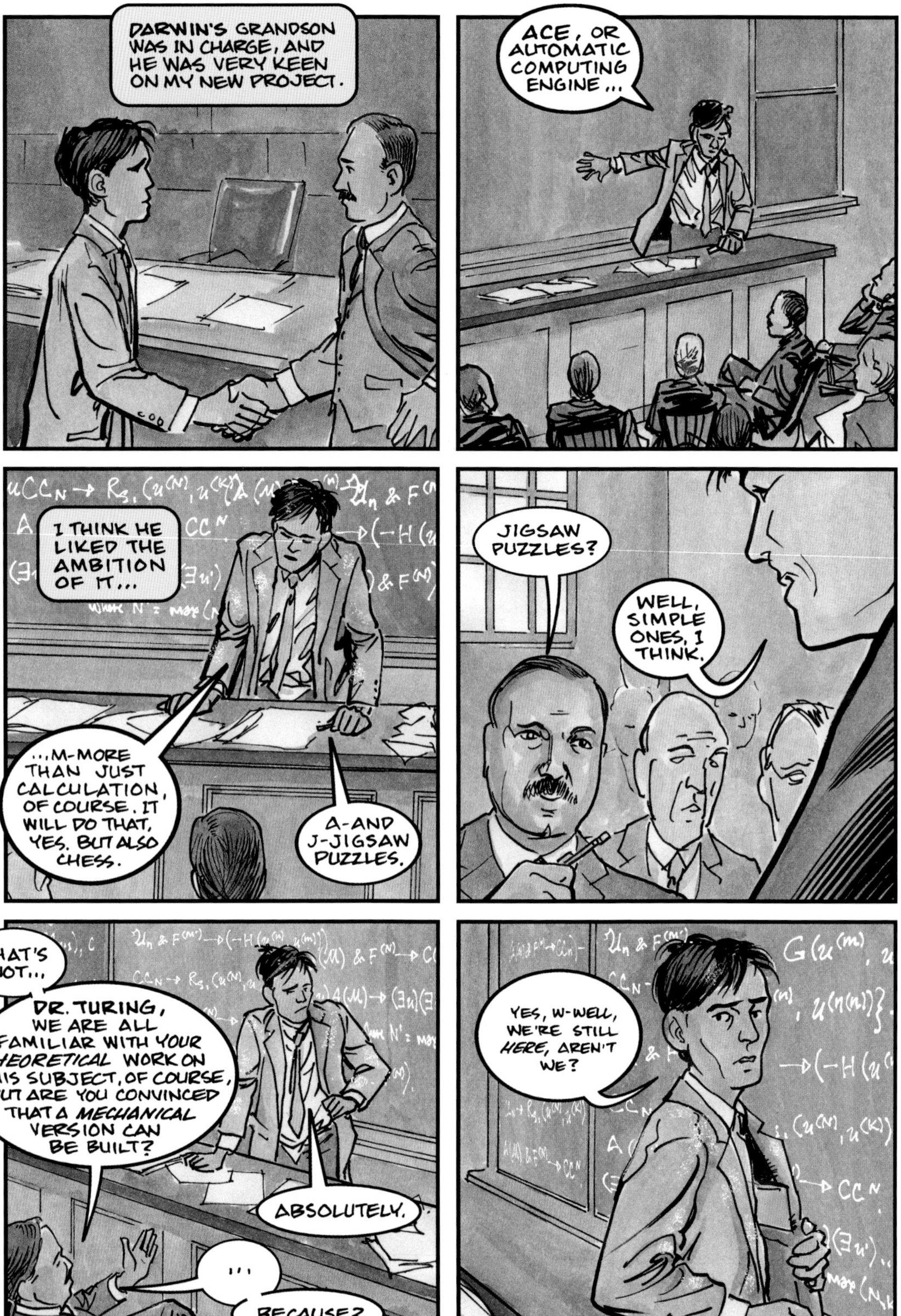
DARWIN'S GRANDSON WAS IN CHARGE, AND HE WAS VERY KEEN ON MY NEW PROJECT.
ACE, OR AUTOMATIC COMPUTING ENGINE...
I THINK HE LIKED THE AMBITION OF IT...
...M-MORE THAN JUST CALCULATION, OF COURSE. IT WILL DO THAT, YES. BUT ALSO CHESS.
A-AND J-JIGSAW PUZZLES.
JIGSAW PUZZLES?
WELL, SIMPLE ONES, I THINK.
THAT'S NOT...
DR. TURING, WE ARE ALL FAMILIAR WITH YOUR *THEORETICAL* WORK ON THIS SUBJECT, OF COURSE, BUT ARE YOU CONVINCED THAT A *MECHANICAL* VERSION CAN BE BUILT?
ABSOLUTELY.
...
BECAUSE?
YES, W-WELL, WE'RE STILL *HERE*, AREN'T WE?

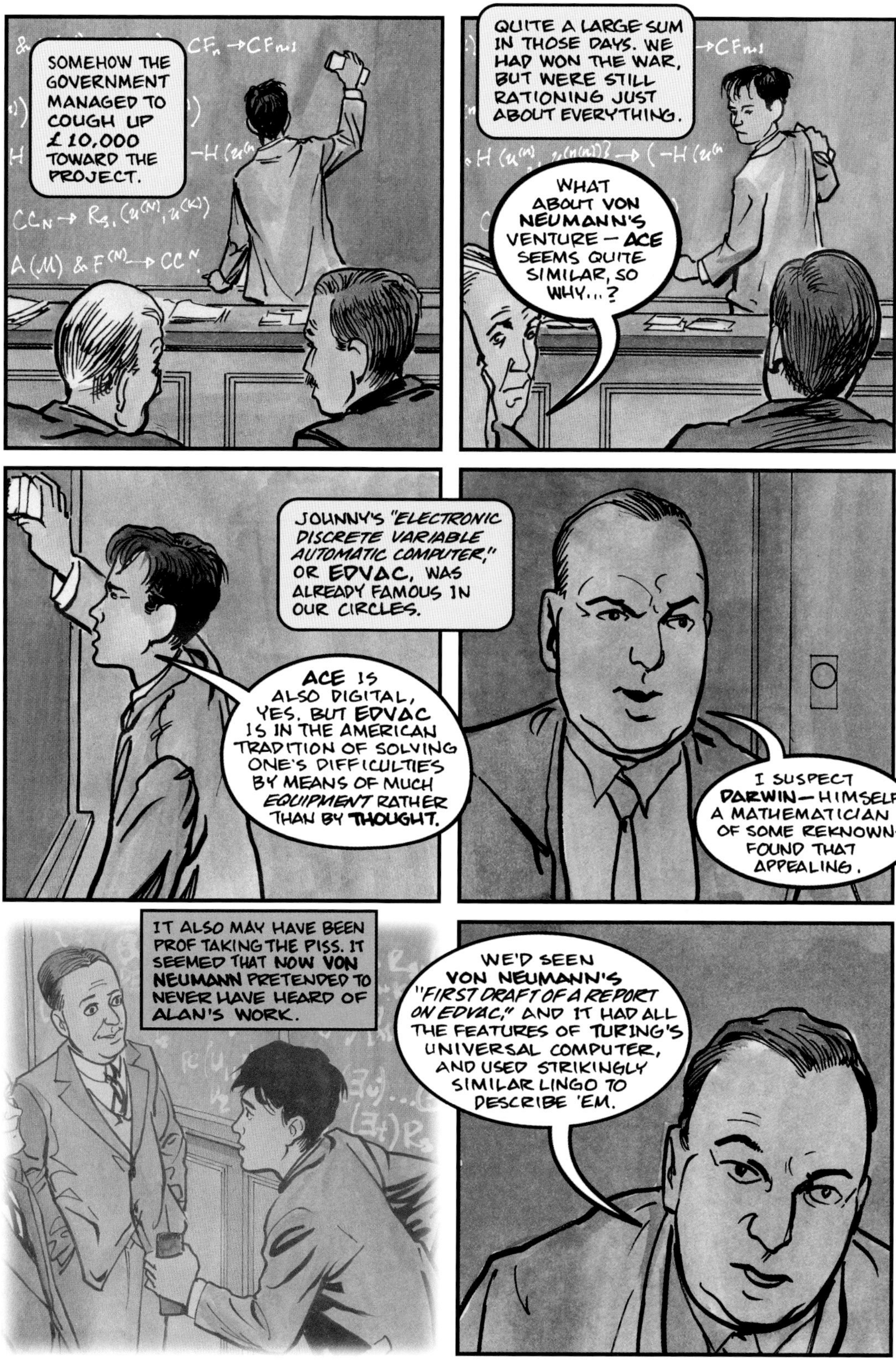
SOMEHOW THE GOVERNMENT MANAGED TO COUGH UP £10,000 TOWARD THE PROJECT.
QUITE A LARGE SUM IN THOSE DAYS. WE HAD WON THE WAR, BUT WERE STILL RATIONING JUST ABOUT EVERYTHING.
WHAT ABOUT VON NEUMANN'S VENTURE—ACE SEEMS QUITE SIMILAR, SO WHY...?
JOHNNY'S "ELECTRONIC DISCRETE VARIABLE AUTOMATIC COMPUTER," OR EDVAC, WAS ALREADY FAMOUS IN OUR CIRCLES.
ACE IS ALSO DIGITAL, YES. BUT EDVAC IS IN THE AMERICAN TRADITION OF SOLVING ONE'S DIFFICULTIES BY MEANS OF MUCH EQUIPMENT RATHER THAN BY THOUGHT.
I SUSPECT DARWIN—HIMSELF A MATHEMATICIAN OF SOME REKNOWN—FOUND THAT APPEALING.
IT ALSO MAY HAVE BEEN PROF TAKING THE PISS. IT SEEMED THAT NOW VON NEUMANN PRETENDED TO NEVER HAVE HEARD OF ALAN'S WORK.
WE'D SEEN VON NEUMANN'S "FIRST DRAFT OF A REPORT ON EDVAC," AND IT HAD ALL THE FEATURES OF TURING'S UNIVERSAL COMPUTER, AND USED STRIKINGLY SIMILAR LINGO TO DESCRIBE 'EM.

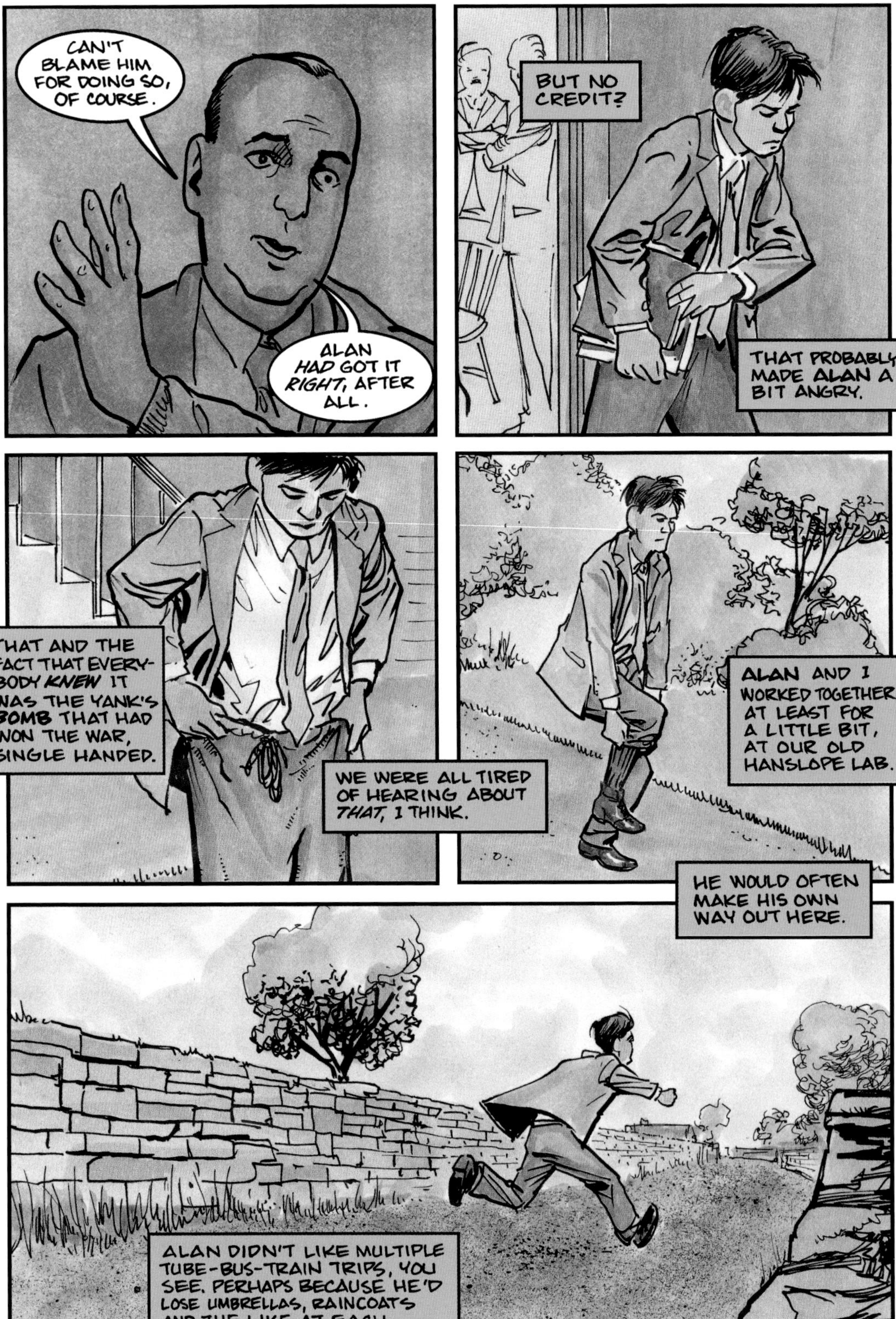
CAN'T BLAME HIM FOR DOING SO, OF COURSE.
ALAN HAD GOT IT *RIGHT*, AFTER ALL.
BUT NO CREDIT?
THAT PROBABLY MADE **ALAN** A BIT ANGRY.
THAT AND THE FACT THAT EVERYBODY ***KNEW*** IT WAS THE YANK'S **BOMB** THAT HAD WON THE WAR, SINGLE HANDED.
WE WERE ALL TIRED OF HEARING ABOUT *THAT*, I THINK.
ALAN AND I WORKED TOGETHER, AT LEAST FOR A LITTLE BIT, AT OUR OLD HANSLOPE LAB.
HE WOULD OFTEN MAKE HIS OWN WAY OUT HERE.
ALAN DIDN'T LIKE MULTIPLE TUBE-BUS-TRAIN TRIPS, YOU SEE. PERHAPS BECAUSE HE'D LOSE UMBRELLAS, RAINCOATS AND THE LIKE AT EACH CONNECTION.

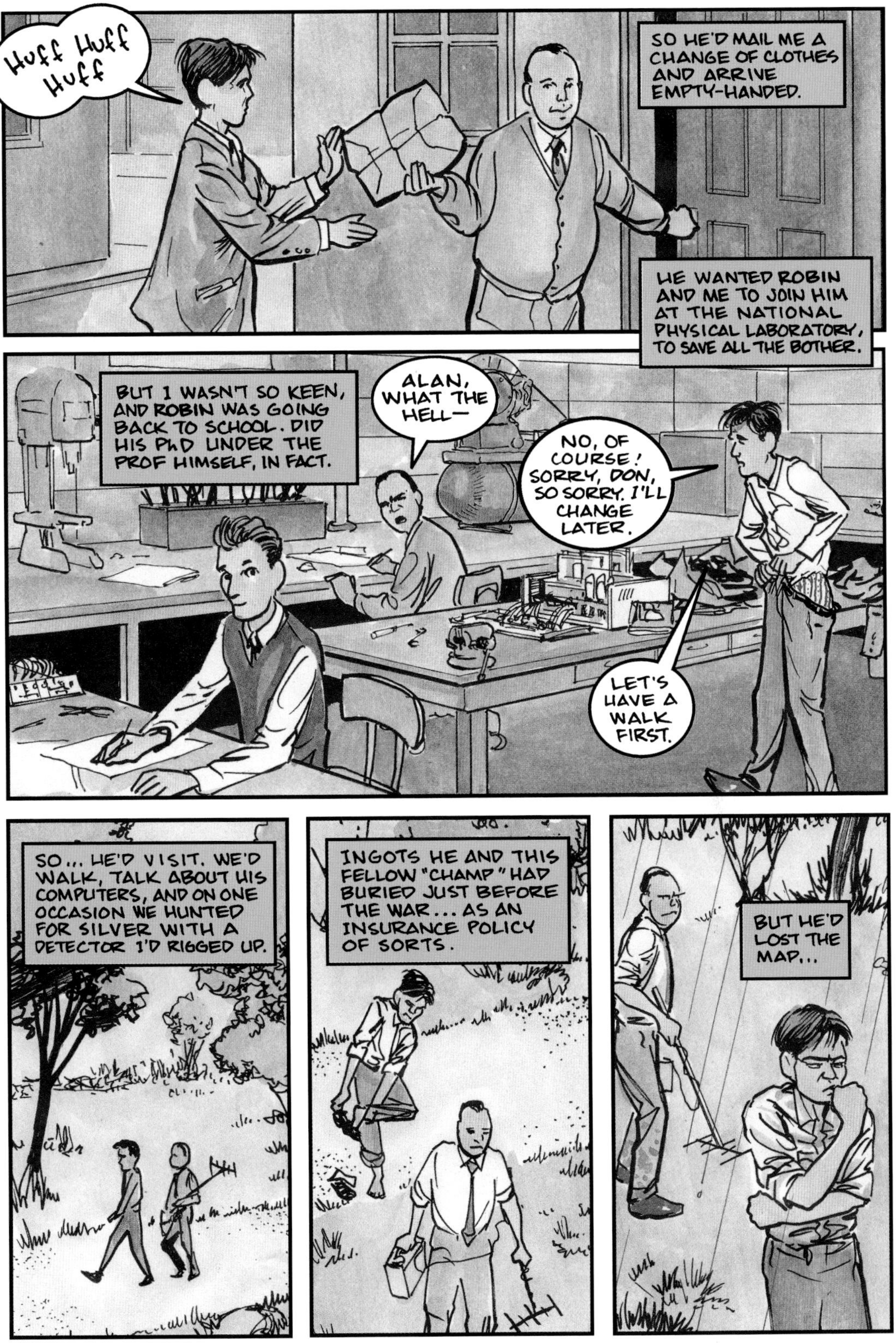
Huff Huff Huff
SO HE'D MAIL ME A CHANGE OF CLOTHES AND ARRIVE EMPTY-HANDED.
HE WANTED ROBIN AND ME TO JOIN HIM AT THE NATIONAL PHYSICAL LABORATORY, TO SAVE ALL THE BOTHER.
BUT I WASN'T SO KEEN, AND ROBIN WAS GOING BACK TO SCHOOL. DID HIS PhD UNDER THE PROF HIMSELF, IN FACT.
ALAN, WHAT THE HELL—
NO, OF COURSE! SORRY, DON, SO SORRY. I'LL CHANGE LATER.
LET'S HAVE A WALK FIRST.
SO... HE'D VISIT. WE'D WALK, TALK ABOUT HIS COMPUTERS, AND ON ONE OCCASION WE HUNTED FOR SILVER WITH A DETECTOR I'D RIGGED UP.
INGOTS HE AND THIS FELLOW "CHAMP" HAD BURIED JUST BEFORE THE WAR... AS AN INSURANCE POLICY OF SORTS.
BUT HE'D LOST THE MAP...

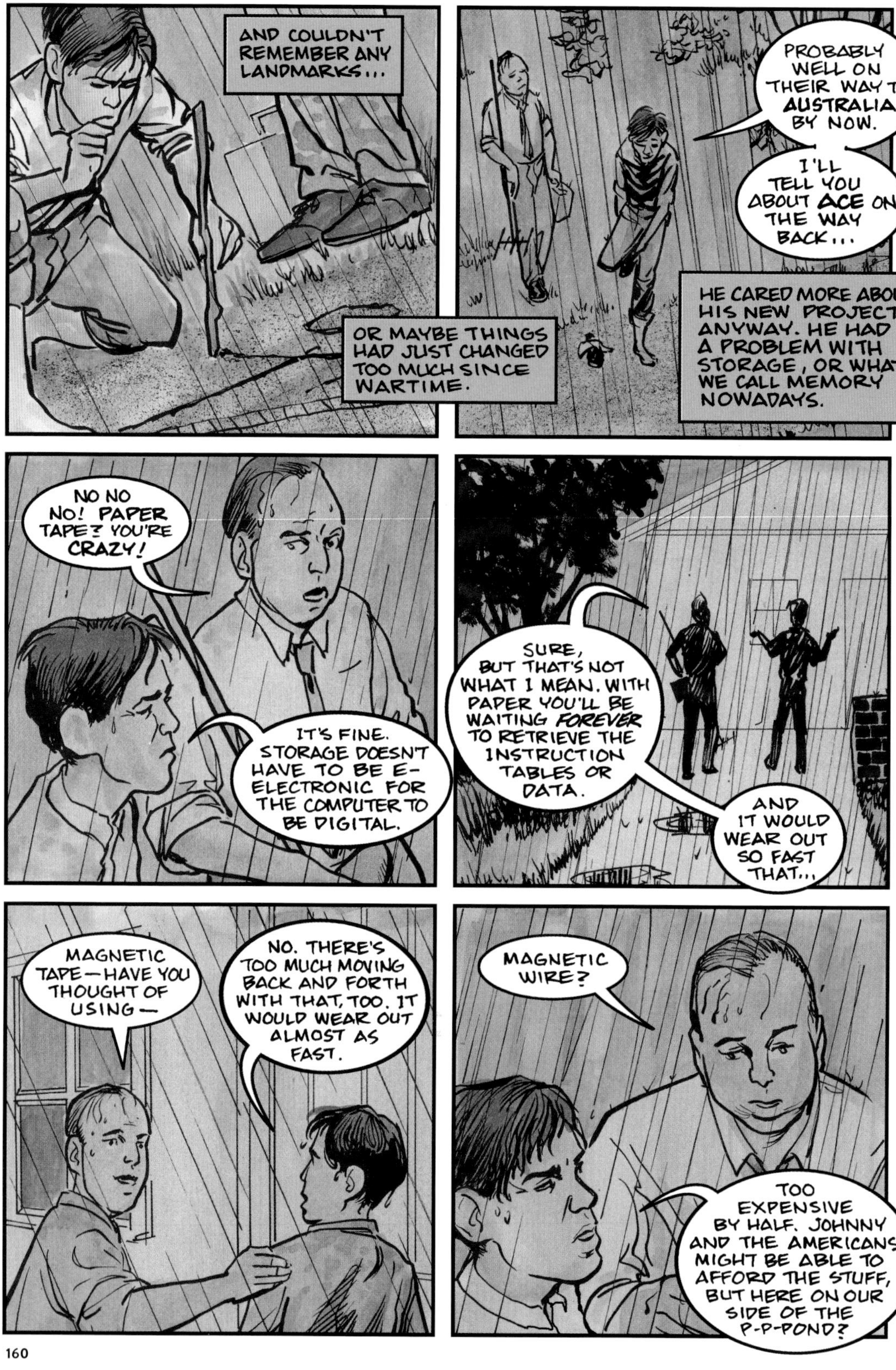
AND COULDN'T REMEMBER ANY LANDMARKS...
OR MAYBE THINGS HAD JUST CHANGED TOO MUCH SINCE WARTIME.
PROBABLY WELL ON THEIR WAY TO AUSTRALIA BY NOW.
I'LL TELL YOU ABOUT ACE ON THE WAY BACK...
HE CARED MORE ABOUT HIS NEW PROJECT, ANYWAY. HE HAD A PROBLEM WITH STORAGE, OR WHAT WE CALL MEMORY NOWADAYS.
NO NO NO! PAPER TAPE? YOU'RE CRAZY!
IT'S FINE. STORAGE DOESN'T HAVE TO BE E-ELECTRONIC FOR THE COMPUTER TO BE DIGITAL.
SURE, BUT THAT'S NOT WHAT I MEAN. WITH PAPER YOU'LL BE WAITING FOREVER TO RETRIEVE THE INSTRUCTION TABLES OR DATA.
AND IT WOULD WEAR OUT SO FAST THAT...
MAGNETIC TAPE—HAVE YOU THOUGHT OF USING—
NO. THERE'S TOO MUCH MOVING BACK AND FORTH WITH THAT, TOO. IT WOULD WEAR OUT ALMOST AS FAST.
MAGNETIC WIRE?
TOO EXPENSIVE BY HALF. JOHNNY AND THE AMERICANS MIGHT BE ABLE TO AFFORD THE STUFF, BUT HERE ON OUR SIDE OF THE P-P-POND?

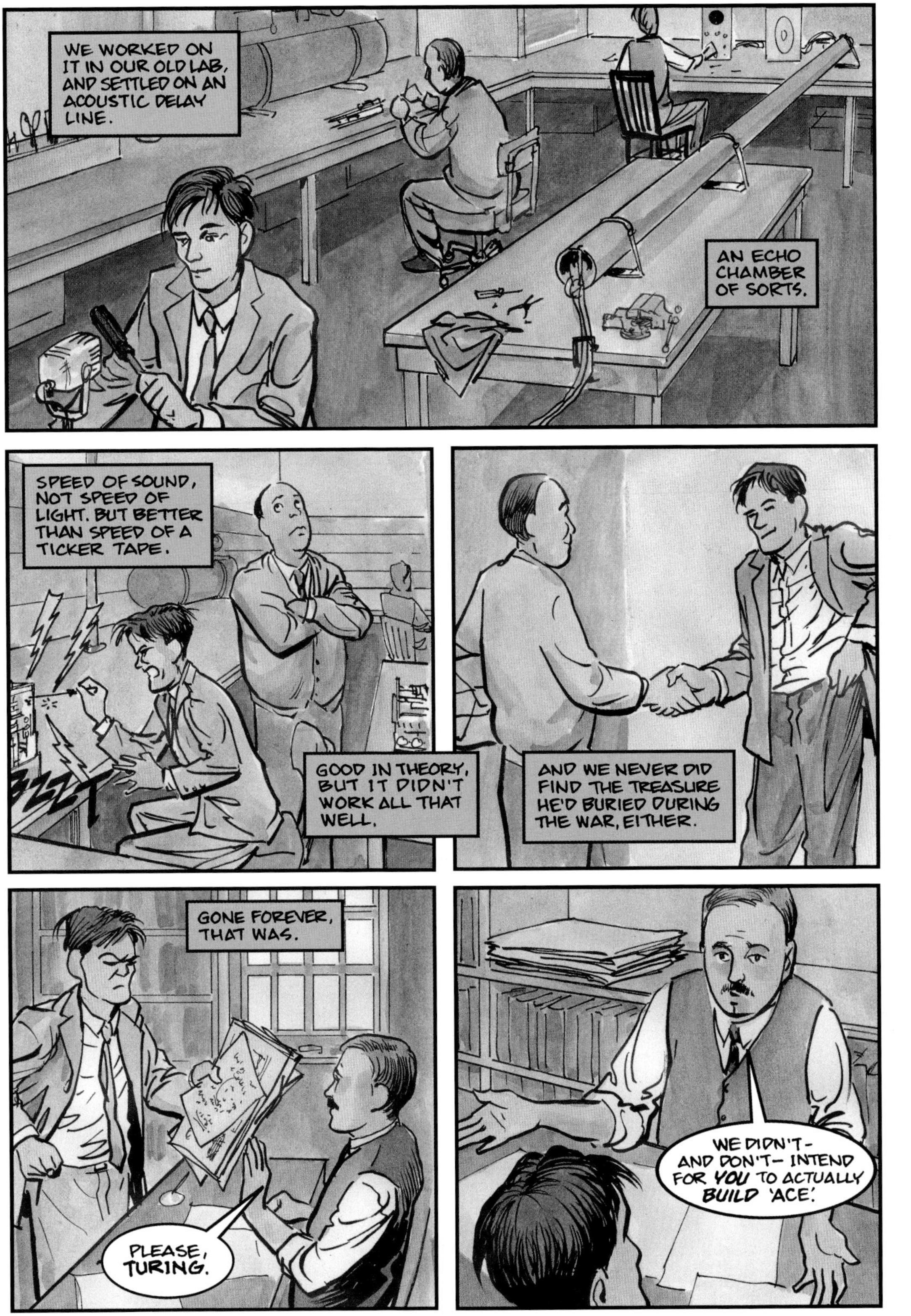
WE WORKED ON IT IN OUR OLD LAB, AND SETTLED ON AN ACOUSTIC DELAY LINE.
AN ECHO CHAMBER OF SORTS.
SPEED OF SOUND, NOT SPEED OF LIGHT. BUT BETTER THAN SPEED OF A TICKER TAPE.
BZZZT
GOOD IN THEORY, BUT IT DIDN'T WORK ALL THAT WELL.
AND WE NEVER DID FIND THE TREASURE HE'D BURIED DURING THE WAR, EITHER.
GONE FOREVER, THAT WAS.
PLEASE, TURING.
WE DIDN'T- AND DON'T- INTEND FOR ***YOU*** TO ACTUALLY ***BUILD*** 'ACE'.

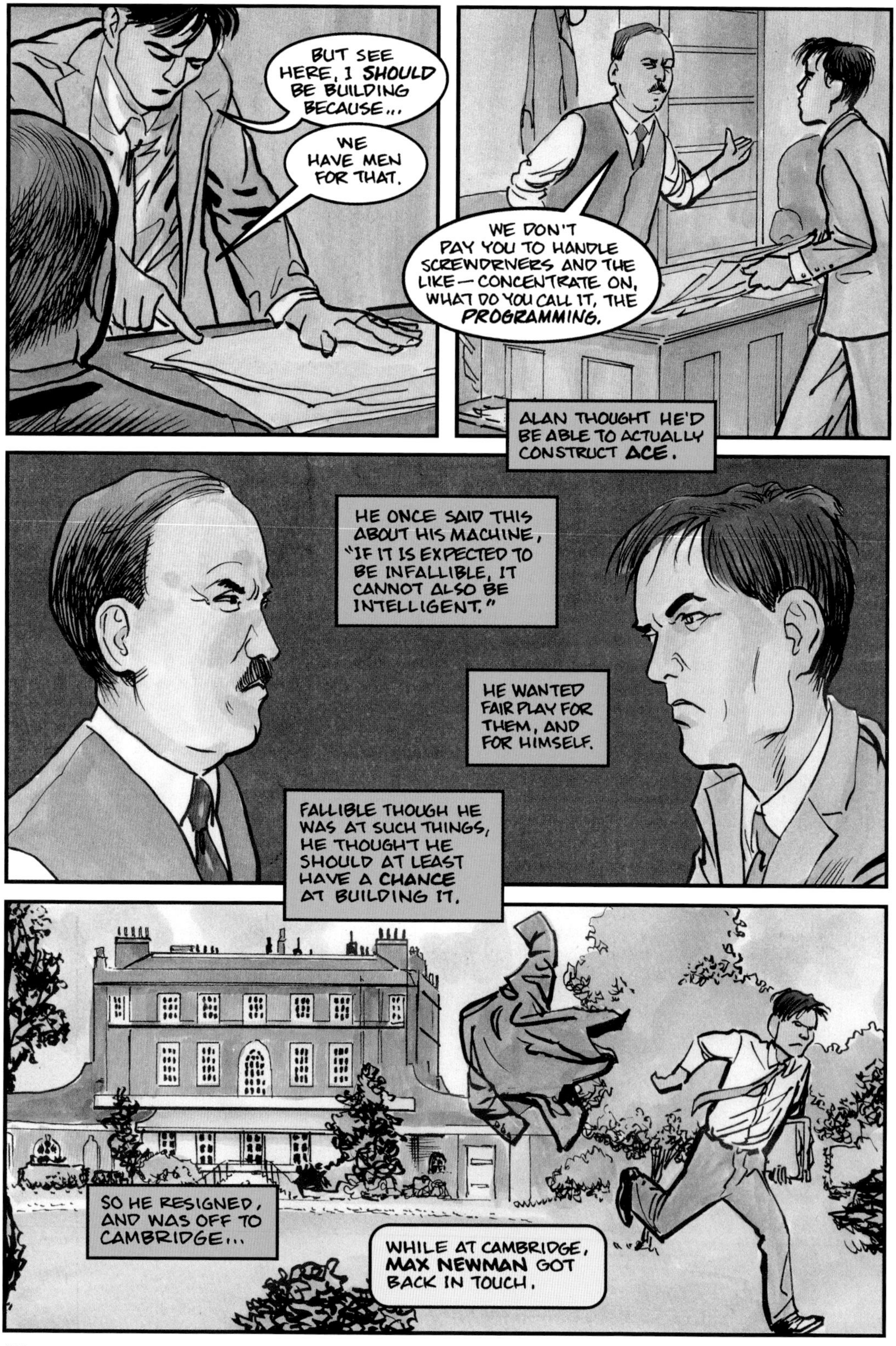
BUT SEE HERE, I SHOULD BE BUILDING BECAUSE...
WE HAVE MEN FOR THAT.
WE DON'T PAY YOU TO HANDLE SCREWDRIVERS AND THE LIKE— CONCENTRATE ON, WHAT DO YOU CALL IT, THE PROGRAMMING.
ALAN THOUGHT HE'D BE ABLE TO ACTUALLY CONSTRUCT ACE.
HE ONCE SAID THIS ABOUT HIS MACHINE, "IF IT IS EXPECTED TO BE INFALLIBLE, IT CANNOT ALSO BE INTELLIGENT."
HE WANTED FAIR PLAY FOR THEM, AND FOR HIMSELF.
FALLIBLE THOUGH HE WAS AT SUCH THINGS, HE THOUGHT HE SHOULD AT LEAST HAVE A CHANCE AT BUILDING IT.
SO HE RESIGNED, AND WAS OFF TO CAMBRIDGE...
WHILE AT CAMBRIDGE, MAX NEWMAN GOT BACK IN TOUCH.

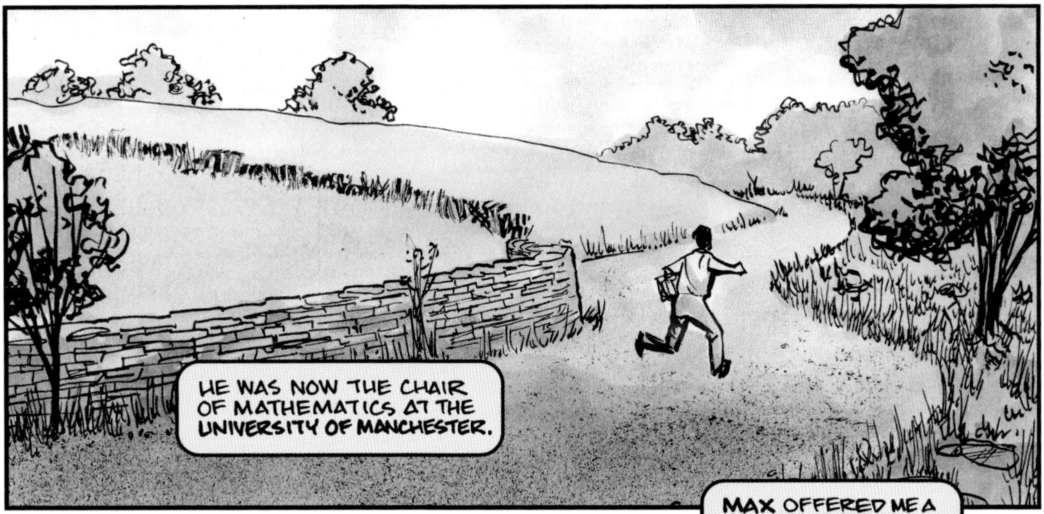
HE WAS NOW THE CHAIR OF MATHEMATICS AT THE UNIVERSITY OF MANCHESTER.

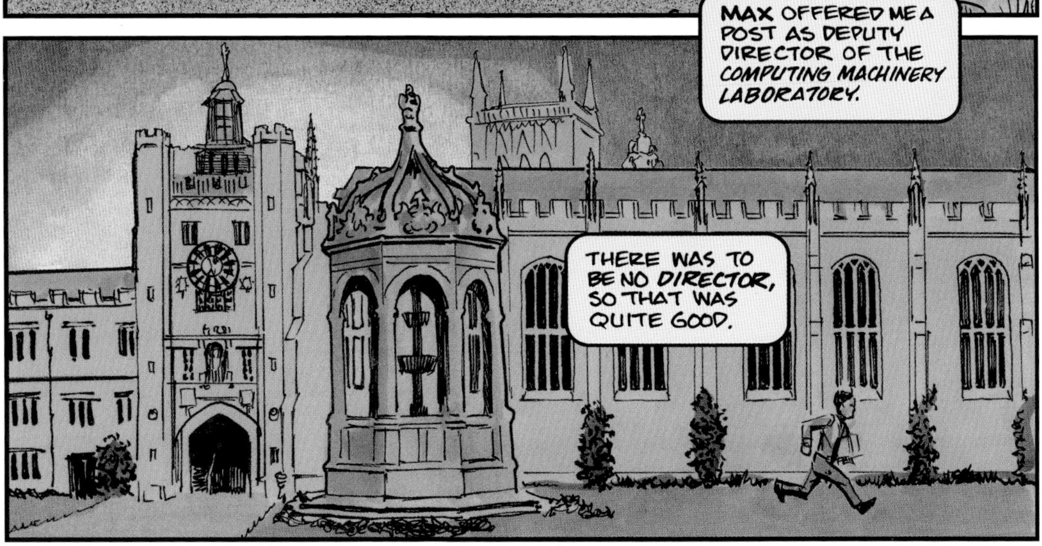
MAX OFFERED ME A POST AS DEPUTY DIRECTOR OF THE COMPUTING MACHINERY LABORATORY.
THERE WAS TO BE NO DIRECTOR, SO THAT WAS QUITE GOOD.

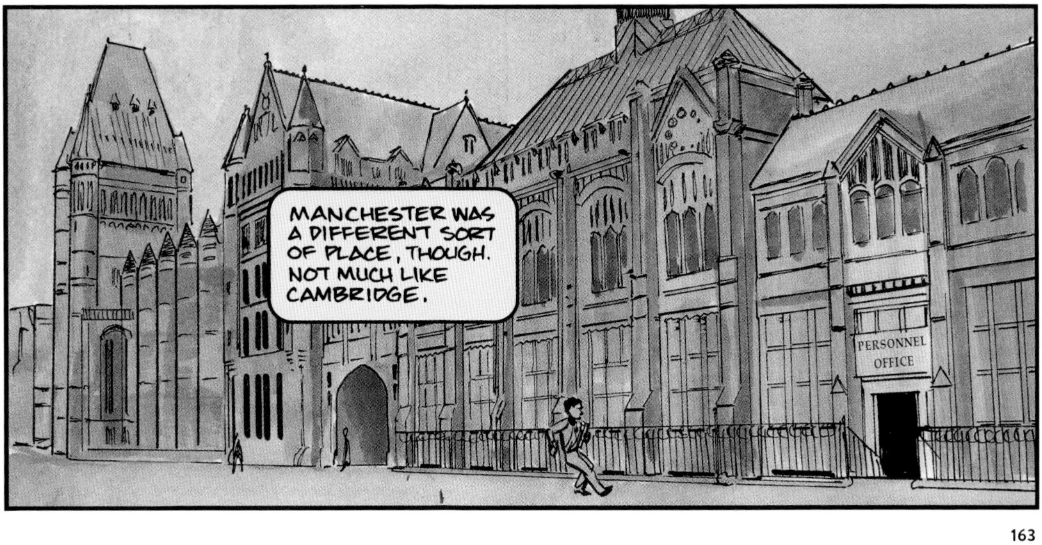
MANCHESTER WAS A DIFFERENT SORT OF PLACE, THOUGH. NOT MUCH LIKE CAMBRIDGE.
PERSONNEL OFFICE

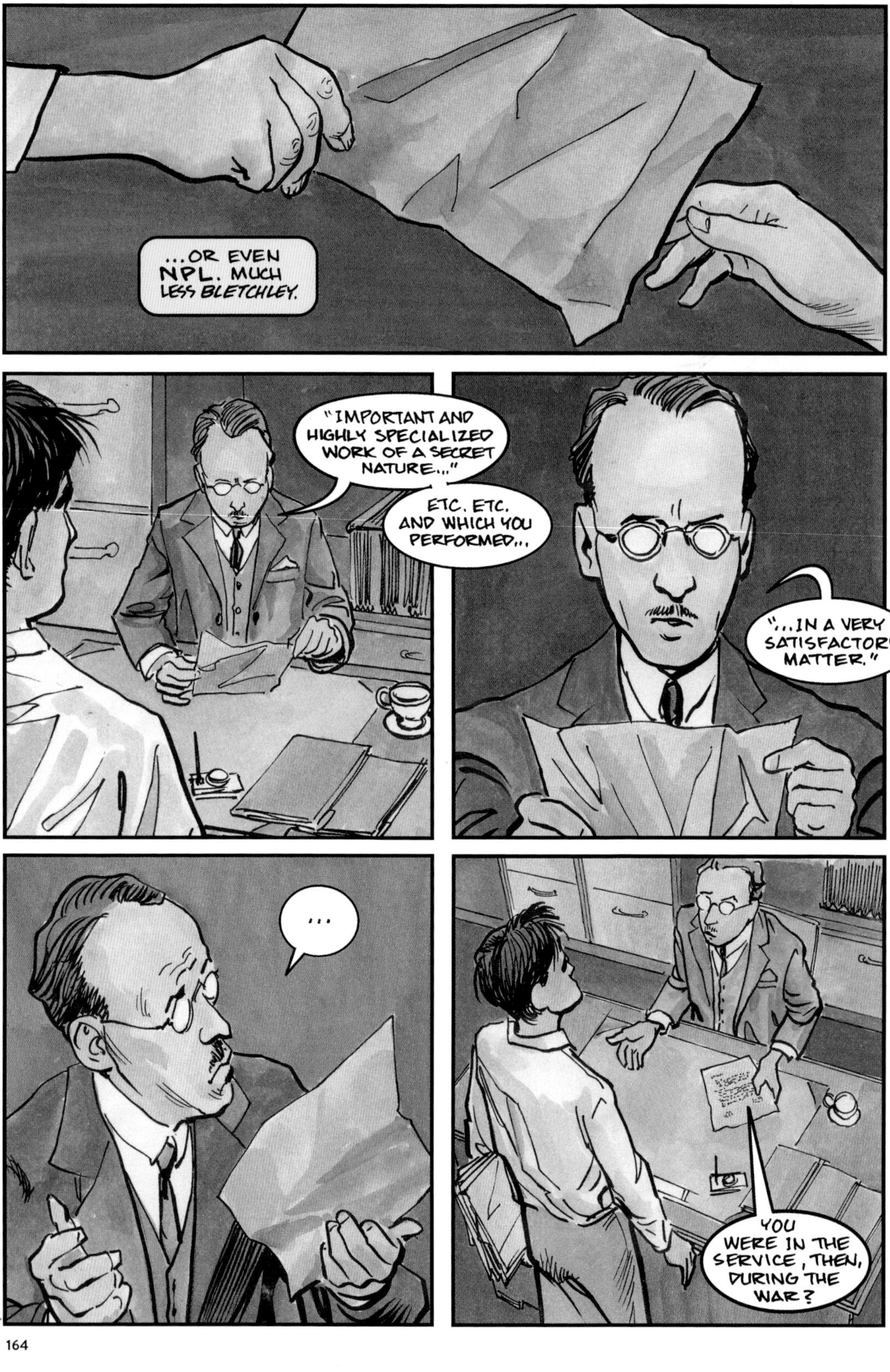
...OR EVEN NPL. MUCH LESS BLETCHLEY.
"IMPORTANT AND HIGHLY SPECIALIZED WORK OF A SECRET NATURE..."
ETC. ETC. AND WHICH YOU PERFORMED...
"...IN A VERY SATISFACTORY MATTER."
...
YOU WERE IN THE SERVICE, THEN, DURING THE WAR?

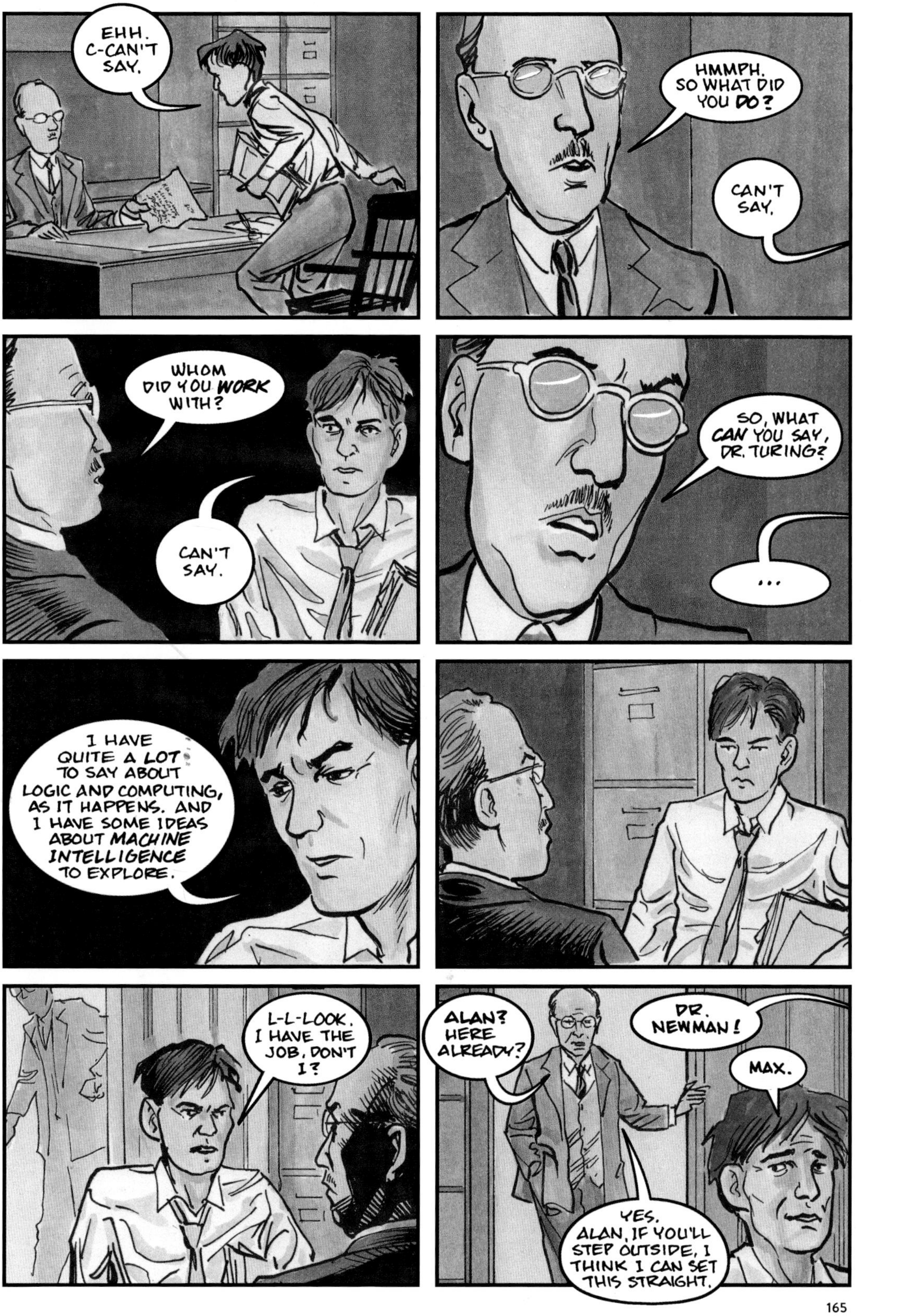
EHH. C-CAN'T SAY.
HMMPH. SO WHAT DID YOU DO?
CAN'T SAY.
WHOM DID YOU WORK WITH?
CAN'T SAY.
SO, WHAT CAN YOU SAY, DR. TURING?
...
I HAVE QUITE A LOT TO SAY ABOUT LOGIC AND COMPUTING, AS IT HAPPENS. AND I HAVE SOME IDEAS ABOUT MACHINE INTELLIGENCE TO EXPLORE.
L-L-LOOK. I HAVE THE JOB, DON'T I?
ALAN? HERE ALREADY?
DR. NEWMAN!
MAX.
YES. ALAN, IF YOU'LL STEP OUTSIDE, I THINK I CAN SET THIS STRAIGHT.

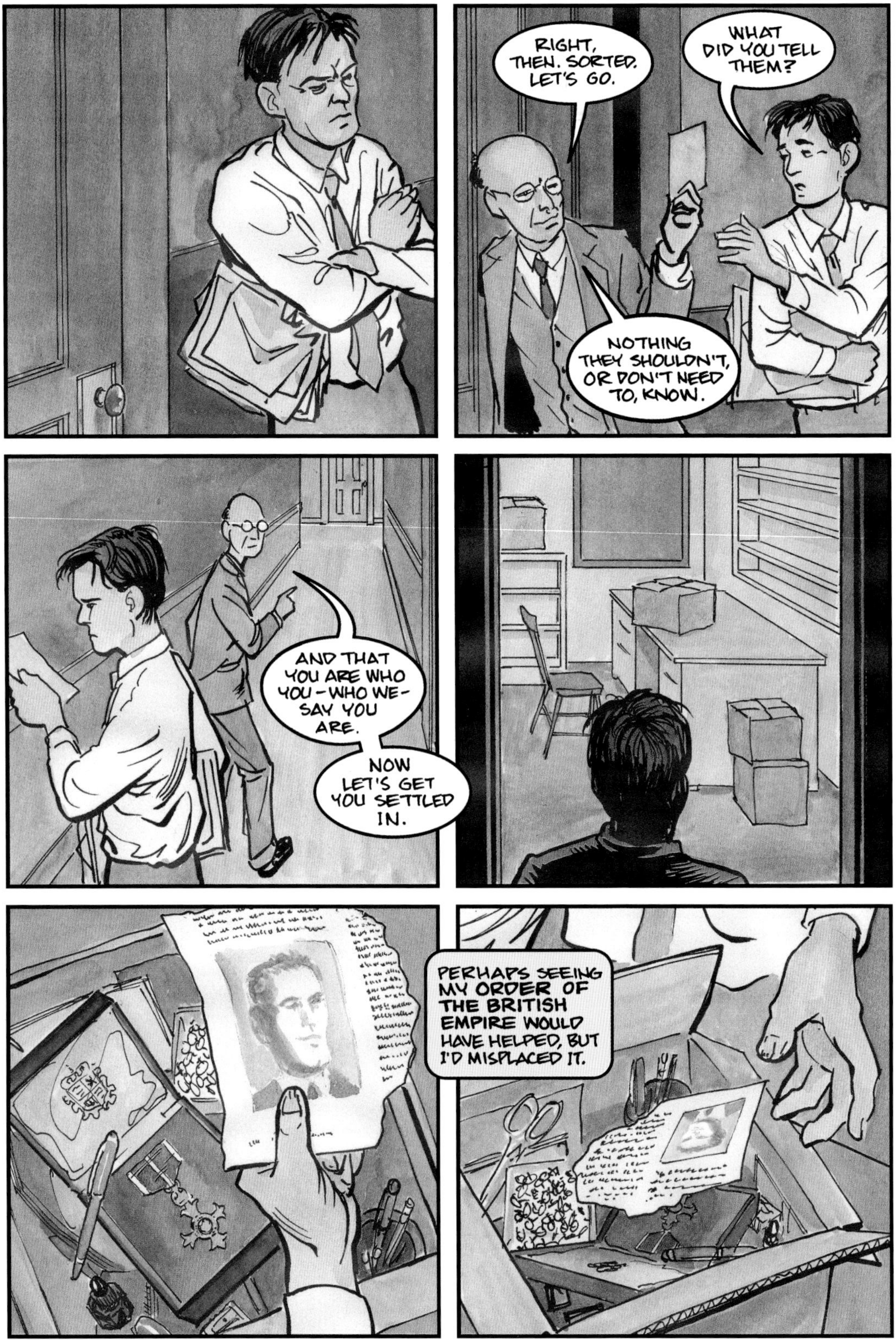

RIGHT, THEN. SORTED. LET'S GO.
WHAT DID YOU TELL THEM?
NOTHING THEY SHOULDN'T, OR DON'T NEED TO, KNOW.
AND THAT YOU ARE WHO YOU - WHO WE - SAY YOU ARE.
NOW LET'S GET YOU SETTLED IN.
PERHAPS SEEING MY ORDER OF THE BRITISH EMPIRE WOULD HAVE HELPED, BUT I'D MISPLACED IT.

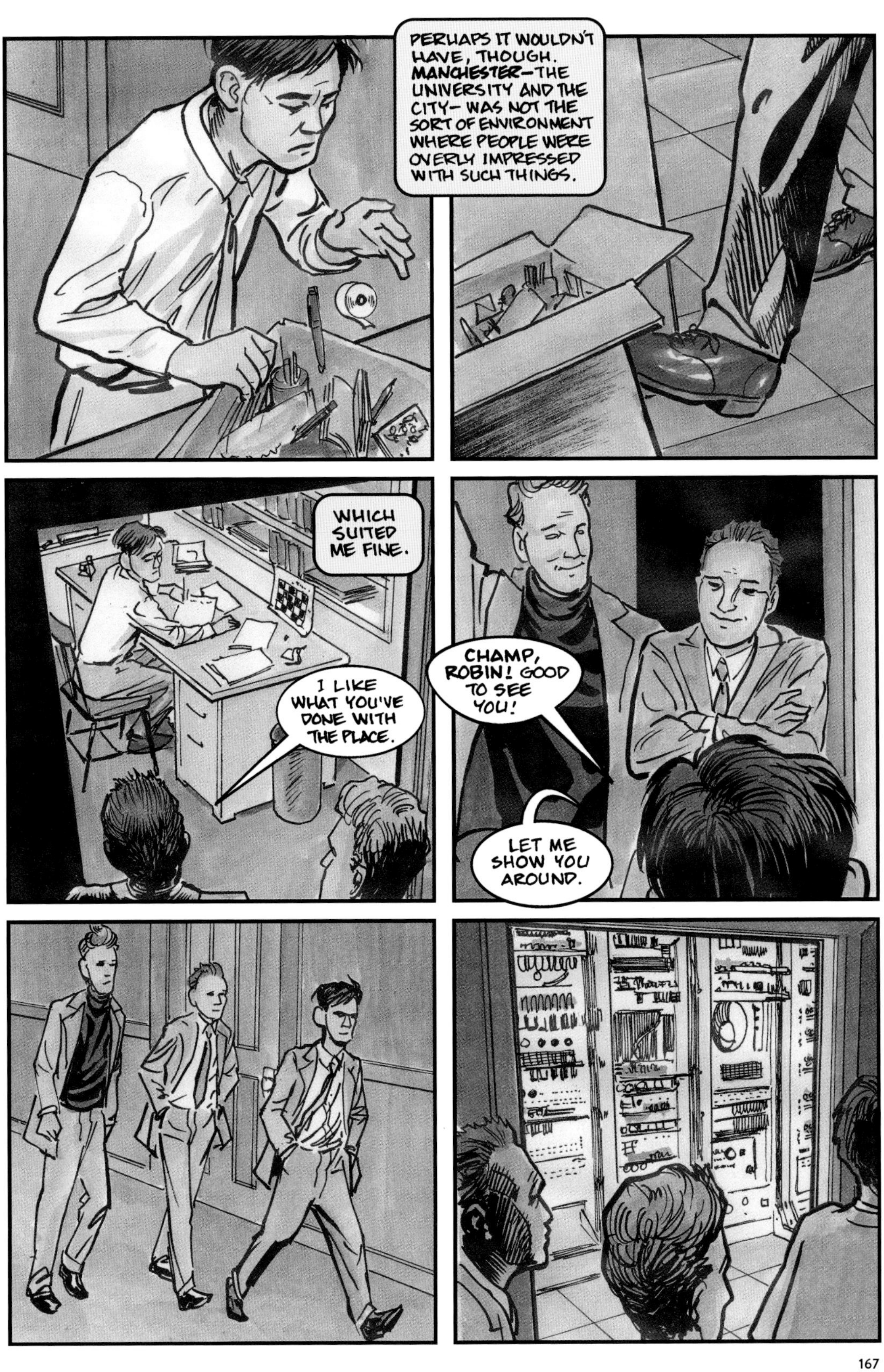
PERHAPS IT WOULDN'T HAVE, THOUGH. MANCHESTER—THE UNIVERSITY AND THE CITY— WAS NOT THE SORT OF ENVIRONMENT WHERE PEOPLE WERE OVERLY IMPRESSED WITH SUCH THINGS.
WHICH SUITED ME FINE.
I LIKE WHAT YOU'VE DONE WITH THE PLACE.
CHAMP, ROBIN! GOOD TO SEE YOU!
LET ME SHOW YOU AROUND.

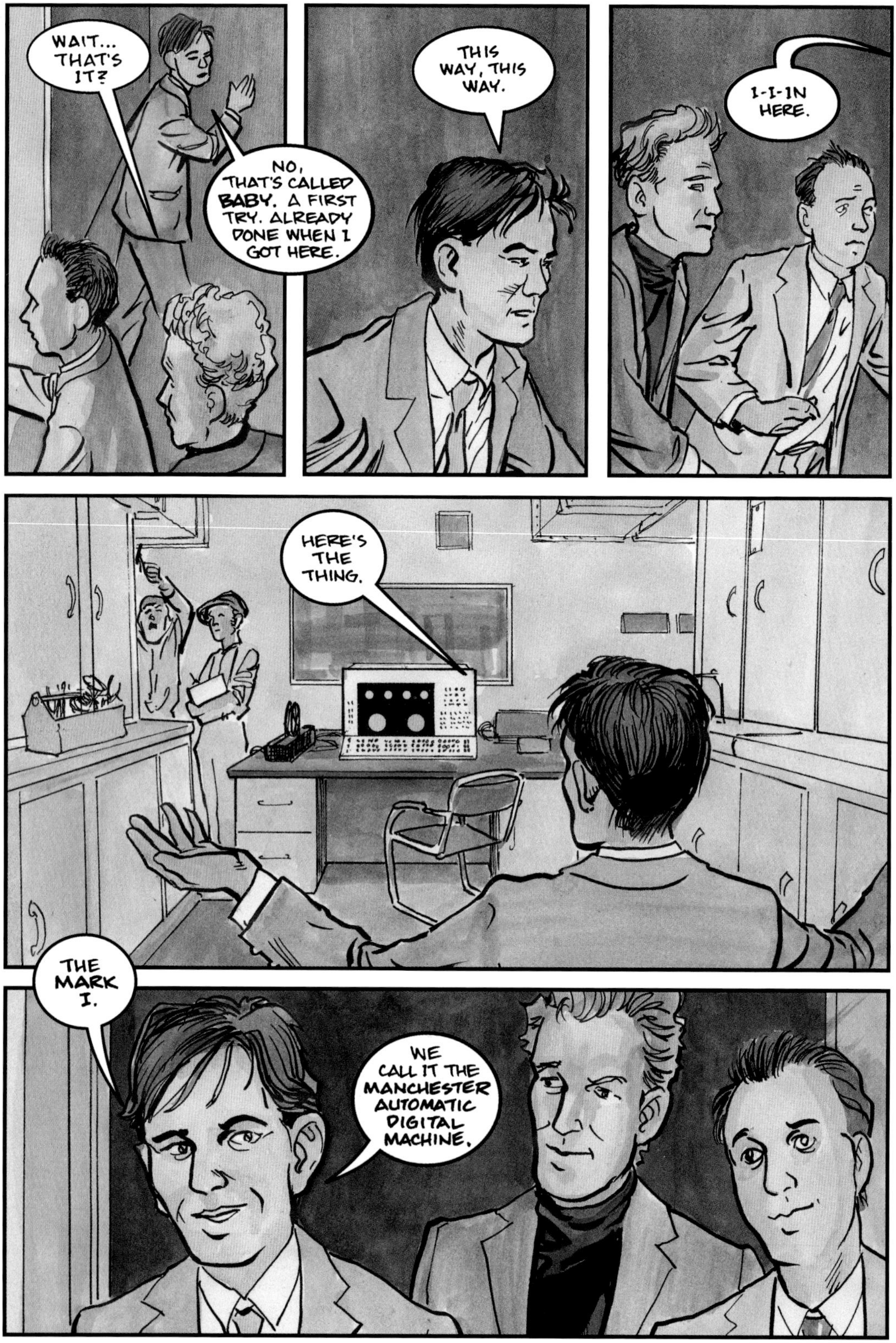
WAIT... THAT'S IT?
NO, THAT'S CALLED BABY. A FIRST TRY. ALREADY DONE WHEN I GOT HERE.
THIS WAY, THIS WAY.
I-I-IN HERE.
HERE'S THE THING.
THE MARK I.
WE CALL IT THE MANCHESTER AUTOMATIC DIGITAL MACHINE.

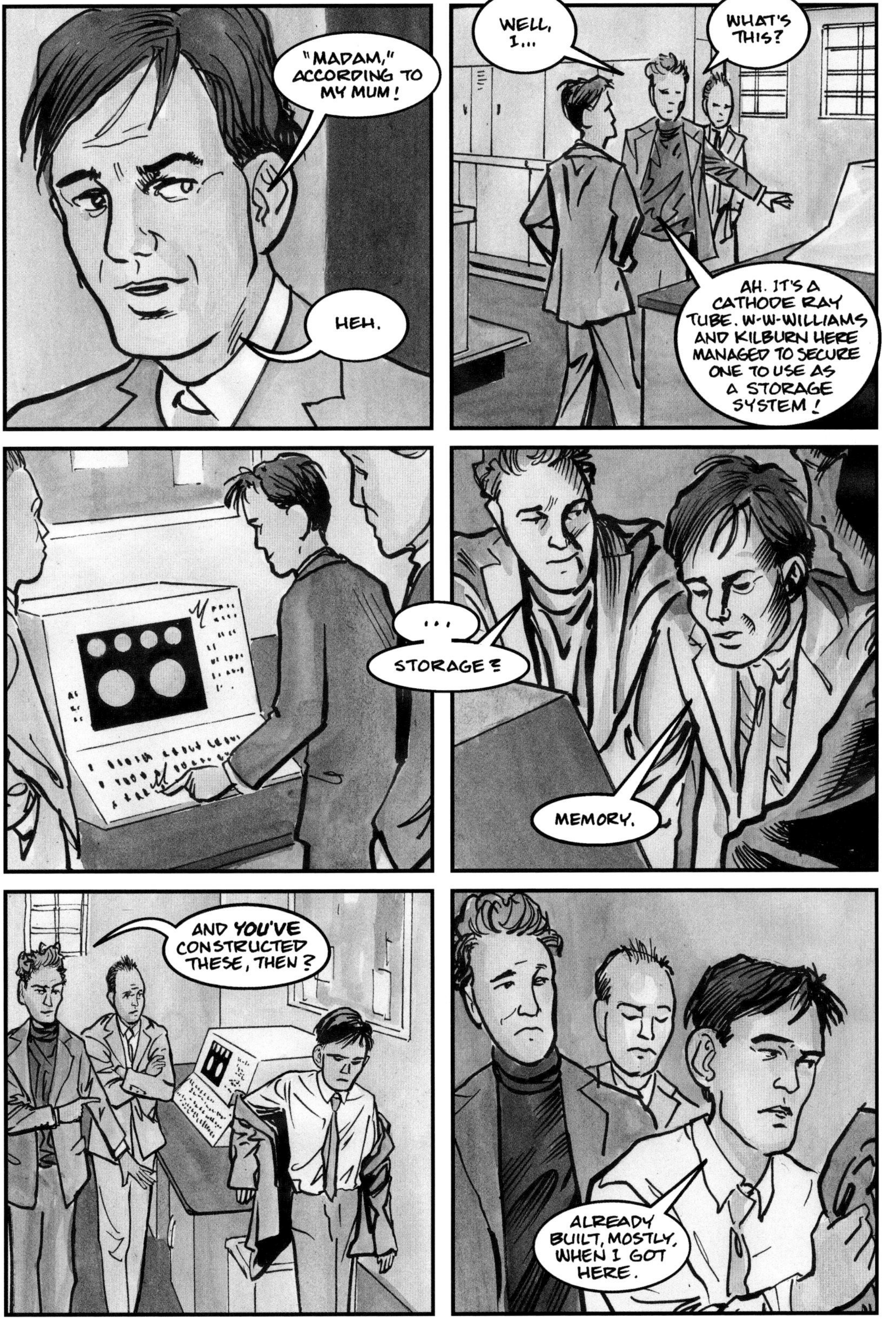
"MADAM," ACCORDING TO MY MUM!
HEH.
WELL, I...
WHAT'S THIS?
AH. IT'S A CATHODE RAY TUBE. W-W-WILLIAMS AND KILBURN HERE MANAGED TO SECURE ONE TO USE AS A STORAGE SYSTEM!
...
STORAGE?
MEMORY.
AND YOU'VE CONSTRUCTED THESE, THEN?
ALREADY BUILT, MOSTLY, WHEN I GOT HERE.

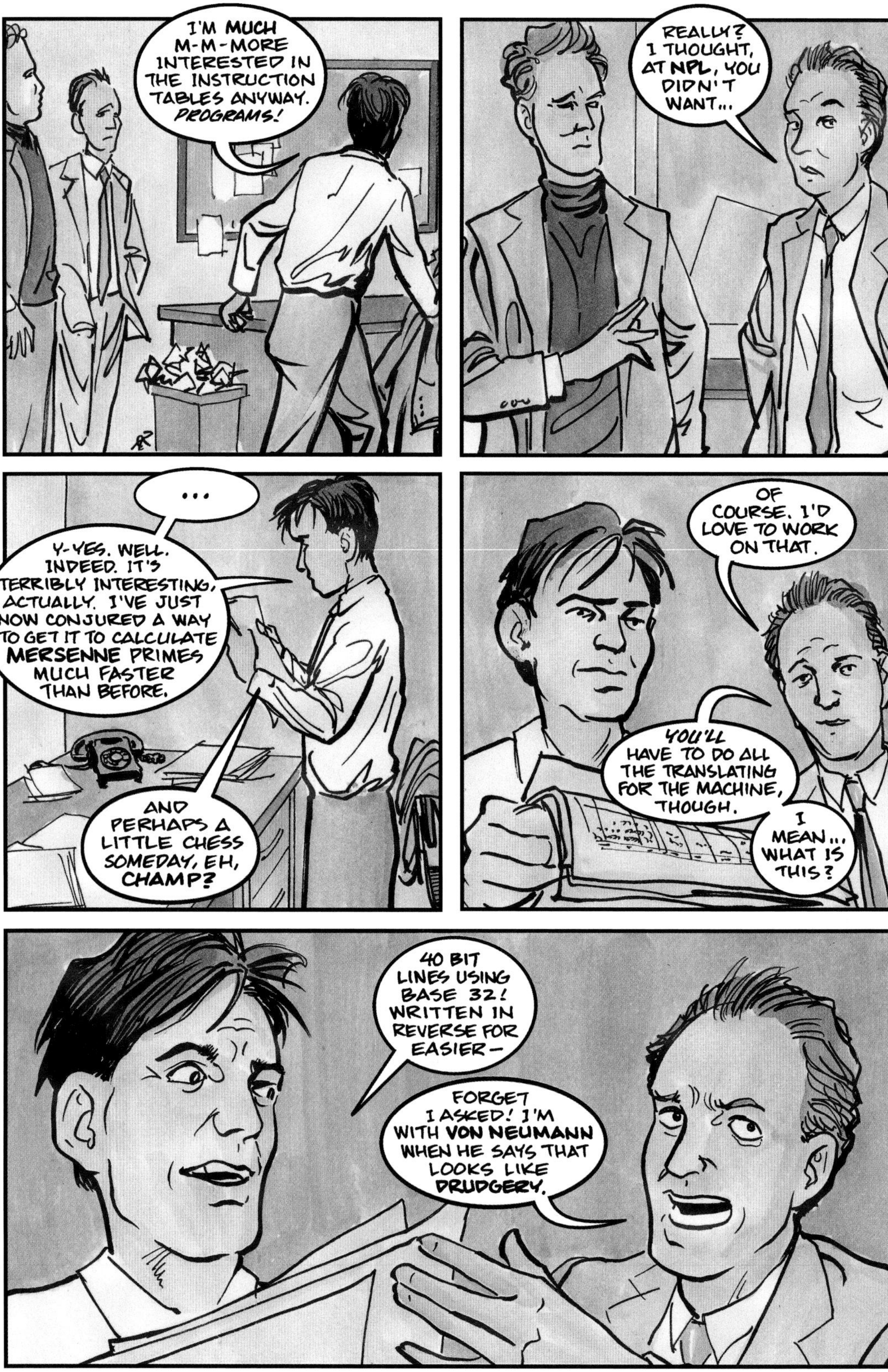

I'M MUCH M-M-MORE INTERESTED IN THE INSTRUCTION TABLES ANYWAY. PROGRAMS!
REALLY? I THOUGHT, AT NPL, YOU DIDN'T WANT...
...
Y-YES. WELL. INDEED. IT'S TERRIBLY INTERESTING, ACTUALLY. I'VE JUST NOW CONJURED A WAY TO GET IT TO CALCULATE MERSENNE PRIMES MUCH FASTER THAN BEFORE.
AND PERHAPS A LITTLE CHESS SOMEDAY, EH, CHAMP?
OF COURSE. I'D LOVE TO WORK ON THAT.
YOU'LL HAVE TO DO ALL THE TRANSLATING FOR THE MACHINE, THOUGH.
I MEAN... WHAT IS THIS?
40 BIT LINES USING BASE 32! WRITTEN IN REVERSE FOR EASIER—
FORGET I ASKED! I'M WITH VON NEUMANN WHEN HE SAYS THAT LOOKS LIKE DRUDGERY.

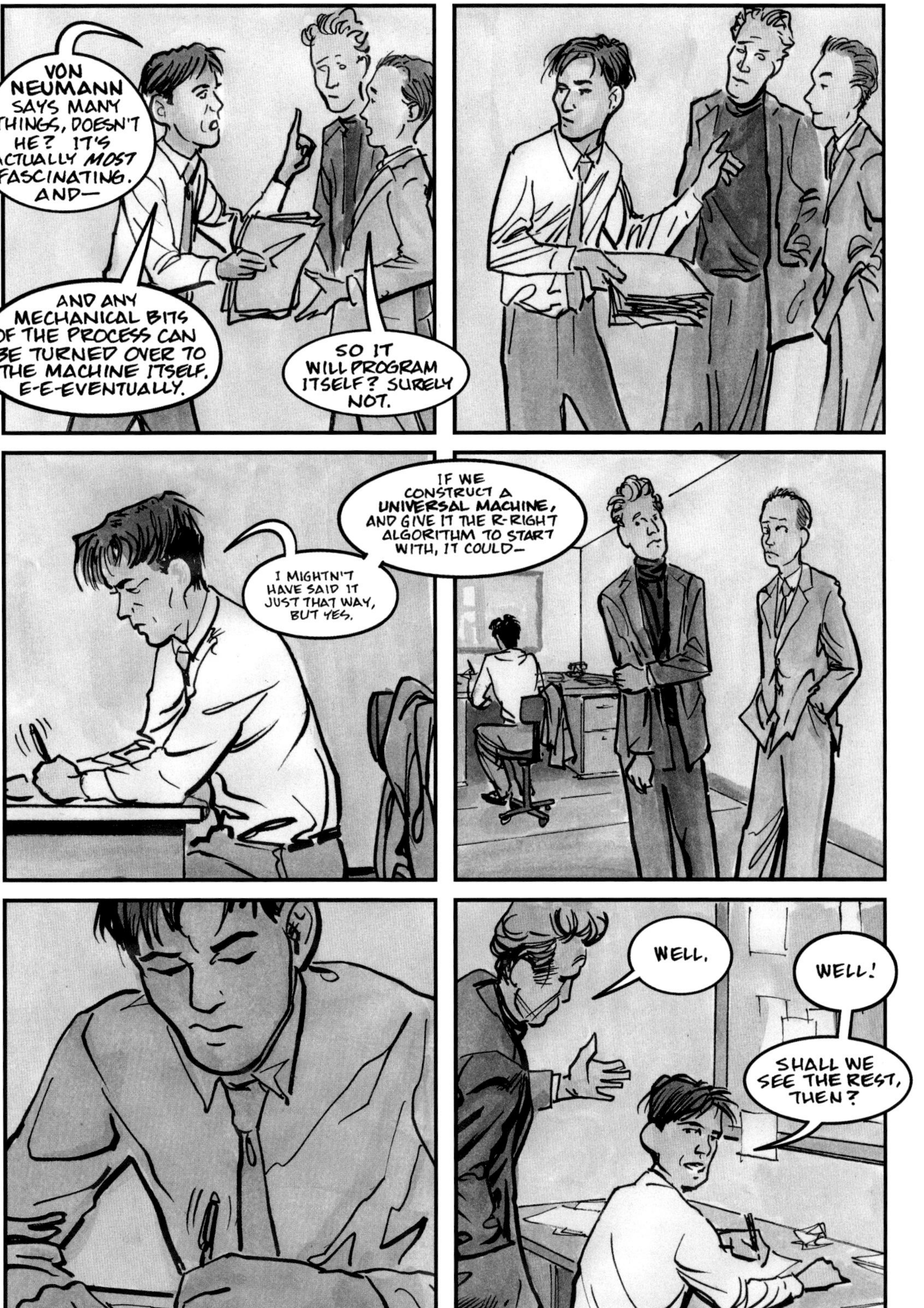
VON NEUMANN SAYS MANY THINGS, DOESN'T HE? IT'S ACTUALLY *MOST* FASCINATING. AND—
AND ANY MECHANICAL BITS OF THE PROCESS CAN BE TURNED OVER TO THE MACHINE ITSELF. E-E-EVENTUALLY.
SO IT WILL PROGRAM ITSELF? SURELY NOT.
IF WE CONSTRUCT A **UNIVERSAL MACHINE**, AND GIVE IT THE R-RIGHT ALGORITHM TO START WITH, IT COULD—
I MIGHTN'T HAVE SAID IT JUST THAT WAY, BUT YES.
WELL.
WELL!
SHALL WE SEE THE REST, THEN?

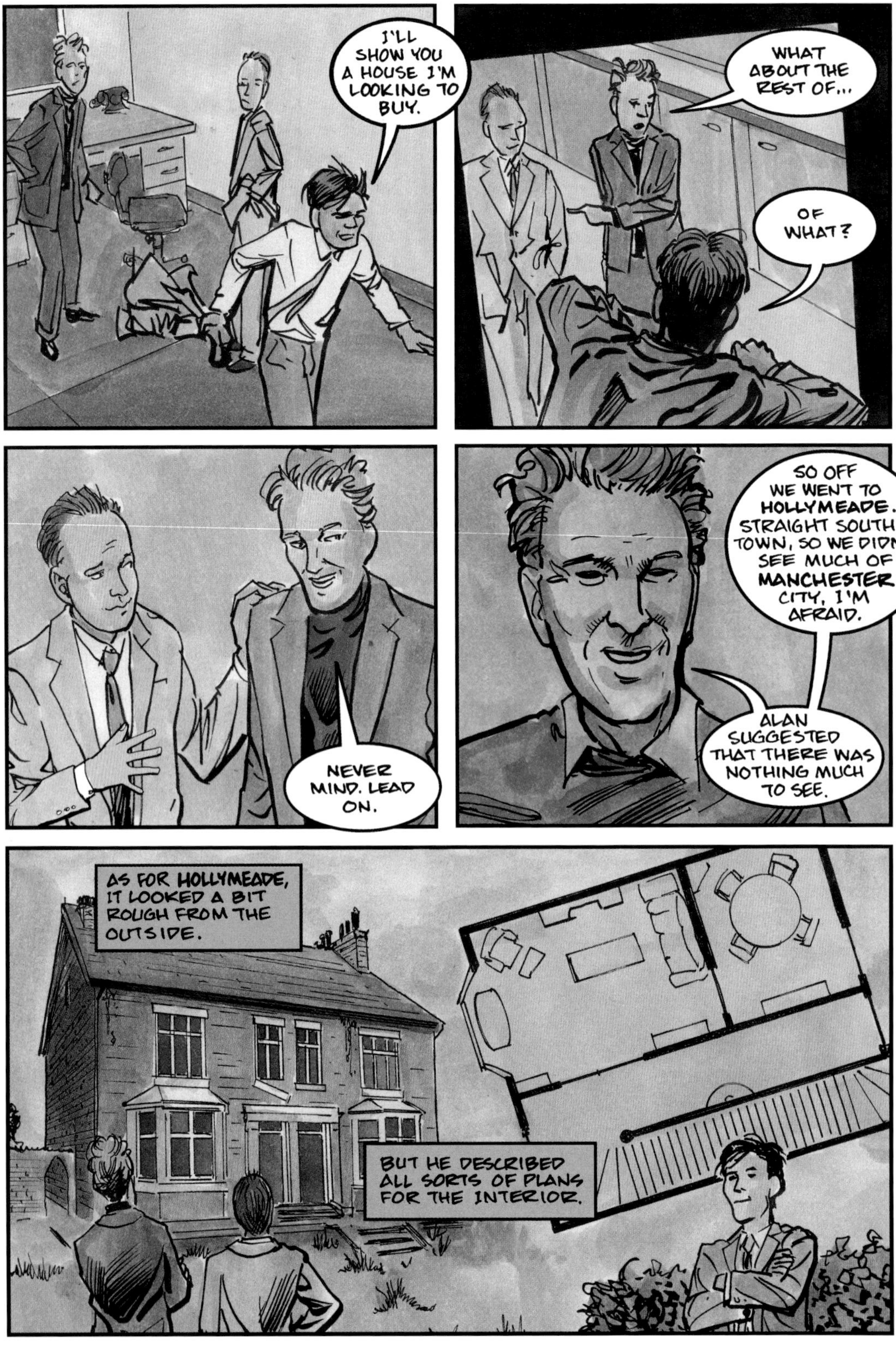
I'LL SHOW YOU A HOUSE I'M LOOKING TO BUY.
WHAT ABOUT THE REST OF...
OF WHAT?
NEVER MIND. LEAD ON.
SO OFF WE WENT TO HOLLYMEADE. STRAIGHT SOUTH OF TOWN, SO WE DIDN'T SEE MUCH OF MANCHESTER CITY, I'M AFRAID.
ALAN SUGGESTED THAT THERE WAS NOTHING MUCH TO SEE.
AS FOR HOLLYMEADE, IT LOOKED A BIT ROUGH FROM THE OUTSIDE.
BUT HE DESCRIBED ALL SORTS OF PLANS FOR THE INTERIOR.

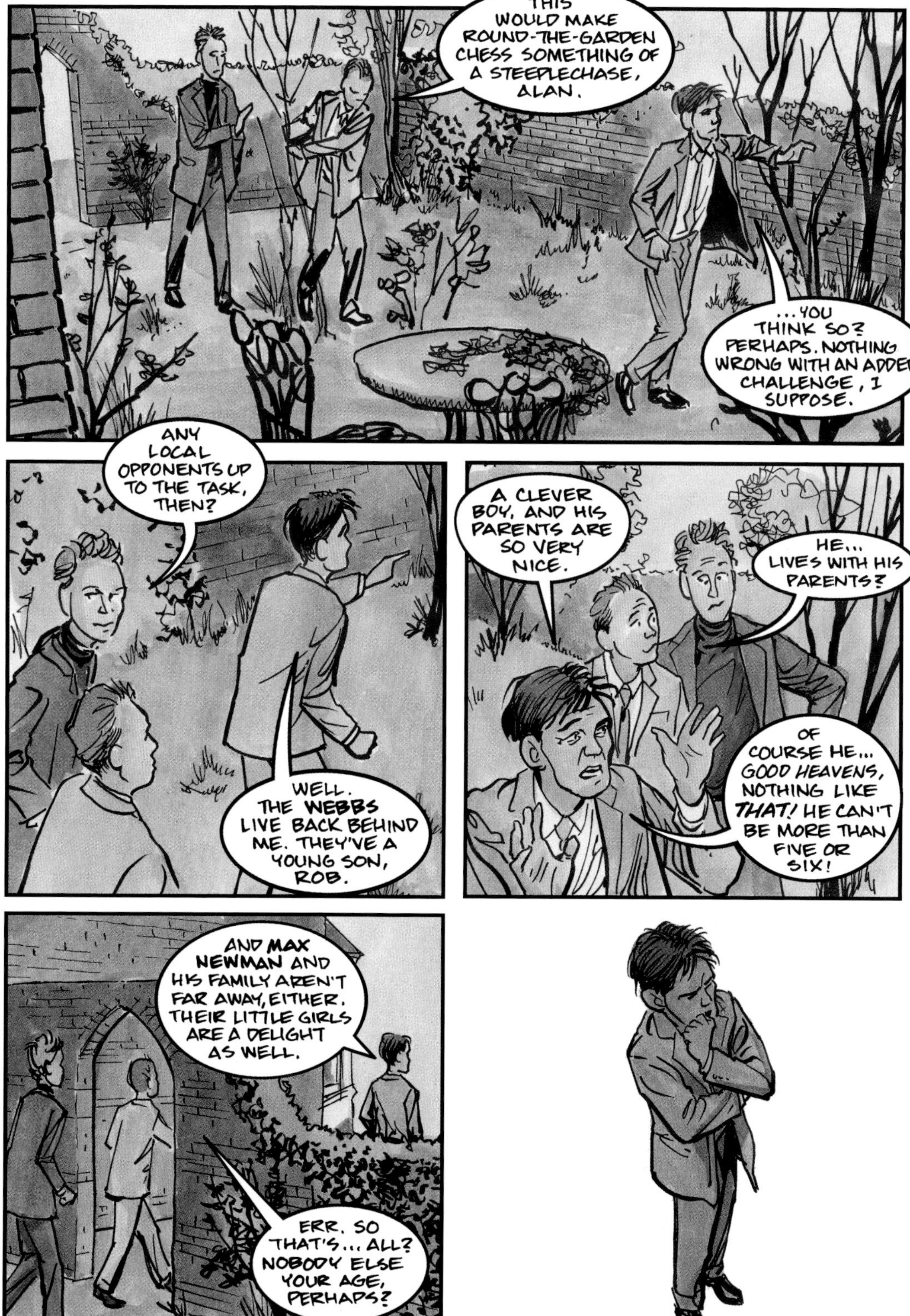
THIS WOULD MAKE ROUND-THE-GARDEN CHESS SOMETHING OF A STEEPLECHASE, ALAN.
...YOU THINK SO? PERHAPS. NOTHING WRONG WITH AN ADDED CHALLENGE, I SUPPOSE.
ANY LOCAL OPPONENTS UP TO THE TASK, THEN?
WELL. THE WEBBS LIVE BACK BEHIND ME. THEY'VE A YOUNG SON, ROB.
A CLEVER BOY, AND HIS PARENTS ARE SO VERY NICE.
HE... LIVES WITH HIS PARENTS?
OF COURSE HE... GOOD HEAVENS, NOTHING LIKE THAT! HE CAN'T BE MORE THAN FIVE OR SIX!
AND MAX NEWMAN AND HIS FAMILY AREN'T FAR AWAY, EITHER. THEIR LITTLE GIRLS ARE A DELIGHT AS WELL.
ERR. SO THAT'S... ALL? NOBODY ELSE YOUR AGE, PERHAPS?

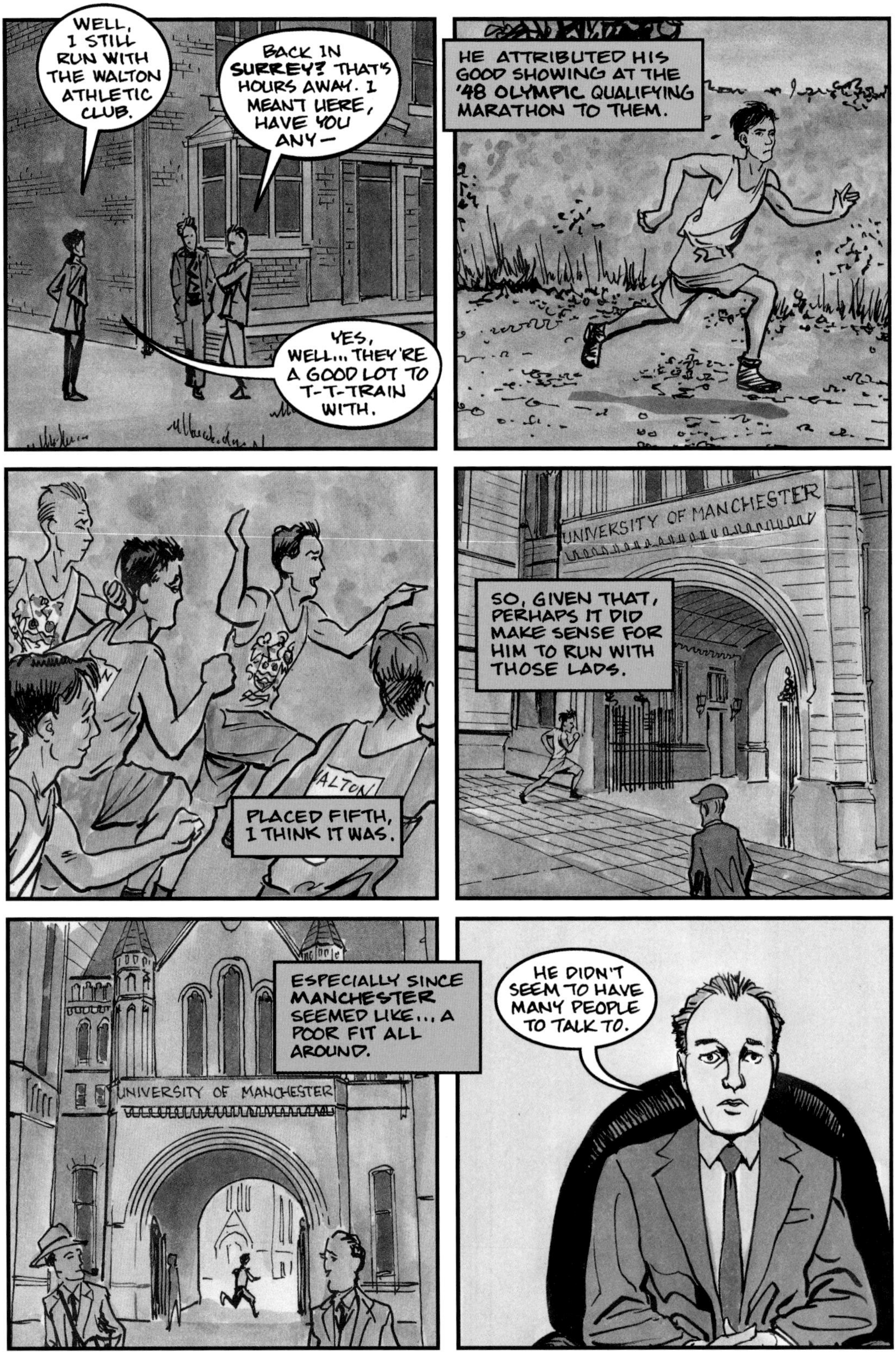
WELL, I STILL RUN WITH THE WALTON ATHLETIC CLUB.
BACK IN SURREY? THAT'S HOURS AWAY. I MEANT HERE, HAVE YOU ANY—
YES, WELL... THEY'RE A GOOD LOT TO T-T-TRAIN WITH.
HE ATTRIBUTED HIS GOOD SHOWING AT THE '48 OLYMPIC QUALIFYING MARATHON TO THEM.
WALTON
PLACED FIFTH, I THINK IT WAS.
UNIVERSITY OF MANCHESTER
SO, GIVEN THAT, PERHAPS IT DID MAKE SENSE FOR HIM TO RUN WITH THOSE LADS.
ESPECIALLY SINCE MANCHESTER SEEMED LIKE... A POOR FIT ALL AROUND.
UNIVERSITY OF MANCHESTER
HE DIDN'T SEEM TO HAVE MANY PEOPLE TO TALK TO.

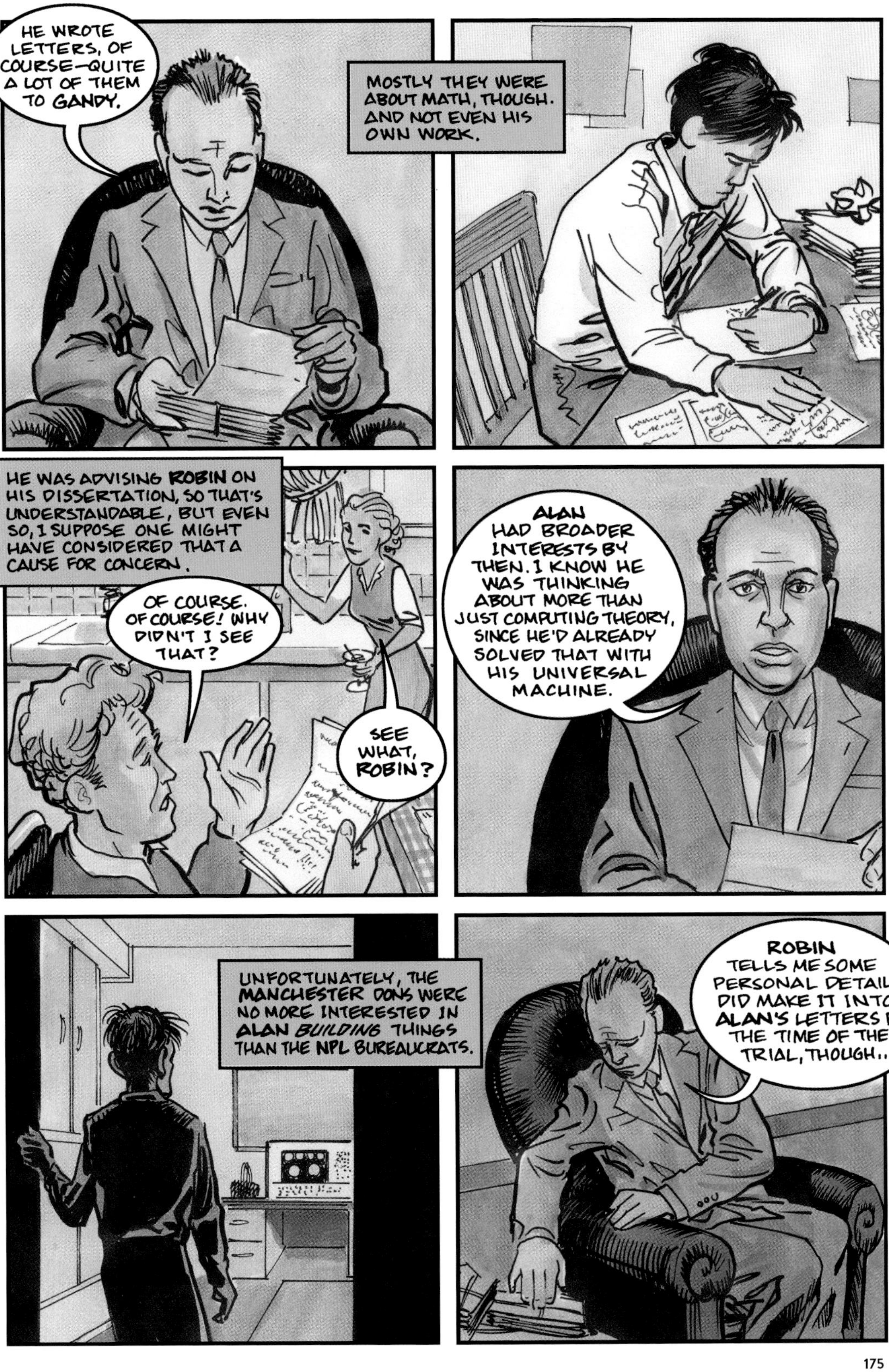

HE WROTE LETTERS, OF COURSE—QUITE A LOT OF THEM TO GANDY.
MOSTLY THEY WERE ABOUT MATH, THOUGH. AND NOT EVEN HIS OWN WORK.
HE WAS ADVISING ROBIN ON HIS DISSERTATION, SO THAT'S UNDERSTANDABLE, BUT EVEN SO, I SUPPOSE ONE MIGHT HAVE CONSIDERED THAT A CAUSE FOR CONCERN.
OF COURSE. OF COURSE! WHY DIDN'T I SEE THAT?
SEE WHAT, ROBIN?
ALAN HAD BROADER INTERESTS BY THEN. I KNOW HE WAS THINKING ABOUT MORE THAN JUST COMPUTING THEORY, SINCE HE'D ALREADY SOLVED THAT WITH HIS UNIVERSAL MACHINE.
UNFORTUNATELY, THE MANCHESTER DONS WERE NO MORE INTERESTED IN ALAN BUILDING THINGS THAN THE NPL BUREAUCRATS.
ROBIN TELLS ME SOME PERSONAL DETAILS DID MAKE IT INTO ALAN'S LETTERS BY THE TIME OF THE TRIAL, THOUGH...

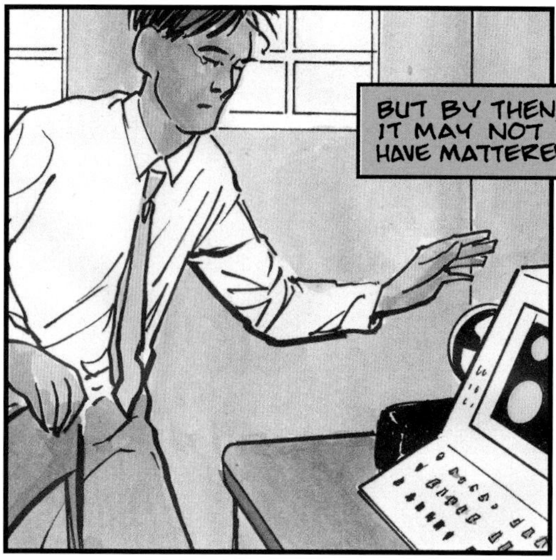
BUT BY THEN, IT MAY NOT HAVE MATTERED.

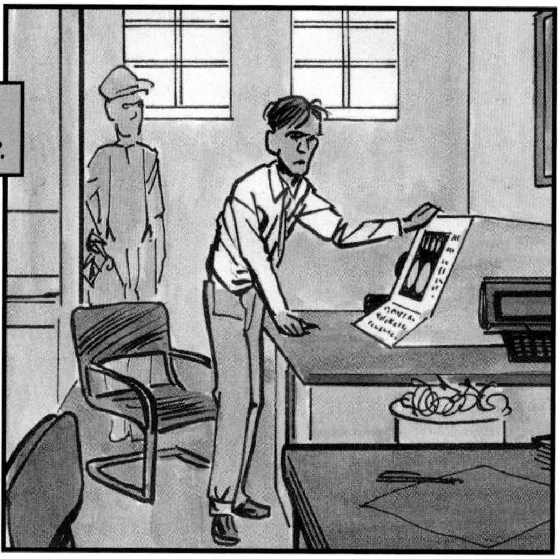

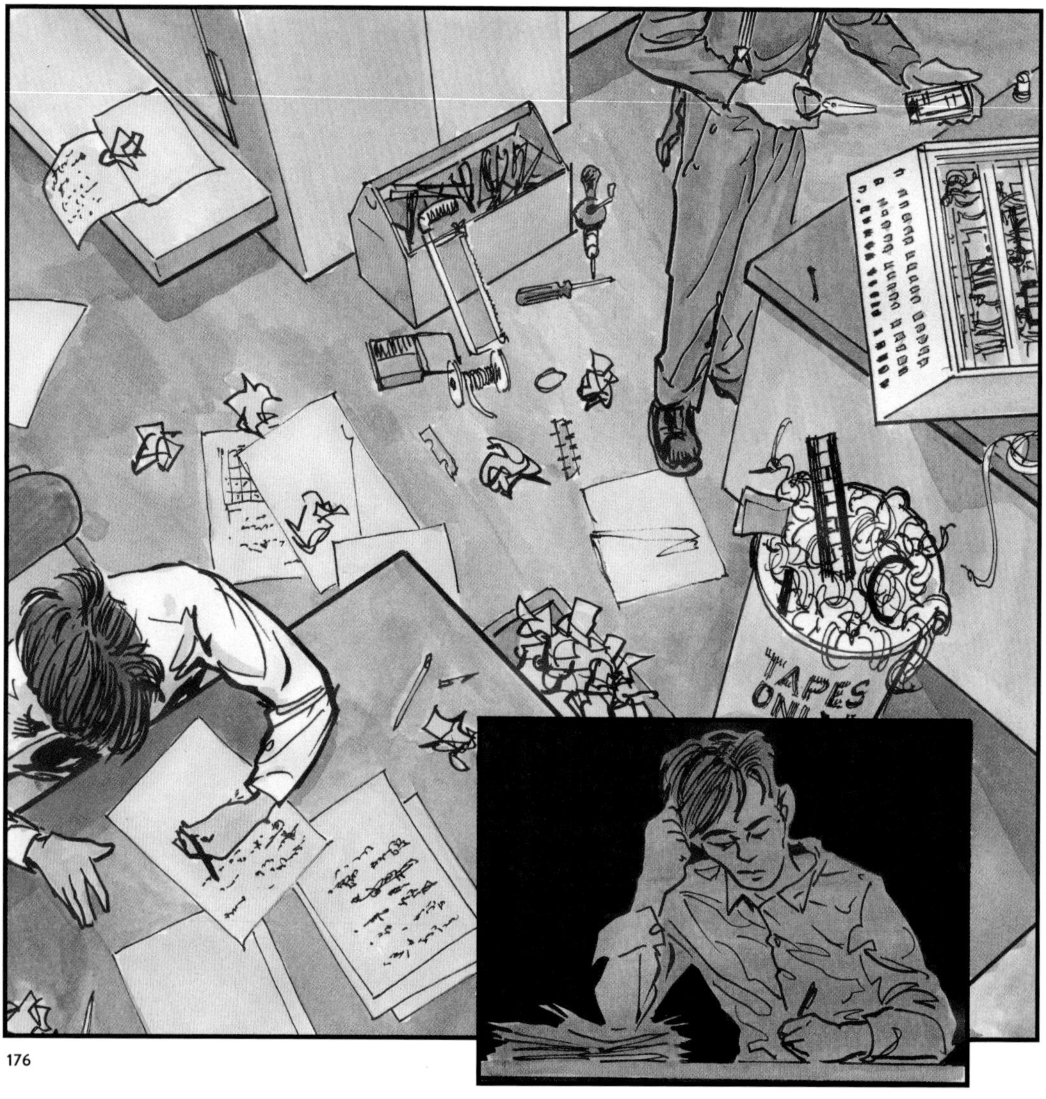
TAPES

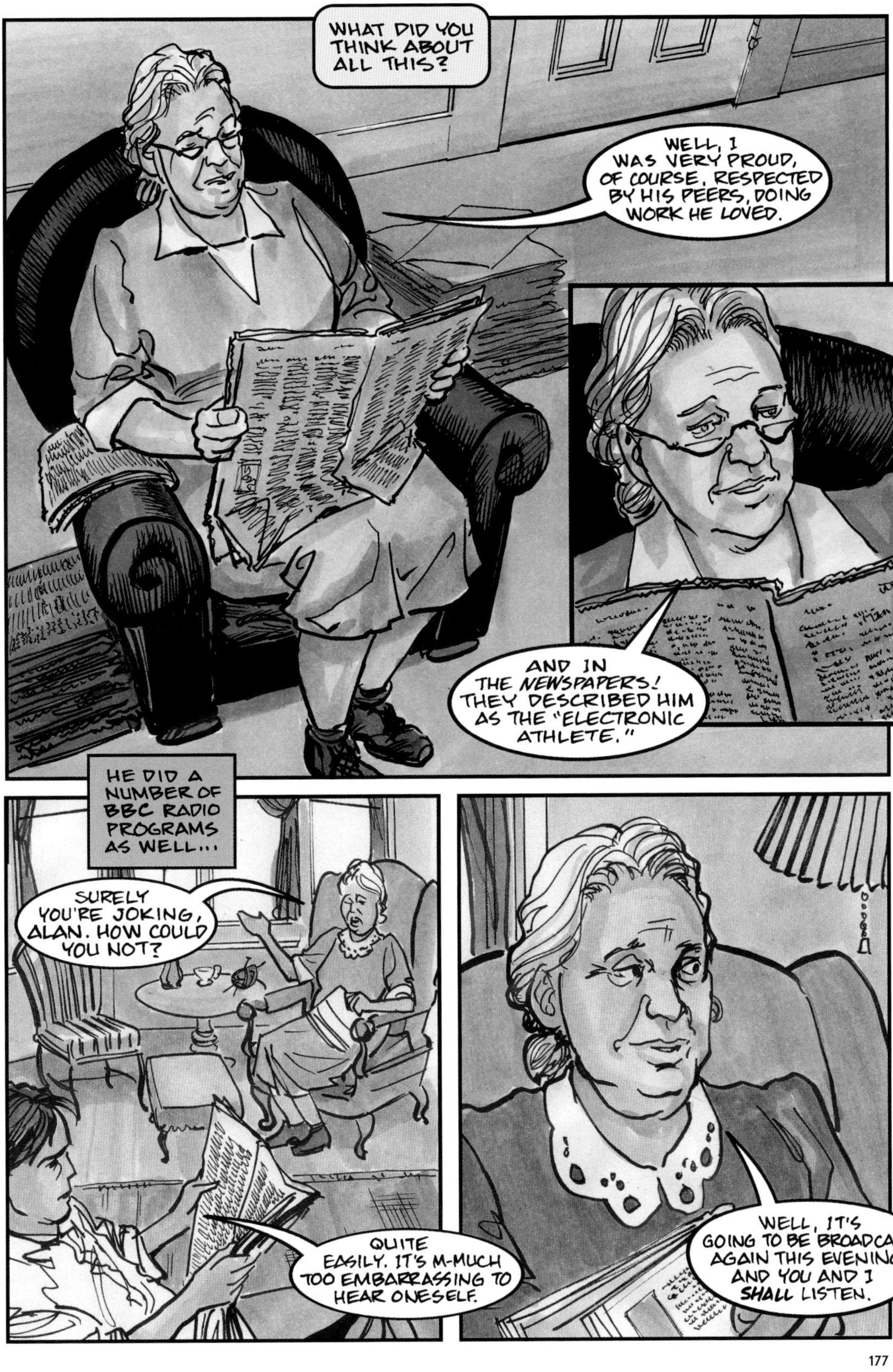
WHAT DID YOU THINK ABOUT ALL THIS?
WELL, I WAS VERY PROUD, OF COURSE. RESPECTED BY HIS PEERS, DOING WORK HE LOVED.
AND IN THE *NEWSPAPERS!* THEY DESCRIBED HIM AS THE "ELECTRONIC ATHLETE."
HE DID A NUMBER OF BBC RADIO PROGRAMS AS WELL...
SURELY YOU'RE JOKING, ALAN. HOW COULD YOU NOT?
QUITE EASILY. IT'S M-MUCH TOO EMBARRASSING TO HEAR ONESELF.
WELL, IT'S GOING TO BE BROADCAST AGAIN THIS EVENING, AND YOU AND I **SHALL** LISTEN.

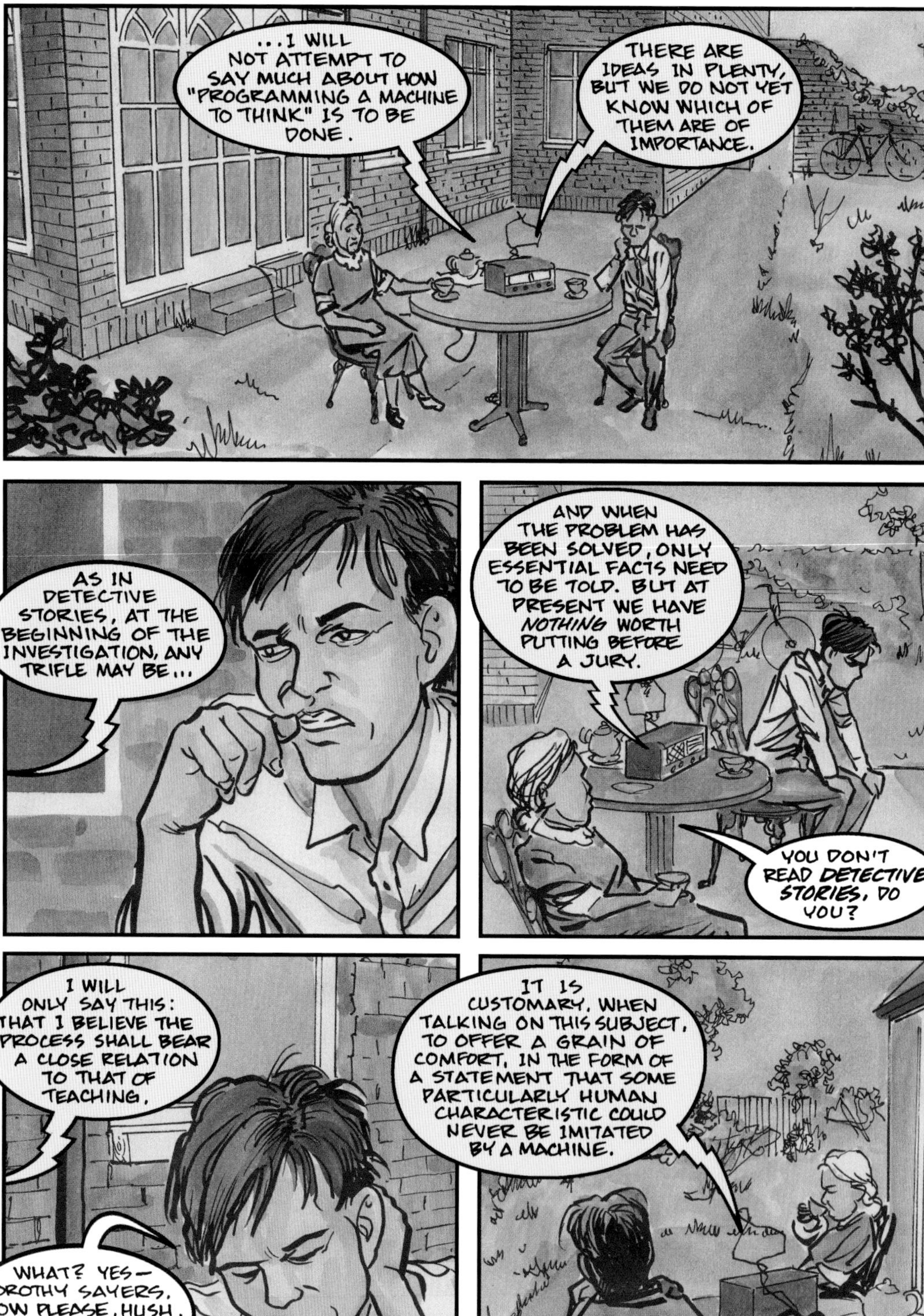
...I WILL NOT ATTEMPT TO SAY MUCH ABOUT HOW "PROGRAMMING A MACHINE TO THINK" IS TO BE DONE.
THERE ARE IDEAS IN PLENTY, BUT WE DO NOT YET KNOW WHICH OF THEM ARE OF IMPORTANCE.
AS IN DETECTIVE STORIES, AT THE BEGINNING OF THE INVESTIGATION, ANY TRIFLE MAY BE...
AND WHEN THE PROBLEM HAS BEEN SOLVED, ONLY ESSENTIAL FACTS NEED TO BE TOLD. BUT AT PRESENT WE HAVE *NOTHING* WORTH PUTTING BEFORE A JURY.
YOU DON'T READ ***DETECTIVE STORIES***, DO YOU?
I WILL ONLY SAY THIS: THAT I BELIEVE THE PROCESS SHALL BEAR A CLOSE RELATION TO THAT OF TEACHING.
WHAT? YES— DOROTHY SAYERS. NOW PLEASE, HUSH. I'LL ONLY ENDURE THIS MISERY ONCE!
IT IS CUSTOMARY, WHEN TALKING ON THIS SUBJECT, TO OFFER A GRAIN OF COMFORT, IN THE FORM OF A STATEMENT THAT SOME PARTICULARLY HUMAN CHARACTERISTIC COULD NEVER BE IMITATED BY A MACHINE.

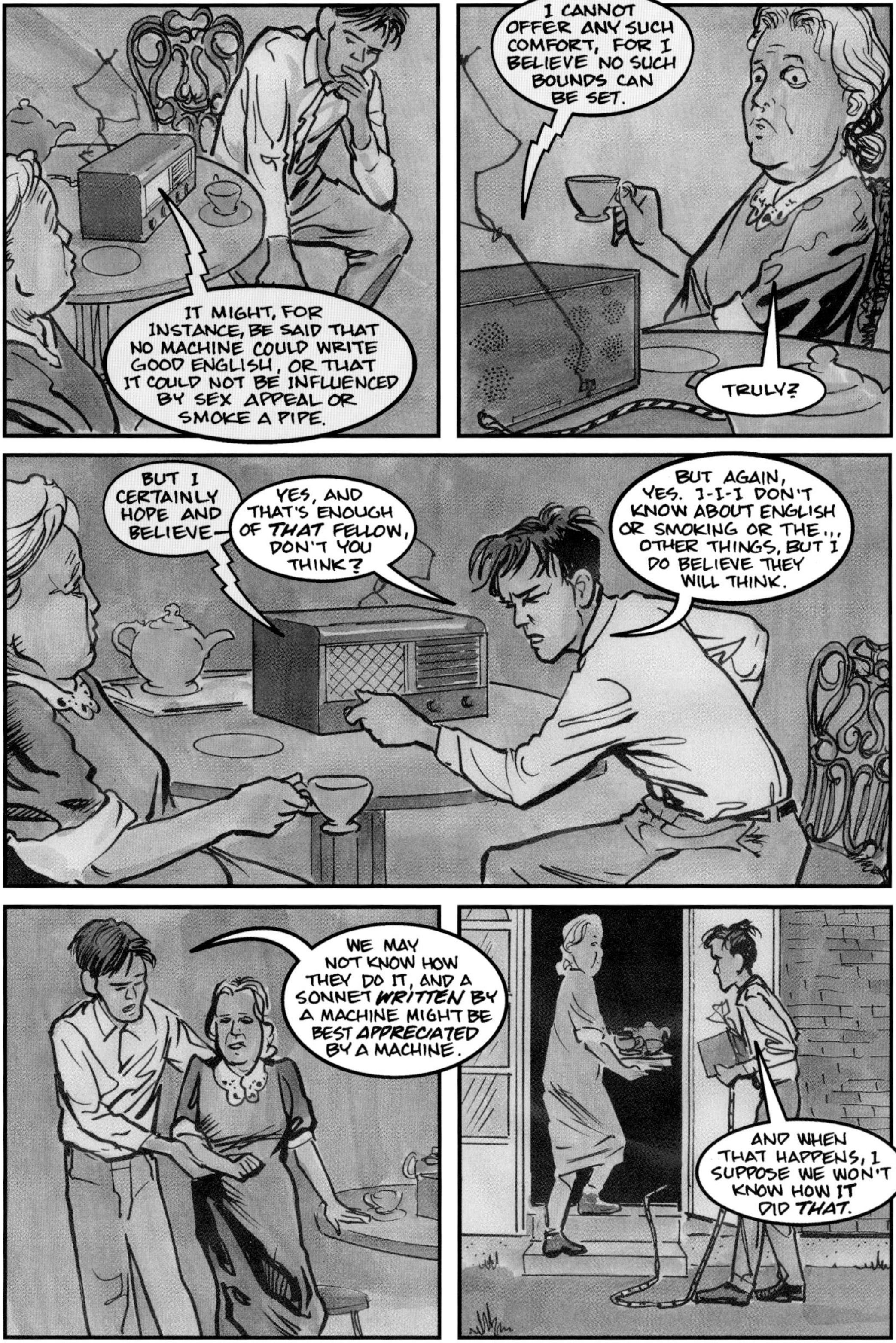
IT MIGHT, FOR INSTANCE, BE SAID THAT NO MACHINE COULD WRITE GOOD ENGLISH, OR THAT IT COULD NOT BE INFLUENCED BY SEX APPEAL OR SMOKE A PIPE.
I CANNOT OFFER ANY SUCH COMFORT, FOR I BELIEVE NO SUCH BOUNDS CAN BE SET.
TRULY?
BUT I CERTAINLY HOPE AND BELIEVE—
YES, AND THAT'S ENOUGH OF THAT FELLOW, DON'T YOU THINK?
BUT AGAIN, YES. I-I-I DON'T KNOW ABOUT ENGLISH OR SMOKING OR THE... OTHER THINGS, BUT I DO BELIEVE THEY WILL THINK.
WE MAY NOT KNOW HOW THEY DO IT, AND A SONNET WRITTEN BY A MACHINE MIGHT BE BEST APPRECIATED BY A MACHINE.
AND WHEN THAT HAPPENS, I SUPPOSE WE WON'T KNOW HOW IT DID THAT.

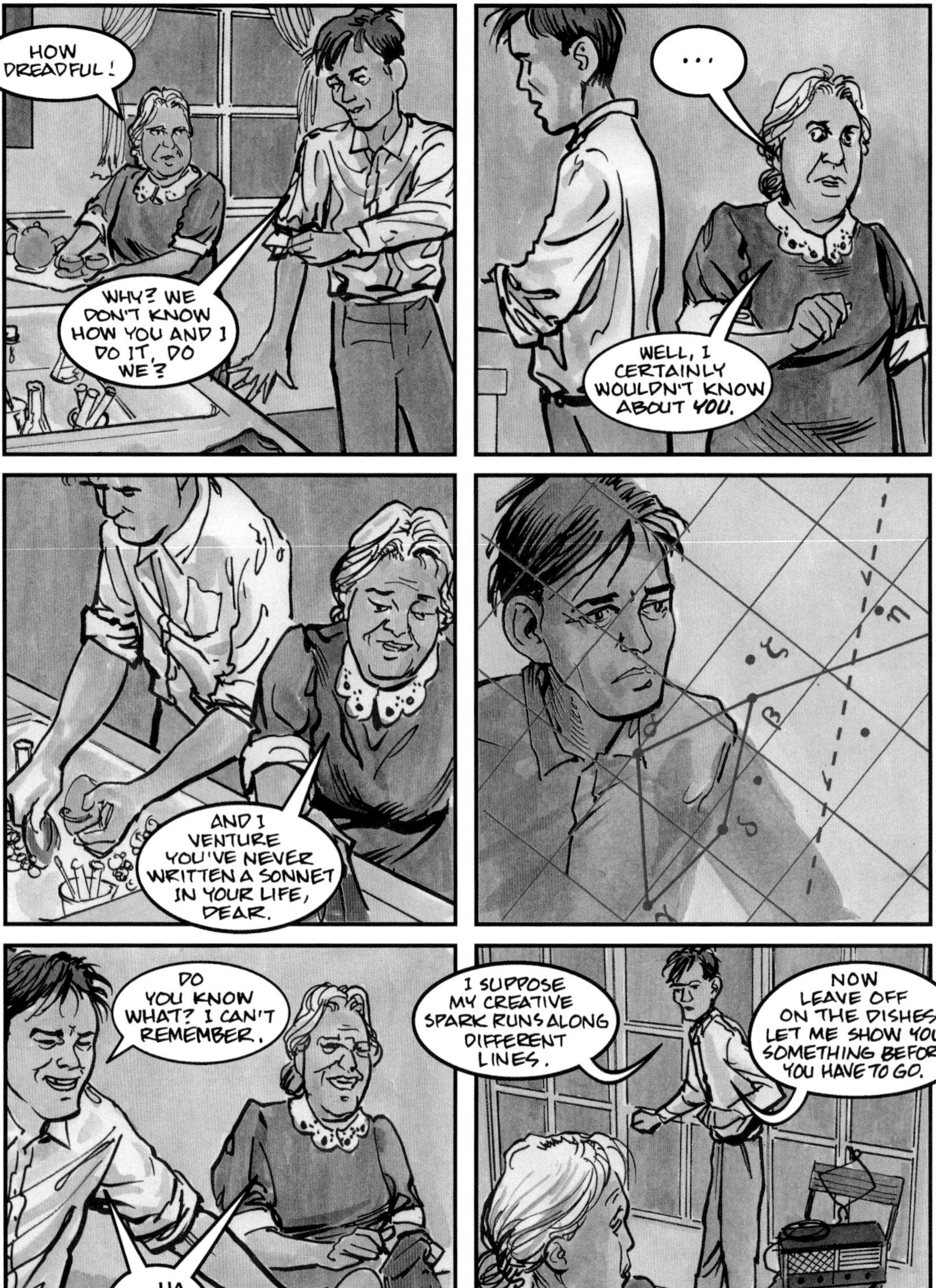
HOW DREADFUL!
WHY? WE DON'T KNOW HOW YOU AND I DO IT, DO WE?
...
WELL, I CERTAINLY WOULDN'T KNOW ABOUT *YOU*.
AND I VENTURE YOU'VE NEVER WRITTEN A SONNET IN YOUR LIFE, DEAR.
DO YOU KNOW WHAT? I CAN'T REMEMBER.
HA HA HA HA
I SUPPOSE MY CREATIVE SPARK RUNS ALONG DIFFERENT LINES.
NOW LEAVE OFF ON THE DISHES, LET ME SHOW YOU SOMETHING BEFORE YOU HAVE TO GO.

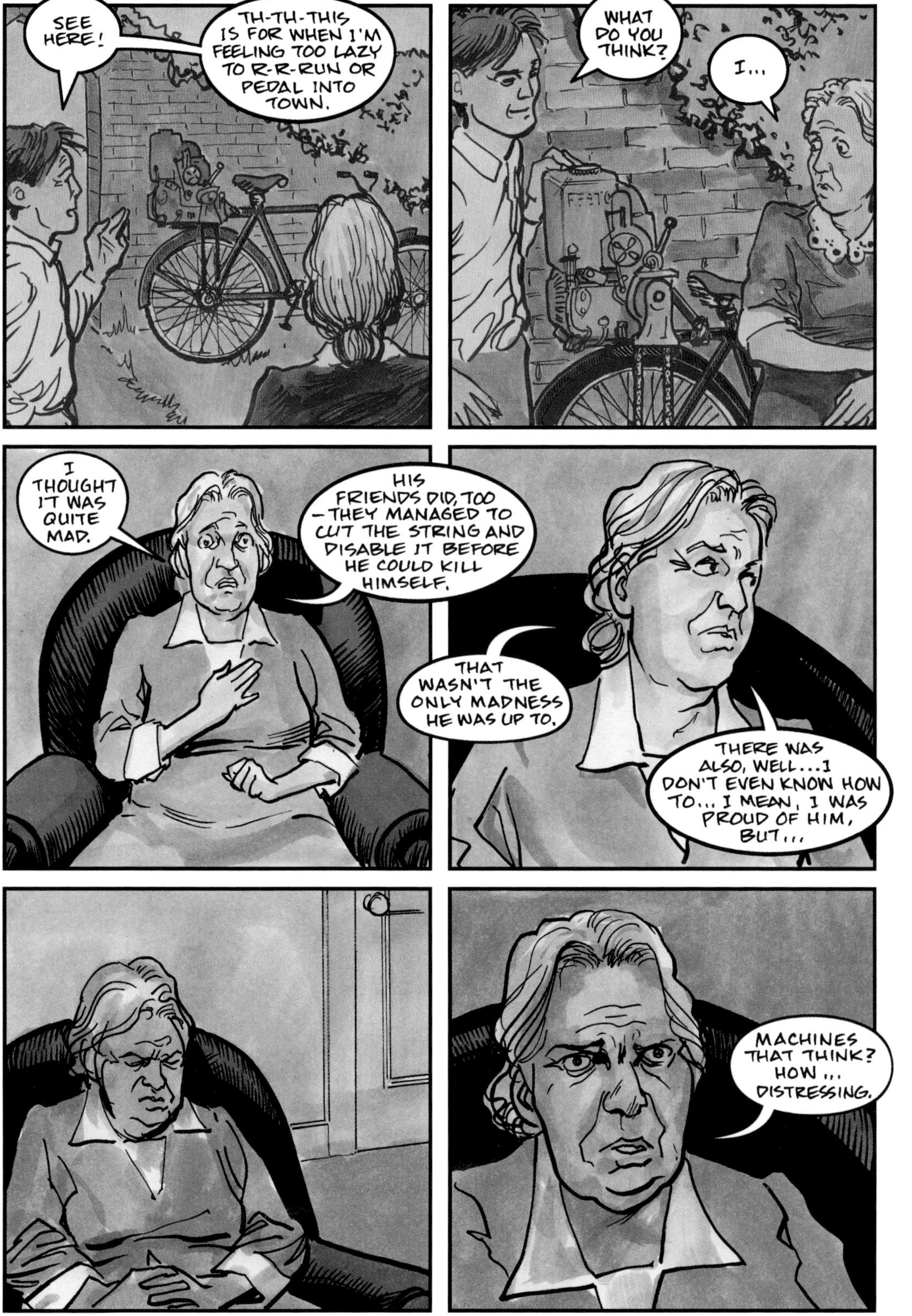
SEE HERE!
TH-TH-THIS IS FOR WHEN I'M FEELING TOO LAZY TO R-R-RUN OR PEDAL INTO TOWN.
WHAT DO YOU THINK?
I...
I THOUGHT IT WAS QUITE MAD.
HIS FRIENDS DID, TOO —THEY MANAGED TO CUT THE STRING AND DISABLE IT BEFORE HE COULD KILL HIMSELF.
THAT WASN'T THE ONLY MADNESS HE WAS UP TO.
THERE WAS ALSO, WELL... I DON'T EVEN KNOW HOW TO... I MEAN, I WAS PROUD OF HIM, BUT...
MACHINES THAT THINK? HOW... DISTRESSING.

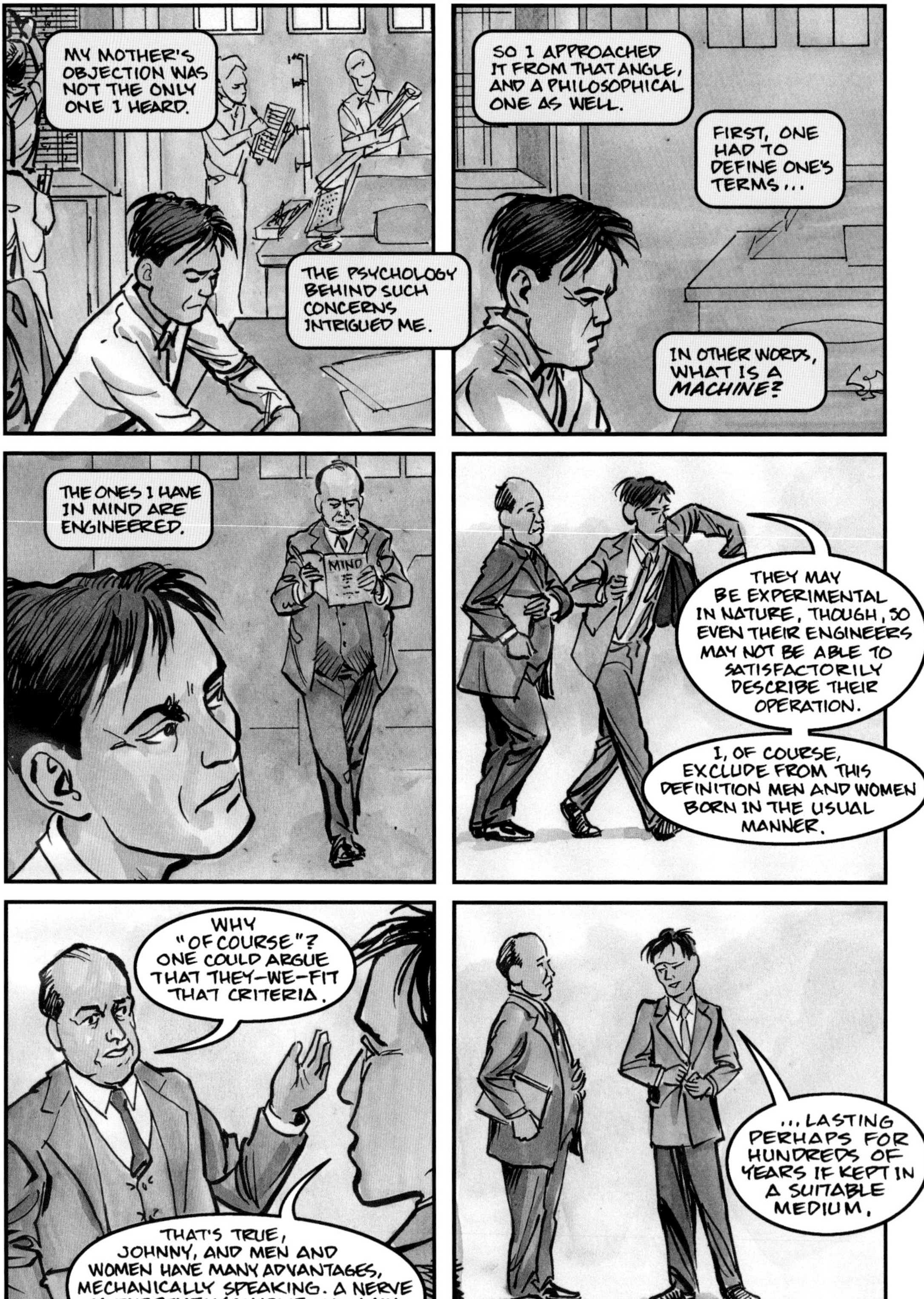

MY MOTHER'S OBJECTION WAS NOT THE ONLY ONE I HEARD.
THE PSYCHOLOGY BEHIND SUCH CONCERNS INTRIGUED ME.
SO I APPROACHED IT FROM THAT ANGLE, AND A PHILOSOPHICAL ONE AS WELL.
FIRST, ONE HAD TO DEFINE ONE'S TERMS...
IN OTHER WORDS, WHAT IS A *MACHINE*?
THE ONES I HAVE IN MIND ARE ENGINEERED.
MIND
THEY MAY BE EXPERIMENTAL IN NATURE, THOUGH, SO EVEN THEIR ENGINEERS MAY NOT BE ABLE TO SATISFACTORILY DESCRIBE THEIR OPERATION.
I, OF COURSE, EXCLUDE FROM THIS DEFINITION MEN AND WOMEN BORN IN THE USUAL MANNER.
WHY "OF COURSE"? ONE COULD ARGUE THAT THEY—WE—FIT THAT CRITERIA.
THAT'S TRUE, JOHNNY, AND MEN AND WOMEN HAVE MANY ADVANTAGES, MECHANICALLY SPEAKING. A NERVE IS EXTREMELY COMPACT, HAS LOW ENERGY CONSUMPTION, AND DOES NOT WEAR OUT...
...LASTING PERHAPS FOR HUNDREDS OF YEARS IF KEPT IN A SUITABLE MEDIUM,

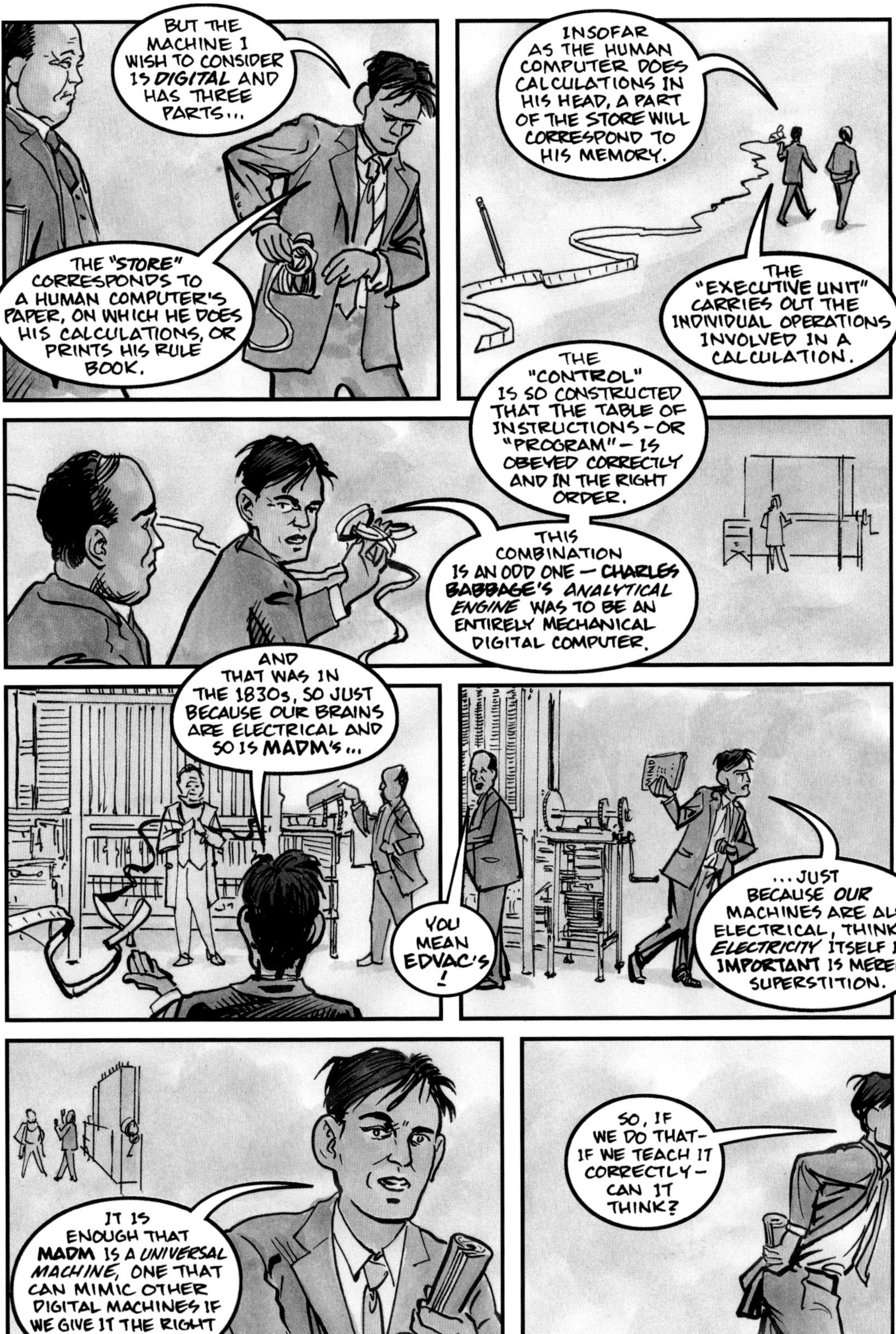
BUT THE MACHINE I WISH TO CONSIDER IS DIGITAL AND HAS THREE PARTS...
THE "STORE" CORRESPONDS TO A HUMAN COMPUTER'S PAPER, ON WHICH HE DOES HIS CALCULATIONS, OR PRINTS HIS RULE BOOK.
INSOFAR AS THE HUMAN COMPUTER DOES CALCULATIONS IN HIS HEAD, A PART OF THE STORE WILL CORRESPOND TO HIS MEMORY.
THE "EXECUTIVE UNIT" CARRIES OUT THE INDIVIDUAL OPERATIONS INVOLVED IN A CALCULATION.
THE "CONTROL" IS SO CONSTRUCTED THAT THE TABLE OF INSTRUCTIONS - OR "PROGRAM" - IS OBEYED CORRECTLY AND IN THE RIGHT ORDER.
THIS COMBINATION IS AN ODD ONE — CHARLES BABBAGE'S ANALYTICAL ENGINE WAS TO BE AN ENTIRELY MECHANICAL DIGITAL COMPUTER.
AND THAT WAS IN THE 1830s, SO JUST BECAUSE OUR BRAINS ARE ELECTRICAL AND SO IS MADM's...
YOU MEAN EDVAC'S!
...JUST BECAUSE OUR MACHINES ARE ALSO ELECTRICAL, THINKING ELECTRICITY ITSELF IS IMPORTANT IS MERELY SUPERSTITION.
IT IS ENOUGH THAT MADM IS A UNIVERSAL MACHINE, ONE THAT CAN MIMIC OTHER DIGITAL MACHINES IF WE GIVE IT THE RIGHT PROGRAM.
SO, IF WE DO THAT- IF WE TEACH IT CORRECTLY - CAN IT THINK?

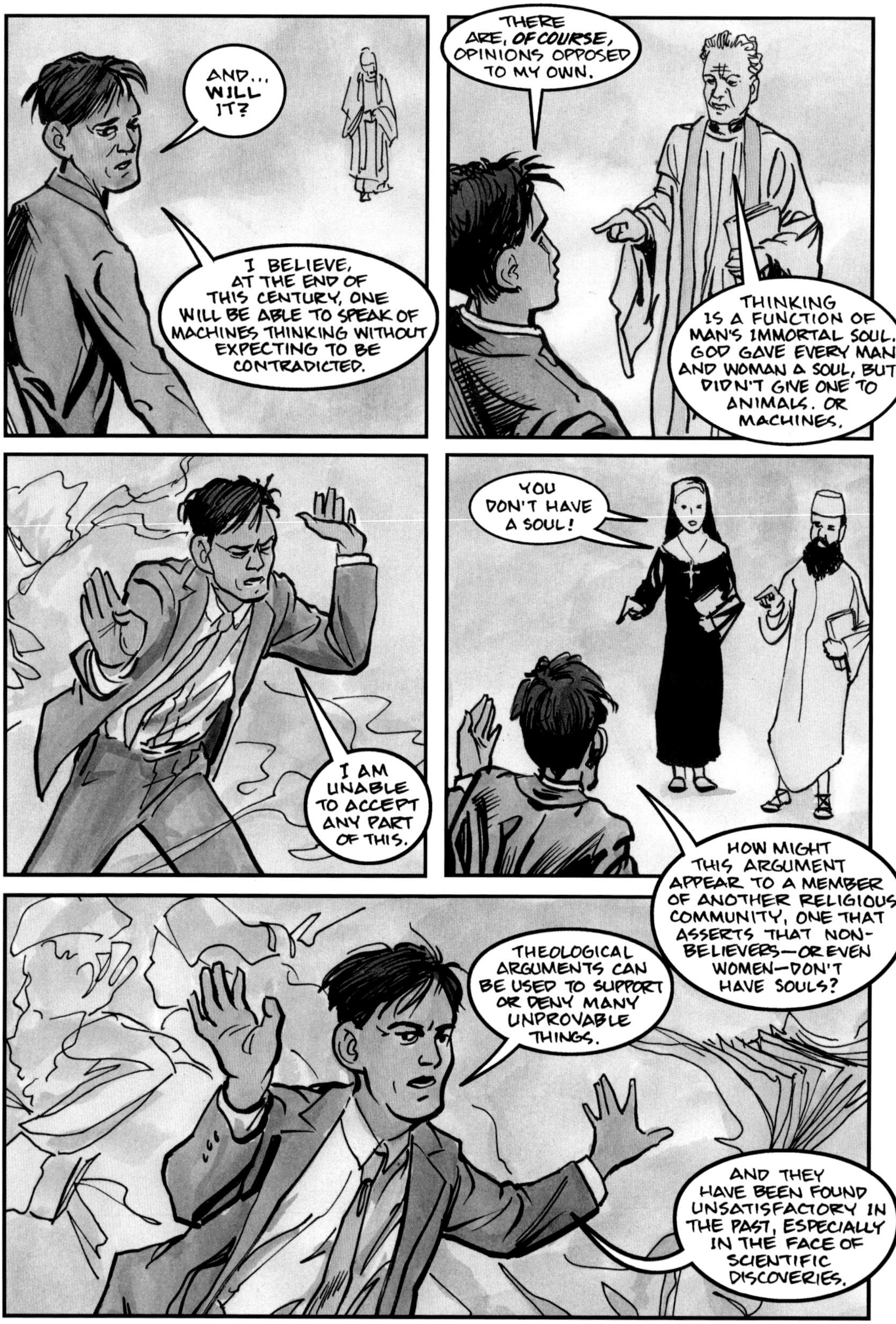
AND... WILL IT?
I BELIEVE, AT THE END OF THIS CENTURY, ONE WILL BE ABLE TO SPEAK OF MACHINES THINKING WITHOUT EXPECTING TO BE CONTRADICTED.
THERE ARE, OF COURSE, OPINIONS OPPOSED TO MY OWN.
THINKING IS A FUNCTION OF MAN'S IMMORTAL SOUL. GOD GAVE EVERY MAN AND WOMAN A SOUL, BUT DIDN'T GIVE ONE TO ANIMALS. OR MACHINES.
I AM UNABLE TO ACCEPT ANY PART OF THIS.
YOU DON'T HAVE A SOUL!
HOW MIGHT THIS ARGUMENT APPEAR TO A MEMBER OF ANOTHER RELIGIOUS COMMUNITY, ONE THAT ASSERTS THAT NON-BELIEVERS—OR EVEN WOMEN—DON'T HAVE SOULS?
THEOLOGICAL ARGUMENTS CAN BE USED TO SUPPORT OR DENY MANY UNPROVABLE THINGS.
AND THEY HAVE BEEN FOUND UNSATISFACTORY IN THE PAST, ESPECIALLY IN THE FACE OF SCIENTIFIC DISCOVERIES.

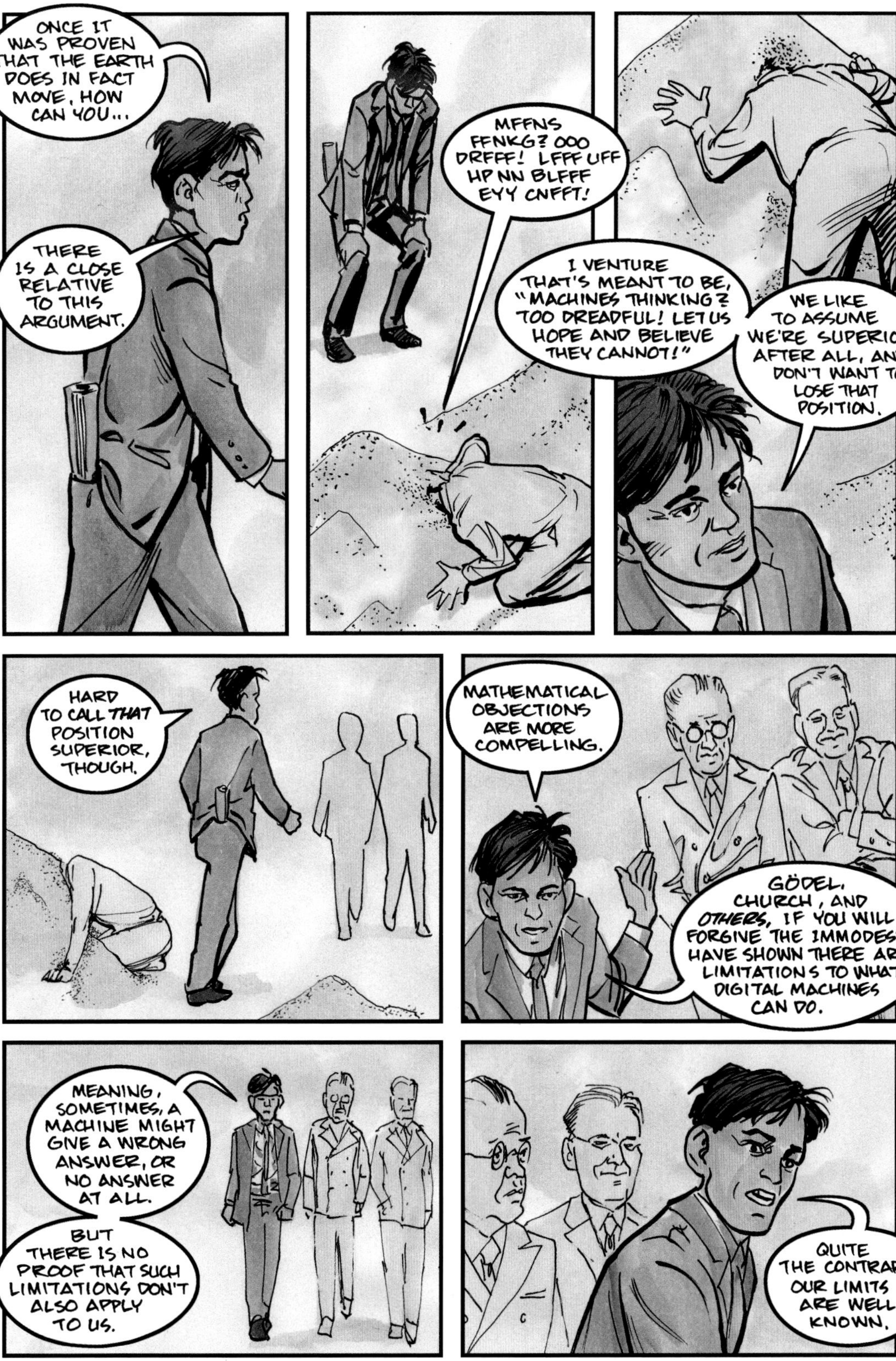
ONCE IT WAS PROVEN THAT THE EARTH DOES IN FACT MOVE, HOW CAN YOU...
THERE IS A CLOSE RELATIVE TO THIS ARGUMENT.
MFFNS FFNKG? OOO DRFFF! LFFF UFF HP NN BLFFF EYY CNFFT!
I VENTURE THAT'S MEANT TO BE, "MACHINES THINKING? TOO DREADFUL! LET US HOPE AND BELIEVE THEY CANNOT!"
WE LIKE TO ASSUME WE'RE SUPERIOR, AFTER ALL, AND DON'T WANT TO LOSE THAT POSITION.
HARD TO CALL *THAT* POSITION SUPERIOR, THOUGH.
MATHEMATICAL OBJECTIONS ARE MORE COMPELLING.
GÖDEL, CHURCH, AND *OTHERS*, IF YOU WILL FORGIVE THE IMMODESTY, HAVE SHOWN THERE ARE LIMITATIONS TO WHAT DIGITAL MACHINES CAN DO.
MEANING, SOMETIMES, A MACHINE MIGHT GIVE A WRONG ANSWER, OR NO ANSWER AT ALL.
BUT THERE IS NO PROOF THAT SUCH LIMITATIONS DON'T ALSO APPLY TO US.
QUITE THE CONTRARY. OUR LIMITS ARE WELL KNOWN.

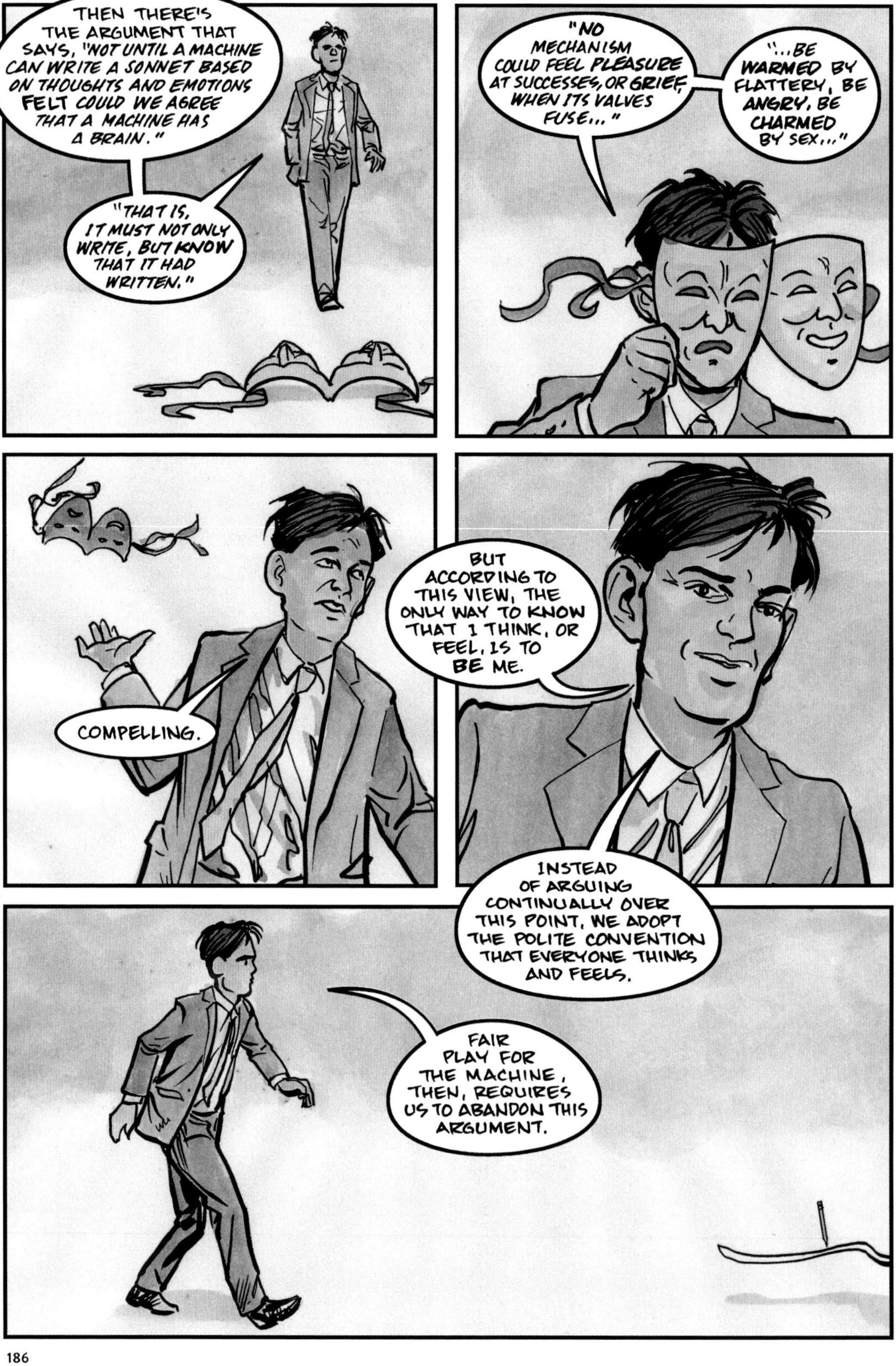
THEN THERE'S THE ARGUMENT THAT SAYS, "NOT UNTIL A MACHINE CAN WRITE A SONNET BASED ON THOUGHTS AND EMOTIONS FELT COULD WE AGREE THAT A MACHINE HAS A BRAIN."
"THAT IS, IT MUST NOT ONLY WRITE, BUT KNOW THAT IT HAD WRITTEN."
"NO MECHANISM COULD FEEL PLEASURE AT SUCCESSES, OR GRIEF, WHEN ITS VALVES FUSE..."
"...BE WARMED BY FLATTERY, BE ANGRY, BE CHARMED BY SEX..."
COMPELLING.
BUT ACCORDING TO THIS VIEW, THE ONLY WAY TO KNOW THAT I THINK, OR FEEL, IS TO BE ME.
INSTEAD OF ARGUING CONTINUALLY OVER THIS POINT, WE ADOPT THE POLITE CONVENTION THAT EVERYONE THINKS AND FEELS.
FAIR PLAY FOR THE MACHINE, THEN, REQUIRES US TO ABANDON THIS ARGUMENT.

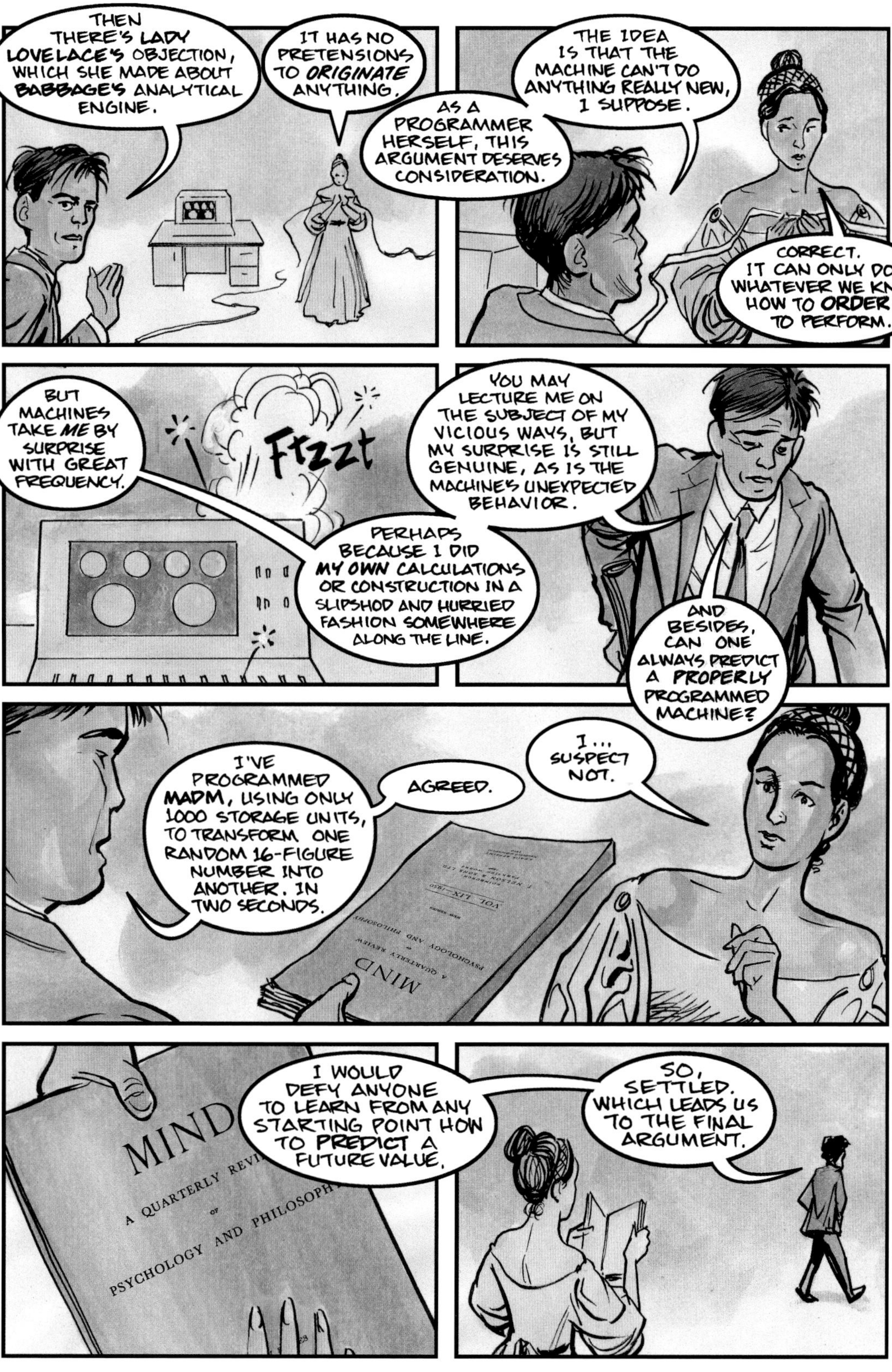
THEN THERE'S LADY LOVELACE'S OBJECTION, WHICH SHE MADE ABOUT BABBAGE'S ANALYTICAL ENGINE.
IT HAS NO PRETENSIONS TO ORIGINATE ANYTHING.
THE IDEA IS THAT THE MACHINE CAN'T DO ANYTHING REALLY NEW, I SUPPOSE.
AS A PROGRAMMER HERSELF, THIS ARGUMENT DESERVES CONSIDERATION.
CORRECT. IT CAN ONLY DO WHATEVER WE KNOW HOW TO ORDER IT TO PERFORM.
BUT MACHINES TAKE ME BY SURPRISE WITH GREAT FREQUENCY.
Ftzzt
PERHAPS BECAUSE I DID MY OWN CALCULATIONS OR CONSTRUCTION IN A SLIPSHOD AND HURRIED FASHION SOMEWHERE ALONG THE LINE.
YOU MAY LECTURE ME ON THE SUBJECT OF MY VICIOUS WAYS, BUT MY SURPRISE IS STILL GENUINE, AS IS THE MACHINE'S UNEXPECTED BEHAVIOR.
AND BESIDES, CAN ONE ALWAYS PREDICT A PROPERLY PROGRAMMED MACHINE?
I... SUSPECT NOT.
AGREED.
I'VE PROGRAMMED MADM, USING ONLY 1000 STORAGE UNITS, TO TRANSFORM ONE RANDOM 16-FIGURE NUMBER INTO ANOTHER. IN TWO SECONDS.
MIND
I WOULD DEFY ANYONE TO LEARN FROM ANY STARTING POINT HOW TO PREDICT A FUTURE VALUE.
SO, SETTLED. WHICH LEADS US TO THE FINAL ARGUMENT.

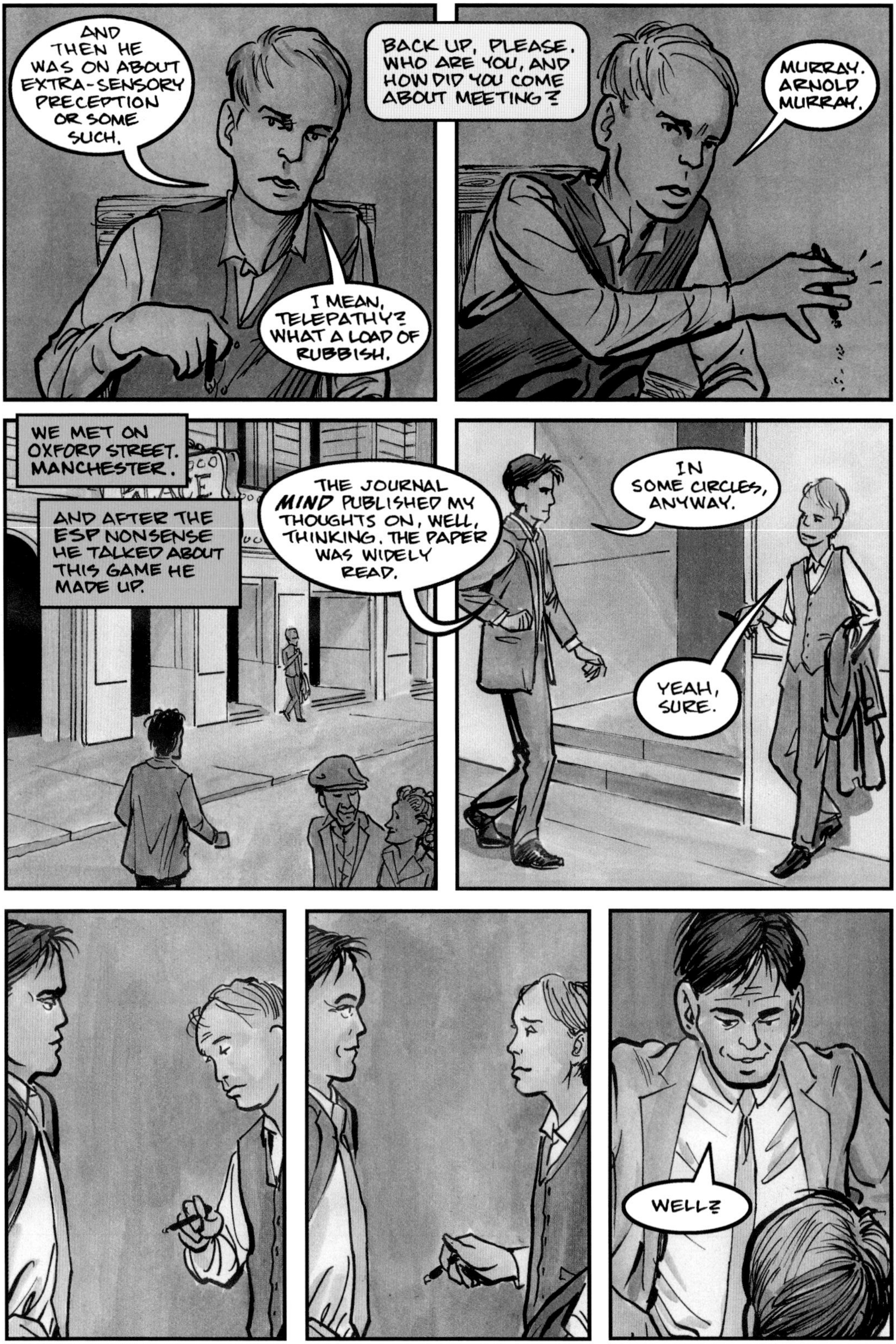
AND THEN HE WAS ON ABOUT EXTRA-SENSORY PRECEPTION OR SOME SUCH.
I MEAN, TELEPATHY? WHAT A LOAD OF RUBBISH.
BACK UP, PLEASE. WHO ARE YOU, AND HOW DID YOU COME ABOUT MEETING?
MURRAY. ARNOLD MURRAY.
WE MET ON OXFORD STREET. MANCHESTER.
AND AFTER THE ESP NONSENSE HE TALKED ABOUT THIS GAME HE MADE UP.
THE JOURNAL MIND PUBLISHED MY THOUGHTS ON, WELL, THINKING. THE PAPER WAS WIDELY READ.
IN SOME CIRCLES, ANYWAY.
YEAH, SURE.
WELL?

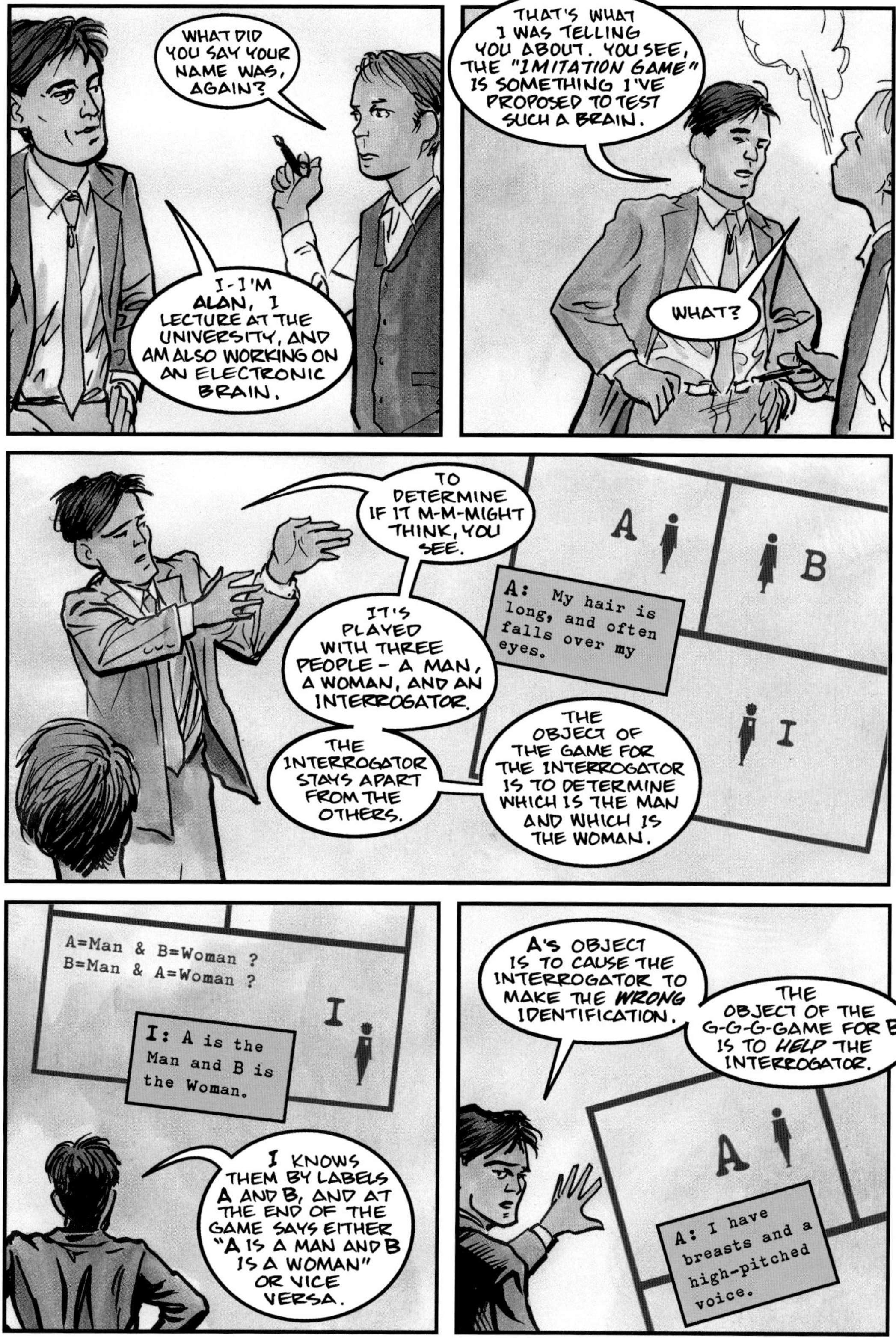
WHAT DID YOU SAY YOUR NAME WAS, AGAIN?
I-I'M ALAN, I LECTURE AT THE UNIVERSITY, AND AM ALSO WORKING ON AN ELECTRONIC BRAIN.
THAT'S WHAT I WAS TELLING YOU ABOUT. YOU SEE, THE "IMITATION GAME" IS SOMETHING I'VE PROPOSED TO TEST SUCH A BRAIN.
WHAT?
TO DETERMINE IF IT M-M-MIGHT THINK, YOU SEE.
A
B
A: My hair is long, and often falls over my eyes.
IT'S PLAYED WITH THREE PEOPLE - A MAN, A WOMAN, AND AN INTERROGATOR.
I
THE INTERROGATOR STAYS APART FROM THE OTHERS.
THE OBJECT OF THE GAME FOR THE INTERROGATOR IS TO DETERMINE WHICH IS THE MAN AND WHICH IS THE WOMAN.
A=Man & B=Woman ?
B=Man & A=Woman ?
I
I: A is the Man and B is the Woman.
I KNOWS THEM BY LABELS A AND B, AND AT THE END OF THE GAME SAYS EITHER "A IS A MAN AND B IS A WOMAN" OR VICE VERSA.
A'S OBJECT IS TO CAUSE THE INTERROGATOR TO MAKE THE WRONG IDENTIFICATION.
THE OBJECT OF THE G-G-G-GAME FOR B IS TO HELP THE INTERROGATOR.
A
A: I have breasts and a high-pitched voice.

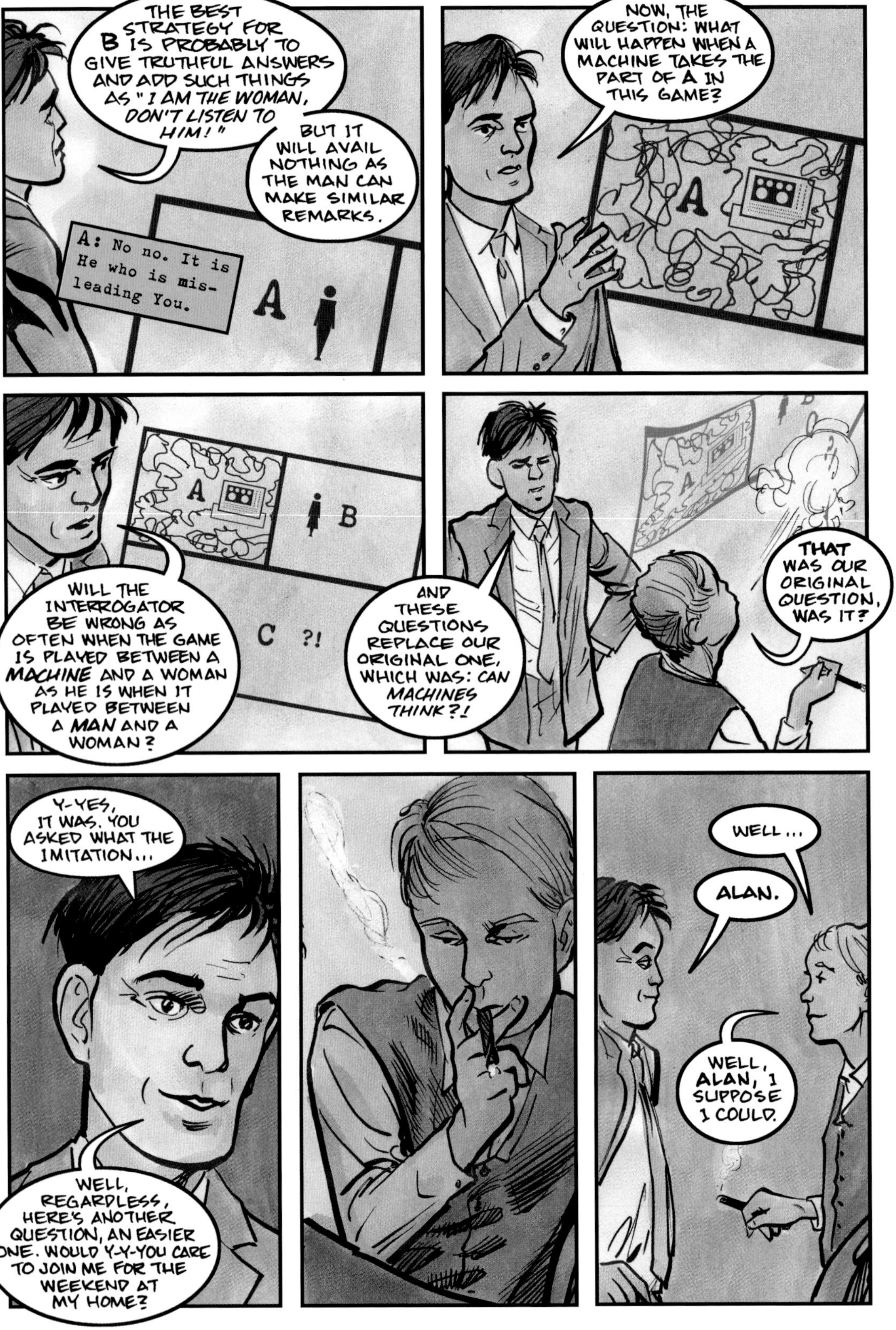
THE BEST STRATEGY FOR B IS PROBABLY TO GIVE TRUTHFUL ANSWERS AND ADD SUCH THINGS AS "I AM THE WOMAN, DON'T LISTEN TO HIM!"
BUT IT WILL AVAIL NOTHING AS THE MAN CAN MAKE SIMILAR REMARKS.
A: No no. It is He who is misleading You.
A
NOW, THE QUESTION: WHAT WILL HAPPEN WHEN A MACHINE TAKES THE PART OF A IN THIS GAME?
A
A
B
C ?!
WILL THE INTERROGATOR BE WRONG AS OFTEN WHEN THE GAME IS PLAYED BETWEEN A MACHINE AND A WOMAN AS HE IS WHEN IT PLAYED BETWEEN A MAN AND A WOMAN?
AND THESE QUESTIONS REPLACE OUR ORIGINAL ONE, WHICH WAS: CAN MACHINES THINK?!
THAT WAS OUR ORIGINAL QUESTION, WAS IT?
Y-YES, IT WAS. YOU ASKED WHAT THE IMITATION...
WELL, REGARDLESS, HERE'S ANOTHER QUESTION, AN EASIER ONE. WOULD Y-Y-YOU CARE TO JOIN ME FOR THE WEEKEND AT MY HOME?
WELL...
ALAN.
WELL, ALAN, I SUPPOSE I COULD.

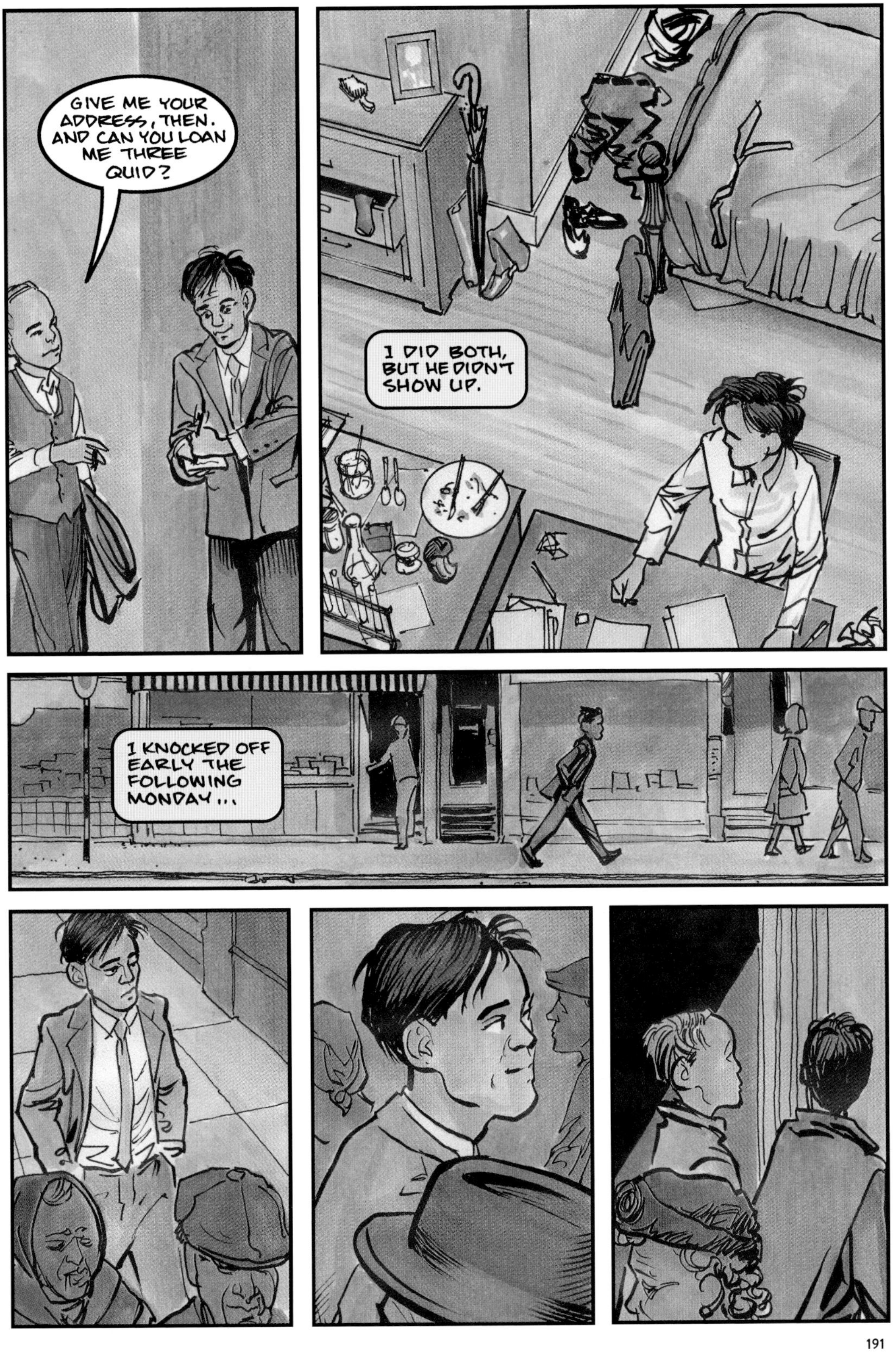
GIVE ME YOUR ADDRESS, THEN. AND CAN YOU LOAN ME THREE QUID?
I DID BOTH, BUT HE DIDN'T SHOW UP.
I KNOCKED OFF EARLY THE FOLLOWING MONDAY...

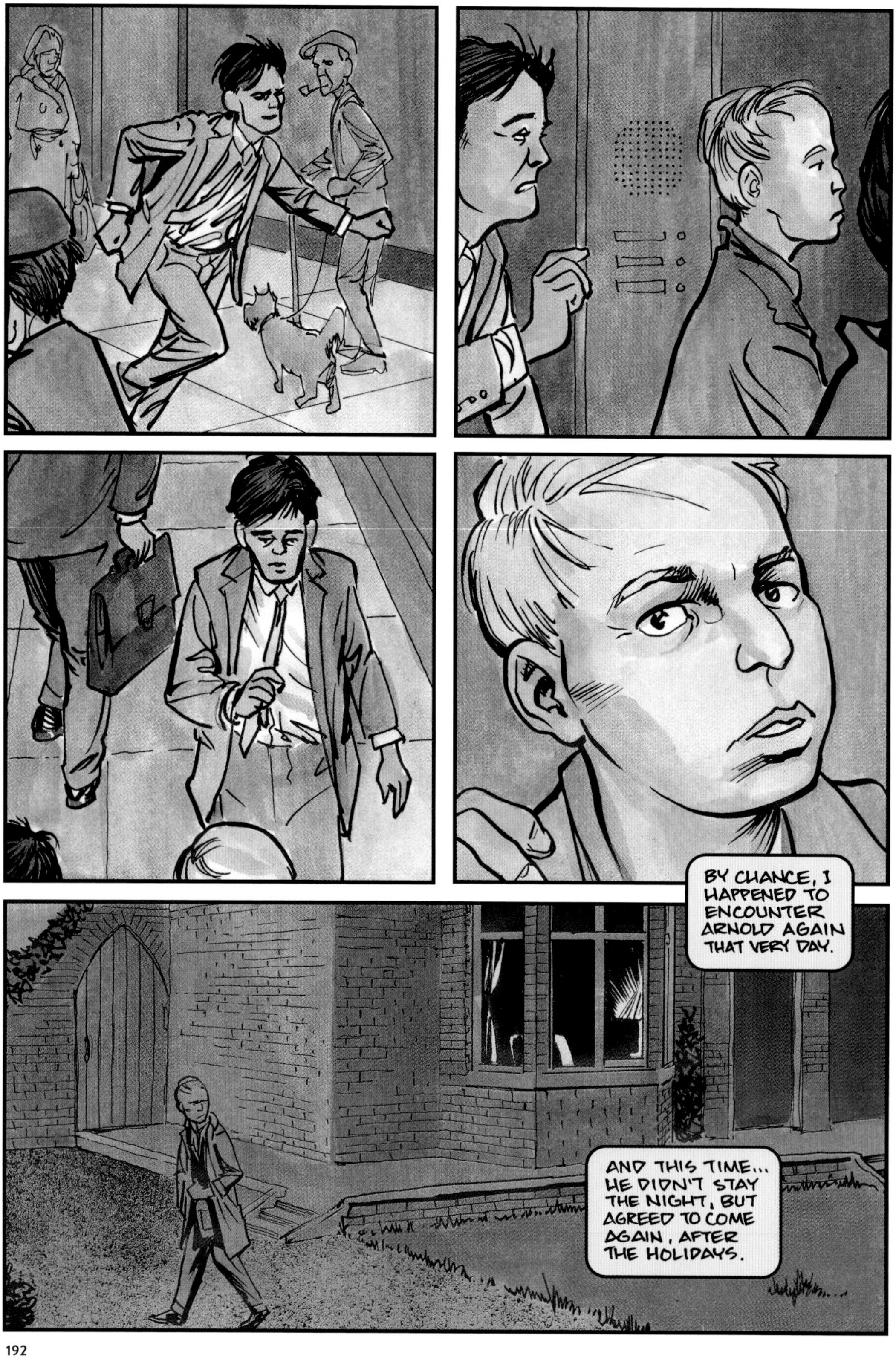
BY CHANCE, I HAPPENED TO ENCOUNTER ARNOLD AGAIN THAT VERY DAY.
AND THIS TIME... HE DIDN'T STAY THE NIGHT, BUT AGREED TO COME AGAIN, AFTER THE HOLIDAYS.

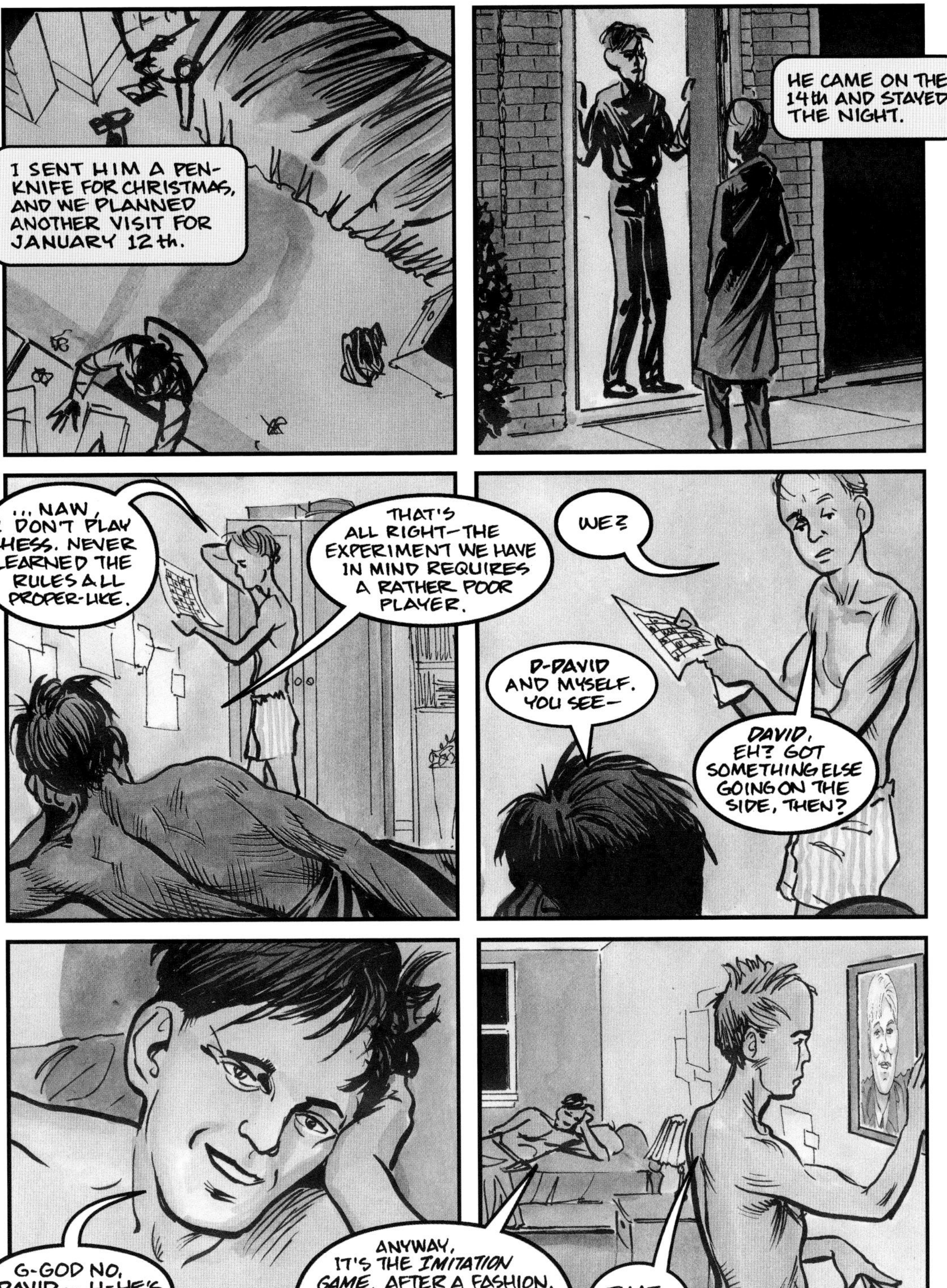

I SENT HIM A PEN-KNIFE FOR CHRISTMAS, AND WE PLANNED ANOTHER VISIT FOR JANUARY 12th.
HE CAME ON THE 14th AND STAYED THE NIGHT.
...NAW, I DON'T PLAY CHESS. NEVER LEARNED THE RULES ALL PROPER-LIKE.
THAT'S ALL RIGHT—THE EXPERIMENT WE HAVE IN MIND REQUIRES A RATHER POOR PLAYER.
WE?
D-DAVID AND MYSELF. YOU SEE—
DAVID, EH? GOT SOMETHING ELSE GOING ON THE SIDE, THEN?
G-GOD NO, DAVID... H-HE'S AN OLD FRIEND. COLLEAGUE, REALLY.
ANYWAY, IT'S THE *IMITATION GAME*, AFTER A FASHION. YOU SEE, WHAT IF WE COMMUNICATED THE MACHINE'S MOVE AND YOURS TO AN OBSERVER, COULD HE TELL—
THAT AGAIN. LISTEN.

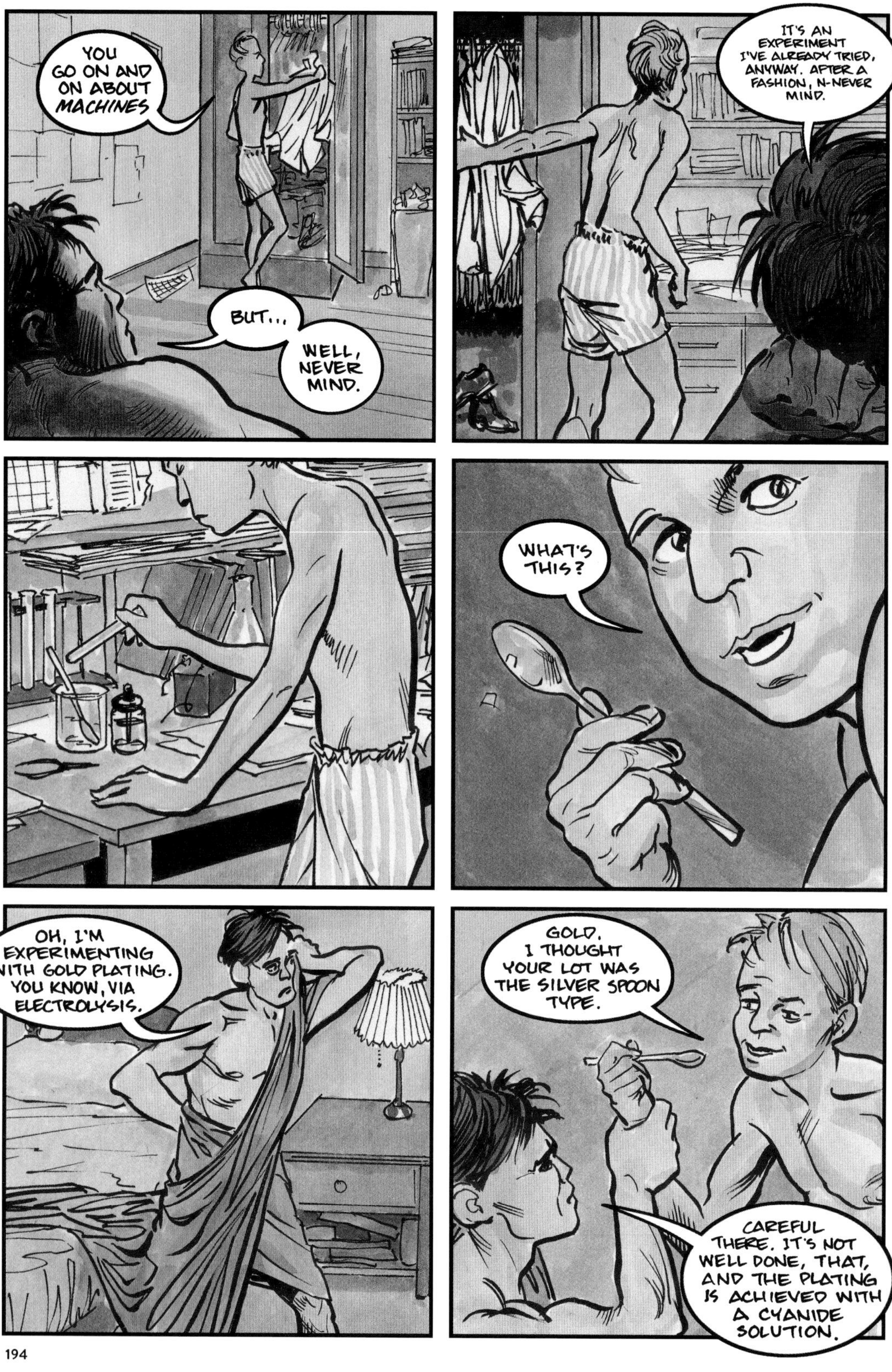
YOU GO ON AND ON ABOUT *MACHINES*
BUT...
WELL, NEVER MIND.
IT'S AN EXPERIMENT I'VE ALREADY TRIED, ANYWAY. AFTER A FASHION, N-NEVER MIND.
WHAT'S THIS?
OH, I'M EXPERIMENTING WITH GOLD PLATING. YOU KNOW, VIA ELECTROLYSIS.
GOLD. I THOUGHT YOUR LOT WAS THE SILVER SPOON TYPE.
CAREFUL THERE. IT'S NOT WELL DONE, THAT, AND THE PLATING IS ACHIEVED WITH A CYANIDE SOLUTION.

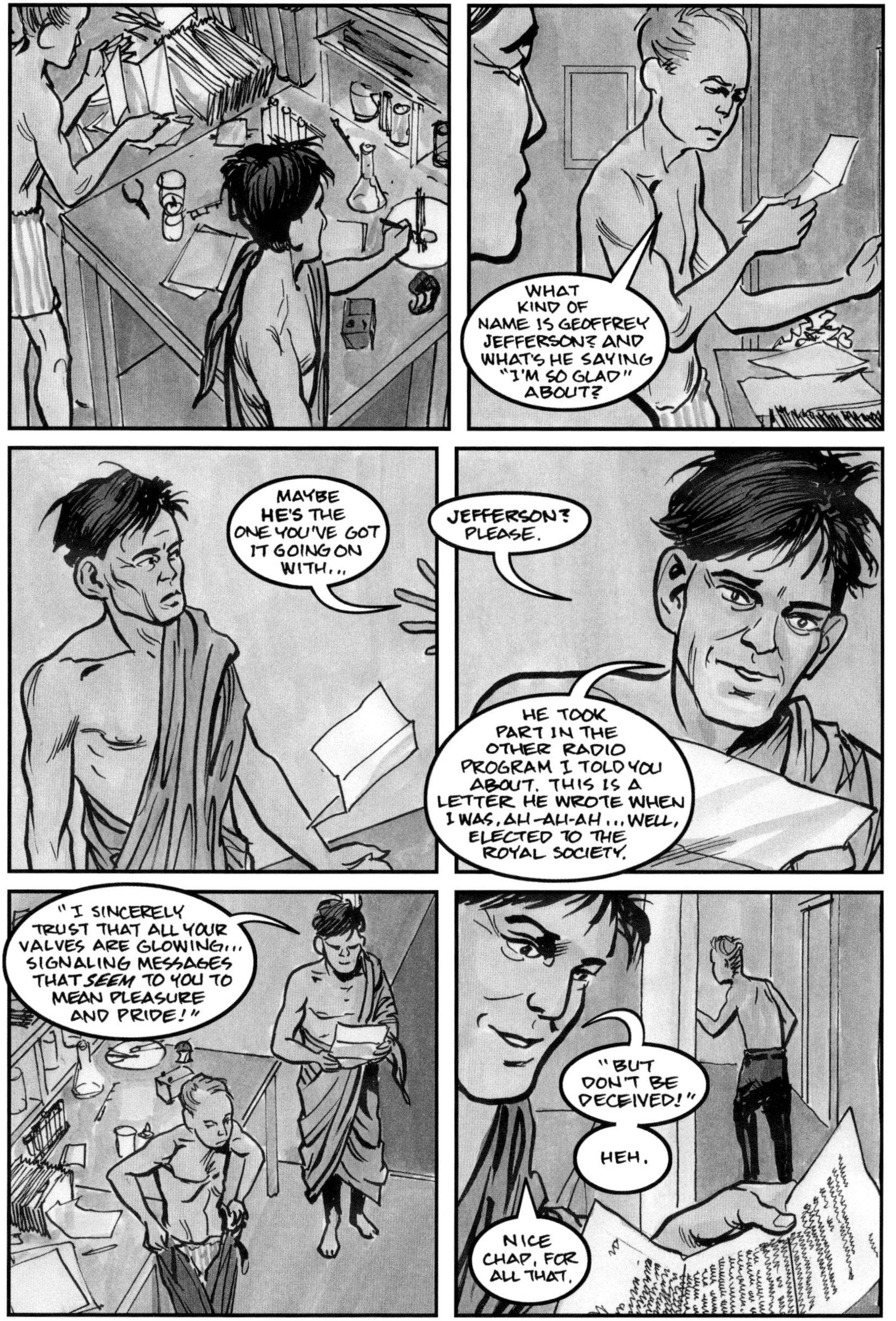
WHAT KIND OF NAME IS GEOFFREY JEFFERSON? AND WHAT'S HE SAYING "I'M SO GLAD" ABOUT?
MAYBE HE'S THE ONE YOU'VE GOT IT GOING ON WITH...
JEFFERSON? PLEASE.
HE TOOK PART IN THE OTHER RADIO PROGRAM I TOLD YOU ABOUT. THIS IS A LETTER HE WROTE WHEN I WAS, AH-AH-AH... WELL, ELECTED TO THE ROYAL SOCIETY.
"I SINCERELY TRUST THAT ALL YOUR VALVES ARE GLOWING... SIGNALING MESSAGES THAT *SEEM* TO YOU TO MEAN PLEASURE AND PRIDE!"
"BUT DON'T BE DECEIVED!"
HEH.
NICE CHAP, FOR ALL THAT.

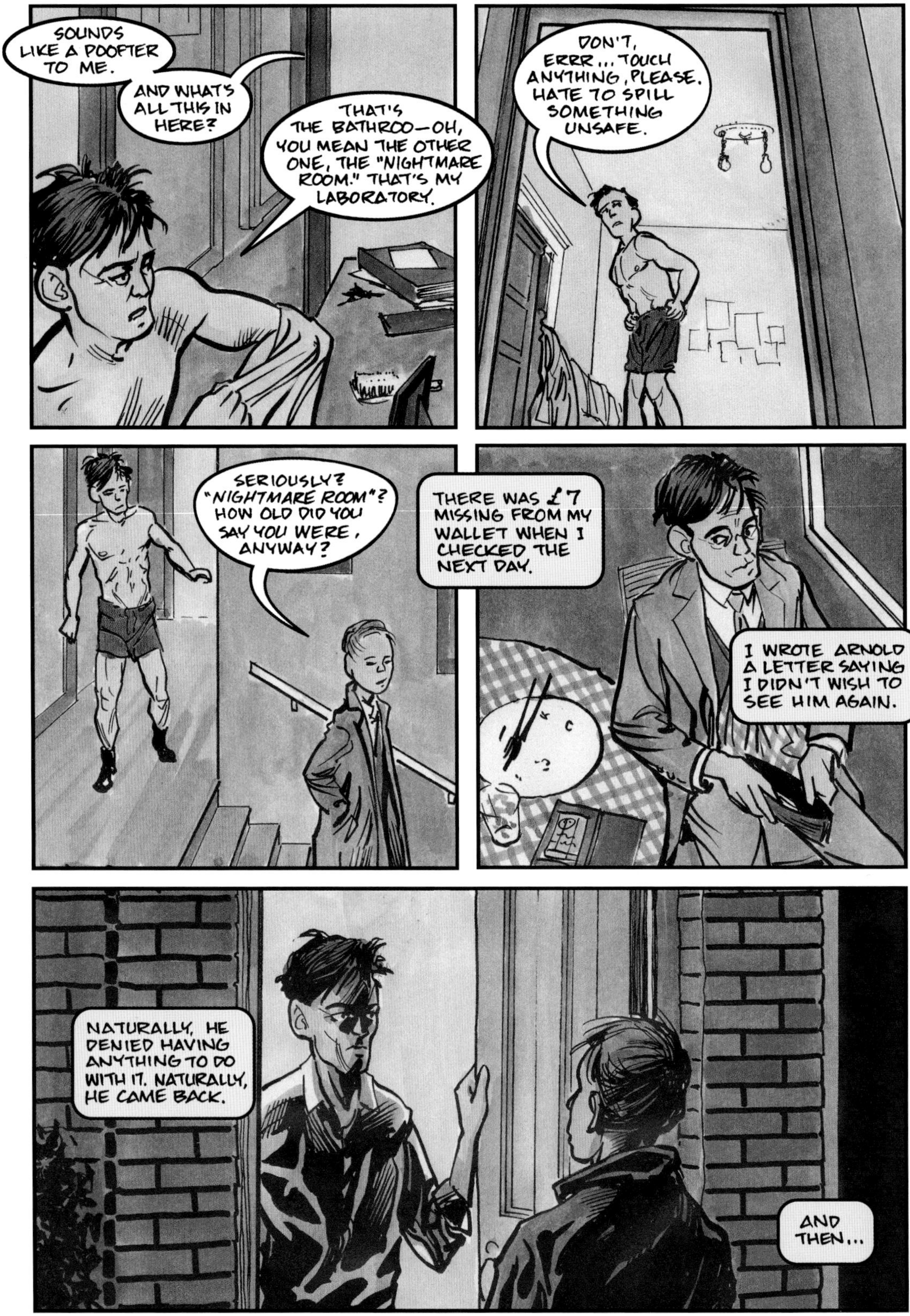
SOUNDS LIKE A POOFTER TO ME.
AND WHAT'S ALL THIS IN HERE?
THAT'S THE BATHROO—OH, YOU MEAN THE OTHER ONE, THE "NIGHTMARE ROOM." THAT'S MY LABORATORY.
DON'T, ERRR... TOUCH ANYTHING, PLEASE. HATE TO SPILL SOMETHING UNSAFE.
SERIOUSLY? "NIGHTMARE ROOM"? HOW OLD DID YOU SAY YOU WERE, ANYWAY?
THERE WAS £7 MISSING FROM MY WALLET WHEN I CHECKED THE NEXT DAY.
I WROTE ARNOLD A LETTER SAYING I DIDN'T WISH TO SEE HIM AGAIN.
NATURALLY, HE DENIED HAVING ANYTHING TO DO WITH IT. NATURALLY, HE CAME BACK.
AND THEN...

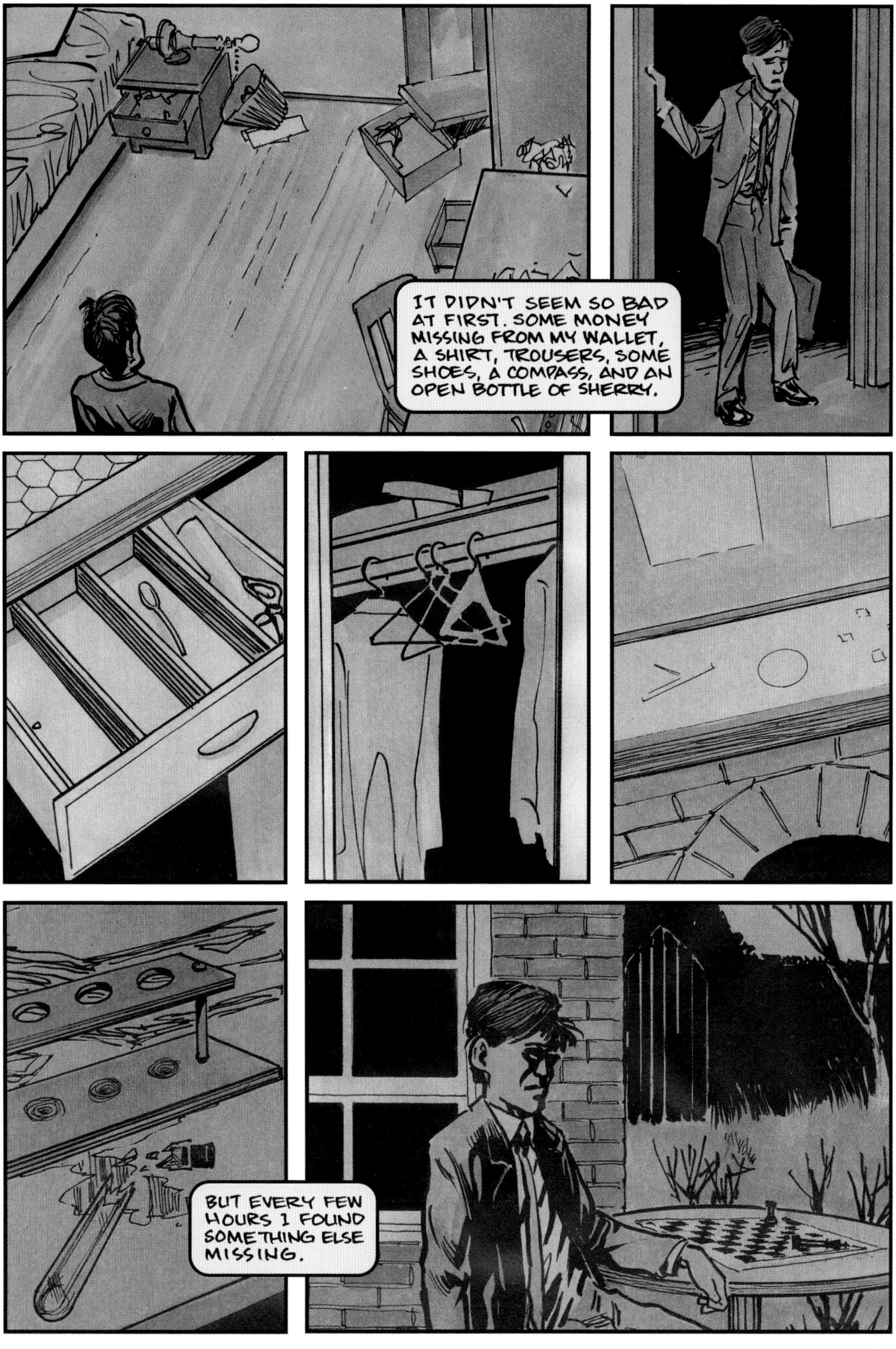
IT DIDN'T SEEM SO BAD AT FIRST. SOME MONEY MISSING FROM MY WALLET, A SHIRT, TROUSERS, SOME SHOES, A COMPASS, AND AN OPEN BOTTLE OF SHERRY.
BUT EVERY FEW HOURS I FOUND SOMETHING ELSE MISSING.

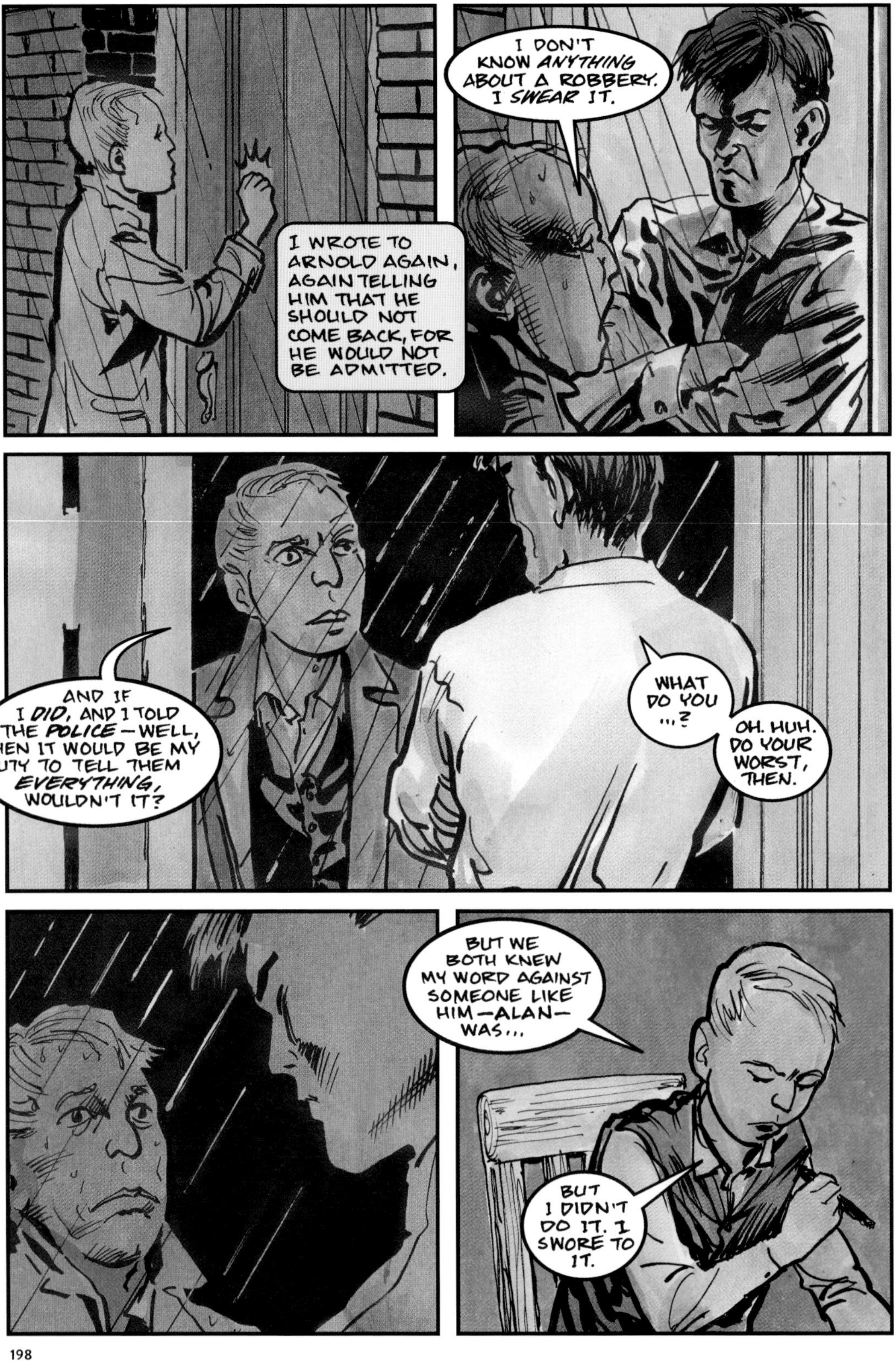
I WROTE TO ARNOLD AGAIN, AGAIN TELLING HIM THAT HE SHOULD NOT COME BACK, FOR HE WOULD NOT BE ADMITTED.
I DON'T KNOW ANYTHING ABOUT A ROBBERY. I SWEAR IT.
AND IF I DID, AND I TOLD THE POLICE—WELL, THEN IT WOULD BE MY DUTY TO TELL THEM EVERYTHING, WOULDN'T IT?
WHAT DO YOU ...?
OH. HUH. DO YOUR WORST, THEN.
BUT WE BOTH KNEW MY WORD AGAINST SOMEONE LIKE HIM—ALAN—WAS...
BUT I DIDN'T DO IT. I SWORE TO IT.

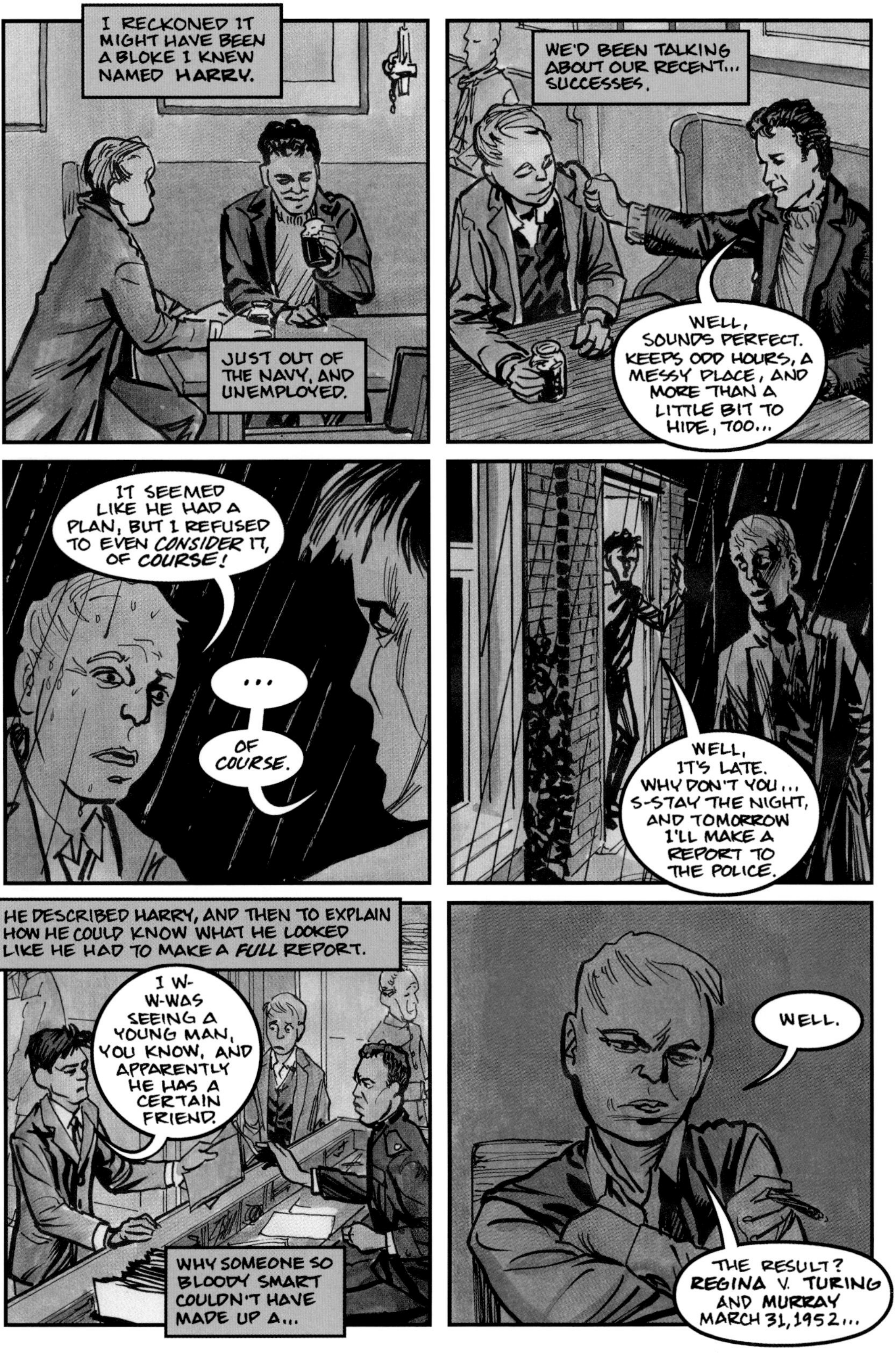
I RECKONED IT MIGHT HAVE BEEN A BLOKE I KNEW NAMED HARRY.
JUST OUT OF THE NAVY, AND UNEMPLOYED.
WE'D BEEN TALKING ABOUT OUR RECENT... SUCCESSES.
WELL, SOUNDS PERFECT. KEEPS ODD HOURS, A MESSY PLACE, AND MORE THAN A LITTLE BIT TO HIDE, TOO...
IT SEEMED LIKE HE HAD A PLAN, BUT I REFUSED TO EVEN *CONSIDER* IT, OF COURSE!
...
OF COURSE.
WELL, IT'S LATE. WHY DON'T YOU... S-STAY THE NIGHT, AND TOMORROW I'LL MAKE A REPORT TO THE POLICE.
HE DESCRIBED HARRY, AND THEN TO EXPLAIN HOW HE COULD KNOW WHAT HE LOOKED LIKE HE HAD TO MAKE A *FULL* REPORT.
I W-W-WAS SEEING A YOUNG MAN, YOU KNOW, AND APPARENTLY HE HAS A CERTAIN FRIEND.
WHY SOMEONE SO BLOODY SMART COULDN'T HAVE MADE UP A...
WELL.
THE RESULT? REGINA V. TURING AND MURRAY MARCH 31, 1952...

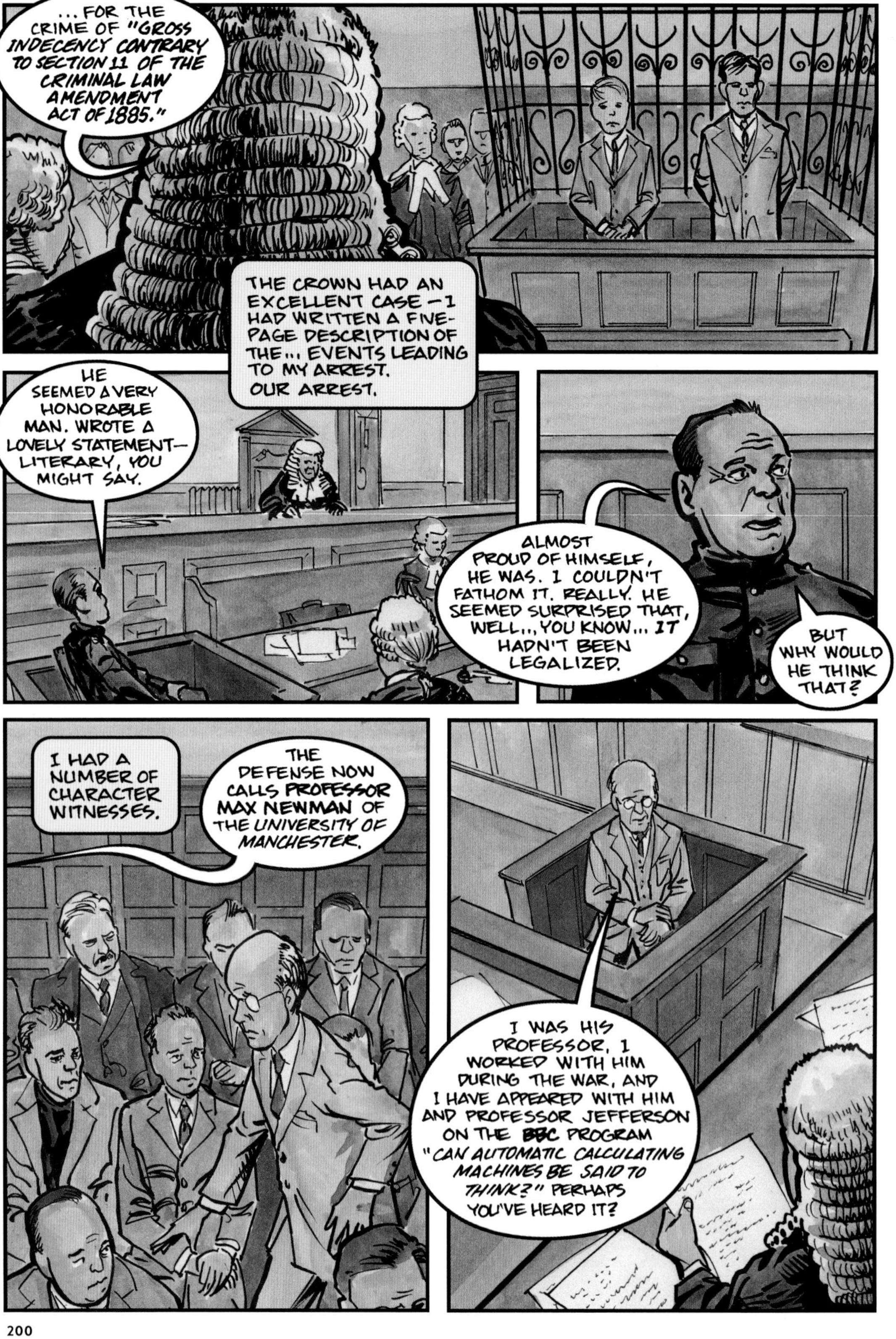
...FOR THE CRIME OF "GROSS INDECENCY CONTRARY TO SECTION 11 OF THE CRIMINAL LAW AMENDMENT ACT OF 1885."
THE CROWN HAD AN EXCELLENT CASE—I HAD WRITTEN A FIVE-PAGE DESCRIPTION OF THE... EVENTS LEADING TO MY ARREST. OUR ARREST.
HE SEEMED A VERY HONORABLE MAN. WROTE A LOVELY STATEMENT—LITERARY, YOU MIGHT SAY.
ALMOST PROUD OF HIMSELF, HE WAS. I COULDN'T FATHOM IT. REALLY. HE SEEMED SURPRISED THAT, WELL... YOU KNOW... IT HADN'T BEEN LEGALIZED.
BUT WHY WOULD HE THINK THAT?
I HAD A NUMBER OF CHARACTER WITNESSES.
THE DEFENSE NOW CALLS PROFESSOR MAX NEWMAN OF THE UNIVERSITY OF MANCHESTER.
I WAS HIS PROFESSOR, I WORKED WITH HIM DURING THE WAR, AND I HAVE APPEARED WITH HIM AND PROFESSOR JEFFERSON ON THE BBC PROGRAM "CAN AUTOMATIC CALCULATING MACHINES BE SAID TO THINK?" PERHAPS YOU'VE HEARD IT?

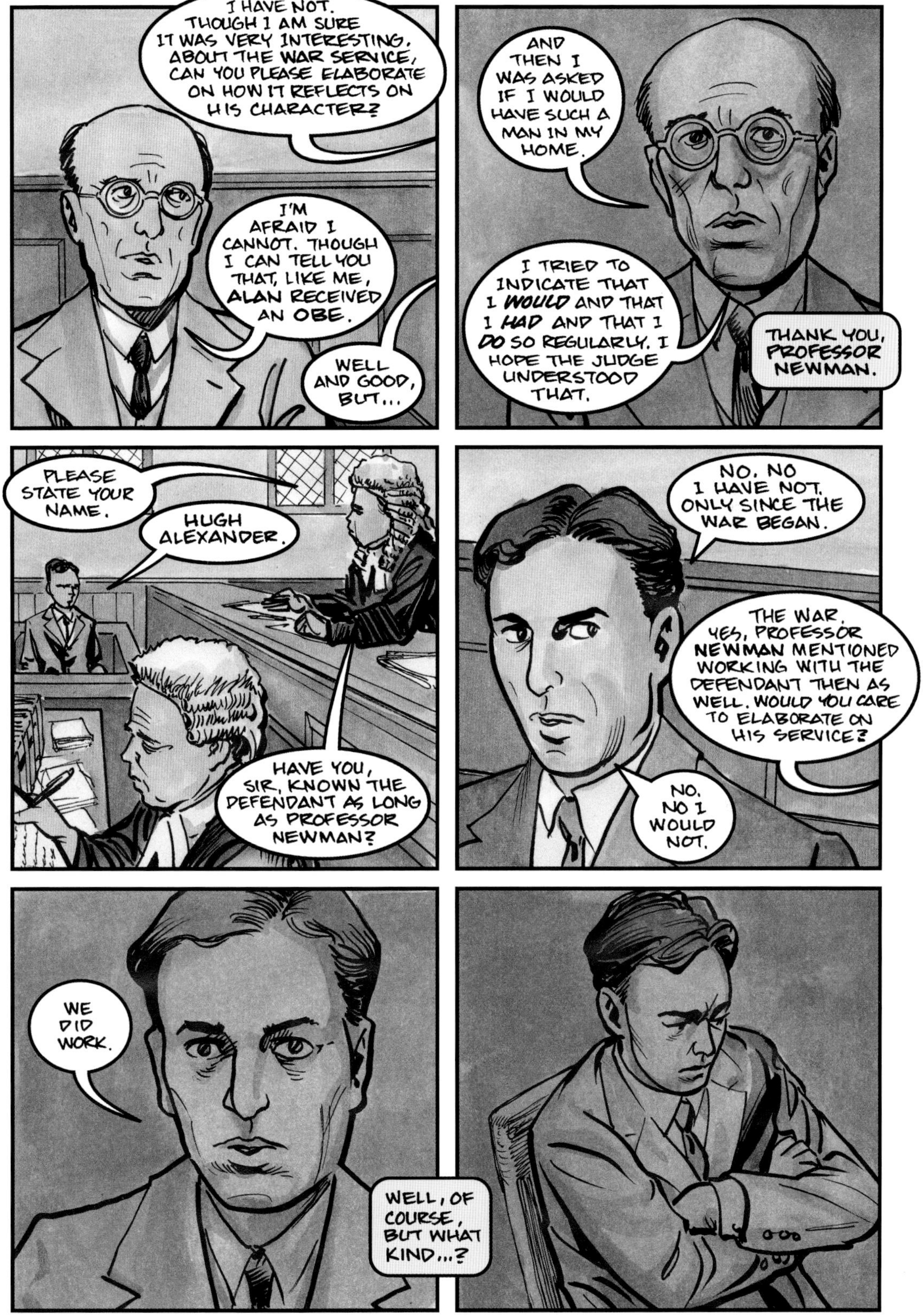
I HAVE NOT. THOUGH I AM SURE IT WAS VERY INTERESTING. ABOUT THE WAR SERVICE, CAN YOU PLEASE ELABORATE ON HOW IT REFLECTS ON HIS CHARACTER?
I'M AFRAID I CANNOT. THOUGH I CAN TELL YOU THAT, LIKE ME, ALAN RECEIVED AN OBE.
WELL AND GOOD, BUT...
AND THEN I WAS ASKED IF I WOULD HAVE SUCH A MAN IN MY HOME.
I TRIED TO INDICATE THAT I WOULD AND THAT I HAD AND THAT I DO SO REGULARLY. I HOPE THE JUDGE UNDERSTOOD THAT.
THANK YOU, PROFESSOR NEWMAN.
PLEASE STATE YOUR NAME.
HUGH ALEXANDER.
HAVE YOU, SIR, KNOWN THE DEFENDANT AS LONG AS PROFESSOR NEWMAN?
NO. NO I HAVE NOT. ONLY SINCE THE WAR BEGAN.
THE WAR. YES, PROFESSOR NEWMAN MENTIONED WORKING WITH THE DEFENDANT THEN AS WELL. WOULD YOU CARE TO ELABORATE ON HIS SERVICE?
NO. NO I WOULD NOT.
WE DID WORK.
WELL, OF COURSE, BUT WHAT KIND...?

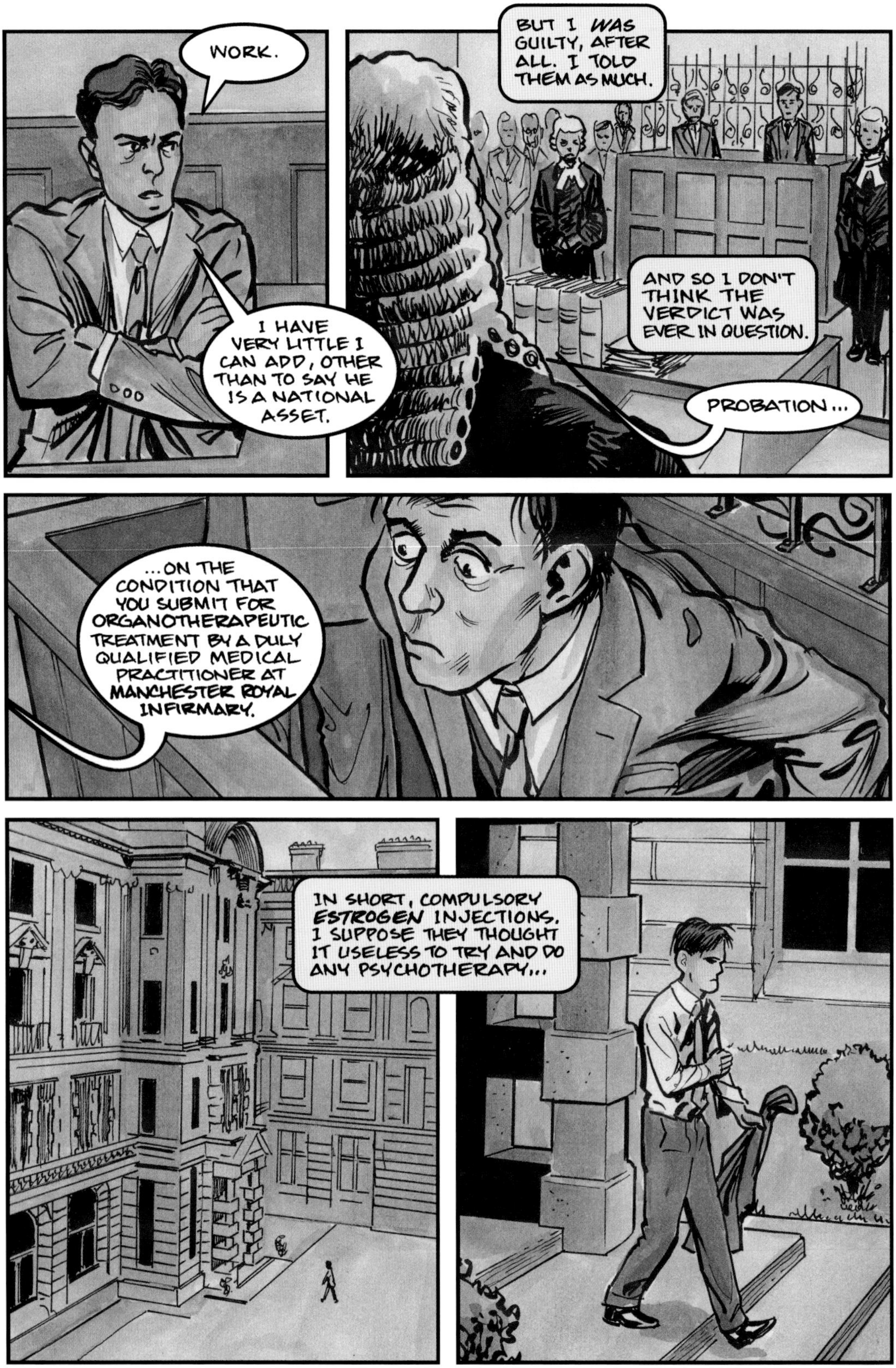
WORK.
I HAVE VERY LITTLE I CAN ADD, OTHER THAN TO SAY HE IS A NATIONAL ASSET.
BUT I WAS GUILTY, AFTER ALL. I TOLD THEM AS MUCH.
AND SO I DON'T THINK THE VERDICT WAS EVER IN QUESTION.
PROBATION...
...ON THE CONDITION THAT YOU SUBMIT FOR ORGANOTHERAPEUTIC TREATMENT BY A DULY QUALIFIED MEDICAL PRACTITIONER AT MANCHESTER ROYAL INFIRMARY.
IN SHORT, COMPULSORY ESTROGEN INJECTIONS. I SUPPOSE THEY THOUGHT IT USELESS TO TRY AND DO ANY PSYCHOTHERAPY...

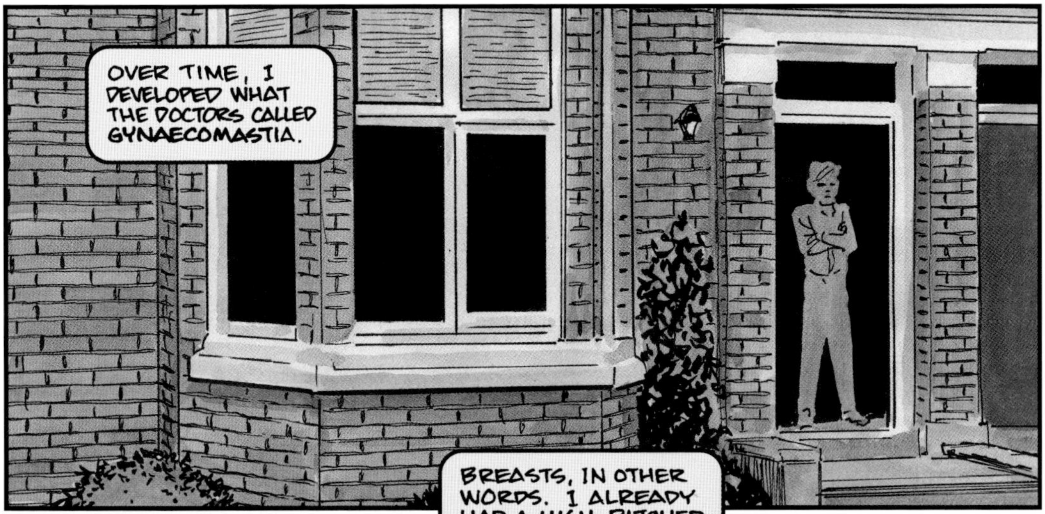
OVER TIME, I DEVELOPED WHAT THE DOCTORS CALLED GYNAECOMASTIA.
BREASTS, IN OTHER WORDS. I ALREADY HAD A HIGH-PITCHED VOICE.

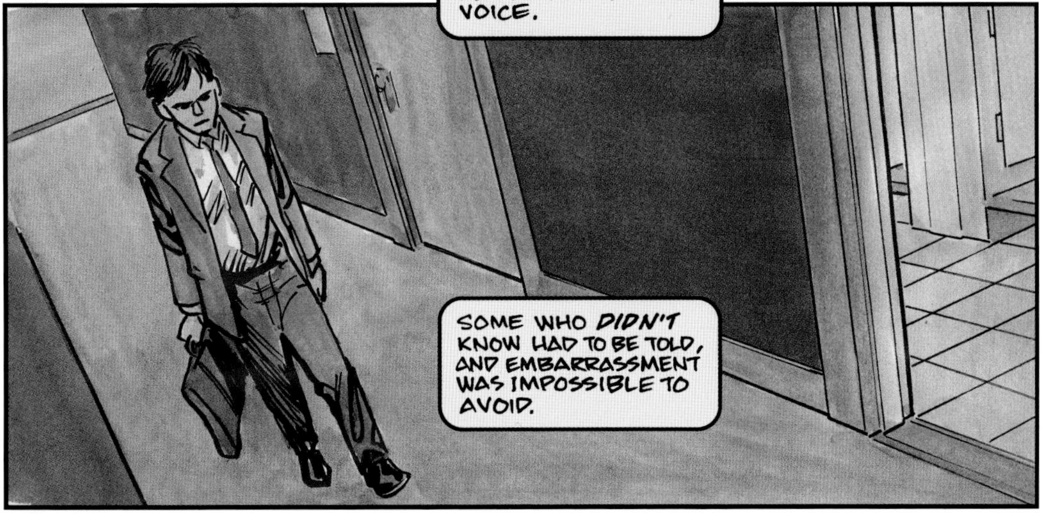
SOME WHO *DIDN'T* KNOW HAD TO BE TOLD, AND EMBARRASSMENT WAS IMPOSSIBLE TO AVOID.

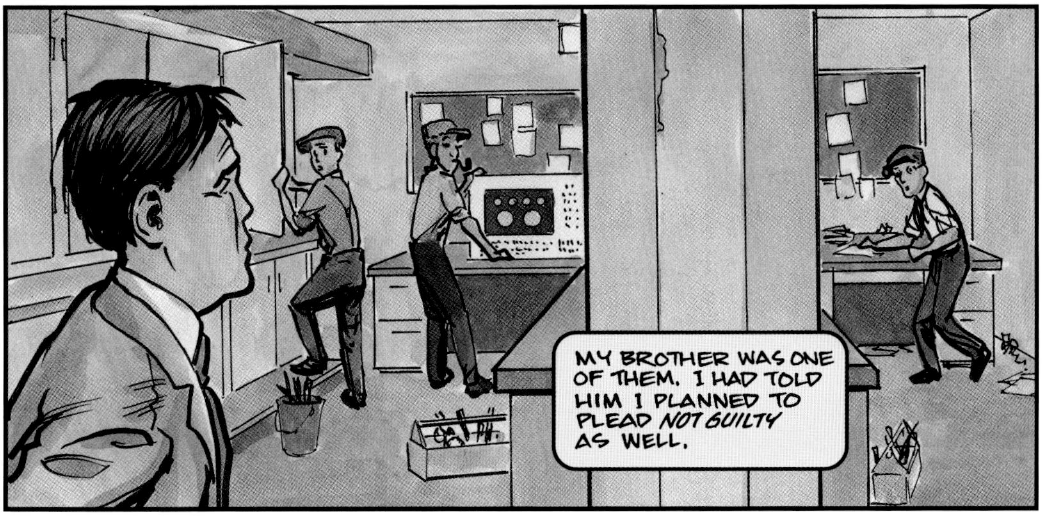
MY BROTHER WAS ONE OF THEM. I HAD TOLD HIM I PLANNED TO PLEAD *NOT GUILTY* AS WELL.

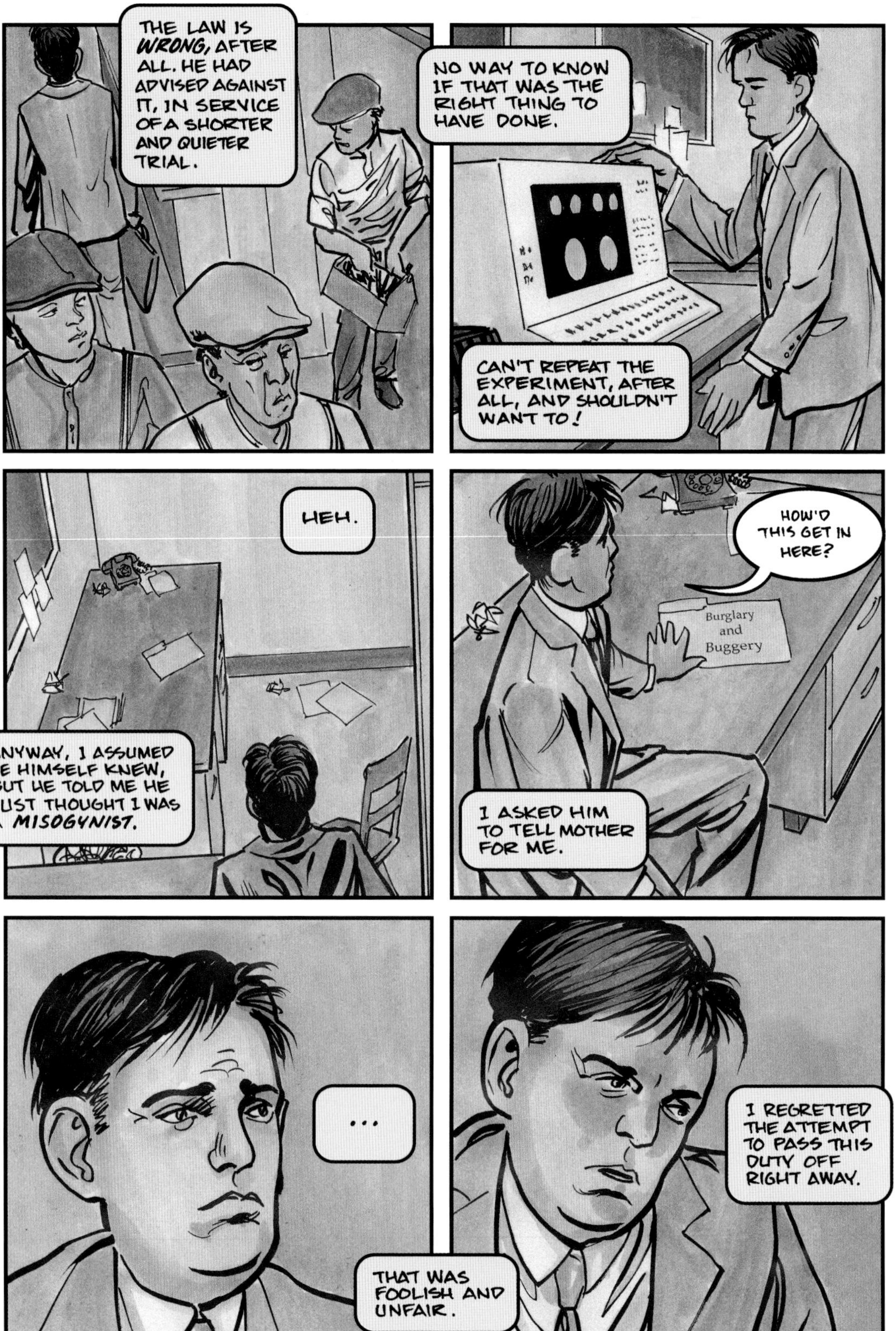
THE LAW IS *WRONG*, AFTER ALL. HE HAD ADVISED AGAINST IT, IN SERVICE OF A SHORTER AND QUIETER TRIAL.
NO WAY TO KNOW IF THAT WAS THE RIGHT THING TO HAVE DONE.
CAN'T REPEAT THE EXPERIMENT, AFTER ALL, AND SHOULDN'T WANT TO!
HEH.
ANYWAY, I ASSUMED HE HIMSELF KNEW, BUT HE TOLD ME HE JUST THOUGHT I WAS A *MISOGYNIST*.
HOW'D THIS GET IN HERE?
Burglary and Buggery
I ASKED HIM TO TELL MOTHER FOR ME.
...
THAT WAS FOOLISH AND UNFAIR.
I REGRETTED THE ATTEMPT TO PASS THIS DUTY OFF RIGHT AWAY.

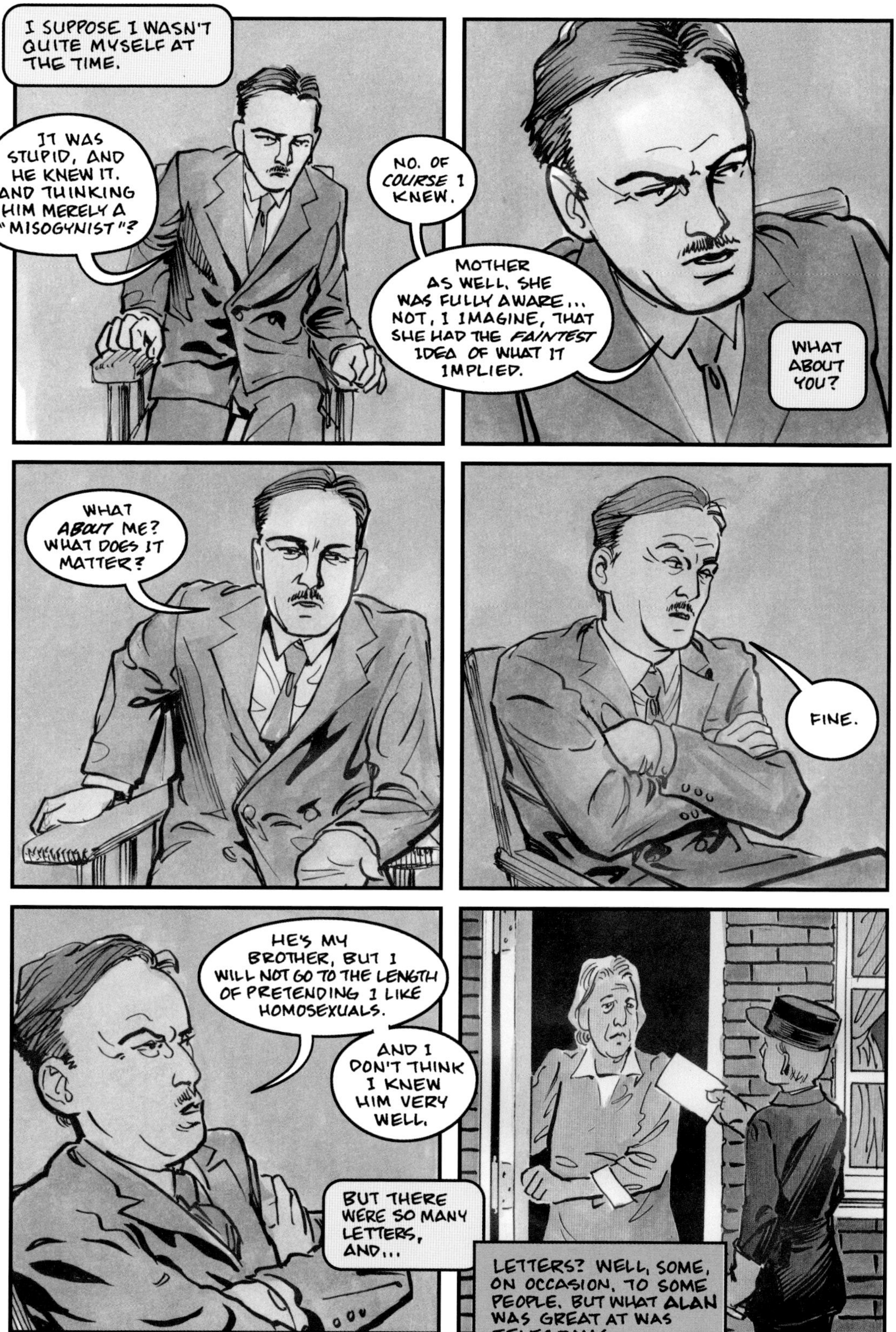

I SUPPOSE I WASN'T QUITE MYSELF AT THE TIME.
IT WAS STUPID, AND HE KNEW IT. AND THINKING HIM MERELY A "MISOGYNIST"?
NO. OF *COURSE* I KNEW.
MOTHER AS WELL. SHE WAS FULLY AWARE... NOT, I IMAGINE, THAT SHE HAD THE *FAINTEST* IDEA OF WHAT IT IMPLIED.
WHAT ABOUT YOU?
WHAT *ABOUT* ME? WHAT DOES IT MATTER?
FINE.
HE'S MY BROTHER, BUT I WILL NOT GO TO THE LENGTH OF PRETENDING I LIKE HOMOSEXUALS.
AND I DON'T THINK I KNEW HIM VERY WELL.
BUT THERE WERE SO MANY LETTERS, AND...
LETTERS? WELL, SOME, ON OCCASION, TO SOME PEOPLE. BUT WHAT ALAN WAS GREAT AT WAS TELEGRAMS.

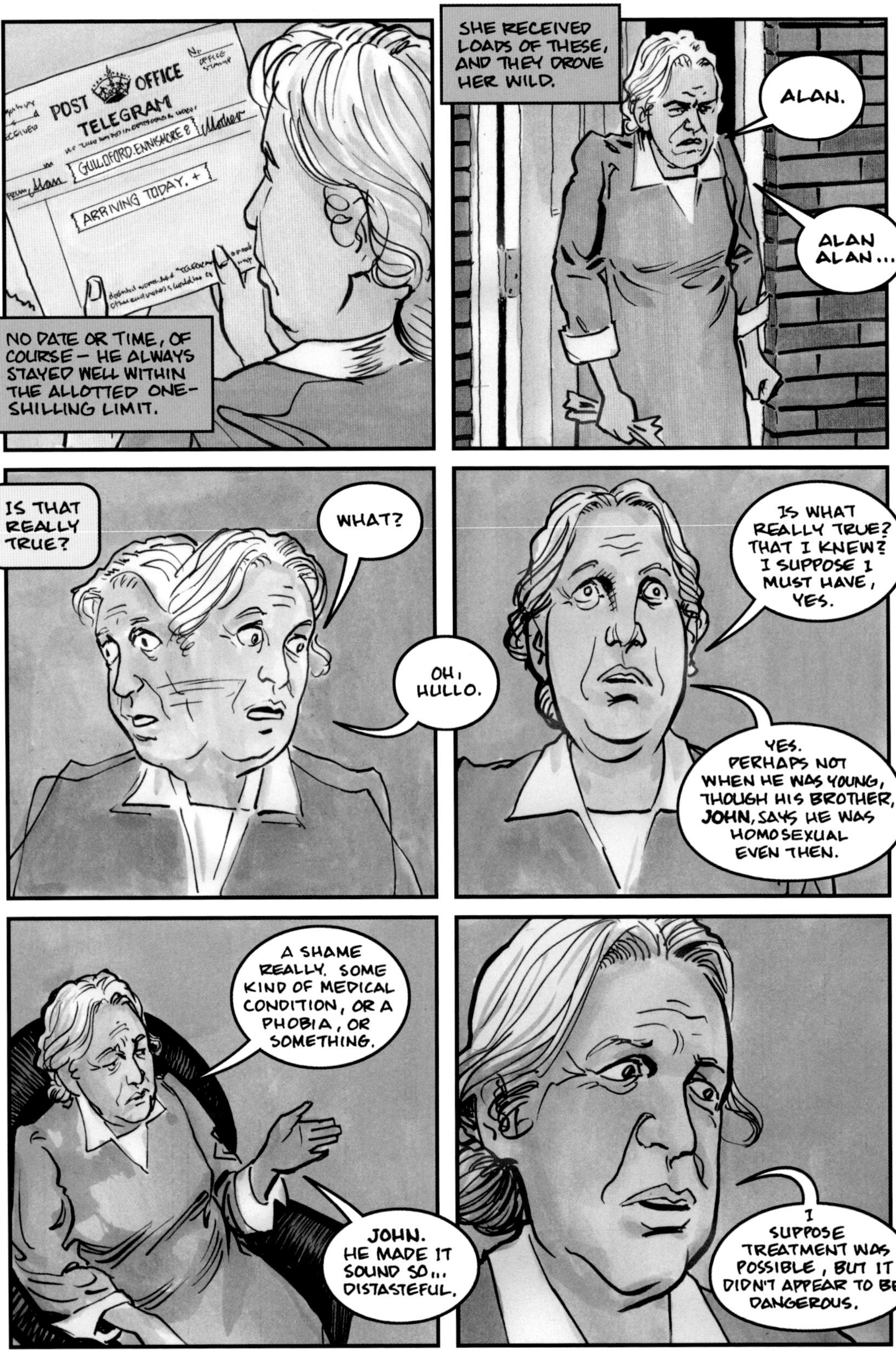

POST OFFICE
TELEGRAM
GUILDFORD.ENNISMORE 8
Mother
ARRIVING TODAY. +
NO DATE OR TIME, OF COURSE – HE ALWAYS STAYED WELL WITHIN THE ALLOTTED ONE-SHILLING LIMIT.
SHE RECEIVED LOADS OF THESE, AND THEY DROVE HER WILD.
ALAN.
ALAN ALAN...
IS THAT REALLY TRUE?
WHAT?
OH, HULLO.
IS WHAT REALLY TRUE? THAT I KNEW? I SUPPOSE I MUST HAVE, YES.
YES. PERHAPS NOT WHEN HE WAS YOUNG, THOUGH HIS BROTHER, **JOHN**, SAYS HE WAS HOMOSEXUAL EVEN THEN.
A SHAME REALLY. SOME KIND OF MEDICAL CONDITION, OR A PHOBIA, OR SOMETHING.
JOHN. HE MADE IT SOUND SO... DISTASTEFUL.
I SUPPOSE TREATMENT WAS POSSIBLE, BUT IT DIDN'T APPEAR TO BE DANGEROUS.

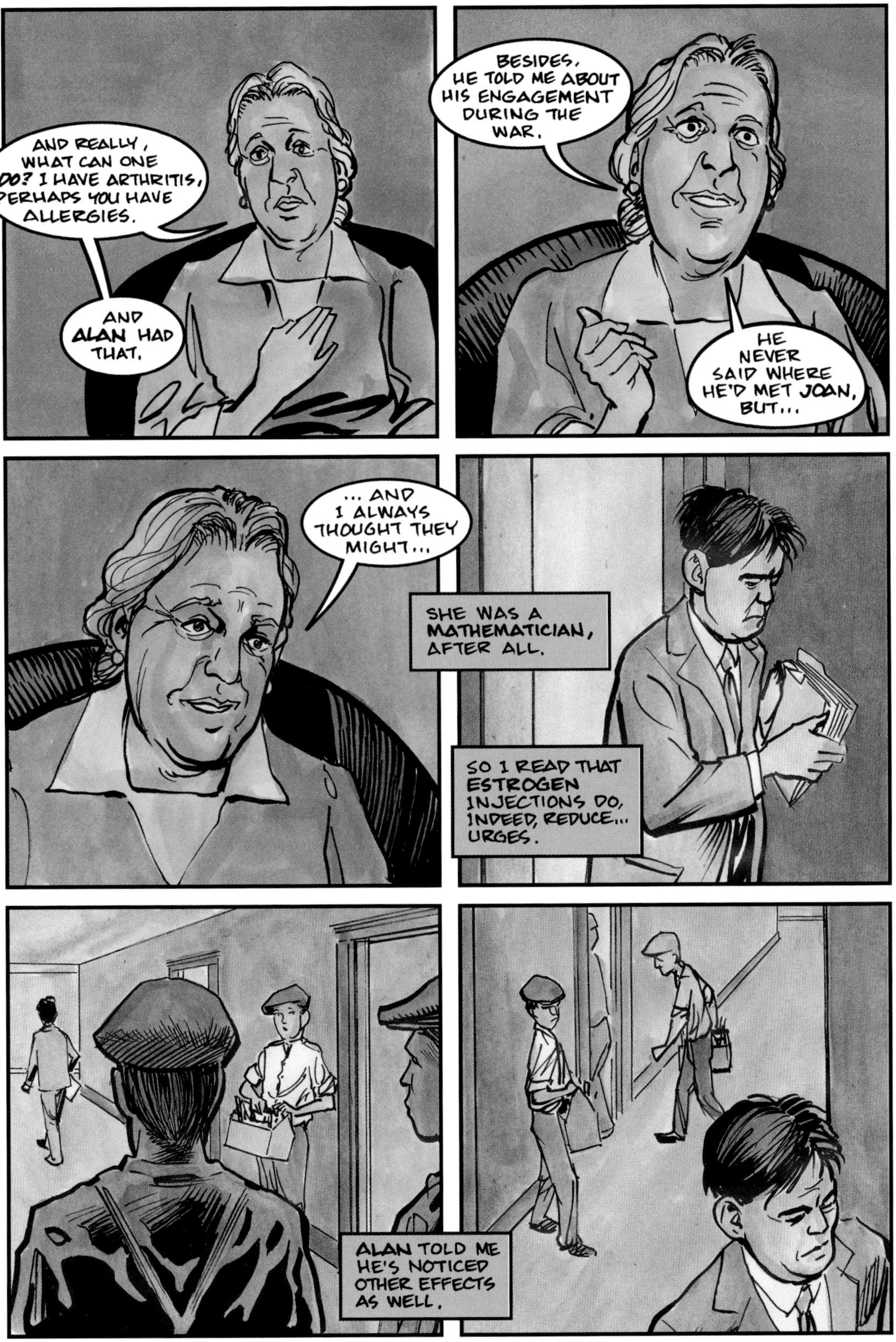
AND REALLY, WHAT CAN ONE DO? I HAVE ARTHRITIS, PERHAPS YOU HAVE ALLERGIES.
AND ALAN HAD THAT.
BESIDES, HE TOLD ME ABOUT HIS ENGAGEMENT DURING THE WAR.
HE NEVER SAID WHERE HE'D MET JOAN, BUT...
... AND I ALWAYS THOUGHT THEY MIGHT...
SHE WAS A MATHEMATICIAN, AFTER ALL.
SO I READ THAT ESTROGEN INJECTIONS DO, INDEED, REDUCE... URGES.
ALAN TOLD ME HE'S NOTICED OTHER EFFECTS AS WELL.

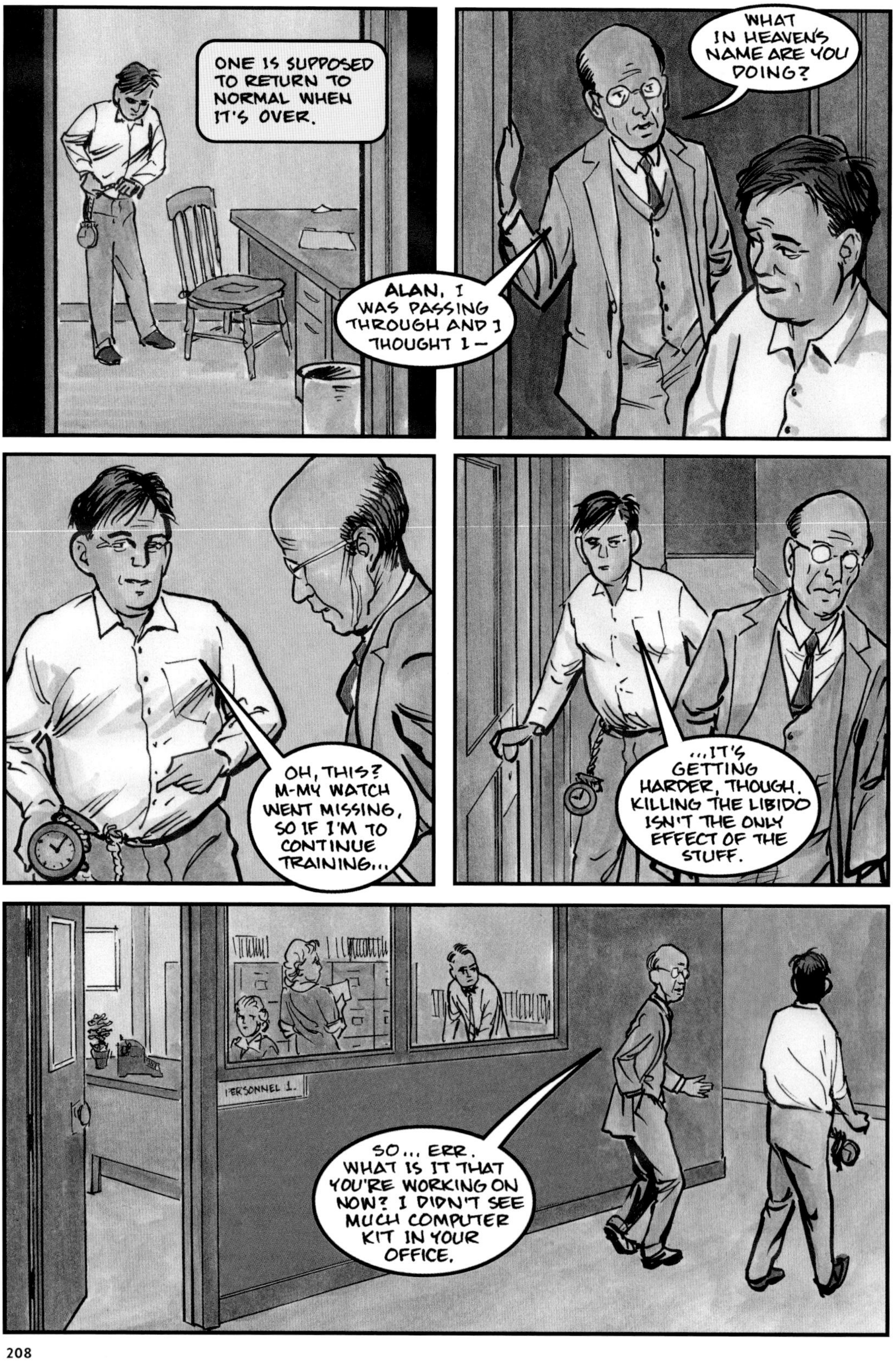
ONE IS SUPPOSED TO RETURN TO NORMAL WHEN IT'S OVER.
WHAT IN HEAVEN'S NAME ARE YOU DOING?
ALAN, I WAS PASSING THROUGH AND I THOUGHT I—
OH, THIS? M-MY WATCH WENT MISSING, SO IF I'M TO CONTINUE TRAINING...
...IT'S GETTING HARDER, THOUGH. KILLING THE LIBIDO ISN'T THE ONLY EFFECT OF THE STUFF.
PERSONNEL 1.
SO... ERR. WHAT IS IT THAT YOU'RE WORKING ON NOW? I DIDN'T SEE MUCH COMPUTER KIT IN YOUR OFFICE.

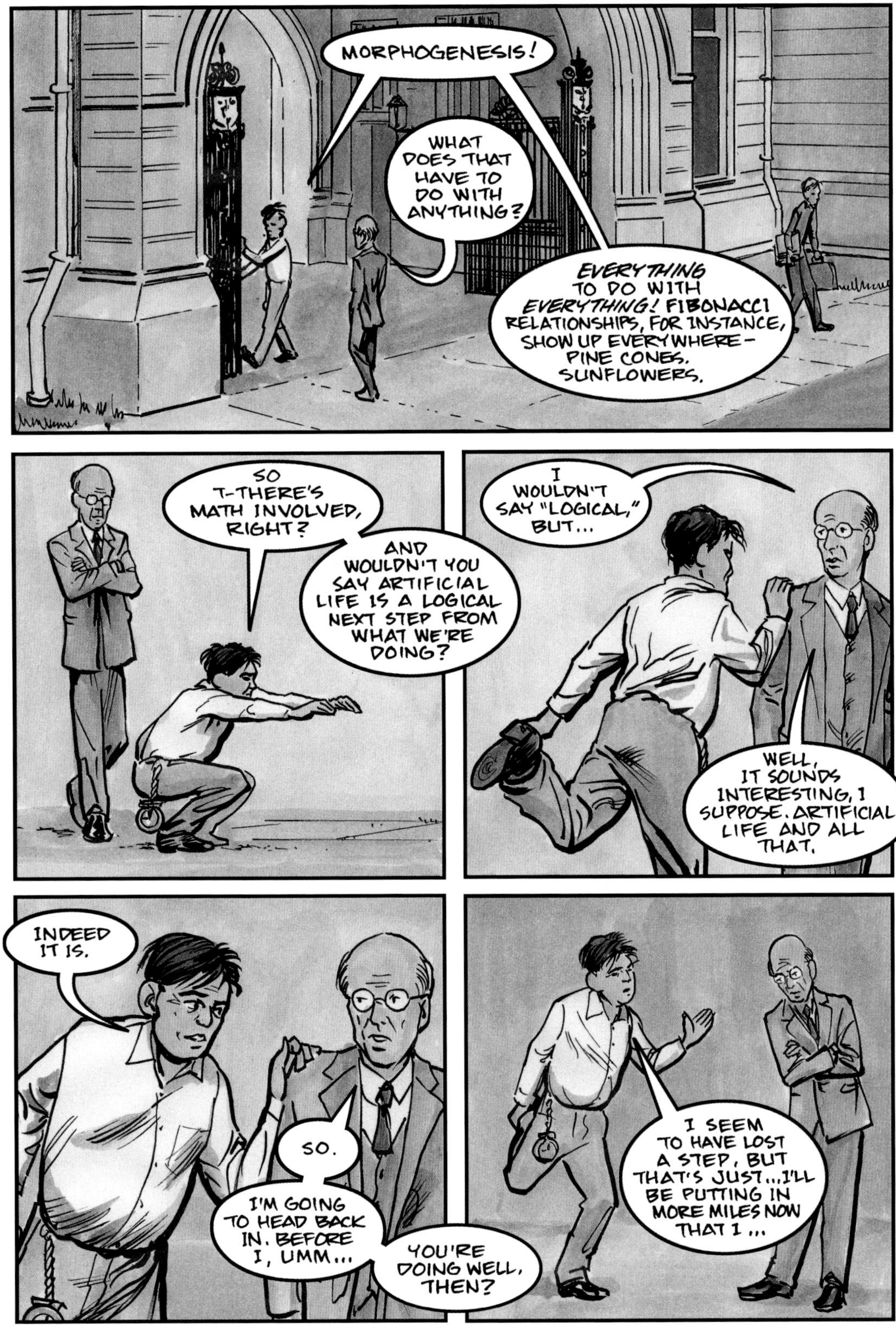
MORPHOGENESIS!
WHAT DOES THAT HAVE TO DO WITH ANYTHING?
EVERYTHING TO DO WITH EVERYTHING! FIBONACCI RELATIONSHIPS, FOR INSTANCE, SHOW UP EVERYWHERE— PINE CONES. SUNFLOWERS.
SO T-THERE'S MATH INVOLVED, RIGHT?
AND WOULDN'T YOU SAY ARTIFICIAL LIFE IS A LOGICAL NEXT STEP FROM WHAT WE'RE DOING?
I WOULDN'T SAY "LOGICAL," BUT...
WELL, IT SOUNDS INTERESTING, I SUPPOSE. ARTIFICIAL LIFE AND ALL THAT.
INDEED IT IS.
SO.
I'M GOING TO HEAD BACK IN. BEFORE I, UMM...
YOU'RE DOING WELL, THEN?
I SEEM TO HAVE LOST A STEP, BUT THAT'S JUST...I'LL BE PUTTING IN MORE MILES NOW THAT I ...

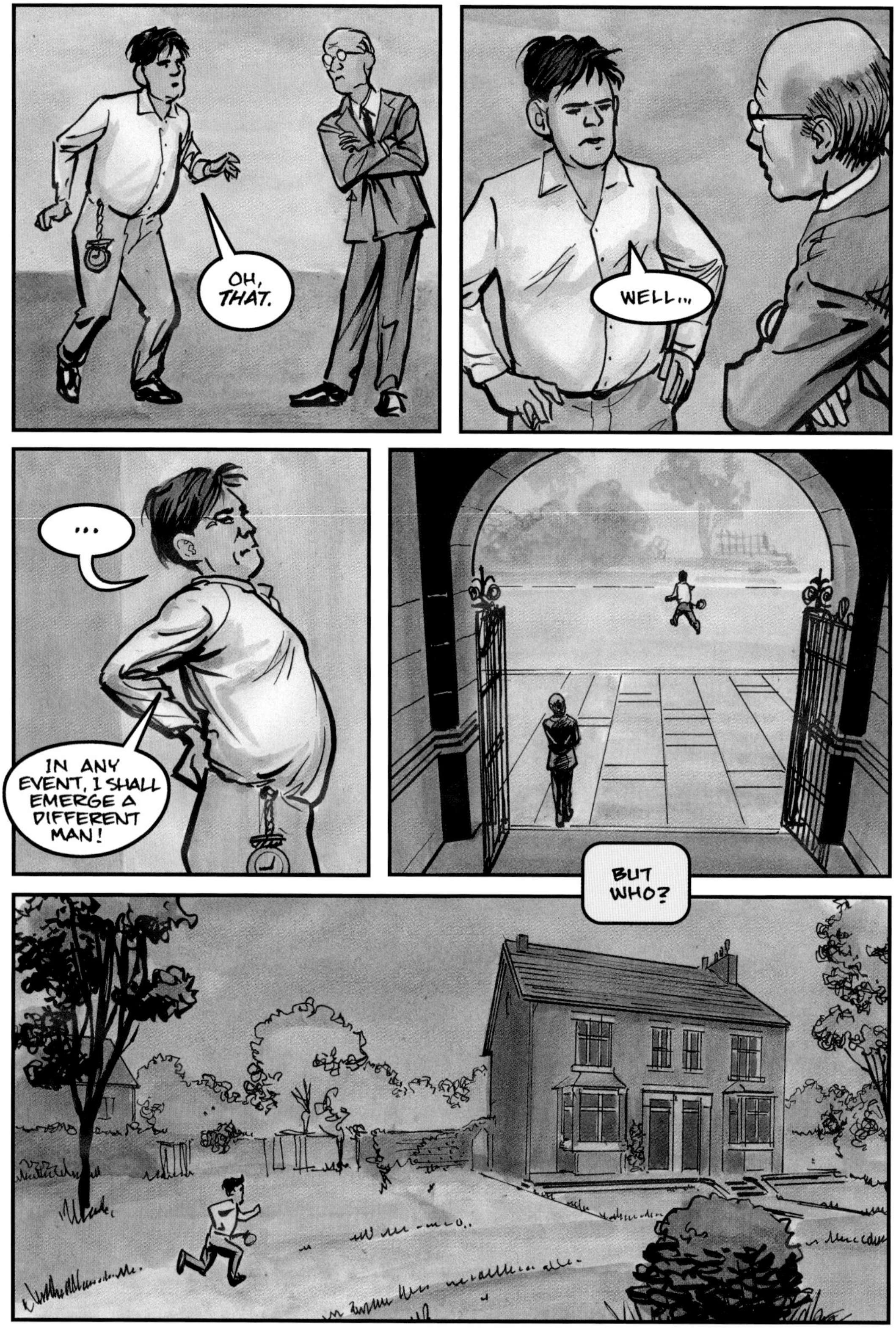
OH, THAT.
WELL...
...
IN ANY EVENT, I SHALL EMERGE A DIFFERENT MAN!
BUT WHO?

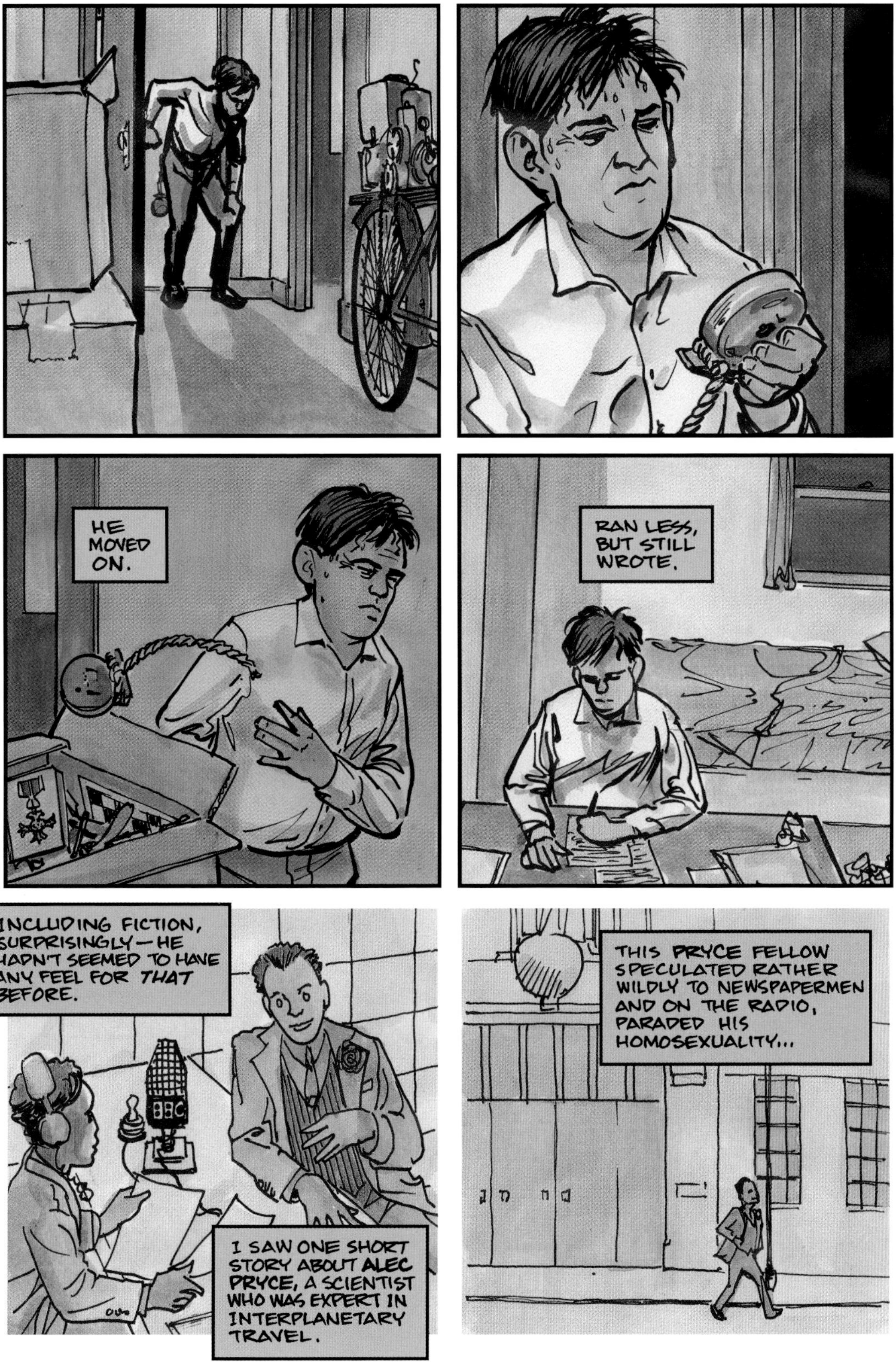
HE MOVED ON.
RAN LESS, BUT STILL WROTE.
INCLUDING FICTION, SURPRISINGLY—HE HADN'T SEEMED TO HAVE ANY FEEL FOR *THAT* BEFORE.
BBC
I SAW ONE SHORT STORY ABOUT **ALEC PRYCE**, A SCIENTIST WHO WAS EXPERT IN INTERPLANETARY TRAVEL.
THIS **PRYCE** FELLOW SPECULATED RATHER WILDLY TO NEWSPAPERMEN AND ON THE RADIO, PARADED HIS HOMOSEXUALITY...

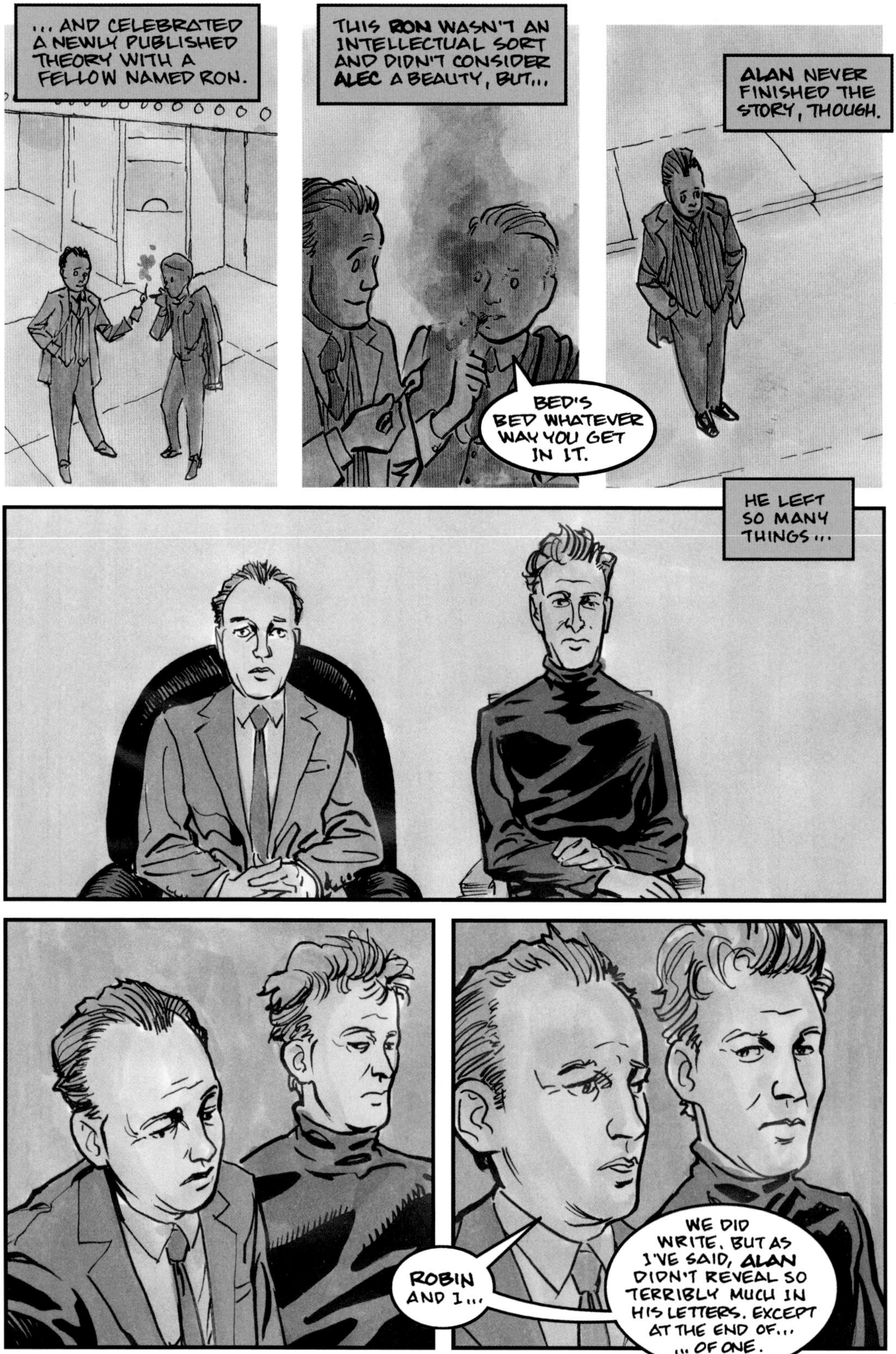
... AND CELEBRATED A NEWLY PUBLISHED THEORY WITH A FELLOW NAMED RON.
THIS RON WASN'T AN INTELLECTUAL SORT AND DIDN'T CONSIDER ALEC A BEAUTY, BUT...
BED'S BED WHATEVER WAY YOU GET IN IT.
ALAN NEVER FINISHED THE STORY, THOUGH.
HE LEFT SO MANY THINGS...
ROBIN AND I...
WE DID WRITE, BUT AS I'VE SAID, ALAN DIDN'T REVEAL SO TERRIBLY MUCH IN HIS LETTERS. EXCEPT AT THE END OF...
... OF ONE.

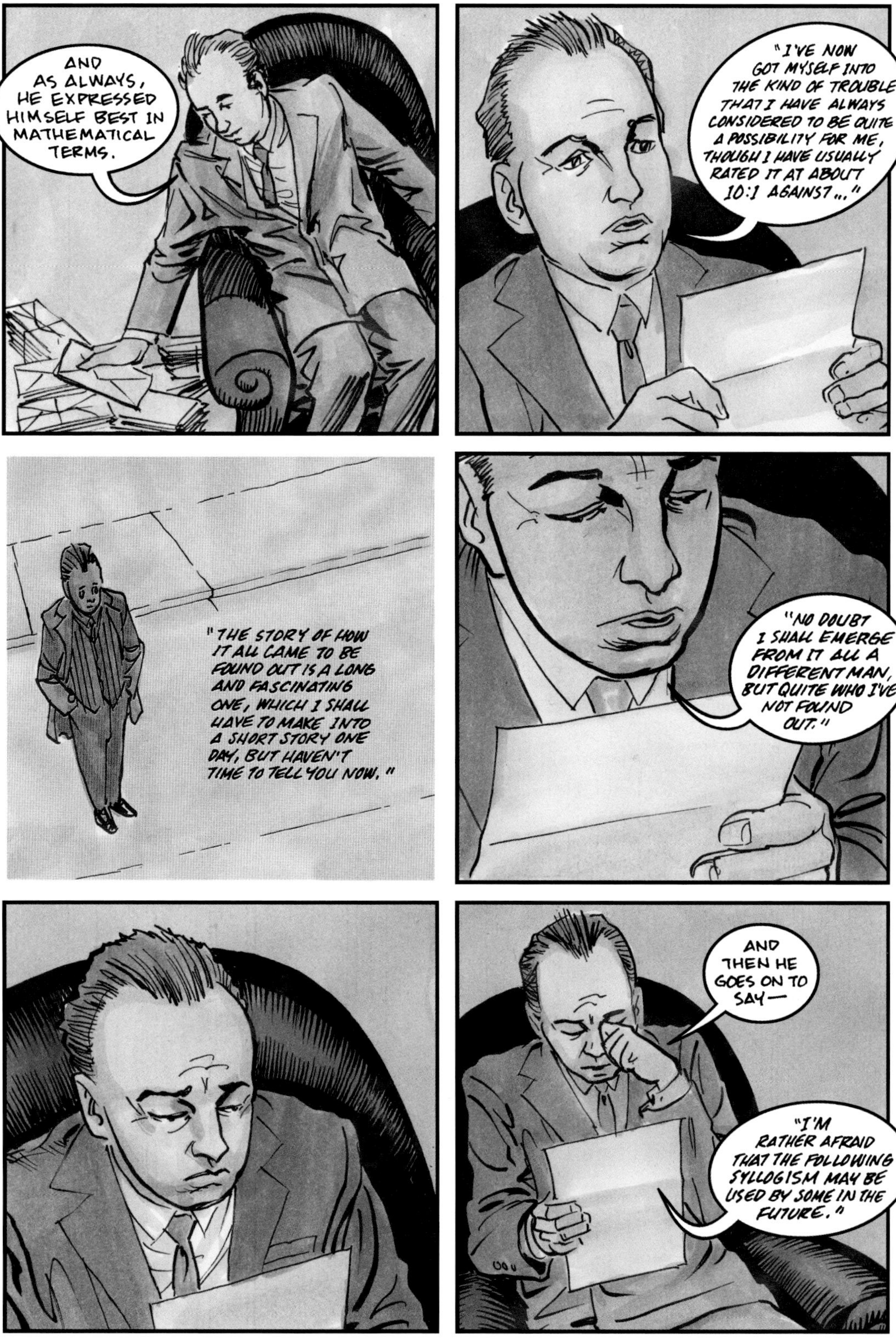
AND AS ALWAYS, HE EXPRESSED HIMSELF BEST IN MATHEMATICAL TERMS.
"I'VE NOW GOT MYSELF INTO THE KIND OF TROUBLE THAT I HAVE ALWAYS CONSIDERED TO BE QUITE A POSSIBILITY FOR ME, THOUGH I HAVE USUALLY RATED IT AT ABOUT 10:1 AGAINST..."
"THE STORY OF HOW IT ALL CAME TO BE FOUND OUT IS A LONG AND FASCINATING ONE, WHICH I SHALL HAVE TO MAKE INTO A SHORT STORY ONE DAY, BUT HAVEN'T TIME TO TELL YOU NOW."
"NO DOUBT I SHALL EMERGE FROM IT ALL A DIFFERENT MAN, BUT QUITE WHO I'VE NOT FOUND OUT."
AND THEN HE GOES ON TO SAY—
"I'M RATHER AFRAID THAT THE FOLLOWING SYLLOGISM MAY BE USED BY SOME IN THE FUTURE."

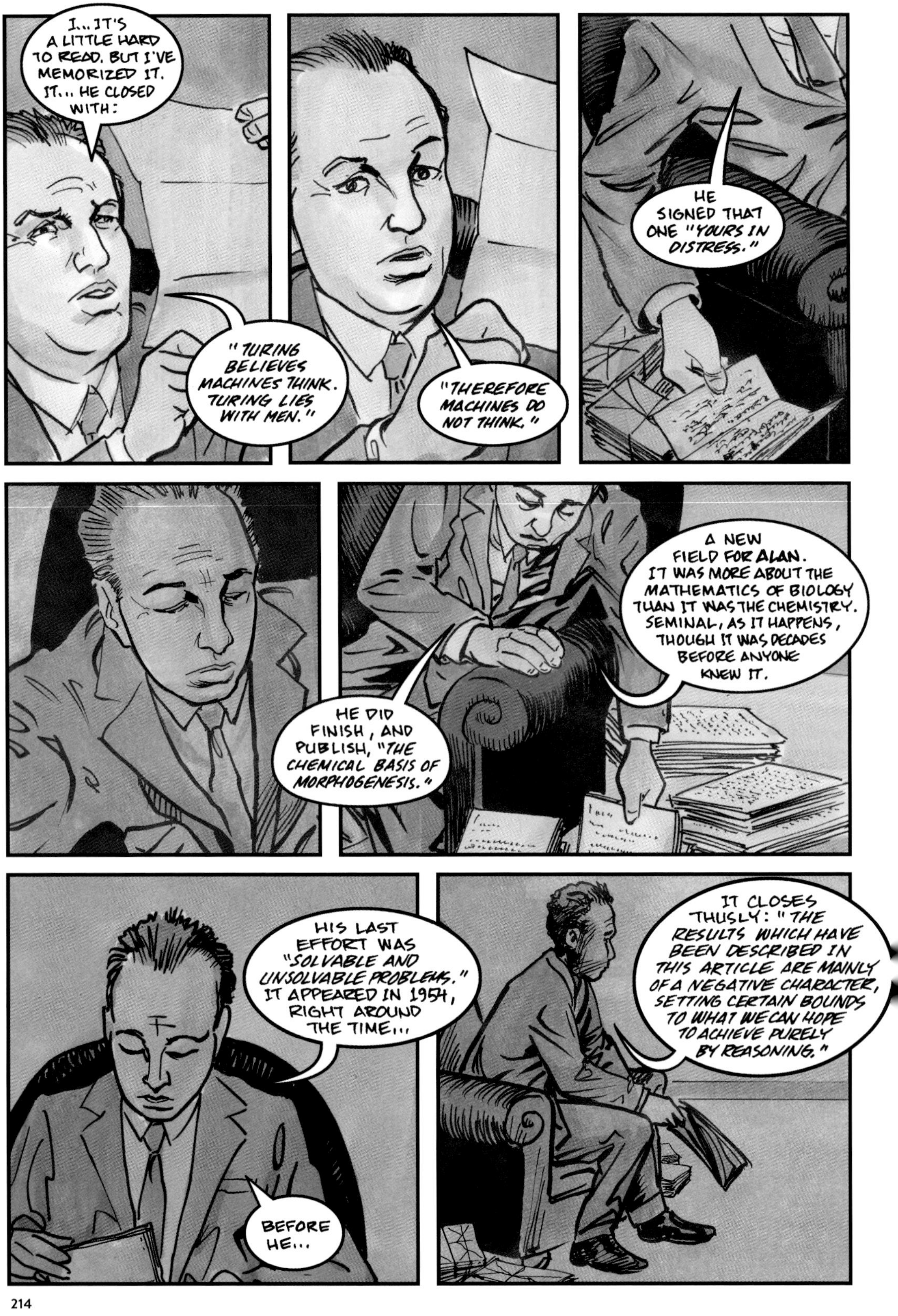
I... IT'S A LITTLE HARD TO READ. BUT I'VE MEMORIZED IT. IT... HE CLOSED WITH:
"TURING BELIEVES MACHINES THINK. TURING LIES WITH MEN."
"THEREFORE MACHINES DO NOT THINK."
HE SIGNED THAT ONE "YOURS IN DISTRESS."
A NEW FIELD FOR ALAN. IT WAS MORE ABOUT THE MATHEMATICS OF BIOLOGY THAN IT WAS THE CHEMISTRY. SEMINAL, AS IT HAPPENS, THOUGH IT WAS DECADES BEFORE ANYONE KNEW IT.
HE DID FINISH, AND PUBLISH, "THE CHEMICAL BASIS OF MORPHOGENESIS."
HIS LAST EFFORT WAS "SOLVABLE AND UNSOLVABLE PROBLEMS." IT APPEARED IN 1954, RIGHT AROUND THE TIME...
BEFORE HE...
IT CLOSES THUSLY: "THE RESULTS WHICH HAVE BEEN DESCRIBED IN THIS ARTICLE ARE MAINLY OF A NEGATIVE CHARACTER, SETTING CERTAIN BOUNDS TO WHAT WE CAN HOPE TO ACHIEVE PURELY BY REASONING."

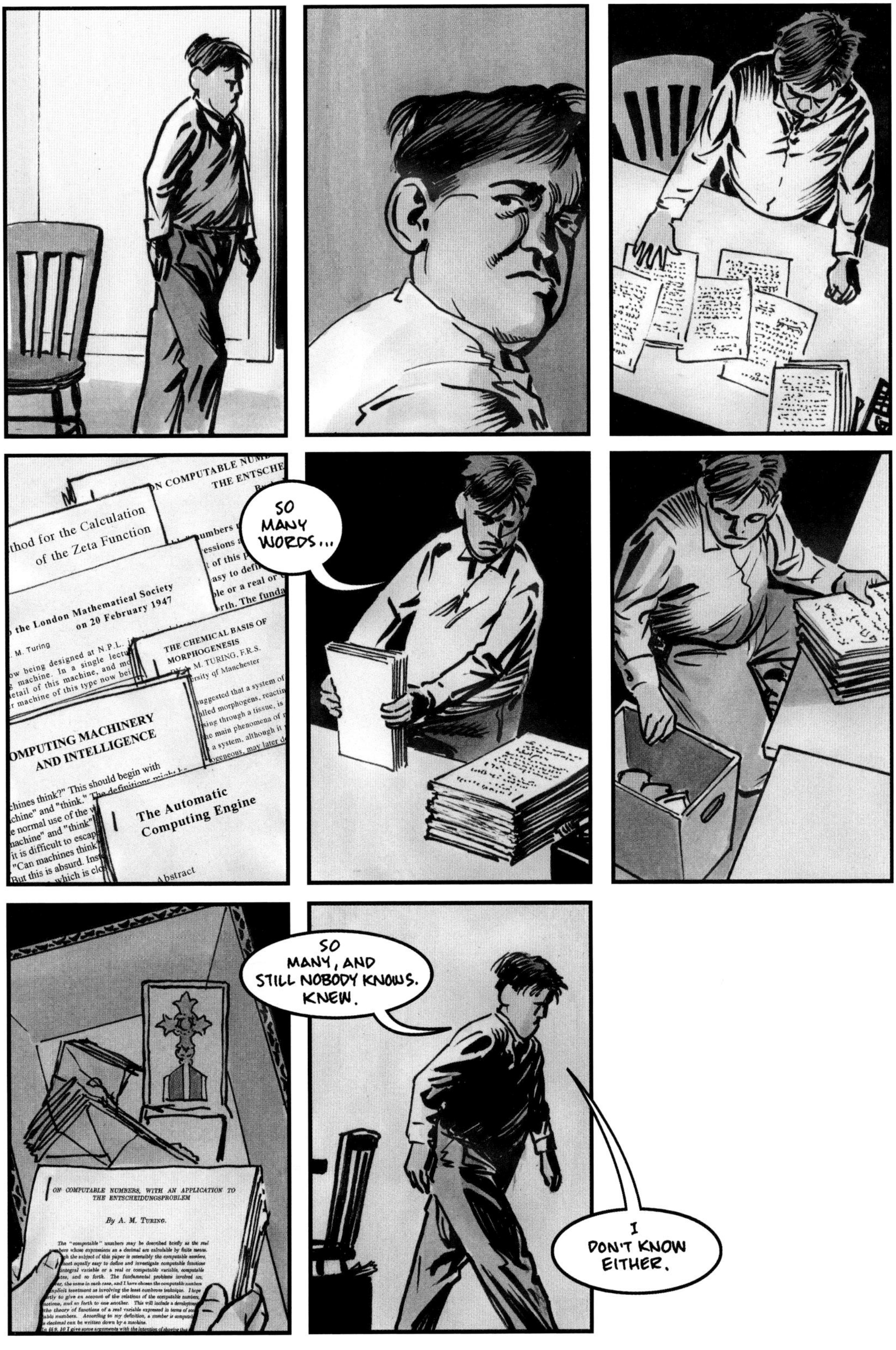

of the Zeta Function
on 20 February 1947
THE CHEMICAL BASIS OF MORPHOGENESIS
The Automatic Computing Engine
Abstract
SO MANY WORDS...
ON COMPUTABLE NUMBERS, WITH AN APPLICATION TO THE ENTSCHEIDUNGSPROBLEM
By A. M. TURING.
SO MANY, AND STILL NOBODY KNOWS. KNEW.
I DON'T KNOW EITHER.

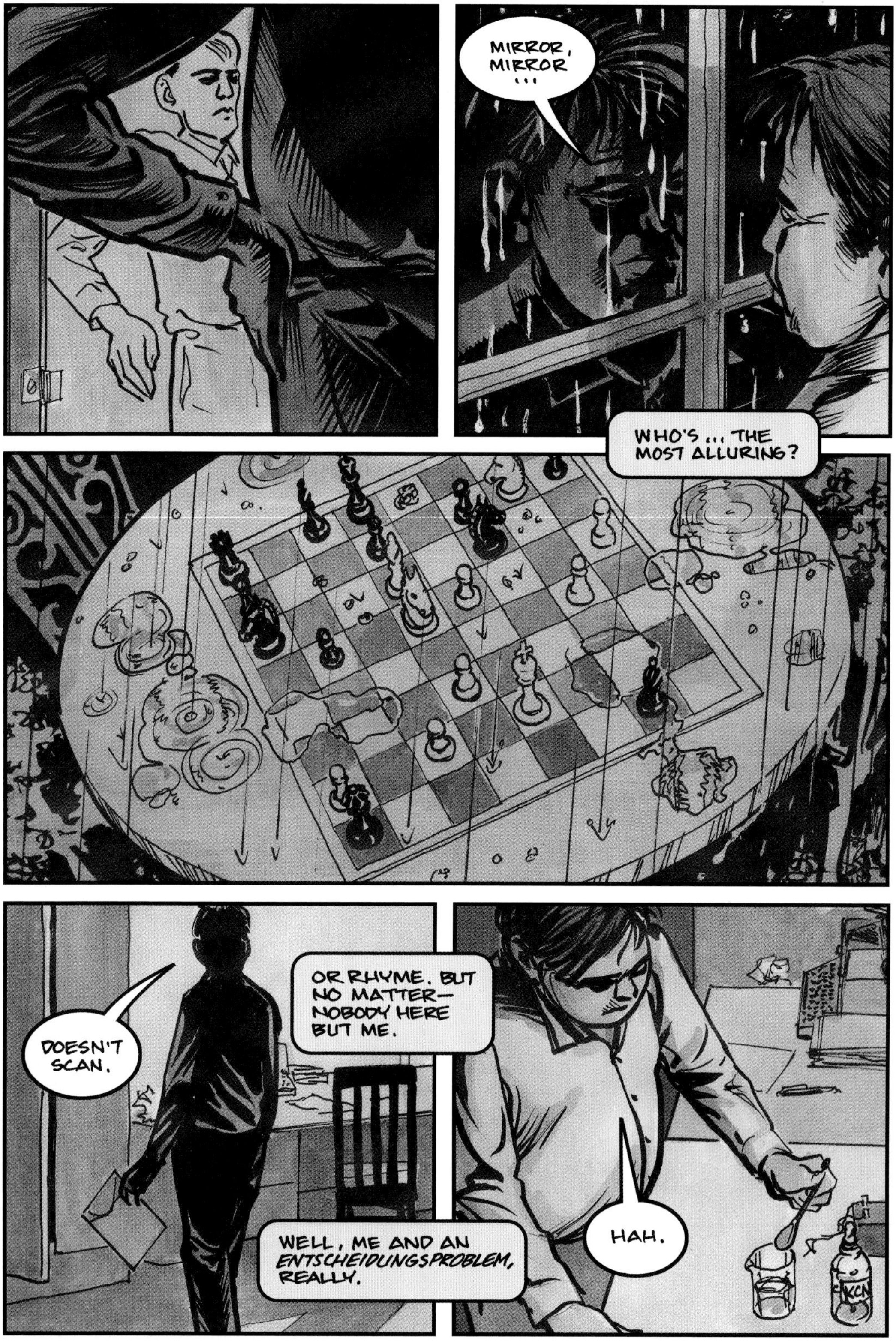
MIRROR, MIRROR ...
WHO'S ... THE MOST ALLURING?
DOESN'T SCAN.
OR RHYME. BUT NO MATTER— NOBODY HERE BUT ME.
WELL, ME AND AN *ENTSCHEIDUNGSPROBLEM*, REALLY.
HAH.

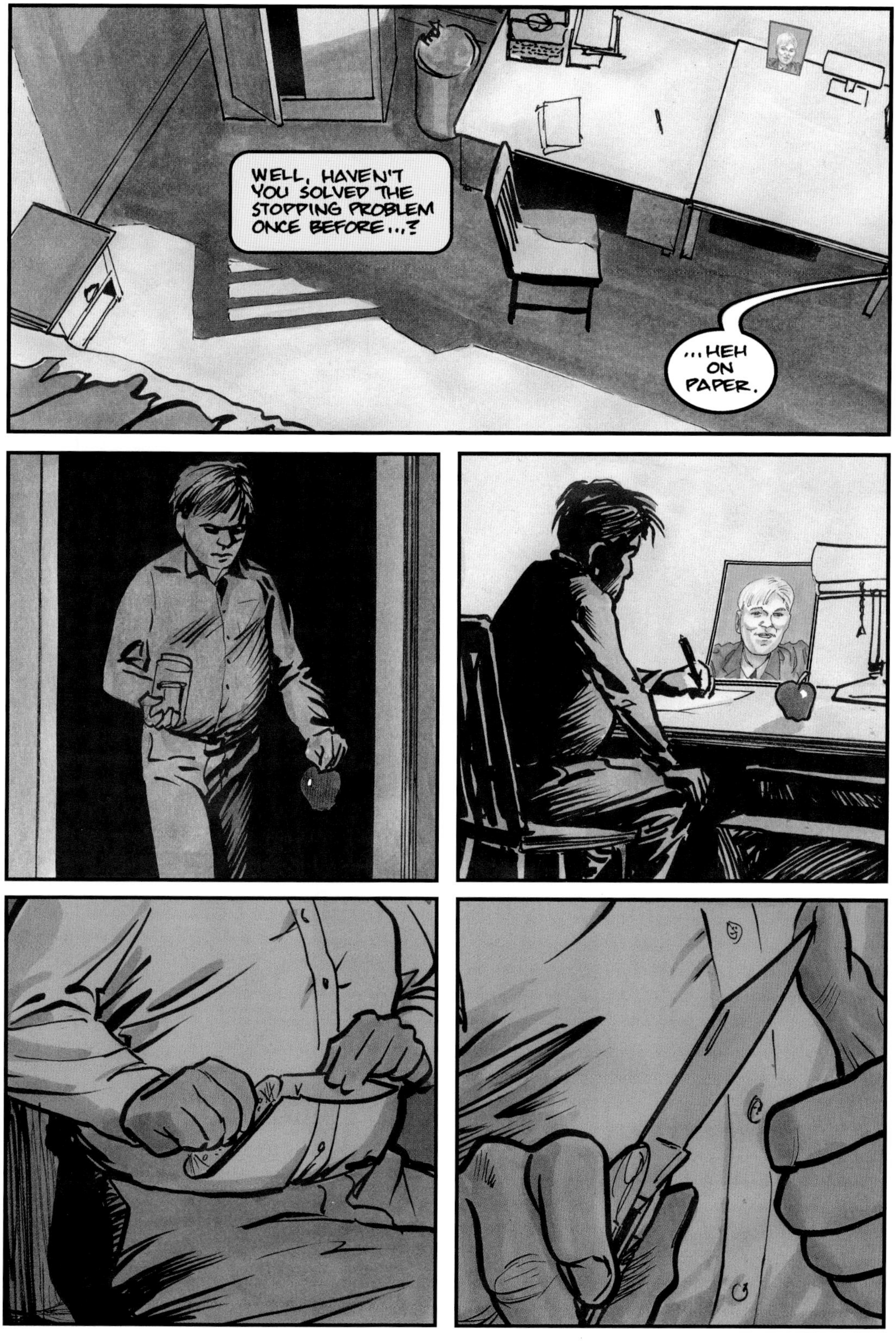
WELL, HAVEN'T YOU SOLVED THE STOPPING PROBLEM ONCE BEFORE...?
...HEH ON PAPER.

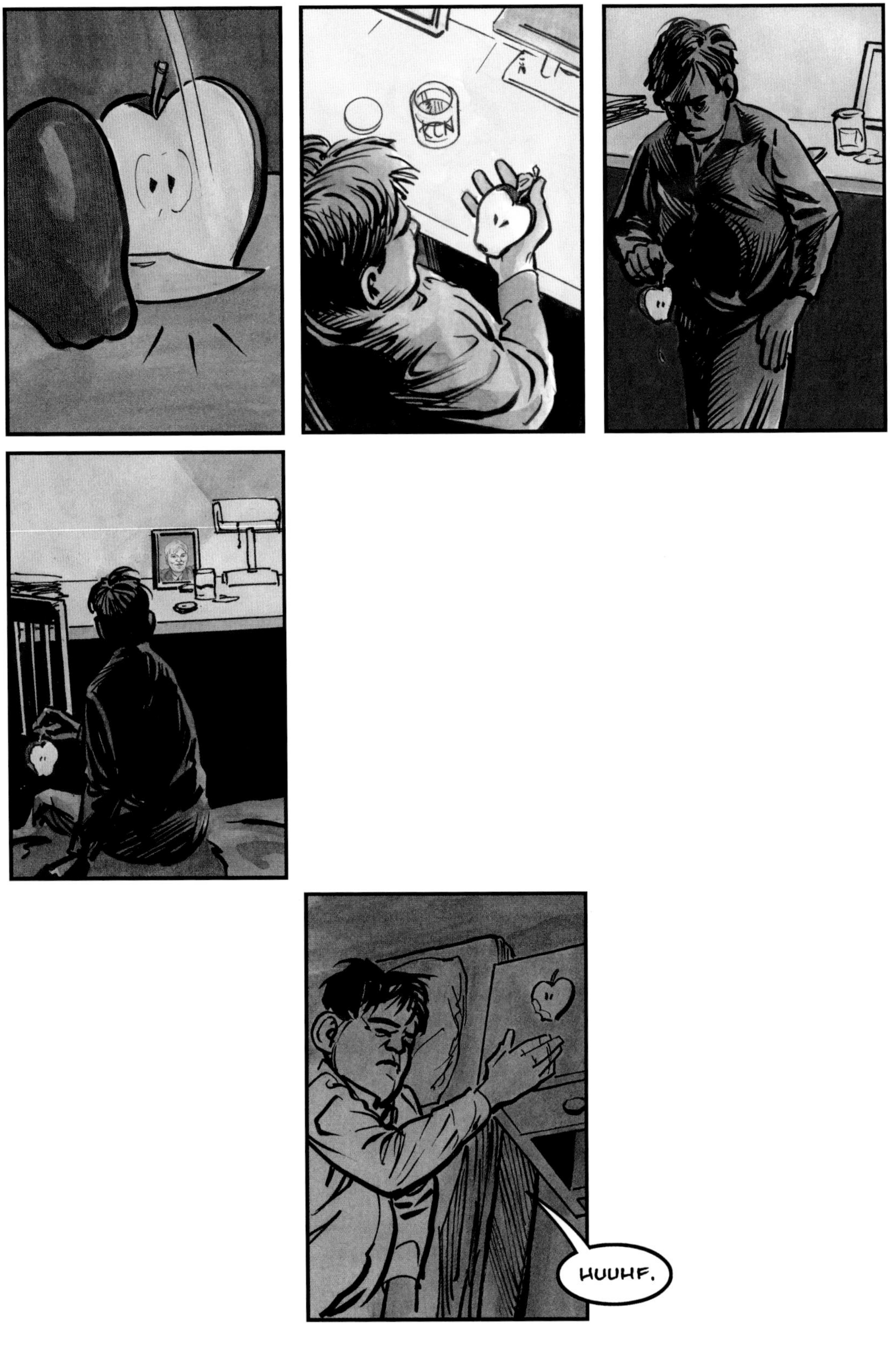
KCN
HUUHF.

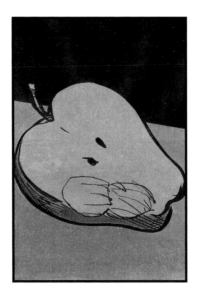

MRS. CLAYTON, HIS
HOUSEKEEPER, FOUND
HIS BODY THE NEXT
EVENING.

AUTHOR'S NOTE

On September 10, 2009, British prime minister Gordon Brown, acknowledging a petition started by John Graham-Cumming, released a statement apologizing to Alan Turing on behalf of the British government. It closed with, "We're sorry. You deserved so much better." Four years later, on December 24, 2013, Queen Elizabeth II granted Turing a pardon under the Royal Prerogative of Mercy. It read:

> NOW KNOW YE that We, in consideration of circumstances humbly represented unto Us, are Graciously pleased to extend Our Grace and Mercy unto the said Alan Mathison Turing and to grant him Our Free Pardon posthumously in respect of the said convictions . . .

The pardon and apology (refreshing for its simplicity and humanity) are steps toward addressing the tragedy of Turing's prosecution, but it's hard not to see them as being the least the government could do, and as coming much too late. I also imagine Turing would find the idea of being extended Grace and Mercy puzzling and would reply, "Thank you. Now what about everyone else convicted under this law?"

We'll never know, and his death remains a puzzling tragedy as well. I wrote the script for *The Imitation Game* between 2007 and 2010 and continued reshaping it through 2011. At the time, B. Jack Copeland's book *Turing: Pioneer of the Information Age* had yet to be published, so I took the coroner's report regarding suicide as the cause of Turing's death as a given. I'm in good company there; many of Turing's friends and colleagues agreed with this conclusion. But Copeland doesn't. Based on documents he uncovered, Copeland presents an alternate theory. He thinks an accidental death from inhalation of cyanide fumes is more likely. He also posits a third scenario . . . Though I think it's less likely than either accident or suicide, I encourage you to read his book to learn more about that, and his reasoning.

When an earlier version of this story was posted online, it featured a less equivocal depiction of the last few hours of Turing's life than what you see here. My original script had left what Turing did (or did not do) to the apple open to question, and we've returned to that original and more ambiguous ending for a number of reasons. First, beyond acknowledging this new information, having the official version almost, but not quite, prevail in a story with so many narrators presenting so many different viewpoints has great appeal. Second, I still think suicide is the more likely scenario. To the limited extent that I was able to get inside Turing's head in the course of writing this book— and it's very limited, because, if nothing else, I'm not a genius—I find a decisive act by Turing at least as plausible as an accidental death.

Should you read our *Imitation Game* as pure and objective history, then? Maybe not. (Just so you know, the parts where Turing wanders through mist and encounters, among others, Lady Ada Lovelace and Charles Babbage aren't supported by a preponderance of evidence, either.) Is what we've depicted here plausible? I think so, but as Copeland puts it: "The exact circumstances of Turing's death may always remain unclear." They may become clear at some point; history is a living thing, constantly subject to changing attitudes and new information coming to light. So ongoing concern and debate about the cause of his death is not the worst fate for his legacy.

Most important, though, is to remember what his death cost him in the first place. And what it cost us . . . For myself, I wish I lived in a world that benefited from decades more of Alan Turing, alive and well, thinking and discovering.

BIBLIOGRAPHY AND RECOMMENDED READING

The main character of this story is just as much "A" of Turing's famous test as he is "B." That leaves you—and Turing himself—as the Interrogators whose job is to decide who the real Alan Mathison Turing was from the many versions of him you meet in *The Imitation Game*. To help you out, and to help in separating fact from the small fictions we introduce, there are many other sources to consult. Here are the most important ones we used to construct this story:

AMT: The Turing Digital Archive at http://www.turingarchive.org. The Digital Archive provides access to original manuscripts, letters, and other documents in Turing's own hand, as well as supplementary material.

AMTst: *Alan M. Turing* by Sara Turing (Cambridge: W. Heffer & Sons, Ltd., 1959). Read this book along with Hodges (below, cited as ATTE) and you'll know the boy, the man, and his work.

AMT100: *Alan M. Turing, Centenary Edition* by Sara Turing with an introduction by Martin Davis and afterword by John Turing (Cambridge: Cambridge University Press, 1959, 2012). His brother John's contribution and commentary is revealing.

ATAC: *Alan Turing's Automatic Computing Engine: The Master Codebreaker's Struggle to Build the Modern Computer* edited by B. Jack Copeland (Oxford: Oxford University Press, 2005).

ATD: *Action This Day* edited by Ralph Erskine and Michael Smith (London: Bantam Press, 2001). For the facsimile of Churchill's memo, and what was apparently the first use of the titular, now famous sticker.

ATLaL: *Alan Turing: Life and Legacy of a Great Thinker* edited by Christof Teuscher (Berlin: Springer-Verlag, 2004).

ATTE: *Alan Turing: The Enigma* by Andrew Hodges (New York: Simon & Schuster, 1983). Required reading. Hodges's book is complete, well written, and satisfying. I read it more than a decade before I began writing comics about scientists, and I look forward to reading it again someday. For this story I used it as an encyclopedic dictionary of all things Turing, though I often found myself reading pages at a time when I had only meant to do a quick fact check. Bonus: Hodges structured his index entry on Turing to read like a short biography, something I only noticed after I'd constructed my own timeline and narrative. I'd never seen that done before, and it's a great and subtle trick.

AWmd: *Angus Wilson: A Biography* by Margaret Drabble (London: Secker & Warburg, 1995).

BoW: *Battle of Wits: The Complete Story of Codebreaking in World War II* by Stephen Budiansky (New York: Free Press, 2000).

BPAIS: *Bletchley Park: An Inmate's Story* by James Thirsk (Bromley: Galago, 2002).

BPe: Bletchley Park Exhibits, visited September 12, 2007.

BPP: *Bletchley Park People: Churchill's Geese that Never Cackled* by Marion Hill (Gloucestershire: Sutton Publishing Ltd., 2004).

Cfhas: *Codebreakers: The Inside Story of Bletchley Park* edited by F. H. Hinsley and Alan Strip (Oxford: Oxford University Press, 1993). Specifically, Joan Murray (née Clarke): "Hut 8 and Naval Enigma, Part I" and Diana Payne: "The Bombes."

CMaI: "Computing Machinery and Intelligence" by A. M. Turing, *Mind*, VIX (236), October 1950, 433–460. More required reading. Don't let its pedigree fool you, or scare you—this is a readable and, better still, enjoyable scholarly article.

Dmb: *Dilly: The Man Who Broke Enigmas* by Mavis Batey (London: Dialogue, 2009). A firsthand account from one of Dilly's "harem," supplemented with excellent additional sources.

ES92: *The Enigma Symposium 1992* edited by Hugh Skillen (Middlesex: Hugh Skillen, 1992).

EtB: *Enigma: The Battle for the Code* by Hugh Sebag-Montefiore (New York: Wiley, 2000).

EUB: *Enigma U-Boats: Breaking the Code* by Jak P. Mallmann Showell (Shepperton: Ian Allen Publishing, 2000).

EV: *Enigma Variations: Love, War & Bletchley Park* by Irene Young (Edinburgh: Mainstream Publishing, 1990).

HoMC: *A History of Manchester Computers* by Simon H. Lavington (Manchester: NCC Publications, 1975). Useful visual reference.

MRaE: *Mathematical Recreations and Essays* by W. W. Rouse Ball (London: Macmillan, 1920). One of Turing's favorite books.

OCN: "On Computable Numbers, with an Application to the Entscheidungsproblem" by A. M. Turing, *Proceedings of the London Mathematical Society*, Series 2, Volume 42, 1937, 230–265.

ORcm: "Operation Ruthless" by C. Morgan, http://www.flickr.com/photos/nationalarchives/4016834826 and http://www.flickr.com/photos/nationalarchives/4016068701. Ian Fleming, James Bond's creator, teams up with Alan Turing. Really.

PBat: "Prof's Book" by Alan Turing, http://www.alanturing.net/profs_book.

SLaD: *The Strange Life and Death of Dr. Turing*, written and directed by Christopher Sykes, BBC2 Horizon/WGBH Nova, 50 minutes, originally aired March 9, 1992. An excellent introduction to Turing and a useful visual reference, with glimpses of the adult Joan Clarke and Donald Bayley as a bonus. Andrew Hodges gets plenty of screen time as well. http://youtu.be/gyusnGbBSHE and http://youtu.be/5LHFzNMgWzw.

StE: *Seizing the Enigma: The Race to Break the German U-Boat Codes, 1939–1943* by David Kahn (Boston: Houghton Mifflin, 1991).

SX: *Station X: The Codebreakers of Bletchley Park* by Michael Smith (London: Channel 4 Books, 1998).

TET: *The Essential Turing: Seminal Writings in Computing, Logic, Philosophy, Artificial Intelligence, and Artificial Life plus The Secrets of Enigma* edited by B. Jack Copeland (Oxford: Oxford University Press, 2004). The title speaks the truth. Contains all of

Turing's important scientific works. Mostly used as a source for quotations from Turing's original papers, but the readable commentary and useful context it provides was invaluable.

THSS: *The Hut Six Story: Breaking the Enigma Codes* by Gordon Welchman (New York: McGraw-Hill, 1982).

TjC: *Turing: Pioneer of the Information Age* by B. Jack Copeland (Oxford: Oxford University Press, 2012).

TMWK: *The Man Who Knew Too Much: Alan Turing and the Invention of the Computer* by David Leavitt (New York: W.W. Norton, 2006).

TSWoCF-S: *The Secret War of Charles Fraser-Smith: The Q Gadget Wizard of World War II* by Charles Fraser-Smith with Gerald McKnight and Sandy Lesberg (London: Michael Joseph, 1981). A different perspective on the Fleming pinch (see pages 102–104) from the man who supplied most of the secret gadgets used in WWII . . . and was the inspiration for "Q" in the James Bond series.

TUC: *The Universal Computer: The Road from Leibniz to Turing* by Martin Davis (New York: W.W. Norton, 2000). Working through Davis's chapter on Turing brought me to my basic understanding of Turing's first great discovery and his work on the Universal Machine.

WKtS: *We Kept the Secret: Now It Can Be Told* edited by Gwendoline Page (Norfolk: Geo. R. Reeve, Ltd., 2002).

WLoF: *Wittgenstein's Lectures on the Foundations of Mathematics, Cambridge 1939* edited by Cora Diamond (Chicago: The University of Chicago Press, 1989).

NOTES AND REFERENCES

These take the form of page.panel, so the first reference you see below tells you that page 6, panel 1 is based on information on page 346 of *Alan Turing: The Enigma*. (More or less, that is, since the reference may also inform nearby panels as well. These annotations come from my original script, which we occasionally deviated from to improve the storytelling. Where and how are left for you as an exercise in decryption.) Sources from the Turing Digital Archive are cited as "AMT/folder_name/item_in_folder/specific_location."

Regarding the title pages: As is obvious in the last instance—and much less so for the first two—they're all built around the opening paragraphs of "Computing Machinery and Intelligence" . . . first in binary, then as a crib for a running key cipher, and finally as plain text.

006.1 = ATTE: 346
007.3 = AMTst: 19
008.4 = AMTst: 17
008.5 = AMTst: 20; AMT/K/1/2
009.1 = AMTst: 18
009.3 = The book is Edwin Brewster's *Natural Wonders Every Child Should Know*.
009.4 = AMTst: 11, 13
010.1 = AMTst: 21
010.3 = AMTst: 22
011.3 = AMTst: 25, 39; AMT/K/1/17
012.4 = AMTst: 27
012.5 = AMTst: 29–30
012.6 = AMTst: 13–14, 27–28
015.5 = ATTE: 48
016.2 = ATTE: 39–41
016.5 = ATTE: 42
020.6 = ATTE: 44
021.3 = ATTE: 45
022.1 = ATTE: 46–47
022.2 = AMT/K/1/20
022.4 = AMTst: 36
023.1 = ATTE: 49–50
023.2 = ATTE: 51
023.3 = Turing is making a "soccer net via Navajo."
024.3 = King's College's motto is *Veritas et Utilitas*, which translates as "Truth and Usefulness."
025.1 = AMTst: 41; ATTE: 89

026.1 = ATTE: 67; AMT/K/1/25
027.4 = AMTst: 43
030.6 = TMWK: 20
031.1 = AMTst: 113; TMWK: 20
036.1 = AMT100: 152–53
037.3 = ATTE: 94; AMTst
038.1 = TMWK: 52–53
039.1 = TMWK: 34–36, 42–44
040.3 and on = There's no evidence that Turing's stutter would disappear when he talked about his research, but it seemed appropriate to reflect the clarity of his writing in his style of speech.
040.5 = "On Computable Numbers" as reprinted in TET, with help from TUC's gloss of the paper.
046.1 = AMTst: 48–49
048.1 = TET: 85–87; OCN
049.3 = AMT/K/1/38
049.4 = AMT/K/1/28
050.3 = TMWK: 106–7,114
050.6 = AMT/K/1/41
051.5 = AMTst: 51; AMT/K/1/41
052.2 = TET: 127; AMT/K/1/42
052.4 = TMWK: 117–19; AMT/K/1/42
053.1 = AMT/K/1/42
054.1 = TMWK: 125
054.3 = AMT/K/1/43
054.4 = TMWK: 119; TET: 127
054.5 = AMT/K/1/43
056.1 = AMTst: 52; TET: 130; AMT/K/1/44
058.2 = TET: 128; TMWK: 133–34; ATLaL: 46
058.4 = AMT/K/1/43; TMWK: 159; ATLaL: 46
059.1 = TET: 128; AMT/K/1/61; This is Will Jones, who we're fictionally (and namelessly) introducing into the story before Turing actually met him on his trip back to the States.
059.2 = AMTst: 54
059.5 = AMT/K/1/56; AMT/K/1/59; TET: 132
060.1 = TET: 134
060.5 = ATTE: 149; Later Alan's chubbier hand will do something similar.
061.1 = ATTE: 149
061.5 = WLoF: 95; Included here because Wittgenstein anticipates the objection Lady Ada makes, which you see later in the story (page 187). I'm paraphrasing and also modifying the chronology a bit so as to

juxtapose the truly academic philosophizing with the very next part, where Turing enters the war.

062.1 = Dmb: 47

062.2 = TMWK: 139, 141; ATTE: 151; A lot of this scene is fictionalized, since there's not much available on Turing and his early Government Code & Cypher School days. So, we played up the emphasis on spying and linguistics, and omitted (which is also plausible) emphasis on the use of automation or even mathematical analysis here, since the early days of the code-breaking effort relied heavily on more traditional methods.

063.4 = AMTst: 67

069.3 = ATTE: 209; BPP: 68–69

072.3 = Though we have the guards call Turing a "scientist" here, they probably called him a "boffin" instead. This bit of slang was used at Bletchley and many other military operations to describe—with a mix of affection, admiration, and (probably, on occasion, like we see here) exasperation—researchers doing their bit to win the war by using their brains rather than their brawn.

076.5–6 = BPe; WKtS: 46; I'm told that some Bletchley Park tour guides now tell visitors that the Wrens may have merely "turned up their cuffs" against the heat—and that the guides then demonstrate this with marvelous reserve. At the time I visited, they didn't treat undressing as a rumor, and Gwendoline Page, herself a Wren at Bletchley Park, mentions Wrens undressing when talking about her work on Colossus.

077.6 = Dmb: 88

078.2 = Dmb: 86

085.1 = ATLaL: 443

086.6 = Dmb: 32

087.3 = TMWK: 182

089.5 = AMT100: xiii

092.2 = AMT/C/30 for the full treatise; PBat.

094.5 = Dmb: 72, 94

098.3 = TUC: 172; StE: 100

099.3 = Dmb: 21, 136–37; TMWK: 178

101.1 = TET: 258–59; Yes, that's Ian "007" Fleming.

101.4 = EUB: 8

103.1 = ORcm; Dmb: 84, 112–13

105.1 = SX: 63

106.2 = Dmb: various

106.3 = Dmb: 106

106.4 = Dmb: 94

106.5 = TET: 260

107.1 = ATTE: 206–8; SlaD

110.5 = BPP: 65

111.3,5 = In case you didn't catch it, Turing and Alexander are in the midst of a variation of "The Immortal Game," as originally played between Adolf Anderssen and Lionel Kieseritzky in 1851.

112.1 = SLaD; BPP; Dmb; SX

112.6 = AMT/K/1/70; Tjc: 75; ATTE: 216

114.1 = The description of this trip in AMT/K/1/70 is the only instance where Sara Turing blacked out something from one of her son's letters so completely that it's now unreadable.

114.3 = ATTE: 26, "The Ballad of Reading Gaol" by Oscar Wilde.

115.1 = SX: 78 for the facts, but most of this is imagined.

119.6 = BPP: 40–41

121.3 = StE: 94–95

124.5 = TET: 338; We left out Stuart Milner-Barry here as a nod to simplicity, and gave his line to an indignant Dilly Knox instead.

125.3 = TET: 336

126.2 = Dmb: 66, 157

126.5 = EUB: 88; SX: 114

127.1 = Dmb: 133

127.4 = EUB: 88–92; BPP

131.6 = Ken Lacroix and Gordon Connel were also in the boat with Brown.

132.2 = Dmb: 147

132.3 = EUB: 33 re. instructions to U-boat sailors.

133.3 = TMWK: 192–93

133.5 = Dmb: 140 for the Lewis Carroll connection.

134.4 = ATLaL: 471; TUC: 174

135.4 = TET: 353; ATTE: 271; BPP: 123

135.7 = TMWK: 194

137.1 = TMWK: 196; ATTE: 282–84

144.4 = SX: 172

145.2 = WKtS: 84; BPP: 132–33

156.2 = AMT/C/32 for the full report on ACE.

157.3 = TUC: 188; TET

157.6 = TUC: 182

158.4 = AMTst: 60, 86

159.3 = ATTE: 479; BPP: 68

160.2 = AMT100: 157

160.3 = TMWK: 208

161.1 = TMWK: 209–10

162.2 = TMWK: 201–2

162.3 = TMWK: 204–5; TET: 354–75; TUC: 191

162.5 = TET: 209

163.2 = TET: 3

166.5 = ATLaL: 165

167.3 = AMTst: 87

168.4 = AMT/B/32 for his programmer's handbook.

169.2 = TMWK: 219

170.5 = TMWK: 233; TUC: 192

175.1 = AMT/D, AMT/C for general letter-writing background.

175.5 = AMTst: 91

177.2 = AMTst: 80

177.3 = AMT/B/5, 6 for transcripts; TET: 476.

178.1 = TET: 484–86

179.4 = AMTst: 91

179.5 = AMTst: 98

181.1 = AMTst: 60

  182 = MaI for the next few pages.

188.3 = ATTE: 449–50; SLaD

191.1 = ATTE: 453

191.3 = ATTE: 450 for Turing being stood up and going back to Oxford . . .
        all the rest is imagined.

193.1 = ATTE: 450

193.3 = ATTE: 388 re. Turochamp's (lack of) prowess.

193.4 = ATLaL: 168

194.2 = TET: 431 for "experiment I've already tried."

195.5 = AMTst: 103

196.1 = AMTst: 115

196.4 = ATTE: 453–54

197.1 = ATTE: 454 for burglary; his actual statements downplay its
        seriousness, so here we've edited them to make it seem as serious as it
        was.

199.1 = ATTE: 455

  200 = Also at the trial were, of course, Turing's attorney G. Lind-Smith and
        Emlyn Hooson, who represented Murray.

200.3 = ATTE: 457, 463, 471–72

200.5 = TET: 494

202.2 = ATTE: 473

203.1 = ATTE: 472

203.3 = ATTE: 476

203.3 = ATTE: 463–64

205.2,4 = AMT100: 147

205.6 = AMT100: 159

206.5 = AMT100: 147

208.1 = AMTst: 113 for the alarm clock, though probably used anachronistically;
SLaD

209.1 = TET: 510

210.3 = AMT/D/14a

211.1 = AMTst: 60

211.5 = AMT/A/13

213.2 = AMT/D/14a; though note that this was a letter to Norman Routledge,
not Robin or Champ.

214.1 = http://www.turingarchive.org/browse.php/C/24, e.g. page 67

216.3 = The final position of "The Immortal Game," were it played all the way
to completion.

218 = Yes, the panel layout here purposely mimics a glider from John
Conway's "Game of Life"

222 = Sara Turing never knew details of her son's service during World War
II. None of the Bletchley Park geese cackled until after their work was
partially declassified in the 1970s.

Author's Note = http://www.telegraph.co.uk/news/politics/gordon-brown/6170112/
Gordon-Brown-Im-proud-to-say-sorry-to-a-real-war-hero.html and
https://www.gov.uk/government/news/royal-pardon-for-ww2-code-
breaker-dr-alan-turing.

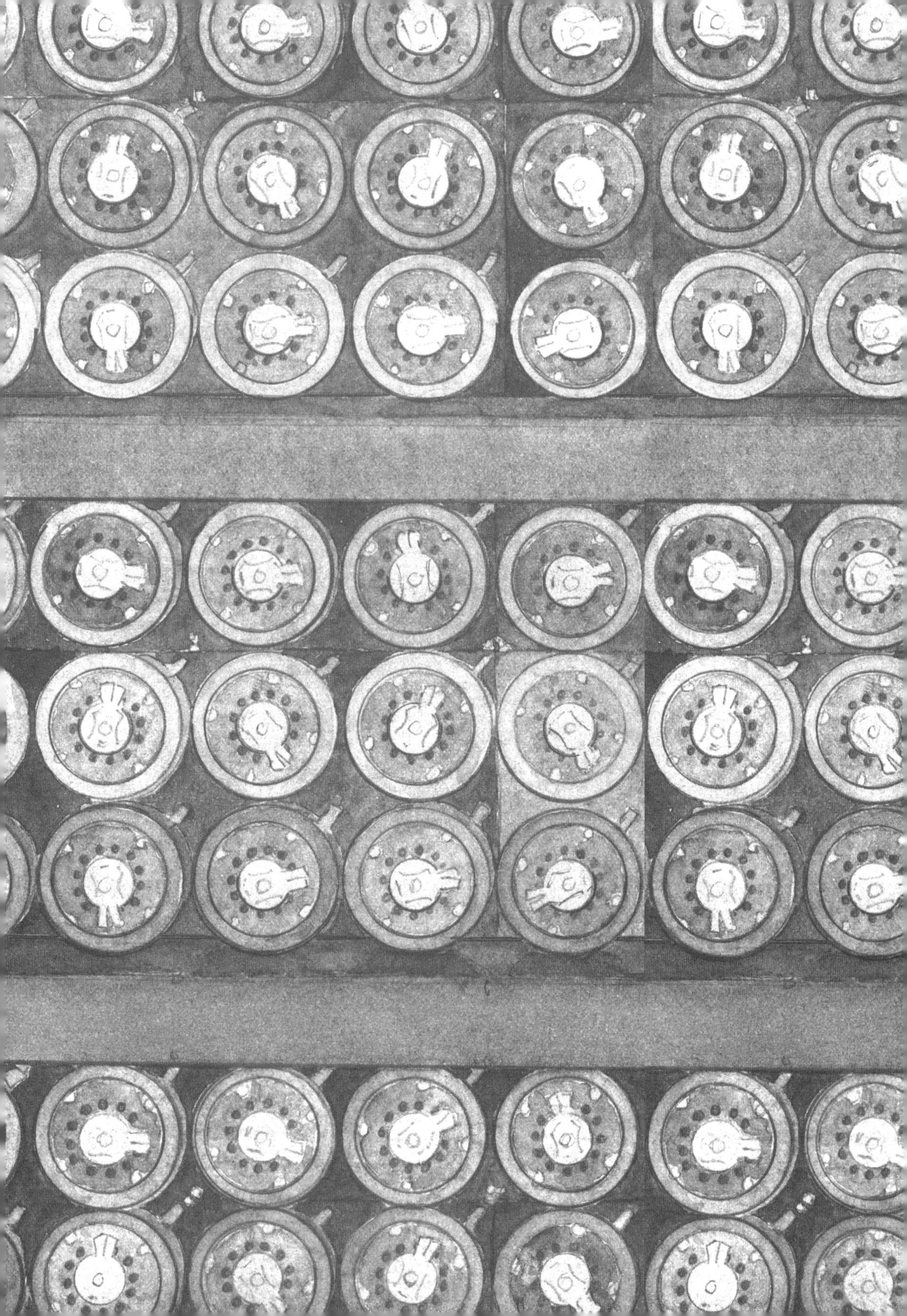

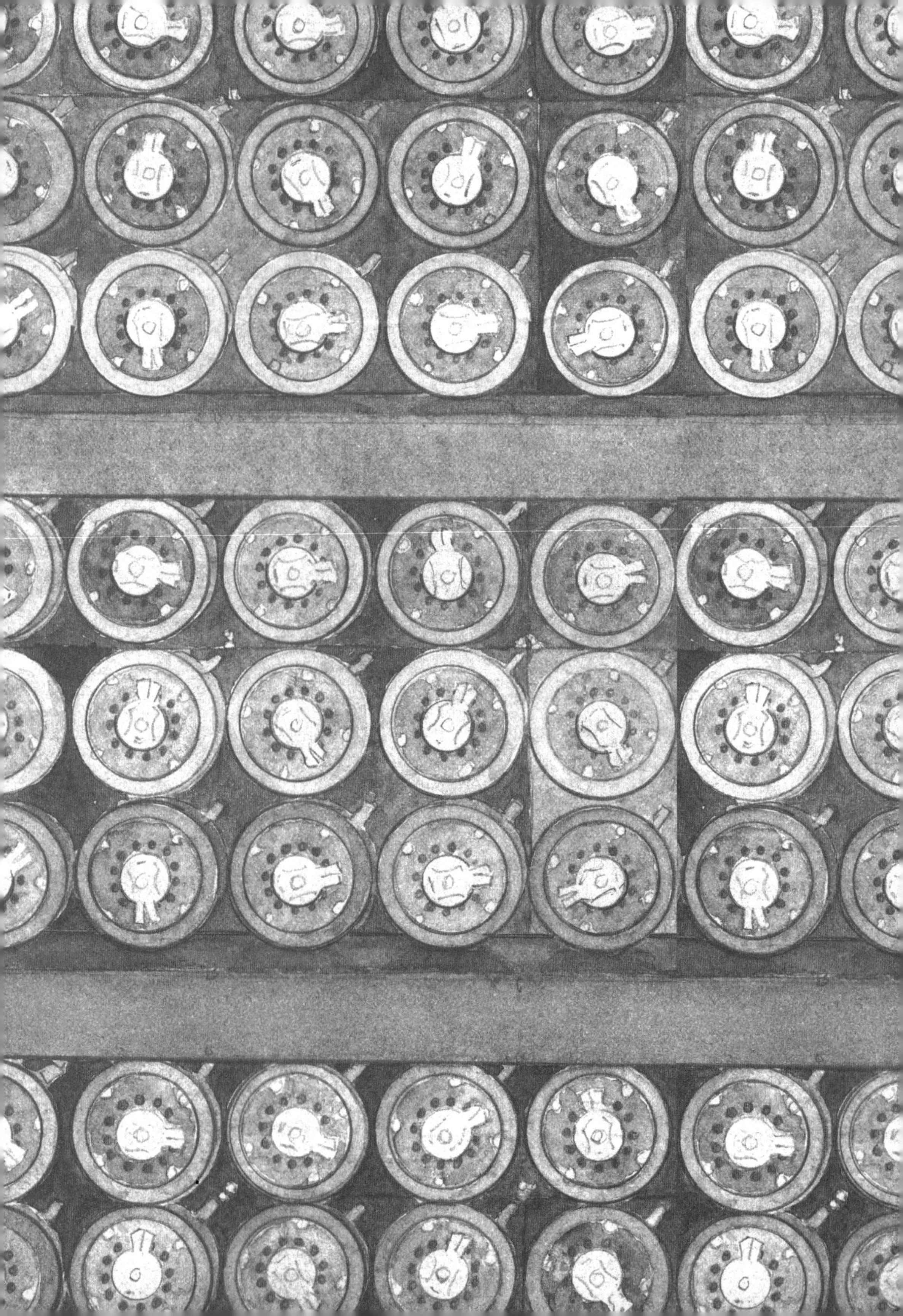